HISTORICAL DICTIONARIES OF LITERATURE AND THE ARTS

Jon Woronoff, Series Editor

1. *Science Fiction Literature*, by Brian Stableford, 2004.
2. *Hong Kong Cinema*, by Lisa Odham Stokes, 2007.
3. *American Radio Soap Operas*, by Jim Cox, 2005.
4. *Japanese Traditional Theatre*, by Samuel L. Leiter, 2006.
5. *Fantasy Literature*, by Brian Stableford, 2005.
6. *Australian and New Zealand Cinema*, by Albert Moran and Errol Vieth, 2006.
7. *African-American Television*, by Kathleen Fearn-Banks, 2006.
8. *Lesbian Literature*, by Meredith Miller, 2006.
9. *Scandinavian Literature and Theater*, by Jan Sjåvik, 2006.
10. *British Radio*, by Seán Street, 2006.
11. *German Theater*, by William Grange, 2006.
12. *African American Cinema*, by S. Torriano Berry and Venise Berry, 2006.
13. *Sacred Music*, by Joseph P. Swain, 2006.
14. *Russian Theater*, by Laurence Senelick, 2007.
15. *French Cinema*, by Dayna Oscherwitz and MaryEllen Higgins, 2007.
16. *Postmodernist Literature and Theater*, by Fran Mason, 2007.
17. *Irish Cinema*, by Roderick Flynn and Pat Brereton, 2007.
18. *Australian Radio and Television*, by Albert Moran and Chris Keating, 2007.
19. *Polish Cinema*, by Marek Haltof, 2007.
20. *Old-Time Radio*, by Robert C. Reinehr and Jon D. Swartz, 2008.
21. *Renaissance Art*, by Lilian H. Zirpolo, 2008.
22. *Broadway Musical*, by William A. Everett and Paul R. Laird, 2008.
23. *American Theater: Modernism*, by James Fisher and Felicia Hardison Londré, 2008.
24. *German Cinema*, by Robert C. Reimer and Carol J. Reimer, 2008.

Historical Dictionary of German Cinema

Robert C. Reimer
Carol J. Reimer

Historical Dictionaries of
Literature and the Arts, No. 24

The Scarecrow Press, Inc.
Lanham, Maryland • Toronto • Plymouth, UK
2008

SCARECROW PRESS, INC.

Published in the United States of America
by Scarecrow Press, Inc.
A wholly owned subsidiary of
The Rowman & Littlefield Publishing Group, Inc.
4501 Forbes Boulevard, Suite 200, Lanham, Maryland 20706
www.scarecrowpress.com

Estover Road
Plymouth PL6 7PY
United Kingdom

British Library Cataloguing in Publication Information Available

Library of Congress Cataloging-in-Publication Data

Reimer, Robert C. (Robert Charles), 1943–
  Historical dictionary of German cinema / Robert C. Reimer, Carol J. Reimer.
    p. cm. — (Historical dictionaries of literature and the arts ; no. 24)
  Includes bibliographical references.
  ISBN-13: 978-0-8108-5623-3 (cloth : alk. paper)
  ISBN-10: 0-8108-5623-9 (cloth : alk. paper)
  1. Motion pictures–Germany–Dictionaries. I. Reimer, Carol J. II. Title.
PN1993.5.G3R417 2008
  791.4309430³–dc22   2007037524

∞™ The paper used in this publication meets the minimum requirements of
American National Standard for Information Sciences—Permanence of Paper
for Printed Library Materials, ANSI/NISO Z39.48-1992.
Manufactured in the United States of America.

For Kirstin Reimer and Karl Reimer

Contents

Editor's Foreword

Every national cinema is different, but in some ways German cinema would seem to be even more distinctive than most. Part of this can be traced to its relatively long history. Among the earliest to get started and now well over a century old, German cinema has gone through many phases, some determined by history, such as the Weimar period, the Third Reich, the fragmentation after World War II, and the postreunification era. It is old enough that the so-called New German Cinema lies several decades back, and German cinema has since reinvented itself, as it had repeatedly in the past and will do again hopefully in the future. Unlike most other national cinemas, it has also gone through two phases of acute split personality, first when some of the best actors and directors fled Nazism, and then again during the period of the two Germanies, East and West. On top of all this, German cinema includes the cinema of Germany, and Austria, and even part of Switzerland. Certainly this is more than enough to generate an extremely varied cinema. On the whole it is rather good, sometimes even excellent, with films known and admired worldwide, but it has also produced some rather tendentious films and others that were simply kitsch. And there is no question that many of its actors, directors, and producers enjoy an international reputation. So this is certainly a cinema to contend with.

But it is also an extremely difficult cinema to grasp and make sense of. This makes the task of writing a handy guide all the more difficult, yet all the more important. This series is therefore greatly enriched by the latest addition, a *Historical Dictionary of German Cinema,* which manages to encapsulate the unusual length, breadth, and variety. The long history is much easier to follow thanks to the extensive chronology. The different periods and styles are then neatly summed up in the introduction. The dictionary section disaggregates, focusing on some of the most notable films, actors, directors, production companies, and government agencies, as well as an assortment of other related items. The range of these entries is impressive, and it is selective in providing the necessary elements to piece together this amazingly variegated national cinema, showing many of its finest but not hiding some of its more dubious moments. In conclusion, realizing that there is so much more to know, it directs the reader toward other related works and Internet resources.

This volume was written by two scholars of German cinema, Robert C. Reimer and Carol J. Reimer. Robert C. Reimer is a professor of German, and until 2007, when he became chair of the Department of Languages and Culture Studies, was director of UNC Charlotte's Film Studies program. Carol J. Reimer has an M.L.S. and is a collection development associate at the J. Murrey Atkins Library of UNC Charlotte. The Reimers were introduced to German film while living in Stuttgart, Germany, in the late 1960s, a turbulent period in which the New German Cinema was competing for viewer allegiance with commercial cinema, derogatorily known as "Opas Kino." It was also a period when there was an awakened awareness of the films of the Third Reich. While viewing three or more works a week from different eras and in different styles, the Reimers developed an understanding of the diversity of German film, which now, after three subsequent extended residencies in Germany, includes Weimar, East German, and recent German film. Robert and Carol Reimer have produced a broad canvas that shows the length and breadth of German film. Thanks to this book it will be much easier than before to appreciate one of the world's great cinemas.

Preface

German film is diverse and multifaceted. This volume can only suggest the richness of a film tradition that includes five distinct German governments (Wilhelmine Germany, the Weimar Republic, the Third Reich, the Federal Republic of Germany, and the German Democratic Republic), two national industries (Germany and Austria), and a myriad of styles and production methods. Paradoxically, the political disruptions that have produced these distinct film eras, as well as the natural inclination of artists to rebel and create new styles, allow for construction of a narrative of German film. Disjuncture generates distinct points of separation and yet also highlights continuities between the ruptures.

This introduction can only outline the richness of German film. Yet we hope that its broad canvas will lead students and scholars of cinema to appreciate the complex nature of German film and not only direct them to the answers they seek in the dictionary, but also help them formulate the questions that still need examination. Entries in the dictionary are accordingly written to provide the basic information about the director, film, or concept and also to suggest avenues of research that may ultimately lead to answers for vexing questions: What exactly is German film, and how does it differ from the film of other national cinemas?

We could not include all personalities engaged in the production of German film. We have instead focused on directors, actors, and classic films, as these are topics for which information is most often sought. Our concept for inclusion has been broad, encompassing directors and actors of mainstream, alternative, and experimental film from 1895 to the present. The choice of films that received their own entry is subjective, but not arbitrary, as they represent those films that have become part of the lore of German cinema or created public debate at the time of their release. We have also included a few major cinematographers, particularly if they were instrumental in creating a film's style. The same criterion was used for the few composers who have received an entry. Producers are included who were important for the wider distribution of German film. Always we asked who or what is German. In the end, we included people, concepts, and products of those who got a significant start in Germany, even if they subsequently had important careers in other national cinemas, including working in Hollywood.

The work is framed by a chronology that follows the historical events crucial to future development of German film and an appendix that lists the 100 most significant German films, chosen by a panel of critics, directors, actors, and producers in the German film industry. The chronology cannot be in dispute, as these are the events that are recorded. But our choices may be disputed, as important events are inevitably left out. We have focused on major developments in technology, implementation of national film policies, and premiers of significant films. Also included are national and international historical events that greatly affected the direction and development of German film. We have avoided creating a necrology; thus, except for the death of Rainer Werner Fassbinder, whose death one could argue had a profound affect on German film of the 1980s, no obituaries are present. The appendix of 100 significant films, like any such list, is arbitrary. But similar to the "best" lists that have appeared in Britain, France, and America, the ranking of films aids in defining German film's national character by revealing what the creators of German cinema consider important.

We would like to thank Kirstin Reimer and Kimberley Hewitt for reading the manuscript and for their insightful suggestions. We also thank the people in film archives who helped us locate the stills that were chosen to give a sense of the diversity of Germany film: Daniele Guerlain at Transit Film, Olivia Just at the Deutsches Filminstitut, Manja Meister at DEFA, Robert Münkel at the Murnau-Stiftung, and Ulla Niehaus at Ulrike Ottinger Filmproduktion, among others. Finally, we thank Jon Woronoff for his suggestions on style and content of the finished volume.

Acronyms and Abbreviations

€	symbol for the euro, Germany's currency
AG	Aktiengesellschaft (limited stock company)
aka	also known as
BRD	Bundesrepublik Deutschland (Federal Republic of Germany)
Bufa	Bild- und Filmamt
Co.	Compagnie (company)
DDR	Deutsche Demokratische Republik (German Democratic Republic)
DEFA	Deutsche Film Aktiengesellschaft (East German film company)
DM	Deutsche Mark (German Mark, currency before the Euro)
FRG	Federal Republic of Germany (West Germany)
FSK	Freiwillige Selbstkontrolle (voluntary film control system)
BFI	British Film Institute
GDR	German Democratic Republic (East Germany)
GmbH	Gesellschaft mit beschränkter Haftung (limited stock company)
KG	Kommanditgesellschaft (limited partnership)
NATO	North Atlantic Treaty Organization
NGC	New German Cinema
Parufamet	Paramount-Ufa-Metro (American and German film partnership)
SED	Sozialistische Einheitspartei Deutschlands (German Unity Party)
SA	Sturmabteilung (Storm Troopers, also known in English as Brown Shirts)

SS	Schutzstaffel (literally, "protective squadron")
U-Boot (U-boat)	Unterseeboot (literally "undersea boat" or submarine)
Ufa	Universum Film AG (sometimes UFA)
VEB	Volkseigenerbetrieb (literally "enterprise owned by the people")

Chronology

1895 German brothers Max and Emil Skladanowsky demonstrated their "bioscop" projection system, which used two alternating apparatuses to project images onto a screen. This historic first was eclipsed a month later, when the French brothers Louis and Auguste Lumière premiered their superior system in Paris.

1898 Oskar Messter, a pioneer in manufacturing cameras and projectors, published a catalog of 84 film titles in order to provide films to the exhibitors who purchased his equipment.

1899 Otto Pritzkow opened a movie house in Berlin, the first recorded permanent movie house in Germany.

1903 **August:** Messter produced the first *Ton-Bilder* (sound images), thus introducing the first sound movies. Generally ahead of other early film industry moguls, Messter's system used a special mechanism to synchronize a gramophone and a projector.

1904 **August:** The premier of *Der Raubmord am Spandauer Schifffahrtskanal bei Berlin* (*Robbery and Murder in the Spandau Shipping Canal near Berlin*) anticipated the direction of narrative film, based on one of America's first genre films, *The Great Train Robbery* (1903). *Der Raubmord* had sufficient imitators to call forth demands for censorship a few years later.

1905 **May:** Official statistics reported that Berlin had 16 permanent movie houses, suggesting the growing popularity of film attendance, at least in big cities.

1906 **January:** Henny Porten, future producer and star, made her first film, *Meißner Porzellan* (*Meissen Porcellan*), a *Ton-Bild* production, for Messter. **March:** For 20,000 marks Paul Davidson founded Allgemeine

Kinematographen-Theater Gesellschaft GmbH in Frankfurt with the intention of establishing movie houses throughout Germany, most of which he called Union Theater. His firm later became Germany's first public movie company, Projektions-Aktiengesellschaft Union (Pagu). **May:** The first censorship laws were established. Henceforth all films required a license for public exhibition. **16 October:** Shoemaker Wilhelm Voigt donned the uniform of a military captain and organized a passport for himself in city hall. The incident inspired more than 10 films, some as early as 1907.

1909   4 September: Davidson opened his first Union Theater in the Grand Hotel on Berlin's famed Alexanderplatz. The facility had its own orchestra, a staple of all major film productions.

1910   28 November: Asta Nielsen, one of Germany's four leading ladies of silent film, made her debut in the Danish production *Abgründe* (*The Abyss*).

1911   January: Dr. Albert Hellwig called for stronger film censorship to combat what he called trashy films, but to no avail, as violence and eroticism continued to be a draw, especially in Berlin.

1913   *Der Andere* (*The Other*, Max Mack) and *Der Student von Prag* (*The Student of Prague*, Stellan Rye and Paul Wegener) premiered in Berlin 31 January and 22 August, respectively. The gothic tale and motif of the doppelgänger soon became staples of Germany's art cinema. **3 October:** *Die Insel der Seligen* (*The Island of the Blessed*), directed by Max Reinhardt, Germany's leading theater director, premiered in Union Theater on the Kurfürstendamm. The 1,000 seats, architectural design, and location impressed moviegoers and signified the growing importance of film in the city.

1914   3 October: Oskar Messter produced the first Messter-Woche newsreel. It reported on the war and government events. **December 15:** The German Ministry of War forbade movies that did not correspond to the seriousness of the times.

1915   15 January: *Der Golem* (*The Golem*), Henrik Galeen's gothic tale of a clay statue come to life, premiered. The film was followed by several sequels during the 1910s and a remake in 1920, *Der Golem, wie er in die welt kam* (*The Golem: How He Came into the World*, Carl

Boese and Paul Wegener). Wegener played the monster in both the original and remake.

1917   31 January: The Ministry of War established the Bild- und Filmamt (Bufa), an office for setting up film branches on the war front. In addition to supplying troops with movies, Bufa oversaw newsreel footage of the war, distributed Agfa's film stock to filmmakers, and oversaw film imports and exports. **2 March:** *Es werde Licht* (*Let There Be Light*), Richard Oswald's film on syphilis, ushered in a wave of sex enlightenment films. **18 December:** Emil Gerhard Strauß, the director of the Deutsche Bank, formed a consortium of interests and raised 25 million marks to create Universum-Film AG (Ufa), a film studio that became famous producing the best works of German film's golden age in the 1920s and infamous for its productions during the Third Reich, 1933–1945.

1918   11 November: World War I ended, creating a vacuum in government control that brought chaos to Germany. The trauma of the lost war, nascent revolution, and general misery at home was reflected in a new wave of horror films, including Robert Wiene's *Das Cabinet des Dr. Caligari* (*The Cabinet of Dr. Caligari*, 1920), Fritz Lang's *Der müde Tod* (*Destiny*, 1921), and Friedrich Wilhelm Murnau's *Nosferatu* (*Nosferatu*, 1922). **12 November:** A government council abolished censorship. Until controls were reinstated a few years later, the German film industry produced a number of erotic movies whose provocative themes resulted in a backlash from Germany's religious leaders.

1919   28 May: Not all of the erotica was exploitative. Richard Oswald continued to make sex enlightenment films that were meant to engage the audience in discourse about the need for change. His *Anders als die Andern* (*Different from the Others*) was directed at repealing paragraph 175 of the penal code, which made homosexuality a crime. **31 May:** The first edition of *Film-Kurier* appeared. It became the most important medium for discussing the popular arts. During the Third Reich it became a mouthpiece for Nazi propaganda, promoting the regime's agenda. Later that year, an illustrated version also appeared. **18 September:** Ernst Lubitsch's *Madame Dubarry* (*Passion*) premiered at the grand opening of the Ufa-Palast am Zoo, anticipating the important role film would play in the popular culture of the Weimar

Republic and starring two of Germany's biggest actors of the 1920s, Emil Jannings and Pola Negri.

1920 **27 February:** *Das Cabinet des Dr. Caligari* (*The Cabinet of Dr. Caligari*) premiered. It remains a unique example of German film expressionism. **12 May:** Censorship was reintroduced at a federal and state level. Henceforth all films had to be screened by an examining board to receive a permit. **29 June:** Two of Europe's leading studios, the French Decla KG and the German Deutsche Bioscop AG, merged to form Decla-Bioscop AG.

1921 **7 October:** *Der müde Tod* (*Destiny*) premiered. Directed by Fritz Lang from a screenplay by Thea von Harbou, the film continued German cinema's fascination with the macabre. **11 October:** Decla-Bioscop merged into Universum Film AG (Ufa), bringing heavy debts that burdened the giant film company for the rest of the 1920s. **11 December:** *Hintertreppe* (*Backstairs*, Paul Leni and Leopold Jessner), a pessimistic melodrama, premiered. As dark and brooding as most gothic tales but without the creatures, the movie's success offered an alternate genre for reflecting the despair of Weimar Germany in the early 1920s.

1922 **31 January:** *Fridericus Rex* (*Fridericus Rex*, Arzén von Cserépy) premiered. The film was the first of four to appear over the next two years, all starring Otto Gebühr, who continued playing Frederick the Great through 1942. **4 March:** *Nosferatu: eine Symphonie des Grauens* (*Nosferatu*, Friedrich Wilhelm Murnau) premiered. **17 September:** Physicist Jo Engl and mechanical engineers Joseph Massolle and Hans Vogt introduced their Tri-Ergon Process, which affixed sound to the film strip and thus made synchronized sound films possible. Unfortunately the process failed during a demonstration two years later. Thus Hollywood and not Germany produced the first sound film, *The Jazz Singer* (Alan Crosland, 1927), starring Al Jolson.

1923 **16 November:** Germany's rampant inflation was curtailed through currency reform, allowing for the country's eventual economic recovery, reflected also in the development of German film.

1924 **14 February:** *Siegfrieds Tod* (*Siegfried's Death*), the first part of Fritz Lang's monumental film, *Die Nibelungen*, based on the legend of the Nibelungen, premiered in Berlin with orchestral accompaniment.

The most expensive film to date for Universum Film AG (Ufa), the second part, *Kriemhilds Rache* (*Kriemhild's Revenge*), followed on **26 April**. **17 September:** Ufa merged the newsreels *Deulig-Woche* and *Messter-Woche* to create the *Ufa-Wochenschau*, a newsreel that became an important propaganda tool during the Third Reich. **19 December:** To stave off bankruptcy, Ufa joined in a partnership with Paramount and Metro-Goldwyn-Mayer, through which they were to cooperate in showing each other's films. The new venture, dubbed Parufamet, worked to the disadvantage of the German studio, necessitating another bailout a few years later. **23 December:** Friedrich Wilhelm Murnau's *Der letzte Mann* (*The Last Laugh*) premiered. Starring Emil Jannings, the film also introduced the innovative camera work of Karl Freund, whose evocative and fluid style reduced the need for intertitles in the film.

1926   29 April: Sergei Eisenstein's *Battleship* Potemkin premiered at the Apollo Theater in Berlin. The Soviet film unleashed a month-long debate over its revolutionary content. In spite of that content, Joseph Goebbels, later minister of propaganda under Adolf Hitler, extolled the film's power and asked German filmmakers to emulate its emotional impact.

1927   10 January: *Metropolis* (*Metropolis*) premiered at the Ufa-Palast in Berlin. With a score for full orchestra by Gottfried Huppertz, monumental sets, a cast of thousands of extras, and a length of two and one-half hours, the film exceeded the cost of Fritz Lang's *Nibelungen*, until then the most expensive production of Universum Film AG (Ufa). **28 March:** Ufa was taken over by a consortium controlled by Alfred Hugenberg, a conservative German publisher.

1929   9 February: The premier of *Die Büchse der Pandora* (*Pandora's Box*, Georg Wilhelm Pabst) made American Louise Brooks an internationally acclaimed star. **13 March:** The two studios specializing in sound production, Ton-bild-Syndikat AG and Klangfilm GmbH, merged to form Tobis-Klangfilm, a leader with Universum Film AG (Ufa) in the pioneering of sound film in Germany. **21 December:** Arnold Fanck's *Die weiße Hölle von Piz Palü* (*The White Hell of Pitz Palu*), starring Leni Riefenstahl, played for the grand opening of the Ufa-Palast in Hamburg. It had 2,667 seats, making it the largest movie theater in Europe. **30 December:** *Mutter Krausens Fahrt ins Glück*

(*Mother Krause's Journey to Happiness*), a film made to raise social awareness of the situation of the working poor, premiered. It was one of the few films of the Far Left to achieve critical success. It was also one of the last important silent films. Four decades later, Rainer Werner Fassbinder paid homage to the film in *Mutter Küsters' Fahrt zum Himmel* (*Mother Küsters Goes to Heaven*, 1975).

1930 1 April: *Der blaue Engel* (*The Blue Angel*, Josef von Sternberg) premiered in Berlin. Although billed as an Emil Jannings movie, the film's sensation was Marlene Dietrich. **23 May:** Georg Wilhelm Pabst's *Westfront 1918* (*Comrades of 1918*) premiered to international acclaim. A pacifist war drama, the film was banned after the Nazis came to power in 1933. *Stoßtrupp 1917* (*Shock Troop 1917*, Hans Zöberlein and Ludwig Schmid-Wildy 1934) presented a Nazi counterpoint to the film.

1931 19 February: *Die Dreigroschenoper* (*The Threepenny Opera*), Georg Wilhelm Pabst's adaptation of Bertolt Brecht's musical, opened after the playwright lost a suit alleging distortion of his original concept. **11 May:** *M* (*M*), Fritz Lang's masterpiece about a child murderer, opened in Berlin. Voted German film's most important movie in 1994, *M* gave its star Peter Lorre international recognition and also typecast him as a maniacal killer. **28 November:** *Mädchen in Uniform* (*Girls in Uniform*, Leontine Sagan) was released. Banned two years later by the Nazis because of its homosexual theme, the film later became a cult classic.

1932 24 March: Leni Riefenstahl made her debut as director with *Das blaue Licht* (*The Blue Light*), a mountain film that showcased the director's striking beauty. **14 May:** *Kuhle Wampe oder Wem gehört die Welt?* (*Kuhle Wampe*, aka *Whither Germany?* Slatan Dudow) premiered in Moscow. Because of its content, which criticized Germany's social institutions, the film had to submit to major changes demanded by the censors. *Kuhle Wampe* was banned once the Nazis came to power.

1933 30 January: President Hindenburg named Adolf Hitler chancellor. Shortly thereafter the Nazis took over the government through a series of political maneuvers. **13 March:** Joseph Goebbels was named minister of propaganda, a position that gave him control of the film industry as well as the other arts. **28 March:** Goebbels made the first of his many speeches to members of the film establishment. He called for reforming German film from the roots but at the same time assured those present they had nothing to fear from his reforms. **14 July:** A new law decreed that in future only members of the Filmkammer (Film Guild) could be engaged in anything to do with producing, distributing, or exhibiting film. Only small-town exhibitors were exempted from joining. As applications from the industry's Jewish members were not accepted, the law effectively banned Jews from working in film. **11 September:** *Hitlerjunge Quex* (*Hitler Youth Quex*, Hans Steinhoff) premiered in Munich. Owing to the nature of the film as a vehicle for propaganda, Adolph Hitler was in attendance.

1934   16 February: The office of the film director was given power to precensor movies. Films could henceforth be banned at any stage in their production, from idea to finished film.

1935   28 March: *Triumph des Willens* (*Triumph of the Will*), Leni Riefenstahl's documentary of the 1934 rally of National Socialists in Nuremberg, premiered with Adolf Hitler and Joseph Goebbels in the audience. The film established Riefenstahl as an accomplished documentary filmmaker, but the blatant propaganda of its message saddled her with the reputation of being Hitler's director.

1936   18 September: *Glückskinder* (*Lucky Kids*, Paul Martin) premiered. The film was made in response to Goebbels's admonition that German filmmakers should try to copy Hollywood's style. *Glückskinder* is a screwball comedy in the manner of *It Happened One Night* (Frank Capra, 1934). **26 November:** Goebbels decreed that henceforth art criticism had to limit itself to film description and eschew any evaluation of the film's merits.

1937   19 March: The National Socialist government completed its takeover of the German film industry by creating the Cautio Treuhandgesellschaft, a trust that took controlling interest of Universum Film AG (Ufa) and established dummy concerns to oversee film production.

1938   20 April: *Olympia. Teil I: Fest der Völker, Teil II: Fest der Schönheit* (*Olympia. Part I: Festival of the People, Part II: Festival of Beauty*), premiered in Berlin with Adolf Hitler in the audience. The film employed 44 cameramen. **9 November:** The SA militia, reputedly supported by the government, staged a pogrom throughout Germany against Jewish shopkeepers and synagogues. The night, in which stores were looted and people mistreated and even killed, became known as Kristallnacht, or Night of Broken Glass.

1939 1 September: German soldiers, disguised as Polish soldiers, faked an attack on a German radio station in Gleiwitz (Gliwice) and used the manufactured incident to attack Poland, thereby starting World War II.

1940 5 September: *Jud Süß* (*Jew Süss*, Veit Harlan), the most notoriously anti-Semitic narrative film of the Third Reich, premiered in Venice, Italy. The film's virulently anti-Semitic sentiments brought the film's director and principle actors into disrepute after the collapse of the Third Reich, with few being able to restart their careers after the war. The film's closing words, "Juden raus" ("Out with the Jews"), reflected the Nazi policy of deporting the Jews to concentration camps. **28 November:** *Der ewige Jude* (*The Eternal Jew*, Fritz Hippler) premiered in Berlin. The most overtly anti-Semitic of the National Socialist films, *Der ewige Jude,* represented a documentary complement to *Jud Süß*, using distortions and fabrications to represent the Jews as a danger to Germany.

1941 4 April: *Ohm Krüger* (*Ohm Krüger*, Hans Steinhoff) earned the title "Film der Nation" (Film of the Nation). Emil Jannings starred as a freedom fighter during the Boer War. One of the film's set pieces showed German citizens being herded into a concentration camp, a cruel example of Nazi cynicism in light of their deportation of Jews to the camps. **29 August:** Wolfgang Liebeneiner's *Ich klage an* (*I Accuse*) premiered. The film's theme of a person's right to die relocated the debate of euthanasia of the mentally retarded and physically disabled, a policy opposed by Germany's religious leaders, to a more acceptable discourse on mercy killing of the terminally ill. **31 August:** *Heimkehr* (*Homecoming*, Gustav Ucicky) premiered in Italy, at the Venice Film Festival. Ucicky paid homage to Eisenstein's *The Battleship* Potemkin, one of Joseph Goebbels's favorite films, by staging a scene similar to the massacre on the Odessa Steps. **7 November:** The actor Joachim Gottschalk and his family committed suicide before the wife and child could be deported to a concentration camp. The incident became the subject of one of Germany's major postwar films, *Ehe im Schatten* (*Marriage in the Shadows*, Kurt Maetzig, 1947).

1942   10 January: All film companies, including Wien-Film (Viennese-Film), were merged into the newly created Ufa-Film GmbH. **12 June:** *Die große Liebe* (*The Great Love*, Rolf Hansen) premiered with Zarah Leander in the lead role. The film became one of the Third Reich's biggest commercial successes, seen by 27 million viewers.

1943   2 February: The Battle of Stalingrad ended with the total defeat of the German Sixth Army, creating a mood of despair among the populace. Joseph Goebbels's propaganda policies combatted pessimism with films whose stories called for persevering until the end (*Durchhaltung*). The Battle of Stalingrad became the subject of popular postwar films. Among these are the German films *Hunde, wollt ihr ewig leben?* (*Dogs, Do You Want to Live Forever?* Frank Wisbar, 1959), *Der Arzt von Stalingrad* (*The Doctor of Stalingrad*, Géza von Radványi, 1958), and *Stalingrad* (*Stalingrad*, Joseph Vilsmaier, 1992). **25 June:** Helmut Käutner's *Romanze in Moll* (*Romance in a Minor Key*) premiered. Joseph Goebbels thought the film defeatist. Viewers liked its romantic mood. After the war French critics declared it a beautiful love story.

1945   30 January: *Kolberg* (*Kolberg*), a prestige project that had obsessed Joseph Goebbels for years, premiered behind enemy lines, as Germany found the Allies pressing from both fronts. Speaking to a group of film dignitaries before the premier, Goebbels asked them how they wanted to be remembered in the future, as the heroes depicted in *Kolberg* or as cowards. **1 May:** Joseph and Magda Goebbels murdered their children and then committed suicide rather than be captured by the Allies. The incident is depicted in chilling detail by Oliver Hirschbiegel in *Der Untergang* (*The Downfall*, 2004). **8 May:** The war in Europe ended. The film industry had been totally destroyed and took several years to recover completely.

1946   17 May: The Deutsche Film Aktiengesellschaft (DEFA) was established in the old film studios in Babelsberg, in the Soviet sector of Germany. The newly formed company remained under Soviet management until 1953, at which time it passed into East German control. **15 October:** The first postwar German film, *Die Mörder sind unter uns* (*The Murderers Are among Us*), premiered. Wolfgang Staudte, who directed the film, was turned down by the Allies in the Western sectors before finally receiving a license from the Soviets. **20 December:** *Sag die Wahrheit (Tell the Truth)* was the first postwar film to be licensed by the Western sectors. Helmut Weiss's comedy used a screenplay written during the Third Reich.

1947 **3 October:** *Ehe im Schatten (Marriage in the Shadows*, Kurt Maetzig) premiered in Berlin. Produced by DEFA, the film continued the Soviet-controlled studio's interest in confronting the past.

1949 **March–April:** Veit Harlan, director of *Jud Süß*, one of the Third Reich's few openly anti-Semitic works, went on trial for crimes against humanity and was acquitted. Gustaf Grüdgens and Wolfgang Liebeneiner testified on his behalf. **24 May:** The constitution of the Federal Republic of Germany (West Germany) became effective. Created out of the American, French, and British sectors, the new country's film policies would develop differently than those in the German Democratic Republic (East Germany), a country that was established **7 October** out of the Soviet sector. **18 July:** The West German film industry created the Freiwillige Selbstkontrolle Filmwirtschaft (FSK), a self-censoring film body modeled after the Hayes Commission in America. **14 December:** The Spitzenorganisation der Filmwirtschaft (SPIO) was founded to represent the interests of West German film. The organization oversaw the activity of the FSK.

1950 **15 May:** *Unter den Brücken (Under the Bridges*, Helmut Käutner), finished in the last year of the Third Reich, premiered six years after its completion. French, Swiss, and German critics praised the film's lyrical tone and neorealistic style. **7 September:** *Schwarzwaldmädel (The Black Forest Girl*, Hans Deppe) became the biggest commercial success of the postwar period. Its theme of nostalgia began a wave of Heimat films, movies that helped viewers flee the problems and worries of postwar Germany by offering them romantic idylls set in the German countryside, pre-1918 Germany, or both.

1951 **18 January:** *Die Sünderin (The Sinner*, Willi Forst) premiered against protests from West Germany's conservative and religious leaders. The film made Hildegard Knef an international star. **31 March:** West Germany created a film subsidy policy that would be revised repeatedly over the next five decades. The first version underwrote 35 percent of production costs for films deemed worthy of support by a committee of the Ministry of the Interior. Between 1951 and 1953, 93 films were supported. **6 June:** The German Film Prize for excellence in various aspects of filmmaking was awarded for the first time. *Das doppelte Löttchen* (*Two Times Lotte*), directed by Josef von Báky, won as best film. **6–18 June:** An International Film Festival took place in Berlin. The Berlin Film festival would become an annual event and rival the festivals in Venice and Cannes in importance.

1952   17–18 September: Participants at a film conference in East Germany, in keeping with the tenets of socialist realism, discussed the need for making their films optimistic and oriented to the future.

1953   9 June: The film subsidization policy was changed to underwrite up to 100 percent of a film's production costs. Within two years, the policy had cost 21 million marks.

1954   9 March: *Ernst Thälmann – Sohn seiner Klasse* (*Ernst Thälmann: Son of His Class*, Kurt Maetzig), the first part of DEFA's prestige film on the life of the German communist hero Ernst Thälmann, premiered in East Berlin. The second film, *Ernst Thälmann – Führer seiner Klasse* (*Ernst Thälmann: Leader of His Class*), followed at the beginning of October 1955. **27–30 October:** The first West German festival of short films took place in Oberhausen, in the state of North Rhine-Westfalia. The festival became an annual event, best known as the origin of the Oberhausen Manifesto in 1962. **1 November:** East Germany established a film school in Babelsberg, the Deutsche Hochschule für Filmkunst. In 1969 the name was changed to Deutsche Hochschule für Film und Fernsehen to reflect the growing importance of television, and in 1985 the name of the country's premier director, Konrad Wolf, was affixed to the title in memory of his contributions to East German film.

1955   11–17 September: The Kultur- und Dokumentarfilmwoche, which was to become East Germany's most important international film festival, took place in Leipzig.

1956   27 September: Georg Tresler's *Die Halbstarken* (*Teenage Wolfpack*, aka *The Hooligans*) premiered in Essen. One year later East Germany followed with its own youth film, *Berlin – Ecke Schönhauser* (*Berlin: Schönhauser Corner*, Gerhard Klein).

1957   January: The first edition of *Filmkritik*, edited by Theodor Kotulla and Enno Patalas, was published in Munich. The journal became an important voice for film criticism during the 1960s and 1970s, the years of New German Cinema. It ceased publication in 1984. **27 July:** West Germany passed a law proscribing attendance at movies by children under six. The law set further age restrictions of 12, 16, and 18 years of age, depending on film content.

1958   3–5 July: A film conference in East Berlin called for more social realism in film and less social criticism.

1959   22 October: Bernhard Wicki's *Die Brücke* (*The Bridge*) premiered in Mannheim. The antiwar film told of a group of schoolboys who were drafted into the war effort in the last days of fighting. It became an international success.

1961   25 June: Reflecting the state of German film at the time, no awards were given for best film or director at the annual awards ceremony. **13 August:** The East German government erected a wall on the border between East and West Berlin. The presence of the Berlin Wall gave occasion for American President John Kennedy to proclaim that everyone was a resident of Berlin (26 June 1963) and for President Ronald Reagan to admonish Mikhail Gorbachev to tear down the wall (12 June 1987).

1962   28 February: At the 8th Oberhausen Kurzfilmtage, a new generation of filmmakers declared that the old cinema was dead, and they were prepared to create movies as they should be made. Among the signers was Alexander Kluge, the intellectual leader of Young German Cinema (later New German Cinema). **12 December:** The success of *Der Schatz im Silbersee* (*The Treasure in Silver Lake*, Harald Reinl) led to a new genre, the Karl May film, German-made Westerns based on the best-selling books of nineteenth-century author Karl May.

1963   10 April: *Nackt unter Wölfen* (*Naked among Wolves*, Frank Beyer) premiered in East Berlin. The film tells of a young boy protected by inmates from being murdered by concentration camp authorities. **30 November:** The first Kommunales Kino or community cinema was opened in Munich. The community cinemas became important venues for playing the films of Germany's alternative filmmakers.

1965 **1 February:** The Kuratorium Junger Deutscher Film e.V. was established in Munich, creating a pool of money to subsidize films by new directors. **16–18 December:** A meeting of the Central Committee of the East German Communist Party (The 11th Plenum des Zentralkomitees der SED) criticized German filmmakers for betraying the spirit of socialism. Leaders singled out for particularly harsh words the films *Das Kaninchen bin ich* (*I Am the Rabbit*, Kurt Maetzig), and *Denk bloß nicht, ich heule* (*Just Don't Think I'll Cry*, Frank Vogel).

1966 **3 February:** The Friedrich-Wilhelm-Murnau-Stiftung, a trust for the preservation of German film, was established in Wiesbaden. The trust has become an important source for German film research. **20 May:** Volker Schlöndorff's *Der junge Törless* (*The Young Törless*) premiered at the Cannes Film Festival in France. Although it was not the first film of the new wave of German films, many see Schlöndorff's film as the beginning of a new era of German filmmaking. **30 June:** *Spur der Steine* (*Trace of Stones*, Frank Beyer) had a brief run in East Berlin before being banned and joining the list of Verbotsfilme that were not seen until 1989.

1967 **28 May:** The Hofer Filmtage, a film festival in the town of Hof, held its inaugural program. The festival had no central theme other than to spotlight all types of films from Germany and abroad, giving particular attention to films by new directors.

1968 **1 January:** A new system of subsidies was created, overseen by the Filmförderungsanstalt (federal film board). Filmmakers received assistance determined by the commercial or critical success of previous projects. **3 February:** *Chronik der Anna Magdalena Bach* (*Chronicle of Anna Magdalene Bach*, Jean-Marie Straub and Danièle Huillet) premiered. After being turned down for assistance by the subsidy selection committee, the filmmaker received funds from a nonprofit corporation set up by Alexander Kluge, Enno Patalas, and Volker Schlöndorff.

1970 **26 June–7 July:** Michael Verhoeven's anti-Vietnam film *o.k.* (*o.k.*) created a controversy at the Berlin Film Festival because of its subject matter, the rape of a young Vietnamese woman by a band of American soldiers. **18 April:** A group of directors founded the Filmverlag der Autoren to help distribute German films. The organization helped New German Film gain an international reputation. **April–July:** The experimental nature of the new wave of German filmmakers led to the opening of a pub for the showing of films. For a modest entry fee patrons could put together their own program from 22 short films by the founders, Ula Stöckl and Edgar Reitz.

1972   29 December: *Aguirre, der Zorn Gottes* (*Aguirre, the Wrath of God*) premiered in Cologne. The film teamed director Werner Herzog with the eccentric actor Klaus Kinski in the first of five films. Their turbulent collaboration became the subject of a documentary by Herzog, *Mein liebster Feind – Klaus Kinski* (*My Best Fiend*, 1999).

1973   29 April: The most popular film of DEFA's history, *Die Legende von Paul und Paula* (*The Legend of Paul and Paula*, Heiner Carow), premiered in East Germany. Twenty-five years later, Leander Haußmann paid homage to the film by casting actor Winfried Glatzeder in a cameo and reprising a scene in which he tries to break in a door with an axe.

1974   June: The first edition of the feminist film journal *Frauen und Film* appeared in West Berlin. Published by Helke Sander, the journal championed women filmmakers and discussed feminist film theory. **22 December:** *Jakob der Lügner* (*Jacob the Liar*, Frank Beyer) premiered on East German television. It was the only East German film ever nominated for an Academy Award in the Best Foreign Film category.

1975   29 June: Bernhard Sinkel's social-political satire, *Lina Braake oder Die Interessen der Bank können nicht die Interessen sein, die Lina Braake hat* (*Lina Braake or The Interests of the Bank Cannot Be the Same as the Interests of Lina Braake*), premiered at the Berlin Film Festival. The film reflected the growing dissatisfaction with the status quo of Germany's conservative government. **9 October:** *Die verlorene Ehre der Katharina Blum* (*The Lost Honor of Katharina Blum*, Volker Schlöndorff and Margarethe von Trotta) divided the Left and Right after its premier. Based on the eponymous political novella by Heinrich Böll, the film was a cinematic broadside against the Springer Publishing Company and its government supporters. **4 November:** The system of film subsidies was enhanced through an agreement with the television networks, in which they would finance films for exclusive broadcast rights after two years.

1976   2 February: *Newsweek* magazine published a title story on New German Cinema, "The German Film Boom." Similar articles in *Time* and America's leading newspapers elevated the status of German film in America. Within a short period German film became a subdiscipline in German studies. **4 March:** Wim Wenders's buddy film *Im Lauf der Zeit* (*Kings of the Road*) premiered in West Berlin. The film reflected the love-hate relationship of German filmmakers with American culture.

1977 21–22 September: Hans-Jürgen Syberberg's *Hitler, ein Film aus Deutschland* (*Hitler, a Film from Germany*) premiered in London.

1978 3 March: *Deutschland im Herbst* (*Germany in Autumn*), an omnibus film directed by a consortium of Germany's leading filmmakers, premiered at the Berlin Film Festival. The film documented the political malaise among the Left caused by three events in the autumn of 1977: the kidnapping and eventual murder of industrialist Hanns-Martin Schleyer by members of the Red Army Faction; the failed hijacking of a plane to Mogadishu; and the supposed suicides of Andreas Baader, Gudrun Enslin, and Jean-Carl Raspe in Stammheim prison. **6 October:** *Messer im Kopf* (*Knife in the Head*, Reinhard Hauff) continued New German Cinema's focus on terrorism and political institutions in West Germany.

1979 20 February: Rainer Werner Fassbinder's *Die Ehe der Maria Braun* (*The Marriage of Maria Braun*) premiered at the beginning of the Berlin Film Festival. In retrospect, the film represents the apogee of Fassbinder's career and the films of New German cinema. **27 February:** *David* (*David*, Peter Lilienthal) premiered at the end of the Berlin festival. One of the first West German films to deal with Jewish persecution under the Nazis, the film won the Golden Bear. **3 May:** *Die Blechtrommel* (*The Tin Drum*, Volker Schlöndorff), based on the eponymous novel by Günter Grass, premiered in West Germany. The film won the Golden Palm Award at the Cannes Film Festival in France and also won an Academy Award for Best Foreign Film, the first feature film from Germany to be so honored. **1 July:** The film subsidy law was revised, raising the seat tax on moviegoers and forming a nine-member commission to oversee approval of projects. **21 November:** Women working in the film industry founded the Verband der Filmarbeiterinnen e.V, an organization to further the interests of women in the various branches of film, which included access to subsidies, jobs in film, and acceptances to film schools.

1981   27 August: The Bundesland (federal state) of Bavaria announced a subsidy program to promote the Bavarian film industry. In subsequent years, most German states established similar programs. **18 September:** *Das Boot* (*The Boat*, Wolfgang Petersen) premiered in Munich. At the time, the film was the most expensive German film ever made.

1982   7 March: Konrad Wolf, East Germany's most innovative and critically successful director, died. Wolf knew how to reconcile the disjuncture between government restrictions on artists and the artist's responsibility to be true to his art. **10 June:** Rainer Werner Fassbinder, the most critically successful director of New German Cinema, died. Fassbinder had become an unofficial catalyst of new wave German cinema. **30 October:** The premier of Herbert Achternbusch's *Das Gespenst* (*The Ghost*) created controversy when the FSK, the film commission overseeing the release of films, asked that the film be banned. The minister of the interior refused to release to Achternbusch the grant subsidy, which he had been awarded to make the movie. The event caused a reformation of film policies in Germany, which together with the void created by Fassbinder's death, diminished German film's reputation as a source of auteur cinema and led to what many film historians interpret as the end of New German Cinema.

1984   6 April: *Die unendliche Geschichte* (*The Neverending Story*, Wolfgang Petersen) premiered in Munich. Its cost of DM 60,000,000 eclipsed that of *Das Boot*, until then the most expensive German production. The film was made in English and anticipated a trend of German film to eschew art house pictures in favor of movies that could be successful in international wide release. **19 May:** Wim Wenders's *Paris, Texas* won the Golden Palm in Cannes. The movie marked Wenders's attempt to merge art cinema with international success by filming in English and using well-known stars. **June:** Book publisher edition text + kritik began publishing *Cinegraph*, a loose-leaf film historical compendium of the life and work of Germans associated with filmmaking. **30 June–1 July:** *Heimat*, Edgar Reitz's monumental made-for-television film, premiered at the Munich Film Festival. It told the fictional history of Schabbach, a small town in the Hunsrück region of Germany.

1985 **18 July:** The comedy *Otto – Der Film* (*Otto: The Film*, Xaver Schwarzenberger and Otto Waalkes) premiered. Produced for DM 6,000,000, the film earned 12 times that in box office receipts and led to a wave of German comedies. **25 October:** Dorris Dörrie's *Männer* (*Men*) premiered in Hof. The film was a phenomenal success and made Dörrie one of German film's leading directors.

1987 **17 May:** *Der Himmel über Berlin* (*Wings of Desire*, Wim Wenders) premiered at the Cannes Film Festival in France. The film won international acclaim and achieved cult status among cineastes, winning the German film industry's Award in Gold for Best Picture.

1989 **9 November:** The Berlin Wall was opened, allowing for free movement between the two German states. The scene has been captured in films as diverse as *Ich bin meine eigene Frau* (*I Am My Own Woman*, Rosa von Praunheim, 1992), *Herr Lehmann* (*Mr. Lehmann*, Leander Haußmann, 2003) and *Good Bye, Lenin!* (*Good Bye Lenin!* Wolfgang Becker, 2003).

1990 **14 February:** *Das Schreckliche Mädchen* (*The Nasty Girl*) premiered at the Berlin Film Festival. The film's story, about a young woman's attempts to bring to light the truth of her town's involvement in the atrocities of the Third Reich, brought the director Michael Verhoeven international acclaim. **3 October:** The two German states, The Federal Republic of Germany (West Germany) and The German Democratic Republic (East Germany), were united under the West German constitution.

1992 **18 January:** *Europa Europa*, which had been released in France in 1990, won a Golden Globe for Best Film. The film had created a controversy in Germany after the German jury that selects the country's nominee for the Academy Award competition in the Best Foreign Film category passed over Agnieszka Holland's dark comedy. **11 March:** The political comedy *Schtonk* (*Schtonk*, Helmut Dietl), about forged Hitler diaries, premiered in Munich. The film was a box office success, was nominated for an Academy Award as Best Foreign Film, and won the German film industry's Award in Gold. **25 August:** Volker Schlöndorff, who began his film career in New German Cinema, became director of the newly created Studio Babelsberg GmbH. **October:** The first number of *KINtop* was published. The appearance of this annual volume on early film history pointed to the growing acceptance of film studies in the German academic community.

1993 1 January: German film subsidization policies were revised once again in an attempt to combat the growing influence of Hollywood, whose films had 80 percent of German screens in the early 1990s. **18 February:** *Abgeschminkt* (*Making Up!* Katja von Garnier) premiered. The film, which was the director's final degree project in film school, became a phenomenal success and created a wave of romantic comedies that lasted throughout the 1990s.

1994 6 October: The relationship comedy *Der bewegte Mann* (*Maybe . . . Maybe Not*, Sönke Wortmann) premiered. It continued the phenomenal success of Katja Riemann, the star of *Abgeschminkt!*, and made Til Schweiger an international star. **November:** The Deutscher Kinematheksverbund (German Film Society) released a list of the 100 most significant German films on the occasion of the 100th anniversary of the birth of motion pictures. Fritz Lang's *M* was number one. (See "100 Most Significant Films" at the end of the book for other movie titles).

1996 4 July: *Jenseits der Stille* (*Beyond Silence*, Caroline Link) premiered in Munich. The movie's uplifting tone signaled a new era for the reputation of German film abroad, generally viewed outside Germany as pessimistic and dark.

1997 2–5 October: A conference to reexamine films produced by DEFA, organized by the University of Massachusetts, raised the profile of films from East Germany and brought them wider recognition.

1998 29 April: Film policy was changed once again, eliminating the obligation of television networks to contribute to the production of films. **20 August:** *Lola rennt* (*Run Lola Run*, Tom Tykwer) premiered in Berlin, giving German film a boost throughout the world.

2000 June–July: The Stiftung Deutsche Kinemathek (German Cinema Foundation) moved into new facilities at Germany's Potsdamer Platz, a showcase of urban renewal after unification of the two German states. In addition to movie auditoriums and meeting rooms, the new facility contains a film museum of the origins of film in Germany and a tribute display to Marlene Dietrich.

2001   22 June: The name of the German award for honoring those in the film industry was changed from Film Award in Gold and Film Award in Silver to Lola in Gold and Lola in Silver. **19 October:** *Der Schuh des Manitu* (*Manitou's Shoe*, Michael Herbig) premiered. The film was both parody of and homage to the Winnetou films of the 1960s. It became the highest grossing German film since 1945.

2002   14 June: Caroline Link's *Nirgendwo in Afrika* (*Nowhere in Africa*) won a Lola in Gold from the German film industry. The nostalgic movie, about a Jewish family that escapes persecution by immigrating to Africa, won an Oscar for Best Foreign Film the next year.

2003   6 June: *Good Bye, Lenin!* (Wolfgang Becker) won a Lola in Gold for Best Film. The film tapped into a wave of nostalgia for the German Democratic Republic. **8 September:** The Deutsche Filmakademie (German Film Academy) was founded in Berlin. The Academy was given the responsibility of promoting German film and was put in charge of the awards ceremony.

2004   5–15 February: Fatih Akin's *Gegen die Wand* (*Head-On*) premiered at the Berlin Film Festival. Akin's film won a Golden Bear, the first German film to win in 18 years. **17 May:** *Die fetten Jahre sind vorbei* (*The Edukators*, Hans Weingartner) was the first German film to be in competition in Cannes in 11 years. Although it did not win, the film was well-received by critics and the public. **16 September:** *Der Untergang* (*The Downfall*, Oliver Hirschbiegel) premiered in Germany, occasioning once again national debate about the past.

2005   24 February: *Sophie Scholl – Die letzten Tage* (*Sophie Scholl: The Final Days*, Marc Rothemund) opened to critical and popular acclaim in Germany. One of a number of films in the late 1990s and early 2000s to revisit the past and the subject of collective guilt for Nazi crimes, *Sophie Scholl* was nominated for an academy Award as Best Foreign Film.

2006   23 March: *Das Leben der Anderen* (*The Lives of Others*, Florian Henckel von Donnersmarck) premiered. Over the next year the film became the most honored German production in decades, being nominated for or winning most of the West's top awards for its director and cast, culminating in an Oscar for Best Foreign Film.

2007 **11 January:** Dani Levy's *Mein Führer – Die wirklich wahrste Wahrheit über Adolf Hitler* (*Mein Führer: The Truly Truest Truth about Adolf Hitler*) premiered, causing debate about the appropriateness of broad comedy in confronting Germany's past. Defenders of the film pointed to Charles Chaplin's *The Great Dictator*, Ernst Lubitsch's *To Be or Not to Be*, and Roberto Benigni's *La vita è bella* (*Life Is Beautiful*, 1997) in support of the film.

Introduction

German film has a rich and extensive history. The mobility of people engaged in film during the silent era, the diaspora of German talent that occurred because of the rise of National Socialism, and the lure of fame in Hollywood almost since the advent of this new art form, has dispersed directors, actors, cinematographers, and technical talent everywhere films are made. Paradoxically, the ubiquitous presence of German film makes it transparent. Do we any longer see the shadows of German expressionism in the films noirs of 1940s and 1950s Hollywood? Can we recognize the fascist aesthetic of such films as *Starship Troopers* as originating in Nazi cinema, or a parody of **Leni Riefenstahl**'s *Triumph of the Will* in *Star Wars* or *Jewel of the Nile*? Would we be able to trace the sophisticated cynicism of Preston Sturges to the silent films of **Ernst Lubitsch** or recognize **Peter Lorre**'s portrayals in 1950s horror films as self-parodies of his first cinematic role in *M*? Does the evocative cinematography of **Michael Ballhaus** contribute anything German to his Hollywood films, and is a film like **Wolfgang Petersen**'s *Troy* more successful in Germany than in the United States because it exhibits the director's German sensibility?

Truly German film encompasses more than films from Germany or in the German language. It embraces immigrants to Germany in the 1910s and 1920s to take part in one of the world's most vibrant film cultures; it welcomes Hollywood actors appearing in the films of the directors of the New German Cinema in the 1970s. It exports but never lets go of actors on loan to Hollywood. It engages in coproductions with its partners in the European Union and beyond. It speaks English, yet looks German. It speaks German, yet could have been made in Hollywood. The film history that follows and the subsequent entries consider the complexity of the question "What is German cinema?" and offers an overview of the many facets of Germany's film culture.

1

BEGINNINGS

The history of motion pictures in Germany presents a paradox. Max and Emil **Skladanowsky** had invented the Bioscop projector. Their invention ran strips of film through two apparatuses that alternated the exposure of the film frames, improving the illusion of movement produced by systems then in use. By eliminating the rotating drums with slits of the zoetrope, praxinoscope, and *théâtre optique*, the projected movement could be shown to a larger audience and for a longer duration. The Skladanowskys introduced their invention in July 1895 at the Gasthaus Sello, a tavern in Pankow, a suburb of Berlin. A few months later they had a successful evening of projected motion in the Wintergarten, a Berlin theater. The evening's show consisted of nine films, showing, among other spectacles, a village folkdance, an acrobatic act, a boxing kangaroo, and a fight. In January 1896 their show was to play the Folies Bergere in Paris, but the exhibition was canceled because their technology had become obsolete. The Bioscop had been replaced by a projection system of Auguste and Louis Lumière, which used only one projector. Thus, although the German inventors could claim to be the first film exhibitors using a continuous projection system, the technology for what was to be a new art form came from elsewhere. Whether this fact disadvantaged Germany in the development of a film industry is difficult to say, but France, the United States, Italy, and Denmark made an impact in international cinema long before Germany.

Even though slow in reaching an international market, film production thrived domestically, with the formation, dissolution, and merging of companies. One of the first and certainly the most successful in the early years was a conglomeration of vertical film enterprises forged by **Oskar Messter**, who brought together various branches of filmmaking, from manufacture of equipment to production of films to exhibition. Messter adapted the Maltese cross for his projectors, after a design by Max Gliewe, and became one of the largest producers of projection equipment in Europe. He also produced film shorts, newsreels, and feature films. His motivation for beginning film production was simple: he needed to create product for his projectors. Many of the first reels were simply documentations of routine events and affairs of state. Titles such as *Am Brandenburgertor in Berlin* (*At the Brandenburg Gate in Berlin*, 1896), *Schlittschuläufer auf der West-Eisbahn* (*Skaters on the West-Ice*

Rink, 1896), *Die zahmen Affen mit ihrem Wärter* (*Tame Monkeys with their Handler*, 1897), and *Vor der Albert-Brücke* (*In Front of the Albert Bridge in Dresden*, 1897) reflect the same desire to document the everyday as the French pioneers, the Lumières, whose early films include *La sortie des usines Lumière* (*Employees Leaving the Lumière Factory*, 1895) and *Arrivée des congressistes à Neuville-sur-Saône* (*The Photographical Congress Arrives in Lyon*, 1895). But his early documentaries also included official events: *Stapellauf vom Kreuzer* Wilhelm der Große (*Launching of the Cruiser* Wilhelm the Great, 1897), *Seine Majestät Kaiser Wilhelm II. In Stettin* (*His Majesty William II in Stettin*, 1897), and *Die Deutsche Kaiser-Familie* (*The German Emperor's Family*, 1897).

In the early 1900s, Messter synchronized his projector with an Edison gramophone to produce sound pictures with his Biophon. The movies told short, simple stories through musical numbers. Technical problems with synchronization of film image and disc recording led to abandonment of the sound films until technology had improved in the 1920s, when the German film industry would again be innovative in sound movies. One of these early sound films was *Meißner Porzellan* (*Meißen Porcelain*, 1906) with **Henny Porten**, who, with Messter as her producer, became the first star of German film. By 1910, she was appearing in short features that told stories; these were simple melodramas of love-sick young women, family tragedies, but also comedies of error. Porten had a natural relationship with the camera that created a sentimental or experiential bond with viewers, which popularized the medium in Germany and gave it international élan.

Messter and Porten were of course not the sole force behind the growth of German film. Much of their early work was spectacle in nature, a performance or an exhibition in front of a camera. Film offered more than spectacle in the early years; it offered excitement, the immediacy of violence, emotion, tragedy. Film historian Curt Riess describes 250 films in Berlin in 1910 as containing 97 murders, 45 suicides, 51 infidelities, 12 seductions, 22 abductions, 25 drunks, and 45 prostitutes. The promise of mayhem and vice drew more and more viewers to the movie houses, which were appearing literally overnight throughout Berlin and other cities. Such morally questionable fare also gave theaters in Germany a reputation as locales for the under classes, which the respectable did not frequent. This was in contrast to France and other

European countries, where film was seen as an art form. German authorities became sufficiently worried that they set up a censorship review board in 1911, which required that cities prescreen films before exhibition and forbid those with objectionable content. As the boards were local, censorship was by city. Consequently films not shown in one city might be shown somewhere else, Berlin being the most liberal city in this regard.

The year 1913 is often seen as crucial for German film. Two films were released at that time, *Der Andere* (*The Other*, Max Mack) and *Der Student von Prag* (*The Student of Prague*, Stellan Rye and **Paul Wegener**), which introduced more complex stories and thus created awareness of film's potential as a serious dramatic medium. They also introduced a dark, sometimes gothic, element into German cinema that gave these works their reputation as brooding, pessimistic, and tragic, a reputation that was to be reinforced 60 years later by the films of **New German Cinema**. Both *Der Andere* and *Der Student von Prag* introduce the themes of the doppelgänger and monstrous other into German film, which persisted throughout the silent era. They were followed by *Der Golem* (*The Golem*, **Henrik Galeen** and Wegener, 1915), its sequels, and the six-part series *Homunculus* (Otto Rippert, 1916). The fascination with the occult on the one hand and obsession with abuse of power on the other seem a direct reflection of the era, a headlong rush into war and the disillusionment that quickly set in.

At the same time that German film was discovering its darker side, it was developing its commercial potential, producing comedies, mysteries, and melodramas. Porten continued making her films about young women in distress, seduced by callous men and her own naiveté. In addition to melodrama, comedy was important to the beginning of German film. Scantily clad women, cross-dressing, bad jokes, and pratfalls were a staple of burlesque theater. Film's ability to capture spectacle allowed stage routines to be adapted to film, either taking them over without change or adding minimal stories. **Ernst Lubitsch**, who was later to become one of Germany's and then Hollywood's successful directors, began his career with a series of slapstick comedies. Drawing upon his experience as a clumsy store clerk in his father's clothier business, Lubitsch developed the persona of Kommis Moritz, a schlemiel who dropped rolls of cloth, knocked over mannequins, and created havoc in other ways. He eventually tired of comedy because, as he said in later years, he had imagined a role as actor to be more than playing a fool (quoted in Curt Riess, *Das gab's nur einmal*, Frankfurt, Berlin, Vienna: Ullstein, 1985). Yet he continued to play comedic roles throughout the 1910s. At the end of the decade he turned to directing, focusing on dramatic films such as *Carmen* (*Gypsy Blood*, 1918), which portrays the passionate Gypsy of Prosper Mérimée's mid-nineteenth-century novel, and *Madame Dubarry* (*Passion*, 1919), the story of Louis XV's mistress. Lubitsch's blend of historical scope and private passion in these films contributed to Germany's reputation for quality films in the silent era. His choice of subject matter also reflected early cinema's inclination to adapt literary classics as a means to elevate the intellectual merit of the art form. Moreover, this early interest in adapting good literature anticipates the preference for the classics of later generations, from the Nazis in the 1930s to the postwar directors of the 1950s to the directors of New German Cinema in the 1960s and 1970s.

From its beginnings, the film industry has been a commercial business. Messter, Porten, Lubitsch, and the other pioneers of German film made films to earn money, and films that entertained and offered diversion were more likely to appeal to large audiences. Film was also to be a tool to educate viewers and to deliver a point of view. General Erich Ludendorff was one of the first to recognize the value of motion pictures for propaganda. He helped create Germany's first national film office, the Bild-und Filmamt (Bufa), which was to make propaganda films about the war. Other producers were also active in filming news footage of the war for their newsreels. Messter, for example, produced the *Messter-Woche*, but his news actualities focused on nonmilitary subjects. Bufa's films were no different. Instead of war coverage, they covered military parades and inspections of ships and equipment, avoiding images of combat.

The idea that film could be effective for Germany's image abroad was strong, however, and others continued working toward a consolidated production company. Emil Georg von Strauß, director of the Deutsche Bank, undertook an initiative to form a studio conglomerate that would, when completed, create the largest film studio in Germany. Working with industry leaders, the new company, **Universum-Film AG** (Ufa) merged the companies of David Oliver, Paul Davidson, and Messter; it also bought up shares in Austrian, Swiss, and Dutch firms. The new company's vertical integration reached into every aspect of the film industry: production, distribution, and exhibition. In 1921 Ufa bought a controlling share in Decla-Bioscop (*see* BIOSCOP GMBH BERLIN), Germany's second largest company, helping it to become synonymous with German film from 1917 to 1945.

THE WEIMAR PERIOD: 1918–1933

German film thrived after World War I. Developing a trend begun during the early years of film, the industry took two directions, producing sufficient commercial product to satiate demand for comedy, mystery, and adventure, and at the same time nurturing what later became known as the art film, films that had appeal for an audience that preferred theater, literature, and occasion for thought. The 1920s were the golden years of cinema for the entire film industry. The fact that films were silent, or at least had no dialogue, as they almost always had musical accompaniment, meant films could be distributed worldwide and allowed their stars to become internationally recognized. The United States, Italy, and France retained their active film production, but now Germany had joined their ranks, eclipsing Italy and at times surpassing even France's reputation as a leader. While the commercial success was certainly due to the quickly produced comedies, thrillers, and melodramas that were among the 600 films produced annually, the reputation for quality at the time and for film history rests with a few artistic works per year.

Weimar cinema is associated with directors, actors, cameramen, and writers who contributed styles, themes, and genres to film history, influencing not only films in 1920s Germany but elsewhere, and later generations as well. The first major picture after the armistice in 1918 was *Das Cabinet des Dr. Caligari* (*The Cabinet of Dr. Caligari*, **Robert Wiene**, 1920), a horror film that continued the gothic tradition begun by Galeen, Wegener, and others. After the war, however, films of murder, mistrust, and general malaise had additional significance, as mirrors of conditions in postwar Germany. *Dr. Caligari* was to have been an indictment of the misuse of authority that had caused the death of millions. Only the producers' timidity about openly criticizing government officials softened the film with a frame that attributed the horror to the delusions of a sanitarium inmate. The film nonetheless retained its power to comment on the dysfunction of the time. Expressionist sets mimicked the art of German painters and their emphasis on diagonals, shadows, and abstract forms. Exaggerated gestures, acting that called attention to itself, and trancelike stares suggested a nation unable to work through national trauma. *Dr. Caligari* was a phenomenon, both because of its popularity and because it was never successfully repeated. When Wiene tried to repeat his experiment in abstract cinema with later films, they failed. While no other directors tried to duplicate his style of complete artifice, they borrowed his themes. *Der müde Tod* (*Destiny*, **Fritz Lang**, 1921) adapts the myth of Orpheus and Eurydice to postwar Weimar, focusing on a woman who journeys to the underworld to bring back her dead lover, perhaps fallen in the just-ended war. *Nosferatu, eine Symphonie des Grauens* (*Nosferatu*, **Friedrich Wilhelm Murnau**, 1922) adapts Bram Stoker's *Dracula*, but privileges scenes of rats, plague, and death over the sexual themes of the novel, reflecting the prevalence of wounded veterans, refugees from the East, and victims of Spanish influenza that were present in the early years of the new republic.

The films made in the first five years of the Weimar Republic, by Ufa and Decla-Bioscop (after 1921 part of Ufa), made producers and directors heady with success. **Erich Pommer**, director of production at the studio after 1923, sanctioned expensive films by directors who had had previous successes: Lang had made the two-part series *Die Spinnen* (*The Spiders*, 1919/1920) and the two-part cycle *Die Nibelungen* (1924); Murnau had directed *Phantom* (*Phantom*, 1922) and *Der letzte Mann* (*The Last Laugh*, 1924). *Die Nibelungen* and *Der letzte Mann* in particular had given German film parity with Hollywood in quality, and the domestic and international box office of the two films was also good. But they had also been expensive. Lang's vision of the Germanic legend of Siegfried and Kriemhild featured monumental sets, thousands of extras, a motorized dragon, a symphonic score, and special effects, whose costs were not recouped. Moreover his next film, *Metropolis* (*Metropolis*, 1927), cost even more: four times what Lang had promised the studio it would. Murnau's *Tartüff* and *Faust*, both 1926, were prestige films. In retrospect the films are excellent adaptations of classics of French and German literature, but they nonetheless failed to appeal to the general viewer, who wanted action, and to the literary-oriented, who felt it sacrilege to violate classic literature by adapting it to a medium of sensations.

As a result of the financial debacles, Ufa faced financial difficulties and turned to Hollywood for help. The studio entered into a partnership with Paramount and Metro-Goldwyn Mayer that became the joint company Parufamet. As part of the agreement, the American studios would infuse Ufa with money to help it forego bankruptcy, and in return Ufa agreed to make 40 films and accept 40 films from America annually and to open 75 percent of Ufa screens to Parufamet's productions. The American companies in return agreed to play the German films in their theaters but without any firm guarantees. While the agreement saved Ufa from immediate bankruptcy, it eventually doomed the studio to seeking another bailout. The American studios for their part rejected German films for their theaters, and Ufa screens in Germany were dominated by movies from Paramount and MGM. Rescue this time came from Alfred Hugenberg, Germany's largest media magnate. Hugenberg wanted to extend the influence of his publishing empire, and movies offered him that opportunity. Not long after the purchase, though, it became clear that Ufa was in more serious financial difficulties than had been thought. The Parufamet agreement continued to place strain on the German company. Finally Ludwig Klitsch, a member of the board, negotiated new terms, which returned Ufa to profitability.

Ufa was also helped in regaining market share by the sound motion picture. Seen at first as a fad by Ufa leaders, sound movies were introduced to Germany by **Tobis-Film**. Sound had always been a part of film. Early in the medium's history, Messter had pioneered technology that synchronized sound and image, but the method was too imperfect to have lasting effect. In the early 1920s, Joseph Engl, Joseph Masolle, and Hans Vogt invented a method in which a sound strip was placed on the film, thus ensuring good synchronization. Their company, Tri-Ergon, worked with Ufa to produce the first sound film in 1925; but equipment breakdown led to abandonment of the project until Hollywood released *The Jazz Singer* (1927), credited with being the first commercially successful sound film. Tri-Ergon thereafter merged into a new company, Ton-Bild-Syndikat (Tobis), which entered into a cartel arrangement with Klangfilm AG, creating a partnership that controlled equipment for recording and playback. Klangfilm also entered into an agreement with Ufa, thus giving the company the technology to become a leader in the production of sound movies. Ufa, having entered into an arrangement with American sound studios that carved up potential markets, became the most successful purveyor of sound film in the early years, producing some of the major films of the era. By creating different language versions for its major titles, Ufa solved what could have been a major problem for the European market; for unlike silent films, sound films could not automatically be understood in multiple countries. Ufa's solution was to film in multiple languages during the same film-shoot. After a scene in one language was done filming, the same set was used to film in another language; sometimes the same actors and directors were used; sometimes new ones had to be brought in if accents or language fluency hindered filming. *Der blaue Engel* (*The Blue Angel*, Josef von Sternberg, 1930), *Der Kongreß tanzt* (*The Congress Dances*, Erik Charell, 1931), and *Die Dreigroschenoper* (*The Threepenny Opera*, **Georg Wilhelm Pabst**, 1931), among a number of other big-budget works, were all filmed in this manner.

THE THIRD REICH 1933–1945

The National Socialists came to power in January 1933. In the confrontational politics that defined the Weimar Republic, however, they had been exerting indirect influence on the cinema through disruptions of left-leaning films and patronage of ideologically conservative ones. One of the most notorious incidents involved the American film *All Quiet on the Western Front* (Lewis Milestone, 1930) based on Erich Maria Remarque's novel *Im Westen nichts Neues*, a pacifist war story told from the perspective of German soldiers. Although the novel had been read by millions and its depictions verified as authentic representations of the war by German officers, the film met with right-wing resistance. Demonstrations by brown-shirted Nazi paramilitary units disrupted exhibition of *All Quiet on the Western Front* at its premier in Berlin in 1931. Historians question the spontaneity of the disruptions and attribute them to political agitation by Joseph Goebbels, who denounced the film as "unpatriotic" and "Jewish." According to reports, Nazis had bought half of the tickets to the second showing of the movie. When the police tried to quell the disturbance caused by exploding stink bombs and the freeing of a pack of white mice in the auditorium, paramilitary thugs overwhelmed the police. Subsequently, rather than crack down on the Nazis, the government banned the film. Yet when a similar incident arose with exhibition of a right-wing film, *Das Flötenkonzert von Sanssouci* (*The Flute Concert of Sanssouci*, Gustav Ucicky, 1930), the police evicted the left-wing protestors and allowed the movie to continue.

The skirmishes between the Nazis and the communists in the movie houses merely reflected what was happening daily in the streets. Aside from these occurrences, film in the last years of the Weimar Republic represented conservative and liberal thinking and produced films to appeal to both Right and Left. Purely communist films were limited to the productions of Prometheus-Film GmbH, a small underfunded company dedicated to making films for and about the working classes. They had made *Mutter Krausens Fahrt ins Glück* (*Mother Krause's Journey to Happiness*, Phil Jutzi, 1929), a pessimistic film about unemployment and suicide (one of the last so-called **Zille-films**), among other movies from a socialist perspective. In 1931–1932 Prometheus and Präsens-Film-Verleih GmbH produced *Kuhle Wampe oder Wem gehört die Welt?* (*Kuhle Wampe*, aka *Whither Germany?* **Slatan Dudow**, 1932), an agit-prop exploration of growing unemployment in Germany in the early 1930s. The film was banned by the Weimar government, which had been growing progressively more conservative, ostensibly for maligning the government and being child-unfriendly. In one scene the main female character fantasizes about the difficulties having a child will cause her. The producers undertook cuts, but not until the second round of edits was the film allowed to be shown, by which time the cuts had made part of the film's story difficult to follow. Six months after approval, the Nazis were in power and banned the film again.

Joseph Goebbels believed in the power of film. He declared Sergei Eisenstein's *The Battleship* Potemkin (1925) a masterpiece and believed German film should strive to emulate its emotionally produced political effect on viewers. He also publicly criticized German filmmakers for making inferior films. When he first became minister of propaganda with the Nazi takeover of Germany, Goebbels assured members of the film industry they need not be fearful of his policies. His audience may have indeed felt there was no cause to worry, as the films he mentioned in his talk as his favorites had been directed by Jewish filmmakers and moreover focused on themes of adultery, individualism, and rebellion. Within a month of his speech, however, Jews were being purged from the industry; within three months a general ban against employing Jews was in place. At the same time, films from the

Weimar Republic and from abroad that had visibly Jewish influence were banned from exhibition. One year later, in January 1934, the government decreed that everyone working in film, from production to distribution to exhibition (mom and pop type movie houses were exempt), had to join the Reichsfilmkammer (Ministry of Film) to continue working in the industry. Jews could not be members of this organization, which finished the process of excluding them from film work.

Film under Nazi leadership did not become a monolith immediately after Adolf Hitler came to power. Goebbels exerted control to ban Jewish participation, and he instituted a policy of precensorship, by requiring that projects be submitted to a film advisor in the Ministry of Film. In spite of such precensorship requirements, studios retained a degree of autonomy, deciding which films to produce within the prescribed rules. The minister of propaganda was fond of using a metaphor of an orchestra to describe his film policy, explaining that not all members of an orchestra play the same instrument but also that no one has the right to play whatever music he wants during a concert. Ufa, Tobis-Film, and Bavaria-Film, the three largest studios, continued as separate studios until 1937, even though they were subject to tight management by the minister of propaganda. Even after 1937 the separate companies retained some autonomy over their film production. Not until the early 1940s did Ufa subsume the other studios. Such freedom within the system notwithstanding, Goebbels exercised almost total control of what was produced and, once it was produced, what could be released to be shown on German screens. He suggested stories and actors. Conversely, he also vetoed ideas and stars. The actress Margot Hielscher reputedly received fewer parts after turning down Goebbels's advances. According to **Leni Riefenstahl** she had to seek Hitler's intervention after Goebbels had rejected her as director of *Triumph des Willens* (*Triumph of the Will*, 1935).

If companies retained autonomy in their choice of films to produce, viewers had little to none in what they saw. Besides the censorship of German films from the Weimar Republic, foreign films were also banned, sometimes because they had Jews in the cast, sometimes because of the themes. The American film *Nana*, for example, was banned because its story tells of a soldier visiting a prostitute, which violated the military's sensibilities and honor code. Ten years later, **Helmut Käutner** had trouble getting his film *Große Freiheit # 7* (*Port of Freedom*, 1944) approved for the same reason, until Admiral Dönitz intervened, suggesting that sailors sometimes visit prostitutes. The number of movies coming from America declined steadily until 1939, after which there was a universal ban on importing films from Hollywood. From early in the takeover, Goebbels voiced an opinion on the state of German films. He criticized their quality and suggested they stop showing Nazis marching across the screen, referring to his dislike of two German films at the time, *S.A. Mann Brand* (*S.A. Man Brand*, Franz Seitz, 1933) and *Hans Westmar* (*Hans Westmar*, Franz Wenzlar, 1933), which portray the brown shirts marching, fighting, and arresting scores of citizens. The only film depicting the brown shirts to win his approval was *Hitlerjunge Quex* (*Hitler Youth Quex*, Hans Steinhoff, 1933), which, like Goebbels's favorite movie *Battleship* Potemkin, uses the language of film to appeal to the emotions of the audience. *Hitlerjunge Quex* places Nazi symbolism in the background, allowing the apotheosis that closes the film to develop from the story rather than be superimposed from without, as Goebbels had apparently found to be the problem with the films of Seitz and Wenzlar.

In his speeches, Goebbels again and again praised the potential for films to teach. Beginning in 1934, short cultural–political films became mandatory viewing by members of the Hitlerjugend, to which most youth belonged. In addition the German newsreel (*see DIE DEUTSCHE WOCHENSCHAU*), which Ufa, Tobis-Film, and Fox continued to produce after the Nazis came to power, directed public attention to what the Nazis considered newsworthy. The documentary **Der ewige Jude** (*The Eternal Jew*, Fritz Hippler, 1940) had a double purpose. On the one hand it appealed to strains of anti-Semitism among viewers in order to build support for the Nazis' program of persecution against the Jews. On the other hand the film represented Jewish culture as a danger that had to be eliminated. Yet whenever Goebbels spoke of cinema's power to inform the public, he warned about making obviously tendentious and manipulative movies. His comment on avoiding overt symbols of Nazi militarism, mentioned above, was made in 1933. Four years later he admonished an audience of film professionals that "the moment that propaganda becomes visible, it loses its effect." Four years after that, in 1941, when the war had been underway for two years, he encouraged his listeners to edify their viewers since art "prepares them [the people] for life" but he cautioned that "it is advisable to disguise the didactic objective." Considering Goebbels's remarks, it is hardly surprising that most of the 1,100 feature films made while the

Nazis were in power were not explicit propaganda. Certainly, they reflected the conservative values of Nazi ideology, and they portrayed characters in accord with accepted stereotypes for positively and negatively valued characters. Removed from the historical context, however, many of the films could be enjoyed as entertainment, which is perhaps why they had a second life on German television after the war.

IMMEDIATE POSTWAR YEARS 1945–1949

By the end of the war in Europe, 8 May 1945, German film production had stopped. The studio at **Babelsberg** lay in ruins. Members of the film community were dead, imprisoned, or discredited. Veit Harlan, the most notorious of the directors in the Third Reich, was put on trial for crimes against humanity, for which he was acquitted in 1949, when he also received permission to again work in film. Directors and actors who could show that their actions were beyond reproach still had no work, as there was no financial support for making films. Moreover, films required a license of approval from the Allies, who had divided Germany into four sectors, one each for the United States, France, Britain, and the Soviet Union. In the first few months, the Allies were not approving any projects.

The narrative of German film after the war almost immediately divides along political lines. One line follows the development of film in the Soviet-occupied Eastern zone, which was to become the German Democratic Republic (GDR or East Germany); the other follows the development of film in the American, French, and British sectors, which were to become the Federal Republic of Germany (FRG or West Germany). The East German narrative ends in 1990 with the dissolution of the GDR, but East Germany's filmmakers of course have continued to work in united Germany's film production. Until 1990, though, **East German film** showed less political diversity than film in the West, owing to state control of the medium. Nonetheless, films from the GDR exhibit variety and tackle important social issues. West German film, on the other hand, exhibits diversity and variety, but until the late 1960s it tended to avoid direct confrontation with sociopolitical issues.

Film in the Soviet sector received immediate support from the Russians, who in May 1946 granted a license to a consortium of filmmakers, including **Kurt Maetzig**, to found the Deutsche Film Aktiengesellschaft (DEFA), which continued under direct Soviet control until 1953. In October of that year the Soviets granted permission to **Wolfgang Staudte** for *Die Mörder sind unter uns* (*The Murderers Are among Us*), after he had been turned down by the Americans, French, and British. Filmed among Berlin's ruins, giving rise to the term **rubble film**, *Die Mörder sind unter uns* is an early attempt to examine Germany's psychological and emotional state after the collapse of the Third Reich and revelation of its crimes. DEFA, with Soviet approval, continued to make a few films each year, almost always revisiting the fascist past and its resonance in the present. That same year the studio released *Irgendwo in Berlin* (*Somewhere in Berlin*, Gerhard Lamprecht), also a rubble film. Lamprecht's film was more upbeat, encouraging Germans to rebuild their lives and their cities. A year later, DEFA released *Ehe im Schatten* (*Marriage in the Shadows*, Maetzig), a look at the tragic human cost of the Holocaust.

Unlike the Soviets, the Western sector Allies did not immediately allow resumption of film production. American, French, and British film companies had a backlog of films that they hoped could fill the screens in the areas those countries controlled. Hollywood film distributors in particular had hundreds of films that could be circulated, and their exhibition became part of an American film policy. Authorities saw film as a way to reverse the ideological imprint left by a decade of Nazi propaganda. On the one hand, they thought this could be accomplished by requiring Germans to watch newsreels or documentaries of the atrocities committed in the concentration camps. The apparent plan was to shame viewers into accepting democracy. One such film, *Die Todesmühlen* (*Deathmills*, 1945), for example, reminds the German viewers that they "bear heavy crosses now . . . the crosses of the millions crucified in Nazi death mills!" (quoted in Heidi Fehrenbach, *Cinema in Democratizing Germany*, Chapel Hill and London: University of North Carolina Press, 1995). On the other hand, authorities believed American films could present positive models of democracy that viewers would be willing to emulate. Both assumptions were wrong. Many viewers resented both the negative and positive approach to indoctrination, and within a year German filmmakers in the Western sectors had also resumed work.

The first production, *Sag die Wahrheit* (*Tell the Truth*, Helmut Weiss, 1946), a comedy about infidelity, is representative of West German film in the years after the war. While some films would confront the impact of recent history on contemporary postwar life, many diverted viewer attention into fantasy and light romance, and those that did reference the war years often framed it in comedy or fantasy. The story of Käutner's *In jenen Tagen* (*In Those Days*, 1947) is narrated by an automobile as it passes from one owner to another during the years 1933 to 1945. His *Der Apfel is ab* (*The Apple Is Gone*, 1948) parodies the story of Adam and Eve. Rudolf Jugert asks if a new form of entertainment might not be needed in postwar Germany in *Film ohne Titel* (*Film without Title*, 1948), and in Berliner Ballade (*The Ballad of Berlin*, 1948), Robert A. Stemmle uses comedy to follow a man trying to get his life back together in Berlin. These films, though, do not reflect avoidance of the past, just another avenue for dealing with reintegration issues.

The variety of films in the West and their often lighthearted, non-tendentious approach to history resulted at least in part from the dissolution of any central film studio or system. Unlike the Soviet-controlled DEFA, film studios in the West were independent, subject to be sure to Allied licensure, but also subject to commercial considerations. Central Cinema Corporation (CCC) was the first studio founded, by Artur Brauner in 1946, but it did not get a license to produce until 1949. In the next several decades, though, it made over 250 films. Filmaufbau, founded by director Rolf Thiele, among others, made 90 films between 1948 and 1960. Realfilm was founded in 1947 and made 30 films during the next decade. By the end of the decade all these companies were making serious films as well as the more lighthearted romances with which they started.

DEALING WITH THE PAST: EAST GERMAN FILMS IN THE 1950S

The Western Allies approved a constitution for the FRG in May 1949, and the Soviets approved one for the GDR later in 1949, making the reality of two German states official and the differences in subject matter, film style, and ideological underpinnings more pronounced. East German film presented a paradox. DEFA continued the tendency exhibited in the East's first releases to be openly critical about the past; confronting audiences with fascist abuse of power, German war crimes, and cowardly acts of acquiescence but also heroic acts of resistance. The films stressed atrocities that were committed against the Soviets but also included early attempts at coming to terms with the wholesale murder of Europe's Jews. At the same time East German film was tightly controlled by a film board that could stop a project at any stage of development, just as had been the case under National Socialism. Moreover, at times during the 40 years of DEFA's existence the rules were changed, requiring directors to conform to a new style or thematic preference. The films produced in this fashion understandably acquired subtexts that separated East Germans from the crimes, or at least made clear how the GDR had distanced itself from the past. They also implicitly and sometimes explicitly drew a parallel from Nazi Germany to the FRG and the Western Allies, in particular the United States.

From the beginning, film in East Germany had a mission to help the country realize a new socialist state. The motivating metaphor for the GDR, and by extension for filmmakers, was that the country was an experiment in changing human behavior to be unselfish, cooperative, and above all optimistic, to believe that life would continually improve. *Irgendwo in Berlin* ends with a depressed man brought back to high spirits by his ten-year-old son, who organizes an entire neighborhood to rebuild the man's workshop, which had been totally destroyed by air raids. As a paradigm for future work, the movie won out over more experimental or formalistic movies, just as progressive film practices in the 1920s in the Soviet Union had yielded to the more prosaic style of social realism. Movie heroes came from the working classes, style favored classical cinema over experimental films, and government criticism and criticism of socialism were absent.

The quality of the films at the time could be high and the ideology minimal. Moreover, the number of filmmakers willing to work for the system suggests support for the rules as necessary to realize a better future for the GDR. Richard Groschopp directed two films typical of the era: *Familie Benthin* (Family Benthin, codirector Slatan Dudow, 1950) contrasts the ethical values of West and East, condemning black market activities. *Modell Bianka* (*The Bianka Pattern*, 1951) is a romantic comedy about the advantages of working together to achieve objectives. Staudte's success in East Germany offered evidence that one could create good movies even with state controls. Working in both the GDR and FRG, Staudte addressed the past at a time when directors in the West preferred to avoid confronting history. Yet he did not subscribe to a totally East German view. To be sure, films such as *Rotation* (*Rotation*, 1949) and *Der Untertan* (*The Kaiser's Lackey*, aka *The Subject*, 1951) have political tendencies; they nonetheless reflect a humanistic world view rather than a specifically socialist one.

By 1953 the East German regime was calling for less tendentious material. The Central Committee of the Sozialistische Einheitspartei Deutschlands (SED) called for films to be more optimistic. Walter Ulbricht, the political leader of East Germany, was asking that films start including personal topics of interest to viewers. Film production increased from 5 films to 15 and more per year in the 1950s; topics indeed became more commercial; Henny Porten, a major star from the 1920s living in the West, made two films for DEFA, including *Das Fräulein von Scuderi* (*Madame von Scuderi*, Eugen York, 1955), whose director also worked in the West; the production was moreover coproduced with a Swedish studio. Films from the period reflected a liberalization that favored comedies, literary adaptations, and even musicals as long as there was some sociopolitical commentary and nothing that could be construed as critical of communism or the GDR. Western imports were also brought in to fill a demand for film entertainment. In 1954 DEFA's first prestige project appeared, *Ernst Thälmann – Sohn seiner Klasse* (*Ernst Thälmann: Son of His Class*, Maetzig, 1954) and *Ernst Thälmann – Führer seiner Klasser* (*Ernst Thälmann: Leader of His Class*, Maetzig, 1955), films that celebrate the legendary communist martyr; but by the middle 1960s the thaw was over, and East German films were again subject to strict regulation.

AVOIDING THE PAST:
WEST GERMAN FILM IN THE 1950S

In the 1950s, West German film moved even further away from looking at the past critically. To be fair, the Third Reich years were not ignored completely, at least not as concerns World War II. A number of directors made **war films**, but their approach was uncritical. The harshest critics of the war movies called them self-serving, intended to rehabilitate the German military at a time when Chancellor Konrad Adenauer prepared for West Germany's entrance into the North Atlantic Treaty Organization

(NATO). Works such as *08/15* (Paul May, 1954/1955), *Haie und kleine Fische* (*Sharks and Small Fish*, **Frank Wisbar**, 1957), and *Der Arzt von Stalingrad* (*The Doctor of Stalingrad*, Géza von Radványi, 1958), among others, portray soldiers as brave, honorable men who were fulfilling their patriotic duty. The only nonwar film to examine life under the Nazis, *Wir Wunderkinder* (*Aren't We Wonderful?* **Kurt Hoffmann**, 1958), did not appear until the end of the decade, and it too was faulted for trivializing National Socialism rather than coming to terms with it and also for failing to examine the ordinary citizen's role in support of Nazism.

In place of critical examination of the past, West German films in the 1950s helped viewers escape from thinking about their role in what had occurred. The most popular genres were romantic comedies, musicals, detective fiction, and **Heimatfilme** (films about hearth and home). The most popular actors were names familiar to the public from the Nazi era, performers who had managed to remain aloof from Nazism even while enjoying successful careers: **Hans Albers**, **Heinz Rühmann**, **Marika Rökk**, among others. In 1948 Rökk had won the first Bambi, an award based on popularity. She was to win it again and again over the next few decades; Rühmann was to win the Bambi 14 times between 1962 and 1990. The most popular directors too had gotten their start during the Third Reich. Käutner, Hoffmann, **Paul Verhoeven**, and **Wolfgang Liebeneiner** are but a few of the directors who resumed successful careers after the war. The works of these men under the Nazis for the most part entertained rather than supported National Socialist ideology; thus it was easy for them to resume their careers. Hoffmann made some of the decade's favorite comedies: *Das fliegende Klassenzimmer* (*The Flying Classroom*, 1954), a children's classic; *Bekenntnisse des Hochstaplers Felix Krull* (*Confessions of Felix Krull*, 1957), based on a Thomas Mann novel; and *Das Wirtshaus im Spessart* (*The Spessart Inn*, 1958), a Heimat comedy. Käutner made *Der Hauptmann von Köpenick* (*The Captain of Köpenick*, 1956) with Rühmann, which became a classic comedy. He also made some of the era's more politically critical films: *Die letzte Brücke* (*The Last Bridge*, 1954), a partisan war film starring **Maria Schell**; *Des Teufels General* (*The Devil's General*, 1955), based on Carl Zuckmayer's play and asking if an act of treason that could have ended the war sooner was not an act of courage; and *Himmel ohne Sterne* (*Sky without Stars*, 1955), a thriller introducing 1950s heartthrob **Horst Buchholz** and taking place in the no-man's zone between the two German states. Liebeneiner made *Die Trapp-Familie* (*The Trapp Family*, 1956), the musical that gave rise to Richard Rogers's and Oscar Hammerstein's Broadway musical *Sound of Music* (1959).

The 1950s were not without critically acclaimed films and also not without controversy. *Die Sünderin* (*The Sinner*, **Willi Forst**, 1951) created a scandal because of its theme of prostitution and suicide and a nude scene by its star, **Hildegard Knef**. The Catholic Church in particular editorialized against the film in its publications and warned parishioners from the pulpit about patronizing the movie. Ever since 1949 the FRG had had a censorship policy that relied on self-policing by the film industry. The Freiwillige Selbstkontrolle der Filmwirtschaft (FSK) was set up to unite the Bundesländer (federal states), religious institutions, and film studios behind one policy. Modeled after the Hayes Code used in Hollywood, the FSK could ban films or release them with age restrictions. *Die Sünderin* was deemed acceptable to those age 16 and older (changed to age 18 in 1957). Both the Protestant and Catholic Churches thought the film should have been banned outright. Individual communities also objected to its distribution and kept it from screens in their locales. Taken to court by the film industry, the communities lost, the courts ruling that the FSK's decisions needed to be followed in order to protect artistic freedom (related on FSK homepage).

Several other films in the 1950s proved an exception to the predominance of comedies, war films, and films of the Heimat. *Die Halbstarken* and *Die Frühreifen* were strongly influenced by the wave of teenagers-in-trouble movies appearing in the United States, among them *The Wild One* (László Benedek, 1953), *Blackboard Jungle* (Richard Brooks, 1955), and *Rebel without a Cause* (Nicholas Ray, 1955). *Die Halbstarken* (*Teenage Wolfpack* aka *The Hooligans*, Georg Tressler, 1956) starred Buchholz, who had become a sensation since *Himmel ohne Sterne*. In *Die Halbstarken* Buchholz plays a juvenile delinquent with the American name Freddy and wears tight black leather pants and jacket, the uniform of the lost generation in America, England, and France in the 1950s. Freddy's rebellion, unlike that of his counterparts in the American movies, has a political rather than existential basis. He and his cohorts question the hypocrisy of a generation that had supported

Hitler and yet now told their children how to conduct their lives. The GDR also experienced the phenomenon of the youth film at the same time. *Berlin—Ecke Schönhauser* (*Berlin: Schönhauser Corner*, Gerhard Klein, 1957) was one of several youth films set in East Berlin. In the case of Klein's film, the state eventually takes over the role of the absent parents, but not before the same problems and tragedies of the Hollywood and West German counterparts occur.

GERMAN FILM'S SECOND GOLDEN ERA

West German Cinema 1960–1975

In the 1960s and 1970s national cinemas created a new vision of film as both entertainment and art. Although movie house attendance was declining as the popularity of television increased, films achieved high status in popular culture, competing with theater for educated audiences. Britain, France, America, Germany, and, in the 1980s, Australia, all enjoyed a new wave of filmmaking, producing movies that rejected the cinema of the previous decade, questioned the status quo in society and government, and challenged viewers to think about identity and values. Directors in the two German states defined their countries' respective cinemas through themes, style, and political texts, which continued to diverge, a process begun in the previous decade.

The new wave in West Germany, known first as Junger Deutscher Film (**Young German Cinema**) and then Neuer Deutscher Film (New German Cinema), grew out of the **Oberhausen Manifesto**, a demand issued in 1962 at the Oberhausen Film Festival. The document, which was signed by 26 filmmakers, including **Alexander Kluge**, Herbert Vesely, and **Edgar Reitz**, called for rethinking and restructuring film policies in the FRG and declared the old cinema dead. The immediate result was underwhelming. The movement started well, with *Das Brot der frühen Jahre* (*The Bread of Those Years*, 1962), Vesely's critical look at Germany's past. The film won six film industry awards, including for Best Feature Film and Best Director, and is often considered the start of the new wave. This was a change from 1961, when no film or director was chosen to be honored with an award. Also in 1962, Reitz and his colleagues founded a film school in Ulm. Yet the rest of that year's film production promised a continuation of the past. *Der Schatz im Silbersee* (*The Treasure in Silver Lake*, **Harald Reinl**) was representative of films for the year. Based on a novel by Karl May, the film broke attendance records and initiated a new genre, the **Winnetou films**, which offered an ahistorical look at America's Old West.

The new generation of German filmmakers needed a system of financial support before their movement could have an effect on the quality of German film. By 1965 the idea of a more demanding cinema was gaining support with critics, students, and the government, even if not with the general public. Consequently the cultural ministry created the **Kuratorium Junger Deutscher Film** e. V. (Young German Film Board) to offer financial incentives to filmmakers. Administered by the federal government until 1968 and thereafter by the individual Bundesländer, the trustees on the Film Board awarded interest-free loans that were to be paid back from earnings. In the eyes of some critics, especially the commercial film companies, the system encouraged esoteric projects that had little to no commercial appeal. Application of the law for film subsidies for first projects was moved to the state level. At the federal level the cultural ministry created the **Filmförderungsanstalt** (federal film board), which increased the amount of the subsidies but tied grants to ticket sales. That is, future projects depended on the financial rather than merely critical success of previous ones. In addition to the two film boards, filmmakers in Germany had two other major sources for support. As in countries such as France, England, and more recently the United States, television networks provided money for films, receiving exclusive broadcast rights after a predetermined theatrical release. Another source of funds was the Federal Ministry of the Interior, which gave monetary awards for excellence to filmmakers. The amount of subsidy depended on the category in which the award was granted. Some variation of these subsidy programs continues to exist, with the stipends for the film awards ranging from €10,000 to €500,000.

As in any system of competitive grants, complaints have been frequent. Success in receiving a financial award from the boards necessarily depends on the preferences of the few individuals who make the decision. In the eyes of many this has encouraged safe movies, prestigious films based on literary sources, and has discouraged experimentation. To be sure, if one examines the films from the 1960s and 1970s one will find an abundance of movies based on classical works of literature.

While these can be experimental projects, such as *Katz und Maus* (*Cat and Mouse*, Hansjügen Pohland, 1967) or Fassbinder's *Fontane Effi Briest* (*Effi Briest*, 1974), they are more often conventional adaptations, often excellent, but no different than what filmmakers of the previous generation had done. Moreover, films that critics later praised received no funding at the time because they were considered not commercial, such as *Chronik der Anna Magdalena Bach* (*Chronicle of Anna Magdalena Bach*, **Jean-Marie Straub** and **Danièle Huillet**, 1968), an experiment in minimalist cinema. In addition, producers of the radically political film *Deutschland im Herbst* (*Germany in Autumn*, 1978) never applied for money because they suspected that the nature of their topic, terrorism in Germany, would preclude receiving a government subsidy. Such films fared better with television and the awards system. Even esoteric or experimental films were broadcast, although not always in prime time, and regardless of its radical theme, *Deutschland im Herbst* won an Award in Gold (*see* FILM AWARDS).

Two other important institutions also promoted New German Cinema, with varying success: the **Filmverlag der Autoren** and the Kommunales Kino (community cinema). The former was founded by 13 filmmakers, including **Wim Wenders**, **Hans W. Geissendörfer**, and **Peter Lilienthal**, in 1971 to produce films for an alternative film audience. After only one year, the Filmverlag was heavily in debt and had to be refinanced. Rather than produce films, the group now focused on domestic and international distribution, aggressively marketing films and giving German film the high status it enjoyed in the 1970s and early 1980s. Fassbinder, **Werner Herzog**, Wenders, and a dozen other directors became recognized as the creators of a new German film voice. After a time the Filmverlag began distributing more commercial German films, which Oberhausen adherents would have eschewed, and eventually even non-German films, such as those of Woody Allen. In 1999 Kinowelt Medien AG, a commercial film distributor, bought the Filmverlag der Autoren and used its name in its alternative film subsidiary, Arthaus Filmverleih.

The Kommunales Kino was created to serve as a complementary force to the Filmverlag and specialized in exhibiting alternative films. The first such communal cinema opened in Frankfurt in 1971 to create a venue for specialized or art films. Soon thereafter cinemas for independent films opened in Hamburg, Stuttgart, and other major cities. The

Kommunales Kino serves the same purpose as the art house theaters in the United States, providing a venue for films that might not otherwise receive screen play. In contrast to France, where French films are guaranteed a certain percentage of theatrical bookings, Germany offers no such blanket protection. As a result, cinemas play mostly Hollywood films, and some French and British movies. Comedies are an exception to this rule, for they not only receive wide distribution, they are often the box office leaders. Art films, in contrast, receive limited engagements in small theaters, even in the larger cities. Their main exposure comes through television and DVD, but even in the case of DVDs, release is limited and in the case of television they do not play in prime time.

West German Cinema 1975–1990

By the mid to late 1970s in West Germany, directors were benefiting from and responding to the changes wrought by the new wave and the Oberhausen Manifesto. The call for more thoughtful films resonated with the political activism of the 1970s to create New German Cinema's most acclaimed films and help German filmmakers regain the reputation they had had for excellence in the 1920s in Weimar. The rebirth of a meaningful film culture also created political controversy. On the one hand individual German states set up museums, archives, and programs of study that nurtured German film. On the other hand the boards that oversaw the new institutions tended to be conservative and objected to the leftist content of many of the films. Moreover, the commercial potential of the movies was often limited by their experimental nature or political tone. Throughout the 1970s and well into the 1980s West German film had multiple personalities. Political films such as *Lina Braake* (Bernhard Sinkel, 1975) and *Die Verlorene ehre der Katharina Blum* (*The Lost Honor of Katharina Blum*, **Volker Schlöndorff** and **Margarethe von Trotta**, 1975) were able to bridge the gap between art house fare and commercial success, proving popular with young people and leftist intellectuals but crossing over into a wider audience. Nonetheless, both drew protests from Germany's Right.

Other films did not reach beyond the art house, even when they won awards. *Hitler, ein Film aus Deutschland* (*Hitler, a Film from Germany*, **Hans-Jürgen Syberberg**, 1977) stages Nazi Germany as a seven-hour

Wagnerian puppet opera. The film mystified viewers, confounded social critics on the Left and Right, and delighted international viewers, who were embracing Herzog, Fassbinder, and Schlöndorff, among others, while their compatriots received them with tepid enthusiasm. *Deutschland im Herbst* (*Germany in Autumn*, 1978) angered the establishment because of its sympathetic treatment of the terrorist phenomenon active in Germany throughout the 1970s. But if Fassbinder upset viewers with his segment of *Deutschland im Herbst*, which portrays him as a paranoid drug user, abusing himself in a corner and berating his mother in an interview, he won their favor with **Die Ehe der Maria Braun** (*The Marriage of Maria Braun*) a year later. Schlöndorff meanwhile accomplished the seemingly impossible when his film *Die Blechtrommel* (*The Tin Drum*, 1979) won the academy award for Best Foreign Film, the first time the Oscar had been awarded to a German film. Consequently, and perhaps coincidentally, Schlöndorff seemed to fall from favor with the art house, or auteur, directors, directing thereafter films with bigger budgets. Fassbinder on the other hand followed *Die Ehe der Maria Braun* with *Berlin Alexanderplatz* (*Berlin Alexanderplatz*, 1980), a 15-hour adaptation for television of the eponymous Alfred Döblin novel. Praised in Italy at the Venice Film Festival, it unleashed controversy at home because of scenes that were drastically underlit and content that was too graphic at the time for television. The film was banished to the after prime time grave hour. The biggest scandal was caused by *Das Gespenst* (*The Ghost*, **Herbert Achternbusch**, 1982), a film that depicts Christ coming down from the cross and wandering through contemporary Bavaria with a mother superior. Achternbusch had received a promise of a subsidy for the film from the Filmförderungsanstalt (federal film board), which was withdrawn amid the complaints that surrounded the release of the movie.

The controversy surrounding Achternbusch's *Das Gespenst* reflects half of an equation that caused a crisis in West German film in 1982. Withdrawal of a subsidy that had been granted signaled that approval bodies would be less liberal in approving projects. This was also the year in which Fassbinder died. Not a signatory of the Oberhausen Manifesto, as he was only 17 in 1962, Fassbinder had nonetheless served as its symbolic leader since the mid-1970s. Although Wim Wenders would eventually take over that role of unofficial top auteur, German film would not recover its international reputation as an exciting film culture for over a decade. Wenders's *Paris, Texas* (1984) and *Der Himmel über Berlin* (*Wings of Desire*, 1987) received international acclaim, but they were hybrid films of a sort as they cast American actors, were shot entirely or partly in English, and exhibited the high production values that one expected from the films of major European studios and the correspondingly large profits one hoped to make.

Paradigmatic of the change in attitude in the films that received acclaim in the 1980s were two films from Bavaria Studio: *Das Boot* (*The Boat*, 1981), which had been released the year before Fassbinder's death, and *Die unendliche Geschichte* (*The Neverending Story*, 1984). Their success brought director Wolfgang Petersen a major Hollywood contract. It is not that no one was making auteur cinema in the 1980s in Germany; it is that recognition was going to the more commercial enterprises. Nevertheless, von Trotta, Herzog, **Helke Sanders**, **Helma Sanders-Brahms**, and a number of other independent directors continued making small budget films whose content and style appealed to limited, initiated audiences. **Rosa von Praunheim**, one of the directors most outside the mainstream, made films primarily for Germany's gay and underground community, distributed mainly to large metropolitan areas, including New York, San Francisco, and London. The same was true for the films of **Monika Treut**, whose focus was the lesbian community. **Ulrike Ottinger** addressed feminist issues in lengthy, stylistically demanding narrative films. The movies of these directors remained in the underground, appealing to an alternative cinema audience, only rarely crossing over even into the independent mainstream, let alone showing commercial viability. That their films are known at all to international audiences is almost entirely due to film festivals and retrospectives that were sponsored by the Goethe Institute and Germany's Ministry of Culture.

Other independent auteur directors followed the lead of Wenders and Schlöndorff, creating thoughtful films that were accessible to a general art house audience, and even sometimes achieving broader success. **Percy Adlon**'s *Zuckerbaby* (*Sugarbaby*, 1985) and *Out of Rosenheim* (*Bagdad Café*, 1987) became cult favorites by focusing on the psychological and social aspects of personal relationships, eschewing history, politics, terrorism, and experimentation. **Doris Dörrie** similarly examined a marital relationship in *Männer* (*Men*, 1985), which became the top German moneymaker of the year and achieved international status for its director. This, with Adlon's films, exemplifies the new attitude about German auteur movies, that they could be inoffensive and nonconfrontational and yet have relevance for contemporary social situations.

East Germany 1960–1990

Owing to the totalitarian nature of the communist regime, cinema in East Germany developed differently than in West Germany. Nevertheless, East German films have an importance in German film history similar to the works of New German Cinema, albeit they do not always receive the same recognition. From 1959 to 1990 DEFA released 700 films, plus more than 2,000 documentaries and short films. The paradigm of the 1950s, which favored larger than life heroes working to defeat fascism and promote a socialist utopia, was replaced by a more realistic view of socialist life, one that was not critical of socialism or the state but revealed nonetheless the difficulties individuals faced within the East German system to achieve self-fulfillment. One of the earliest films to anticipate a thaw in strict adherence to a socialist code of filmmaking was *Verwirrung der Liebe* (*Confusion of Love*, 1959) by Slatan Dudow, the elder statesman of communist film. Revealing Dudow's origins as a leftist filmmaker from Weimar cinema's experimental days, *Verwirrung der Liebe* includes nudity, unusual in the prudish GDR, and veiled but clear criticism of the lofty ideals of the Fifth Party Conference of the SED, which had called for the worker to be integrated more naturally into the cultural life of the nation. Except that the nude scene had to be reshot, putting the actors in bathing suits, the film received wide release. With the exception of Dudow's work and films by **Konrad Wolf**, **Heiner Carow**, and **Frank Beyer**, DEFA's feature films focused mainly on satisfying the regime's requirements of political content and less on crafting films of high quality.

Quality became an important issue early in 1961, when filmmakers began meeting with members of the party elite, pointing out the lack of interesting subjects and production values. The construction of the Berlin Wall in the summer of that year, rather than slowing the nascent reform of cinema, temporarily encouraged it. Some historians theorize that once officials had a barrier to prevent mass exodus from the country, they became less worried about previously questionable themes. The early years after the Berlin Wall was built witnessed some refreshing films. One such was *Auf der Sonnenseite* (*On the Sunnyside*, Ralf Kirsten, 1962), a romantic comedy with strong undercurrents of contemporary life. It could also be seen as a precursor of the numerous DEFA films that tended to empower women in sexual politics. Kirsten's *Beschreibung eines Sommers* (*Description of a Summer*, 1963), a romantic drama, confronted the moral prudery of contemporary East German society. A young woman, fleeing a bad marriage, has a fling with a lothario and manages to set the ground rules for a more meaningful relationship. Wolf's *Der geteilte Himmel* (*Divided Heaven*, 1964) is the best known of the films made during the temporary thaw. Based on the eponymous novel by Christa Wolf (no relation to the director), *Der geteilte Himmel* confronted the tragic reality of having to choose between love and one's country.

Liberalization ended in 1965 at the Eleventh Conference of the Central Committee of the SED. The plenary session, which was supposed to focus on economic matters, turned instead into an attack on filmmakers. The thaw in artistic freedom that many had anticipated turned instead into a crackdown on the film industry. Eventually 12 films were banned, even though they had previously been approved by authorities after careful consideration of their content. Two were singled out as especially egregious affronts to building a socialist utopia, *Das Kaninchen bin ich* (*I Am the Rabbit*, Maetzig, 1965) and *Denk bloß, nicht ich heule* (*Just Don't Think I'll Cry*, Frank Vogel, 1965). The primary criticism was that the films fostered a defeatist attitude by portraying the representatives of East German institutions as corrupt, even though neither film criticizes the government, the form of government, or political leaders. Maetzig and Vogel's films were joined by 10 others, all banned for similar reasons. *Spur der Steine* (*Trace of Stones*, Beyer, 1966), which had a brief release before it was pulled from exhibition, was one of DEFA's prestige films, having received one of the highest budgets that year. Yet it too dared suggest that life in East Germany was not perfect. The GDR's leaders accepted that there were problems in the system and people's lives were not perfect, but they believed that films ought to have closure, showing that people's problems could be solved within the framework of the country's socialist institutions. The banned films, known later as Verbotsfilme (forbidden films), leave matters unresolved. The films were finally shown in 1990 after the fall of the Berlin Wall. Although important documents of the social and political mood of the country when they were made, their subjects seemed dated in 1990. Viewership was small, and once their novelty as forbidden artifacts wore off, they disappeared from public exhibition.

After 1965, film retreated into apolitical fantasy, both to avoid controversy and to attract a larger audience to the movies, which were now, as in the West, receiving competition from television. DEFA copied two successful West German formula films, the Western and the teenage musical. Trying to capture the success of West Germany's Winnetou films, which were based on nineteenth-century pop culture icon Karl May, DEFA produced its own films about American Indians (Indianerfilme). They differed though in that they replaced West German filmmakers' ahistorical picture of benevolent policies toward Indians with an overtly critical text of American practices. The musicals, however, eschewed politics. Modeled after the musicals so popular in West Germany and America at the time, the films were an attempt to capture the East German youth market, reproducing Hollywood's style and stories. Musicals such as *Heißer Sommer* (*Hot Summer*, Joachim Hasler, 1968) and *Hochzeitsnacht im Regen* (*Wedding Night in the Rain*, Horst Seeman, 1968) cast pop music icons in the main roles and gave precedence to singing over story development.

After Erich Honecker became leader of the East German state, film policies were liberalized once again. Topics revolved around daily concerns, focusing on the problems people have in coping with relations at home and at work. *Die Legende von Paul und Paula* (*The Legend of Paul and Paula*, Carow, 1973) demonstrates how much leeway directors had been granted. The film contained nudity, bedroom scenes, and adultery, which, although they were present in earlier films, were certainly never treated with the frankness of Carow's work. Moreover, the characters are unhappy. Paul is a social climber who finds that working as a bureaucrat gives him little satisfaction. Paula is an eccentric, trying to find self-fulfillment as a woman in a system in which the reality of emancipation runs behind official policy. *Die Legende von Paul und Paula* became DEFA's biggest box office hit, owing to its actors and the zaniness of the story. Other films that benefited from liberalization were not as offbeat but achieved equal recognition. Wolf's *Goya* (1971) explores the conflict between artist and state; his *Solo Sunny* (1980) follows a would-be singer trying to forge a career in Berlin. Beyer's *Das Versteck* (*The Hiding Place*, 1977) examines the relationship between a woman and her egotistical ex-husband.

Film policies continued to be liberal during the 1980s, but the period produced few remarkable films. DEFA's major directors provided exceptions, however. Wolf's *Solo Sunny* was one; Frank Beyer's *Der Aufenthalt* (*The Turning Point*, 1982) was another. Beyer's film reexamined Germany's historical guilt at the same time that there was a revival of interest in the past in West Germany. Beyer continued confronting the past in *Der Bruch* (*The Breach*, 1989). For the most part the greater distance from the past in the years before the Wall fell allowed more irony and less ideological certainty in the films of the late 1980s than in earlier East German films dealing with Nazism. One of the last DEFA films, Carow's *Coming Out* (1989), deals with the topic of homosexuality, subject matter that was unusual in an East German film, even though homosexuality was not illegal in the communist state. Released after the fall of the Berlin Wall but before unification of the two German states, *Coming Out* reflects the liberalization that had occurred in East German film production by the time the regime was dissolved.

GERMAN CINEMA LOOKS ABROAD: THE 1990S AND 2000S

Domestic cinema during the 1990s and 2000s has been dominated by the paradigm for success: make audiences laugh and make them feel good about themselves, their problems, and the past. Beginning in the mid-1990s, Germany produced an abundance of comedies of all varieties: slapstick, situational, ironic, and romantic. Starring attractive actors, the best known being **Katja Riemann**, **Til Schweiger**, **Franka Potente**, **Moritz Bleibtreu**, and **Joachim Król**, and directed by a new generation that found humor in all situations, **Helmut Dietl** and Sönke Wortmann, among others, the boom in comedies and feel-good movies brought cinema goers back into theaters to see German films, guaranteed international distribution for at least the bigger successes, and allowed for life after the theatrical run by having recognizable titles go to DVD.

Comparing a few movies of the earlier period with those of the 1990s and 2000s provides evidence for the change in film style, content, and primarily tone. Fassbinder ended *Die Ehe der Maria Braun* with a radio play-by-play of the end of the world cup soccer championship of 1954, when Germany beat Hungary. The contrast in the film between the euphoria of victory and despair over the past's influence on the present produces uncomfortable irony in viewers. Barely 20 years later, the director, Wortman, influenced no doubt by the then upcoming world cup soccer championship in Berlin 2006, directed *Das Wunder von Bern* (*The Miracle of Bern*, 2003), using the soccer championship as background for reconciliation between father and son. His film produces a feel-good ending that elicits a smile and tears of joy from viewers rather than the discomfort viewers feel at Fassbinder's ending.

Dark comedies reveal a similar shift in tone. Adlon ends *Zuckerbaby* with an ambivalent scene that viewers can read as a gesture signifying that the main character either wants to meet a new lover or plans to jump in front of a subway driven by her ex-lover. Dörrie's *Keiner liebt mich* (*Nobody Loves Me*, 1994), also about a woman looking for love, ends with the woman discarding a coffin and dancing with a possible new lover to Edith Piaf's "Non, je ne regrette rien." The number 23, a running gag in the movie, signifies that she has indeed found her mate. Other directors were equally adept at producing a comfortable feeling of happiness, even in noncomedies. *Jenseits der Stille* (*Beyond Silence*, Caroline Link, 1996) involves a young woman's relationship with her deaf parents. After the death of her mother, she becomes estranged from her father, who does not want her pursuing a career in music. Link ends the film with the father in attendance at the girl's successful audition for music school. *Nirgendwo in Afrika* (*Nowhere in Africa*, 2001), also by Link, ends its story about Jewish persecution with a return of a Jewish family, whose parents have perished in the concentration camps, to postwar Germany, willing to try to reintegrate into German society.

Film has grown in importance in Germany since Alexander Kluge and his colleagues first signed the Oberhausen Manifesto declaring the old cinema dead and calling for a renewal of German film. Kluge and the other new wave directors might not agree with some of the recent occurrences in the German film landscape, in particular its pursuit of commercial success by emulating Hollywood themes and style. Nonetheless, they would recognize that German film has matured into one of Europe's leading national cinemas. Its importance can be seen in the establishment of film schools and museums, acceptance of film studies as an academic subject at universities, archival preservation of classic films, and growing international success. Awareness of the importance of German film in film history has led to other initiatives as well. In 1995, for the 100th anniversary of the birth of film, Das Deutsche Kinematheksverbund (an umbrella organization of film museums) commissioned filmmakers to name the 100 most important German films. After 2005, T-Online and filmportal.de began to augment the list with post-1995 works that had won awards from the German film industry. Those awards themselves received a new name. Previously called the "Filmband in Gold" (film strip in gold), film awards were renamed the "Lola," alluding to *Der blaue Engel*, whose main character is called Lola Lola and is played by film diva **Marlene Dietrich**; *Lola* (Fassbinder, 1981), an homage to the Sternberg classic; and *Lola rennt* (*Run Lola Run*, **Tom Tykwer**, 1998), a film that changed the way the German and international public saw German film. Film's growing importance in Germany is further evidenced by the generating of a film canon for schools. In 2003, the German Education Ministry asked 15 directors, pedagogues, critics, and historians to create a list of films that schools should teach. They settled on 35 films, including 7 German features: *Nosferatu* (Murnau, 1922), *M* (Lang, 1931), *Emil und die Detektive* (*Emil and the Detectives*, Lamprecht, 1931), *Die Brücke* (*The Bridge*, **Bernhard Wicki**, 1959), *Ich war neunzehn* (*I Was Nineteen*, Wolf, 1968), *Alice in den Städten* (*Alice in the Cities*, Wenders, 1974), and *Die Ehe der Maria Braun*.

The Dictionary

– A –

ACHTERNBUSCH, HERBERT (1938–). Little known outside of Germany, Herbert Achternbusch is the quintessential filmmaker of **New German Cinema**. His films represent in the extreme the anti-establishment ethos that gives the works of the post-Oberhausen generation their vitality and strength. At the same time, Achternbusch tests the limits of alienating and distancing his viewers, leading them to either love or hate his films.

Shooting mainly in Super-8 and then blowing his films up to 16mm or 35mm for exhibition, Achternbusch writes, directs, produces, and stars in his films, giving them that auteur stamp of individuality and consistent vision so valued by fans of experimental art films. He uses the genre of the *Heimatfilm* to parody and satirize the empty and cold human landscapes of Bavaria, an area Germans and the rest of the world usually associate with scenic beauty, beer halls, oompah music, and *gemütlichkeit* (coziness or comfort in the familiar). The absurdity of his situations and style has occasioned comparisons with Charlie Chaplin, the Marx Brothers, W. C. Fields, and Jerry Lewis. His major debt, however, is to Karl Valentin, a Bavarian humorist.

Bierkampf (*Beer Chase*, 1976/1977) exemplifies the serious and yet zany nature of Achternbusch's themes and style. In this film, a man steals a police uniform to gain authority and thus win for himself some self-esteem. He is pursued through the grounds of the Oktoberfest by his wife, his brother-in-law, and the policeman whose uniform he has stolen until he finally shoots himself. Achternbusch uses a handheld camera, seemingly non sequitur sequencing, and *cinema verité* style to reflect the chaos both at the festival and in the man's thinking.

Achternbusch's film *Das Gespenst* (*The Ghost*, 1982) exposed the unliberal policies of the German film industry's subsidization program. The film shows Jesus Christ getting down from the cross and wandering through town with a nun, having various experiences. Outraged by the blasphemy that he believed he saw in the film, in 1983 Minister of the Interior Friedrich Fleischmann refused to pay Achternbusch the last half of a state film award he had won the year before. Eventually the courts ruled that he had to release the money. Achternbusch took advantage of the controversy surrounding his film to decry the use of public funds to subsidize what he viewed as only marginally valid artists. Film critics likewise used the controversy to debate the current state of German cinema, and were not always favorable to Achternbusch's art. Hans C. Blumenberg, for example, wrote that amateur production values, opportunism, and overproduction were killing the German film as much as censorship or the commercial film industry. Peter Buchka simply declared that "the German film is dead."

Rather than conform to the desires of the state to get funding, Achternbusch's reaction has been to continue parodying German society and its institutions in such later films as *Heilt Hitler* (*Heal Hitler!* 1986), *Wohin?* (*Whereto?* 1988), *Ich bin da, ich bin da* (*I'm Here, I'm Here*, 1993), and most recently *Neue Freiheit – keine Jobs* (*Newfound Freedom, No Jobs* 1998). As in his earlier films, in *Neue Freiheit* Achternbusch takes on the political establishment, as evident on a demonstration poster in the film, which reads, "Who will free me from Helmut Kohl? He hunts through Europe like Hitler's last dog." *See also* NEW GERMAN CINEMA.

ADLON, PERCY (1935–). Best known at home and abroad for his comedies starring Marianne Sägebrecht—*Zuckerbaby* (*Sugarbaby*, 1985), *Out of Rosenheim* (*Bagdad Café*, 1987), and *Rosalie Goes Shopping* (1989)—Percy Adlon was a successful television documentarist of literary portraits before he directed his first feature films, *Céleste* (1981), based on the memoirs of Marcel Proust's last housekeeper, and *Fünf letzte Tage* (*Five Last Days*, 1982), an intimate portrait of the imprisonment of Sophie Scholl, one of the members of The White Rose, a student group opposed to Adolf Hitler and the Nazis. Adlon's early films, his documentaries, and the films with

Sägebrecht are character studies, most often of emotionally strong women who are nevertheless lonely. *Zuckerbaby*, for example, tells the story of an overweight mortician's assistant who seduces an attractive younger man with her mothering and culinary skills. The success of the film in the alternative film market in the United States led to a popular remake for American television, *Babycakes* (1989), starring Ricki Lake. *Out of Rosenheim* tells about the growing relationship between a German woman (Sägebrecht) abandoned by her husband in the desert and the African American owner (CCH Pounder) of a run-down cafe who is likewise alone, having thrown her husband out of the house. *Out of Rosenheim* was also remade by Hollywood as a television series, starring Jean Stapleton and Whoopi Goldberg (CBS, Fall 1990). Adlon's *Salmonberries* (1991), starring k.d. lang and Rosa Zech, is a sensitive portrayal of the relationship between two women in Alaska. Although it has been critically acclaimed, it has not found the popular success of his movies with Sägebrecht. More recent films, such as *Younger and Younger* (1993) and *Hawaiian Gardens* (2001), in spite of strong international casts, have encountered a lukewarm reception from critics and the general public. Adlon's most recent work has him returning to his origins as a documentarist. His Koenigs Kugel (*Koenigs Sphere*, 2003) studies the history of a bronze fountain by Bavarian sculptor Fritz Koenig. The fountain once stood in the courtyard of the Twin Towers, and its damaged remains were later reassembled in New York's Battery Park.

ADORF, MARIO (1930–). Mario Adorf first gained wide attention as a psychotic mass murderer in **Robert Siodmak's** *Nachts, wenn der Teufel kam* (*The Devil Strikes at Night*, 1957), a role that won him a federal film award as best new actor and typecast him as a villain. Years later Adorf lamented: "This role was my fate. . . . Afterwards I was typecast as an evil criminal, I was the personification of villainy in German films." The actor's broad facial features, thick neck, and stocky build contributed to his screen persona of movie heavy. Eventually, Adorf broke from the mold, appearing in comedies in Germany and France. In the 1970s, he was embraced by the directors of **New German Cinema**. His major roles in this regard were as the bullying police inspector, Kommissar Beizmenne, in *Die verlorene Ehre der Katharina Blum* (*The Lost Honor of Katharina Blum*,

Volker Schlöndorff and **Margarethe von Trotta**, 1975) and as the father of Oskar Matzerath in Schlöndorff's *Die Blechtrommel* (*The Tin Drum*, 1979). Adorf also appeared in Sam Peckinpah's *Major Dundee* (1965). Among the many awards he has won during his acting career are a Bambi (1977) for Best Actor; a Film Award in Gold (1992) from the Deutsche Filmakademie (German Film Academy) for Best Actor for his role in *Pizza Colonia* (*Pizza Colonia*, 1991); and a lifetime achievement award (2004), also from the German Film Academy (*see* **film awards**). Adorf's recent work has been mainly on German television. Non-German audiences may be familiar with his work in English-language movies, including *Try This One for Size* (Guy Hamilton, 1989) and *Smilla's Sense of Snow* (Bille August, 1997).

AKIN, FATIH (1973–). A young Turkish woman in Fatih Akin's *Im Juli* (*In July*, 2000) romanticizes about a rendezvous she plans in Istanbul under a bridge that separates the European and Asian sides of the city. She is speaking across the table with a young German man who believes she is his soul mate. The camera moves slowly in on a painting showing the bridge, in the middle a lamppost separating two benches. The scene sums up Akin's fascination with the paradox of cultural divisions: they truly exist, but only if we allow them to. *Im Juli* tells a comedic tale of a young man who travels across Europe chasing the woman of his dreams, overlooking the young woman at home who is in love with him. Starring **Moritz Bleibtreu**, the film deviates from Akin's acclaimed *Gegen die Wand* (*Head-On*, 2004) and his first feature, *Kurz und Schmerzlos* (*Short Sharp Shock*, 1998) in tone and genre, but as in those films, his focus on Europe's multiculturalism never wavers.

Kurz und Schmerzlos (literally, "short and painless") elaborates ideas on second-generation immigrants to Germany that Akin began in his short films *Sensin – Du bist es* (*Sensin . . . You're the One!*, 1995) and *Getürkt* (*Weed*, 1996). *Kurz und Schmerzlos* is a youth crime film, reminiscent of other films in the genre such as Martin Scorsese's *Mean Streets* (1973), Eloy de la Iglesia's *Colegas* (*Pals*, 1982), and Mathieu Kassowitz's *La Heine* (*Hate*, 1995). Like *Mean Streets*, Akin's film focuses on the underbelly of a large city, in this case Hamburg. Similar to *Colegas*, the film tells a story about the tensions of young love. And like *La Heine*, *Kurz und Schmerzlos* is set in the immigrant community. The film focuses on the lives of a Turk, who has just gotten out of prison and wants to go straight; a Serb, who wants to join the Albanian mafia; and a Greek, who goes along with the Serb's plans to escalate their criminal activities.

Gegen die Wand (literally, "against the wall") dominated the German **Film Awards** the year of its release, winning best in five categories: actor, actress, cinematography, directing, and film. The title refers on the one level to a suicidal attempt by crashing a car against a brick wall. On another level, it refers to the two lead characters and their clashes with family, life, and cultural difference. On a third level, the metaphor of going against something head-on refers to the growing awareness of cultural difference brought about by an increase in immigration of non-European cultures. *Gegen die Wand* is the most Turkish of Akin's films, in the sense that the cultural clashes are between generations of Turkish immigrants, not between Germans and Turks. Akin explores the impact of the Turkish diaspora on Turkish traditions through his suicidal characters, who are lonely, bored, addicted to drugs, and searching for identity.

Akin's style resembles that of the directors of **New German Cinema**, especially **Rainer Werner Fassbinder**, in the direct nature of the images, the outsider milieu of the characters, and the interest in social and familial conflict. His penchant for abundant dialogue, inclusion of contemporary ethnic music, and general likeability of his characters put his own stamp on the films. His music tracks, which highlight Turkish traditional and contemporary songs, label his films as Turkish-German. In 2005, he directed the documentary *Crossing the Bridge: The Sound of Istanbul*, in which his camera reveals the life, beauty, and diversity of Istanbul backed by a soundtrack of traditional folk music, Romani music, and Turkish rap. His 2007 film *Auf der anderen Seite* (*The Edge of Heaven*) intertwines several stories in a complex narrative of cultural and generational conflict. Set in Turkey and Germany, the film won best screenplay at the 2007 Cannes Film Festival and was nominated as Germany's entry in the Best Foreign Film category of the Academy Awards.

ALBERS, HANS (1891–1960). Hans Albers got his start in German silent films. His muscular physique and good looks made him ideal as a con artist, seducer, charmer, and lover. His deep voice allowed him to move into talkies, where he developed into a leading man. He is perhaps best known to Americans for his role as Mazeppa, the strong man in *Der blaue Engel* (*The Blue Angel*, 1930) who attracts Lola (**Marlene Dietrich**) and causes her husband, Professor Rath (**Emil Jannings**), to have an emotional breakdown. During the Third Reich, Albers had a successful career as a leading man in dramas and romances, his best-known role being as Baron Münchhausen in **Josef von Báky**'s 1943 film *Münchhausen* (*The Adventures of Baron Munchhausen*). After the war, Albers was able to continue his career, and in his later years he became a well-known character actor.

ALEXANDER, PETER (1926–). Peter Alexander gained fame in the 1950s and 1960s as a singer of Schlagermusik (sometimes mistakenly called top-40 music), a style of popular music characterized by an upbeat tempo, easy to sing melody, and romantic lyrics. Although most Western countries had their version of this music—Patti Page in the 1950s in America and Tom Jones in England in the 1960s, for example—Schlagermusik was particularly popular in Germany and lives on in German television shows that highlight nostalgia. Alexander's success as a singer was mirrored in over 40 musical comedies, in which he sang the tunes for which he was best known, creating a symbiosis between record and movie, where his songs sold tickets to the movie and the movies helped sell his records.

One of Alexander's better-known roles was as Viennese aristocrat Graf Bobby Pinelski, based on the object of ethnically charged Polish jokes: *Die Abenteuer des Grafen Bobby* (*The Adventures of Count Bobby*, Géza von Cziffra, 1961), *Das süße Leben des Grafen Bobby* (*The Sweet Life of Count Bobby*, von Cziffra, 1962), and *Grafen Bobby, der Schrecken des wilden Westens* (*Count Bobby, the Terror of the Wild West*, Paul Martin, 1965). The films mixed visual elaborations of the jokes with Alexander's song interludes. Also popular were two films he did in the film series *Die Lümmel von der ersten Bank* (*Cut-ups in the First Row*): *Zum Teufel mit der Penne* (*To Hell with School*, Werner Jakobs, 1968) and *Hurra, die Schule brennt* (*Hurrah, the School Is Burning*, Jakobs, 1969). Both films also starred Heintje (Heintje Simons), a 13–year-old teenage heartthrob of the 1960s.

ALLGEIER, SEPP (1895–1968). Cinematographer Sepp Allgeier began his career as assistant cameraman to **Arnold Fanck** on **mountain films**. This led to his being lead cameraman on Fanck's *Das Wunder des Schneeschuhs* (*The Miracle of the Snow Shoe*, 1920), the beginning of a long series of mountain films he and Fanck made together, among them *Der heilige Berg* (*The Sacred Mountain*, 1926), *Die weiße Hölle von Piz Palü* (*The White Hell of Pitz Palu*, 1929), and *Stürme über dem Mont Blanc* (*Avalanche*, 1930), all starring **Leni Riefenstahl**. Mountain films pit man against the elements, setting their narratives of love amid the grandeur of snow-covered mountains. As cocreator with Fanck of the mountain film, Allgeier gave the genre its sense of danger and excitement. His camera was tied to snowshoes, raced down mountains, got buried in snow, and otherwise captured the sensuous feel of the outdoors. Allgeier also worked with **Luis Trenker**, another director of mountain films and other films of adventure. For Trenker, he continued to capture the beauty of the outdoors in films such as *Berge in Flammen* (*Mountains on Fire*, 1931); *Der Rebell* (1932), released with a slightly different cast as *The Rebel* in 1933; and *Der Berg ruft* (*The Mountain Calls*, 1938).

Allgeier became Riefenstahl's head cinematographer on her propaganda masterpiece *Triumph des Willens* (*Triumph of the Will*, 1935), a film that had 18 other cameramen. Allgeier is credited with creating the mass dynamics that give the film its monumental effect. As a member of Riefenstahl's team on the front in Poland, Allgeier also contributed to the weekly newsreels that were compiled by Fritz Hippler from his headquarters in Berlin. After the war, he worked as cameraman for German television, continuing to excel in documentaries shot outdoors on location. *See also* MOUNTAIN FILM.

ANDRA, FERN (1895–1974). Born in the United States, Fern Andra became one of the most popular German actresses in the 1910s and early 1920s in Germany. Like **Asta Nielsen** and **Henny Porten**, Andra chose roles that suited her public persona, in her case that of an athletic beauty. She grew up in front of the camera, appearing in her first film in New York, *Uncle Tom's Cabin* (1901), at the age of six. Shortly thereafter she made films in England, before going to first Vienna and then Berlin to gain stardom. Andra starred in two genres, the circus film, owing to her beginnings as part of a circus troupe, and the sentimental melodrama. In the latter, she exploited her beauty in roles that called for overcoming adversity. Andra was a shrewd businesswoman who knew how to promote her films. After 1915, she produced, wrote, and directed many of her movies. She ended her film career in the late 1920s in England after her brand of ingénue heroine had gone out of style in Germany.

ANGST, RICHARD (1905–1984). In a career that spanned five decades, Richard Angst worked as cinematographer for the biggest names in film entertainment, including **Arnold Fanck**, **Kurt Hoffmann**, and Paul Martin. During the Third Reich, he also worked with Hans Steinhoff on some of the National Socialists' less propaganda-laden works: *Die Geierwally* (*Geierwally*, 1940), based on a novel by Wilhelmine von Hillern (1875) and turned into an opera by Alfredo Catalani (1892), and *Rembrandt* (*Rembrandt*, 1942), one of many National Socialist films about European artists, scientists, and political leaders. Although better known for his outdoor work, Angst's cinematography of light and shadow captures the mood of the Dutch painter's works.

As a fanatical mountain climber and outdoorsman, Angst was naturally drawn to Fanck's **mountain films** in the 1920s and early 1930s. Recruited initially by **Sepp Allgeier**, Fanck's main cinematographer, Angst worked on such films as *Der große Sprung* (*The Big Jump*, 1927), *Die weiße Hölle vom Piz Palü* (*The White Hell of Pitz Palu*, 1929), *Stürme über Mont Blanc* (*Avalanche*, 1930), and *S.O.S. Eisberg* (*S.O.S. Iceberg*, 1933), all films that placed man at the mercy of the grandeur and fierceness of nature. Although Allgeier is generally credited with the look of the mountain films, Angst's mountaineering skills added to the dangerous stunts that created the excitement of the genre.

In the 1950s, Angst was chief cameraman on that decade's major films: *Wirtshaus im Spessart* (*Spessart Inn*, 1955) and *Wir Wunderkinder* (*Aren't We Wonderful?*, 1958), both by Hoffmann; *Peter schießt den Vogel ab* (*Peter Shoots down the Bird*, Géza Cziffra, 1959); and *La Paloma* (*Martin*, 1959). With the exception of *Wir Wunderkinder*, the films are escapist fare, used as vehicles for singing and comedy. Hoffman's *Wir Wunderkinder* is a satire of proto-Nazism,

Nazism, and neo-Nazism, spanning the years 1914 to the mid-1950s. Angst's ability to capture atmosphere through the camera is once again evident in *Wir Wunderkinder*, as it was in *Rembrandt*. The other films are well-lit musicals, of which there were many made during the 1950s by Angst and others, and none of which reveals an especially notable style. *See also* MOUNTAIN FILM.

ARNHEIM, RUDOLF (1904–2007). Rudolf Arnheim was one of the pioneers of formalist film theory. In his book *Film als Kunst* (*Film as Art*, 1933), Arnheim suggested that the very essence of film is to be found in its limited abilities to reproduce reality. That is, a filmed object or activity gains its aesthetic dimension, and thus its meaning, precisely because it is perceived differently than if it were being viewed in person. Thus Arnheim, unlike another German film theorist, the realist **Siegfried Kracauer**, decried technical innovations such as sound and color because they gave movies a greater sense of realism, detracting from their artistic possibilities. For Arnheim, film reached its zenith during the silent era, a time when directors had to work within the limitations of silence and black and white in their attempts to give artistic expression to the world. Arnheim immigrated to America in 1940, teaching first at Sarah Lawrence University and later at Harvard University.

AUFKLÄRUNGSFILM. The *Aufklärungsfilm*, literally "film of enlightenment," may refer to any film that educates its viewers, especially on controversial topics. In actuality, though, the term refers to films with sexual topics. These run the gamut from truly educational works to sexual exploitation movies. Although films of sexual education occur throughout film history, there have been two major periods, both marked by a relaxation in censorship policies that led to more sexually oriented material.

After World War I ended in 1918, Germany was beset with problems of poverty, revolution, and general disillusionment. The Weimar government had not yet solidified its power base, and individual cities were subject for a short period to soviet-style coups. In the chaos that prevailed during this time, censorship of films was abandoned, and film companies produced sexually oriented films that had previously been forbidden. The most notorious titles of these early sex films included *Der Weg, der zur Verdammnis führt II – Hyänen der Lust* (*Way to Damnation II: Hyenas of Lust*, Otto Rippert, 1919) and *Aus eines Mannes Mädchenjahre* (*From a Man's Maidenhood*, Karl Grune and Paul Legband, 1919), the former about unbridled sexuality, the latter about hermaphroditism. In addition to the number of exploitative titles, a number of genuine sexual enlightenment films were also made, many by **Richard Oswald**, one of the German film industry's most successful producers and directors of the 1910s. His films included the four-part series *Es werde Licht* (*Let There Be Light*, 1917/1918), the first episodes about venereal disease, the last a plea to reform Paragraph 218, the law outlawing abortion in Germany, a controversial topic throughout the 1920s. He also did films on prostitution, including *Die Prostitution. Teil I: Das gelbe Haus, Teil II: Die sich verkaufen* (*Prostitution, Part 1: The Yellow House, Part 2: Those Who Sell Themselves*, 1919) One of his most controversial films was *Anders als die Andern* (*Different from the Others*), about homosexuality. It joined other voices of the time that were advocating repeal of paragraph 175 of the penal code, which made homosexuality a crime.

The late 1960s, the time of the so-called sexual revolution, brought another wave of sexually oriented films, again dressed up as documentaries of sex education. Oswalt Kolle produced and wrote the most successful series, a group of films focusing on humans as sexual beings. Titles include *Das Wunder der Liebe* (*The Miracle of Love*, Franz Josef Gottlieb, 1968), *Oswalt Kolle: Deine Frau, das unbekannte Wesen* (*Your Wife, the Unknown Creature*, Alexis Neve, 1969), *Oswalt Kolle: Dein Mann, das unbekannte Wesen* (*Your Husband, the Unknown Creature*, Werner M. Lenz, 1970), and *Oswalt Kolle: Was ist eigentlich Pornographie* (*What Exactly Is Pornography*, Kolle, 1971), among others. Kolle's films, documentary in nature, were influenced by two internationally successful Swedish films of the time, *I Am Curious, Yellow* (Vilgot Sjöman, 1967) and *I Am Curious, Blue* (Sjöman, 1968), in which a young woman travels through Sweden searching for her political, national, and most important, sexual nature. Kolle's films never enjoyed the notoriety of the Swedish movies, perhaps because they approached the subject of sexuality with awe-infused reverence instead of the irony with which Sjöman looked at sex. Other directors from the late 1960s and early

1970s were equally as irreverent as their Swedish colleague, but without the explicit nature of his sex scenes. Erich F. Bender's *Helga* (1967) and *Helga und Michael* (*Helga and Michael*, 1968) focus on sexual education for teenagers, made palatable by wrapping the lessons in a love story and appealing young characters.

Whereas the reinstatement of censorship laws in 1920 ended the sexually oriented films during the Weimar Republic, the second wave of sex films died from the public becoming satiated with and eventually tired of soft-core sex films, which seemed to dominate German screens in the late 1960s. The films used mistaken identity, double entendres, vulgar language, and above all nudity to reflect the liberal and liberated sexual mores of the time. They no longer hid the sex behind enlightenment, and thus the genre turned from enlightenment to entertainment.

AUSTRIAN CINEMA. Austrian directors, actors, cinematographers, writers, and producers have played a part in international cinema since 1895, the beginning of the film industry. Yet it is difficult to identify with precision the exact nature of Austrian cinema. From the early days of cinema, film has been a global phenomenon, and directors, actors, and writers, among others, have traveled to where they could find work. For Austrians, this meant moving to Berlin. Thus **Richard Oswald**, a pioneer of cinema and a director whose structured films influenced the filmmakers in the early silent era, moved to Berlin for his film career. Although Austrian by birth, he is one of the many of his countrymen during that era who worked in the German film industry. Two other Viennese, Erich von Stroheim and Josef von Sternberg, began their careers in America. Von Stroheim returned to Europe in the 1930s, making films in France. Von Sternberg was hired by **Erich Pommer** to direct *Der blaue Engel* (*The Blue Angel*, 1930), one of the best-known early German talking films. Karl Grune, another well-known silent film director, whose film *Die Straße* (*The Street*, 1923), about the dangers of street life, influenced a genre of film, also pursued his career in Berlin. Finally, **Carl Mayer**, the writer of *Das Cabinet des Dr. Caligari* (*The Cabinet of Dr. Caligari*, **Robert Wiene**, 1920), German film's best-known silent work, was from Graz, Austria.

Even though most directors in the silent era left Austria to make films elsewhere, a few directors pursued at least part of their career in their homeland. Gustav Ucicky and **Willi Forst**, for example, had successful careers in Germany as well as Austria in the 1920s and 1930s. Forst wrote, directed, and acted in light romances, musicals, and operettas. Films such as *Oh, du lieber Augustin* (*Oh, Dear Augustine*, H. K. Breslauer, 1922) and *Café Elektrik* (*Café Electric*, Gustav Ucicky, 1927), silent films in which he acted, and *Maskerade* (*Masquerade in Vienna*, 1934), *Unfinished Symphony* (*Unfinished Symphony*, 1934), *Burgtheater* (*Burgtheater*, 1936), all of which he directed, show a tendency of Austrian film to favor commercial appeal over artistic pretensions, a tendency also found in Oswald, von Sternberg, Grune, and Ucicky. After the National Socialists annexed Austria to Germany in 1938, Forst's films continued to have an Austrian flavor: *Operette* (*Operetta*, 1940) and *Wiener Blut* (*Vienna Blood*, 1942) stress the Austrian stereotype of music, romance, and relaxed personality. Postwar films likewise traded on the Viennese stereotype: *Wiener Mädel* (*Vienna Maidens*, 1949) and *Wien, du Stadt meiner Träume* (*Vienna, City of My Dreams*, 1957) view Vienna as an Old World city of music and love. Ucicky's films show a similar pattern of being made with a sense of a wider audience in mind. For example, *Pratermizzi* (*Pratermizzi*, 1927), which alludes to a Viennese amusement park (Prater) and a young woman (Mizzi) who works as a cashier at the park's tunnel of love, captures the melodramatic sensationalism of Ucicky's silent films, others of which are *Tingel Tangel* (1927), the title referring to a burlesque club, and *Café Elektrik*, also about night life in the city.

After World War II, Austrian cinema became known as the home of some of the European film industry's biggest stars. As was true during the silent era, however, much of the work of actors such as **Maximillian Schell**, **Maria Schell**, and **Romy Schneider** was for non-Austrian production companies. Maximillian Schell, for example, began his career in West German films before establishing himself as a major presence in Hollywood films. His two contributions to Austrian film were as a director. *Geschichte aus dem Wienerwald* (*Tales from the Vienna Woods*, 1979) creates a quasi anti-Viennese atmosphere that deconstructed the romantic clichés of the Vienna found in the films of Forst, Ucicky, and earlier Austrian directors. Maximillian Schell's other Austrian film, *Meine Schwester Maria* (*My Sister Maria*, 2002) pays homage to his sister Maria Schell, who gained international recognition in *Der Engel mit der Posaune* (*The Angel with the Trumpet*, **Karl Hartl**, 1948). As is true of many of the films that fall within Austrian cinema, *Der Engel mit der Posaune* focused on Austrian history and culture, emphasizing the country's musical heritage. *Nach dem Sturm* (*After the Storm*, Ucicky, 1948) looks at how the life of a young Austrian musician, played by Maria Schell, has been devastated by her incarceration by the Nazis during World War II. Schneider's contribution to Austrian cinema is more extensive than that of the Schells, owing to her association with Marischka, an Austro-Hungarian director of romances and musicals, whose films exploited the Austrian stereotype of music and romance. Starring in several of Marischka's films, Schneider became associated with her portrayal of Empress Elisabeth of Austria (aka Sissy) in a series of films on the ruler. Schneider, too, though, continued her career after a while in West Germany, Hollywood, and finally France.

Films made about Austria's annexation by Germany and its role during World War II and auteur films made after 1970 show evidence of a cohesive body of films that reflect Austrian concerns and show evidence of an Austrian style. As early as 1948, with *Der Engel mit der Posaune* and *Nach dem Sturm*, Austrian cinema began focusing on the historical legacy of the country's complicity in its annexation. Such early *Vergangenheitsbewältigungsfilm* gave a largely uncritical interpretation of the past, similar to early films in both West Germany and East Germany. But like the films in those countries, the Austrian films about the past would gain in critical awareness as the past receded. For example, *Die letzte Brücke* (*The Last Bridge*, **Helmut Käutner**, 1954) examines partisan fighting in Yugoslavia. Although the film is not about Austria's role in the war, Maria Schell's presence in the main role and financing from the Austrian film industry make it an Austrian film. Furthermore, *Die letzte Brücke* contains the binary tendency of postwar films about Austria and the National Socialists: On the one hand, the films acknowledged participation in the crimes of the Nazis; on the other hand, they stressed the individual Austrian's will to resist. Franz Antel, in *Der Bockerer* (*Bockerer*, 1981), tells of a Viennese butcher who openly defies the Nazis. In *Eine Minute Dunkel macht uns nicht blind* (*A Minute of Darkness Will Not Blind Us*, 1986), Susanne Zanke tells the story of real-life resister Schütte Luhotzky, who endured imprisonment for her political opposition. Two years earlier, a consortium of women directors filmed *Küchengespräche* (*Kitchen Talks*, Karin Berger, Elisabeth Holzinger, Charlotte Oodgornikand, Lisbeth N. Trallori, 1984), a documentary. Wolfgang Glück's *38— Auch das war Wien* (*38—Vienna before the Fall*, 1987) portrays a Vienna in which Jews and non-Jews function alongside each other, at least in the theater, until the Nazis march into the country.

In the made-for-television trilogy *Wohin und Zurück* (*Whereto and Back*, 1982–1986), Axel Corti likewise reveals the complicity of non-Jewish Austrians in the Anschluß, or annexation, of Austria into the National Socialist Empire. The first of the films, *An uns glaubt Gott nicht mehr* (*God Does Not Believe in Us Anymore*, 1982), follows a young man staying one step ahead of the Nazis as he flees Vienna, makes his way through France, and escapes to America. The second film *Santa Fe* (1986) shows his life in America, and in the third he returns to Vienna as a soldier helping restore normalcy after the war. The film emphasizes how easily former Nazis and their sympathizers integrated back into leadership in the country, often with the cynical understanding of the Allies. Also working for Austrian television, Karin Brandauer tells the story of a young Roma girl, whose adoption by an Austrian family does not save her from death in Auschwitz because of the prejudices of the family's neighbors and friends. Noted actor **Klaus Maria Brandauer**, Karin Brandauer's husband, also appeared in a series of Austrian, Hungarian, and West German coproductions exploring the roots of fascism. *Mephisto* (1981), based on a novel by Klaus Mann, looks at the phenomenon of opportunism among theater professionals. *Oberst Redl* (*Colonel Redl* 1985) traces the roots of fascism to the protofascist Austro-Hungarian Empire. *Hanussen* (*Hanussen*, 1988), again, explores opportunism among people in the theater, telling the quasi-true, but highly distorted, story of an Austro-Hungarian Jew who passed himself off as non-Jewish and served for a while as Adolf Hitler's mystic consultant. All three films were directed by Hungarian director **István Szabó**, who made a number of German films and whose works show the difficulty of identifying a purely Austrian cinema. The three films starring Brandauer had multinational financing, Austrian as well as German actors, a Hungarian director, and an original German audio track. Two were also based on Austrian personalities, Redl and Hanussen. Yet beyond the themes, nothing identifies them as Austrian cinema.

Film historians generally agree that Austrian cinema benefited from the French New Wave and the **New German Cinema** movements of the 1960s. Just as their French and German colleagues did, Austrian directors rebelled against what they saw as a cinema of lies to create a highly individualized auteur cinema or, in German, Autorenkino. Most prominent of the new wave Austrian directors is **Michael Haneke**, whose films depict a world whose calm, almost emotionless exterior hides a disturbingly violent reality. In *Der siebente Kontinent* (*The Seventh Continent*, 1989), a financially successful, upper-middle-class couple kills themselves and their daughter. In *Benny's Video* (*Benny's Video*, 1992), an adolescent prone to watching violence on television kills a young girl and chops up her body. Haneke's later works reveal how difficult it is identifying even an Austrian auteur cinema. Since 2001 he has made his films in France, with French actors, in the French language, but the preoccupation with violence remains. Austria also remains in the credits as one of the countries producing the film. **Xaver Schwarzenberger**, Franz Novotny, and **Valie Export** are other directors from the new wave whose films help define Austrian cinema of the 1980s and 1990s as experimental. Better known as **Rainer Werner Fassbinder**'s cinematographer, Schwarzenberger has directed a number of films for Austrian television, the venue of choice and maybe necessity for many Austrian directors. Novotny directs for both television and theatrical release. Export is best known for her performance art projects but directed the experimental science fiction film *Unsichtbare Gegner* (*Invisible Adversaries*, 1977), a parody of the American classic *The Invasion of the Body Snatchers* (Don Siegel, 1956).

Austria's best-known auteur, **Georg Wilhelm Pabst**, whose cutting on action and sociopolitical themes exemplify his style, seldom worked in Austria during a career that spanned the 1920s through the 1950s. Thus, although books on Austrian cinema give him prominent mention, he is one more example of the difficulty there is in describing Austrian cinema.

– B –

BABELSBERG STUDIOS. Babelsberg Studios (Studio Babelsberg), located near Berlin, today comprise sound stages, outdoor lots, prop warehouses, and a theme park. The first studio at Babelsberg, a district of Pottsdam, was built by **Bioscop** in 1911, a studio that merged with the French group Decla after World War I. Both were then merged into **Universum Film AG** (Ufa) in 1921. Babelsberg quickly became Germany's Hollywood. Ufa-Stadt (Ufa City), as it came to be known, offered films such as *Metropolis* (**Fritz Lang**, 1927), *Der blaue Engel* (*The Blue Angel*, Josef von Sternberg, 1930), and *Der Kongreß tanzt*, (*Congress Dances*, Erik Charell, 1931) and over 4,000,000 square feet of buildings and lots, including 10 sound studios, synchronization facilities, 250 individual dressing rooms, 2,500 extras, a 255-foot-long and 45-foot-wide small town street with 50 buildings, a 270-foot-long and 66-foot-wide paved city street, a small palace surrounded by a garden, brooks, a pond, 10,000 pieces of furniture, 8,000 costumes, 2,000 wigs, ocean liner furnishings, boat chimneys, and construction equipment and materials for building any number of sets (statistics come from Curt Riess, *Das gab's nur einmal*, vol. 2, 1985). Approximately 1,000 of the 1,100 feature films made by the Nazis used the studios and lots of Babelsberg between 1933 and 1945. After Germany's defeat in World War II, Babelsberg lay in what was to become the German Democratic Republic. The **East German film** studio known as **DEFA** (Deutsche Film Aktiengesellschaft) made many of its feature, children's, and television films on the lot until the East German government was absorbed into a united Germany in 1990. At that time, the studio was put into a trust and subsequently sold to private industry, which has once again made Babelsberg into a competitive studio for international productions. Among the better known of these are *Enemy at the Gates* (Jacques-Annaud, 1993); *Around the World in 80 Days* (Frank Caraci, 2004), starring Jackie Chan; and *V for Vendetta* (James McTeigue, 2005).

BACKUS, GUS (1937–). Gus Backus is one of a number of American singers and actors whose careers flourished in Germany. A member of the 1950s American pop music singing group the Del-Vikings, Backus spent a year in Germany in the military in the late 1950s. In 1961, he had his first hit in Germany and became a singing sensation. Just as his German singing contemporaries, Roy Black and **Peter Alexander**, Backus starred in a number of teenage and 20-something comedies that spotlighted his singing talents and helped sell his records.

BAER, HARRY (1947–). Harry Baer was one of the members of **Rainer Werner Fassbinder**'s *antiteater* in Munich, appearing in the director's *Preparadise sorry now* (*Preparadise Sorry Now*, 1969), an experimental play confronting the relationship between violence and media representation. Baer became a regular performer in Fassbinder's films when the director turned to moviemaking. He played primarily subsidiary roles but had leading parts in *Götter der Pest* (*Gods of the Plague*, 1970), *Pioniere in Ingolstadt* (*Pioneers in Ingolstadt*, 1971), and *Wildwechsel* (*Jail Bait*, aka *Wild Game*, 1973). Baer also starred as Ludwig II in **Hans-Jürgen Syberberg**'s *Ludwig – Requiem für einen jungfräulichen König* (*Ludwig: Requiem for a Virgin King*, 1972), and played in supporting roles in films by **Werner Schroeter** (*Polermo oder Wolfsburg* [*Polermo or Wolfsburg*], 1980), **Doris Dörrie** (*Im Innern des Wals*, [*In the Belly of the Whale*], 1985), and Finnish director Mika Kaurismäki (*Helsinki Napoli All Night Long*, 1987).

BALÁCZS, BÉLA (1884–1949). Béla Baláczs (a pseudonym for Herbert Bauer) was a film theorist and historian as well as the writer of screenplays. His major contributions include *The Visible Man* (1924) and *The Theory of the Film: Character and Growth of a New Art* (1948). Film historian James Monaco described the latter as "one of the most balanced volumes of its kind." Often compared to the Soviet formalists V. I. Pudovkin and Sergei Eisenstein, Baláczs placed less emphasis on abstract montage than they did. In particular, he emphasized the importance of the close-up for showing the essence of things. According to Baláczs all things in a film have symbolic meaning, which he referred to as a thing's physiognomy. Directors cannot show things objectively, that is, stripped of their symbolic importance. They can, however, control how the things appear. Baláczs's theory of the symbolism inherent in all things also influenced his approach to a film's reception. An early practitioner of semiology or the science of signs, he concluded that viewer responses to films and their images are influenced by the cultural values spectators share with the director.

Baláczs's most important screenplays were *Das blaue Licht* (*The Blue Light*, **Leni Riefenstahl**, 1932), *Die Dreigroschenoper* (*The Threepenny Opera*, **Georg Wilhelm Pabst**, 1931), and *Die Abenteuer* *eines Zehnmarkscheines* (*The Adventures of a Ten Mark Bill*, Berthold Viertel, 1926). For the most part, his other scripts were commercial products, a criticism that could also be applied to the *Die Dreigroschenoper* adaptation, from which he distanced himself, often requesting that no screen credit be given. Toward the end of his career Baláczs helped revitalize the film industry in Hungary, the country of his birth.

BALLHAUS, MICHAEL (1935–). Michael Ballhaus, one of Germany's most successful cameramen, began his career in 1960 for German television, often teaming with director **Peter Lilienthal**. In 1971, he worked on **Rainer Werner Fassbinder's** *Whity* (*Whity*, 1971), which began a 10-year association that produced *Angst essen Seele auf* (*Ali: Fear Eats the Soul*, 1974), *Faustrecht der Freiheit* (*Fox and His Friends*, 1975), and *Die Ehe der Maria Braun* (*The Marriage of Maria Braun*, 1979), three of **New German Cinema's** most memorable films. Although it is difficult to determine the exact extent of Ballhaus's contribution to the collaboration, given Fassbinder's control over his productions, Ballhaus is credited with opening Fassbinder's films up, using camera movement and angles to underscore the melodrama in the films. Furthermore, Ballhaus brought a higher degree of craftsmanship to the set. The lighting tends to be more uniform, the sets deeper, and the actors more lively than in the films Fassbinder made before his association with Ballhaus. On his philosophy of cinematography, Ballhaus commented that "one has to utilize all technical possibilities at one's disposal to tell a story."

As did other members of Fassbinder's ensemble, Ballhaus proved that there was life after splitting with the director. After leaving Fassbinder, Ballhaus worked with **Hans W. Geissendörfer**, **Margarethe von Trotta**, and **Volker Schlöndorff** among other members of New German Cinema. In 1982, he was director of photography for John Sayles's *Baby It's You* (1982) and worked with the director again on a Bruce Springsteen video, *I'm on Fire* (1985), for which Ballhaus received a music video award. He has won two German **Film Awards** and has been nominated for three Academy Awards, including one for *Gangs of New York* (2002), directed by Martin Scorsese, with whom Ballhaus has worked on a number of films, most recently *The Departed* (2006).

Ballhaus favors a fluidly moving camera and evocative angles. He assured his reputation as an innovative cameraman with Fassbinder's *Martha* (*Martha*, 1974), in which he used a 360-degree tracking shot. Ballhaus later said Fassbinder should receive the credit for the shot, as he (Ballhaus) was going to stop after 180 degrees. Ballhaus's success and innovative camerawork is reminiscent of **Karl Freund**, another German cinematographer, who after establishing himself on major German productions in the 1920s, went to Hollywood to continue a successful career.

BAMBI. *See* FILM AWARDS.

BAVARIA FILM. During the 1920s, Bavaria Film GmbH, founded in 1919, offered filmmakers an alternative to the **Babelsberg Studios**, Germany's largest film studio. After World War II, the studio gained in importance because the Babelsberg Studios were located in East Germany. Bavaria Film GmbH is particularly important for television, but it is also the location at which **Wolfgang Petersen** shot his first three international hits, *Das Boot* (*The Boat*, 1981), *Die unendliche Geschichte* (*The Neverending Story*, 1984), and *Enemy Mine* (1985). In addition to sound stages and studio lots, Bavaria Film offers a virtual tour of filmmaking and film history similar to the tours in Hollywood studios.

BENNENT, DAVID (1966–). Son of actor **Heinz Bennent**, David Bennent's major role was as Oskar Matzerath, a child who decides to stop growing at the age of three, in **Volker Schlöndorff**'s *Die Blechtrommel* (*The Tin Drum*, 1979). Few readers and critics of the Günter Grass eponymously titled novel (1959) believed Grass's work could ever be filmed, as it required finding an actor who could function as child and adult. Bennent, who has dwarfism and who was 13 at the time, played the part as a precocious child who grows into a young man, but without ever changing physical appearance. Bennent's small physical features limit his roles; but he appeared in the fantasy film *Legend* (Ridley Scott, 1975) and also in Spike Lee's *She Hate Me* (2004).

BENNENT, HEINZ (1921–). Heinz Bennent began acting in films at age 35, after a career as a stage actor. In spite of the late start he has appeared in over 80 films, including some of West Germany's best-known works from **New German Cinema**. His style could be described as the nervous shyness of a man in a position to assert himself who retreats into himself instead. In **Volker Schlöndorff**'s and **Margarethe von Trotta**'s *Die verlorene Ehre der Katharina Blum* (*The Lost Honor of Katharina Blum*, 1975), Bennent played Dr. Blorna, the title character's left-leaning employer and mentor, who is both sympathetic to and distant from Katharina's troubles. In Schlöndorff's *Die Blechtrommel* (*The Tin Drum*, 1979), he plays Greff, a greengrocer who acts as a pied piper to the youth in the area. Bennent also worked for Schlöndorff in the director's episode "Die verschobene Antigone" ("The Deferred Antigone") in *Deutschland im Herbst* (*Germany in Autumn*, 1978), an omnibus film by Germany's leading leftist directors and actors protesting the West German government's actions in several incidents in 1977. Bennent has also acted for Swedish director Ingmar Bergman, in *The Serpent's Egg* (1977) and *Aus dem Leben der Marionetten* (*From the Life of Marionettes*, 1980), two of the director's non-Swedish-language films. Many of Bennent's 80 plus films were made for German television, where he has enjoyed a long and distinguished career.

BERGFILM. See MOUNTAIN FILM.

BERGER, SENTA (1941–). Winner of a Golden Globe award in 1965 for most promising young actress, Senta Berger has had a varied career in Germany, Italy, and the United States as stage, screen, and television actor, singer, and producer. Her Sentana Productions contributed to the growth of **New German Cinema** through its financing of films by her husband, director **Michael Verhoeven**, and other directors.

Berger's U.S. credits include roles in the films *Major Dundee* (Sam Peckinpah, 1964), *The Quiller Memorandum* (Michael Anderson, 1966), *The Ambushers* (Henry Levin, 1967) and *If It's Tuesday, This Must Be Belgium* (Mel Stuart, 1968/1969). In all but the last film, she played the part of a foreign temptress, a role in which she was essentially typecast in much of her German and Italian work as well.

Berger's German credits include Hester Prynne in **Wim Wenders**'s *Der scharlachrote Buchstab* (*The Scarlet Letter*, 1972/1973), musical comedies, and spy thrillers. She has also acted in numerous television films, including the popular miniseries *Kir Royal* (*Kir Royal*, **Helmut Dietl**, 1984–1986), *Die schnelle Gerdi* (*Fast Gerdi*, 1989–2004), *Ärzte: Dr. Schwarz und Dr. Martin* (*Doctors*, 1994–1996), and *Unter Verdacht* (*Under Suspicion*, 2002–2005). Berger plays a cab driver in the Gerdi films, which were directed by her husband Michael Verhoeven. In addition to the Golden Globe, she won a Bambi in 1967 for acting and a **Film Award** in Silver as producer of *Die weiße Rose* (*The White Rose*, Verhoeven, 1982). Together with Verhoeven, she also produced the critically acclaimed and award-winning films *Das schreckliche Mädchen* (*The Nasty Girl*, 1990) and *Mutters Courage* (*My Mother's Courage*, 1995). With the notable exception of a role in *Bin ich Schön?* (*Am I Beautiful?* **Dorris Dörrie**, 1998), Berger's film work since the early 1980s has been for German television.

BERLIN FILM FESTIVAL. Also known as the Berlinale, the Berlin Film Festival was first held June 6–18, 1951. Over the years it has remained one of the three major European film festivals, and its Golden Bear award for top film is as coveted by directors as the Golden Palm of the Cannes Film Festival or the Golden Lion of the Venice Film Festival. It may also be the most film-oriented of the festivals, exhibiting more films than other festivals, albeit most not in competition.

In 1970 the festival was almost disbanded when disagreement broke out over awarding a prize to **Michael Verhoeven**'s *o.k.*, a film about the actual rape and murder of a Vietnamese girl by a band of American GIs. Although this incident was made into a successful Hollywood production 20 years later, starring Michael J. Fox (*Casualties of War*, Brian De Palma, 1989), the topic was too controversial for 1970. The festival ended amid protests and resolutions and with no prizes being awarded. The following year, a new section was opened to serve young directors. In 1986, a less-contentious split occurred over **Reinhard Hauff**'s film *Stammheim* (*Stammheim*), about the imprisonment of the Baader-Meinhof radicals. Jury chair Gina Lolobrigida broke the tie in favor of Hauff's film, awarding it a Golden Bear.

At times German film directors have objected to America's domination at the festival. They perceive Hollywood films as exercising hegemony over German-made ones in German movie theaters and also specifically at the festival. **Volker Schlöndorff**, head of the **Babelsberg Studios**, has decried the number of screens devoted to American films, because they present an American-biased view of the world and history. With the recent revival of German film's competitive quality, beginning with **Tom Tykwer**'s *Lola rennt* (*Run Lola Run*, 1998), German film has won back some of its lost screen presence, including capturing a Golden Bear at the 2004 Berlinale for *Gegen die Wand* (*Head-On*, **Fatih Akin**, 2004) and a Silver Bear at the 2005 Berlinale for *Sophie Scholl – Die letzten Tage* (*Sophie Scholl: The Final Days*, Marc Rothemund, 2005).

BEYER, FRANK (1932–2006). Along with **Kurt Maetzig**, **Heiner Carow**, and **Konrad Wolf**, Frank Beyer gave the cinema of the former German Democratic Republic (GDR) its particular stylistic and thematic character. Seeing their country as pioneering a new socialist Germany, born from the defeat of the Third Reich, the three men, in particular Beyer, felt obligated to attack fascism and bolster East Germans in the building of a new socialist state in the GDR in their films. The films employ the elements of socialist realism: heroic workers, soldiers and peasants, ideological clarity, political tendentiousness, party speeches, solidarity, and guarded optimism. Yet they also experiment with film form, looking for new ways to deliver the socialist message. Thematically, the films of these directors try to come to terms with Germany's Nazi past. Sometimes they attack Nazism directly by focusing on historical situations. At other times, they confront the Nazi legacy by fighting its memory in the present.

Beyer clearly sees his country's past sins with the eyes of someone who was too young to have been involved. His films reveal a mixture of anger, sadness, and curiosity. Over and over he finds his material in the conflict between past and present, fascism and socialism, bad and good. Yet any attempt to pigeonhole his films fails because of his diversity of material and styles. *Fünf Patronenhülsen* (*Five Cartridges*, 1960) takes place during the Spanish Civil War and is an action-packed war film. *Königskinder* (*Royal Children*, 1962), on the other hand, is a love story. But even films with the same setting can be vastly different. Thus, *Nackt unter Wölfen* (*Naked among Wolves*, 1963) presents a naturalistic chronicle of life in a concentration camp, whereas *Jakob der Lügner* (*Jacob the Liar*, 1974) tells a melancholy, poetic story about life in the ghetto. Holding these films together is the director's belief that film must educate but also entertain. Film critic and director Hans C. Blumenberg summarizes the films as "optimistic tragedies about the principle of hope in hopeless times." Yet Beyer's films were not always accepted by authorities. His 1966 film *Spur der Steine* (*Trace of Stones*), for example, was withdrawn by authorities as too critical of East German institutions. Beyer's later career was mostly as a director of television films. *See also* EAST GERMAN FILM.

BIEBRACH, RUDOLF (1866–1938). Actor and director Rudolf Biebrach was an important presence in the silent film era in Germany. After a successful career on stage in a number of German cities, Biebrach directed himself and German silent era superstar **Henny Porten** in *Andreas Hofer* (1909), about the early 19th-century freedom fighter. He returned to stage acting until 1913, when he again worked with Porten in the short *Des Pfarrers Töchterlein* (*The Minister's Daughter*, Adolf Gärtner). Over the next few years, Biebrach appeared with Porten in a number of films produced by **Oskar Messter** and directed by **Carl Froelich**, Curt A. Stark, or himself. Messter's skill as producer and promoter made Porten, Biebrach, Stark, and Froehlich into one of the most successful teams in early film history. Biebrach's career as actor and director continued throughout the 1920s. He also directed a few minor films in the early days of sound and played minor roles in films during the Nazi era, until his death in 1938.

BIOSCOP GMBH BERLIN. Bioscop, one of Germany's first commercial film studios, began producing films in 1899. Named for a projection system invented by **Max Skladanowsky** that had already been superseded by the time of the studio's first production, Bioscop's first films were short documentaries of news events, such as state visits to the emperor, or daily activities like lunching at a restaurant. Some of the early works were invented stories, however. In both documentaries and story films, Bioscop's films paralleled what studios in France, America, and elsewhere were doing. In 1911, Bioscop built a studio that later became the **Babelsberg Studios**. During the

1910s, the studio produced some of Germany's better-known horror or fantasy films, including *Der Student von Prag* (*The Student of Prague*, Stellan Rye and Paul Wegener, 1913), about a young man who sells his mirror image for fame, fortune, and a girl. The film had a sequel, *Der andere Student von Prag* (*The Other Student of Prague*, Emil Albes, 1913/1914), which has been lost. Bioscop also made *Der Golem* (*The Golem*, **Henrik Galeen** and **Paul Wegener**, 1915), about a Jewish legend that tells of a statue that comes to life. This film inspired two sequels, *Der Golem und die Tänzerin* (*The Golem and the Dancer*, Rochus Gliese and Wegener, 1917) and *Alraune und der Golem* (*Alraune and the Golem*, Nils Chrisander, 1919), both of which are lost. The studio also produced the successful *Homunkulus* series (*Homunculus*, Otto Rippert, 1916), about a man created in a laboratory. After World War I, the French studio Decla bought Bioscop and the new studio, Decla-Bioscop, was bought out in the 1920s and merged into **Universum Film AG** (Ufa). Since 1973, a newly founded Bioskop studio (now spelled with a "k") has financed films from its office in Munich.

BIRGEL, WILLY (1891–1973). Willy Birgel was one of the major stars of the Third Reich. His cultivated mannerisms, learned from work on stage, won him roles as officers, aristocrats, and university educated professionals. Birgel played supporting roles in early National Socialist films, including an English prisoner camp commandant in *Ein Mann will nach Deutschland* (*A Man Wants to Go to Germany*, **Paul Wegener**, 1934). The film was one of several made at the time, including *Schlußakkord* (*The Final Chord*, **Douglas Sirk**, 1936) *Heimat* (*Homeland*, **Carl Froelich**, 1938), and *Der verlorene Sohn* (*The Prodigal Son*, **Luis Trenker**, 1934), in which Germans living abroad return home, a motif of importance to the National Socialists, who were trying to forge a new German national identity.

Birgel's roles as aristocrat took two major directions. Sometimes he was part of a love triangle, usually playing the older of the lovers. At other times, he played a cad, a man who misused the power he had over others by virtue of his position. In *Zu neuen Ufern* (*To New Shores*, Sirk, 1936), the first of three movies he made with National Socialist diva **Zarah Leander**, Birgel played an English aristocrat who commits fraud and allows his lover, played by Leander, to go to prison for his crime. In the film *Der Blaufuchs* (*The Blue Fox*, Viktor Tourjansky, 1938), also starring Leander, he shows a more comedic side to his acting. Playing a reluctant lover to Leander's character, rather than betray her husband and his best friend, Birgel plays against type as he tries to resist committing adultery.

In . . . *reitet für Deutschland* (*Riding for Germany*, Arthur Maria Rabenalt, 1941), Birgel plays what became his best-known role, Rittmeister (cavalry captain) Ernst von Brenken, who comes back after a debilitating injury to lead the German equestrian team to a world championship. As with *Ein Mann kommt nach Deutschland*, Birgel's . . . *reitet für Deutschland* contributed to the National Socialist agenda of forging national unity, as did a film he made a year later, *Diesel* (Gerhard Lamprecht, 1943). The movie is about the inventor Rudolf Diesel and is one of a number of films that highlighted the lives of misunderstood German geniuses.

After World War II, Birgel first starred in, and as he got older had supporting parts in, more than 45 theatrical and television films. Among the better known are *Zwischen gestern und morgen* (*Between Yesterday and Tomorrow*, Harald Braun, 1947), a **rubble film** that follows the lives of several people during and after the war, and two films for **New German Cinema**, *Schonzeit für Füchse* (*Close Season on Foxes*, Peter Schamoni, 1966) and *Sommersprossen* (*Freckles*, Helmut Förnbacher, 1968).

BLAUE ENGEL, DER. Undoubtedly one of the most famous German films ever made, *Der blaue Engel* (*The Blue Angel*, 1930) was directed by the Austrian American Josef von Sternberg and starred **Marlene Dietrich**, **Emil Jannings**, and **Kurt Gerron**. It is based on the novel *Professor Unrat oder das Ende eines Tyrannen* (*Small Town Tyrant*, 1905), by Heinrich Mann, but von Sternberg restructured the novel, deemphasizing its social criticism in favor of highlighting the fatal attraction that dance hall performer Lola Lola has for a middle-aged, lonely, inexperienced high school teacher. Although Dietrich, who played Lola Lola, went on to a successful career in Hollywood, she became forever associated with the amoral seductress that she played in *Der blaue Engel*. For Jannings, it was another role in which he would play a character that was degraded and humiliated. The film also serves as an introduction to the atmospheric, cluttered style of von Sternberg. An English-language version of the film was made simultaneously with the German version, a practice that was common in the early 1930s.

The three principle actors in *Der blaue Engel* had widely varying relationships with the Nazi regime that came to power a few years after the film's release. Dietrich followed von Sternberg back to Hollywood, turning down a request by Minister of Propaganda Joseph Goebbels to play a role in the Nazi film industry. Emil Jannings did not return to Hollywood, preferring to pursue his career in Germany, where he enjoyed considerable success under the Nazis. Kurt Gerron, who was Jewish, was sent to the concentration camp Theresienstadt to make a mock documentary that supported Nazi propaganda about their humane treatment of Jews in the camps. When the documentary was finished, he was sent to Auschwitz and murdered.

Der blaue Engel has been remade twice. Edward Dymtryk directed a remake in 1959, which starred **Kurd Jürgens** and May Britt. **Rainer Werner Fassbinder** paid homage to the film in *Lola* (1981), the last film in his postwar trilogy about Germany in the 1950s.

BLEIBTREU, MORITZ (1971–). One of a number of German actors in the 1990s and 2000s to gain international recognition for their good looks, charismatic personalities, and comedic and dramatic acting talent, Moritz Bleibtreu has appeared in over 40 films, 35 of them between 1995 and 2007. The son of actors Monika Bleibtreu and Hans Brenner, Moritz Bleibtreu had acted in small parts in a few films as a child before going to Paris, Rome, and New York to study acting. Bleibtreu moved from supporting to starring roles after playing a petty mobster in *Knockin' on Heaven's Door* (Thomas Jahn, 1997), for which he won an Award in Gold for Best Supporting Actor (*see* **film awards**) from the Deutsche Filmakademie (German Film Academy). Bleibtreu became a major international star playing Manni, the title heroine's boyfriend in *Lola rennt* (*Run Lola Run*, **Tom Tykwer**, 1998). The actor's three-day beard, laconic smile, and charisma gave him major presence in a supportive role and contributed to his persona of a laconic and vulnerable, if slightly edgy, slacker.

Bleibtreu's other major roles have been in *Im Juli* (*In July*, **Fatih Akin**, 2000), *Das Experiment* (*The Experiment*, **Oliver Hirsch-**

biegel, 2001), *Solino* (*Solino*, Akin, 2002), and *Elementarteilchen* (*Elementary Particles*, aka *Atomized*, Oskar Roehler, 2006). *Im Juli* allowed Bleibtreu to develop his vulnerable, light comedic side, as a student teacher who travels across Eastern Europe to Turkey, to meet a woman with whom he has had a brief affair. He is accompanied for much of the trip by a street vendor, who is in love with him but to whom he is oblivious. In *Das Experiment*, Bleibtreu displays dramatic talent in a film based on the Stanford "prisoner experiment" conducted in 1971. Here also, the actor's persona of vulnerability adds to the dramatic tension created when the experiment goes awry. For these two films, Bleibtreu won an Award in Gold in 2001 from the *Deutsche Filmakademie*. In *Solino*, the actor plays the shyer one of two Italian brothers who immigrate to Germany as young boys and who become estranged for a while then, years later, they both fall in love with the same woman. In *Elementarteilchen*, Bleibtreu played against type in a role as a sex addict in a dysfunctional family.

Fluent in English, French, and Italian, in addition to his native German, Bleibtreu has international presence. He played Andreas in Steven Spielberg's *Munich* (2004) and appears in the epic film *The Keeper: The Legend of Omar Khayyam* (Kayvan Mashayekh, 2005). In addition, he appears in *Taking Sides*, an international production directed by Hungarian **István Szabó** about Wilhelm Furtwangler, whose career flourished under National Socialism, and in *Fakiren fra Bilbao* (*The Fakir*, Peter Flinth, 2004), a spooky Danish children's film.

BOHM, HARK (1939–). Hark Bohm is a director, screenwriter, and actor and one of the cofounders of the **Filmverlag der Autoren**. He has been successful as a director of films for and about adolescents, in which he clearly sides with the youth, showing the world of adults from their perspective. Friendship is a major theme in his work, as his heroes struggle to find their own way in the world. Aside from his first feature, *Tschetan, der Indianerjunge* (*Chetan, the Indian Boy*, 1973), set in the old American West, his films have a contemporary setting. Among these are *Nordsee ist Mordsee* (*North Sea Is Dead Sea*, 1976); *Yasemin* (1988), for which he won an Award in Gold for direction (*see* **film awards**); and *Für immer und immer* (*Forever and Always*, 1997). His television film, *Der Fall Vera Brühne* (*The Trial* *of Vera Brühne*, 2001), departs from his usual theme of adolescents to focus on one of Germany's most notorious postwar murder trials.

As an actor, Bohm often plays officious but decent authority figures. His best-known roles internationally are as the heroine's piano accompanist in *Lili Marleen* (*Lili Marleen*, 1981) and the accountant in **Die Ehe der Maria Braun** (*The Marriage of Maria Braun*, 1979), two of **Rainer Werner Fassbinder**'s biggest successes. In addition, he appeared in minor roles in numerous other Fassbinder films, as well as in those of other major directors, including **Helmut Dietl**'s *Schtonk* (*Schtonk*, 1992), **Margarthe von Trotta**'s *Das Versprechen* (*The Promise*, 1995), and **Werner Herzog**'s *Invincible* (2001).

BOIS, CURT (1901–1991). Curt Bois was a child actor, appearing at age seven in the operetta by Leo Fall, *Der fidele Bauer* (*The Merry Farmer*, 1908), about a peasant boy who dreams of becoming a famous composer. The stage musical was also filmed and recorded on a music disc, an early version of sound technology. Bois continued to appear on stage as well as in film, becoming Germany's first child actor. In the early 1920s, he made the transition to adult star, playing in cabarets and films. Bois became known for his transvestite parts, in particular for *Der Jüngling aus der Konfektion* (*The Lad from the Clothing Industry*, Richard Löwenbein, 1926) and *Der Fürst von Pappenheim* (*The Prince of Pappenheim*, aka *The Masked Mannequin*, Richard Eichberg, 1926). During the Third Reich, Bois's characterizations occasioned ridicule from the Nazis, who berated his stage and film persona as perverse, and the film **Der ewige Jude** (*The Eternal Jew*, Fritz Hippler, 1940) contained inserted scenes from his films to ridicule Jewish character. Late in Bois's career, **Wim Wenders** referenced Germany's history and the Holocaust in his film *Der Himmel über Berlin* (*Wings of Desire*, 1987) by casting Bois as the storyteller Homer.

Bois immigrated to Hollywood after the Nazis came to power and had small, but often highly visible, roles in over 30 films, the most memorable being as a pickpocket in Michael Curtiz's *Casablanca* (1942). He returned to Germany in the early 1950s, first to East Germany and then to West Germany, where he appeared in several films, including *Der Spukschloß im Spessart* (*The Haunted Castle in Spessart*, **Kurt Hoffmann**, 1960), a popular musical comedy at the time.

From 1960 until the late 1980s, Bois appeared on German television in both made-for-TV films and the popular miniseries *Kir Royal* (*Kir Royal*, **Helmut Dietl**, 1996).

BOOT, DAS. *Das Boot* (*The Boat*, 1981), directed by **Wolfgang Petersen**, remains one of the most expensive and commercially successful German films in film history. Three versions of the film exist, the original 149-minute theatrical release of 1981; a 1985 five-hour television version that adds back stories for the major characters; and a 209-minute director's cut released in 1997, which allowed Petersen to take advantage of improvements in sound technology. Although a German film, *Das Boot* typifies a big-budget Hollywood concept movie. The visual effects create a horrific death scene of Allied sailors, as a large burning destroyer sinks into the ocean. Interior shots were made from within a small, enclosed elevated chamber, precluding the scene's claustrophobic atmosphere being diminished by camera shots from without. Petersen used three models of the submarine, respectively 67, 11, and 6 meters in length, and also used a full-sized mockup of a submarine's interior. He employed sound effects and precision editing between gauge dials and facial expressions to create the fear and suspense of being trapped underwater. His script included several harrowing escapes, each intensifying the danger of being caught and destroyed. And he included the typical war movie clichés: crew members of different backgrounds, experience, and emotional stability; pregnant girlfriends left at the home front; an embattled, strict, but compassionate captain; and sensitive men destined to be the ones killed. He also included a cliché from German **war films** of the 1950s, for which the film was criticized: The men of the submarine seem to be fighting a war devoid of ideology; indeed, a major scene in the film suggests the men were opposed to the excesses of National Socialism.

Notwithstanding criticism of the film's historical accuracy, Petersen accomplished what no other German director had since the silent era. He created a film that competed successfully with Hollywood's big-budget action films, breaking out of the art cinema ghetto and receiving distribution in America's suburbs. It also competed successfully with Hollywood and indigenous films in the United Kingdom, France, Italy, and Japan, among other countries. It occupied major screens in

Germany at a time when German films had only about 10 percent of screen space. Key to the film's success, besides its being based on the internationally best-selling novel, *Das Boot* (1975), the autobiography of Lothar Gunther Buchheim, was Petersen's telling the story of the submarine crew entirely from their perspective. The film gives humanity to the members of the crew, who were defending National Socialism, which is conventionally, if not universally, considered the epitome of 20th-century evil. The paradox of viewers knowing the men of the submarine had fought for a system that had tried to annihilate the Allies, had perpetrated mass murder of the Jews, and had caused the deaths of millions of its own citizens, and yet sympathizing with these men nonetheless, gives the film its undeniable power. For Petersen gives the men so many enemies that viewers are moved to their side. Allied ships come at them out of the fog like sea monsters; their superiors in the High Command give them impossible orders; their consciences plague them after abandoning a sunken enemy vessel, leaving scores of men to die; and finally, they perish in spite of outwitting the enemy on an escape run through a narrow strait.

BRANDAUER, KLAUS MARIA (1944–). Klaus Maria Brandauer gained international recognition for his portrayal of Hendrik Höfgen, the opportunistic actor obsessed with fame, in the Academy Award–winning film *Mephisto* (**István Szabó**, 1981). Based on the roman à clef by Klaus Mann of the German actor **Gustaf Gründgens**, who was known for the role of Mephisto in the play version of Goethe's *Faust*, the film spotlighted Brandauer's style of acting, from his expressive body language to his ecstatic and dramatic outbursts of emotion. He has successfully reprised his bravura performance in a succession of films dealing with the Nazi or pre-Nazi period, portraying men given to megalomania, including *Oberst Redl* (*Colonel Redl*, Szabó, 1984), *Hanussen* (*Hanussen*, Szabó, 1988), *Das Spinnennetz* (*The Spider's Web*, **Bernhard Wicki**, 1989), and *Georg Elser – Einer aus Deutschland* (*Georg Elser*, aka *Seven Minutes*, Brandauer, 1989).

Brandauer's American credits include the arch-villain Latigo in the James Bond film *Never Say Never Again* (Irvin Kershner, 1983) and Baron Bror von Blixen-Finecke, the unloved husband in *Out of Africa* (Sydney Pollack, 1985), for which he won a New York Critics prize, a Golden Globe (1985), and an Oscar nomination as Best Supporting Actor (1986). Other awards include a Bambi for Best Actor of 1983, and one in 2003 for his cultural contribution through film (*see* **film awards**). He also won an Award in Gold for *Oberst Redl* in 1985, awarded by the Deutsche Filmakademie (German Film Academy), and was nominated for an Emmy for his work in the HBO film *Introducing Dorothy Dandridge* (Martha Coolidge, 1999). *See also* AUSTRIAN CINEMA.

BRAUNER, ARTUR (1918–). Artur Brauner is one of the most important producers of post–World War II German cinema. Through his production company, CCC-Film (Central Cinema Company Film), later called CCC Filmkunst, Brauner produced over 200 feature films, representing all genres and types. After the war, his films confronted the moral and historical issues of Germany's National Socialist past (coming-to-terms films or **Vergangenheitsbewältigungsfilme**), including *Die weiße Rose* (*The White Rose*, **Michael Verhoeven**, 1982), about the protest group of the same name led by Hans and Sophie Scholl, which won a Film Award in Silver from the Deutsche Filmakademie (German Film Academy); *Il Gardino dei Finzi-Contini* (*The Garden of the Finzi Continis*, Vittorio DeSica, 1970), about a wealthy Italian family deported to a concentration camp, which won an Oscar as Best Foreign Film and a Golden Bear at the **Berlin Film Festival**; *Bittere Ernte* (*Angry Harvest*, **Agnieszka Holland**, 1985), about a Polish peasant who hides a Jewish refugee, which was nominated for an Oscar as Best Foreign Film; and *Europa Europa* (Holland, 1990), about a young Jewish boy who hides his Jewish background from the Nazis while serving in the army and attending an elite school for Hitler youth, which won a Golden Globe. Among his other films that are situated during the National Socialist era are *Hanussen* (**István Szabó**, 1988), about an opportunistic clairvoyant eventually killed by the Nazis; *Eine Liebe in Deutschland* (*A Love in Germany*, Andrzej Wajda, 1983), about a German woman and Polish prisoner of war, told in flashback; *Charlotte* (*Charlotte*, Frans Weisz, 1981), about a young artist who was killed in Auschwitz; *Nach Mitternacht* (*After Midnight*, Wolf Gremm, 1981), set in Nazi Germany in 1935; and *Es muss nicht immer Kaviar sein* (*It Doesn't Always Have to Be Caviar*, Géza von Rádvani, 1961), a spy thriller set in Nazi Germany.

Brauner's *Europa Europa* caused a minor film scandal in Germany when the committee responsible for nominating a German film for the Academy Awards failed to nominate it as the German entry, ruling that the film was technically not a German film, but rather a multinational coproduction. Even a petition signed by many of the biggest names in German film, including **Wolfgang Petersen**, **Volker Schlöndorff**, and Michael Verhoeven, and published in trade papers, was unable to dissuade the committee from its decision. Artur Brauner was outspoken in his criticism of members of the committee, accusing them of anti-Semitism and citing statistics that he claimed proved the film was indeed German. Some members of the committee countered that even if that were so, the film was not up to Hollywood's high production standards, an argument that seems to have been refuted when the film won a Golden Globe as Best Foreign Language Film of the year.

BRECHT, BERTOLT (1898–1956). Bertolt Brecht's legacy to cinema is profound, although his direct involvement with the film industry was minimal and limited to writing a few screenplays. Brecht is Germany's best-known playwright of the 20th century, having written 30 plays, among them *Die Dreigroschenoper* (*The Threepenny Opera*, 1928) and *Mutter Courage und ihre Kinder* (*Mother Courage and Her Children*, 1939) and a major work on theater theory, *Kleines Organon für das Theater* (*Little Organon for the Theater*, 1948). His film work includes providing the screenplays for *Die Dreigroschenoper* (*The Threepenny Opera*, aka *The Beggar's Opera*, **Georg Wilhelm Pabst**, 1931), *Kuhle Wampe oder Wem gehört die Welt?* (*Kuhle Wampe*, aka *Whither Germany?* **Slatan Dudow**, 1932), and *Hangmen Also Die* (**Fritz Lang**, 1943). *Die Dreigroschenoper* embroiled Brecht in a lawsuit with the producers of the film. He felt the filmed version distorted the original intent of his play of that title, on which the film is based. *Kuhle Wampe* created controversy through its overt communist material, occasioning protests from the Right in theaters that exhibited the film, and calling forth a ban until cuts were made. *Hangmen Also Die*, the least controversial of his works, fictionalized the assassination of Reinhard Heydrich, the Nazi Reichsprotector of the occupied territories of Czechoslovakia, Bohemia, and Moravia.

Brecht's theories on theater focus on eliminating realism from the stage. At the time he began writing, theater was still influenced by 19th-century realism, for which creating illusion of reality was the ultimate goal of staging plays. Although others in Germany and elsewhere had already begun deconstructing illusionist theater, among them Erwin Piscator (1893–1966), Brecht's plays and writings created a new, militant way to view theater. For Brecht, theater had the responsibility to present the world as it really is, a construct of those in power, and which, as a construct, could be changed. He saw traditional theater as perpetuating the power elite by intimating that the world on stage was inviolate. His theories suggested ways to break this myth by exposing the mechanizations of control. For theater, this meant exposing the artificiality of scenery, bringing musicians out of a concealed position and placing them in full view on stage, writing roles in a way that precluded identification with the characters, laying bare false sentimentality behind actions, questioning actions of all sorts, suggesting actors should not disappear into their parts, and addressing the audience directly, confronting it with its political misconceptions and social prejudices.

The French New Wave of the early 1960s adapted Brecht to cinema in order to break from the tradition of the well-made film, which created false emotions and contrived illusions of reality. Jean-Luc Goddard, in particular, used Brecht's ideas of distancing and alienation to advance a cultural and, eventually, political agenda that differed from, even rebelled against, that of the previous generation of filmmakers. The directors of **New German Cinema** (NGC), whose movement partially grew out of the French New Wave, embraced the idea of alienation in its earliest films. **Jean-Marie Straub** and his partner **Danièle Huillet** reduced cinema to minimal movement and camera work, forcing viewers to focus on what was being conveyed by images and words. **Alexander Kluge**, the intellectual leader of NGC's predecessor **Young German Cinema**, employed disjuncture of imagery and dialectal opposition of visuals and sound to underscore how history is a construct of those in power. **Rainer Werner Fassbinder**, the undisputed leader of New German Cinema, upon whose death the movement lost importance, employed Brechtian distancing to comment on sociopolitical historical issues. In *Katzelmacher* (*Katzelmacher*, 1969), minimalist camera movement and scene changes underscore the emptiness of contemporary youth; in *Angst essen Seele auf* (*Ali: Fear Eats the Soul*, 1974), long takes, exaggerated stares, and artistic framing reveal the loneliness at the heart of Germany's culture in the 1970s; *Fontane Effi Briest* (*Effi Briest*, 1974) uses card title inserts, direct addresses to the audience, slow camera movement, and fade to white to emphasize Germany's fascist beginnings in the Wilhelmine era of the Second Empire. The techniques used by Straub and Huillet, Kluge, Fassbinder, and others in NGC trace directly back to the title cards, exposed scenery, contrasts of lyrics and melodies, and style of acting of Brecht's theories on theater, often abbreviated as Verfremdung (alienation).

BROOKS, LOUISE (1906–1985). American actress Louise Brooks made over 25 films in her career, most of them for American producers. Yet she owes her lasting fame to the two films she made in Germany, *Die Büchse der Pandora* (*Pandora's Box*, 1929) and *Tagebuch einer Verlorenen* (*Diary of a Lost Girl*, 1929), both directed by **Georg Wilhelm Pabst**. Brooks personified independence and lust in Pabst's films. Her sexy appearance in flapper dresses and bobbed hair became the look for a time. But it is the strong content of the films that earned her a reputation as one of the Weimar era's most exciting actors. In *Die Büchse der Pandora*, she played Lulu, an amoral call girl who lives off the men in her life and eventually dies at the hands of Jack the Ripper. In *Tagebuch einer Verlorenen*, she played a young innocent seduced into a life of sin. Brooks returned to Hollywood after making the films for Pabst and retired from acting in the late 1930s, but she remained in the public forum through her writing.

BRÜCKNER, JUTTA (1941–). Jutta Brückner is one of Germany's leading women directors of the 1970s and 1980s. Like other women directors of her generation (**Helke Sander, Helma Sanders-Brahms**, and **Margarethe von Trotta**), born during the early 1940s and coming of age in West Germany during the conservative Adenauer years, Brückner stands on the leading edge of German feminist films. By focusing on such issues as gender identity, self-fulfillment, child bearing and child rearing, and oppression by a male privileged society, Brückner and her colleagues defined the feminist film for a later generation. Her first four films were features made for German television. *Tue recht und scheue niemand – Das leben der Gerda Siepebrink (Do Right and Fear No One: The Life of Gerda Siepebrink,* 1975) chronicles the life of her mother from 1922 to 1975. Using photos and reenactments, Brückner uncovers the mechanisms at work controlling or preventing women's self-realization during the five decades covered by the film. Through the use of interviews and reenactments, in her film *Ein ganz und gar verwahrlostes Mädchen – Ein Tag im Leben der Rita Rischak (A Thoroughly Bedraggled Girl: A Day in the Life of Rita Rischak,* 1977), Brückner gets Rita Rischak to reveal the contradiction in her choices. She is a single mother without adequate education who wants a better life but does not want to see marriage as the only way to achieve economic security. Yet she is too passive to realize her desires.

Hungerjahre (The Hunger Years, 1980), is set during Germany's economic miracle of the 1950s. Like other filmmakers at the time, **Rainer Werner Fassbinder** in *Die Ehe der Maria Braun (The Marriage of Maria Braun,* 1979), Sanders-Brahms in *Deutschland bleiche Mutter (Germany Pale Mother,* 1980), and von Trotta in *Die bleierne Zeit (Marianne and Juliane,* aka *The German Sisters,* 1981), for example, Brückner uses the 1950s as metaphor to examine Germany's wartime past and its radical present (the time of the films), as she focuses on women who seek independence in the patriarchal world of the 1950s. The fourth of these films, *Laufen lernen (Learning to Walk,* 1980), focuses on an early middle-aged housewife who wants to break out of her bourgeois existence.

Brückner's *Die Hitlerkantate (Hitler Cantata,* 2005) takes place during the Third Reich and relates the fictional story of a conductor commissioned to write a cantata for Adolf Hitler's 50th birthday. Not trusting the man's politics, the Nazis assigned a young woman, aspiring to be a composer, to help him but also to spy on him. The film has elements of a conventional love story but also examines anti-Semitism among Germany's educated and suggests how willingly many supported the regime. Deviating from her usual ultrarealistic style, Brückner creates at times the artifice of the stage. Her film was one of many *Vergangenheitsbewältigungsfilme* (coming to terms with the past) that appeared in the wake of the 60th anniversary of National Socialism. Others appearing about the same time were *Der*

Untergang (*The Downfall*, **Oliver Hirschbiegel**, 2004), about Hitler's final days in Berlin; *Sophie Scholl – die letzten Tage* (*Sophie Scholl: The Final Days*, Marc Rothemund, 2005), about the days before Scholl's execution for distributing pamphlets opposed to the National Socialist regime; *Gloomy Sunday – Ein Lied von Liebe und Tod* (*Gloomy Sunday*, Rolf Schübel, 1999), a love story set during the period of the Third Reich, built around a popular composition whose minor key melody was said to be the cause of a rash of suicides; *Edelweißpiraten* (*Edelweiss Pirates*, Niko Brücker, 2004), about young rebels opposed to the Nazis in the Cologne area; *NaPoLa* (*Before the Fall*, Dennis Gansel, 2004), about an elite school for Nazi youth; and *Mein Führer – Die wirklich wahrste Wahrheit über Adolf Hitler* (*Mein Fuehrer: The Truly Truest Truth about Adolf Hitler*, Dani Levy, 2007), a comedy about a Jewish actor who is recruited to help a depressed Adolf Hitler work on a speech to rally the German people as the country faces imminent defeat. *See also FRAUEN-FILM*.

BRÜHL, DANIEL (1978–). Daniel Brühl is one of a few German stars of the 1990s and 2000s who have gained international recognition after achieving early success in Germany. Others are **Franka Potente**, **Moritz Bleibtreu**, **Benno Fürmann**, **Katja Riemann**, and **Til Schweiger**. Brühl, whose father is a television director in Germany, began his career as a teenage actor, achieving his first starring role in *Der Pakt – Wenn Kinder töten* (*The Pact: When Children Kill*, Miguel Alexandre, 1996). The film, loosely based on the story of Hitchcock's *Strangers on a Train*, tells of an abused teenage boy and abused teenage girl who agree to kill each other's abusive parent. The film won several awards for its director. Brühl's breakthrough into theatrical films came in *Schule* (*No More School*, Marco Petry, 2000) a comedic coming-of-age film taking place on the eve of the Abitur (Germany's equivalency to England's A-levels and France's baccalaureate exam, necessary for admission to university).

In 2002 Brühl received one of the German film industry's top honors, the **Film Award** in Gold, for three of his movies that year: *Nichts bereuen* (*No Regrets*, Benjamin Quabeck, 2001), a comedy about a young man who cannot win the girl of his dream until he loses his virginity to another woman; *Das weiße Rauschen* (*White Noise*, Hans

Weingartner, 2001), a drama about a young man's battle with schizophrenia; and *Vaya con Dios* (*Go with God*, Zoltan Spirandelli, 2002), a comedic road movie about three monks whose religious order has closed and who journey to Italy to join their brothers. Brühl again won the Award in Gold in 2003 for *Elefantenherz* (*Heart of an Elephant*, Züli Aladag, 2002), about a young boxer beset with financial and love problems and visited by a crisis of confidence; and *Good Bye, Lenin!* (*Good Bye Lenin!* Wolfgang Becker, 2003). The last-mentioned film gained Brühl international recognition as a young East German man who creates an elaborate fiction with the help of friends and family in order to keep his mother from learning the truth after she awakens from a year-long coma, namely that East Germany has collapsed while she lay unconscious.

Brühl's next three films all received wide distribution, two even receiving international financing. *Die fetten Jahre sind vorbei* (*The Edukators*, Weingartner, 2004) follows three radicals in their early twenties, two men and a woman, while exploring contemporary attitudes in Germany and contrasting them with the idealism of the 68ers, the generation of protesters in the late 1960s who now, having grown rich, have become part of the culture of overconsumption. *Ladies in Lavender* (Charles Dance, 2004) pairs Brühl with venerable British actors Judith Dench, whose character hopes there will be a May–December romance, and Maggie Smith, whose character looks upon her sister's wish as the ultimate folly. In *Joyeux Noël* (*Merry Christmas*, Christian Carion, 2005), Brühl plays a German captain during World War I in a story based on a true incident: At the start of the war Scottish, French, and German soldiers ceased fighting to celebrate Christmas with each other and then refused to take up the battle again until forced to do so by their superiors. In all his films, Brühl plays an essentially decent fellow whose naïveté leads to complications that are not always easy to solve. His smile and vulnerability make him instantly likable as an actor.

BUCHHOLZ, HORST (1933–2003). Although his career in film and television spanned six decades, during which time he made over 80 films, Horst Buchholz is best remembered for his work in the 1950s. For Germans of the postwar generation, he epitomized the generational conflict brought about by World War II. As Freddy, in Georg Tressler's

Die Halbstarken (*Teenage Wolfpack* aka *The Hooligans*, 1956), Buchholz played a troubled youth in the style of James Dean or Marlon Brando. His good looks and sensitive acting style made Buchholz a film idol and also brought him to the attention of Hollywood, where he starred as Chico in the highly successful *The Magnificent Seven* (John Sturges, 1960). The actor considered his roles as Freddy and Chico to be among the best four of his successful career, the other two being as Felix Krull in *Bekenntnisse des Hochstaplers Felix Krull* (*Confessions of Felix Krull* **Kurt Hoffmann**, 1957) and as Korchinsky in *Tiger Bay* (Lee Thompson, 1959). As these four roles suggest, the height of Buchholz's career came between 1956 and 1960. He nonetheless continued to make films in Hollywood and throughout Western Europe, including television productions in Germany and the United States. His American work includes episodes on the television series *Logan's Run* (1977–1978) and *The Return of Captain Nemo* (1978) and the made-for-television movies *Raid on Entebbe* (1976) and *Return to Fantasy Island* (1978). His last memorable role was as the riddle-loving Doctor Lessing in Roberto Benigni's *La vita è Bella* (*Life Is Beautiful*, 1997). Buchholz's awards include an Award in Gold in 1984 as Best Actor for *Wenn ich mich fürchte* (*When I'm Afraid*, Christian Rischert, 1984), a Film Award in Silver in 1956 as Best New Actor for *Himmel ohne Sterne* (*Sky without Stars*, **Helmut Käutner**, 1955), and a Bambi (*see* **film awards**) as Best New Actor in 1956 and 1957.

BUCK, DETLEV (1962–). After making a series of short films, director Detlev Buck gained recognition in Germany with *Karniggels* (*Rabbits*, 1991), a comedy about policemen in a small town. Buck's film was to be one of many German comedies in the 1990s, a mini-wave to which he also contributed *Männerpension* (*Jailbirds*, 1996). The film starred **Til Schweiger**, a box office draw after appearing in *Der bewegte Mann* (*Maybe . . . Maybe Not*, Sönke Wortmann, 1994). *Männerpension*, which also starred Buck, who appears in many of his films and those of other directors, follows two men who have been let out of prison early under the condition that they find a woman who will take them in. The comedy became the most popular film of 1996 and won a Bambi for the director (*see* **film awards**). Two other comedies have been popular with German audiences, *Liebe deine Nächste* (*Love Your Neighbor*, 1998) and *Liebesluder* (*Bundle of Joy*,

2000). The first takes place in the city, where two women of the Salvation Army try to comfort the homeless but are thwarted by a developer, played by **Moritz Bleibtreu**. *Liebesluder*, in contrast, takes place in a small town and is a mix of black comedy and parody. A beautiful young woman comes to town and seduces three men. She subsequently tries to extort money from all three for a supposed pregnancy. The men, however, rather than pay, plan a mild retaliation. The film questions the hypocrisy of tranquil small town Germany, and as such is reminiscent of a *Heimatfilm* or more precisely an anti-*Heimatfilm*.

Buck's films are not profound. The director eschews the psychologizing and politization of his predecessors. But Buck retains complete control over his films, writing, directing, producing, and sometimes acting in them. In this regard, he is a true auteur, similar to Jerry Lewis or Jacques Tati, even if he does not enjoy their reputation. Buck won a **Film Award** in Silver for his portrayal in the comedy *Herr Lehmann* (*Mr. Lehmann*, Leander Haußmann, 2003) of a fanatical sculptor who has a mental breakdown when his work does not sell. He also played a major role in Haußmann's 1999 *Sonnenallee* (*Sonnenallee*), a nostalgic comedy about life in East Germany.

– C –

CABINET DES DR. CALIGARI, DAS. After World War I, two writers, Hans Janowitz, a German-Bohemian (today, the Czech Republic), and **Carl Mayer**, an Austrian, collaborated on a script for a film that was to become synonymous with cinematic expressionism: *Das Cabinet des Dr. Caligari* (*The Cabinet of Dr. Caligari*, **Robert Wiene**, 1920). Based on a news item Janowitz found in a newspaper, the screenplay was a clear indictment of the war and Germany's leaders. The criticism of the government and its role in the deaths of almost two million Germans, however, was lessened by a framing device, not found in the original script, which the writers say they were required to add to get approval for the film.

The visuals of *Dr. Caligari* pay homage to the expressionist movement in painting, especially as practiced in the 1900s and 1910s. The film reproduces reality as if it is being reflected in a fun house mirror.

The distortions don't obscure the objects but rather render them out of shape: Elongated shadows are drawn on walls; streets wind crookedly past even more crooked houses; carnival rides appear at a slant, as if waiting to slide from the screen's canvas; César, Dr. Caligari's monstrous human instrument of murder, climbs through a trapezoid-shaped window into a bedroom whose diagonal lines match the angular shape of the furnishings and the monster's knife. Production designers Walter Reimann, Walter Röhrig, and Hermann Warm, who also did set decoration, created a world that is at once familiar and strange and that speaks to the physical and psychological horrors Germans were still experiencing two years after the end of the war.

On one level, *Das Cabinet des Dr. Caligari* continued a tradition of German gothic horror films of the 1910s, such as *Der Student von Prag* (*The Student of Prague*, Stellan Rye and Paul Wegener, 1913), about a man who sells his mirror image to the devil; *Der Andere* (*The Other*, Max Mack, 1913), a Jekyll and Hyde story of dual personality; *Der Golem* (*The Golem*, **Henrik Galeen** and **Paul Wegener**, 1915), about a clay statue that comes to life and seeks revenge against the villagers for wrongs against the Jewish populace; and the *Homunculus* series (*Homunculus*, Otto Rippert, 1916), about a creature brought to life in a lab who turns to destroying the world that created him. These films were born more out of the English tradition of the gothic tale than a movement of rebellion. Their message was that those who defy the laws of the natural world will necessarily be destroyed by their creations.

On another level *Dr. Caligari* transcended the tradition of the gothic tale by addressing the pessimism prevalent throughout Germany after the war and lasting until the mid-1920s. Although its style of distorted images had only minimal influence on the films that followed, its mood of cultural malaise can be found in post-*Caligari* horror and nonhorror films alike. Some of the better horror films from the period include *Nosferatu, eine Symphonie des Grauens* (*Nosferatu*, **Friedrich Wilhem Murnau**, 1922), which reinvents Bram Stoker's novel *Dracula*, turning it from a story of sexual repression into one of physical suffering and emotional torment. *Der müde Tod* (*Destiny*, **Fritz Lang**, 1921) pays homage to the fallen of World War I by recasting the legend of Orpheus and Eurydice. Lang's film reverses the roles of husband and wife and has a young woman visit the underworld to bring her husband back but decide instead to join him in death.

The beauty and the beast imagery found in *Dr. Caligari* appears again in Hollywood films such as *Frankenstein* (James Whale, 1931). While the hyper-abstract nature of the sets does not affect the look of films that come after, its presentation of danger and reactions to it are repeatedly used to the point of cliché: The monster is unable to kill the woman in her bed once he recognizes her beauty; while the woman is abducted her father and fiancé sleep in the next room, awakening a fraction of a second too late to save her; as in *King Kong* (Merian Cooper and Ernest Schoedsack, 1933) a decade later, the monster carries the woman over rooftops.

The film lends its name to the title of one of the best-known books on German film history, **Siegfried Kracauer**'s *From Caligari to Hitler*, a work that uses the motifs of Wiene's film and those found in other films of the 1920s to construct a protofascist profile of Germans, which could explain the rise of Adolf Hitler and the Nazis. Numerous directors have paid homage to the film, in such movies as *The Cabinet of Dr. Caligari* (Roger Kay, 1962), *Dr. Caligari* (Stephen Sayadian, 1989), and *The Cabinet of Dr. Caligari* (2005). The first two films use the name of the doctor in the original to focus on obsession and evil. The last is a sound remake of the 1920 film, at times using clips from Wiene's film. In 1982, independent filmmaker Peter Sellars directed *The Cabinet of Dr. Ramirez*, an homage to the original, set in present-day America. Financed by a consortium of German, French, American, and British sources, the film combines music and visuals to tell the familiar story of psychological obsession.

CAROW, HEINER (1929–1997). Heiner Carow directed *Die Legende von Paul und Paula* (*The Legend of Paul and Paula*, 1973), the most popular film in the history of **DEFA**, the German Democratic Republic's (**East Germany's) film** studio. The film reflects the temporary liberalization of censorship in communist-controlled East Germany, which witnessed the publication of novels critical, however mildly, of life in the GDR. One of the most successful of these was *Die neuen Leiden des jungen W.* (*The New Sorrows of the Young W.*, 1972), written by Ulrich Plentzdorf, who wrote the screenplay for *Die Legende von Paul und Paula*. Similar to the novel, in which a young man experiences depression that could be found under any ideology, Paul and Paula, who are in their mid to late twenties, confront personal crises rather than political issues. The film's musical soundtrack, by the popular rock group The Puhdys, enhanced the appeal of the movie for young people.

Carow started at DEFA in 1952 directing documentary shorts about meeting production goals and similar topics, but moved to directing feature films on the basis of *Martins Tagebuch* (*Martin's Diary*, 1956), which was honored at the *Dokumentarfilmwoche* (Documentary Film Festival) in Leipzig. He next directed several children's films, which were well received by critics and the public. *Sheriff Teddy* (*Sheriff Teddy*, 1957) belongs to a group of films that became known as the Berlin films for their setting in the East German capital and their similarity in style and theme. The Berlin films, shot in neorealist style, focused on the problems of youth. *Sheriff Teddy* relates the initial loneliness of a boy whose parents move to East Berlin from West Germany. Carow's *Sie nannten ihn Amigo* (*They Called Him Friend*, 1959) is set during World War II and revolves around the attempts of a group of boys to save a young refugee from being caught and reimprisoned in a concentration camp. In *Die Reise nach Sundevit* (*The Trip to Sundevit*, 1966), a lonely boy who lives in a lighthouse with his father befriends some *Jungpioniere* (similar to Boy Scouts) and must find his way to them when he misses a deadline for their excursion.

Carow's films have also called forth controversy. *Die Russen kommen* (*The Russians Are Coming*, aka *Career*, 1971) was banned for almost 20 years. Although the image it portrays of the Russians is essentially positive, the theme of a young Nazi living in fear because of what the approaching Russians might do to him was too controversial in 1971, only three years after the Soviet Army marched into Prague, Czechoslovakia, ending the political liberalization in that country known as the Prague Spring. *Coming Out* (*Coming Out*, 1989) was East Germany's first film to deal with homosexuality. It premiered on 9 November 1989, the night the Berlin Wall fell, obscuring the groundbreaking nature of the film, as by West German film standards, which were soon to become the expected norm, the film was tame. Carow turned to directing for television at the end of his career, commenting after unification of the two German states that he now found himself artistically "being under constant surveillance, subject to the censorship of ratings."

CARRIÈRE, MATHIEU (1950–). Mathieu Carrière has enjoyed a long career in European cinema, appearing in a number of French-German-Italian coproductions. Many of his almost 150 films are features made in France, a country where he studied as a young man. He has also appeared in individual episodes of some of Germany's most popular television crime shows, including *Der Kommisar* (*The Commissioner*, 1969–1976), *Derrick* (*Derrick*, 1974–1998), *Tatort* (*Scene of the Crime*, 1970–), and *Der Alte* (*The Old Man*, 1977–). Carrière's most memorable work occurred in his first films while he was still a teenage actor. In *Tonio Kröger* (*Tonio Kröger*, Rolf Thiele, 1964), Carrière plays the title hero as a child, a bit dreamy, and longing for something more than the bourgeois life of his father but not daring to experience life fully. The parents' catch phrase, "after all we're not Gypsies in a green wagon," which Thomas Mann, who wrote the short story on which the film is based, used as a leitmotif to highlight Tonio's confused artistic longings, here reflects the rebellious mood of the 1960s, in this early example of **Young German Cinema**. Carrière's next film also came from the new wave of German film, **Volker Schlöndorff**'s *Der junge Törless* (*The Young Törless*, 1966). The actor's characterization of a sensitive young man in boarding school further developed the sensitive persona Carrière created in *Tonio Kröger*. Törless has an emotional awakening through his first sexual experience. But he is also cold and analytical, as he becomes complicit, through his silence, in the torture of another student. Carrière acted for Schlöndorff again in *Der Fangschuß* (*Coup de Grâce*, 1976), playing a military officer who seduces a young Prussian noblewoman. Carrière also had a high-profile role that traded on his persona of sensitive masculinity in *Die flambierte Frau* (*A Woman in Flames*, Robert van Ackeren, 1983), an erotic tale of a love affair between a call girl and call boy.

CARSTENSEN, MARGIT (1940–). Margit Carstensen is one of Germany's premier stage actors. Her early career in film was in the films of **Rainer Werner Fassbinder**. As a member of his repertoire of actors, she appeared in leading and supporting roles in 16 of his films.

The raw emotional energy of her performance in *Die bitteren Tränen der Petra von Kant* (*The Bitter Tears of Petra von Kant*, 1972), a filmed stage version of one of Fassbinder's plays, brought Carstensen and Fassbinder international recognition. Carstensen's characterization in the movie of a woman in a failed lesbian affair created her future film persona of an embittered, pinch-faced shrew, a role she plays to perfection in non-Fassbinder films as well. In *Bremer Freiheit* (*Bremen Freedom*, 1972), also a filmed stage production, she plays an abused wife who becomes a serial killer, murdering her baby, husband, parents, friend, and fiancé to eliminate all controls on her life. In Fassbinder's *Satansbraten* (*Satan's Brew*, 1976), Carstensen revealed an absurdly dark side to her spinsterish persona, playing an oversexed devotee of a failed Stefan George-like poet. In the film *Possession* (Andrzej Zulawski, 1981), she again plays a lesbian lover of a schizophrenic woman. The film, banned in England for a decade because of its violence, includes a scene when Margit Gluckmeister (played by Carstensen) has her throat cut in a graphically brutal scene. Carstensen revealed the humorous elements of her embittered persona as a school director in Leander Haußmann's *Sonnenallee* (*Sonnenallee*, 1999), a nostalgic look back at life on this East German street before the fall of the Berlin Wall.

CATALOGUE OF FORBIDDEN FEATURE AND SHORT FILM PRODUCTIONS. National Socialism produced more than 1,100 feature films, the vast majority of which were diversionary in nature rather than propagandistic. After the war, in an attempt to reeducate viewers in the western zones of Germany, under the control of the French, British, and Americans, the Allies created a list of censored or forbidden films on the basis of their thematic content. Films that had overt or covert propaganda, such as showing the Allies in a bad light, exhibiting anti-Semitism, glorifying Nazism, and distorting German history, were the main topics that could land a film on the list. The films of some directors were completely exempt because of their lack of propaganda, while the films of other directors were placed under closer scrutiny. Thus most of **Helmut Käutner**'s films were free to be shown, but his *Auf Wiedersehen, Franziska!* (*Goodbye, Franziska!*, 1941) had to be edited before being released. **Veit Harlan**'s anti-Semitic *Jud Süß* (*Jew Suess*, 1940) has never been released, nor has Fritz Hippler's *Der ewige Jude* (*The Eternal Jew*, 1940). Both films can be shown only within an educational context and must be checked out from a state film archive. Perhaps the best-known film on the list is **Leni Riefenstahl**'s *Triumph des Willens* (*Triumph of the Will*, 1935), a film that, although not available in Germany for public viewings, has become a cult classic in other countries because of its masterful use of propaganda.

CAVEN, INGRID (1938–). Ingrid Caven began her stage career in **Rainer Werner Fassbinder**'s *antiteater*, the minimalist acting initiative that Fassbinder and a number of his friends undertook in the late 1960s. When Fassbinder began directing films, Caven, who was briefly married to the director, became a regular in his troupe of actors. Her most visible role for him was as the other woman in *Händler der Vierjahreszeiten* (*The Merchant of Four Seasons*, 1974), a film about a depressed vegetable peddler who drinks himself to death. Unlike some of the other members of the repertoire company, such as **Hanna Schygulla**, **Margit Carstensen**, **Michael Ballhaus**, or **Irm Hermann**, Caven gained little notice for her film career. Her recognition has come as a singer in the style of **Marlene Dietrich** and Edith Piaf.

– D –

DAGOVER, LIL (1897–1980). Lil Dagover's early role as the mysterious, specterlike Jane in **Robert Wiene**'s *Das Cabinet des Dr. Caligari* (*The Cabinet of Dr. Caligari*, 1920) assured her a place in film history. Her dark beauty and photogenic face also led to roles in many of the classics of Germany's golden age of silent film, including **Fritz Lang**'s *Der müde Tod* (*Destiny*, 1921) and *Dr. Mabuse, der Spieler* (*Dr. Mabues the Gambler*, 1922) and **Friedrich Wilhelm Murnau**'s *Herr Tartüff* (*Tartuffe*, 1925). Her deep, sophisticated-sounding voice allowed Dagover to make the switch to sound motion pictures, where she was often cast as a noble lady or member of royalty. After a number of successful German productions in the early period of sound, Dagover went to Hollywood and appeared in *The Woman from Monte Carlo* (Michael Curtiz, 1932), but she returned to Germany after the film proved unsuccessful.

During the years of the Third Reich, she appeared in a number of films, including *Schlußakkord* (*The Final Chord*, 1936) by noted director Detlev Sierck (later known as **Douglas Sirk**). In 1937, Joseph Goebbels presented her with the distinction of Staatsschauspielerin (Actress of the Nation), an honor given to the more popular German actors and actresses. In 1944, she received the Kriegsverdiestkreuz (war service cross) for entertaining troops at the front from 1939 to 1944, including a tour with her own troupe of actors.

After the war Dagover appeared in some of Germany's more memorable films, including *Die Buddenbrooks* (*The Buddenbrooks*, Alfred Weidenmann, 1959), *Der Fußgänger* (*The Pedestrian*, 1973), *Der Richter und sein Henker* (*End of the Game*, 1975), and *Geschichten aus dem Wienerwald* (*Tales from the Vienna Woods*, 1979), the last three directed by **Maximilian Schell** and in which she traded on her signature noble bearing. In 1954, she won an Award in Silver from the Deutsche Filmakademie (German Film Academy) for her role in *Königliche Hoheit* (*His Royal Highness*, Harald Braun, 1953). For her long and distinguished career in German film, Dagover received an honorary award from the Deutsche Filmakademie in 1962 and a Bambi in 1964 (*see* **film awards**). In 1967, she was awarded a Großes Verdienstkreuz (large service cross) by the Federal Republic of Germany.

DEFA (1946–1992). Deutsche Film-Aktiengesellschaft, or DEFA, was the official film studio of the German Democratic Republic (GDR or East Germany). It was founded in 1946 in the Soviet sector of divided Germany when the Soviets granted a license for film production to a consortium of directors and others in the film industry. Control was gradually turned over to East Germany after the country's establishment in 1949. In 1953, DEFA became a Volkseigener Betrieb (VEB), a company owned by the people of the GDR.

DEFA consisted of several divisions; studios for feature films, newsreels, and documentaries were set up in 1950. An animation studio was added in 1955. DEFA went into receivership when East Germany united with West Germany in 1990. It was dissolved in 1992, with its last film being released in 1993. The studio's first film was *Die Mörder sind unter uns* (*The Murderers Are among Us*, **Wolfgang Staudte**, 1946); its last was *Novalis – Die blaue Blume* (*Novalis – The*

Blue Flower, Herwig Kipping, 1993). Today DEFA's considerable library is overseen by the DEFA-Stiftung; many of its more important films are available through the DEFA Film Library. *See also* EAST GERMAN FILM.

DEPPE, HANS (1897–1969). The director Hans Deppe's career spans two distinct periods in German film history: National Socialism and the films of the 1950s and early 1960s, derisively labeled Opas Kino ("Grampy's cinema") by the signers of the **Oberhausen Manifesto**, the document that ushered in the German new wave of cinema known as **Young German Cinema**. In both periods, Deppe showed a preference for the *Heimatfilm*, a genre based heavily on novels that romanticized village life, tradition, and regional and national identity. The films were favored by Adolf Hitler and the Nazis as a way of identifying the Third Reich with past traditions. Deppe's films were not merely romanticized visions of an idyllic world, however. In *Der Schimmelreiter* (*The Rider of a White Horse*, 1934), based on Theodor Storm's 19th-century novella of the same name, Deppe captures the harsh and untamed nature of the North Sea. The choice of the novella fit into the National Socialist program of portraying the Third Reich as legitimate inheritor of Germany's 19th-century literary legacy. Moreover, Hauke Haien, the story's hero, as a visionary misunderstood by others was the first in a number of heroes that served as stand-ins for Hitler to illustrate the leadership qualities of an often-misunderstood genius. In spite of such subliminal messages, which support Nazi ideology, *Der Schimmelreiter* and the other films Deppe made during the Third Reich were entertaining features whose ideological content is clear only in the context of when they were made.

After the war, the *Heimatfilm* proved an avenue of comfortable escape for a population whose country had been devastated by war. Furthermore, the films offered a substitute home for those Germans who had left the Sudetenland of Czechoslovakia, the formerly German cities in western Poland, and East Germany. Deppe's productions in the early 1950s, *Schwarzwaldmädel* (*The Black Forest Girl*, 1950), *Grün ist die Heide* (*The Heath Is Green*, 1951), and *Wenn der weiße Fliederwieder blüht* (*When the White Lilacs Bloom Again*, 1953) became some of Germany's biggest hits of the decade. The last film led to two more in the series, *Wenn die Alpenrosen blüh'n* (*When the Alpine Roses Bloom*, 1955) and *Solange noch die Rosen blüh'n* (*As Long as the Roses Bloom*, 1956). Not only did *Schwarzwald-mädel* and *Grün ist die Heide* both win a Bambi for their commercial success (*see* **film awards**), they rose above mere escapist fluff through the director's realism, which gave his characters contemporary worries and problems set in an idyllic world.

DEUTSCHE WOCHENSCHAU, DIE. *Die Deutsche Wochenschau* (*German Newsreel*) was created by the National Socialists from the weekly newsreels of **Universum Film AG** (Ufa), **Tobis**, and Fox Studios in 1940. The companies had lost their independence after the Nazis took power in 1933, with censorship of content beginning in 1934. Until 1939, however, studios oversaw production of their films. The Wochenschauzentrale, or newsreel central office, was established in 1939, and the *Wochenschau* name in 1940. In 1938, showing of newsreels had become a requirement for movie houses, which generally placed them between a cultural short and the feature film.

Newsreels had had a long history in Germany. **Max Skladanowsky** and **Oskar Messter**, pioneers in the German film industry, had created clips of news events as early as the late 1890s and early 1900s, usually official ceremonies or shots of the emperor. These, however, were not successful; it was not until World War I and the desire to show news from the front that two news series became popular, *Eiko-Woche* (1914–1918) and *Messter-Woche* (1914–1920). Neither of these showed much of the front though, favoring military parades, scenes of the emperor, and noncombat footage of soldiers. That is, from the beginning, producers of newsreels recognized their potential to not only control content but create news.

In the 1920s newsreels focused more on entertainment than politics. Nonetheless the newsreels of Ufa, Deulig, and Fox revealed rightist or at the least conservative bias. Only the *Emelka-Woche*, with ties to the socialist party, espoused leftist ideology. With the advent of sound, the major companies expanded production, focusing on politics, culture, and sports.

Joseph Goebbels saw the potential of the newsreels to control the thinking and mood of Germany's citizens. He recognized that focus-

ing on entertaining features could create a feeling of security and
well-being that distracted viewers from thinking about politics, and
after 1939, the war. Goebbels was an advocate of film as a means of
propaganda and micromanaged newsreel production, going over
scripts and previewing raw footage. The *Deutsche Wochenschau*
gained in importance after the war began. Army units were each assigned their own film team; Goebbels saw the newsreels as a means
to connect families with the men at the front. Yet the films showed
very little military action. Just as Messter's films during World War I
had done, the newsreels of the Third Reich focused on noncombat situations. A feature of the December newsreel every year until Christmas 1944 was to show the troops decorating their Christmas trees,
following the scenes with families at home doing the same, thus creating a bond between home front and war front.

After the war, German studios continued making newsreels. In the
Soviet zone, which was to become East Germany, one company was
set up to produce all news programs. In the West, several were created for that same purpose. The last East German newsreel appeared
in 1980; the last West German version in 1986.

DIETERLE, WILHELM (1893–1972). At six foot four, Wilhelm Dieterle created an imposing figure in the 1920s, often in proletarian or
working-class roles, starring opposite **Henny Porten** and **Asta
Nielsen** and in films by most of the era's major directors, including
Ewald André Dupont, **Friedrich Wilhelm Murnau**, and Karl
Grune. His more memorable roles as actor include the rejected postman in *Hintertreppe* (*Backstairs*, Leopold Jessner and Paul Leni,
1921), the Russian prince (one of the wax figures) in *Das Wachsfigurenkabinett* (*Waxworks*, Leo Birinsky and Leni, 1924), Gretchen's
brother Valentin in *Faust* (Murnau, 1926), and an agitator in *Die Weber* (*The Weavers*, Frederic Zelnik, 1927), based on Gerhart Hauptmann's proletarian drama. In the late 1920s, Dieterle turned to directing. His *Die Heilige und ihr Narr* (*The Saint and Her Fool*, 1928),
based on a contemporary pulp novel, was the most popular film of
1928 in Germany. His next film, *Geschlecht in Fesseln – Die Sexual-
not der Gefangenen* (*Sex in Chains*, 1928), although tame by today's
standards, presented a controversial look at men in prison, calling for
conjugal visits. Dieterle also directed a few sound films in Germany,

including *Der Tanz geht weiter* (*The Dance Goes On*, 1930). Following the practice at the time of shooting films in several languages, *Der Tanz geht weiter* was the German language version of *Those Who Dance* (William Beaudine, 1930), an early Warner Brothers gangster movie. Shortly thereafter Dieterle left for Hollywood, where he enjoyed a successful career, excelling particularly in the genres of biopics, literary adaptations, and mystery comedies.

DIETL, HELMUT (1944–). Helmut Dietl directed two of the most popular German comedies of the 1990s, *Schtonk* (*Schtonk*, 1992), a parody of journalistic carelessness and sensationalism, and *Rossini* (*Rossini*, 1997), a parody of the film industry. *Schtonk*, an invented German word built on the verb *stinken* (to stink), parodies a news event of 1983, when *Stern*, one of Germany's popular news magazines, published diaries reputed to be written by Adolf Hitler. Dietl uses the incident to satirize the news media's tolerance of shoddy investigative reporting as long as the sensational news that journalists uncover sells newspapers and magazines. Dietl's touch in *Rossini* is lighter, perhaps because the theme is not as immediate. Film people meet at a popular restaurant in Munich to negotiate the rights for a best-selling novel of a reclusive writer. Dietl wrote the screenplay with Patrick Süskind, who at the time was being protective of his recently published best-selling novel, *Das Parfum* (*Perfume*, 1985), insisting it could not be filmed. The film's self-reflexivity has Süskind, producer **Bernd Eichinger**, and other famous film personalities of the day playing characters similar to themselves. *Schtonk* won the Award in Gold (*see* **film awards**) for Best Feature Film, Best Direction, and Best Actor (**Götz George**). *Rossini* won the Award in Gold for Best Feature Film, Best Direction, and Best Editing. *Rossini* also won a Bambi for actor Heiner Lauterbach. Dietl's third film from this period, *Late Night* (*Late Night*, 1999), a parody of television and radio, was not as successful as the other two films.

DIETRICH, MARLENE (1901–1992). From her first major role, that of Lola Lola in *Der blaue Engel* (*The Blue Angel*, Josef von Sternberg, 1930), Marlene Dietrich cultivated her image as every man's sexual fantasy, a femme fatale who was both a liberated woman and subservient wife or lover. Under von Sternberg's direction, Dietrich's screen persona developed from that of an amoral, slightly chubby sexpot, to a self-assured, sophisticated Hollywood love goddess.

At the end of the 1930s, when she felt her believability as seductress was waning, Dietrich left von Sternberg and her sultry roles behind. Beginning with *Destry Rides Again* (George Marshall, 1939), Dietrich developed her screen personality into that of a boisterous, just one of the boys, woman. In the late 1950s, she reinvented her persona one more time, as character actress, appearing in such films as *Witness for the Prosecution* (Billy Wilder, 1957) and *Judgment at Nuremberg* (Stanley Kramer, 1961).

Unanimously critics agree that Dietrich's appeal lay in her shapely thighs, naughty woman image, and androgynous roles. Heinrich Mann, who wrote *Professor Unrat oder das Ende eines Tyrannen* (*Small Town Tyrant*, 1905), the novel used as the source of *Der blaue Engel*, remarked that it was probably "Frau Dietrich's naked thighs" that made her famous. Noted film historian **Siegfried Kracauer** wrote that she represented the "play of unleashed urges." And Wilder clearly counted on the audience being familiar with Dietrich's persona when he cast her as the mysterious woman who disguises herself in a man's raincoat in *Witness for the Prosecution*.

Dietrich also enjoyed a successful career as cabaret singer. Her appearances, which lasted from 1953 into the early 1970s, changed little over the years and traded on her screen image. Dressed in a skintight silver gown, with a fox stole around her shoulders or dragged behind her, Dietrich flirted outrageously with her audience. Her performances always included her numbers from *Der blaue Engel*, "Ich bin die fesche Lola" ("My Name Is Naughty Lola") and "Ich bin von Kopf bis Fuß auf Liebe eingestellt" ("Falling in Love Again"), her signature song.

Although it is difficult to separate the mythical character of German resistance that Dietrich made herself into from the reality of savvy film star, the record is clear on several matters. She did indeed leave Germany, although probably more to further her career than to flee Nazism. Moreover, she never went back to Germany as long as Adolf Hitler was in power, and she became a U.S. citizen and entertained American troops in her efforts to oppose Hitler. Many Germans never forgave Dietrich for what they viewed as an act of treason and booed her return to Germany. Nonetheless, she continued to include the song "Ich hab' noch einen Koffer in Berlin" ("I Still Have a Suitcase in Berlin") in her cabaret performances and requested that she be buried in that city.

DOMRÖSE, ANGELIKA (1941–). Angelika Domröse was one of East Germany's most popular stage, film, and television actors until her emigration from the German Democratic Republic to West Germany in 1980. Her reputation today rests primarily on one film, *Die Legende von Paul und Paula* (*The Legend of Paul and Paula*, **Heiner Carow**, 1973). The most successful **East German film** of **DEFA**'s history, *Die Legende von Paul und Paula* owes its success to its stars Domröse and **Winfried Glatzeder**. Domröse in particular gives the movie its freshness. Playing Paula as part flower child, part ingénue, and part manic lover, Domröse imparts to an otherwise low-budget East German love story a degree of sensuality and eroticism. Her other memorable roles include her first role, as a young girl in **Slatan Dudow**'s *Verwirrung der Liebe* (*Confusion of Love*, 1959), a controversial romantic comedy that questioned East Germany's progress toward a utopian society, and a made-for-television adaptation of Theodor Fontane's *Effi Briest* (*Effi Briest*, Wolfgang Luderer, 1968/1969), in which she played the title character.

In 1980, after a successful career primarily in television films, Domröse had to leave East Germany because of her support for poet and protest singer Wolf Biermann, whose criticism of East German politics had made him persona non grata and lost him his East German citizenship. In West Germany, Domröse has appeared on German television in a number of popular series, including two episodes of the crime show *Der Alte* (*The Old Man*, 1977–) and three of *Polizeiruf 110* (*Precinct 110*, 1971–). *Polizeiruf 110*, East Germany's most popular crime show, had started in the GDR as an answer to West Germany's *Tatort* (*Scene of the Crime*, 1970–). It ran from 1971 until unification in 1990, when it was picked up by German television, alternating with *Tatort*. Domröse played Inspector Vera Bilewski in three episodes between 1994 and 1998.

DÖRRIE, DORIS (1955–). Doris Dörrie achieved recognition with *Männer* (*Men*, 1985), a modest comedy that was a surprise hit in Germany and abroad. So successful was the film that *Der Spiegel*, Germany's leading news magazine, placed the director on its cover, an unusual tribute from the intellectually oriented news weekly. *Männer* sold five and a half million tickets in Germany, in a market dominated by Hollywood films and in which a German film at the time was considered a success at 100,000 tickets.

Dörrie followed *Männer* with a succession of other successful comedies. Although none was as popular as *Männer*, her series of light, entertaining films has made her arguably the most commercially successful woman director in German film history, and also one of only a few post–**New German Cinema** directors (**Tom Tykwer, Helmut Dietl, Percy Adlon**, and **Oliver Hirschbiegel** are others) to receive critical and public acclaim.

Männer is a screwball comedy with a feminist twist, reflecting the change that took place in gender stereotyping in the 1980s in Hollywood and Western European films. The film owes its acceptance by public and critics both to its story—a cuckolded husband moves in with his wife's lover in order to split the two up—and to Dörrie's considerable talent as a director. The film has an original and clever screenplay, fast-paced staging, witty dialogue, and natural, unforced acting. Moreover, the film seems to have tapped into a cynicism in Germany and elsewhere (*Männer* was an art house hit in the United States) about the sincerity of the commitment of the 1960s generation. The husband, a product of the 1968 student movement in Germany, has sold out and become a yuppie. The lover has retained his lifestyle as a 1960s dropout, which is what attracts the wife to him. However, when tempted with the promise of a fast sports car and an upper middle class lifestyle, he cuts his hair, buys expensive clothes, and gets a high-paying job in an advertising firm.

Dörrie's later films continue to satirize gender roles, hetero- and homosexual relationships, and the commitment of the upwardly mobile in those relationships. Her greatest successes after *Männer* have been *Keiner liebt mich* (*Nobody Loves Me*, 1994), about a woman turning 30 who despairs of ever finding a husband and her relationship with a gay African German; *Erleuchtung garantiert* (*Enlightenment Guaranteed*, 2000), about two brothers who enter a Buddhist monastery in Japan to find themselves; and *Nackt* (*Naked*, 2002), about two couples who bet that if blindfolded they would not be able to determine who was their spouse.

Dörrie's philosophy of filmmaking is that directors can make successful films with good stories and appealing characters without compromising their integrity as filmmakers. Her one misstep has been *Me and Him* (*Ich und er*, 1988), a Hollywood production starring Griffin Dunne that came after her success with *Männer*. The film flopped in the United States but was a major success in Germany. It has been cited as an example of German humor being unexportable, although its afterlife on American cable television suggests that the film's puerile sexual humor may have simply been before its time.

Dörrie's filmography also includes *Im Innern des Wals* (*In the Belly of the Whale*, 1985), a film about abusive relationships; *Paradies* (*Paradise*, 1986), a dark comedy of obsessive love; *Geld* (*Money*, 1989), about a woman who breaks out of a rut by robbing a bank; and *Bin ich schön?* (*Am I Beautiful?* 1998), a comedy that follows a set of couples as they work through troubled relationships. All of these films, and those mentioned previously, are based on short stories by the director, an accomplished writer, whose works appear in German and English. In her film, *Der Fischer und seine Frau* (*The Fisherman and His Wife*, 2005), Dörrie returns to the screwball-style satire of her hit *Männer* as she explores how money and success can ruin a good marriage. Not surprisingly, critics see elements of Billy Wilder in her work. Dörrie herself cites the influence of John Cassavetes and Martin Scorsese. Influences of New German Cinema, however, are remarkably not prominent in her films.

DUDOW, SLATAN (1903–1963). Bulgarian born Slatan Dudow had a successful career after World War II in East Germany, where he directed films that adhered closely to Communist Party ideology, such as *Stärker als die Nacht* (*Stronger Than the Night*, 1954) and *Der Hauptmann von Köln* (*The Captain of Cologne*, 1956). Yet he is best known for *Kuhle Wampe oder Wem gehört die Welt?* (*Kuhle Wampe*, aka *Whither Germany?*, 1932). Working closely with **Bertolt Brecht**, who wrote the screenplay for the film and for whom he had worked in the theater, Dudow created the only purely communist-inspired feature film of the Weimar Republic. Indeed, in the first years after Adolf Hitler's rise to power, the Nazis used the film as an example of all that was wrong with the Weimar era.

In *Kuhle Wampe*, Dudow combines the social problems of Weimar street films with the tone of proletariat theater, acquired from his work with an agitation-propaganda troupe. Dudow begins his film with the suicide of a young man unable to find work, a familiar theme in Weimar cinema, and ends it with a portentous march as young communists sing of solidarity and the future. In between the tragic beginning and triumphal end, the director includes evictions, bureaucratic indifference to the workers, working class despair, and an unwanted pregnancy. The communist sports rally, which ends the third and final scene of the film, infuses the youthful participants at the event with the knowledge of their power and potential. The scene is also ironically similar to the way that the Nazis exploited images of athletics in their films. *See also* EAST GERMAN FILM.

DUPONT, EWALD ANDRÉ (1891–1956). Ewald André Dupont, usually credited as E. A. Dupont, began his film career in the late 1910s writing screenplays for **Richard Oswald** and Joe May, directors of highly popular detective films. By 1918, he was directing his own films, including major productions starring **Henny Porten**, one of the silent film era's leading German actors. Dupont achieved his greatest success in 1925 with the internationally celebrated *Varieté* (*Jealousy*), starring **Emil Jannings**. With the help of cameraman **Karl Freund**, who had worked for **Friedrich Wilhelm Murnau** on *Der letzte Mann* (*The Last Laugh*, 1924), Dupont fashioned a motion picture dynamic that mimicked the high drama of circus trapeze acts. At times, Freund located the camera on the swinging trapeze, and at other times he placed it directly beneath, creating a sensation of dizzying motion. The film's critical and popular acceptance gained Dupont an invitation to Hollywood, where he directed *Love Me and the World Is Mine* (1927), but the Viennese milieu of the film failed to resonate with American audiences. After the film's failure, Dupont returned to Europe, making films in England and Germany. With the advent of sound, he introduced the practice of shooting a film in two or three languages, bringing in a new set of actors to repeat in a different language a just-completed scene. Thus he directed the three films *Les deux mondes*, *Two Worlds*, and *Zwei Welten* in 1930, using the same sets and screenplay but different casts. Dupont returned to

Hollywood after the National Socialists came to power in 1933. Until his death in 1956, he made a number of B movies, but he was unable to regain the critical acclaim he found with his earlier films.

DURCHHALTUNGSFILM. The *Durchhaltungsfilm*, a term that literally means the "seeing-it-through film," refers to a tone found in many films of the Third Reich, made after the defeat of the Sixth Army at the Battle of Stalingrad in the winter of 1942–1943, when it was becoming clear to the Nazi leadership that Germany might lose the war. Two films stand out in the genre: *Die große Liebe* (*The Great Love*, Rolf Hansen, 1942) and *Kolberg* (*Kolberg*, **Veit Harlan**, 1945). *Die große Liebe*, released before the defeat at Stalingrad, starred **Zarah Leander**, one of the Third Reich's biggest personalities. Leander plays Helga Holberg, a singer engaged to an officer. Their love keeps having to be postponed, either because of his injuries or because he is again being sent to the front. The big moments in the film come during musical interludes. Leander, who sang in most of her films, sings two of Nazi Germany's most popular wartime hits: "Ich weiß, es wird eimal ein Wunder geschehen" ("I Know, There Will Be a Miracle") and "Davon geht die Welt nicht unter" ("This Won't Cause the World to End"). Although both songs represent Holberg's response to personal situations in her love life, the political subtext cannot be overlooked—that a miracle might yet give Germany victory or that just because things aren't going well, there's no reason to despair. Holberg sings "Davon geht die Welt nicht unter" to a concert hall full of military men, getting them to link arms and sway side to side, as if at a beer hall rather than in a war.

Kolberg, coming at the end of the war, is more pessimistic in tone. The film was conceived by Joseph Goebbels as a sort of German *Gone with the Wind* (Victor Fleming, 1939) and exhausted financial and human resources at a critical time in the war. Yet its message of fighting to the bitter end had been an obsession with Joseph Goebbels, the minister of propaganda, who in his speeches had started calling for "total war." Set in early 19th-century Germany, *Kolberg* is an allegory of Germany in 1945, exhorting viewers not to give up. At a special screening of the movie before film industry dignitaries, Goebbels admonished his audience that the future would judge them just as viewers at a film judge the characters on screen. "Gentlemen, in 100 years people will show another wonderful color film which depicts the terrible days we are now living through. Don't you want to play a part in this film, to be awakened to a new life in a hundred years? Each of you now has the opportunity to select the part he will play in this film . . . . Stay firm, so that in 100 years the audience does not boo and whistle when you appear on the screen." At the end of *Kolberg*, Nettlebeck consoles his daughter, who has sacrificed her happiness and well-being for the greater good, with similar words: "You have sacrificed everything that you had, Maria, but it wasn't in vain. . . . You are great, Maria. You didn't budge from your spot, you fulfilled your duty, you weren't afraid of dying. You too were victorious, Maria."

– E –

EAST GERMAN FILM. The history of film in the German Democratic Republic (GDR), or East Germany, is bracketed by the limited duration of the political regime producing the films. The GDR existed from 1949 to 1990. During that time, the East German film studio, **DEFA**, which was the sole producer of feature films, made approximately 7,500 films, over 900 of them feature productions, in all genres. With the exception of brief periods when there was a thaw in total government control of filmmaking, productions in the GDR followed a specific educational mission of integrating East Germany's citizens into a socialist workers' state. The interpretation of what that meant and exactly how it could be accomplished evolved during the four decades of the GDR, but the teleological vision remained the same: filmmakers were to contribute to the success of a state in which all workers were fully integrated into the socialist community.

Die Mörder sind unter uns (*The Murderers Are among Us*, **Wolfgang Staudte**, 1946), considered the first East German film, and *Coming Out* (**Heiner Carow**, 1989), one of the last DEFA films, form an exception to the totalitarian picture of films in the GDR. Staudte's film, the first of many that were meant to help Germans come to terms with the past (*see Vergangenheitsbewältigungsfilm*) had difficulty receiving clearance from the authorities in the American, French, and British sectors in Berlin after the war. Officials in the Soviet sector permitted filming, provided Staudte changed the ending of the screenplay. Initially the protagonist was to kill his former commanding officer for war crimes he had committed in Poland. In the ending as approved and filmed, the protagonist's fiancée persuades him to give the war criminal over to the officials to receive justice. But except for the revised ending, there is nothing in the film that points to the official party voice that would be heard in East German films throughout the GDR's and DEFA's existence.

Carow's film likewise stands outside the official party ideology. Considered one of the first GDR films to deal openly with the topic of homosexuality, *Coming Out* was released 9 November 1989, the day that the Berlin Wall fell. That the screenplay had been approved by the censors at DEFA and eventually filmed suggests that the regime was loosening, or perhaps losing, artistic control of film production, as films made before Carow's were still undergoing close scrutiny. It may also be that since the GDR did not openly sanction discrimination against homosexuals, and since the narrative was otherwise government-friendly in that it addressed issues of integration into the socialist community, the film gave no grounds for censorship.

Unlike in the zones of Germany that were to become West Germany, controlled by the Americans, French, and British, film production played an important role in the zone that was to become the GDR. Supported by the Soviets who controlled the eastern sector, filmmakers founded DEFA in 1946 and by 1947 had moved into the old **studios in Babelsberg**, once occupied by **Universum Film AG** (Ufa). From the beginning the governing bodies, first the Soviets and then the Sozialistische Einheitspartei Deutschlands or SED (Socialist Unity Party), which took control of DEFA after the move to Babelsberg, recognized the power of cinema to educate.

In *Irgendwo in Berlin* (*Somewhere in Berlin*, Gerhard Lamprecht, 1946), one of the many films to be set amid the ruins of war (*see* **rubble film**), the on-location set of buildings destroyed by fighting becomes more than an admonition against repeating the past. Lamprecht uses the rubble to focus on the future, encouraging East Germans to rebuild their city in a spirit of idealistic progressivism. *Irgendwo in Berlin* anticipates many of the films of the first decade at DEFA when East Germany was still in its formative stages. **Slatan Dudow**, whose *Kuhle Wampe oder: Wem gehört die Welt?* (*Kuhle Wampe* aka *Whither Germany*, 1932) had anticipated the themes and style of early East German film over a decade before, influenced early DEFA projects. Although the emphasis in Dudow's *Kuhle Wampe* was on ordinary workers who awaken to political awareness, focus shifts in the East German films, which offer lessons on how the workers will build a better social order. In *Unser täglich Brot* (*Our Daily Bread*, 1949), a family struggles in postwar Germany. One son and daughter get jobs in a factory, earning little but contributing to rebuilding the country and economy. Another son, whom the father favors, trades successfully on the black market. Not until the favored son mistakenly mugs the father in a dark street does the father accept the choice of his working children to contribute constructively.

Other films place the struggle between East and West into the center of the film. **Kurt Maetzig**, like Dudow one of the leaders behind East German film, implicates I. G. Farben, a large German industrial firm, in supplying the Nazis with the poison chemicals used in the concentration camps. His film *Der Rat der Götter* (*Advice of the Gods*, 1949/1950) also suggests that the company has continued to develop chemical weapons at its plant in Ludwigshafen in West Germany. Maetzig's *Familie Benthin* (*Benthin Family*, 1950) tells of two brothers whose black marketeering in medical supplies leads to the death of one of them when the medicine necessary to save him is unavailable.

In the mid- and late 1950s, East German directors produced a series of youth-oriented films that resembled the teenage rebel movies appearing in Hollywood and West Germany. The formula used in these films was remarkably similar in all three countries: teenagers, whose parents are absent or otherwise occupied, lead aimless and personally and socially destructive lives. Not until one of the teenagers tragically dies do the youth and the adults awaken to their responsibility. East German director Gerhard Klein and screenwriter Wolfgang Kohlhaase collaborated to give their East German teenage rebel films a distinctly socialist message. Whereas films like the Hollywood *Rebel without a Cause* (Nicholas Ray, 1955) and the West German *Die Halbstarken* (*Teenage Wolfpack*, aka *The Hooligans*, Georg Tressler, 1956) moralize about the responsibility of parents for what has occurred, Klein and Kohlhasse point no fingers. True, the parents in their film, *Berlin – Ecke Schönhauser* (*Berlin: Schönhauser Corner*, 1957) are absent, but their role has been taken over by the state, which recognizes that it will have to work to integrate young people into a socialist society. Ironically, the role the communist state plays in socializing youth is reminiscent of the role National Socialism is seen to have in the life of the hero in the Third Reich film of propaganda *Hitlerjunge Quex* (*Hitler Youth Quex*, Hans Steinhoff, 1933). Quex's mother is dead and his father is an ineffectual communist worker. His welfare is therefore taken care of by the Nazi Party.

East German films of the late 1950s through the 1970s worked through memories of the past, helping viewers cope with the legacy of the Third Reich. **Frank Beyer** and Konrad Wolf saw the past as something that had to be confronted directly in order to approach daily life. Beyer often used World War II, the National Socialist era, and life in the concentration camps to remind viewers of what the Nazis had done and why East Germany was trying to create a new social order. *Nackt unter Wölfen* (*Naked among Wolves*, 1963) portrays ordinary prisoners in a concentration camp who hide a small Jewish boy from authorities. *Jakob der Lügner* (*Jacob the Liar*, 1974) uses humor to show how one man tries to give his friends in a Polish ghetto hope by inventing a radio broadcast that tells of an advancing Russian army that will free them. *Jakob der Lügner* is the only East German film to have been nominated for an Academy Award, as Best Foreign Film.

Wolf's films more easily fit the paradigm of the East German state, a country whose allegiance was to the Soviets rather than its West German neighbor. *Ich war neunzehn* (*I Was Nineteen*, 1968) follows a young German whose father had escaped the Nazis with his family by immigrating to Russia. Returning now as a soldier in the Soviet army, the young man must confront prejudice from his fellow Russian soldiers, who resent a German in their company. At the same time, he must deal with an identity crisis, as a German who is assigned to occupy Germany. In *Mama, ich lebe* (*Mama, I'm Alive*, 1977), Wolf deals with the question of loyalty and issues of identity even more strongly. The story revolves around three captured German soldiers who slowly realize their captors are not the enemy and join them in the fight against their comrades in the Nazi army.

Not all films belonged to the category of helping viewers cope with the past. Film adaptations of classics and children's films enjoyed success throughout the DEFA era. Directors adapted literary works in the conventional style preferred by East German authorities. Wolfgang Luderer's *Effi Briest* (*Effi Briest*, 1968/1969) tells Theodor Fontane's tale of adultery in Wihelmine Germany as melodrama, critical of the bourgeois morality that leads to Effi's transgression, banishment, and death. When compared with **Rainer Werner Fassbinder**'s version of only a few years later, Luderer's seems conventional indeed, as Fassbinder used a range of experimental distancing techniques to estrange viewers from the story. Martin Hellberg's *Emilia Galotti* (*Emilia Galotti* 1958), based on Gotthold Ephraim Lessing's play, has fun with the genre of middle class tragedy that the play represents. At one point, he includes a chase scene on horse and coach that is reminiscent of Hollywood Westerns, a distinct oddity in a film set in 18th-century Italy.

Given that DEFA saw the Western as a possible moneymaker, as the **Winnetou films** had been in Germany, perhaps the inclusion of a chase scene in *Emila Galotti* was not that unusual. *Die Söhne der großen Bärin* (*The Sons of the Great Mother Bear*, Josef Mach, 1965), for example, became a success in 1965 and led to a series of films set in the American West. The films, shot on location in Yugoslavia and on studio sets, featured clashes between white settlers or the American military and native Indian tribes. Yugoslav Gojko Mitic, who had appeared as an Indian extra in the West German Winnetou series and would play Winnetou in a revival of the series in the 2000s, starred in over a dozen films, playing a warrior or chief who witnesses, and is often victim of, the deceit of white officials, officers, or settlers. The films thus offered not only entertainment but also a means to deliver anti-American propaganda. Considering, however, that Hollywood's films by the 1960s were hardly more favorable in their portrayal of actions against the American Indians, the East German films were hardly groundbreaking in their criticism of exploitation of America's Indian nations.

In the mid-1960s, East German film encountered a crisis. Earlier in the decade, artists had begun voicing criticism of working under the GDR's restrictions. Novelist Günter Kunert complained sarcastically that authorities took issue with even simple statements such as "winter is cold," declaring them unnecessarily negative. After construction of the Berlin Wall in late summer 1961, however, artists believed that maybe things would change now that the East was sealed off, making the West's decadent lifestyle unreachable and therefore no longer a threat to a country that was losing people to a porous border. Indeed, things did improve for a while. **Konrad Wolf**'s *Der geteilte Himmel* (*Divided Heaven*, 1964), based on Christa Wolf's novel of that title, examines the effect a separated Germany has on a love affair and also the sacrifices that are necessary if a new East German society is to evolve. A year after the film's appearance, the censors cracked down on films no more critical of East German life or dangerous to the regime than Wolf's and banned almost an entire year's film production. The banned films became known as the DDR *Verbotsfilm*, 11 films that focused on the private lives of individuals within the East German state. *Das Kaninchen bin ich* (*I Am the Rabbit*, **Kurt Maetzig**, 1965) is emblematic of the films that were banned because they focused on the real concerns of ordinary people: love affairs, ineffectual bosses, and corrupt officials. Although the films never criticize the government, Communist ideology, or the East German socialist system, leaders saw danger in their criticism. Erich Honecker singled out Maetzig's film, along with *Denk bloß nicht, ich heule* (*Just Don't Think I'll Cry*, Frank Vogel, 1965), as particularly egregious in their transgressions against the integrity of the state. The banned films were finally released in 1990 after dissolution of the GDR.

EHE DER MARIA BRAUN, DIE. **Rainer Werner Fassbinder**'s *Die Ehe der Maria Braun* (*The Marriage of Maria Braun*, 1979) is the best-known film of **New German Cinema**. It is also the most important film to come out of the obsession many directors of the new wave and later have had in helping viewers come to terms with the past (*see* **Vergangenheitsbewältigungsfilm**). *Die Ehe der Maria Braun* is the first film in Fassbinder's trilogy of the 1950s in Germany, a time of economic prosperity, rearmament, and growing self-assuredness. As such the films are often seen as exposés of Germany's coldness, warnings against repeating past mistakes, and metaphors of German history. Yet the films are much more than this. *Die Ehe der Maria Braun*, in particular, functions as an *aide-mémoire*, warning not about the importance of not forgetting the past but admonishing us to recognize how much the past is part of the present.

Die Ehe der Maria Braun begins during the last days of World War II. Maria (**Hanna Schygulla**) and Hermann (Klaus Löwitsch) sign their marriage papers lying on the ground while bombs fall around them. The narrative then moves from 1945 through 1954, as Germans and West Germany recover from wartime defeat and begin to enjoy the recovery known as the Wirtschaftswunder (economic miracle). After Hermann is mistakenly reported killed in action, Maria has an affair first with Bill, a black American officer, part of the occupation forces, and then with Oswald, a German industrialist who had spent the war in exile. Maria is an independent woman who believes she controls her life and her love affairs. Eventually she learns that she has been a pawn in a deal arranged between Oswald, who had a fatal illness, and her husband. If the husband would renounce his love until Oswald died, then he and Maria would each inherit half of his fortune. When Maria discovers that she has not been in control of her life, she kills herself and Hermann by blowing up their house. In the background, we hear that Germany has just won the World Cup Championship of 1954. The film ends with a series of portraits of former German chancellors; notably absent is a portrait of Willy Brandt.

Many understand Fassbinder's film as a metaphor of Germany's economic miracle, which produced abundance for its citizens and contributed to a rise in materialism, making Germans cold. Others interpret the movie as an allegory of West Germany's situation after the war, moving from total dejection to burgeoning power. Still others see Maria as a feminist cipher for women who have been cheated out of their newfound independence as men come back from war. Schygulla's faultless performance as Maria embodies metaphor, allegory, and cipher, showing how she loses her humanity as she gains economic success, only to be disillusioned in the end when she finds her empowerment has been a self-deception.

EICHINGER, BERND (1949–). After taking over the film distributor Neue Constantin in 1979, Bernd Eichinger became Germany's most powerful and successful producer. Not content with restricting his company to film distribution, Eichinger expanded Neue Constantin to include production and even exhibition. After filmmaker **Doris Dörrie** dismissed the failure in the U.S. market of her film *Me and Him* (*Ich und er*, 1988) as being of little importance to her, Eichinger remarked, "Doris is satisfied being known in Schwabing (Munich's Greenwich Village); the whole world is going to know who I am."

And indeed, Eichinger is associated with some of the most commercially successful films that Germany produces.

Eichinger was one of the first European producers willing to compete with American films in Europe and the United States. Although he began his career producing art films—he worked with **Wim Wenders**, **Hans-Jürgen Syberberg**, and **Edgar Reitz**—Eichinger switched to big-budget commercial films in 1981. He seems to have learned from Hollywood that movies are more likely to make a profit if they tell exploitable stories, are based on best-sellers, and use internationally popular stars.

Eichinger's first major film, for example, *Christiane F.—Wir Kinder vom Bahnhof Zoo* (*We Children of Bahnhof Zoo*, Uli Edel, 1981), was based on a diary that achieved cult status among Germany's youth because of its realistic portrayal of teenage drug addiction. The film incorporated an extended concert appearance by David Bowie, thus increasing its chance for success with the youth market. In contrast, *Die unendliche Geschichte* (*The Neverending Story*, 1984) lacked sensational content and international stars, but its source, Michael Ender's international best-seller, and director, **Wolfgang Petersen**, who made the highly successful *Das Boot* (*The Boat*, 1981), guaranteed a market. Similarly, Eichinger's *Der Name der Rose* (*The Name of the Rose*, 1986) capitalized on its source, the Italian best-seller by Umberto Eco; its director, popular French filmmaker Jean-Jacques Annaud; and stars Sean Connery and F. Murray Abraham, to give the film international status.

Eichinger repeated his successful formula of basing films on proven sources in his television productions. Between 1996 and 1998, he had four popular made-for television movies. *Die Halbstarken* (*The Hooligans*, Urs Egger, 1996) was a remake of Georg Tressler's 1956 hit film of the same name. *Das Mädchen Rosemarie* (*A Girl Called Rosemarie*) was produced, written, and directed by Eichinger. The film revisits a 1950s political scandal first filmed by Rolf Thiele in 1958. Eichinger's *Es geschah am hellichten Tag* (*It Happened in Broad Daylight*, Nico Hofmann, 1997), was first filmed in 1958 (Ladislao Vajda) and later turned into a novel by the writer of the screenplay, the critically acclaimed Swiss author Friedrich Dürrenmatt. Dürrenmatt's novel was also the source of the American film *The Pledge* (Sean Penn, 2001), starring Jack Nicholson.

Eichinger produced the highly successful television movie *Opernball* (*Opera Ball*, Urs Egger, 1998) based on Josef Haslinger's bestseller of the same name. His other box office hits include *Der bewegte Mann* (*Maybe . . . Maybe Not*, Sönke Wortmann, 1994), an adaptation of a cult comic book series about homosexuals and starring **Til Schweiger** and **Katja Riemann** at the height of her career. *Der Untergang* (*The Downfall*, **Oliver Hirschbiegel**, 2004) has been Eichinger's most critically acclaimed and also most controversial film to date. As is the case with his other films, *The Downfall* has its source in best-selling books, *Der Untergang: Hitler und das Ende des Dritten Reiches* (*Inside Hitler's Bunker: The Last Days of the Third Reich*, 2002) and *Bis zur letzten Stunde: Hitler's Sekretärin erzählt ihr Leben* (*Until the Final Hour: Hitler's Last Secretary*, 2002), by Traudl Junge and Melissa Müller.

EISBRENNER, WERNER (1908–1981). One of Germany's most prolific film composers, Werner Eisbrenner wrote the music for over 110 films during his 30-odd-year career, 1934–1968. As with most film music from these years, Eisbrenner's compositions recede into the background of the film, underscoring dramatic moments, adding local color, or adding volume to the soundtrack. At times, though, his music becomes a character in the film. In *Titanic* (*Titanic*, Werner Klingler and Herbert Selpin, 1943), Eisbrenner's score rises above the typical background music of the period. Eisbrenner characterizes the classes on board, changing style and tone of the music as each dominates the visuals. During the final catastrophe, no distinctions are made. In the dramatic climax of the film, the music crescendos at the appropriate dramatic moments, as one would expect, but Eisbrenner incorporates the ship's horn, Morse code, and even the song of a canary into the score. When the final disaster occurs and the ship goes down, he brings in an orchestral arrangement of "Nearer My God to Thee," which anecdote says was played at the end by the ship's orchestra, bringing the melody down an octave as the ship's captain opens a port window to let the canary fly to safety.

The composer's score for *Romanze in Moll* (*Romance in a Minor Key*, **Helmut Käutner**, 1943), which he wrote with lyricist Lothar Brühne, likewise becomes part of the movie's narrative. Brühne's simple song of love transmutes from major key to minor key, simple song to operatic composition, and piano to full orchestra as it comments on the film's love affair. In *Große Freiheit # 7* (*Port of Freedom*, Käutner, 1944), the title refers to a street in the red light district of Hamburg, Eisbrenner contrasts simple folk melodies with music hall chansons to characterize the innocence of the young woman who has moved in with her protector and the women of the music hall where he works. At one point, during a waltz melody while the characters are sitting at an outdoor café, a storm approaches. The music crescendos, cymbals clash, horns blast, and people scurry frantically, as if running to find shelter from an air raid, a strange effect in a movie that should otherwise entertain and divert viewers from the war outside the movie house.

Eisbrenner continued his successful career as composer after the war, composing the music for dramas, comedies, and musicals. Among the better known of the films are *Im weißen Rößl* (*The White Horse Inn*, **Willi Forst**, 1952), a romantic operetta with **Peter Alexander**, and *Kinder, Mütter, und ein General* (*Children, Mothers, and a General*, László Benedek 1955), a war film with a minimal score that is most effective in quiet moments on the front, when a harmonica underscores the irony of the danger the teenage soldiers (the children of the title) face. Eisbrenner's score for the two-part film *Die Buddenbrooks* (*The Buddenbrooks*, Alfred Weidenmann, 1959) provides mainly background music for the narrative based on Thomas Mann's family saga.

EISLER, HANNS (1898–1962). Hanns Eisler is one of the 20th century's foremost film composers. His discordant, contrapuntal scores offer a distinct contrast to the harmonic orchestral compositions of the 1940s and 1950s. His jazz-inspired compositions, based on Arnold Schönberg's 12-note scale, distance viewers from the events on screen rather than bring them into the film. In this way, Eisler reflects the aesthetic tradition of **Bertolt Brecht**, with whom he often collaborated. Like Brecht, he believed that art's purpose was to teach, to expose, to reveal the truth, and not to lull viewers into complacency with their lot.

Eisler's theory of film music can be found in a book he cowrote with Theodor Adorno, *Composing for the Films* (1947). Rather than use music to underscore and support what the screen was showing visually, Eisler and Adorno asked that film music provide counterpoint, forging in this way a dialectical relationship with the image. This relationship in turn creates a new idea in the mind of the viewers, one that goes beyond both the visual and aural cues.

Eisler had practiced his theories before publishing them. In *Kuhle Wampe oder Wem gehört die Welt?* (*Kuhle Wampe*, aka *Whither Germany?*, **Slatan Dudow**, 1932), screenplay by Brecht, the composer provides a score that reflects Dudow's and Brecht's Communist ideology. Consisting of three sections, an introduction to the plight of the workers, the unresponsiveness of government bureaucracy to their problems, and the need to empower the working class, Dudow, Brecht, and Eisler create a paradigm of dialectical filmmaking. For the opening scene, which shows young men on bikes racing frantically toward a job opportunity, Eisler provides chaotic, discordant sounds, suggesting the futility of their search. In the next section, Eisler's music accompanies Brecht's lyrics, exposing the sentimentality in its message of love. Discordant notes play as the lovers walk into the woods to words of spring and romance, preparing viewers for the female protagonist's pregnancy. The third act changes the tone and rhythm of the movie. Dudow and Brecht want to show workers that they have the power to change their situation. Eisler's music accordingly reflects this shift by offering a martial-like hymn to the power of the workers, which builds in intensity as young workers march forward in a wall of solidarity.

Eisler immigrated for a brief time to Hollywood. Some of his work, such as the score to *Hangmen Also Die* (1943), directed by fellow émigré **Fritz Lang** and written by Brecht, despite obvious compromises of tonality that Eisler makes to Hollywood studio tastes, maintains his insistence that music be integrated into the film and not serve as mere aural filler. This was also true of his other scores, particularly *None but the Lonely Heart* (Clifford Odets, 1944), for which he received an Oscar nomination for best musical score. Eisler, who was under surveillance by the House Un-American Activities Committee of the U.S. Senate and appeared before Congress to answer questions about his loyalty to the government, was deported in 1948. His subsequent work in East Germany and France reflects the style of his earlier films. His score for *Nuit et brouillard* (*Night and Fog*, Alain Resnais, 1955) offers contrapuntal jazz piano to images of the Auschwitz concentration camp.

EISNER, LOTTE (1896–1983). Lotte Eisner, film critic and historian, wrote film criticism for the *Film-Kurier*, a leading film daily (later semiweekly) which covered film news during the German film industry's so-called golden age during the Weimar Republic. She fled to France when Adolf Hitler came to power in Germany in 1933, spent time there in a concentration camp after the Nazis occupied the north of France, and later escaped to the south of France. Eisner was an assistant to Henri Langlois, founder of the Cinématèque in Paris, and a personal friend to **Friedrich Wilhelm Murnau** and **Fritz Lang**, and wrote the definitive work on German expressionist film, *The Haunted Screen* (*L'Ecran Démonique*, 1952).

In 1974 **Werner Herzog**, having just completed his film *Jeder für sich und Gott gegen alle* (*The Enigma of Kaspar Hauser*), walked from Munich to Paris to Eisner's sickbed. There he received her blessing and, more important, her assurance that German film was indeed "legitimate German culture" and that he and his contemporaries in **New German Cinema** (NGC) were following in the footsteps of the great film directors of the Weimar Republic: **Ernst Lubitsch**, Fritz Lang, and Friedrich Wilhelm Murnau. It was as if she were establishing a history for German cinema that went from Weimar through the exiles to the directors of NGC, completely bypassing the film production of the Third Reich and thus giving them no role in German film history.

Of Herzog's pilgrimage Thomas Elsaesser writes: "Lotte Eisner, thanks to Herzog, became the super-mother of the New German Cinema and of a film history conceived as family melodrama, whose key figure is, precisely, the abandoned child."

EUROPA EUROPA. After being turned down in 1991 by a German committee that nominates German-language films for the Best Foreign Language Film category of the Academy Awards, **Agnieszka Holland**'s 1990 *Europa Europa* (known in German as *Hitlerjunge Salomon* [*Hitler Youth Solomon*], 1991) became one of the most successful German films in the United States, demonstrating that all publicity is good. The nominating committee felt that as Holland was Polish, the film was not German. Moreover they felt that its quality was not up to Hollywood standards. Yet the committee had nominated Holland's film *Bittere Ernte* (*Angry Harvest*, 1985) in this category in 1986, and not all of the actors were German. Holland claimed that the judges had been influenced by the film's historical theme, the Holocaust, and not its country of origin. The movie, which follows the adventures of a teenage Jewish boy who hides from the Nazis in plain sight in an elite school for Hitler youth, eventually won a Golden Globe as Best Foreign Film, among other honors. *See also* HOLOCAUST IN FEATURE FILMS.

***EWIGE JUDE*, *DER*.** Of over 1,100 feature films made by the Nazis between 1933 and 1945, very few were overt propaganda. Fewer still were overtly anti-Semitic. Yet the few films that placed anti-Jewish rhetoric and sentiment in the foreground were vicious indeed. *Der ewige Jude* (*The Eternal Jew*, Fritz Hippler, 1940) is considered by cultural historians to be one of the vilest representations of Jewish culture and is still banned from public exhibition in Germany.

Der ewige Jude* was released in 1940, the same year as ***Jud Süß*** (*Jew Süss*, **Veit Harlan**), a year after World War II had begun, and a time when Germany was intensifying its propaganda against the Allied nations: England, France, the Soviet Union, and soon America. At the same time, Germany was increasing its anti-Jewish rhetoric, attributing the war and the world's problems to a Jewish conspiracy. *Der ewige Jude* and *Jud Süß* worked in tandem to increase the level of anti-Semitism among viewers. *Der ewige Jude* was mandatory for some groups, including soldiers engaged in arresting and transporting Jews from occupied countries, and schoolchildren, for whom more graphic scenes had been edited. *Jud Süß*, while not mandatory viewing, was ensured a large audience by virtue of its star-studded cast. Four of the Third Reich's biggest stars played the major roles: **Ferdinand Marian**, **Heinrich George**, **Kristina Söderbaum**, and **Werner Krauss**.

Although the films were different in nature, one a compilation documentary and the other a fictional narrative, *Der ewige Jude* and *Jud Süß* employed similar stylistic and thematic means to manipulate viewers against Jews. Both films make Jewish culture strange and dangerous. *Der ewige Jude* presents the Jewish ritual of slaughter as animal cruelty and anathema to German values. It misuses statistics, inventing percentage figures in order to libel Europe's Jews as criminals. It quotes scenes from true documentaries in contexts opposite from their original purpose and references Hollywood and Yiddish narrative fictions as factual evidence of Jewish culture and morality. Finally, the film implies that there are Jews throughout Germany who go unnoticed because they are good at disguising themselves as German. In similar fashion, *Jud Süß* represents Jewish life as being non-German. Family values, business ethics, and personal morality are compared, always to the disadvantage of Jewish culture. A pivotal scene in the movie suggests to viewers that Jews are not always easy to recognize, and calls on Germans to be more vigilant about the others among them. Finally, the film implies that Germany will be a better country without the Jews.

Der ewige Jude and Jud Süß joined several other movies of the period that in retrospect can be seen as preparing the Germans for the transporting of Europe's Jews to the concentration camps and their eventual murder. In 1939, Hans H. Zerlett's *Robert und Bertram* (*Robert and Bertram*) escalated stereotyping of Jews as criminals, as confidence men who would rather cheat than work. The 1940 cultural short *Das Opfer* (*The Sacrifice*) called for euthanizing Germany's mentally retarded population. *Die Rothschilds* (*The Rothschilds*, Erich Waschneck) also appeared in 1940. The film is a complementary feature narrative to *Der ewige Jude*, focusing on the same idée fixe as other Nazi films, the anti-Semitic theme that the Jews were engaged in an international conspiracy to control the world, financed by Jewish banking houses. The 1941 film *Ich klage an* (*I Accuse*, **Wolfgang Liebeneiner**) disguised the policy of euthanasia of the mentally handicapped, which had been opposed by religious leaders, as assisted suicide of the terminally ill.

After the war, Liebeneiner, Hippler, and Veit Harlan were blacklisted, as was Werner Krauss. Marian committed suicide. Harlan was put on trial for crimes against humanity, but was acquitted in 1950. *See also* CATALOGUE OF FORBIDDEN FEATURE AND SHORT FILM PRODUCTIONS.

EXPORT, VALIE (1940–). Valie Export (born Waltraud Lehner), a prominent Austrian artist, became known in the 1960s primarily for her avant-garde experiments with video and multimedia. She worked to expand the syntax of film; to increase its repertoire of possibilities for expression; and to expose the power relationships that exist between director and spectator, artist and audience, or society and its citizens. Her primary focus has been on how these relationships affect women. In one of her performance art pieces, she projected lights up on a screen that spectators then had to try to hit by bouncing balls off paddles. Other early performance films include sexual imagery, for example *Tapp- und Tast-Kino* (*Tap and Touch Cinema*, 1968), in which Export invited participants to put their hands into a box that was strapped to her chest. The box represented a screen and the participants were feeling the image on the "screen," which in this case were her naked breasts.

Export's first feature film, *Unsichtbare Gegner* (*Invisible Adversaries*, 1977), has achieved cult status among cineastes. Outwardly a parody of the Don Siegel science fiction classic *Invasion of the Body Snatchers* (1956), the film profiles the schizophrenia of its heroine, who hears voices telling her of an invasion that may be real and may be a result of the oppression she suffers at the hands of a male-dominated society. The film also parodies the traditional portrayal of women by artists, reflecting Export's interest and involvement in the Austrian and international feminist movements. In 2000, Export won the Oskar Kokoschka award for her action artworks. This award is given to a major Austrian artist every two years. *See also* AUSTRIAN CINEMA.

EXPORT UNION DES DEUTSCHEN FILMS. *See* GERMAN FILMS SERVICE.

– F –

FANCK, ARNOLD (1889–1974). Arnold Fanck's fame rests on two singular contributions to German film: He created a genre that became known as the **mountain film**, and in one of these mountain films he introduced **Leni Riefenstahl** to motion pictures, subsequently starring her in five more of his features.

Fanck was an avid skier, hiker, and nature lover who began his film career making documentaries of hiking and skiing. In 1926, he directed *Der heilige Berg* (*Sacred Mountain*), starring Leni Riefenstahl as a free-spirited dancer loved by two men. The melodrama was just a pretext, however, to juxtapose his human actors against the real star of this and his other mountain films, the violent power and grandeur of nature. Fanck created images of intense beauty by using camera location, the natural light of the outdoors, and effective montage sequences. Although the mountains often extracted sacrifice from those who dared climb them, they also allowed these chosen individuals an occasional victory.

Fanck's mountain films, most made before Adolf Hitler's rise to power, romanticized rugged individualism and, not surprisingly, were reputed favorites of Hitler. For his part, however, Fanck maintained that he never supported the Nazi Party or Nazi ideology. He never joined the Nazi Party, and although he continued making films under the Nazi regime, these were often documentaries far removed from the propaganda of his most famous protégée, Riefenstahl. Only once does he seem to have championed the party line, when he made *Ein Robinson* (*Robinson* 1941), a film that told of an exiled soldier returning to the Reich, the homeland, after years of absence. Two other well-known films by Fanck are *Die weiße Hölle von Piz Palü* (*White Hell of Pitz Palu*, 1929), codirected with **Georg Wilhelm Pabst**, and *S.O.S. Eisberg* (*S.O.S. Eisberg*, 1933), which takes place on an ice floe rather than a mountain top. Both films starred Riefenstahl. *See also* ALLGEIER, SEPP; ANGST, RICHARD.

FAROCKI, HARUN (1944–). Film critic and filmmaker Harun Farocki emerged from the **Young German Cinema** movement in the 1960s to become Germany's most philosophical, inventive, and original filmmaker. In his film essays, which vary in length from just a few minutes to an hour, Farocki juxtaposes preexisting images from feature films, commercial advertising, newsreel archives, computer monitors, and similar media sources in order to move viewers to see the images afresh. For him, there are no new images, only new ways to show existing ones.

Farocki's films are not abstract exercises in objectivity. His topics, as well as the images he uses to portray them, are chosen for their content, which comments on the nature of the filmed image, the manner in which viewers receive the image, and the way the image comments on the world. His work is very much influenced by the theories of the production of art as espoused by Germany's influential leftist thinkers, including social philosopher Theodor Adorno and drama theorist and playwright **Bertolt Brecht**.

In trying to get viewers to see, Farocki employs all methods of estrangement and distancing. About his film *Nicht löschbares Feuer* (*Inextinguishable Fire*, 1969), he wrote: "How can we show you napalm in action? And how can we show you the injuries caused by napalm? If we show you pictures of napalm burns, you'll close your eyes. First you'll close your eyes to the pictures. Then you'll close your eyes to the memory. Then you'll close your eyes to the facts. Then you'll close your eyes to the entire context." Farocki's dilemma is the same one faced by Alain Resnais in *Hiroshima mon amour* (1959), when he struggled to find a way to approach the horror of the dropping of the atom bomb on Hiroshima. Farocki's solution is similar also, to approach human suffering through images that allow viewers to put the memory of pain and destruction together in their minds, rather than show and narrate explicit images. In this way, Farocki moves beyond re-creating human suffering, which can never be understood if not experienced directly. He shows the origins of the chemical compound that eventually becomes napalm, asking who carries the moral responsibility for the dropping of this chemical on human populations.

Farocki's sociopolitical criticism is evident in his other films as well. In *Videogramme einer Revolution* (*Videogram of a Revolution*, 1992), he reconstructs the downfall of Romanian dictator Nicolae Ceausescu using television footage, including the live feeds before they are edited for broadcast. The result is a filmic essay on how news is created, how we no longer see the truth of an event but only how the event is presented. In *Arbeiter verlassen die Fabrik* (*Workers Leaving the Factory*, 1995), Farocki pays homage to Louis Lumière's *La sortie des usines Lumière* (*Employees Leaving the Lumière Factory*, 1895). Beginning with images from the film, he then shows clips from films showing workers leaving other factories, including Ford Motors in Detroit. He also includes a clip of strikebreakers trying to enter a factory. These joyless images present work as something to escape from, as something that controls the workers. *Stilleben* (*Still Life*, 1997) looks at how art has become a commodity. Here, Farocki examines a number of paintings by moving his camera around them, showing the painted images from different points of view. The result is an exposé on how images no longer depict reality but have become part of the world around us. We understand them through the associative images they produce in us.

FASSBINDER, RAINER WERNER (1945–1982). Rainer Werner Fassbinder, the most productive and most controversial filmmaker in the **New German Cinema**, directed more than 40 films before his death in 1982 of a drug overdose. He also wrote the screenplays for many of his films and acted in his own films and those of other directors. Many feel that his death marked the end of New German Cinema.

Fassbinder's films are about outsiders: disaffected youth, homosexuals, immigrant workers, women, the unemployed, the insane, and addicts. His themes of sexual repression, infidelity, emotional blackmail, and forsaken love—drawn from his favorite directors, **Douglas Sirk**, Josef von Sternberg, Raoul Walsh, and Billy Wilder, among others—are set in a middle class or lower middle class milieu. His characters mistreat others and are themselves mistreated in their desperate attempts to find love or recognition of any sort. Always in the background is a repressive social and political structure, reminding viewers, regardless of the actual period in which the story takes place, of the fascism of Nazi Germany and, in Fassbinder's view, of fascism's echo in contemporary Germany.

Fassbinder's early films were static, employing an almost immobile camera, sparse sets, staged movement, and amateurish acting. Their minimalist style, influenced by European directors such as **Jean-Marie Straub**, angered some critics, who saw films such as *Katzelmacher* (*Katzelmacher*, 1969) and *Warum läuft Herr R. amok?* (*Why Does Mr. R. Run Amok?*, 1970) as slow, naive, and boring. Other critics recognized Fassbinder's talent and viewed him as a leader of the new cinema being made in Germany. The director's breakthrough to a larger public came with *Angst essen Seele auf* (*Ali: Fear Eats the Soul*, 1974) and *Fontane Effi Briest* (*Effi Briest*, 1974). *Angst essen Seele auf*, about a German cleaning lady who marries a Moroccan about 15 years younger than she, offers viewers not only an accessible and highly melodramatic love story—the film is loosely based on Douglas Sirk's *All That Heaven Allows* (1955)—but also a look at the repressive nature of the German lower middle class. *Effi Briest*, based on a novel by Theodor Fontane that has long been part of the school curriculum, reflects similar social repression, in this case during Wilhelmine Germany.

Angst essen Seele auf and *Fontane Effi Briest* represent two facets of Fassbinder's production, the first a melodramatically charged love story that reaches the emotions, and the second an experimental retelling of a classic that speaks to the intellect. As different as the films are, however, both display the director's bag of tricks that have become his trademark: reflections in mirrors, characters framed by doorways or confined to the upper part of a frame by obstacles placed beneath, dramatic lighting, shadows, bizarre colors, choreographed movement, and self-conscious actors.

Throughout his film career, Fassbinder preferred working with the ensemble of actors he met at Munich's action-theater in 1968 and with whom he formed the experimental *antiteater* when the action-theater failed. In *Warnung vor einer heiligen Nutte* (*Beware of a Holy Whore*, 1971), the director mirrors the love–hate relationship that according to biographical accounts by several members of his acting troupe existed between him and his film team. Other regular actors in his films included **Kurt Raab**, **Margit Carstensen**, **Ingrid Caven**, **Irm Hermann**, **Hanna Schygulla**, **Harry Baer**, **Gottfried John**, **Günther Kaufmann**, **Volker Spengler**, **Brigitte Mira**, and his mother, Lilo Pempeit.

Other highlights of Fassbinder's career include *Die bitteren Tränen der Petra von Kant* (*The Bitter Tears of Petra von Kant*, 1972), based on Fassbinder's play about the emotionally damaging end of a lesbian affair; the multiepisode television film *Berlin Alexanderplatz* (*Berlin Alexanderplatz*, 1979/1980), based on Alfred Döblin's 1929 novel and considered by some critics to be Fassbinder's masterpiece; **Die Ehe der Maria Braun** (*The Marriage of Maria Braun*, 1979), *Lola* (1981), and *Die Sehnsucht der Veronika Voss* (*Veronika Voss*, 1982), three films about the emotional and spiritual cost of Germany's Wirtschaftswunder, the name given to the rapid economic development that occurred in the mid-1950s in West Germany; and finally the multi-million-dollar extravaganza *Lili Marleen* (1981), about song diva Lale Andersen, who entertained German troops during World War II with the popular song that gives the movie its name. Fassbinder's most commercially successful film, in Germany and worldwide—including the United States—was *Die Ehe der Maria*

Braun; this melodrama serves as a paradigm of Fassbinder's total output. Set in the immediate postwar years, 1945–1954, the film makes far-reaching connections between Nazi Germany, postwar development, and Germany at the time of the film's release. *See also* BRECHT, BERTOLT.

FECHNER, EBERHARD (1926–1992). Until his death in 1992, Eberhard Fechner was Germany's leading documentary filmmaker. In films that covered a range of political, social, and historical issues, Fechner constructed narrative dialogues out of interviews he conducted with average German citizens, probing the relationship between the lives of ordinary humans and sociopolitical history. In *Klassenphoto* (*Class Photo*, 1970), for example, he interviews the surviving members of a pre–World War II school class 25 years after the end of the war. Fechner edits the responses in a way that creates individual private histories, which are inexorably tied to the public or political history of Germany. The director never distorts his subjects or their words, but rather he permits them to tell their stories to the camera unadorned by interpretation. Gradually, viewers learn the relationship between individual actions and the course of history.

Other documentaries by Fechner, which likewise show how private histories always occur against the larger backdrop of political history, include *Unter Denkmalschutz – Erinnerungen aus einem Frankfurter Bürgerhaus* (*Historic Building: Memories from a Frankfurt Apartment Building*, 1975), about historic preservation and historical memory; *Der Prozeß – Eine Darstellung des Majdanek-Vefahrens in Düsseldorf* (*The Trial: Presentation of the Majdanek Concentration Camp Trial in Düsseldorf*, 1984), about the trial of war criminals who were active in the concentration camp in Majdanek; *Damenstift* (*Home for Ladies*, 1983), about a home for elderly women; and *Die Comedian Harmonists* (*The Comedian Harmonists*, 1977), interviews with the surviving members of the popular singing group, whose career and eventual persecution by the Nazis was also the subject of Joseph Vilsmaier's narrative feature of the same name.

Fechner successfully transferred his documentary style to two television miniseries: *Tadellöser & Wolff* (*My Country, Right or Wrong*, 1975) and *Ein Kapitel für sich* (*A Chapter by Itself*, 1979), both based on autobiographical novels by Walter Kempowski. *Tadellöser &*

Wolff traces the life of a bourgeois family during the Third Reich. *Ein Kapitel für sich* follows the same family through the early postwar years. In both films, Fechner examines the culpability of the ordinary citizen in the events that occurred under the Nazis, suggesting that regardless of how decent members of the Kempowski family were and regardless of the distance they kept from the Nazi government, they bear responsibility for what occurred during the Third Reich. *See also VERGANGENHITSBEWÄLTIGUNGSFILM.*

FELMY, HANSJÖRG (1931–2007). Hansjörg Felmy's boyish good looks and charm helped him create his persona in the 1950s of a German Everyman—honest and well-intentioned but possessed of weaknesses that explain, while not excusing, Germany's troubled past. In such **war films** as *Der Stern von Afrika* (*Star of Africa*, Alfred Weidenmann, 1957) and *Haie und kleine Fische* (*Sharks and Small Fish*, **Frank Wisbar**, 1957), Felmy portrayed officers who were troubled by the war but whose sense of duty and patriotism moved them to support it nonetheless. In a sense, he was the conscience of his adult audience at the time the films were released, suggesting they should not have gone along with the Nazis, maybe did not want to go along with the policies, but had no choice because of their loyalty to Germany.

Felmy's signature role came as Hans Boeckel in **Kurt Hoffmann**'s *Wir Wunderkinder* (*Aren't We Wonderful?*, 1958), a biting satire of Germany from 1913 to 1955. Felmy plays an essentially decent German who because of his trust of others finds himself in political difficulties. The film is especially critical of his reluctance to recognize the danger of the Nazis and his compliance with their policies, including going to war, although his views are precisely the opposite. As a stand-in for the ordinary German, Boeckel represents the reluctant fellow traveler, whose silence lent support to the crimes of the Nazis. After the war, when Boeckel finds courage and finally opposes the Nazis by exposing their presence in 1950s Germany, the film makes clear his actions come too late. Bruno Tiches, the Nazi he exposes, is destroyed not by Boekel's articles but by a malfunctioning elevator: Tiches falls down the elevator shaft.

Felmy's other important films include *Schachnovelle* (*Brainwashed*, Gerd Oswald, 1960), in which he plays against type, portraying a dedicated Nazi officer; *Die Buddenbrooks* (*The Buddenbrooks*,

Weidenmann, 1959), in which he plays Thomas Buddenbrooks, the son torn between his practical and artistic inclinations; and *Tatort* (*Scene of the Crime*, 1970–), in which he starred as Detective Commissioner Heinz Haferkamp in 20 episodes of Germany's longest-running crime show.

FILM AWARDS. The Bambi, a small deer-shaped award named after the fawn in Walt Disney's classic animated movie *Bambi*, is the oldest of several German film honors and was first awarded in 1948 by the magazine *Film-Revue*. Since 1968, a jury of editors at Burda-Verlag has determined the recipients based on reader polls of their magazine *Bild und Funk* but also considering artistic merit. Previous winners have included **Hanna Schygulla**, **Wim Wenders**, Ingmar Bergman, and Ottokar Runze.

The major film awards are the Deutsche Filmpreise (German film awards), until 1999 known as the Bundesfilmpreise, and are awarded by the Deutsche Filmakademie (German Film Academy). These awards, originally selected by a jury of peers in the German film industry and since 2005 by members of the German Film Academy, are presented annually to best films in three categories—feature film, children's film, and documentary—and to the best achievement in individual categories, including direction, cinematography, acting, editing, and set design. As with Hollywood's Academy Awards, there is also an honor for lifetime achievement. In each of the film categories, two works may be awarded, the Lola in Silver and the Lola in Gold. These awards were previously called the Filmband in Gold (filmstrip in gold) and Filmband in Silber (filmstrip in silver) because of their resemblance to a strip of film, but in 1999 the award was redesigned as a statue with a female shape and was renamed the Lola, an homage to the films *Der blaue Engel* (*The Blue Angel*, Josef von Sternberg, 1930), *Lola* (**Rainer Werner Fassbinder**, 1980), and *Lola rennt* (*Run Lola Run*, **Tom Tykwer**, 1998), whose heroines are named Lola. In the past, there was also an award for extraordinarily meritorious films. The award was in the shape of a bowl and named appropriately the *goldene Schale* (golden bowl). The nominated films receive monetary awards as well as the statue. In 2007, the nominated feature films each received €250,000; the silver awards were for €400,000, and the winning film received €500,000. The awards for the other film categories were slightly lower. Winners in individual categories received €10,000.

Two other prestigious awards are the Golden and Silver Bears, awarded at the **Berlin Film Festival**, and the Max Ophüls Prize, named for director **Max Ophüls** and awarded for promising new director at the Saarbrücken Film Festival.

FILMFÖRDERUNGSANSTALT. In 1967, the West German Parliament passed the Film Subsidy Bill establishing the Filmförderungsanstalt (federal film board), whose mission statement calls for fostering the making of quality films through a system of subsidies and the promotion of German films in Germany and abroad. Financed without government taxes, the Filmförderungsanstalt, which is a partner in **German Films Service + Marketing GmbH**, receives its budget through levies on film admissions and video sales. Subsidies take the form of direct grants and interest-free loans, all or a portion of which may be forgiven. The list of those who are eligible to receive funds is broad and includes directors and producers—who receive the largest share of funds—film distributors, movie house owners, and those wanting training in acting or technical aspects of filmmaking. The major criterion for directors, producers, distributors, and exhibitors is that they have a record of success with previous films. The system of subsidies provided effectively replaced an earlier system of support, direct loans provided by the **Kuratorium Junger Deutscher Film** (Film Board of **Young German Cinema**), which was active in the first years after the **Oberhausen Manifesto** created the German new wave.

FILM-KURIER. *Film-Kurier* was the German film industry's most important trade publication from its inception in 1919 until its discontinuation in 1945. Appearing daily in newspaper format, it reported on present and future film projects, ran film critiques and interviews with film personalities, and also covered theater and sports. Its articles were directed both at a general readership interested in film and at people in the industry. During the Third Reich, the publication played a role in directing reception of the films through ads, proclaiming a film's popularity, and presenting feature articles. The propaganda ministry under Joseph Goebbels had forbidden film critics from criticizing films, requiring them instead to describe and explain the films to the public in accordance with National Socialist ideology. As a result writers praised, in particular, film projects favored by the government. The companion publication, the *Illustrierter Filmkurier*, was sold in movie theaters as an additional source of revenue for the company. During the National Socialist era, the *Illustrierter Filmkurier* focused in particular on those films of interest to the regime's propaganda efforts. *Die Rothschilds* (*The Rothschilds*, Erich Wanderschek, 1940) and *Jud Süß* (*Jew Süss*, **Veit Harlan**, 1940), for example, two of the Nazi's major anti-Semitic films (*see **Der ewige Jude***), were cover stories for the publication.

FILMVERLAG DER AUTOREN. Recognizing the importance of distribution if they were to change the viewing habits of moviegoers, filmmakers of **New German Cinema** founded the Filmverlag der Autoren (Authors' Film Publishing Group) in 1971, to distribute their independent films. The initial members, among whom were **Hark Bohm**, **Hans W. Geissendörfer**, **Peter Lilienthal**, and **Wim Wenders**, modeled their distribution cooperative after the Verlag der Autoren, a German literary and theatrical publishing group. Other members included **Rainer Werner Fassbinder**, **Edgar Reitz**, **Alexander Kluge**, and **Reinhard Hauff**.

In tandem with initiatives begun by the **Oberhausen** movement of **Young German Cinema**, support from the **Kuratorium Junger Deutscher Film**, grants from the **Filmförderungsanstalt** (federal film board), and financing from television, the Filmverlag der Autoren boosted the visibility and prestige of West German cinema internationally. In 1985, the Filmverlag was sold to the independent producer-distributor Futura Films.

FISCHER, OTTO WILHELM (1915–2004). Otto Wilhelm Fischer, known as O. W. Fischer, was one of the most popular and highest paid film stars in Germany in the late postwar period (1950–1963). He won a Bambi (*see **film awards***) in the years 1953–1955 and again in 1958–1961. He won an Award in Silver from the Deutsche Filmakademie (German Film Academy) for his role as the mad king in *Ludwig II* (*Ludwig*, **Helmut Käutner**) in 1955, an Award in Gold for his acting in *Helden* (*Heroes*, Franz Wirth, 1958), and a career achievement award in 1977, also from the German Film Academy. He again won a Bambi in 1987. Fischer owed his popularity to his good looks and to good roles. In his first postwar films, he played opposite **Maria Schell**, Germany's leading actress at the time. In 1955, his role as King Ludwig in Käutner's *Ludwig II* established his acting skills as encompassing more than romantic gentlemen and comedic lovers. In all his roles, however, whether romantic, comedic, or melodramatic, Fischer portrayed a new type of hero, a man not afraid to show his vulnerability. His characters could at times be weak and at other times strong; they could be dreamers who were also realists; they had childlike and even feminine traits; and they could be erotic while also being straightlaced. In short, he played a hero that German audiences needed to see after the heroes presented to them during the Nazi years.

In 1957, Fischer received the starring role in the American film *My Man Godfrey* (Henry Koster), but he was replaced by David Niven after 16 days of shooting because of irreconcilable differences with the director. Later Fischer acknowledged that he had to give up the part because of memory loss. He nevertheless continued to appear in theatrical films throughout the 1960s and in several television films in the 1970s. His last major appearance was in 1986 in the television movie *Auferstehung in Lugano* (*Uprising in Lugano*, Edgar von Heeringen).

FLEISCHMANN, PETER (1937–). Peter Fleischmann, one of the directors of **New German Cinema**, has less visibility than his fellow filmmakers. Today, besides his work for the **Babelsberg Studios**, Fleischmann is known for his anti-*Heimatfilm Jagdszenen aus Niederbayern* (*Hunting Scenes from Lower Bavaria*, 1969). The film was a revelation at the time of its release, both for the way it deconstructed the idyll of village life, exposing the dangers of the *Heimat* (home, homeland, but implying the place one feels secure), and also for its contrast with so many of the films of the 1960s, an era of sex comedies, sentimental melodramas, and commercially safe films.

FORST, WILLI (1903–1980). Willi Forst was an Austrian actor and director whose strength lay in musical comedy. He began his film career in the 1920s, appearing opposite **Marlene Dietrich** in *Café Elektric* (*Café Electric*, Gustav Ucicky, 1927) and *Gefahren der Brautzeit*

(*Dangers of the Engagement Period*, Fred Sauer, 1929). A brief appearance in an early sound film, *Atlantic* (**Ewald André Dupont**, 1929), in which he breaks down while singing a song as the ship he is on sinks, cemented his reputation as an actor who could move audiences to tears. His first film as director, *Maskerade* (*Masquerade in Vienna*, 1934), in which he demythologizes fin de siècle romanticism, became a worldwide success and generated the Hollywood remake *Escapade* (Robert Z. Leonard, 1935).

Forst's major success as actor and director occurred in the early 1930s, when he appeared in and made a number of musical comedy films in the style of Viennese operettas. After 1938, when Austria became part of the German Third Reich, Forst continued to make films in Austria, claiming after the war that his films were a form of personal protest against National Socialism. The Viennese historical epics that comprise this period in his life are filled with charm and gallantry, made, according to Forst, to make people happy.

After the defeat of National Socialism in World War II, Forst directed *Die Sünderin* (*The Sinner*, 1951). The film, in which **Hildegard Knef** plays a prostitute who helps a dying artist commit suicide before taking her own life, brought forth strong protest from Germany's church leaders and the country's press. The campaign against the film eventually led to its commercial success (it had reportedly not been doing well at the box office) and also gave Knef international recognition. In spite of the film's success, Forst was never able to regain the reputation he had had with his earlier films, and he withdrew from filmmaking in 1957, explaining that it is "better to go than to be asked to go." *See also* AUSTRIAN CINEMA.

FRAUENFILM. The term *Frauenfilm* ("women's film") refers to films about women, which generally but not necessarily are made for women and may be directed by either a male or female filmmaker. The *Frauenfilm* does not constitute a genre per se. Rather it may be a melodrama, documentary, or romantic comedy, among other film forms. The term can be pejorative, describing films that make viewers tear up, or positive, referring to films that have social or political importance.

The most active advocate in Germany for the *Frauenfilm* as sociopolitical statement has been the film journal *Frauen und Film*, founded by **Helke Sander** in 1974 and now appearing irregularly. Two important sociopolitical women's films have been *Die Ehe der Maria Braun* (*The Marriage of Maria Braun*, **Rainer Werner Fassbinder**, 1979) and *Deutschland bleiche Mutter* (*Germany Pale Mother*, **Helma Sanders-Brahms**, 1980), which examine the role of women in postwar Germany from a feminist perspective.

Besides Sander and Sanders-Brahms, other feminist directors include **Jutta Brückner, Margarethe von Trotta, Ulrike Ottinger, Valie Export**, and **Monika Treut**. Brückner, like Sander and Sanders-Brahms, examines the absence of power among women in 1950s West Germany in *Hungerjahre* (*Years of Hunger*, 1980). Von Trotta focuses on the political helplessness of women in such works as *Die verlorene Ehre der Katharina Blum* (*The Lost Honor of Katharina Blum*, 1975), which she codirected with **Volker Schlöndorff**, *Das zweite Erwachen der Christa Klages* (*The Second Awakening of Christa Klages* 1978), and *Die bleierne Zeit* (*Marianne and Juilane*, 1981). The films show an escalation in political awareness of the female protagonist, from Katharina's naiveté to Christa's political activism to Marianne's terrorist activities.

Valie Export and Monika Treut create controversial essays on female sexuality. Export works in the medium of performance art. Treut directs soft-core sexual movies that make a spectacle of the female body in an attempt to demystify it.

FREUND, KARL (1890–1969). Karl Freund was Germany's most important director of photography during the golden age of silent film, the mid-1920s. Working with movie legends such as **Ernst Lubitsch, Fritz Lang**, Carl Dreyer, **Ewald André Dupont**, and **Friedrich Wilhelm Murnau**, Freund brought to their films his eye for lighting effects, unusual perspectives, and innovative camera movement.

Without question Freund's greatest contribution to the film canon came with his camera work for *Der letzte Mann* (*The Last Laugh*, Murnau, 1924) and *Varieté* (*Jealousy*, Dupont, 1925). In *Der letzte Mann*, Freund mounted the camera on his stomach in order to follow the action more freely. Critics agree that the result was a film in which the camera becomes an actor, commenting as much on the action as any subtitles could. Indeed, Freund's subjective camera eliminates the need for subtitles until the very end of the film. After *Der letzte Mann*, Freund continued innovative camera movement in Dupont's *Varieté*. Here he mounted the camera on a trapeze and also on the floor directly below it in order to capture the dizzying and terrifying work of the trapeze artist. In 1927, Freund worked with Lang on **Metropolis** and with **Walter Ruttmann** on *Berlin – Die Sinfonie der Großstadt* (*Berlin: Symphony of a Great City*), two of the best-known films of the Weimar Republic.

Freund immigrated to Hollywood in 1931, where his chiaroscuro lighting effects created the frightening atmosphere in Tod Browning's *Dracula* (1931) and Robert Florey's *Murders in the Rue Morgue* (1932), before directing his own horror film, *The Mummy* (1933). Freund is sometimes credited with suggesting the final scene in Lewis Milestone's *All Quiet on the Western Front* (1931), in which the hero is shot while reaching for a butterfly. In 1937, he won an Oscar for his camera work on *The Good Earth* (Sidney Franklin).

Freund spent the final part of his career in television, working as supervising photographer for Desilu studios on over 400 episodes of *I Love Lucy*. Together with Desi Arnaz, he developed a three-camera system and the necessary overhead lighting, which allowed three 35mm cameras to shoot simultaneously. The process allowed this and subsequent television series to be put on film in front of a live audience. Until this time, live television shows were simply filmed for archival purposes by one stationary camera, rendering the finished product unsuitable for rebroadcast.

In 1965, Freund received an Award in Gold (*see* **film awards**) for career achievement from the Deutsche Filmakademie (German Film Academy).

FRITSCH, WILLY (1901–1973). Willy Fritsch's film career spanned five decades, from the 1920s to the 1960s, and represents three film eras: silent and early sound films of the Weimar Republic (1918–1933), National Socialist films of the Third Reich (1933–1945), and films of the postwar, pre–**New German Cinema** period (1945–1962). His first film was *Miß Venus* (*Miss Venus*, Ludwig Czerny, 1921); his last was *Das habe ich von Papa gelernt* (*I Learned It from Father*, Axel von Ambesser, 1964). Fritsch's good looks, charm, and unforced acting, which were already on display in the film operetta *Miß Venus* and still evident in his last film, made him one of Germany's most popular film stars. His greatest success came in the12 films he made with **Lilian Harvey**, beginning with the silent *Die keusche Susanne* (*The Innocent Susanne*, Richard Eichberg, 1926) and ending with *Frau am Steuer* (*Woman at the Wheel*, Paul Martin, 1939), after which Harvey left Germany and Fritsch joined the Nazi Party.

Fritsch and Harvey were dubbed the country's *Traumpaar* ("dream couple") by the German press, and they were reputedly a couple off screen as well as on. Together Fritsch and Harvey recorded a number of the songs from their musicals, a symbiosis that increased their popularity and sold records and tickets. The best known of their films are *Die Drei von der Tankstelle* (*Three from the Gas Station*, Wilhelm Thiele, 1930), *Der Kongreß tanzt* (*Congress Dances*, Erik Charell, 1931), both made during the Weimar years, and *Glückskinder* (*Lucky Kids*, Paul Martin, 1936), made under National Socialism. *Glückskinder* was made in answer to Joseph Goebbels's admonition that Germany's film industry needed to make films that could compete with those coming from Hollywood. It was a quasi remake of the successful film *It Happened One Night* (Frank Capra, 1934), starring Clark Gable. In the film's big production number, Fritsch muses that he wishes that he were Clark Gable, while Lilian Harvey wishes to be Mickey Mouse. Most of the films Fritsch made under the Nazi regime were lighthearted, entertaining fare. Toward the end of World War II, however, he made the militaristic *Junge Adler* (*Young Eagles*, Alfred Weidenmann, 1944), a film that reflects Joseph Goebbels's public admonition to fight to the bitter end. (*See* **Durchhaltungs-film**).

Fritsch's postwar career never achieved the success he had in the Weimar Republic or the Third Reich. He appeared in a number of nostalgic musical films, playing an older version of the charming rogue from the earlier part of his career. In 1965, he was honored by the Deutsche Filmakademie with an honorary award for a distinguished career.

FRÖBE, GERT (1913–1988). Although he began his film career at the age of 35 in 1954, Gert Fröbe (Karl-Gerhard Fröber) appeared in over 100 films in the next three decades. Known primarily as a character actor, Fröbe was good at portraying an average German citizen in postwar films. His career work includes comedies, dramas, and *Heimatfilme*, among other genres, for German, French, Italian, British, and American productions. After playing Schrott, a serial killer, in *Es geschah am hellichten Tag* (*It Happened in Broad Daylight*, Ladislao Vajda, 1958)—based on Friedrich Dürrenmatt's novel of that name, which also provided the source for *The Pledge* (Sean Penn, 2001)—Fröbe received more notable roles. He played the detective commissioner in two Mabuse films, *Die 1000 Augen des Dr. Mabuse* (*The Thousand Eyes of Dr. Mabuse*, **Fritz Lang**, 1960) and *Das Testament des Dr. Mabuse* (*The Testament of Dr. Mabuse*, Werner Klingler, 1962), an attempt to capitalize on Lang's classic crime series. Two of his most memorable roles are as an abusive, alcoholic husband and father in *Via Mala* (*Via Mala*, Paul May, 1961) and as James Bond's nemesis Auric Goldfinger in *Goldfinger* (Guy Hamilton, 1964).

FROBOESS, CORNELIA (1943–). Cornelia (Conny) Froboess began acting in films as a child in the early 1950s. Her success, however, came with a series of musicals she made in the late 1950s, some with **Peter Kraus**, with whom studio publicity and the tabloids linked her romantically. *Wenn die Conny mit dem Peter* (*When Conny and Peter Do It Together*, Fritz Umgelter, 1958) and *Conny und Peter machen Musik* (*Conny and Peter Make Music*, Werner Jacobs, 1960) established the singers/actors as West Germany's singing film couple. Their success and popularity with German teenagers mirrored that of Annette Funicello and Frankie Avalon, who epitomized the Hollywood teen musical in the mid-1960s. Froboess also appeared in numerous musicals without Kraus during the late 1950s and early 1960s. While her later career never achieved the same degree of success as her teenage films, she has had notable roles, including that of Henriette in *Die Sehnsucht der Veronika Voss* (*Veronika Voss*, 1982). In this third film of **Rainer Werner Fassbinder**'s postwar trilogy, Froboess plays a woman who watches as her partner entangles himself in a relationship with a faded actress. In the 1990s and 2000s, Froboess has made frequent guest appearances on German television series. She also played the mother of Martin Brest (**Til Schweiger**), a criminal looking for happiness before he dies, in the crime comedy *Knockin' on Heaven's Door* (*Knockin' on Heaven's*

Door, Thomas Jahn, 1997), one of the many comedies German directors made during the film comedy wave of the 1990s.

FROELICH, CARL (1875–1953). Carl Froelich is one of the pioneers of early German cinema. He worked as producer, writer, cinematographer, and director; his films display good technological values for the period, suggest a preference for themes involving the upper middle class and professionals, and reveal a tendency to national patriotism. He established movie houses for soldiers and also produced newsreels about action at the front. After World War I, he merged his production company with that of **Henny Porten** and directed her in a number of silent films in the mid to late 1920s. Froelich's production company made the first full-length German sound film, *Die Nacht gehört uns* (*The Night Is Ours*, 1929), with **Hans Albers**. The film was codirected by French director Henry Roussel and was the German version of the French film *La nuit est à nous* (1930), on which the two directors assisted Roger Lion. Froelich also directed a number of films during the Third Reich. Most of these were entertaining diversions, but the nationalism Froelich exhibited in his films during World War I is evident in some of his National Socialist works. The story of *Heimat* (*Homeland*, 1938), which starred **Zarah Leander** and **Heinrich George**, revolves around a world-famous diva (Leander) who reconciles with her father (George) for the sake of her daughter, reinforcing the conservatism of National Socialist values of family and homeland. But many of Froelich's films were similar to his *Es war eine rauschende Ballnacht* (*The Life and Loves of Tschaikovsky*, 1939), a light drama portraying the composer Peter Tschaikovsky's tumultuous life.

FRÖHLICH, GUSTAV (1902–1987). Gustav Fröhlich remained a popular German actor from the silent films of the 1920s through the films of the postwar years, acting in over 100 films and also, late in his career, appearing on German television. His best-known role is as Freder Frederson, the rebellious son in **Fritz Lang**'s *Metropolis* (*Metropolis*, 1927). Arguably, had he never appeared in another role, he would be remembered for his expressionistic acting in the film, which has him running with one arm outstretched, in a Christ-like pose splayed across a huge menacing clock, and holding his hand up to his brow and staggering backward, watching in horror as the machines of Metropolis explode. Fröhlich was introduced to a whole new generation of fans when Giorgio Moroder restored *Metropolis* in 1984. The rock soundtrack and color, which Moroder added to the film, made it a cult hit, with video outtakes containing Fröhlich appearing on the MTV television network.

Although *Metropolis* may have assured Fröhlich's cult status in later years, he was always a popular actor, never typecast in a particular role. He combined good looks with impulsiveness, yet also ordinariness, which allowed him to play a number of different types — Bohemian artist, jealous lover, medieval knight, and immigrant — yet all with audience appeal. He appeared in a number of films during the Third Reich until he was called into service in 1941. He reputedly also had personal difficulties with Joseph Goebbels, after the minister of propaganda began an affair with Fröhlich's lover at the time, Czech actress Lída Baarová. In 1950, Fröhlich played a terminally ill painter who is helped to die by **Hildegard Knef's** character in *Die Sünderin* (*The Sinner*, **Willi Forst**, 1951). Although the film was not successful at first, it gained notoriety when the Catholic Church and the German press condemned the film as immoral, which occasioned its wider release. Fröhlich also directed several films, none of which achieved wide recognition. In 1973, he received an honorary award from the Deutsche Filmakademie (German Film Academy) for his contributions to German film.

FÜRMANN, BENNO (1972–). Benno Fürmann is one of several German actors who gained recognition in the 1990s. Like his contemporaries, **Franka Potente**, **Til Schweiger**, **Daniel Brühl**, and **Moritz Bleibtreu**, among others, Fürmann benefited from being cast in high-quality productions with commercial appeal. Fürmann's breakthrough came with his role as boxer Gustav "Bubi" Scholz in *Die Bubi Scholz Story* (*The Bubi Scholz Story*, Roland Suso Richter, 1998). Scholz, a popular German middleweight fighter in the late 1950s and early 1960s, was convicted of negligent homicide in 1984 after shooting his wife while he was in an alcoholic stupor. Fürmann won the German equivalent of an Emmy that year as best actor in the made-for-television movie. His first major theatrical film was *Freunde* (*Friends*, Martin Eigler, 2000), a thriller that pits former friends against each other when one becomes a cop and the other a petty criminal. Gritty in the fashion of an early Martin Scorsese movie, *Freunde* led to *Kanak Attack* (Lars Becker, 2000), a film of 13 mini-stories about gangland thugs. These films, as well as his turn as the alcoholic Scholz, established Fürmann as a good-looking but edgy male lead. In *Der Krieger und die Kaiserin* (*The Princess and the Warrior*, **Tom Tykwer**, 2000), Fürmann plays Bodo Riemer—a young man who saves the life of a woman run down by a truck—as a tightly wound spring ready to violently release its tension. In *Nackt* (*Naked*, **Doris Dörrie**, 2002), a film about three couples in various stages of their romances, Fürmann's character retains his masculine anger, never revealing a softer, feminine side as the other two male leads do. Fürmann plays against type in *Joyeux Noël* (*Merry Christmas*, Christian Carion, 2005), in which he appears as an opera singer who performs on the front during a lull in fighting.

– G –

GALEEN, HENRIK (1881–1949). Henrik Galeen worked as writer, assistant director, or director on Germany's best-known horror films during the silent era. In 1913, he reputedly worked as assistant director on *Der Student von Prag* (*The Student of Prague*, Stellan Rye and Paul Wegener), which he remade in 1926. In 1914, he directed his first major film with **Paul Wegener** as codirector, *Der Golem* (*The Golem*), based on a Jewish legend of a clay statue that comes to life and seeks revenge for perceived wrongs. Galeen wrote the screenplay for the film's remake, *Der Golem, wie er in die Welt kam* (*The Golem: How He Came into the World*, Wegener and Carl Boese, 1920), which told the same story but without bringing the legend into the 20th century. Galeen also wrote the screenplays for *Nosferatu, eine Symphonie des Grauens* (*Nosferatu*, **Friedrich Wilhelm Murnau**, 1922) and *Das Wachsfigurenkabinett* (*Waxworks*, Leo Birinsky and Paul Leni, 1924), a horror film built around the tales of three wax figures. In 1928, Galeen directed *Alraune* (*A Daughter of Destiny*), a mix of the Frankenstein and *Homunculus* (*Homunculus*) legends, themselves made into countless films, in which an artificially created woman seeks revenge on her creator. Although never as famous as Murnau or as well-known as Wegener or **Robert Wiene**, Galeen can be seen as one of the major influences on German film expressionism. His preference for expressionist symbolism turns the gothic tale of a doppelgänger in his 1926 version of *Der Student von Prag* into a shattered search for identity. In the final scene of the film, after the student shoots his mirror image and falls to the floor dying, all that remains is his reflection in a broken piece of glass.

GANZ, BRUNO (1941–). Bruno Ganz may forever be remembered as the actor who gave a human face to evil. Playing Adolf Hitler in the **Oliver Hirschbiegel** film *Der Untergang* (*The Downfall*, 2004), Ganz portrayed the leader of the National Socialists and Germany's Third Reich as an ordinary man, suffering from Parkinson's, charming in the presence of women, and prone to violent outbursts among his generals and ministers. His portrayal created controversy among Germany's critics, but reviews outside Germany generally praised his work.

Ganz's acting in *Der Untergang* reveals the intelligence he brings to his roles. Before playing Hitler, he had already created a number of memorable characters, at first on the stage and starting in 1976 on film. In the 1970s, Bruno Ganz was one of the most prominent protagonists on the German stage, having starred in plays by William Shakespeare, **Bertolt Brecht**, Henrik Ibsen, Heinrich von Kleist, and **Peter Handke**. In 1976, his role in Eric Rohmer's *Die Marquise von O.* (*The Marquise of O.*), based on a short story by Kleist, brought him an Award in Gold (*see* **film awards**) and international recognition. It also made him a star of **New German Cinema** (NGC). His most notable roles from this period were as the terminally ill framemaker-turned-assassin who is befriended by Dennis Hopper's character in *Der amerikanische Freund* (*The American Friend*, **Wim Wenders**, 1977); as a microbiologist in *Messer im Kopf* (*Knife in the Head*, **Reinhard Hauff**, 1978), who tries to regain his memory and reestablish his identity after being shot in the head by a policeman; and as Jonathan in *Nosferatu – Phantom der Nacht* (*Nosferatu the Vampyre*, 1979), **Werner Herzog**'s remake of the 1922 horror classic by **Friedrich Wilhelm Murnau.**

Ganz's most renowned role before *Der Untergang* was as the angel Damiel in Wenders's post-NGC film *Der Himmel über Berlin* (*Wings *of Desire*, 1987), a part that broadened his international fame and which he reprised in *In weiter Ferne, so nah!* (*Faraway, So Close!*, 1993). Like a number of European actors, Ganz is fluent in English, French, and Italian. Among his over 70 films, not counting television roles, Ganz has therefore appeared in French, Italian, Swiss, Spanish, Dutch, Australian, and American productions, including *Lumière* (*Lumiere*, Jeanne Moreau, 1976), *Dans la ville blanche* (*In the White City*, Alain Tanner, 1983), *Pane e tulipani* (*Bread and Tulips*, Silvio Soldini, 2000), *The Boys from Brazil* (Franklin J. Schaffner, 1978), and *The Manchurian Candidate* (Jonathan Demme, 2004).

Ganz is a physical actor who has a good relationship with the camera. Some critics, especially early in his career, felt that he was too mannered and self-conscious, perhaps a carryover from his stage work. Yet, as his portrayal of Hitler demonstrates, he can lose himself in a role, and with accent, voice modulation, and movement create the illusion of natural acting. In an interview with Richard Raskin about his role as the angel Damiel in *Der Himmel über Berlin*, Ganz remarked that he had to play the part without affect, as angels are not given to psychological problems. "I mean there is just no acting. What you deliver is physical presence."

GEBÜHR, OTTO (1877–1954). Otto Gebühr acted in over 70 feature films during his four decades in film, but his likeness to the figure of the King of Prussia in Adolph Menzel's painting *Der Flötenspieler von Sanssouci* (*The Flute Player of Sanssouci*, 1852) typecast him throughout his career as Frederick the Great. He played the part in 16 films and numerous times in stage plays. One of the more memorable film portrayals was in the four-part *Fridericus Rex* (Arzén von Cserépy, 1922–1923) in which Gebühr played Frederick II from his days as crown prince until he became "der alte Fritz" (the affectionate nickname his subjects called him when he was an old man). Arguably his greatest success as Frederick the Great came under the Nazis, when he played Frederick II in **Veit Harlan**'s big-budget production *Der große König* (*The Great King*, 1942), an undisguised hymn to the Prussian leader's genius. Harlan draws the parallels between Prussia and Germany, Frederick the Great and Adolf Hitler, broadly enough that they cannot be overlooked. After Germany's defeat and the end of the Third Reich, Gebühr resumed his acting career in West Germany, appearing in dramas, romances, comedies, and *Heimatfilme*. The best known of these was *Grün ist die Heide* (*The Heath Is Green*, **Hans Deppe**, 1951), a mixture of idyllic country life and postwar realism.

GEISSENDÖRFER, HANS W. (1941–). One of the founding members of the **Filmverlag der Autoren**, Hans W. Geissendörfer has never enjoyed the international success of his peers in **New German Cinema**. After an auspicious beginning with his original telling of the vampire tale in *Jonathan* (1970), which won him an Award in Silver (*see* **film awards**) from the Deutsche Filmakademie (German Film Academy) as Best New Talent, Geissendörfer, like the more critically and commercially successful **Volker Schlöndorff** and others of his peers, directed a series of films based on literary sources: *Die gläserne Zelle* (*The Glass Cell*, 1978), *Der Zauberberg* (*The Magic Mountain*, 1982), and *Ediths Tagebuch* (*Edith's Diary*, 1983). *Die gläserne Zelle*, based on a mystery by Patricia Highsmith, won an Award in Gold from the German Film Academy and an Oscar nomination for Best Foreign Film. *Der Zauberberg*, based on the novel by Thomas Mann, won an Award in Silver. Geissendörfer is the producer and sometimes director for *Lindenstraße* (*Lindenstreet*, 1985–), Germany's longest-running soap opera. In 1993, Geissendörfer had international success with his film *Justiz* (*Justice*, 1993), based on the novel of the same name by Friedrich Dürrenmatt. After a long period without directing any feature films, he released *Schneeland* (*Snowland*, 2005), which has won international awards and had its U.S. premier at the Sundance Film Festival. *Schneeland* tells a love story while also dealing with taboo subjects such as child molestation and incest.

GEORGE, GÖTZ (1938–). Son of actor **Heinrich George**, Götz George (Götz Schulz) began acting as a teenager. His first film roles were in musical comedies, including the *Heimatfilm Wenn der weiße Flieder wieder blüht* (*When the White Lilacs Bloom Again*, **Hans Deppe**, 1953), with **Romy Schneider**. George's breakthrough to dramatic recognition came with his role in *Kirmes* (*The Fair*, aka *Death Carousel*, **Wolfgang Staudte**, 1960) as Robert, who as a deserter during the war is hounded to death by his village. George became a star with his role in *Der Schatz im Silbersee* (*The Treasure in Silver Lake*, Harald Reinl, 1962), the first of the **Winnetou films**, the successful film series based on the popular novels of Karl May. *Der Schatz im Silbersee* and two other Western films, *Unter Geiern* (*Frontier Hellcat*, Alfred Vohrer,1964) and *Winnetou und das Halbblut Apanatschi* (*Half-Breed*, Harald Philipp, 1966), established George as an action hero who reportedly did most of his own stunts. George also played more demanding roles, for example, the prisoner in *Mensch und Bestie* (*Man and Beast*, Edwin Zbonek, 1963), who escapes a camp in order to save fellow prisoners, only to be shot and killed by his brother, an officer of the Schutzstaffel (SS).

George is one of 10 actors in postwar Germany who have been honored with a special permanent exhibit in the film museum in Berlin. In his 50 years as an actor, he has appeared in over 100 films, including some of Germany's most commercially and critically successful movies and television shows. He has won numerous **film awards**, including the Bambi in 1962, 1984, and 1987. In addition to the popular Winnetou films that established him as an action hero, George has a deserved reputation as a comedian. His portrayal of a newsman for *Stern* magazine, a cross between a serious news journal and the boulevard press, in *Schtonk* (*Schtonk*, **Helmut Dietl**, 1992), captured the news media's willingness to sacrifice accuracy in order to scoop one's rivals. The film is based on an actual event, the publication of diaries falsely attributed to Adolf Hitler. George plays newsman Hermann Willié with broad humor and bravura. His comic turn in *Rossini* (*Rossini*, 1997) satirizes a director desperately trying to get the rights to a supposedly unfilmable novel.

Comedic roles are, however, an exception to most of George's work. German viewers are more likely to recognize him as Horst Schimanski, one of the most successful and identifiable detectives on German television. Similar to the degree with which Telly Savalas became associated with his role as Kojak or Peter Falk with his role as Columbo in the detective series named after their characters, George assured his place in film history portraying a tough as nails cop in Germany's longest running crime show *Tatort* (*Scene of the Crime*, 1970–). The character was later spun off into its own series, *Schimanski*. Playing against his comic personas of arrogant fool or courageous cop, George appeared in *Der Totmacher* (*Deathmaker*, Romuald Karmakar, 1995) as Fritz Haarmann, a serial killer in 1920s Germany who killed 20 boys, at times eating their flesh. George won an Award in Gold as Best Actor of 1995 for his performance.

GEORGE, HEINRICH (1893–1946). Heinrich George is best remembered for his support of National Socialism. As one of the Third Reich's most popular stars, he appeared in several of their more egregiously propagandist efforts, including *Hitlerjunge Quex* (*Hitler Youth Quex*, Hans Steinhoff, 1933), *Jud Süß* (*Jew Süss*, **Veit Harlan**, 1940), *Die Degenhardts* (*The Degenhardts*, Werner Klingler, 1944), and *Kolberg* (*Kolberg*, Harlan, 1945). Captured by the Soviets after the war, George died in the concentration camp in Sachsenhausen.

Hitlerjunge Quex, the first of his National Socialist films, portrayed George's character, the young hero Heini Völker's father, as undergoing a conversion to the Nazi cause. The elder Völker had been a staunch communist who believed in the international solidarity of all workers. In a scene that is crucial to the film's reception as a vehicle to raise national consciousness and increase allegiance to the National Socialist cause, George's character retreats from his son's life, acceding his parental responsibility to the leader of the Hitler Youth. The elder Völker's onscreen embrace of Nazism reflected the actor's own acceptance of the new regime. During the Weimar years, George's politics had tended to favor leftist positions, at least as suggested by the roles he had. He had played the foreman in **Metropolis** (*Metropolis*, **Fritz Lang**, 1927), who only reluctantly accepts the hand of his boss after the city has been almost destroyed. In other films, George played criminals, down-on-their-luck proletarians, and other members of the lower class. His role as Franz Biberkopf in *Berlin Alexanderplatz* (*Berlin Alexanderplatz*, **Phil Jutzi**, 1931), based on Alfred Döblin's novel of that title, showcased George's ability to play inarticulate and down-on-their-luck individuals. In *Menschen hinter Gittern* (*Men Behind Bars*, Pál Fejös, 1931), the German-language version of MGM's *The Big House* (George W. Hill, 1930), he played a machine gun killer; but George also played articulate, compassionate characters, such as the writer Emile Zola in *Dreyfus* (*Dreyfus*, **Richard Oswald**, 1930), portrayed as a passionate humanist fighting anti-Semitism through his writing and speeches.

With the noted exception of the father in *Hitlerjunge Quex*, George played the passionate speaker more than the inarticulate worker. In his most notorious role, as Karl Alexander, Duke of Württemberg, in *Jud Süß*, he played an autocratic ruler, willing to trade the well-being of his subjects to Jud Süß Oppenheimer in return for funds to support a ballet and therby keep his mistress happy. In *Die Degenhardts* he represents a hardworking German bureaucrat, who even after being forced into retirement recognizes the importance of keeping the family morale up as the war continues to worsen. George's most emotive role was as Nettlebeck, mayor of the town under siege by Napoleon in *Kolberg*. In the final scene of the movie, he makes an impassioned speech to his daughter, saying that their sacrifice has not been too much to ask of them, that suffering is necessary to make a people great. The film stands as the ultimate ***Durchhaltungsfilm*** suggesting to viewers that fighting even to death serves a noble cause.

GERMAN FILMS SERVICE + MARKETING GMBH. Begun in 1954 as a promotional unit of the German film industry, German Films Service + Marketing GmbH, until 2004 known as the Export Union des Deutschen Films, organizes German film festivals outside Germany, publishes informational material, and promotes German films worldwide. It publishes *German Films* (before 2004 published under the title *Kino*), a quarterly report on recent movie releases as well as short essays and portraits on topics and people important to the German film industry. The quarterlies are combined into an annual once a year, which in addition to the information on recent films includes a list of German films since 1946 and the person(s) holding foreign rights to the film. The German Films Service also has a Web site, www.german-films.de, which among other features provides attendance statistics on movies in German theaters, a list of the 100 most significant German films, news releases, and festival information.

GERRON, KURT (1897–1944). Kurt Gerron was a popular supporting actor during the 1920s. Because of his portly stature he most often portrayed comedic or shady figures. His most memorable role was as Kiepert, the magician in Josef von Sternberg's ***Der blaue Engel*** (*The Blue Angel*, 1930). Feeling himself belittled by Professor

Rath, the film's main character, Kiepert manipulates the man's downfall. Gerron switched to directing films in the late 1920s and filmed cabaret programs. He also directed comic **Heinz Rühmann** in *Meine Frau, Die Hochstaplerin* (*My Wife, the Con Artist*, 1931), in one of that actor's early successes.

In 1944 the Nazis forced Gerron, whom they had taken prisoner and incarcerated at Theresienstadt, to direct a film about life at the camp, *Der Führer schenkt den Juden eine Stadt* (*Hitler Gives a City to the Jews*, 1944). Theresienstadt served the National Socialists as a model camp to deceive the Red Cross and other humanitarian visitors into believing that the Jews were being treated humanely. Gerron's film, which was never shown in its completed form, portrayed life as idyllic, with soccer games, children's pageants, decent food, and meaningful work. After completion of the pseudo-documentary, Gerron and actors in the film were sent to Auschwitz and murdered in the gas chambers. The making of the film is the subject of the fictional *Czech Transport z raje* (*Transport from Paradise*, Zbynek Brynych, 1962) and the documentary of Gerron's career, *Prisoner of Paradise* (Malcolm Clarke and Stuart Sender, 2002). *See also* HOLOCAUST IN FEATURE FILMS.

GEYER, KARL A. (1880–1964). Karl A. Geyer was a pioneer in transforming filmmaking from an individual undertaking to an industrial enterprise. In 1911, he founded the Kino-Kopier-Gesellschaft, a company that specialized in duplicating film. Prior to this time, films had to be copied individually in a laborious hand-copying procedure. Geyer's company mechanized the process. In the early 1920s, working with several sound technicians, the company worked on sound film and perfected an optical sound process still used today. Kino-Kopier-Gesellschaft became Geyer-Werke AG in 1926 and operated until the end of World War II. After a few years on hiatus, the company again began postproduction work on film. Today, the company founded by Geyer is part of Germany's largest postproduction conglomerate, CinePostproduction GmbH. & Co. KG.

GLATZEDER, WINFRIED (1945–). Winfried Glatzeder has been an established actor in Germany since the mid-1960s. He began his career in East Germany, moved with his family in the early 1980s to

West Germany, and since unification of the two German states has acted in the repertoire company of the Theater am Kurfürstendamm in Berlin. Glatzeder's dark hair, tall thin physique, and rugged face made him a theater and film idol. His characters can be dangerous or edgy, but also sentimental. His most visible role was as Paul in *Die Legende von Paul und Paula* (*The Legend of Paul and Paula*, **Heiner Carow**, 1973), one of East Germany's most commercially successful films. Playing an ambitious bureaucrat who falls in love with a free-spirited woman, Paul at first chooses his career over love. Eventually he discovers the importance of Paula for his life and chops down her door with an axe. A reprisal of the scene 26 years later in *Sonnenallee* (*Sonnenallee*, Leander Haußmann, 1999), in which Glatzeder's character comes out of his apartment to lend an axe to another character, suggests how popular the film and Glatzeder were.

Glatzeder's other memorable theatrical films include *Vergeßt Mozart* (*Forget Mozart*, Miloslav Luther, 1985), a mystery about Mozart's death that was shot on the same set as *Amadeus* (Milos Forman, 1984), the big-budget Hollywood film on the life of the composer. Glatzeder played Salieri, the composer who was more popular than Mozart but nonetheless stood in his shadow. Glatzeder had a supporting role in *Die Boxerin* (*The Girl Boxer*, Catharina Deus, 2005), which many critics compared unfavorably to *Million Dollar Baby* (Clint Eastwood, 2004). In the 1980s, 1990s, and 2000s, Glatzeder has been active on German television, appearing in many of Germany's favorite crime series, including as inspector Ernst Roiter in 13 episodes of *Tatort* (*Scene of the Crime* 1970–), Germany's longest-running cop show. *See also* EAST GERMAN FILM.

GLAWOGGER, MICHAEL (1959–). Michael Glawogger is one of Austria's leading documentary filmmakers. His style is characterized by regard for high aesthetic values: meaningful editing, striking visuals, and disturbing themes. Glawogger focuses on the exploited, the underprivileged, and those who refuse to think critically in societies throughout the world. Two of his documentaries, *Megacities* (*Megacities*, 1998) and *Workingman's Death* (*Workingman's Death*, 2005), travel the globe to reveal the misery of the underprivileged. *Megacities* looks at a shirt maker in Mumbai, a grifter in New York City, a stripper in Mexico, and petty juvenile thieves in Moscow, to create a feeling of hopelessness among those who missed out on the riches of the global economy. In *Workingman's Death*, he films laborers who engage in dangerous underpaid jobs out of desperation to survive economically. Among his subjects are coal miners in the Ukraine, workers in a sulfur extraction pit in Indonesia, welders dismantling ships in Pakistan, and butchers in an abattoir in Nigeria.

In both these films, the stories are told separately but united through editing. For example, in *Workingman's Death* Glawogger matches visuals of the dangerous extraction of coal from mines in the Ukraine with the digging out of the sulfur from a mountainside quarry in Indonesia; the blood sacrifice of a sheep in the Indonesian segment with scenes in the Nigerian slaughterhouse; the torches from shipyard scenes in Pakistan with the torches in a Chinese factory. Evident in the director's choice of thematic materials is a desire to expose society's exploitation of workers; at the same time his imagery and the lyrical editing reveal his humanist understanding of the dignity of work.

Other Glawogger documentaries include *Frankreich, wir kommen* (*France, Here We Come!* 1999), a look at the world cup soccer championship in France from the perspective of Austrian fans, and *Zur Lage – Österreich in sechs Kapiteln* (*State of the Union: Austria in Six Chapters*, 2002), an omnibus film in which four directors, one of them Glawogger, interview Austrians about their lives and their opinion of Austria's growing multiculturalism.

Glawogger's feature-length narrative films reveal a similar preoccupation with people living on the fringes of society, but not always with the same humanistic eye. In *Nacktschnecken* (*Slugs*, 2004), the director lampoons sex comedies through three college students looking to score big with a porno film. At times sexually explicit, the movie chronicles the difficulties the three buddies have performing sexually in front of a camera. *Slumming* (*Slumming*, 2006) tells a story of two yuppie friends who like visiting lower-class venues and playing jokes on the unfortunate people they find there. One of their favorite tricks is to film up women's skirts and then share the videos. Another prank sees them transporting a drunken struggling poet to Czechoslovakia and stranding him there to find his own way back. Critics have been divided on whether the nastiness of the lead characters leads to laughter or disgust. *See also* AUSTRIAN CINEMA.

GOTTSCHALK, THOMAS (1950–). Thomas Gottschalk is one of Germany's most popular television entertainers. As host of the variety show *Wetten, dass . . . !* he is known for his humor and prominent facial features. His large nose gave rise to two comedies in the 1980s, *Die Supernasen* (*Supernoses*, Dieter Pröttel, 1983) and *Zwei Nasen tanken Super* (*Supernoses II*, Pröttel, 1984). Although generally panned by the critics, the films' slapstick comedy was very successful with the German public. Gottschalk has appeared in American films, including *Sister Act II: Back in the Habit* (Bill Duke, 1993), as Father Wolfgang. He played the lead in **Helmut Dietl**'s *Late Show* (*Late Show*, 1999), the third in Dietl's films satirizing excesses in the media.

GRIEM, HELMUT (1932–2004). After winning a Bambi (*see* **film awards**) as Most Promising Young Artist in 1960 for his role as a young lieutenant in *Fabrik der Offiziere* (*Officer Factory*, **Frank Wisbar**), Helmut Griem's career seemed assured. At the time, though, German film was in a crisis caused in part by the low quality of films being produced and in part by competition from television. Griem had to wait until the end of the decade to get the recognition he seemed destined for. In 1969, Luchino Visconti cast Griem in the role of Aschenbach, an officer in the Schutzstaffel or SS, in *La caduta degli dei* (*The Damned*), a film about the purging of the Nazis' private army, also known as the Sturmabteilung or SA, in a mass murder that became known as "the night of the long knives." In 1972, Bob Fosse cast him in *Cabaret* as Baron Maximilian von Heune, a bisexual, wealthy industrialist who seduces the major characters, Sally Bowles (Liza Minnelli) and Brian Roberts (Michael York). Griem's characterization of the Baron in *Cabaret* and SS-Officer Aschenbach in *La caduta degli dei* capitalize on his almost stereotypical Germanic features—blond hair, blue eyes, good looks, and strong will—which allow him to dominate others.

Griem also acted in a number of films of the **New German Cinema**, including *Die Moral der Ruth Halbfass* (*The Moral of Ruth Halbfass*, **Volker Schlöndorff**, 1972), *Ansicht eines Clowns* (*Face of a Clown*, Vojtěch Jasný, 1976), *Kaltgestellt* (*Put on Ice*, Bernhard Sinkel, 1979), and *Berlin Alexanderplatz* (*Berlin Alexanderplatz*, **Rainer Werner Fassbinder**, 1980), a television miniseries that also was released as a feature movie. After 1990 and until his death, Griem acted mainly in television films and miniseries.

GRÜNDGENS, GUSTAF (1899–1963). Although Gustaf Gründgens is best known for his signature role as Mephisto in Goethe's *Faust*, his theater and film career reflects a diverse repertoire of roles. He was active in German theater and film for close to five decades. In the 1920s, he was typecast as a character of dubious morals, playing seducer, cynic, and con artist among other roles. His best-known role from the 1930s is that of the head of the criminal ring in the thriller *M* (*M*, **Fritz Lang**, 1931).

During the Third Reich, Gründgens acted in a number of films, including *Der Tanz auf dem Vulkan* (*Dance on the Volcano*, Hans Steinhoff, 1938), considered by some film historians to be a disguised criticism of totalitarian government, and *Ohm Krüger* (*Ohm Krüger*, Hans Steinhoff, 1941), considered by most film historians to be one of the more overtly propagandistic of Nazi films. In *Der Tanz auf dem Vulkan*, Gründgens sings the film's primary song, "Die Nacht ist nicht allein zum Schlafen da" ("The Night Isn't Just for Sleeping"), implying that not only is it also there for love-making but for revolution as well. *Ohm Krüger* tells of the Boer War (1899–1902) from the Boers' perspective, depicting the British as cruel and cold-blooded killers. In what must be described as unintentional irony, the film depicts German civilians being herded into prison camps secured by barbed wire and also shows them being ruthlessly gunned down as they descend a slope, similar to the Odessa Steps scene in *The Battleship* Potemkin (Sergei M. Eisenstein, 1925), one of Joseph Goebbels's favorite films.

Gründgens directorial output includes mostly films of entertainment, such as *Der Schritt vom Wege* (*Step from the Path*, 1939), an adaptation of German novelist Theodor Fontane's *Effi Briest*, written in 1895 at the height of Germany's Second Empire under Kaiser Wilhelm II. In 1940, however, he filmed *Zwei Welten* (*Two Worlds*), a film about youthful volunteers helping with a harvest, a not very well disguised call to Germany's youth to support the war effort.

Gründgen's successful rise under the Nazis—by 1934 he was a director in the Prussian State Theater and in 1935 was named managing director of the Prussian State Theater—is the subject of Klaus Mann's novel *Mephisto* (1936). Although Mann, Gründgen's former brother-in-law, denied any relationship between his protagonist Hendrik Höfgen and Gründgens, the novel is clearly a roman á clef. It presents its protagonist as the prototype of a career opportunist and chronicles his collaboration with the Nazis to advance his career, events that are remarkably similar to Gründgens. No German publisher dared a German edition of the novel before 1965, and that edition was banned upon request by Gründgens's heirs. In 1981, it was made into an internationally successful film, *Mephisto*, by **István Szabó**.

– H –

HANDKE, PETER (1942–). Peter Handke is perhaps more famous for his dramas and essays than his screenplays, but those he has written reveal poetic language whose lyric quality is without equal in postwar German film. Handke's public recognition came in 1966 when, in an open forum, he criticized writers in the literary circle Gruppe 47, whose membership comprised the best-known and most-respected writers in the German language. Handke's plays are infused with profundities about the nature of language in creating identity. His best-known screenplay was for **Wim Wenders**'s *Der Himmel über Berlin* (*Wings of Desire*, 1987), a film about an angel who becomes mortal in order to experience human sensations. The opening sequence in the biblical cadence of 1 Corinthians, Chapter 10, reminds viewers of what it is like to be a child. Other films directed by Wenders for which Handke wrote the screenplays are *Die Angst des Tormanns beim elf Meter* (*The Goalie's Anxiety at the Penalty Kick*, 1972), based on Hanke's novel of the same title, and *Falsche Bewegung* (*False Movement*, aka *The Wrong Movement*, 1975), based on Johann Wolfgang von Goethe's late 18th-century novel. Handke also wrote and directed the **New German Cinema** film *Die linkshändige Frau* (*The Left-Handed Woman*, 1978), based on his novel, in which a woman rejects the cultural and linguistic constraints society places on her.

HANEKE, MICHAEL (1942–). Arguably Austria's greatest director of the 1990s and 2000s, Michael Haneke is also the country's most controversial and enigmatic. Born in Germany but raised and schooled in Vienna, Haneke began his career directing films for West German and then Austrian television. His first feature film, *Der siebente Kontinent* (*The Seventh Continent*, 1989), suggests that life has lost meaning for the professional middle class and provides a cold analysis of the consequences. *Der siebente Kontinent* introduces the themes—boredom, coldness, lack of communication, meaningless violence—and style—long takes, static camera work, abrupt edits, detached acting, shocking visuals, withholding of information—of Haneke's subsequent films. At one point, the family takes the car to a drive-through car wash. Filmed from inside the car, viewers sit through what seems an interminable stream of water hitting the windows, brushes cleaning away dirt, and no dialogue. The young daughter in the family, in a desperate attempt to elicit some reaction from her parents, pretends to be blind. The continent of the title represents escape as promised in billboard ads exhorting people to come to Australia. It is also a play on English language speakers' confusion of Australia and Austria, offering one of the few release valves from the tension of the movie's inevitable violent end.

Der siebente Kontinent studies the malaise afflicting the film's family; it offers no explanation for their depression or their horrific response to it. In contrast, Haneke's next film, *Benny's Video* (*Benny's Video*, 1992), places responsibility for the brutalization of society on the preponderance of violence in television and other media. The absence of parental guidance also receives some blame. *Benny's Video* centers on a teenage boy whose room serves as a metaphor for the intrusion of media into our lives. Benny delights in watching images of violence. He also delights in watching himself watch images of violence, capturing his reactions to what he views by means of a camera and monitor. After he kills a girlfriend, whom he has invited to watch a video of him slaughtering a pig, his parents find a tape of the killing and attempt to suppress it. *Funny Games* (*Funny Games*, 1997) intensifies the brutalization of one individual by another. A family is held captive in their vacation home by two psychotic killers who force them to play sadistic games. Much of the action occurs in the dark or off-camera, forcing viewers to imagine the horrors that are taking place.

Michael Haneke's critical success with his early films in Germany has led to European productions in French, in which he continues his obsession with analyzing violence in today's world. In *Code inconnu: Récit incomplet de divers voyages* (*Code Unknown*, 2000), Haneke's elliptical style forces viewers to fill in missing information when he abruptly edits from one sequence to the next. The story follows several characters whose paths cross in situations that escalate from trivial, thoughtless acts to individual suffering. At one point, Haneke places a film within his film (the main character is an actress), in which viewers see a woman being lured to an apartment and then locked up and left to starve. *La Pianiste* (*The Piano Player*, aka *The Piano Teacher*, 2001) follows an affair between a perfectionist piano teacher and a university student. The student is at first repulsed by the sadomasochistic games the piano teacher wants to play, but his curiosity moves him to participate nonetheless. *Le temps du Loup* (*The Time of the Wolf*, 2003) takes place in the near future after an unspecified disaster has reduced the population to scavenging for food. Cinematographer Jürgen Jürges, who worked with Haneke on *Funny Games* and *Code inconnu*, again films entire sequences in the dark, forcing viewers to imagine what transpires on the screen. *Caché* (*Hidden*, 2005), Haneke's most critically and commercially successful film, opens with an extended take of the outside of an apartment house. While credits are typed across the scene, a stationary camera focuses on a row of balconies of an apartment house. Only later does the film reveal the apartment is being secretly videotaped and the tapes delivered to its inhabitants in a plain envelope.

Code inconnu, *Le temps du loup*, and *Caché* offer a departure of sorts from Haneke's Austrian films, in that he seems to be asking why people in a rich culture are violent; why they do not communicate with each other; whether there is hope. *Code inconnu*, for example, suggests people would help each other but do not know how. *Le temps du loup* suggests that the world is waiting for a sacrificial offering and then pulls back before a child offers himself for the good of the whole. *Caché* traces problems back to historical animosities, suggesting that the Algerian war is responsible for the tragedy in the film. All of Haneke's films, though, whether made in Austria or France, are guaranteed to shock, turn stomachs, and sometimes alienate viewers from watching. *See also* AUSTRIAN CINEMA.

HANSEN, JOACHIM (1930–2007). A matinee idol of the 1950s and 1960s in West Germany, Joachim Hansen appeared in **war films**, crime dramas, filmed Shakespeare productions, and films of nostalgia (*see Heimatfilm*). His breakthrough came in *Der Stern von Afrika* (*The Star of Africa*, Alfred Weidenmann, 1957), as a pilot in the Nazi Air Force during World War II who becomes a hero because of his courageous but daredevil flying in the campaign in North Africa. During a leave he falls in love with a student and slowly begins to doubt the sense of the war and his actions. In *Hunde, wollt ihr ewig leben?* (*Dogs, Do You Want to Live Forever?* **Frank Wisbar**, 1959), Hansen plays Lieutenant Wisse, an idealistic officer who begins to doubt the course of the war and the righteousness of the cause, but continues to fight to protect his men. In a scene that highlights his disillusionment with Nazism but his allegiance to the military, he shoots and kills a superior officer who is trying to escape the Battle of Stalingrad. Hansen's other major roles include that of the young son in *Und ewig singen die Wälder* (*Beyond Sing the Woods*, Paul May, 1959), who cannot avert tragedy in a family feud. He reprised the role in the film's sequel, *Das Erbe von Björndal* (*The Legacy of Björndal*, Gustav Ucicky, 1960), in which young Dag and his new wife have to face obstacles while operating their farm. Both films were based on Norwegian Trygve Gulbranssen's popular novels about life on the land at the beginning of the 20th century, a favorite period for the *Heimat* genre. Hansen also played an officer in *Lebensborn* (*Ordered to Love*, Werner Klingler, 1961), who befriends a young woman sent to the Nazi camp where young girls were paired with officers to propagate the Nazi Aryan ideal.

HARFOUCH, CORINNA (1954–). Corinna Harfouch began her career in an episode of *Polizeiruf 110* (*Precinct 110*, 1971–), the successful East German crime series that eventually merged with West Germany's *Tatort* (*Scene of the Crime*, 1970–) after the Berlin Wall fell. Subsequently she starred in a number of films for **DEFA**, never achieving the recognition that others of her fellow actors received. She continued to act on West German television and in a number of nonmajor productions until she played Magda Goebbels in **Oliver Hirschbiegel**'s *Der Untergang* (*The Downfall*, 2004), about Adolf Hitler's last days in his Berlin bunker. Harfouch's portrayal of a woman so steadfast in her belief in Hitler's new order that she murdered her children rather than have them live in a world without National Socialism was chilling. Other roles in some of Germany's more successful films have been as the mother of one of the convicts in *Knockin' on Heaven's Door* (*Knockin' on Heaven's Door*, Thomas Jahn, 1997), and as the title character in the made-for-television film *Der Fall Vera Brühne* (*The Trial of Vera Brühne*, **Hark Bohm**, 2001). The film was based on one of Germany's most notorious murder cases, which ended in a life sentence for Brühne, accused of killing her lover and his housekeeper. *See also* EAST GERMAN FILM; *VERGANGENHEITSBEWÄLTIGUNGSFILM*.

HARLAN, VEIT (1899–1964). Veit Harlan gained his place in German film history through his adroit use of emotional effects to increase the Nazi propaganda value of his films. While many actors, directors, and screen writers during the Third Reich could be accused of opportunism or cowardice in their acquiescence to the demands of Joseph Goebbels, Harlan seemed committed to trumpeting the Nazi cause in his films. In his film *Der Herrscher* (*The Ruler*, 1937), for example, based on the Gerhart Hauptmann play *Vor Sonnenuntergang* (*Before Sunset*, 1932), Harlan changed a tragic love story of an old man and a young girl into a hymn to Nazi ideology. In other films as well, he adapted his material to National Socialist ideology. Thus he set Theodor Storm's novella *Immensee* (*Bees' Lake*, 1943) in contemporary times and emphasized the element of self-denial beyond the level it reaches in Storm's work. If the work already had ideological tendencies, he increased the propaganda effect through melodramatic dialogue and soliloquy. After the war, when Harlan defended himself against charges of war crimes, he cited coercion as the motivation for making the notoriously anti-Semitic film *Jud Süß* (*Jew Süss*, 1940). Other witnesses, however, testified that he had made the film more anti-Semitic than required to satisfy the propaganda ministry.

Although he made a number of films under the Nazis, and directed several more after being acquitted of war crimes after the war, Harlan is remembered primarily for two works: *Jew Süß* and *Kolberg* (*Kolberg*, 1943–1944). The first was based on the historical figure Joseph Süß-Oppenheimer, who helped finance the Duke of Würettemberg's government. The real Süß was a problematic figure whose hubris led to a tragic end. His story had already been the subject of Lion Feuchtwanger's Novel *Jud Süß* (1925) and the English film *Jew Süss* (aka *Power*, Lothar Mendes, 1934), both showing Süss as a tragic rather than an evil figure. Harlan, in contrast, distorts the historical facts. His Süß becomes the devil incarnate, interested in violating German women and bringing down the government. The film was reportedly shown to officers of the Schutzstaffel (SS) to increase their hatred of Jews. After the war, it was supposedly used by Arab militants as propaganda against Israel. Harlan had to stand trial because of the anti-Semitism in the film, but since there was no evidence that he had willingly included the more scurrilous sentiments of the film, he was acquitted.

Harlan's other major film, *Kolberg*, was a pet project of Goebbels, who in 1943 commissioned a film about a last-stand battle against Napoleon in 1813 at the town of Kolberg. The film cost eight million marks, a considerable sum at the time, and according to film historians used more extras than the historical battle had participants. Goebbels wanted a film that would encourage Germans not to lose hope in final victory and to fight to the bitter end. Accordingly, Harlan uses his historical figures as surrogates for Goebbels and Adolf Hitler, distorting history in order to end the film on an optimistic note, making one more plea that Germans not give up. Maria's father tells her as they stand overlooking their destroyed village: "Death is overcome . . . . More importantly, we are reborn in pain. If someone endures great pain, he is a great person. You are a great person, Maria. You remained and did your duty." The father and Maria were played by **Heinrich George** and **Kristina Söderbaum**, two of Nazi Germany's biggest stars. *See also* CATALOGUE OF FORBIDDEN FEATURE AND SHORT FILM PRODUCTIONS; *DURCHHALTUNGSFILM*.

HARTL, KARL (1899–1978). Karl Hartl was an Austrian director and producer whose major works included action and science fiction films and chamber dramas. *F.P.1 antwortet nicht (F.P.1 Doesn't Answer*, 1932) and *Gold (Gold*, 1934) adapted two sci-fi novels of Hans Dominik, an author who wrote futuristic works in the vein of Jules Verne and H. G. Wells. As was common for major productions of the day, both films appeared in German, French, and English. All were directed by Hartl, which was not as common at that time, as dual versions often had a different director. The three versions of *F.P.1 antwortet nicht* starred three of the major actors of the time as the pilot hero Ellisen—**Hans Albers** in the German-language version, Charles Boyer in the French version (*I.F.1 ne répond plus*), and **Conrad Veidt** in the English film (*F.P.1*). Hartl became head of the Viennese production company Wien-Film after the Nazis, having annexed Austria in 1938, shortly thereafter collapsed the country's independent companies into one. Reportedly Hartl used his considerable influence to curtail the degree of propaganda projects. After the war, Hartl's last major film was *Der Engel mit der Posaune* (*The Angel with the Trumpet*, 1948), which followed an Austrian family of musicians from the first part of the 20th century and the Austro-Hungarian Empire through the end of World War II. Hartl's style is characterized by a preference for large spaces, which give room for broad camera movement, crane shots, and monumental sets. Yet he was also proficient in directing quiet chamber dramas. *See also* AUSTRIAN CINEMA.

HARVEY, LILIAN (1906–1968). London-born Lilian Harvey was one of Germany's leading film stars in the 1920s and 1930s. In silent films, she played liberated women in the flapper image of postwar Germany. As sound arrived she gravitated to operetta-like musicals. Harvey teamed with **Willy Fritsch** in two silent and 10 sound films between 1926 and 1939, including *Die Drei von der Tankstelle* (*Three from the Gas Station*, Wilhelm Thiele, 1930) and *Der Kongreß tanzt* (*Congress Dances*, Erik Charell, 1931), two of the most popular films of the era. The latter, shot simultaneously in German, French, and English, as was the custom early in the sound era for major films, starred Harvey, who was fluent in the three languages in all versions. Fritsch appeared only in the German-language film. Henri Garat played opposite Harvey in the English and French films.

Harvey and Fritsch first acted together in *Die keusche Susanne* (*The Innocent Susanne*, Richard Eichberg, 1926), and they soon became Germany's favorite screen couple, being dubbed the country's "dream couple" by the film press. When sound arrived and they made the first of their musicals together, their popularity increased, helped along by the recordings they made of songs from their movies. Harvey's popularity occasioned an invitation from Hollywood, but her four films in America, among them *I Am Suzanne* (Rowland V. Lee, 1933) and *My Lips Betray* (John G. Blystone, 1933), failed to appeal to audiences and critics. She therefore returned to Germany, where she was able to resume her successful collaboration with Fritsch. In 1936, the pair made *Glückskinder* (*Lucky Kids*, Paul Martin), an attempt to remake and capture the popularity of *It Happened One Night* (Frank Capra, 1934) and establish Fritsch and Harvey as Germany's Clark Gable and Claudette Colbert, the stars of the American film.

Harvey worked with Fritsch for the last time in *Frau am Steuer* (*Woman at the Wheel*, Paul Martin, 1939), after which she left Germany. She spent the years of World War II in exile in America, touring with Noel Coward's *Blithe Spirit* and other plays. Her attempts to rekindle her career after the war met with little success.

HAUFF, REINHARD (1939–). Reinhard Hauff interrupted his directorial career in 1993 to become president of the Deutsche Film- und Fernsehakademie (German Film and Television Academy) in Berlin. By then he had gained a reputation as one of the more conventionally realistic filmmakers of **New German Cinema**. Although he has never gained the international stature of other conventionally realistic directors such as **Volker Schlöndorff** or **Wolfgang Petersen**, Hauff has always been popular in Germany, owing perhaps to the accessibility and timeliness of his films. For example, the film *Messer im Kopf* (*Knife in the Head*, 1978), the sole film to achieve wide international distribution, examines loss of memory against a background of terrorist activities, a concern for many Germans in the 1970s. *Messer im Kopf* tells the story of an ordinary man drawn into an existential situation not of his making. The fictional narrative of a man trying to reconstruct the events leading up to his being shot in the head by a policeman engages the audience's interest in the politics behind the situation. In addition, **Bruno Ganz**'s sensitive portrayal of the main character makes the man likable and vulnerable, allowing viewers to identify with him as victim, caught in the middle between authorities and terrorists.

Other films that received attention in Germany but not abroad are *Mathias Kneißl* (*Mathias Kneissl*, 1970), about a 19th-century German Robin Hood; *Die Verrohung des Franz Blum (The Brutalization of Franz Blum*, 1974), about a convict who becomes as brutal as the prisoners who brutalize him; *Paule Pauländer (Paule Pauländer*, 1976), about a tragic conflict between a father and son; and *Stammheim (Stammheim* 1982), about the imprisonment of the Baader-Meinhof radical activists. The film received a "Golden Bear" at the **Berlin Film Festival.** In 2005, Hauff received an honorary award from the Deutsche Filmakademie for his mentoring of young directors in his position as president of the Deutsche Film- und Fernsehenakademie in Berlin.

HEIMAT—EINE DEUTSCHE CHRONIK (HEIMAT: A CHRONI-CLE OF GERMANY, **1984).** **Edgar Reitz** conceived this miniseries as an answer to the American television miniseries *Holocaust* (Marvin J. Chomsky, 1978), which played on German television in 1979. The American series achieved high ratings and provoked a sociopolitical debate on German collective responsibility and memory for the genocidal policies of the Nazis. Reitz believed that Hollywood's aesthetic of suspense, attractive characters, and historical clichés would distort Germany's past, and the history of ordinary citizens. *Heimat* unfolds in 11 episodes and runs just over 15 hours, following three generations of the Wiegand and Simon families. It focuses primarily on the second generation, headed eventually by the matriarch Maria Wiegand Simon, who is 17 years old when the first episode begins.

Heimat engages viewers on both a formal and contextual level. On the one hand, the film is formally complex and self-reflexive. Reitz alternates between shooting in black and white and full color, using color for scenes he wants to emphasize. He inserts authentic-looking photographs of the characters to recap what has occurred in earlier episodes, a technique that helped give the Wiegand and Simon families the feel of a real family and that may explain why so many tourists came to the Hunsrück region of Germany looking for Schabbach, the fictional home of these fictional people. The film also provides a running history of technological development in the 20th century, including automobiles, airplanes, radio, television, photography, and cinema. On the other hand, the film plays like a soap opera, a chronicle of the lives and loves of the various members of the family, including birth and death, marriage and divorce, generosity of spirit and opportunistic selfishness. There are characters to like and characters to dislike, and the episodes always give a reason to come back the next week.

Heimat is not without its faults, which add to its importance as a historical document in its own right. The miniseries works through a very problematic history. Predating by two years the Historikerstreit, or public debate on National Socialism along revisionist lines, the series suggests that Nazism was not that terrible, or at least that it left most Germans untouched. Indeed, Nazism is represented in the village of Schabbach by the least likable of the characters and also by an outsider, a woman who marries into the family. Neither plays much of a role once the war is over. In fact, the woman disappears entirely, as does any recognition of what occurred. In this regard, *Heimat* is a forerunner of a trend that remembers the past through romantic eyes. Joseph Vilsmaier's *Herbstmilch (Autumn Milk,* 1989), Christian Wagner's and Thomas Mauch's *Wallers letzter Gang (Waller's Last Walk,* 1988), and **Hans W. Geissendörfer**'s *Gudrun (Gudrun,* 1992) all turn a personal nostalgic eye on the past.

The success of *Heimat* has led to three sequels: *Die zweite Heimat – Chronik einer Jugend (Heimat II: A Chronicle of a Generation,* 1992), *Heimat 3—Chronik einer Zeitwende (Heimat 3: A Chronicle of Beginnings and Endings,* 2004), and *Heimat-Fragmente: Die Frauen (Heimat-Fragments: The Women,* 2006). Although neither the second nor third installments in the series achieved the recognition afforded the first *Heimat,* both have been successful with critics and viewers. The fourth installment has been less successful with critics and public.

Heimat II continues the formal and contextual elements begun in the first installment. Cinematographers Gernot Roll, Gerard Vandenberg, and Christian Reitz, as in *Heimat,* alternate between black and white and color and also combine the two, with objects within the black and white screen highlighted through use of color. The screenplay follows the soap opera format of the original, again rising above the clichés of the genre through psychologically developed characterizations. Comprising 13 episodes and running 25 hours, even in its theatrical release, the film is not a continuing sequel to the original. Rather, it fills in gaps in the first film's story. In episode nine of *Heimat,* Hermann, Maria Simon's youngest son, leaves home in 1960 after a love affair, vowing never to fall in love again and never to return to Schabbach. *Heimat* then jumps to 1982. *Heimat II* follows Simon from 1960 to 1970 as he studies music in Munich, befriends other artists, becomes a composer, and forsakes his vow of no more love by marrying and then having several affairs. As in *Heimat*, personal stories play against a backdrop of history. Rather than the grand scope of the first series, which focuses on actual epochs such as the Third Reich, World War II, and the so-called economic miracle, *Heimat II* emphasizes the personal scope of history, including the students' movement, feminism, free love, and radicalism. Simon's life and that of his friends unfold within the defining liberal to radical ethos of the 1960s.

Heimat 3 continues Simon's story, but set against a broader historical background than the second film. Jumping to 1989, *Heimat 3* opens with Simon in Berlin, conducting the Berlin Philharmonic as the Berlin Wall falls, signaling the end of a divided Germany. Cinematographers Thomas Mauch and Christian Reitz capture the theatrical look of the first two films, once again using both black and white and color photography. The story again follows a soap opera format, even more so than the other films. Historical events are again moved to the forefront as in the first series and as the years 1989–2000 warrant. The story also returns to Schabbach, site of the first series. With Simon as the central figure, as Maria was in the first film, *Heimat 3* introduces characters that some critics have said border on cliché. Hermann employs Ossies (the belittling term West Germans used to describe their countrymen from the defunct East Germany) to build his house. Also introduced are an orphan from Bosnia, an unwed mother from Russia, and entrepreneurs taking advantage of the fall of the Berlin Wall. Whereas the mood of *Heimat* is nostalgic and that of *Heimat II* is hopeful, the mood of *Heimat 3* is apprehensive. The characters are optimistic in the beginning, Germany's victory in the 1990 World Cup soccer match offering the perfect metaphor for their euphoria. By the end of the decade though, as the millennium nears, optimism has turned to pessimism, a mood swing visually present in the total eclipse of the sun in 1999. The ending shot of Lulu, Hermann's daughter, staring out a window during a New Year's party suggests that the younger generation faces an uncertain future. It also prepares viewers for the sequel.

Heimat-Fragmente: Die Frauen departs from the other three series in the epic in that it does not narrate a linear story with the emotional and affective clichés of the others. Employing a framing device, shot by the director's son Christian Reitz, the film focuses on the women of the first three *Heimat* films. It narrates their stories through fragments, philosophical musings of the last of the Simon women, Lulu, who appeared at the end of *Heimat 3* staring out a window on New Year's Eve. *Heimat-Fragmente* uses outtakes from the other films as well as new material to give a more introspective examination of memory.

The first three installments in the *Heimat* saga contain 30 episodes and run 52 hours. They played on television but also had theatrical releases in Germany and abroad and are available on DVD. The fourth film adds 146 minutes. There has not been a more far-reaching, ambitious, or culturally successful miniseries on German television.

HEIMATFILM. Narrowly defined, *Heimatfilm* refers to a uniquely German genre that developed from a tradition of *Heimat* (homeland or home village) literature. Set in a village, a *Heimatfilm* has at the center of its narrative a loner who becomes a folk hero by helping the peasantry in their fight against the landowners. The story is often complicated by a love affair between the peasant hero and the daughter of the most powerful of the landowners. More broadly defined, the term refers to any film about village life that focuses on the strength of the peasants and the beauty of the landscape. Owing to the superficiality of many of the films, the term is usually pejorative. The heyday of the genre was in the 1950s. Two of the better-known films from that era are **Hans Deppe**'s *Schwarzwaldmädel* (*The Black Forest Girl*, 1950) and *Grün ist die Heide* (*The Heath Is Green*, 1951).

In the late 1960s and early 1970s, several **New German Cinema** directors parodied the idyllic settings, naive peasants, and happy endings of the *Heimatfilm*. The hero of **Peter Fleischmann**'s *Jagdszenen aus Niederbayern* (*Hunting Scenes from Lower Bavaria*, 1969) is an ex-convict suspected of molesting a young boy in the village and subsequently hunted down by an angry peasant mob. The villagers in **Volker Schlöndorff**'s *Der plötzliche Reichtum der armen Leute von Kombach* (*The Sudden Wealth of the Poor People of Kombach*, 1970) succeed in robbing a tax shipment after five botched attempts only to be arrested, tried, and hanged when they begin spending the money. **Edgar Reitz** paid homage to the genre in his television film series

Heimat – Eine deutsche Chronik (*Heimat: A Chronicle of Germany*, 1984), set in a small fictional village in the Hünsrück area of Germany. He revisits the town in *Die zweite Heimat—Chronik einer Jugend* (*Heimat II: A Chronicle of a Generation*, 1992), *Heimat 3— Chronik einer Zeitwende* (*Heimat 3: A Chronicle of Endings and Beginnings*, 2004), and *Heimat-Fragmente: Die Frauen* (*Heimat-Fragments: The Women*, 2006).

The late 1980s and early 1990s witnessed yet another revival of the *Heimatfilm*: Joseph Vilsmaier's *Herbstmilch* (*Autumn Milk*, 1989), about the normalcy of peasant life under the Nazis, and Franz X. Bogner's *Madame Bäurin* (*Madame Bäurin*, 1993), about love on a Bavarian farm during World War I. In both films, the farmers best the city dwellers, and everyone lives happily ever after. In *Schlafes Bruder* (*Brother of Sleep*, 1995), Vilsmaier reprises the negative vision of village life as seen in the films of New German Cinema.

HELM, BRIGITTE (1908–1996). Brigitte Helm played the part of vamp extraordinaire in some of the best-known silent films of the late 1920s and sound films of the early 1930s. Her dual role in **Fritz Lang**'s silent classic *Metropolis* (*Metropolis*, 1927) as the virtuous Maria and her doppelgänger, the evil robot Maria, created a persona that Helm exploited in most of her films. She was at once exotic and plain, erotic and innocent, sinful and virtuous. Helping children escape their flooding city, Helm portrays her character as a frantic mother, rushing one way and then another, willing to sacrifice for her brood. As the rampaging Maria she twists her mouth and screws up her face in a hideous laugh as she leads the children's parents to ruin. In *Alraune* (*A Daughter of Destiny*, 1928), Helm plays the title character, a woman created in a lab. Her facial expressions again help her embody a lascivious seductress whose fame goes beyond Germany. Helm played the role twice, in **Henrik Galeen**'s silent version of 1928 and then again in a sound version directed by **Richard Oswald** in 1930. Helm also worked with **Georg Wilhelm Pabst**, who had directed **Louise Brooks** in her erotic thrillers. In *Die Liebe der Jeanne Ney* (*The Loves of Jeanne Ney*, 1927), she plays against type and portrays a sensitive blind girl. In *Abwege* (*Desire*, aka *The Devious Path*, 1928), she plays a sexually frustrated married woman, an erotic temptress looking for excitement.

In sound films, Helm played Antinea in the German (*Die Herrin von Atlantis*, 1932), English (*The Mistress of Atlantis*, 1932), and French (*L'Atlantide*, 1932) versions of the story of Atlantis, all three directed by Pabst. She has few lines in the films and not much screen time, but when present she dominates the scene, as when lounging on a divan while receiving visitors. Helm withdrew from films in the mid-1930s.

HERLTH, ROBERT (1893–1962). Working with fellow art director Walter Röhrig, Robert Herlth created the distinctive look of some of the best-known films of the1920s and 1930s. Herlth and Röhrig created sets and costumes of ornate richness, period accuracy, and stylistic unity that contributed to German silent film being considered a golden age of movies. Some of the pair's most striking work appeared in **Fritz Lang**'s *Der müde Tod* (*Destiny*, 1921), in which a long, high wall dwarfs characters and creates an existential barrier between the living and the dead. Their lower class apartment complex, with tenements and inner courtyard, in **Friedrich Wilhelm Murnau**'s *Der letzte Mann* (*The Last Laugh*, 1924), emphasizes an unbridgeable divide behind the haves of the hotel world and the have-nots of the working class. In *Herr Tartüff* (*Tartuffe*, Murnau, 1925), they re-created the rococo world of 18th-century France and in *Faust* (*Faust*, Murnau, 1926), the superstitious feel of 16th-century Germany. In sound film, they constructed an elaborate town for *Der Kongreß tanzt* (*The Congress Dances*, Erik Charell, 1931), which allowed the director to do an extended sequence of the film's lead as she rides in an open coach from town square to villa, passing vegetable stalls, town hall, row houses, city gates, and peasant cottages. The scene creates a contrast of artificial and realistic settings that matches the story and music. In *Morgenrot* (*Dawn*, Vernon Sewell and Gustav Ucicky, 1933), Herlth and Röhrig reproduced the interior of a submarine for a tale of men trapped in a boat with too few diving apparatuses to rescue all the men. After World War II, Herlth designed sets mainly for musicals and romances. His art direction for *Die Buddenbrooks* (*The Buddenbrooks*, Alfred Weidenmann, 1959) re-created the patrician houses of late 19th-century northern Germany described in the Thomas Mann novel on which the film is based.

HERMANN, IRM (1942–). Irm Hermann belonged to the *antiteater*, **Rainer Werner Fassbinder**'s experimental theater ensemble that stripped productions to the minimum needed: an elevated platform, actors, and a script. Hermann stayed with Fassbinder's repertoire players when he began making films in the late 1960s. Before breaking with the director in 1975, she had appeared in more than 20 of his productions. Herman received mostly supporting roles in Fassbinder's films, usually playing an uptight, sexually repressed petit bourgeois. In her first major role for Fassbinder, a landlady and innkeeper in *Katzelmacher* (*Katzelmacher*, 1969), she perfected the persona of an angry, parsimonious, and emotionally cold woman who subjected others to her will. This was a role she varied only slightly throughout her work for Fassbinder. For his part, Fassbinder reportedly delighted in humiliating Hermann by refusing to star her in his films and offering her only negative roles. When she did receive a starring part, as the wife in *Händler der Vierjahreszeiten* (*The Merchant of Four Seasons*, 1972), she played an expanded version of the shrew she played in the other films.

After leaving Fassbinder in 1975, although she appeared in several of his films after that date, Hermann expanded her range, revealing herself as a versatile actor, at home in comedic, melodramatic, and serious dramatic parts. She portrays Else Gebel, a woman who shared a cell with Sophie Scholl before Scholl's execution for treason, in **Percy Adlon**'s *Fünf letzte Tage* (*Five Last Days*, 1982). Escaping from her cinematic persona, Hermann here plays a devout Christian truly troubled by Nazi policies but feeling powerless to change anything. Her conversations with Scholl reveal the religious convictions that drove women like Scholl to protest even at the cost of their lives.

Hermann has had supporting roles in the films of many of Germany's auteur and alternative directors, those once associated with **New German Cinema** and others who came later. In experimental filmmaker **Ulrike Ottinger**'s *Johanna d'Arc of Mongolia* (*Joan of Arc of Mongolia*, 1989), she again plays a prim woman, a schoolteacher, but without the shrewish quality of her earlier characterizations of a repressed woman. Hermann also had a supporting role in Ottinger's *Dorian Gray im Spiegel der Boulevardpresse* (*The Image of Dorian Gray in the Yellow Press*, 1984), a pastiche that mixes opera, German expressionism, and lesbianism in a satire of West Germany's media. She has appeared in the films of **Werner Herzog** (*Woyzeck* [*Woyzeck*], 1979), **Herbert Achternbusch** (*Hades* [*Hades*], 1995), **Hans W. Geissendörfer** (*Ediths Tagebuch* [*Edith's Diary*], 1983), and Christoph Schlingensief (*120 Tage von Bottrop* [*120 Days of Bottrop*], 1997). Hermann also appears regularly on German television in miniseries and made-for-television movies. For her roles in *Händler der Vierjahreszeiten* and *Fünf letzte Tage*, she won Germany's highest acting honor, the Award in Gold (*see* **film awards**) in 1972 and 1982, respectively.

HERZOG, WERNER (1942–). The films of Werner Herzog (born Werner H. Stiptik), together with those of **Rainer Werner Fassbinder**, **Wim Wenders**, and **Volker Schlöndorff**, gave international visibility in the 1970s to the group of filmmakers known as **New German Cinema** (NGC). While one can argue that New German Cinema ended with the death of Fassbinder as directors choose less politically charged themes and achieve the production values of mainstream cinema, thus making them commercially viable, Herzog's films continue to display his allegiance to a cinema of ideas. His films, like those of his contemporaries in NGC, have won many awards at film festivals, including Best Debut Film at the **Berlin Film Festival**, for *Lebenszeichen* (*Signs of Life*, 1968), and Best Director at the Cannes Film Festival, for *Fitzcarraldo* (*Fitzcarraldo*, 1982). In 2006, the Director's Guild of America gave him an award for Outstanding Directorial Achievement in Documentary for his film *Grizzly Man* (2005).

Herzog is a visionary and a dreamer who has said of his work: "We are surrounded by worn-out images, and we deserve new ones. . . . I am one of the ones who try to find those images." His films, whether narrative or documentary, full-length or short, are hauntingly beautiful, replete with images of primeval forests, desolate landscapes, misty seas, and fog-covered mountains. His human subjects, whether fictional or documentary, are as strange and forbidding as his landscapes, and just as endangered. In his early feature film *Lebenszeichen*, his protagonist goes mad in an isolated and lonely Greek town. In the documentary *Grizzly Man*, made almost 40 years later, grizzly bear expert Timothy Treadwell and his companion are devoured by a grizzly. Characters aren't always endangered, but they are always unusually exotic, at least in Western culture. *Wodaabe—Die Hirten der Sonne* (*Herdsmen of the Sun*, 1989) travels to sub-Sahran Africa to study the dating rituals of the Wodaabe tribe, which places extreme emphasis on the physical beauty of men.

Herzog's films are psychological studies of people in extremis, of outsiders and misfits driven to the physical and mental boundaries of human endurance. As mentioned, his first feature-length film, *Lebenszeichen*, portrays the breakdown of a German soldier who, recuperating on a Greek island, takes over a munitions depot and threatens to blow up the surrounding area. In *Auch Zwerge haben klein angefangen* (*Even Dwarves Started Small*, 1970), arguably the most bizarre of Herzog's films, a group of dwarves imprisoned on an island rebel against the authorities who oversee their normal-sized environment. In *Woyzeck* (*Woyzeck*, 1974), based on Georg Büchner's unfinished 1837 play of the same name, Woyzeck, taunted by voices and suspicious of the fidelity of his common-law wife Maria, stabs her to death, a scene that Herzog renders aesthetically beautiful by filming in slow motion, setting the movements to Baroque music, and keeping the worst of the violence just below the lens of the camera.

Psychological distortion, physical deformation, and emotional dysfunction form the aesthetic structure of Herzog films. His best-known film, *Aguirre, der Zorn Gottes* (*Aguirre, the Wrath of God*, 1972), relates the adventures of a band of conquistadors as they descend the Andes Mountains and raft down the Amazon River. The film is an homage to the developing madness found in Joseph Conrad's novel *Heart of Darkness*. As the film ends, Aguirre, the leader of the exploration party, stands on a raft that is floating in circles, holding his daughter's dead body, as he proclaims that with her he will found El Dorado. The tableau of madness is completed as the camera pulls away and we see how the raft is overrun with monkeys. *Stroszek* (*Stroszek*, 1977) depicts a man destroyed by debt who commits suicide on a ski lift. As the lift goes around, the film cuts to the man's truck, which he has left in gear with its steering wheel pulled to one side so that the vehicle circles in the street. Then the film cuts to a chicken in a carnival amusement that is forced to dance on a turntable in hopes of receiving a bit of corn.

Herzog prefers shooting on location to lend his films authenticity. *Aguirre*, for example, was shot in the Amazon jungle. The director reportedly had to threaten the lead actor, **Klaus Kinski**, at gunpoint to complete the picture, an incident confirmed in Herzog's later documentary about his relationship with the volatile Kinski, *Mein liebster Feind – Klaus Kinski* (*My Best Fiend*, 1999). The title refers to their tumultuous relationship during the making of five films and the often murderous roles that Kinski assumed, especially his role as Count Dracula in Herzog's *Nosferatu—Phantom der Nacht* (*Nosferatu the Vampire*, a remake of **Friedrich Wilhelm Murnau**'s *Nosferatu, eine Symphoie des Grauens* [*Nosferatu*, 1922]). Such harsh conditions of shooting were repeated for two other Herzog/Kinski projects, *Fitzcarraldo* (*Fitzcarraldo*, 1982) and *Cobra Verde* (*Slave Coast*, 1987).

Since the late 1980s, Herzog has focused more on documentaries or documentary-like biographies than fictional films. Among these are *Little Dieter Needs to Fly* (1997), which Herzog turned into the feature film *Rescue Dawn* (2006), starring Christian Bale; as well as *Rad der Zeit* (*Wheel of Time*, 2003), *The White Diamond* (*The White Diamond*, 2004), and *Grizzly Man*.

HIRSCHBIEGEL, OLIVER (1957–). Oliver Hirschbiegel began his career directing police dramas and mysteries for German and Austrian television. His work includes episodes for *Tatort* (*Scene of the Crime*, 1970–) and *Kommisar Rex* (*Inspector Rex*, 1994–2004), respectively Germany's and Austria's long-running crime shows. The feature film *Das Experiment* (*The Experiment*, 2001) was Hirschbiegel's first theatrical feature and received excellent reviews in Germany and abroad. The film offers a fictional account of an actual experiment conducted at Stanford University in 1971, in which a researcher divided a group of men into prisoners and prison guards and studied the dynamic of their relationship. The researcher stopped the experiment after guards and prisoners started to lose control of the situation. In the film, Hirschbiegel continues the experiment beyond where the researchers aborted the study for safety concerns. He projects how the situation might have played itself out if no one had intervened.

Hirschbiegel's greatest success, and one of the most successful German films in the 2000s, was *Der Untergang* (*The Downfall*, 2004), a film about the last 10 days of Adolf Hitler's life in his bunker in Berlin. Based on two books, Joachim Fest's *Der Untergang: Hitler und das Ende des Dritten Reiches* (*Inside Hitler's Bunker: The Last Days of the Third Reich*, 2002) and the memoirs of Hitler's secretary, *Bis zur letzten Stunde: Hitler's Sekretärin erzählt ihr Leben* (*Until the Final Hour: Hitler's Last Secretary*, 2002), *Der Untergang* created a sensation among Germany's intellectuals. **Bruno Ganz**'s portrayal of Hitler as an ordinary man, suffering from Parkinson's disease and given to outbursts of emotions but also moments of introspection, humanized the dictator more than any previous film. Some critics accused the film of trivializing or belittling the suffering and horror perpetrated by Hitler and the Nazis on the Jews and other groups. On the one hand the film captures honestly the desperation that governed the actions of Hitler, his ministers, and his generals in the last few days. On the other hand, the absence of sufficient historical context to interpret the events during this period pulls one into the film rather than distancing one from what is occurring. Not until Magda Goebbels kills her children, holding the jaw of one shut so that the poison will go down, is one sufficiently distanced from the story to remember the tragedy this period in history caused.

As if in answer to critics of *Der Untergang*, Hirschbiegel next directed a one-man movie about a Jew growing up in postwar Germany. *Ein ganz gewöhnlicher Jude* (*A Very Ordinary Jew*, 2005) films a Jewish man in his apartment as he formulates a refusal to an invitation to speak to a German high school class about his experiences as a Jew in Germany. The man considers even the formulation of the invitation to speak "on being a Jew" an effrontery. But as he rehearses his negative response he realizes just how difficult it is to be the carrier of the past, to be forever representing, protecting against, and explaining being Jewish in a post-Holocaust world. In *Mein letzter Film* (*My Last Film*, 2002), Hirschbiegel offers an intimate portrait of Marie, an aging actress, who has decided that the film we are viewing will be her last. The movie presents actress Hannelore Elsner in a one-woman tour de force as she packs things into a suitcase, reminiscing about the three loves in her life: a director, an artist, and an athlete. *See also* HOLOCAUST IN FEATURE FILMS; *VERGANGENHEITSBEWÄLTIGUNGSFILM*.

HOFFMANN, KURT (1910–2001). Kurt Hoffmann was one of Germany's most successful directors of film comedies. He began his career during the Third Reich with, among others, four films starring the comedian **Heinz Rühmann**, in which he showed his penchant for romantic comedy as well as slapstick. The best-known film of his collaboration with Rühmann, *Quax, der Bruchpilot* (*Quax, the Stunt Pilot*, 1941), embeds obvious propaganda for military recruitment within a slapstick story of an incompetent pilot in training school who unwittingly becomes a hero.

Hoffmann's major breakthrough as a director came after the war. Following a false start directing dramas, Hoffmann returned to comedy and had a string of successes through the 1960s. His strength lay in adapting contemporary novels to the visual requirements of film. Of his literary adaptations, *Bekenntnisse des Hochstaplers Felix Krull* (*Confessions of Felix Krull*, 1957), based on Thomas Mann's novel of the same name, is arguably his best known, as the film introduced **Horst Buchholz** and won a **Film Award** in Gold as Best Film from the Deutsche Filmakademie (German Film Academy) and a Golden Globe as Best Foreign-Language Film. Hoffmann also successfully adapted two best-selling novels by Erich Kästner, *Das fliegende Klassenzimmer* (*The Flying Classroom*, 1954) and *Drei Männer im Schnee* (*Three Men in the Snow*, 1955).

In 1958, at a time when most German filmmakers avoided references to Germany's National Socialist past, Hoffmann satirized his countrymen's proclivity for obedience to uniforms and authority in *Wir Wunderkinder* (*Aren't We Wonderful?*), based on the novel of the same name by Hugo Hartung. The film tracks the careers of two young men, one a democratic idealist, the other an economic opportunist, from the eve of World War I in Germany (1914) through the German economic miracle (1958). Using slapstick, romantic comedy, parody, and cabaret skits, Hoffmann lampoons Germany's postwar pieties, exposing the roots of Nazism in pre-Third Reich Germany and the remnants of Nazism in postwar Germany. By casting cabaret artists Wolfgang Müller and Wolfgang Neuss as two balladeers whose songs bridge the years that the film covers, Hoffmann crafts a modern day morality play. The film at times delivers its message in heavy-handed fashion, ending with a warning to the living that real life does not always end as happily as this film.

HOLLAENDER, FRIEDRICH (1896–1976) (Frederick Hollander, US). During his career Friedrich Hollaender composed songs, incidental, and stock music for over 200 films. Although he began as a classical musician, he switched to popular music during the 1920s in Germany, composing for cabarets and theatrical revues. Having worked with **Marlene Dietrich** in stage shows, Hollaender accompanied Dietrich in her audition for *Der blaue Engel* (*The Blue Angel*, Josef von Sternberg, 1930) at the actress's request. Because of this, he ended up composing the music for the film, whose songs include some of the most memorable evergreens in the German film repertoire: "Ich bin von Kopf bis Fuß auf Liebe eingestellt" ("Falling in Love Again") "Ich bin die fesche Lola" ("My Name Is Naughty Lola"), and "Nimm dich in Acht vor blonden Frauen" ("Beware of Blondes"). Hollaender's music and lyrics and Dietrich's style of singing created the persona of an unsentimental, amoral seductress that the actress portrayed in almost all of her films. "Ich bin von Kopf bis Fuss auf Liebe eingestellt" became Dietrich's signature song, and she never failed in her concert appearances to honor Hollaender for his part in her career. In 1933, after the Nazis rose to power, Hollaender, who was Jewish, immigrated to the United States. There he again worked with Dietrich, composing, among other songs, "The Boys in the Back Room," for *Destry Rides Again* (George Marshall, 1939).

HOLLAND, AGNIESZKA (1949–). Agnieszka Holland was born in Poland and has made most of her movies in Poland, France, and the United States. She did, however, make two German films: *Bittere Ernte* (*Angry Harvest*, 1985), which was nominated for an Academy Award as an entry from West Germany in the Best Foreign Film category, and *Europa Europa* (1990), which the German jury refused to nominate in that same category because Holland was not German. The committee's refusal to nominate the movie, which is known in Germany as *Hitlerjunge Salomon* (*Hitler Youth Solomon*), created a controversy among critics, members of the nominating jury, and producers of the film. *See also* HOLOCAUST IN FEATURE FILMS; *VERGANGENHEITSBEWÄLTIGUNGSFILM*.

HOLOCAUST IN FEATURE FILMS. The Holocaust, the Nazi program of systematically murdering Europe's Jews, as well as the Sinti and Roma peoples, homosexuals, and the mentally and physically disabled, had a profound impact on the history and politics of the West lasting into the 21st century. Not surprisingly, the national film industries of Western and Eastern Europe and of Hollywood turned again and again to cinematic portrayals of the Third Reich in order to come to terms with the horrific events of that era. While many of the non-German productions focused on the genocidal policies of Adolf Hitler and the National Socialists, German films for the most part did not. Instead, they offered solace to viewers by suggesting they too were victims of a ruthless regime (*see* ***Vergangenheitsbewältigungsfilm***). Nevertheless, a small but significant number of German films addressed the genocidal policies of the Nazis, sometimes directly but most often indirectly. Moreover, films on the Holocaust from America, Holland, France, and Poland, among other countries, even though not German productions, received exposure in German theaters and on German television, giving German viewers a means to confront their country's past.

Three films made shortly after the end of World War II offered a hopeful beginning to how German film would remember the past. *Die Mörder sind unter uns* (*The Murderers Are among Us*, **Wolfgang Staudte**, 1946) included a shot of a newspaper headline, albeit only briefly, that read "2,000,000 Gassed." *Ehe im Schatten* (*Marriage in the Shadows*, **Kurt Maetzig**, 1947) is based on the life of Joachim Gottschalk, an Aryan actor who committed suicide with his Jewish wife and child rather than see them deported to a concentration camp. *Lang ist der Weg* (*Long Is the Road*, Herbert B. Fredersdorf and Marek Goldstein, 1947), an American–German coproduction, follows a young man who hides from the Nazis within Germany, loses his family to Auschwitz, but in the end is reunited with his mother and looks forward to living in a Jewish state in Palestine. In spite of this auspicious beginning in coming to terms with crimes of the past, subsequent films in the 1950s and 1960s in West Germany and the 1950s in East Germany focused on different aspects of the National Socialist legacy than the Holocaust. Those made in West Germany focused on the war itself, helping to rehabilitate the ordinary soldier by showing him as a victim of the Nazi leadership (*see* **war films**). Films in East Germany took as their point of departure the need to differentiate the new Socialist Germany from the fascist policies not only of the past, but also of the West (*see* **East German Film**).

In 1979 the American miniseries *Holocaust* (Marvin J. Chomsky, 1978) played on German television to a wide audience. The event led to renewed interest in the Holocaust among Germans and initiated public discourse on Germany's past and the concomitant issues of generational and collective guilt. Even before *Holocaust* appeared, however, there had been increased awareness of the crimes of the Third Reich. In East Germany, *Nackt unter Wölfen* (*Naked among Wolves*, **Frank Beyer**, 1963) told the story of a group of men in a concentration camp, hiding a young boy who if discovered by officials would be killed. Twelve years later Beyer set a film in a Jewish ghetto in *Jakob der Lügner* (*Jacob the Liar*), a dark comedy that relates how a Jewish man encourages others to keep believing they will be rescued by lying to them about radio broadcasts and suggesting that the Allies are near. *Der vorletzte Akt—Brundibar* (*The Second to the Last Act: Brundibar*, Walter Krüttner, 1965) reconstructs a children's opera that was performed in Theresienstadt, the camp used by the Nazis to deceive the International Red Cross about conditions in and purpose of the camps. Theresienstadt figures in several other films as well. A 1991 VHS recording of *Der Führer schenkt den Juden eine Stadt* (*The Führer Gives a City to the Jews*, Kurt Gerron, 1944), a film that was never released by the Nazis, becomes nevertheless a self-indictment of their policies more than 45 years after the film was shot. The Czech film *Transport z raje* (*Transport from Paradise*, Zbynek Brynych, 1962) reenacts life in Theresienstadt while Gerron was making the film about the camp. *Prisoner of Paradise* (Malcolm Clarke and Stuart Sender, 2002) is a documentary of Gerron's life and also tells about the time when he made the film and shortly thereafter, when he was deported to Auschwitz and murdered. To be sure, neither of the last two films is German produced.

A number of German films that began appearing at the time *Holocaust* was broadcast look at the plight of individual Jews as they flee the Nazis. *David* (**Peter Lilienthal**, 1979), released two months after the German premier of *Holocaust*, portrays a young Jewish man who survives the genocide by hiding among the Nazis after his family is deported to Auschwitz. *Charlotte* (Frans Weisz, 1981), based on a true story, follows a young woman painter who flees to France and is subsequently arrested and deported to Auschwitz, where she perishes. Axel Corti's *An uns glaubt Gott nicht mehr* (*God Does Not Believe in Us Anymore*, 1982) follows an Austrian adolescent Jew as he flees to Prague, then to Paris, and finally to the South of France after his father is brutally murdered at the hands of Nazi thugs. In *Regentropfen* (*Raindrops*, Michael Hoffmann and Harry Raymon, 1982), a young boy and his family escape persecution by sailing to America, only to be denied entry because of the father's incipient tuberculosis. The Swiss film *Das Boot ist voll* (*The Boat Is Full*, Markus Imhoof, 1980) tells of several families who escape to neutral Switzerland, only to be deported back to Germany and certain death in the camps. Finally, **Europa Europa** (**Agnieszka Holland**, 1990) tells of a young Jewish man who escapes the Nazis by hiding in plain sight at an elite school for Hitler Youth. As excellent as these films are in portraying the tragedies of individuals, because they focus on personal narratives, they can merely suggest the enormity of what occurred under the Nazis.

In contrast, German documentaries emphasize the universal suffering that was brought about by the genocidal program of the National Socialists. *Die Wannseekonferenz* (*The Wannsee Conference*, Heinz Schirk, 1984) reconstructs discussions that took place at a conference of Nazi leaders in February 1942 in Wannsee, a suburb of Berlin. As a reconstruction, the film is not a true documentary but rather a fictionalized account of what might have transpired. Its release in 1984 reflected the political discourse that ensued after a debate among historians on the nature of the Holocaust. Briefly described, the debate centered on whether the Holocaust was of intentional design, as portrayed in the film, or whether it was more functional, a visceral response to the threat from the Soviet Union. Another film, which countered revisionist arguments, was the documentary *Der gelbe Stern* (*The Yellow Star*, Dieter Hildebrandt, 1980). This film focuses on the atrocities committed against the Jews, highlighting how the atrocities of the Holocaust were witnessed by much of the world and yet little was done to prevent their being carried out. The film *Es ging Tag und Nacht, liebes Kind: Zigeuner (Sinti) in Auschwitz* (*It Went On Day and Night, Dear Child: Gypsies (Sinti) in Auschwitz*, **Katrin Seybold**, 1982) documents the genocidal policies of the Nazis against the Sinti or gypsies. Moreover the film asserts that official policies of discrimination still existed at the time the movie was released. The late Austrian filmmaker Karin Brandauer likewise portrays anti-Sinti and

Roma policies in her film *Sidonie*, focusing on the fate of one pread-
olescent girl who dies after deportation to a camp.

If one includes references to persecution, whether camps are central
to the film or even visible, the number of Holocaust films made by Germans totals more than 50. These range from brief but striking references
in films to depictions of life in the camps. As noted, *Die Mörder sind
unter uns* flashes a headline on the screen that 2,000,000 have been
gassed. *Ich war neunzehn* (*I Was Nineteen*, **Konrad Wolf**, 1968) asks
the question of how the Holocaust happened and how one can reconcile
to others that the German language includes both Goethe and
Auschwitz. Other films focus on the non-Jewish aspects of the Holocaust. *Kalmenhofkinder* (*Children of Kalmenhof*, Nikolaus Tscheschner,
1990) looks at how the disabled were treated. *Ich bin meine eigene Frau*
(*I Am My Own Woman*, **Rosa von Praunheim**, 1992), a biography of
the transvestite Charlotte von Mahlsdorf, depicts persecution by both
the Nazis and the East Germans. *Invincible* (**Werner Herzog**, 2001)
tells a fantastical story about a Jewish strong man who portrayed an
Aryan in the stage spectacles of Erik Jan Hanussen, himself an opportunistic Jewish magician and impresario entertaining the Nazis. In *Der
letzte Zug* (*The Last Train*, Joseph Vilsmaier, 2006) two women escape
from a train transporting them and other Berlin Jews to Auschwitz.
Sixty years later, they meet at a conference in Wannsee and reminisce
how they were the only ones in their train car to escape. *Nirgendwo in
Afrika* (*Nowhere in Africa*, Caroline Link, 2001) alludes to the Holocaust most profoundly by registering the absence of those killed in the
camps. A young couple and their daughter who have escaped persecution by fleeing to a new life in Africa learn through letters and news reports of the death of their families and friends. Dani Levy's *Mein
Führer: Die wirklich wahrste Wahrheit über Adolf Hitler* (*Mein Führer:
The Truly Truest Truth about Adolf Hitler*, 2007) delivers a farce that
traces the Holocaust in part back to Hitler's unhappy childhood.

HOPPE, MARIANNE (1909–2002). Marianne Hoppe was a successful
and distinguished stage, film, and television actor for almost six
decades. She began her career in Nazi Germany, where her popularity
rivaled that of male stars **Hans Albers** and **Heinz Rühmann**. Hoppe's
style is characterized by charm, independence, and elegance. In her
most successful roles for the Third Reich, she embodied a German
Everywoman, willing to sacrifice her happiness for the country, but

not necessarily her independent spirit. Hoppe played Effi Briest, the heroine of Theodor Fontane's novel, as a naive ingénue who learns to be independent of her controlling husband. The film, whose title was changed from the novel's *Effi Briest* to *Der Schritt vom Wege* (*Step from the Path*, **Gustaf Gründgens**, 1939) in order to emphasize Effi's transgression, nonetheless sympathizes with her act, given the unheroic portrayal of her husband.

Although Hoppe's films for the Third Reich are classified as entertainment, and she never appeared in the more egregiously propagandistic productions, her films sometimes reflected Nazi ideology. In *Der Herrscher* (*The Ruler*, **Veit Harlan**, 1937), loosely based on Gerhart Hauptmann's tragedy *Vor Sonnenuntergang* (*Before Sunset*, 1932), Hoppe plays a young secretary who plans to marry a 70-year-old patriarch. In the play, when the patriarch's children protest, the old man commits suicide. However, in the film he disinherits his children and donates his munitions factory to the German people, with an obligation to rebuild the German economy. The nationalistic spirit evident in *Der Herrscher* is more strongly present in *Auf Wiedersehen, Franziska!* (*Goodbye, Franziska!*, **Helmut Käutner**, 1941). When her husband, a globetrotting photographic reporter, is drafted into the military and is reluctant to serve, Hoppe's character reminds him about his duty to his family and country and admonishes him that he must serve. The scene was considered sufficiently pro-Nazi that the Allies required it be cut before the movie was released for viewing in postwar Germany (*see* **Catalogue of Forbidden Feature and Short Film Productions**).

Hoppe's greatest film from the Third Reich period was *Romanze in Moll* (*Romance in a Minor Key*, Käutner, 1943), a film that was almost banned by Minister of Propaganda Goebbels, who believed that the film was too defeatist. Madeleine, the character played by Hoppe, has an affair with a composer, which the boss of her husband and friend of the composer threatens to expose to her spouse if she does not submit to him. The film was especially successful after the war with French film critics, who saw it as an exception, along with Käutner's *Unter den Brücken* (*Under the Bridges*, 1945), to the Nazi's ideologically colored films.

After the war, Hoppe continued to have a successful stage and film career. Much of her film work was for German television, where she acted in some of West Germany's popular series, including the crime show *Der Kommissar* (*The Commissioner*, 1969–1976). She had a supporting role in *Ten Little Indians* (George Pollack, 1965), in which she played Elsa Grohmann, who with her husband, played by **Mario Adorf**, are caretakers of the house where Agatha Christie's mystery takes place. She also appeared as Wilhelm Meister's mother in **Wim Wenders**'s *Falsche Bewegung* (*False Movement*, 1975).

HÖRBIGER, PAUL (1894–1981). Paul Hörbiger played the archetypal Viennese in almost 300 films: charming, music loving, and sentimental. Although he began in silent films, he gained recognition in sound films, where he could engage his musical talents. He appeared in comedies, operettas, and films set in Vienna or requiring a Viennese character. The titles of his movies suggest an actor who was typecast as a cliché: *Zwei Herzen im Dreivierteltakt* (*Two Hearts in Waltz Time*, Géza von Bolváry, 1930), *Paprika* (*Paprika*, Carl Boese, 1932), *Walzerkrieg* (*The War of the Waltzes*, Ludwig Berger, 1933), *Königswalzer* (*The Royal Waltz*, Herbert Maisch, 1935), *Operette* (*Operetta*, **Willi Forst** and **Karl Hartl**, 1940), *Schwarzwaldmädel* (*The Black Forest Girl*, **Hans Deppe**, 1950), *Das tanzende Herz* (*The Dancing Heart*, **Wolfgang Lieberneirer**, 1953), *An der schönen blauen Donau* (*On the Beautiful Blue Danube*, Hans Schweikert, 1955), *Tanze mit mir in den Morgen* (*Dance with Me into the Morning*, Peter Dörre, 1962), and *Sing, aber spiel nicht mit mir* (*Sing, but Don't Play with Me*, Kurt Nachmann, 1963).

Although most of Hörbiger's films were in the vein of the titles mentioned above, he also appeared in some of the better-known films of the 1930s and 1940s. He plays a singer in *Der Kongreß tanzt* (*The Congress Dances*, Erik Charell, 1931), one of the most popular musicals of the early sound era, and a composer in *Liebelei* (*Flirtation*, **Max Ophüls**, 1933), based on an Austrian writer's turn-of-the-century Viennese play. He played opposite **Zarah Leander**, one of the Nazi era's most popular divas, in *Heimat* (*Homeland*, **Carl Froelich**, 1938), *Der Blaufuchs* (*The Blue Fox*, Viktor Tourjansky, 1938), and *Die große Liebe* (*The Great Love*, Rolf Hansen, 1942). While *Der Blaufuchs* was an apolitical entertainment, both *Heimat* and *Die große Liebe* fit well within the Nazis' ideological program. In *Heimat*, Hörbiger plays an organist whose playing is instrumental to the heroine's reconciliation with her father, a metaphor for the wayward German's coming home to the

Reich. He also has one of the political speeches in the film, which despite taking place at the end of the 19th century alludes to the momentous changes in Germany of the 1930s: "But you do know of this other world [one with values and traditions], Mister von Schwartze. It is ascending with new visions and a new honor. It touches our hearts and cannot be stopped even by you." In *Die große Liebe*, a film about surviving against terrible odds (*see Durchhaltungsfilm*), Hörbiger's character embodies the spirit of sacrifice as he renounces his love for the heroine, realizing that life does not always turn out as we want.

After the war, in addition to scores of musical comedies and romances, Hörbiger appeared in Orson Welles's *The Third Man* (1949), a classic Welles tale about greed and corruption in postwar Vienna, and **Helmut Käutner**'s *Epilog: Das Geheimnis der Orplid* (*The Secret of the Orplid*, 1950), an experiment in point-of-view storytelling. *See also* AUSTRIAN CINEMA.

HUILLET, DANIÈLE. *See* STRAUB, JEAN-MARIE.

HUPPERTZ, GOTTFRIED (1887–1937). Composer Gottfried Huppertz created scores for three of the silent era's most important films: *Die Nibelungen: Siegfrieds Tod* (*Siegfried's Death*, 1924), *Die Nibelungen: Kriemhilds Rache* (*Kriemhild's Revenge*, 1924), and *Metropolis* (*Metropolis*, 1927), three silent era masterpieces directed by **Fritz Lang**. Although called silent films, movies in the 1910s and 1920s were not without music, often supplied by an organist or pianist following a book of suggested tunes. Major films often had individual scores performed by full orchestras at their premiers in first-run theaters in Berlin, Paris, New York, and London. Huppertz's scores for Lang's movies were therefore serious compositions, akin to symphonic compositions. Huppertz used copious melodies in his movies; was a master of the leitmotif, melodic lines dedicated to a particular character, object, or idea; and showed a preference for extended passages. His music has been called derivative of Richard Wagner and Bruckner, two late romantic composers. Huppertz's score to *Metropolis* was lost until the early 2000s, when the British Film Institute remastered the movie and added the original music back to the film. Until then, 16mm and then VHS copies of the film could be found with at least five different music tracks.

– I –

IMHOOF, MARKUS (1941–). Markus Imhoof is arguably Switzerland's most important German-language film director. He began as a documentarist, focusing on controversial issues often associated with the Left. *Rondo* (*Rondo*, 1968) looked at the prison system in Switzerland, implying that for the Swiss, incarceration as a form of punishment and means of deterrence was more important than integrating released prisoners back into society. *Ormenis 199+69* (*Ormenis 199+69*, 1969), the title referring to the horse Imhoof rode when he was in the Swiss military, examines the role and treatment of horses in the cavalry and suggests the unit should be disbanded. Before the film could be screened publicly, Imhoof had to edit out material that veterans' groups found objectionable. The film was not shown in unedited form to the public until 2002. *Rondo* had likewise been banned, but it was released by 1975. *Volksmund – oder man ist was man isst* (*Vernacular—One Is What One Eats*, 1972) documents eating, showing fat people, skinny people, gorging, banquets, and other activities suggestive of food. Imhoof avoids contrasting scarcity of food with plenitude or starving societies with well-fed ones. Instead, he allows food and eating to become a metaphor for consumption, for people's desire or need to consume. At one point, the film muses that most cultures seem to envision paradise as a place of unconstrained eating.

Imhoof's narrative films show the same particular interest in Swiss culture and politics as his documentaries. He received international recognition for his narrative feature *Das Boot ist voll* (*The Boat Is Full*, 1980), a film that exposed the downside of Switzerland's neutrality during World War II. In 1942, a group of Jewish refugees fled across the German border to Switzerland, only to be returned to Germany and death in the concentration camps. The official reason for the return was a law that forbade granting asylum solely on the basis of race or ethnicity. Imhoof's film suggests that the public's xenophobic fear of being overrun by outsiders and anti-Semitism contributed to the rejection of the refugees. Imhoof's film appeared at the time other films were helping viewers come to terms with the Nazi era (*see* **Vergangenheitsbewältigungsfilm**) but was the first Swiss film to do so.

Imhoof's *Die Reise* (*The Journey*, 1986) examines terrorism as it appeared in the late 1960s and was practiced by the Red Army Faction or the Baader-Meinhof Group, named after Andreas Baader and Ulrike Meinhof, two of its leaders. Similar to **Margarethe von Trotta**'s analysis of terrorism in *Die bleierne Zeit* (*Marianne and Juliane*, 1981), Imhoof locates the roots of terrorism in the conflict between the generation of parents that lived their formative years under the Nazis and the generation of children that never received an explanation from their parents of their role in the Third Reich. Imhoof's *Der Berg* (*The Mountain*, 1990) provides a psychological study of three individuals stranded at the top of a mountain with provisions for only two to survive. As are his other works, *Der Berg* is driven by a tension between the extraordinary nature of the situation and the reality of the emotions. This paradox of creating realism from the fantastic is even more striking in *Flammen im Paradies* (*Fire in Paradise*, 1997), a film whose exotic visuals are reminiscent of **Werner Herzog**'s *Aguirre, der Zorn Gottes* (*Aguirre, the Wrath of God*, 1972). Imhoof here provides a psychological study of a young woman who is promised in marriage but switches places with a woman bound for India. The movie follows her journey to independence and eventual happiness.

INTERNATIONALE HOFER FILMTAGE (HOF INTERNATIONAL FILM FESTIVAL). After the **Berlin Film Festival**, this is perhaps the best known of Germany's many film festivals. (Other festivals are held at Emden, Leipzig, Cologne, Saarbrücken, Mannheim, Munich, and Oberhausen.) Originally billed as "the smallest film festival in the world" and labeled the "home of film" by **Wim Wenders**, the Hof event was started in 1967 by Uwe Brander and Heinz Badewitz as an occasion to show friends their work. The festival has grown to the point that today it spotlights films from new directors as well as established filmmakers, theatrical as well as television films, feature length movies as well as shorts, and films from abroad as well as those from Germany. Particular emphasis is given to German films from new or first-time directors. In spite of its growth, the festival retains small-town friendliness by sponsoring a soccer game every year between those who work in film and a local team.

– J –

JANNINGS, EMIL (1884–1950). One of silent film's greatest actors, Emil Jannings has never had an equal in the ability to portray suffering on screen. For his role of demoted bank clerk in *The Way of All Flesh* (Victor Fleming, 1927) and his role of an ex-Czarist general reduced to playing bit parts in Hollywood movies in *The Last Command* (Josef von Sternberg, 1928), Jannings won the first Academy Award for acting.

By the time he had won the Academy Award, Jannings was already a master at portraying humiliation on screen. He starred as the wronged man in *Varieté* (*Jealousy*, **Ewald André Dupont**, 1925) and as the demoted doorman in *Der letzte Mann* (*The Last Laugh*, **Friedrich Wilhem Murnau**, 1924). His characterization in *Der letzte Mann* of a doorman reduced to attending a lavatory illustrates Jannings's superb acting skills. In the film, he uses mime and gesticulation, facial expression, and body movement to convey the damage to his psyche that his demotion has caused. His movements and facial expressions were the perfect complement to the roving camera of **Karl Freund**, the film's cinematographer, and the fluid film language of Murnau, allowing the film to tell its story with only one intertitle, which appears at the end of the film to explain the added happy ending.

With the introduction of talking pictures, Jannings returned from Hollywood to Germany. To help him reestablish his career there, he asked Josef von Sternberg to direct him in ***Der blaue Engel*** (*The Blue Angel*, 1930), the film that made **Marlene Dietrich** a star and for which most later generations know him. His role in this adaptation of Heinrich Mann's novel *Professor Unrat oder das Ende eines Tyrannen* (*Small Town Tyrant*, 1905) reprises the role of a wronged man whose passion and jealousy lead to his ultimate degradation and downfall. Set in the same lower middle class milieu as most of Jannings's films, *Der blaue Engel* allowed the actor to use his melodious voice to underscore his great physical acting abilities.

Jannings continued his successful career under the Nazis. By cultivating roles that called for idealism and authority, he was able to become one of the Culture Ministry's star vehicles, advancing even to

State Actor. After the war, Jannings was blacklisted for a while but was eventually declared denazified. However, because of poor health he never acted again. In 2004, Jannings's hometown of Rorschach, Switzerland, was to honor the actor with a star (similar to those on the Hollywood Walk of Fame), but rescinded the honor when his role in the Nazi film industry was revealed.

JOHN, GOTTFRIED (1942–). Gottfried John gained recognition as the title character in *Carlos* (*Carlos*, **Hans W. Geissendörfer**, 1970), an adaptation of the Friedrich Schiller classic *Don Carlos* (1787) as a Western. His lanky body, long face, and broken nose suggested to one entertainment weekly publication that "ugly was in again." In any case, John became a regular in **Rainer Werner Fassbinder**'s troupe of film and stage actors. His most memorable role was as Willi, the husband of Maria's friend in *Die Ehe der Maria Braun* (*The Marriage of Maria Braun*, 1979), his drawn out, tired-looking face adding to the feeling of 1950s malaise created by the film. His portrayal of Anton Seitz, a Jewish real estate agent, in Fassbinder's *In einem Jahr mit 13 Monden* (*In a Year of 13 Moons*, 1978), revealed John's darkly comedic side. In addition to the eight films he made with Fassbinder, John has played a supporting role in more than 70 other theatrical and made-for-television films. He had a major supporting role in **Volker Schlöndorff**'s *Der Unhold* (*The Ogre*, 1996), one of the many German-produced films about the Third Reich (*see* **Vergangenheitsbewältigungsfilm**). John befriends a simple man, played by John Malkovich, who has been taken prisoner by the Nazis. John's Hollywood parts include the Russian villain in the James Bond thriller *Goldeneye* (Martin Campbell, 1995) and a crazy missionary who adds a touch of absurdity to *Proof of Life* (Taylor Hackford, 2000).

JUD SÜß. Directed by **Veit Harlan**, *Jud Süß* (*Jew Süss*, 1940) represents one of a handful of the anti-Semitic films produced by the Nazis to prepare Germans for the disappearance of Jews from Germany. Along with *Der ewige Jude* (*The Eternal Jew*, Fritz Hippler, 1940), *Robert und Bertram* (*Robert and Bertram*, Hans H. Zerlett, 1939), and *Die Rothschilds* (*The Rothschilds*, Erich Waschneck, 1940), *Jud Süß* was meant to fortify already anti-Semitic feelings among the populace and the prevailing anti-Jewish policies of the government.

Harlan's film is based loosely on Lion Feuchtwanger's essentially philo-Semitic novel, *Jud Süß* (1925), a psychological study of obsession with power. The book had already been filmed by German filmmaker Lothar Mendes working in England. The English film followed Feuchtwanger's characterization fairly closely, emphasizing what drove Süß Oppenheimer to form an alliance with the Duke of Württemberg and commit acts that could be viewed as treasonous. Harlan recast Oppenheimer's obsession with power as an obsession with bringing down Germany. Structuring his film as an 18th-century bourgeois tragedy, in which virtuous middle class citizens fight to wrest control of their lives from a greedy, despotic ruler, as in *Emilia Galotti* (*Emilia Galotti*, Gotthold Ephraim Lessing, 1772) or *Kabale und Liebe* (*Intrigue and Love*, Friedrich Schiller, 1784). Süß takes on the role of an evil opportunistic adviser to the duke, who is too weak to see through the cunning of his Jewish adversary. *Jud Süß* creates a polar world, in which all positive values, such as love of family, chastity, patriotism, frugality, and honesty, reside in Germans, and all negative values, such as debauchery, wanderlust, sexuality, profligate spending, and duplicity, are located in Jews. The film furthermore delivers a strong message that the Jews took over Germany once, at least in Württemberg, and that driving them out was the right and only course of action open to Germany. Viewers in 1940 could hardly have overlooked the obvious parallels the film was trying to make with Nazi Germany's current situation.

Most of Germany's big stars acted in *Jud Süß*. Matinee idol **Ferdinand Marian** played Süß, perhaps a mistake in casting as he reportedly received love letters for his portrayal of the hot-blooded Süß. **Werner Krauss** played multiple Jewish roles in the film, displaying disdain for Gentile values in all his parts and adopting a stereotypical speech pattern that characterizes German Jews negatively. **Heinrich George** played the duke as too weak to fight Jewish encroachment. **Kristina Söderbaum** portrayed the daughter as an ingénue, flattered by Jud Süß's attention at first until it was too late to prevent his raping her. Her subsequent suicide reflected the Nazi ideology of the only recourse to her having been violated. After the war, the participants in the film came under close scrutiny by the Allies assessing war crimes.

Harlan effectively argued that he and the others were forced to make the film and were exonerated. Only George was imprisoned, in Sachsenhausen, a former Nazi camp used by the Russians after the war. *See also* CATALOGUE OF FORBIDDEN FEATURE AND SHORT FILM PRODUCTIONS.

JÜRGENS, CURD (1915–1982). For an actor whom Francois Truffaut reputedly called "one of the four worst actors in the world," Curd Jürgens (1915–1982) had a remarkably successful international career. In German, Austrian, and French films he was often cast as a sophisticated man of the world, a charming rogue and lover, and he appeared with the 1950s French sex goddess Brigitte Bardot in *Et Dieu . . . créa la femme* (*. . . And God Created Woman*, Roger Vadim, 1956), and with **Maria Schell** in *Der Engel mit der Posaune* (*The Angel with the Trumpet*, **Karl Hartl**, 1948).

His role as General Harras in *Des Teufels General* (*The Devil's General*, **Helmut Käutner**, 1955), based on Carl Zuckmayer's antifascist play of the same name, brought him international recognition and also typecast him in the eyes of Hollywood as a Teutonic adversary. His major American roles include German officers in *The Enemy Below* (Dick Powell, 1957) and *The Longest Day* (**Bernhard Wicki** et al., 1961); Colonel Prokoszny in *Me and the Colonel* (Peter Glenville, 1958), starring Danny Kaye and based on the play by Franz Werfel; and the villain in the James Bond thriller *The Spy Who Loved Me* (Lewis Gilbert, 1977). During his career he appeared in over 160 films, several of them during the Nazi era, during which he seemed to have a promising career until arrested and interned in a concentration camp when he angered **Joseph Goebbels** by being insubordinate. After the war, he became an Austrian citizen.

JUTZI, PHIL (1896–1946). Phil Jutzi, who for a while in the early 1920s used the first name Piel until sued by actor **Harry Piel**, was an important leftist director of the silent era. His breakthrough as a moviemaker of the proletariat came with *Kindertragödie* (*Children's Tragedy*, 1927), a tendentious study of starving children, which gained its impact from Jutzi's gritty realism. The daily misery that the poor must accept is even more pronounced in *Ums tägliche Brot* (*Hunger im Waldenburg*, 1929). Filmed as a quasi documentary, it shows the hopeless situation of coal miners and weavers in the Waldenburg area. When a young man's luck finally seems to change, he is pushed down stairs and in his hunger-weakened condition dies. *Mutter Krausens Fahrt ins Glück* (*Mother Krause's Journey to Happiness*, 1929) is Jutzi's best-known and best-executed work. The film blends agit-prop realism with melodrama to tell the story of an elderly woman driven to suicide by despair about her situation. Her daughter, however, together with her politically active partner, fights for a better life. The film's mixture of despair and message influenced **Slatan Dudow**'s *Kuhle Wampe oder? Wem gehört die Welt* (*Kuhle Wampe*, a.k.a. *Whither Germany?* 1932), the most successful German communist film of its period.

At the beginning of the sound era, before National Socialist rule, Jutzi directed *Berlin Alexanderplatz* (*Berlin Alexanderplatz*, 1931), starring **Heinrich George** and based on Alfred Döblin's realist novel about the city of Berlin. Jutzi pared down the lengthy, multifaceted novel to the story of Franz Biberkopf, a man whose life cycles continually downward. Jutzi's preference for on-location shooting, begun in his silent films, continued in his early sound films. (**Rainer Werner Fassbinder** remade both *Mutter Krausens Fahrt ins Gluck*, as *Mutter Küsters' Fahrt zum Himmel* [*Mother Küsters Goes to Heaven*, 1975], and *Berlin Alexanderplatz* [*Berlin Alexanderplatz*, 1980], the latter as a 15-hour made-for television miniseries, as compared to Jutzi's two-hour movie.)

Jutzi made a number of films for the National Socialists, having quit the Communist Party at the end of the 1920s and joined the Nazi Party in 1933. Owing, however, to the themes and style of his early films, which were sympathetic to the Left and therefore banned once the Nazis came to power, Jutzi was allowed to make only film shorts.

– K –

KAUFMANN, GÜNTHER (1947–). Günther Kaufmann was a member of **Rainer Werner Fassbinder**'s troupe of actors. As an African-American German, with a German mother and G.I. father, Kaufmann was pigeonholed into mostly parts requiring a black American soldier. His flat American accent when speaking English betrayed his

German origins, but Fassbinder cast him nonetheless in the role of a G.I. in his postwar trilogy of films *Die Ehe der Maria Braun* (*The Marriage of Maria Braun*, 1979), *Die Sehnsucht der Veronika Voss* (*Veronika Voss*, 1982), and *Lola* (*Lola*, 1981). Although the roles were small, encompassing barely two minutes of screen time, they provided the catalyst to turning points in the movies. In *Die Ehe der Maria Braun*, Kaufmann's character's indecent and vulgarly stated proposal to Maria releases a torrent of profanity from her that awakens the interest of her soon to be benefactor. As Veronika's drug dealer, he precipitates the former film diva's tailspin into dependency. At the beginning of his association with Fassbinder, while engaged in an affair with him, Kaufmann received larger roles, including that of the title character in *Whity* (*Whity*, 1971), in which he plays a mixed-race butler to a wealthy family in Southwest America at the end of the 19th century. Aside from playing in Fassbinder's films, Kaufmann has appeared in small roles on German television. He was accused of murder in 2002 and sentenced to 15 years' imprisonment but received a pardon when it was discovered that he had perjured himself and admitted guilt to protect his wife, who had committed the crime, a story line similar to that of *Die Ehe der Maria Braun*. *See also* NEW GERMAN CINEMA.

KÄUTNER, HELMUT (1908–1980). Helmut Käutner began his directorial career in Nazi Germany in 1939, after having appeared as an actor in several films and also having written for, and performed in, cabaret. His films avoid overt political propaganda, focusing instead on social criticism. They are considered by most film historians and critics to be the best produced during the Third Reich. Their technical polish, lyrical narration, and creative stories assured that they would be funded, even without political messages. Nonetheless, Käutner's talent did not make his films immune from censorship or guarantee that they would be released.

Käutner's first film, *Kitty und die Weltkonferenz* (*Kitty and the World Conference*, 1939), takes place against a backdrop of international diplomacy. Its satirical look at diplomacy gives the movie a light, screwball tone, reminiscent of American directors Frank Capra and Howard Hawks. In spite of the film's popularity, it was withdrawn after war broke out in late summer 1939, as Goebbels felt the film presented too favorable an image of England. *Romanze in Moll* (*Romance in a Minor Key*, 1943), Käutner's best-known film from this period, also ran into censorship difficulties. The story, which ends with the suicide of the film's heroine, was too depressing for Goebbels, who wanted films to cheer viewers. However, the movie's success with critics outside Germany led to its eventual release in Germany as well, where it was equally well received by audiences. *Große Freiheit # 7* (*Port of Freedom*, 1944) ran afoul of the censors for its setting, the red light district in the port city of Hamburg. The film was eventually released outside Germany, in countries under German control. Käutner's only film to openly support National Socialism, *Auf Wiedersehen, Franziska!* (*Goodbye, Franziska!* 1941), got him into difficulties with the Allies after the war. On the one hand the values in the film are merely those of a conservative ideology, extolling the virtues of family life and placing the national over the international community. On the other hand, the last sequence of the film reminds Germans of their patriotic duty to support the war effort. After the war, the ending sequence placed the film on a list of movies banned for exhibition by the Allies. The film was removed from the list after Käutner convinced officials that the propaganda sequence in no way reflected his political ideology and was added at the request of officials. He convinced them by cutting out the sequence and demonstrating that the story remained unaffected.

Käutner's work after World War II disappointed critics, who felt that the director never fulfilled the promise many saw in *Romanze in Moll* and especially in *Unter den Brücken* (*Under the Bridges*, 1945), a film that is reminiscent of French poetic realism. Although approved by National Socialist censors, it was not released until after Germany's defeat and elicited comments of astonishment at its freshness and apolitical nature. In contrast to the freshness of his early films, many critics find Käutner's postwar work too filled with compromises, particularly disappointing considering the source. Reviewers wanted Käutner to attack the problems of postwar Germany, and they felt he was avoiding the important issues. Critic Walter Schmieding wrote in 1961, for example, that the director's "compromises would be easier to accept if they were not coming from someone who sees the real problems . . . but he sees them more sharply and more clearly than all others."

The criticism notwithstanding, Käutner was politically and socially engaged in his postwar films. *Epilog: Das Geheimnis der Orplid* (*The Secret of the Orplid*, 1950) examines postwar international intrigue in a taut political thriller. *Die letzte Brücke* (*The Last Bridge*, 1954), a war film about partisans in Yugoslavia, starring **Maria Schell** in one of her finest performances, asks questions about patriotism and treason. *Des Teufels General* (*The Devil's General*, 1954–1955) again questions the concepts of patriotism and treason, as it focuses on crimes committed under the Nazis. Based on the play of the same name by Carl Zuckmayer, the film elevated **Curd Jürgens** to international stardom. However, Käutner's greatest success in the postwar years was a comedy about the German adoration of men in uniform, *Der Hauptmann von Köpenick* (*The Captain of Köpenick*, 1956), also based on a Zuckmayer play and starring **Heinz Rühmann**, who reprises his role from another Käutner film, *Kleider machen Leute* (*Clothes Make the Man*, 1940). The film won awards from the Deutsche Filmakademie (German Film Academy), a Bambi, and a German critics' prize for best film. It was Germany's first postwar success in the United States and played in 53 countries. The incident on which the film is based occurred in 1906, when shoemaker Wilhelm Voigt donned the uniform of a military captain and organized a passport for himself in city hall. It inspired more than 10 films, some as early as 1907, of which Käutner's is the best known and most popular. The most unusual version was made in 2001, directed by Katharina Thalbach, who also played the male lead. Slatan Dudow, an East German, directed the most political version, *Der Hauptmann von Köln* (*The Captain of Cologne*), in which he relocated the action to West Germany in the service of cold war rhetoric.

In the 1950s Käutner had a brief career in Hollywood, making two films: *The Restless Years* (1957) and *Stranger in My Arms* (1957). About these films the director commented: "They were what I call unfortunate hybrids. They were too European for Americans and too American for Europeans." Both however starred Sandra Dee, an American sweetheart at the time, and an indication of the importance of Käutner's film projects. In 1973, Käutner received a **Film Award** in Gold for his contributions to the German film industry. In 1975, he received an Award in Gold for his portrayal of the title character in **Hans-Jürgen Syberberg**'s *Karl May* (*Karl May*, 1974). In spite of public acclaim, young critics at the Oberhausen Film Festival in 1961 named his films *Schwarzer Kies* (*Black Pebbles*, 1961) and *Der Traum von Lieschen Müller* (*The Dream of Lieschen Müller*, 1961), the year's worst achievement by a known director.

KEKELLI, SIBEL (1980–). After a career in pornographic films, Sibel Kekilli broke into mainstream German film with her role as an independent Turkish woman in *Gegen die Wand* (*Head-On*, **Fatih Akin**, 2004). Kekilli's attractive presence on screen allows viewers to sympathize with her even when she is at her most unsympathetic, as when provoking others through screaming, threatening suicide to get what she wants, or being vulgarly erotic. In *Der letzte Zug* (*The Last Train*, Joseph Vilsmaier and Dana Várová, 2006), Kekelli plays Ruth Zilbermann, a woman who survived the Holocaust by escaping from a transport to Auschwitz. Here she projects the quiet desperation of a woman who must survive in an environment of hostility. In *Eve Dönüs* (*Home Coming*, Ömer Ugur, 2006), Kekilli again plays a Turkish woman, married to a man interrogated and wrongfully jailed for terrorism.

KERN, PETER (1949–). Peter Kern began his career in **New German Cinema**, where his corpulence suited him for the German new wave's preference for outsiders. He was cast mostly in supporting roles, but had the lead in *Flammende Herzen* (*Flaming Hearts*, Walter Bockmayer and Rolf Bührmann, 1978), a film about a lonely man named Peter who wins a trip to New York City. In New York, he becomes a fish out of water, even after being befriended by a German couple, whose German-American Club festivities provide some of the absurd humor in the film. His friendship with a stripper at first promises salvation for Peter but ends in disaster when he wins a cow and his new girlfriend objects to walking around with an animal. The film, which mixes the absurd with the serious, allows Kern to reveal a man whose absurdity leads to true pathos.

Kern has had supporting roles in the films of many of West Germany's auteur or independent filmmakers. He had multiple roles in **Hans-Jürgen Syberberg**'s *Hitler, ein Film aus Deutschland* (*Hitler, a Film from Germany*, 1977), played a hormone specialist in **Monika Treut**'s *Die Jungfrauenmaschine* (*The Virgin Machine*, 1988), and played a Yiddish actor in **Ulrike Ottinger**'s *Johanna d'Arc of Mongolia* (*Joan of Arc of Mongolia*, 1989). Kern is also an independent producer and director of primarily low-budget films.

KINO: GERMAN FILM. A film magazine started by Ronald Holloway and his wife, actress Dorothea Moritz, in 1979 with a subsidy from the **Filmförderungsanstalt** (federal film board), *Kino: German Film* (not to be confused with *Kino*, the title before 2004 of *German Films*, the publication of **German Films Service + Marketing GmbH**), appears three or four times annually, with special issues appearing irregularly. The publication contains reports of film festivals, interviews, and movie and book reviews. The federal film board stopped its subsidy in 1981, requiring the Holloways to finance the publication through subscriptions and assistance from *inter nationes* (a government supported cultural institution) and subsequently from the Goethe Institute, after it absorbed this organization. The Holloways write most of the reviews and have expanded the publication to include special issues on films of Eastern Europe. Ron Holloway also covered German film for *Variety* in Berlin.

KINSKI, KLAUS (1926–1991). Klaus Kinski was a fiend extraordinaire of German stage and screen throughout his career. His grand gestures, mannerisms, and extreme emotions typecast him as an obsessive, terrifying monster or sympathetic psychotic in a series of films in Italy, Germany, and the United States. He appeared in over 130 films and although he often took roles just to get money to finance his poetry readings and stage projects, Kinski was in a number of highly acclaimed films. Early in his career he appeared in films that for their day were unusual in their willingness to bring up Germany's recent past: *Morituri* (*Morituri*, Eugen York, 1948), *Kinder, Mütter, und ein General* (*Children, Mothers, and a General*, László Benedek, 1955), and *Hanussen* (*Hanussen*, **Otto Wilhelm Fischer**, 1955). In the 1950s, he also appeared in **Helmut Käutner**'s *Ludwig II* (*Ludwig*, 1955) and **Douglas Sirk**'s *A Time to Love and a Time to Die* (1958).

The films Kinski made under **Werner Herzog** are his most memorable, both for the range in acting that he achieves and because of the volatile relationship the two men had with each other on the sets of the films. Documented in *Mein liebster Feind—Klaus Kinski* (*My Best Fiend*, 1999), Herzog's documentary on their relationship, the director and actor engaged in mind games, each antagonizing the other until verbal and sometimes physical violence broke out. Kinski said of Herzog that he was "an Adolf Hitler," and there were reports that the director kept his actors from rebelling in the Amazon jungle only by holding a gun on them, an event included in *Mein liebster Feind*. Yet Herzog's megalomania only seems to have brought Kinski to new heights of emotionalism as the crazed dictatorial conquistador in *Aguirre, der Zorn Gottes* (*Aguirre, the Wrath of God*, 1972); the hideous, yet erotic, monster of *Nosferatu—Phantom der Nacht* (*Nosferatu the Vampyre*, 1979); and the exploited, psychotic soldier in *Woyzeck* (*Woyzeck*, 1979), who is driven to murdering his common-law wife because of the voices in his head. Other films made with Herzog include *Fitzcarraldo* (*Fitzcarraldo*, 1982) and *Cobra Verde* (*Slave Coast*, 1987).

Among Kinski's non-German credits are *Per qualche dollaro in più* (*For a Few Dollars More*, Sergio Leone, 1965), as a hunchback; *Dr. Zhivago* (David Lean, 1965), *Marquis de Sade: Justine* (Jesus Franco, 1969), as de Sade; *Jack the Ripper* (Jesus Franco, 1975), as the murderous title character; and *The Little Drummer Girl* (George Roy Hill, 1983–1984), as a Mossad agent. Kinski won an Award in Gold (*see* **film awards**) from the Deutsche Filmakademie (German Film Academy) in 1979 for his role as the vampire in Herzog's *Nosferatu. See also* NEW GERMAN CINEMA.

KINSKI, NASTASSIA (1959–). Daughter of legendary film actor **Klaus Kinski**, Nastassia Kinski appeared in several films, including **Wim Wenders**'s *Falsche Bewegung* (*False Movement*, 1975), before gaining wide exposure as a troubled teen in *Tatort—Reifezeugnis* (*For Your Eyes Only*, **Wolfgang Petersen**, 1976) an episode of *Tatort* (*Scene of the Crime*, 1970–), a popular and long-running German detective series. She won international recognition when cast as the title character in Roman Polanski's *Tess*, based on Thomas Hardy's novel *Tess of the D'Urbervilles*, for which she won a Golden Globe as best newcomer in 1981.

After *Tess*, Kinski seemed assured of a good career in motion pictures. In 1982, she starred as the cat woman in Paul Schrader's *Cat*

People, a successful remake of the 1942 film by Jacques Tourneur, starring legendary French actress Simone Simon. *Cat People* allowed Kinski to showcase her developing persona of erotic yet vulnerable innocent, on display again in Wenders's *Paris, Texas* (1984), in which she plays a woman who abandons husband and child and ends up working in an erotic peep show before being reunited with her child. Kinski's success in these two movies, however, was not repeated. Since 1984 she has appeared in over 50 films in Germany, France, Italy, Canada, and the United States. Many of these are made-for-television movies, and others can be classified as B or nonmajor productions. Exceptions to this are Wenders's art film *In weiter Ferne, so nah!* (*Faraway, So Close!*, 1993), in which she plays Raphaela, one of the angels overseeing humankind, and *Les liaisons dangereuses* (*Dangerous Liaisons*, Josée Dayan, 2003), a big-budget television miniseries based on Choderlos de Laclos's epistolary novel of 1782, which has been filmed more than 10 times.

KLUGE, ALEXANDER (1932–). Alexander Kluge is unquestionably the intellectual force behind **Young German Cinema**, the new wave in German filmmaking initiated at the Oberhausen Film Festival in 1962 with the proclamation of new rules for cinema, known since as the **Oberhausen Manifesto**. As one of the signers of the manifesto, Kluge, a practicing lawyer, used his knowledge of the law, his skills as a writer, and his training as a filmmaker—he had assisted **Fritz Lang** when that director returned briefly to Germany in the 1950s— to gain international recognition and respect for alternative German cinema. As a member of various film advisory boards, Kluge was instrumental in persuading government cultural agencies to subsidize German filmmaking.

In his essays on film, Kluge championed a new type of cinema for German directors. Influenced by the political films of French director Jean-Luc Godard, Kluge called for a cinema of association, of contrasting visual and aural images, reminiscent of the montage theories of Sergei Eisenstein and Vsevolod Pudovkin, the Russian film pioneers of the 1920s, but going beyond their dialectical model of "thesis plus antithesis equals synthesis." Kluge wanted to do more than direct viewers into synthetic images; he wanted to create a new way for viewers to see. From often contradictory bits and pieces of visual and aural imagery, the viewer is to construct the ultimate meaning of the film: Kluge's film theory held that "the film is put together in the viewer's head, and is not a work of art that exists for its own sake on the screen."

Kluge is a director's director. As such, his works have garnered awards, influenced other directors, and elicited praise from film historians, but they have not had the commercial success of the films of **Rainer Werner Fassbinder** or **Wim Wenders**, two filmmakers very much influenced by him. The distribution of his films in the United States has been limited mainly to showings in metropolitan areas and retrospective screenings sponsored by the Goethe Institute or other cultural institutions. His films' innovative narrative techniques, however, earn for Kluge a leading position in German cinema.

Most well-known and most accessible to viewers is Kluge's *Abschied von gestern*, (*Yesterday Girl*, 1966), a breakthrough film for the Young German Cinema that won the Silver Lion award at the Venice Film Festival and an Award in Gold (*see* **film awards**) from the Deutsche Filmakademie (German Film Academy). The film contains most of the stylistic features that were to become Kluge's trademarks: handheld camera, off-center framing of characters, lay acting, contrasting aural and visual tracks, and associative editing of images. The themes in *Abschied von gestern* also recur in his other films. For example, the influence of the past on the present, generational conflict, political confrontation, and the contrast between public and private discourse provide the major content of the multivoiced *Die Artisten in der Zirkuskuppel: Ratlos* (*Artists under the Bigtop: Perplexed*, 1968), a film that indeed perplexed many critics because of its loose structure and abundance of metanarrative texts. Nonetheless it won a Golden Lion at the Venice Film Festival.

Kluge's other important films include the omnibus film *Deutschland im Herbst* (*Germany in Autumn*, 1978), for which Kluge directed an episode. *Deutschland im Herbst* was a response from the country's leading leftist filmmakers to reflect and memorialize the political climate in Germany following a series of incidents involving suspected terrorists. *Der starke Ferdinand* (*Strongman Ferdinand*, 1976) is a tragicomic film about a fascistic security guard who turns to terrorism, and *Die Patriotin* (*The Patriot* 1979) is about a teacher who rejects the historical materials available to her for teaching. *Die Patriotin* won an

Award in Silver from the Deutsche Filmakademie. Kluge gave up filmmaking in the late 1980s. He no longer wanted to be an auteur, as he felt films should be made in collaboration with others, but he also wanted to devote his time to producing cultural programs and news documentaries for German television.

KNEF, HILDEGARD (1925–2002). Hildegard Knef (also billed as Hildegard Neff) became a star with her first major film role as Susanne Wallner in *Die Mörder sind unter uns* (*The Murderers Are among Us*, **Wolfgang Staudte**, 1946). In this **rubble film**, which takes place among the ruins of Berlin in postwar Germany, Knef embodies the optimism and spirit of justice that Germans would require to come to terms with the past and rebuild their country. The actress appeared in two more rubble films, *Zwischen gestern und morgen* (*Between Yesterday and Tomorrow*, Harald Braun, 1947) and *Film ohne Titel* (*Film without a Title*, Rudolf Jugert, 1948), before causing a sensation in Germany when she appeared nude in a scene in *Die Sünderin* (*The Sinner*, **Willi Forst**, 1951), a film about a woman who prostitutes herself in order to support a terminally ill artist, whom she finally assists in a suicide. Religious institutions and much of the press saw the nudity and the themes of prostitution and euthanasia as affronts to moral values and condemned the film, no doubt increasing its commercial success. The notoriety Knef gained by appearing in the film brought her an invitation to Hollywood, where she appeared in *Decision before Dawn* (Anatole Litvak, 1951), which takes place in Germany in the final months of World War II. A *New York Times* film critic wrote of the film: "As a watery-eyed hostess in a German café Hildegard Neff is affecting, too, conveying the pathos of desertion without making any piteous appeals."

In the early 1950s Knef appeared in several Hollywood films, playing sultry women. Because of her sensuous yet aloof persona and throaty voice, she was often compared to **Marlene Dietrich** and Greta Garbo. Yet Knef's American film career never developed the potential that many predicted. Her best film of the period is arguably *The Snows of Kilimanjaro* (Henry King, 1952), in which she sang two Cole Porter tunes, indicating the direction that her later career would take. In 1955, she was invited by Porter to star in his Broadway show *Silk Stockings*, a musical version of Ninotchka, Garbo's signature role. The play and Knef were a hit, running for two and a half years. In the 1960s, Knef became a cabaret singer in the style of Dietrich, and after her 1970 autobiography, *Der geschenkte Gaul* (*The Gift Horse*), became a best-seller in Germany and the United States, she was quoted in *Variety* as saying "I shall never do another movie unless poverty forces me to." She broke her vow a number of times though, most notably in *Jeder stirbt für sich allein* (*Everyone Dies His Own Death*, Alfred Vohrer, 1976), in which she plays a mother in Nazi Germany opposed to the regime. In 1977, Knef received an Award in Gold (*see* **film awards**) from the Deutsche Filmakademie (German Film Academy) in recognition of her life's achievement in film. Knef acted up to her death in 2002, appearing in films and television shows in America and Germany.

KNUTH, GUSTAV (1901–1987). Gustav Knuth began acting during the Third Reich, playing men who were the opposite of the heroic, strapping ideal of the Nazis. His characters were generally shy and withdrawn. Two of his major roles during this time were in films that were not in general release until after the Third Reich was defeated. In *Große Freiheit # 7* (*Port of Freedom*, **Helmut Käutner**, 1944), he plays a shy sailor who finds love in a cabaret in the Reeperbahn, the red light district of Hamburg where the street of the title is located. The film was released only in German-occupied lands, not in Germany itself, because of the setting. In *Unter den Brücken* (*Under the Bridges*, 1945), considered by many critics to be Käutner's best movie, Knuth played a sensitive boatman in a love triangle consisting of two tugboat operators and their girlfriend. Knuth shows impeccable timing in the film's choreographed set pieces, when his character walks in and around a restaurant and then a museum, not realizing his rival is present. In Käutner's *Himmel ohne Sterne* (*Sky without Stars*, 1955), he plays the father of the lead character trying to get to West Berlin. In the three decades after the war, Knuth appeared in character roles in over 100 films. Two of his better-remembered were as a slick theater director in *Der Raub der Sabinerinnen* (*The Abduction of the Sabin Women*, **Kurt Hoffmann**, 1954), a farcical comedy that displayed Knuth's comic timing, as did many of his postwar films, and in *Die Mücke* (*The Mosquito*, Walter Reisch, 1954), in which he portrayed a weapons dealer on the black market, one of the few times he played a negative character. Knuth also appeared in supporting roles in the *Sissi* films (*see* **Schneider, Romy**); in *08/15* (*08/15*, Paul May, 1955), one of the many **war films** of the 1950s focusing on enlisted men rather than Nazism; and in numerous television shows.

KRACAUER, SIEGFRIED (1889–1966). Siegfried Kracauer was a film theorist and historian whose two major works, *From Caligari to Hitler* (1947) and *Theory of Film: The Redemption of Physical Reality* (1960), have become part of the canon of film history. In the first, Kracauer analyzes the films of the Weimar Republic (1918–1933), constructing from them a fascinating psychogram of the German people that purports to demonstrate that the country was destined to produce an Adolf Hitler. Kracauer's conclusions are sometimes simplistic and his arguments circular. His work has nonetheless remained an important source of information about German film in the 1920s and early 1930s. Kracauer describes and analyses dozens of films classified according to content. These include *Fridericus Rex* films, street films, **mountain films**, and horror films.

In *Theory of Film: The Redemption of Reality*, using Italian neorealism as a point of departure, Kracauer develops an ethical theory of filmmaking based on the precepts of realism. Unlike **Rudolf Arnheim**, the other major German film theorist, who believed that the motion picture must exploit its inability to reproduce reality, Kracauer prescribed reproducing reality and life as closely as possible. As with Arnheim's work, the book suffers from the author's dogmatic insistence that films must follow a realist paradigm—for Arnheim it was a formalist paradigm—if they are to be worth viewing. In spite of its limitations, *Theory of Film* remains an important statement of the realist principle of filmmaking and also offers a thorough analysis of Italian neorealism.

KRAUS, PETER (1939–). Peter Kraus (Peter Siegfried Krausenecker) is a pop singer-actor contemporary to Roy Black, **Gus Backus**, **Peter Alexander**, and Heintje, whose film careers rested primarily on their popularity as singers in a number of West German musicals of the late 1950s and the 1960s. Kraus had appeared as a teenager in such popular films as *Das fliegende Klassenzimmer* (*The Flying Classroom*, **Kurt Hoffmann**, 1954), based on Erich Kästner's children's crime thriller of the same title, and *Die Frühreifen* (*The Rowdies*, **Josef von Báky**, 1957), one of several teenage delinquent dramas in the 1950s. But it was not until he was paired with **Cornelia Froboess** in *Wenn die Conny mit dem Peter* (*When Conny and Peter Do It Together*, Fritz Umgelter, 1958) and *Conny und Peter machen Musik* (*Conny and Peter Make Music*, Werner Jacobs, 1960) that his popularity soared. Kraus made a number of musicals, most of which featured him singing the latest pop tune or *Schlager*, but appeared in dramas as well, including a role as Josef Strauss in Walt Disney's production of *The Waltz King* (Steve Previn, 1963), a musical biography of Johann Strauss Jr. In 1986, he had a supporting role opposite Froboess in *Der Sommer des Samurai* (*The Summer of the Samurai*, Hans-Christoph Blumenberg), a mystery drama about a German Samurai in search of a stolen sword.

KRAUSS, WERNER (1884–1959). Werner Krauss acted in more than 125 movies between 1914 and 1955, all but a dozen of them before the advent of sound. His portrayal of Dr. Caligari, the deranged psychiatrist in **Robert Wiene**'s *Das Cabinet des Dr. Caligari* (*The Cabinet of Dr. Caligari*, 1920), established him as the foremost expressionist actor of German silent film. His Caligari created a visual cliché of the crazed scientist that has become an icon of Weimar Germany films. In his role as the mad doctor, whose madness turns out to be a figment of the imagination of an inmate in Caligari's mental institution, Krauss exaggerates his crooked body, his crippled gait, and his tortured face to the point of abstractions that perfectly match the abstract shapes of the decor. Other films that demonstrate Krauss's expressionist craft and his ability to use outward appearance to reflect his inner state of being are *Hoffmanns Erzählungen* (*Tales of Hoffmann*, **Richard Oswald**, 1916), *Herr Tartüff* (*Tartuffe*, **Friedrich Wilhelm Murnau**, 1925), *Geheimnisse einer Seele* (*Confessions of a Soul*, **Georg Wilhelm Pabst**, 1926), and *Der Student von Prag* (*The Student of Prague*, **Henrik Galeen**, 1926), in the last of which he plays Scapinelli, the strange man who lends the student Balduin money, only to steal his mirror image.

Although he made only a few films during the Third Reich, Krauss was an important film presence for the Nazis. In 1934, Joseph Goebbels awarded him the title Staatsschauspieler (State Actor), an honor afforded film actors who also acted on stage and whose work contributed to the National Socialist cause. Few in number, Krauss's films during the Third Reich nonetheless included high-profile works that were made by major directors, included other stars, and added to the historical national identity that the Nazis were creating. Thus the actor appeared in *Robert Koch* (*Robert Koch*, Hans Steinhoff, 1939), starring **Emil Jannings**, in *Paracelsus* (*Paracelsus*, **Georg Wilhelm Pabst**, 1943), in which he played the misunderstood title character; and in *Die Entlassung* (*Bismarck's Dismissal*, **Wolfgang Liebeneiner**, 1942), one of several films about the Second Empire's strong-willed chancellor. These films, as well as other biographies of strong personalities fighting the mainstream, were part of a series of heroic National Socialist biographies that critics sometimes see as portraying stand-ins for Adolf Hitler.

Beyond doubt, Krauss's engagement with National Socialism is most evident in **Veit Harlan**'s notorious anti-Semitic film *Jud Süß* (*Jew Süss*, 1940). Playing all the Jewish speaking roles, except that of Süß Oppenheimer, Krauss displays the negative stereotypes of Jews that were familiar to non-Jews at the time from theater and film. As various characters, he speaks nonstandard German, flails the air with his hands when he talks, focuses on money, and presents an untidy appearance. One aspect is positive, however, in that he criticizes Süß Oppenheimer for abandoning the Jewish religion by siding with the Duke of Württemberg. Krauss's work on *Jud Süß*, a film the Allies thought too overtly propagandistic, and which is still not available in Germany, kept him out of films and off the stage immediately after the collapse of the Third Reich, as it did for many of the film's participants. But the actor was able to get work again after 1948, especially on the stage, and was honored in 1954 with the Iffland Ring, Austria's prestigious acting award, and with *das Große Bundesverdienstkreuz* (High Medal of Service), one of Germany's highest honors for public figures.

KRETSCHMANN, THOMAS (1962–). One of a number of young German actors of the 1990s and 2000s to achieve recognition in a revival of German film (*see also* **Bleibtreu, Moritz; Fürmann, Benno; Potente, Franka; Riemann, Katja; and Schweiger, Til**), Thomas Kretschmann received recognition for his role as idealistic

KRÓL, JOACHIM • 181

lieutenant Hans von Witzland in *Stalingrad* (*Stalingrad*, Joseph Vilsmaier, 1993), based on the defeat of the German Sixth Army at Stalingrad, in the battle that signaled the ultimate end of the Third Reich.
Kretschmann's portrayal of an officer whose idealism turns to cynicism and then to depression revealed emotional range that brought
him to the attention of German and international directors, including
those in Hollywood. Kretschmann again portrays a German officer in
U-571 (Jonathan Mostow, 2000), in which he is the captain of a submarine boarded by Americans to capture a decoding device, and in
The Pianist (Roman Polanski, 2002), in which he portrays the only
good German in the film, a captain who befriends a Jewish refugee
hiding from the Nazis. In *Der Untergang* (*The Downfall*, **Oliver
Hirschbiegel**, 2004), Kretschmann plays Hermann Fegelein, the notorious womanizing SS officer, who was Adolf Hitler's brother-in-
law. In addition to his many theatrical films, Kretschmann has appeared in numerous television series, including Germany's crime
show *Derrick* (*Derrick*, 1974–1998), Hollywood's sci-fi *Total Recall
2070* (1999), and the terrorist thriller *24* (2003).

KRÓL, JOACHIM (1957–). Joachim Król's double-take facial expressions, comic timing, and ability to project sincerity make him a
favorite with critics and the public. He received wide recognition after winning an Award in Gold (*see* **film awards**) two years in a row:
in 1993 for portraying an illiterate man who travels with his brother
across Germany to claim an inheritance, in the comedy *Wir können
auch anders* (*No More Mr. Nice Guy*, **Detlev Buck**), and in 1994 for
his role as Norbert in the comedy *Der bewegte Mann* (*Maybe . . .
Maybe Not*, Sönke Wortmann), in which he played the gay roommate
of a heterosexual looking for a place to live. Król has had roles in the
films of Germany's most successful directors. He has played supporting parts for **Doris Dörrie**, **Tom Tykwer**, and **Helmut Dietl**. In
particular, his cheeky airport security guard in Dörrie's *Keiner liebt
mich* (*Nobody Loves Me*, 1994), drunken homeless man in Tykwer's
Lola rennt (*Run Lola Run*, 1998), and introverted author of a best-
seller in Dietl's *Rossini* (*Rossini*, 1997) reveal his range of comedy
from subtle sitcom to farcical slapstick. Król's dramatic roles include
one of the leads in *Gloomy Sunday—Ein Lied von Liebe und Tod*
(*Gloomy Sunday*, Rolf Schübel, 1999), as a club owner involved in a

love triangle during World War II. Król also played Detective Guido Brunetti in the television adaptation of four novels of popular mystery writer Donna Leon (*Donna Leon*, 2000–).

KURATORIUM JUNGER DEUTSCHER FILM. Established in 1965, several years after the proclamation of the **Oberhausen Manifesto**, the Kuratorium Junger Deutscher Film (Young German Film Board) received as its charge to implement the proposals of the Oberhausen directors and to draw funds from the cultural budgets of the federal states. In its first three years, operating with starting capital of 5 million marks, the board sponsored 20 features, including films by **Alexander Kluge**, **Werner Herzog**, and Hansjürgen Pohland. Although support was in the form of loans, generally DM 300,000, in truth the money was often not repaid.

In 1967, after the establishment of the **Filmförderungsanstalt** (federal film board), the Young German Film Board lost its direct funding from the Ministry of Interior and ceased to be an important source of assistance. *See also* NEW GERMAN CINEMA.

– L –

LAMPRECHT, GÜNTER (1930–). Günter Lamprecht has had a long career on German television, appearing in a number of crime shows and thrillers as well as comedies. His bulky physical presence ideally suits him to play character parts, particularly those from the lower middle class. In *Die Ehe der Maria Braun* (*The Marriage of Maria Braun*, **Rainer Werner Fassbinder**, 1979), he played the lusty boarder of Maria's mother as an awkward but welcome lover. His best-known role was as Franz Biberkopf in Fassbinder's epic miniseries *Berlin Alexanderplatz* (*Berlin Alexanderplatz*, 1980), based on Alfred Döblin's novel about an ex-convict trying to rehabilitate himself in 1920s Berlin. Lamprecht portrayed Biberkopf as an inarticulate wretch, whose chance at happiness is thwarted at every turn by circumstances he cannot control. Lamprecht also had supporting roles in the television version of **Wolfgang Petersen**'s *Das Boot* (*The Boat*, 1984) and Joseph Vilsmaier's *Comedian Harmonists* (*The Harmonists*, 1997).

LANDGREBE, GUDRUN (1950–). Gudrun Landgrebe received international recognition for her portrayal of Eva, a divorcee turned call girl, in *Die flambierte Frau* (*A Woman in Flames*, Robert van Ackeren, 1983). Landgrebe's Eva reflects awakening interest in feminism, which appeared later in Germany than France or the United States (*see also* **Brückner, Jutta; Export, Valie;** *Frauenfilm;* **Ottinger, Ulrike; Sander, Helke; Sanders-Brahms, Helma; Treut, Monika; and Von Trotta, Margarethe**). Eva was also a reincarnation of the femme fatale from the 1920s, an independent spirit, self-assured in her sexuality. Although she has played other parts, Landgrebe's screen persona has become associated with that of a woman who wants to control her own destiny.

LANG, FRITZ (1890–1976). Fritz Lang had two distinct and successful careers as a filmmaker: the first from 1919 to 1933 in Germany as the director of silent and early sound films, and the second in Hollywood from 1933 until 1956 as the director of studio films. Before retiring from directing he returned to Germany, making several films that reprised themes from his early silent films. While many critics and film historians feel that his best work was accomplished in Germany, others, in particular French critics of the periodical *Cahiers du cinéma*, believe that his Hollywood films show more of his qualities as an auteur director. Whereas in Germany Lang had control of his films and thus could create according to his personal visions, in Hollywood he had to create within the constraints imposed by the studio system. Whether made in Germany or Hollywood, Lang's films are characterized by an expressionistic style, which he often disavowed having, and a dark and fatalistic tone, even when Hollywood appended a happy ending. Lang is best known for three films from his German period: *Die Nibelungen* (*The Nibelungen*, 1924), *Metropolis* (*Metropolis*, 1927) and *M* (*M*, 1931).

Lang based *Die Nibelungen*, consisting of two separate films, *Siegfrieds Tod* (*Death of Siegfried*) and *Kriemhilds Rache* (*Kriemhild's Revenge*), on the original medieval epic rather than Richard Wagner's opera. Movie legend claims *Die Nibelungen* as Adolf Hitler's favorite film, its rhythmic movements, action scenes, ornamental patterns, monumental architecture, and mythical heroic story appealing to the Nazi love of pageantry, soldierly virtues, inexorable fate, and death. Its influence may be seen in the spectacular party rallies later designed by Albert Speer when the Nazis came to power and in the way **Leni Riefenstahl** manipulates human form in *Triumph des Willens* (*Triumph of the Will*, 1935), her documentation of the Nazi Party rally held in Nuremberg in 1934. In spite of such dubious endorsement of the film's power, however, there is no denying that it is magnificent. Restored prints reveal Lang's genius for manipulating crowd scenes, his eye for spatial relationships, and his effective use of portentous—detractors might call them pretentious—symbols.

When in 1984 Giorgio Moroder recut and colorized *Metropolis*—according to him to restore it to its original form—for re-release, he not only introduced a whole new generation to Lang's visionary genius but also reopened the debate about the film's confused and confusing plot. For although the images and special effects of *Metropolis*, created by **Eugen Schüfftan**, are indeed dazzling, the story about a savior from the upper middle class who is able to unite workers and industrialists is not merely muddled but a bit silly. In addition, the film has some of the most exaggerated acting found in silent film. Spanish filmmaker Luis Buñuel commented that it "was two films glued together by their bellies." And noted film critic and historian **Lotte Eisner**, a lifelong friend of Lang, wrote that the film was "an exaggerated dream of the New York skyline, multiplied a thousand-fold and divested of all reality."

Lang's greatest legacy is *M*, a film based on the Düsseldorf child murderer Peter Kürten and the Hanover serial killer Fritz Haarmann. As directed by Lang in his first sound picture, the story takes on the same themes of fate, ambiguity of good and evil, and revenge found in most of his films. Here, however, using overlapping sound, parallel editing, and foreboding urban landscapes, he crafted a film more focused and unified than any of his silent masterpieces. As played by **Peter Lorre**, the schizophrenic murderer of the Weimar tabloids, here called Becker, is beset by voices that he can quiet only by killing children. The role won Lorre an international following and typecast him as a sinister villain, sometimes maniacal but also vulnerable, a persona he cultivated until his death.

Lang turned down an offer from Joseph Goebbels to head the film office of the Ministry of Propaganda. Leaving behind his wife **Thea von Harbou**, who became a Nazi collaborator and whom he soon afterward divorced, Lang emigrated from Germany, first to France and eventually to Hollywood, where he forged a second career. His American films include anti-German propaganda films such as *Hangmen Also Die* (1943), from a screenplay written by fellow émigré **Bertolt Brecht**, and *Ministry of Fear* (1944). He also directed successful genre films, in particular Westerns and films noirs. One of his more successful films noirs is *The Big Heat* (1953), about the dehumanizing quest for vengeance, a recurring Lang theme since the director's silent film days. After directing the murder mystery *Beyond a Reasonable Doubt* (1956), Lang returned to Europe, directing *Der Tiger von Eschnapur* (*The Tiger of Eschnapur*, 1959) and *Das Indische Grabmal* (*The Indian Tomb*, 1959), both based on the two-part film *Das indische Grabmal* (Joe May, 1921), for which Lang and von Harbou wrote the screenplay. His last film was *Die Tausend Augen des Dr. Mabuse* (*The Thousand Eyes of Dr. Mabuse*, 1960), a return to the mysterious hero of his Weimar films *Dr. Mabuse, der Spieler* (*Dr. Mabuse, the Gambler*, 1922) and *Das Testament des Dr. Mabuse* (*The Testament of Dr. Mabuse*, 1933.)

LEANDER, ZARAH (1902–1981 [birthdate also given as 1900 and 1907]). Zarah Leander began her career in Sweden, where between 1929 and 1936 she gained little notice as a concert singer and actress. After successful appearances in German-language works in Austria, first the stage musical *Axel an der Himmelstür* (*Axel at the Gates of Heaven*, 1936) and then the revue film *Premiere* (*Premiere*, Géza von Bolváry, 1937), **Universum Film AG** (Ufa)—the major German film studio founded in 1917 and brought under National Socialist control during the Third Reich—offered her a major contract. The studio experimented with Leander's hairstyle, makeup, clothes, figure, appearance, and voice, creating a screen persona that was the National Socialist film industry's most glamorous, exotic, and seductive creation. Ufa composed new melodies for her and commissioned Detlev Sierck (**Douglas Sirk**) to direct her in two melodramatic love stories: *Zu neuen Ufern* (*To New Shores*, 1937) and *La Habanera* (*La Habanera*, 1937). For the National Socialist film industry, Leander became a substitute for **Marlene Dietrich** and Greta Garbo, two Weimar-era actresses who had left Germany for Hollywood. Like Dietrich, Leander had a sultry singing voice and sexy presence, and like Garbo, she spoke German with a slight but pleasing Swedish accent.

Leander owes her success only partially to the star treatment she received at Ufa and her makeover as a replacement for Dietrich and Garbo. For in addition to her elegance, beauty, and well-tempered alto voice, she also had no competition from German actresses for the roles she played. Official National Socialist policy prevented German-born actresses from being cast as promiscuous, seductive, and independent women. As a result, roles in which women displayed even a touch of these traits were given to three actresses. **Kristina Söderbaum**, also Swedish, played ingénues who were seduced by men more worldly and sophisticated than she. **Marika Rökk**, a Hungarian who had established her career in New York and London, often played actresses and dancers, professions that were morally suspect. Leander appeared as a free-spirited temptress, in lowcut dresses and with a sultry, seductive voice. Whereas one could feel sorry for the characters Söderbaum played and marvel at the athleticism and energy Rökk brought to her dancing, one could fall in love with Leander. Her persona captured audiences weary of screen portrayals that reflected the National Socialist line of chaste, subservient German women.

As a major film star, however, Leander also served National Socialist ideology, and thus her screen femme fatale never got the man. Indeed, she was famous for her ability to portray resignation and sacrifice as much as passion, offering a role model of sorts to women whose husbands were away at war. Her ability to emote confidence and courage is nowhere more apparent than in *Die große Liebe* (*The Great Love*, Rolf Hansen, 1942). Entertaining a troop of wounded soldiers in France and having heard that Germany had just attacked the Soviet Union, thus expanding the war and pushing off the day she will be reunited with her lover, Leander's screen character sings "Davon geht die Welt nicht unter" ("This Won't Cause the World to End"), as the soldiers link arms and sway back and forth to the music. This song, together with "Ich weiß, es wird einmal ein Wunder geschehen" ("I Know, There Will Be a Miracle"), became Leander's signature melodies, comforting her fans during the war and commenting ironically on the war after Germany's defeat.

After the war, Leander was forbidden to work until 1948. Although she was never able to recapture the success she had had as a film ac-

tress, she remained one of Germany's most popular singers and entertainers until her death. In 1984, **Edgar Reitz** paid Leander homage in
his successful miniseries *Heimat—Eine deutsche Chronik* (*Heimat:
A Chronicle of Germany*), when two of the women in the film sit in
front of a mirror trying to duplicate the Leander hairstyle. Camp
cabaret artists also frequently mimic Leander's persona, singing her
best-known songs and wearing her highly stylized costumes.

LIEBENEINER, WOLFGANG (1905–1987). Wolfgang Liebeneiner
began his career as an actor during the 1930s, playing military officers, lovers, and musicians. His skill as a stage director earned him a
position as film director after smaller studios were brought together
under a larger Nazi umbrella organization and the new studio thought
fresh talent was needed. Liebeneiner displayed technical skill and a
fluid style of filmmaking that placed him above most other directors
of the period and ensured him a successful career after the war.

Liebeneiner, who was important to Nazi film production, directed
films of entertainment but also of propaganda. After the war, he ex-
cused his propaganda efforts by pointing to the fact he never joined
the party and that he had helped Jews escape persecution and out-of-
favor film workers get jobs, which assertions were supported by eye-
witnesses. Nevertheless, his films certainly supported Nazi ideology,
sometimes egregiously so. *Ich klage an* (*I Accuse*, 1941), the most
notorious example, supports the National Socialist program of euthanasia. The film tells of a medical doctor who administers a lethal
dose of medicine to his debilitated wife at her request. In the ensuing
trial for murder, he argues for the humanitarian aspect of his act, and
the National Socialist prosecutorial board argues for a restrictive policy on assisted suicide. Away from its historical context, the film
seems to be a plea consistent with progressive thought current in
Western culture. Looking at the film from its position in history, *Ich
klage an* reveals an ominous subtext. A year earlier, the short cultural
film *Das Opfer* (*The Sacrifice*) called for the euthanasia of the mentally retarded by showing scenes intended to frighten Germans into
accepting a program of sanctioned killing. The plan, however, back-
fired and Germans, in particular church leaders, objected to killing
mentally ill patients. At the time of *Das Opfer*, the government propaganda ministry also released a virulently anti-Semitic film, *Der*

ewige Jude (*The Eternal Jew*, Hippler, 1940), which characterized
Jews as parasites within German culture, similar to how the mentally
disabled had been presented. It is a fair assumption that *Ich klage an*
was a sanitized version of what the government had proposed in *Das
Opfer* and what was going to be proposed at the Wannsee Conference
two years later, a universal killing of Europe's Jews.

As most of Liebeneiner's films contained less egregious propaganda, he continued his career after the end of the war relatively
seamlessly. His 1949 film *Liebe 47* (*Love 47*), based on Wolfgang
Borchert's *Draußen vor der Tür* (*Outside the Door*), reversed the pessimism of the original, in which a man is rejected by everyone when
he returns from war, resulting in his eventual suicide. Liebeneiner,
borrowing from **Wolfgang Staudte**'s *Die Mörder sind unter uns* (*The
Murderers Are among Us*, 1946), turns a potential tragedy into an optimistic ending by allowing the man to find redemption through love.
For the rest of his career, Liebeneiner directed large commercial projects and small intimate films. As if wanting to defend his and other
National Socialist films as nonpropaganda, he made several remakes
in the 1950s, including, *Wenn eine Frau liebt* (*When a Woman Loves*,
1950), based on his film *Versprich mir nichts* (*Promise Me Nothing*,
1937); *Schlußakkord* (*Final Chord*, 1960), based on **Douglas Sirk**'s
1936 film of that title; *Franziska* (*Franziska*, 1959), a remake of **Helmut Käutner**'s *Auf Wiedersehen, Franziska!* (*Goodbye, Franziska!*,
1941); and *Jacqueline* (*Jacquline* 1959), originally filmed as *Nanette*
(*Nanette*, Erich Engel, 1940). Liebeneiner also had tremendous success with two films about the Austrian von Trapp family of singers,
Die Trapp-Familie (*The Trapp Family*, 1956) and *Die Trapp-Familie
in Amerika* (*The Trapp Family in America*, 1958). In the 1970s, he
was active as a director on West German television.

LILIENTHAL, PETER (1929–). Having emigrated from Berlin to
Montevideo, Uruguay, with his parents in 1939 to escape persecution
by the Nazis, Peter Lilienthal returned in 1956 to attend film school. By
the time of *Malatesta* (*Malatesta*, 1970), his first feature film, Lilienthal had directed close to 20 television films, establishing himself as a
director of engaging stories told with a distinct artistic style. Through
his television work and especially his subsequent feature films, he
earned a reputation in Germany as a left of center, liberal director of the

school of **New German Cinema**. In such films as *Es herrscht Ruhe im Land* (*Calm Prevails over the Country*, 1976), *La Insurrección* (*The Uprising*, 1980), and *Das Autogramm* (*The Autograph*, 1985), all winners of federal **film awards**, he champions the rights of the economically and politically oppressed in Latin America.

In spite of his reputation in Germany and his position within New German Cinema, Lilienthal is known in the United States for two films, *Dear Mr. Wonderful* (aka *Ruby's Dream*, 1982), starring Joe Pesci, and *David* (1979), which won a Golden Bear as best film at the **Berlin Film Festival**. Like the better-known *Europa Europa* (**Agnieszka Holland**, 1991), *David* tells the story of a young man who hides from the Nazis and eventually escapes Germany after his family is picked up for deportation to a concentration camp. The situation allows Lilienthal to explore the reaction of his hero under extremely adverse conditions, a theme that recurs in many of his films. The optimistic ending also echoes the hope found in many of his films. Lilienthal is reportedly surprised that many consider him a German director, as most of his feature films were shot outside of Germany. Yet this is understandable, as the bulk of his work has been financed by German production companies, he worked for German television for the first 10 years of his career and again after 1988, he has taught at the Deutsche Film- und Fernsehakademie (German Film and Television Academy), and he was a signer of the **Oberhausen Manifesto**. *See also* HOLOCAUST IN FEATURE FILMS; *VERGANGENHEITSBEWÄLTIGUNGSFILM*.

LINGEN, THEO (1903–1978). Theo Lingen was a character actor who played in more than 225 films between 1930 and his death in 1978. His staccato style of speaking made him instantly recognizable. A very physical actor, Lingen modeled his early roles after French silent actor Max Linder. Sometimes arrogant, sometimes put upon, Lingen's characters are average but uptight bureaucrats visited by catastrophe, which they overcome by the end of the film. He was also adept at playing servants in comedies of the 1930s and 1940s. In the 1950s, he appeared mainly in slapstick films with abundant visual gags, and he developed to mannerist farce his persona, already evident in his earlier films, of a nervous, hysterical individual who is able to unnerve everyone around him.

LOMMEL, ULLI (1944–). Ulli Lommel was a member of **Rainer Werner Fassbinder**'s repertoire troupe of actors, appearing in a dozen of the **New German Cinema** director's films. He played mostly small parts but had an important supporting role opposite **Hanna Schygulla** in Fassbinder's *Fontane Effi Briest* (*Effi Briest*, 1974). Lommel portrays Major Crampus, who has an affair with Effi that precipitates her tragic end, as a distanced, distracted suitor, a persona he relied on in his other films for Fassbinder as well.

Lommel is also a director of low-budget sci-fi, thriller, and slasher films. After the futuristic sci-fi drama *Haytabo* (*Haytabo*, 1971), with American-born Eddie Constantine (who was a cult favorite in France and Germany), he directed *Die Zärtlichkeit der Wölfe* (*The Tenderness of Wolves*, 1973), which tells the story of mass murderer Fritz Haarmann, who was one of the models for the serial killer in *M* (*M*, **Fritz Lang**, 1931). Whereas Lang focused on the psychology behind the murderer, Lömmel takes liberties with the facts and focuses on the homoerotic nature of a man who killed boys to feed them to his friends. Since 1980, Lommel has worked almost exclusively in Hollywood, turning out slasher and adventure films, which he directs, writes, and produces, and in which he often acts. Most have gone straight to video and carry titles such as *Boogeyman* (1980), *Boogeyman II* (1983), *Brain Wave* (1983), *Revenge of the Stolen Stars* (1985), *Bloodsuckers* (1998), and *Zodiac Killer* (2005).

LORRE, PETER (1904–1964). After acting on stage in Vienna and Zürich, Peter Lorre (the stage and screen name for László Loewenstein) relocated to Berlin, where **Bertolt Brecht** cast him in Marieluise Fleissers' *Pioniere in Ingolstadt* (*Pioneers in Ingolstadt*) in 1928, leading to a lifelong friendship between the two men. Lorre's stage work, particularly his starring role in Brecht's *Mann ist Mann* (*Man Is Man*) in Berlin in 1931, brought him the role of the schizophrenic child murderer in **Fritz Lang**'s film *M* (*M*, 1931). His tour de force performance as a mild and gentle man beset by voices that could be stilled only through murdering children won him a Hollywood contract but also typecast him as a psychopathic monster.

Lorre's portrayal of the mild-mannered killer entrenched itself in the public imagination, becoming an icon of evil and danger. Warner Brothers cartoons used the persona and voice in several of its cartoons. Seventy-five years after he played a serial killer and 40 years after his death, Lorre's persona is apparently still recognized, as Tim Burton gave the actor's voice and mannerisms to a creature in *Corpse Bride* (2005). The most notorious appropriation of Lorre's image as the child murderer, however, occurred in the Nazi anti-Semitic film *Der ewige Jude* (*The Eternal Jew*, Fritz Hippler, 1940). In this compilation documentary, Hippler uses music, art, film clips, newsreel footage, and reenactments to create fear and loathing of Jews. At one point, he inserts Lorre's portrayal of the serial killer in *M*, conflating the character with the actor Lorre himself, who was Jewish, suggesting that Jews have dubious morals.

Lorre traded on his image as a psychotic serial killer in *Der Verlorene* (*The Lost One*, 1951), a film he produced and directed and in which he played the starring role. Returning to Germany to direct this film, Lorre intended it as a means to help viewers come to terms with what had transpired during the Third Reich. In the film, Lorre plays a doctor whose gentle demeanor and profession as healer belie his alter ego as a serial killer. The National Socialist authorities know of his crimes but cover them up because they require his assistance in other matters. The film was a critical success. In some ways, however, reprising as it does his persona of gentle and kind mass murderer, the film further solidified Lorre's image as schizophrenic in the minds of the critics and public.

Although Lorre was typecast as a criminal, he played other roles for which he is also known. In the 1930s, he starred in eight comedic mysteries, playing the Asian detective Mr. Moto. In the 1940s, he played nefarious types in several films noirs, most notably in *Casablanca* and *The Maltese Falcon*, both starring Humphrey Bogart. But after the war, his film career faded. In the 1950s, Lorre revived his cinematic success on American television, appearing in episodes of *Alfred Hitchcock Presents*, *Studio 57*, *Schlitz Playhouse of Stars*, and *Climax Mystery Theater*. In the *Climax* series, he played a James Bond villain, Le Chiffre, in the film *Casino Royale* (William H. Brown Jr., 1957). In the 1960s, Lorre parodied his persona in Roger Corman's *Tales of Terrors* (1962) and *The Raven* (1962) and Jacques Tourneur's *The Comedy of Terror* (1963). Although he accepted his screen persona in order to work, Lorre denied that he was in horror films. He described them as films of "psychological terror."

LUBITSCH, ERNST (1892–1947). Ernst Lubitsch contributed brilliantly to film history in two distinct eras: the German silent film of the early 1920s and Hollywood film of the 1930s and 1940s. Beginning his career as an actor in comedy shorts in the 1910s in Germany, he quickly became a successful and respected director, alternating between comedies and costume epics. His early accomplishments brought him to Hollywood by 1923, where he continued to excel in historical dramas. In the 1930s, the sophisticated style of his musicals and comedies, which today form part of Hollywood's classic comedic repertoire, eclipsed his early silent dramatic epics.

Lubitsch's greatest silent films include *Madame Dubarry* (*Passion*, 1919) and *Anna Boleyn* (*Anne Boleyn*, 1920), costume dramas with elaborate sets, name stars, and thousands of extras. The films merge high dramatic form and entertainment, opening them up to a wider audience while at the same time still appealing to intellectuals. Lubitsch's screen epics offered the sweep of historical events, even if largely superficially, and the intimacy of individuals wrestling with private, nonhistorical, problems. These early movies display a visual style that focuses on objects or persons to comment on the emotions underlying the historical action. In these and the other films of his career, Lubitsch's strength lay in his presentation of sexual and psychological relationships and his avoidance of offering moral judgments.

Lubitsch's silent films also include nonhistorical melodramas, often based on literary sources, and comedies. In *Kohlhiesels Töchter* (*Kohlhiesel's Daughters*, 1920), starring **Henny Porten**, he shows his talent for slapstick humor. His filmed versions of operettas before the advent of sound—for example, *The Student Prince in Old Heidelberg* (1927) and *The Marriage Circle* (1923)—display the fluid style and satirical social commentary of his masterpieces of the sound era.

In his Hollywood sound films, Lubitsch added witty dialogue to his already recognizable visual style and clever stories to create what became known as the "Lubitsch touch." Although critics disagree about the precise ingredients of this style, it is accurate to say that the "Lubitsch touch" included his obsession with allowing objects and asides to comment on the story without necessarily showing the accompanying action. It is his way of telling the audience more than he allows them to see and of adding poignancy to happy moments. Lubitsch's best-known films from this era are *Ninotchka* (1939), *The Shop around the Corner* (1940), *To Be or Not to Be* (1942), and *Heaven Can Wait* (1943). All offer clear examples of the Lubitsch style. *Ninotchka* wryly tells about a Russian government official, played by Greta Garbo, who is sent to Paris to bring three emissaries seduced by capitalism back to Moscow, but who herself finds it easy to accept a decadent lifestyle once she falls in love. *The Shop around the Corner*, starring Jimmy Stewart and Margaret Sullavan, comments on the irony of love relationships. *To Be or Not To Be* joins other Hollywood films of the period—such as *The Great Dictator* (Charles Chaplin, 1940) and The Three Stooges' short *You Nazty Spy* (Jules White, 1940)—in lampooning National Socialism while addressing issues some were still unwilling to hear about. Finally, in *Heaven Can Wait*, Lubitsch plays on the power of true love as a philanderer is saved from Hell by the love of his wife. Lubitsch's power to evoke lasting images and stories imprinted these four movies on the popular culture of the time, so much so that all were remade decades later, and Garbo's *Ninotchka* became a pop culture artifact.

– M –

M. The legend surrounding *M*, **Fritz Lang**'s 1931 masterpiece of criminal psychology and the serial killer, reports that the film almost was not made for lack of a studio. It was originally scheduled to be shot at one of the stages at the **Babelsberg Studios**, but Lang was later told the studio was fully booked. After investigating the situation, which seemed strange to him, he discovered that conservatives were pressuring the studio to withhold space. They believed the film, whose tentative title was *Die Mörder sind unter uns* (*The Murderers Are among Us*), to be a political exposé of the Nazis. (After the war, there was indeed a film with this title by **Wolfgang Staudte**, warning about Nazis still present in postwar Germany [*see* **Vergangenheitsbewältigungsfilm**].) By the time the confusion was discovered and the name had been changed, Lang had found a studio and no longer needed space at Babelsberg.

M mirrors not the Nazi presence in Germany but Lang's desire to address the corruption and malaise of a society he saw existing in Germany's larger cities, especially Berlin. Searching for a story around which to illustrate this theme, he asked **Thea von Harbou**, his wife at the time, for a screenplay, but rejected her original ideas in favor of a film about a serial killer of children. Recognizing that no theme could represent the culture's ills more strongly, he used the case of the notorious murderer Peter Kürten, who had been arrested in May 1930 for killing nine people, not all children, and who had taunted police through letters to the newspaper about their inability to capture him. Fritz Haarmann, a serial killer of children in the early 1920s, also served as a model.

Lang's film tells a simple story. A number of children have been murdered, causing anxiety among the populace, which is hurting the reputation of the police, who in turn are harassing average criminals. Both groups undertake to find the killer. The criminals capture him first and put him on trial in a mock court, but before they can execute him, they are interrupted by the police. He is then tried and convicted in a legal court trial, but the film ends before sentence is passed. We hear one of the mothers remark that killing him won't bring their children back.

M's story may be simple, but its structure, visual imagery, and acting are rich in detail and meaning. The story has three separate acts: the murder of one child and the ensuing anguish it creates; the hunt by police and criminals for the killer; and the mock trial. During the first act, Lang develops suspense by withholding gruesome details, using suggestion rather than visual confrontation. A child's rhyme about a killer lurking in their environment introduces both the theme of killing and the naiveté of children in believing that they cannot be affected. An empty staircase introduces the concern of a mother whose child has not come home. An off-key whistle of a melody from the *Peer Gynt Suite* announces the presence of the murderer. A balloon stuck in electrical wires informs about the murder.

The second section is structured through parallel editing as a race between police and criminals. Besides adding a touch of humor to an otherwise dark narrative, the editing suggests the similarities between criminals and cops, which has become a cliché since *M* and was already present in French and German films in the 1910s. Lang cuts between smoke-filled rooms of cops and criminals discussing strategy, searches of premises looking for the murderer, and the two groups as they close in on the final hiding place.

Section three presents the mock trial. It is here that **Peter Lorre**, in his first film, creates his signatory persona. Lorre's bulging eyes, small but slightly pudgy build, and unique voice became synonymous with villainy. As the mock prosecutor, played by **Gustaf Gründgens**, accuses Lorre's character of the murders and pleads for a death sentence, Lorre's character delivers a defense of his actions that calls forth pity and understanding. The murderer confesses to drives that he cannot overcome, to blackouts that occur during the commission of his crimes, and to the remorse he feels afterward. During the extended speech, the camera cuts to criminals in the mock courtroom nodding their heads in agreement. Lorre's extended monologue bursts the narrative of the film and becomes a confession and rationalization of criminal behavior, as his murdering is presented as innate to his being. Almost a decade later, the Nazis would use the scene in *Der ewige Jude* to characterize Jews and justify their anti-Semitic policies.

M was a pioneering film, perhaps the most important German film of the Weimar period. Besides introducing Lorre and reinforcing the parallels cinema found between criminal and police behavior, it presented a model of suspense that would later be found in film noir. Its use of sound in the simple melody that is whistled; its use of symbolism, as in the blind beggar who is the only one who can sense the criminal; and its committed sociopolitical text anticipate crime film tropes that are still found in films and television shows 80 years later.

MACKEBEN, THEO (1897–1953). Film composer Theo Mackeben was a master of tuneful melodies during the Third Reich. Several of his songs became hits when released independently as records or when the sheet music was published. "Die Nacht ist nicht allein zum Schlafen da" ("The Night Isn't Just for Sleeping"), sung by **Gustaf Gründgens** in the film *Tanz auf dem Vulkan* (*Dance on the Volcano*, Hans Steinhoff, 1938), was one such overnight sensation. With lyrics by Otto Ernst Hesse, Mackeben's song runs as a rhythmically upbeat melody throughout the film. The movie concludes as Gründgens, who plays revolutionary Debureau, sings the rebellious last verse on his way to the gallows. Minister of Propaganda Joseph Goebbels had the last verse removed in the versions released independently of the film, as they could be construed as promoting rebellion. Mackeben's song was subsequently recorded by later artists, including **Hildegard Knef** and Udo Lindenberg. Mackeben's other hit tunes in the 1930s included "Nur nicht aus Liebe weinen" ("Just Don't Cry Out for Love") from *Es war eine rauschende Ballnacht* (*The Life and Loves of Tschaikovsky*, **Carl Froelich**, 1939), sung by **Zarah Leander**, and "Du hast Glück bei den Frau'n, Bel ami" ("You're Lucky with Women, My Friend") from *Bel ami* (*Bel Ami*, **Willi Forst**, 1939). Mackeben's songs from the 1930s became evergreens in the repertoires of a number of chanson singers of later generations.

MAETZIG, KURT (1911–). Kurt Maetzig was born in Berlin and studied engineering and then business, earning an advanced degree with his dissertation on cost accounting in a film printing laboratory. In spite of his interest in film—photography and animation were two of his hobbies—Maetzig was kept from working in the film industry during the Third Reich because his mother was Jewish. After the war, he started a film printing laboratory and began directing. Little known outside Germany, Maetzig is nonetheless important to German film. As one of the cofounders of **DEFA**, the **East German film** studio, he contributed to the rebirth of the film industry in the German Democratic Republic (East Germany). He gained recognition for his first film, *Ehe im Schatten* (*Marriage in the Shadows*, 1947). Adapted from the novella *Es wird schon nicht so schlimm* (*It Won't Be That Bad*) by Hans Schweikart, the film tells the real-life story of the actor Joachim Gottschalk, who rather than divorce his Jewish wife commits suicide. The theme attracted Maetzig, whose Jewish mother had also committed suicide. *Ehe im Schatten* was an important film for its time, which along with **Wolfgang Staudte**'s *Die Mörder sind unter uns* (*The Murderers Are among Us*, 1946) was an early attempt at helping Germans come to terms with the legacy of the Third Reich. At a time when the issue was not yet being addressed in film, Maetzig confronted viewers with the reality of their anti-Semitism and how it had destroyed the lives of Jews and non-Jews. Initially very popular and shown in all four sectors of divided Germany, the film's later reception has suffered. **Bertolt Brecht** referred to the film as kitsch, and later critics consider the work overly sentimental. Maetzig himself later distanced himself from the movie's melodramatic story.

Maetzig's films could serve as a paradigm for social realism in film. Intended to raise class consciousness among the workers of the newly founded German Democratic Republic, his films stress the importance of worker solidarity, the strength and the equality of women, the history of the workers' movement, and the uniqueness of the East German experience and experiment. Similar in intent and style to films in other Eastern bloc countries, Maetzig's *Die Buntkarierten* (*Brightly Checkered*, 1949), a chronicle of three generations of a family; *Schlösser und Katen* (*Castles and Cottages*, 1957); and *Roman einer jungen Ehe* (*Story of a Young Couple*, 1952) presented a model for building the new socialist state. Maetzig's early successes led to his being offered DEFA's prestige big-budget movie about Ernst Thälmann, the leader of German communists in the 1920s who was murdered by the Nazis at Buchenwald in 1944. Filmed in color, unusual at the time, the film tells Thälmann's story in two parts, *Ernst Thälmann—Sohn seiner Klasse* (*Ernst Thälmann: Son of His Class*, 1954) and *Ernst Thälmann—Führer seiner Klasse* (*Ernst Thälmann: Leader of His Class*, 1955). Critics have noted the film's ponderous nature and not always accurate portrayal of history, as the film was meant to legitimize the government of the German Democratic Republic as much as narrate the story of a communist hero. *Das Kaninchen bin ich* (*I Am the Rabbit*, 1965) came at a time of supposed cultural liberalization. Yet the film obviously went too far in its criticism of the government, mild as it was, and with other films at the time was banned by the Eleventh Plenum of the Central Committee of the Socialist Unity Party (SED), East Germany's ruling government. The film was finally shown in theaters in 1990, after the collapse of communism in East Germany and the unification of the German states.

MARIAN, FERDINAND (1902–1946). Ferdinand Marian is arguably one of the Nazi film community's few heartthrob actors. His muscular physique, swarthy complexion, and general good looks reportedly generated bags of admiring fan mail even though he played undesirable characters. He was typecast as a likable but destructive scoundrel after his portrayals of Rodolphe Boulanger, the seducer of Emma Bovary in *Madame Bovary* (*Madame Bovary*, Gerhard Lamprecht, 1937), based on Gustave Flaubert's novel (1857), and Don Pedro de Avila, a husband who dominates his wife and child in *La*

Habanera (*La Habanera*, **Douglas Sirk**, 1937). Marian's most recognized and dubious part was in *Jud Süß* (*Jew Süss*, **Veit Harlan**, 1940), in which he played the title character Süß Oppenheimer. In the film, he portrays Oppenheimer as a man who has turned his back on his Jewish heritage, himself seduced by the glitter and glamour of court life, but who, at the same time precipitates the ruin of the town by exorbitant taxation; the death of the duke through financial shenanigans; and the suicide of the heroine, who is distraught after Süß rapes her. Marian also played more sympathetic characters. His composer in *Romanze in Moll* (*Romance in a Minor Key*, **Helmut Käutner**, 1943) recasts the seducer as a sincere lover who, although he steals Madeleine from her husband, is willing to fight a duel over her when she is wronged by a third man. His Cagliostro in *Münchhausen* (*The Adventures of Baron Munchausen*, **Josef von Báky**, 1943) points out the paradox in all his roles. His portrayal of the sorcerer skilled in the occult is clearly inscribed into the segment as negative; he is a man viewers should shun. Yet he remains sympathetic, as if the personalities he portrays never consume the actor.

MATTES, EVA (1954–). Although not as well known outside Germany as other contemporary German actors, Eva Mattes is one of the most prominent and important figures of **New German Cinema**, having made films for most of the new wave's directors. The daughter of Austrian film composer Willy Mattes and Hungarian Austrian dancer and actress Margit Symo, Mattes was an established stage star and had synchronized voices on television before making her film debut in **Michael Verhoeven**'s controversial film *o.k.* (*o.k.*, 1970). Mattes won an Award in Gold from the German film industry as Most Promising Young Actress for her portrayal of Pan Thi Mao, a young peasant girl raped by a band of soldiers. The film created a scandal at the **Berlin Film Festival** because of the subject matter, which was highly critical of American involvement in Vietnam. Twenty years later the story was filmed by Hollywood without incident.

In her early films Mattes usually played a strong-willed adolescent, as in *Mathias Kneißl* (*Mathias Kneissl*, **Reinhard Hauff**, 1971) and *Wildwechsel* (*Jailbait*, **Rainer Werner Fassbinder**, 1972), both award-winning films for the actress. Mattes appeared in several other

Fassbinder films, including *Die bitteren Tränen der Petra von Kant* (*The Bitter Tears of Petra von Kant*, 1972), in which she plays the daughter of a lesbian mother, and *In einem Jahr mit 13 Monden* (*In a Year with 13 Moons*, 1978), in which she is the child of a transsexual father. Although both roles were small, they allowed the actress to exercise her considerable acting skills in dealing with parents whose sexual identity affected their emotional stability. Matte's frequent association with Fassbinder—she also appeared in his *Fontane Effi Briest* (*Effi Briest*, 1974) and *Frauen in New York* (*Women in New York*, 1977)—won her the role of a Fassbinder-like director in *Ein Mann wie EVA* (*A Man Like Eva*, Radu Gabrea, 1984), an anti-homage to the director after his death of a drug overdose. She also had a role in the television short *Warum läuft Herr V. amok?* (*Why Does Mr. V. Run Amok?* Dietrich Brüggemann, 2004). The film is a spoof of cinema, playing on the title of Fassbinder's film *Warum läuft Herr R. amok?* (*Why Does Mr. R. Run Amok?* 1970).

Mattes played equally compelling and award-winning roles for **Werner Herzog**. In *Stroszek* (*Stroszek*, 1979), she appears as a prostitute who immigrates to the United States with her boyfriend to get a fresh start, only to succumb to glib bankers and easy credit. In *Woyzeck* (*Woyzeck*, 1979), she stars as an unfaithful woman murdered by her jealous and schizophrenic common law husband, Woyzeck, played by **Klaus Kinski**.

Mattes has appeared in some of Germany's best-known new wave and post–new wave films. In *Céleste* (*Céleste*, **Percy Adlon**, 1982), she has what some critics consider her best role. Expanding her repertoire beyond young rebels and easy women, Mattes here portrays the supportive, patient, and introverted housekeeper of Marcel Proust as he writes his masterpiece *À la recherche du temps perdu* (*Remembrance of Things Past*, 1913–1922). Others see her most important role as the star of *Deutschland bleiche Mutter* (*Germany Pale Mother*, **Helma Sanders-Brahms**, 1979–1980), in which she plays a young wife who learns to cope with the deprivations of daily life in Nazi Germany without her husband and who after the war must cope with life with him. At the time, the film served as a counter voice to the self-assertive title heroine of Fassbinder's *Die Ehe der Maria Braun* (*The Marriage of Maria Braun*, 1979). Mattes has also had small parts in other films dealing with Germany's past, including

Herbstmilch (*Autumn Milk*, Joseph Vilsmaier, 1989), about the home front in a village during the war; *Das Versprechen* (*The Promise*, **Margarethe von Trotta**, 1995), about life in divided Germany; and *Enemy at the Gates* (Jean-Jacques Annaud, 2001), about famed sniper Vassili Zaitsev.

As a child Mattes dubbed the voice of Timmy Martin, the young boy in the American television series *Lassie*, for German television. Since 2002 she has portrayed detective Klara Blum in the long-running detective series *Tatort* (*Scene of the Crime*, 1970–), whose repertoire list of detectives has been entertaining Germany for more than 35 years.

MAYER, CARL (1894–1944). Carl Mayer wrote the screenplays for many of the silent film era's best-known films. His most famous credits include *Das Cabinet des Dr. Caligari* (*The Cabinet of Dr. Caligari*, **Robert Wiene**, 1920), a tale of horror that pioneered expressionism in German film; *Der letzte Mann* (*The Last Laugh*, **Friedrich Wilhelm Murnau**, 1924), a cautionary study of hubris that set a new standard for cinematic storytelling; and *Sunrise* (Murnau, 1927), a Hollywood production that the French film journal *Cahiers du Cinèma* in 1958 voted "the most beautiful film there is."

Although Mayer gained fame by collaborating with Hans Janowitz on the screenplay for the horror film *Dr. Caligari*, his strength lay in chamber drama, a genre borrowed from theater that adapted the bourgeois tragedies of family dysfunction of dramatists such as Gerhart Hauptmann and Frank Wedekind to the social realities of Weimar Germany. These films, generally but not necessarily situated in a lower middle class milieu, explored the effect of Germany's economic crisis on the lower strata of the working poor, both blue and white collar. Drawing by some accounts on his childhood experiences in a dysfunctional family—his father had committed suicide when Mayer was still young—he wrote the screenplays for a series of these lower middle class tragedies, the best known of which is *Der letzte Mann*, mentioned above. Others include *Hintertreppe* (*Backstairs*, Leopold Jessner and Paul Leni, 1921), about the unrequited love of a postman for a young servant woman who loves another man. When the postman hides letters from the young woman's lover, he precipitates a tragic misunderstanding that ends in the lover's murder, the postman's arrest, and the young woman's suicide. *Scherben* (*Shattered*, Lupu Pick, 1921) and *Sylvester* (*New Year's Eve*, Pick, 1923) are equally as melodramatic. In *Scherben*, the mother of a young woman who has been seduced runs out into the cold and freezes to death, and the father murders the seducer and then turns himself in to the police. *Sylvester* varies the formula a bit by contrasting the world of the rich and that of the poor during a New Year's Eve celebration.

Mayer's style is both lyrical and visual. His scripts, rich in details not only of the plot but also of the psychological and sociological underpinnings of the characters, led cameraman **Karl Freund**, with whom Mayer worked on several movies, to remark that "a script by Carl Mayer was already a film." Indeed there is argument among critics whether he should not be credited with the innovative and fluid style of *Der letzte Mann*. When Murnau went to Hollywood, Mayer accompanied him, writing the screenplays for the director's lyrical masterpiece *Sunrise* (1926) and for *Four Devils* (1929). Because the Nazis had come to power, Mayer, a Jew, upon his return to Europe lived first in France and then England. Although he collaborated on screenplays in both countries, he never achieved the success he had had in Germany.

MESSTER, OSKAR (1866–1943). Oskar Messter was a pioneer of the German film industry who grew a division of his father's optical firm into a major producer of film shorts, newsreels, and narrative feature films in the first two decades of the 20th century. As inventor of the Geneva drive or "Maltese cross," the device in projectors that allows for smooth projection of 35mm film, he allowed for the spread of film exhibition. In order to ensure a supply of films for the buyers of his projectors with the new technology, Messter began producing films in the late 1890s, becoming in a sense the court filmographer for Wilhelm II, Germany's emperor. In the early 1900s, he combined his projector with an Edison gramophone and made tone movies, shorts that featured music. In the 1910s, Messter began an association with **Henny Porten**, which helped make her into one of the decade's biggest film stars. During the war years, 1914–1918, Messter again served the government by producing newsreels of the war. At the time, he also started lobbying the government for a greater role for cinema in the commercial enterprises of the nation. His argument that Germany was wasting a valuable propaganda resource led eventually to the creation of **Universum Film AG** (Ufa), a conglomerate studio that combined smaller studios, including Messter's, under one umbrella.

METROPOLIS. *Metropolis* (1927), directed by **Fritz Lang** with screenplay by Lang and **Thea von Harbou**, is recognized as a pioneering science fiction film and at the same time a confusion of themes and subtexts. The film reflects 1920s modernity in its ambivalence to science and technology, social justice, the city, and feminism. Its themes of doppelgänger, religious fervor, and endangered love are reminiscent of gothic romanticism. Its story of a master class ruling over the workers anticipates both Nazi Germany and Stalinist Russia. Indeed, the film was reportedly a favorite of Adolf Hitler. And finally, the film's visual imagery resonates to the films of the 21st century. Mary Shelley's *Frankenstein*, Hans Dominick's novels of marvelous inventions, expressionist poems of the power and brutality of the city, broadsides against assembly production, sometimes known as Fordism, the growth of a new Brahmin class of citizens replacing the nobility of pre–world war Europe, the skyscrapers of Manhattan, and feminism, all influence and have a role in creating the film's confusion of ideas.

On the one hand, *Metropolis* tells a simple story. In a large city of the future, a small class of men own production and live on the world's surface. A larger group of workers, who tend the machinery that runs the city and creates wealth for the upper class, lives in the depths of the world. In between the two are the machines that keep everyone alive. The head of the wealthy believes he will get more from the workers, who are threatening to strike—led on by Maria, an evangelical do-gooder—if he can goad them into rebelling. When he crushes them, he will have them completely under his control. He asks a mad scientist to construct a robot in the image of the evangelist, who is to then serve as the catalyst of the rebellion. Two things intervene to thwart the plan. First, the wealthy leader's son falls in love with the true Maria and is thus enlisted on the side of the workers. Second, similarly to the prince in Swan Lake and other legends, Freder, the son, cannot tell the difference between the woman he loves and the false image of her. Such confusion causes the false Maria to replace the good Maria and flood the city, endangering the workers' children. It also endangers the wealthy scion, as he is in the city that is being flooded. Eventually the false Maria is burned at the stake, melting back to her robot state; the good Maria is rescued from the evil scientist, who mistook her for his dead wife; and order is restored as the son mediates between his father and the lead worker to find a compromise.

Even a brief summary of the film reveals why, in spite of the film's pioneering style and special effects, its themes cause critics to question its many subtexts. Women are presented only as stereotypes: the virgin or the prostitute. Reflecting the two Marias, other women in the film are party-loving flappers (the Brahmin class) or scatter-brained mothers (the working class). Social conscience is reduced to origins in religious zealotry or sexual desire. The son's role anticipates the literary and filmic cliché of the latter half of the 20th century, that men join causes to sleep with the women behind the cause. The film's end is particularly troubling. As generally interpreted, the father (referred to as "head" in the ending intertitles), the worker (referred to as "hand"), and the son (referred to as "heart"), are premonitions of Hitler, the heart uniting industry and labor. Indeed, if one looks at the imagery of the final moments, the workers are again marching in unison, and the father is back in power. The compromise that the son achieves is essentially a compromise of status quo.

Few viewers have ever seen *Metropolis* as Lang intended. The original 153-minute film, the most expensive of its day for **Universum Film AG** (Ufa), was pulled by the studio shortly after its premier and shortened. Furthermore, viewers have seen various versions of the film. Three master negatives were made available to America, Germany, and outside Germany. Distributors cut these to correspond to their assumption of viewer expectations. The version originally released in America reportedly ran 63 minutes. The movie initially lost money for the studio. Eventually *Metropolis* became a cult favorite of cinema clubs, architecture and physics students, and classic movie fans. Several different 16mm versions of the film circulated before VHS tapes became popular in the 1970s. Tape and finally DVD formats now make at least five different versions available. The films differ slightly in the order of scenes, the inclusion or exclusion of sometimes important narrative material, and most of all the accompanying music. As the original score was lost when the film was released on

16mm, substitute music was added. VHS and DVD copies included even more optional tracks. One can now watch the movie with electronic music, waltzlike tunes, jazz, industrial sounds, 1980s rock, and an orchestral score. The last two are the only ones available for the film in 35mm, as the films with these scores were released theatrically. In 1984, music impresario Giorgio Moroder released the film to theaters with a rock/disco track, colorized scenes, additional footage, and narrative notes. In 2001, the Murnau Stiftung, together with the British Film Institute, remastered the film in order to preserve it and at the same time restore it as near as possible to what viewers in the 1920s saw, at least those who saw it after the premier. The original soundtrack by **Gottfried Huppertz** was also put back in, in an arrangement by Berndt Heller.

MIKESCH, ELFI (1940–). Elfi Mikesch has worked as a cinematographer on the films of Germany's major underground or alternative directors. Often working with video, her films have a sometimes garish color scheme that complements the erotic themes of the films. Mikesch was camerawoman on **Rosa von Praunheim**'s *Ein Virus kennt keine Moral* (*A Virus Knows No Morals*, 1986), a film about the AIDS epidemic; *Anita-Tänze des Lasters* (*Anita—Dances of Vice*, 1987), about a woman who believes she is a reincarnated erotic dancer from 1920s Berlin; and *Der Einstein des Sex* (*The Einstein of Sex*, 1999), about Magnus Hirschfeld, a German who established the field of sexology.

Mikesch's best-known works are for feminist director **Monika Treut**, with whom she also codirected *Verführung: Die grausame Frau* (*Seduction: The Cruel Woman*, 1985). Set in Hamburg's red light district near the city's waterfront, the film focuses on the sadomasochistic world of the sex business. Fast cutting, extreme angles, and bright colors characterize Mikesch's cinematography in the film, which at times seems to exploit the eroticism of pain for its own sake. Mikesch's camerawork for Treut on *Die Jungfrauenmaschine* (*The Virgin Machine*, 1988) and *My Father Is Coming* (1991) likewise emphasizes the spectacle of sex in the films' narratives, through soft focus and erotic framing. Mikesch has served as a camerawoman on several films for **Werner Schroeter**, including *Malina* (*Malina*, 1991). In 1978, she won an Award in Silver for Outstanding Non-

Feature Film (*see* **film awards**) for *Ich denke oft an Hawaii* (*I Often Think of Hawaii*, 1978), about a 16-year-old Berlin student who escapes into a fantasy world of Hawaii as pictured on postcards.

MIRA, BRIGITTE (1910–2005). Brigitte Mira began as a stage actor in operettas and comedies. In film, she received mainly small supporting roles in the 1950s and 1960s. Her first major role came in **Rainer Werner Fassbinder**'s *Angst essen Seele auf* (*Ali: Fears the Soul*, 1974), for which she won an Award in Gold (*see* **film awards**) for her portrayal of Emmi, a lonely widow who falls in love with Ali, a Moroccan guest worker 20 years younger than she. Mira gives a nuanced performance in the role, which requires her to display a range of emotions. Mira again played a working class woman for Fassbinder in *Mutter Küsters' Fahrt zum Himmel* (*Mother Küsters Goes to Heaven*, 1975), about a widow exploited by the media and the Left, who want to gain political hegemony, after her husband dies in an industrial accident. Mira appeared in eight other Fassbinder films in supporting roles. She also had roles in the films of other **New German Cinema** directors, including the maid who befriends Kaspar Hauser in *Jeder für sich und Gott gegen alle* (*The Enigma of Kaspar Hauser*, **Werner Herzog**, 1974) and a role in *Die Zärtlichkeit der Wölfe* (*The Tenderness of Wolves*, **Ulli Lommel**, 1973), about the notorious killer Fritz Haarmann, who was also one of the models for the serial killer in *M* (*M*, **Fritz Lang**, 1931). After the end of New German Cinema, Mira continued to act in theatrical films and on television. She appeared in over 120 films, more than 60 of them made after the age of 70.

MONTEZUMA, MAGDALENA (1943–1982). Magdalena Montezuma was the shrill high priestess of West Germany's underground cinema. As the star, or antistar, of films by **Werner Schroeter**, **Elfi Mikesch**, **Rosa von Praunheim**, and **Ulrike Ottinger**, her exaggerated gestures, imposing and distinctive voice, and dilettante-like bearing made her a cult figure in film circles and an icon of the underground film. For Montezuma, life was a stage. Her mannered style of acting, both expressive and excessive, can be seen not only in the films of Germany's alternative directors—for example, Ottinger's *Dorian Gray im Spiegel der Boulevardpresse* (*The Image of Dorian*

Gray in the Yellow Press, 1984)—but also in small roles in the films of **Rainer Werner Fassbinder**: *Rio das Mortes* (*Rio das Mortes*, 1970), *Warnung vor einer heiligen Nutte* (*Beware of a Holy Whore*, 1971), *Welt am Draht* (*World on a Wire*, 1973), and *Berlin Alexanderplatz* (*Berlin Alexanderplatz*, 1980). Montezuma also had a small part in the cult film *Taxi zum Klo* (*Taxi to the Toilet*, Frank Ripploh, 1981), about the life of a gay schoolteacher in Germany.

Her best-known role, however, was in Ottinger's *Freak Orlando* (*Freak Orlando*, 1981), in which Montezuma played Orlando, a hermaphroditic time traveler, based on Virginia Woolf's *Orlando: A Biography*. In the film, Montezuma wanders from the desert into "Freak City," meeting a number of unusual characters in equally unusual vignettes. The film offers a parody of Western culture's sexism and obsession with consumerism.

MOUNTAIN FILM. The first film about mountain climbing dates to 1903, when mountain climber Frederick Ormiston-Smith produced the documentary *The Ascent of Mont Blanc*, depicting tourists ascending the famous mountain. The mountain film as a genre, however, was popularized by **Arnold Fanck** in the 1920s, in a series of silent and early sound adventure films.

Fanck's *Der heilige Berg* (*The Sacred Mountain*, 1926) is a classic mountain film. Starring **Luis Trenker** as the mountain climber Karl and **Leni Riefenstahl** as the dancer Diotima, who both went on to make their own mountain films, the film provides physically striking actors who endure perilous cold and avalanches in a mountainous setting. The relationship between the two is disturbed by a younger, more virile mountain climber, Vigo, played by Ernst Petersen, who also falls in love with Diotima. The cliffhanger, a requisite part of any mountain film, here has Karl literally holding Vigo's lifeline in his hands, as the latter dangles from a mountainside. In the film biography of Riefenstahl's career, *Die Macht der Bilder: Leni Riefenstahl* (*The Wonderful, Horrible Life of Leni Riefenstahl*, Ray Müller, 1993), the actor/director comments on the hardships she had to endure to satisfy Fanck's insistence on capturing the reality of snow slides.

In his pioneering study of the psychology of German films in the 1920s, **Siegfried Kracauer** theorized that mountain films displayed protofascist tendencies both in the way the camera captured the physical strength and beauty of the actors and the way the stories privileged mountain life (climbing) over the life of the city dwellers. The contrast between mountain residents and city dwellers is particularly marked in the two mountain films Riefenstahl made during her career. *Das blaue Licht* (*The Blue Light*, 1932), about a strange mountain girl shunned by her village, and *Tiefland* (*Lowlands*, 1954), about a Carmen-like Gypsy dancer who marries a simple mountain boy so she can become the mistress of the province's duke, both starred Riefenstahl as a beautiful outsider, misunderstood but clearly superior to all around her. The mountain film continues today, if in changed form, in such Hollywood films as *Vertical Limit* (Martin Campbell, 2000) and *Touching the Void* (Kevin Macdonald, 2003). *See also* ALLGEIER, SEPP; ANGST, RICHARD.

MUELLER-STAHL, ARMIN (1930–). Armin Mueller-Stahl became known for his highly dramatic characters whose tragedy plays out within the everyday. His career has had three main phases, first in the German Democratic Republic (East Germany) until 1980, after that in the Federal Republic of Germany, and most recently in American films.

In East Germany, Mueller-Stahl often starred in the programmatic films of **Frank Beyer**. Two of these, *Nackt unter Wölfen* (*Naked among Wolves*, 1963) and *Jakob der Lügner* (*Jacob the Liar*, 1974), about persecution of the Jews under the Nazis, have become classics of East German cinema. In West Germany, his biggest roles were in *Die Sehnsucht der Veronika Voss* (*Veronika Voss*, 1982) and *Lola* (*Lola*, 1981), which together with *Die Ehe der Maria Braun* (*The Marriage of Maria Braun*, 1979) form **Rainer Werner Fassbinder**'s trilogy about postwar Germany. For his performance in *Lola*, Mueller-Stahl won an Award in Gold as Actor of the Year from the German film industry. In the film, based on Josef von Sternberg's *Der blaue Engel* (*The Blue Angel*, 1930), he plays a building inspector seduced by a prostitute with ambitions to strike it rich in the booming economy of Germany's economic miracle. His controlled analytical style of acting, devoid of pathos, contrasted greatly with the mannered, emotive style of **Emil Jannings** in the original film.

Mueller-Stahl's roles suggest a desire to help viewers understand 20th-century European history, especially German history. In addition to the already-mentioned roles in his early East German work or in the films of Fassbinder, Mueller-Stahl has portrayed men from all walks of life who confront moral dilemmas. In **Agnieszka Holland**'s *Bittere Ernte* (*Angry Harvest*, 1985), he plays a Polish peasant during World War II who hides a Jewish refugee, lying to her about the death of her husband in a failed attempt to win her love. In **István Szabó**'s *Oberst Redl* (*Colonel Redl*, 1985) and **Bernhard Wicki**'s *Das Spinnennetz* (*Spider's Web*, 1989), he plays aristocrats in the protofascist world of the 1910s and 1920s. He again plays an aristocrat in **Volker Schlöndorff**'s *Der Unhold* (*The Ogre*, 1996), set during the Third Reich. Unlike the peasant Leon Wolny in *Bittere Ernte* or Baron von Rastchuk in *Das Spinnennetz*, whose ambivalence to their situation leads to immoral choices, Count Kaltenborn acts righteously, condemning the actions of the Third Reich by supporting the military plot to kill Adolf Hitler on July 20, 1944, and forfeiting his freedom because of his actions. Other German films attempting to come to terms with the years of the Third Reich in which Mueller-Stahl had parts include *Die Mitläufer* (*Fellow Travelers*, Eberhard Itzenplitz and Erwin Leiser, 1985) and *Eine Liebe in Deutschland* (*A Love in Germany*, Andrzej Wajda, 1983). In the latter film, he plays a commander in the Schutzstaffel (SS) in a Polish town.

Mueller-Stahl's American films include *Music Box* (Costa-Gavras, 1989), in which he reprises the roles he played so often in East and West German films, portraying a Hungarian immigrant accused of heinous war crimes. In Barry Levinson's *Avalon* (1990) and Jim Jarmusch's *Night on Earth* (1992), Mueller-Stahl displays his ability to play comedic roles, which was already evident in his East German work. Mueller-Stahl has also appeared in supporting roles in a number of Hollywood and American independent action and science fiction films, including *The Game* (David Fincher, 1997), *The Peacemaker* (Mimi Leder, 1997), *The X-Files* (Rob Bowman, 1998), and *The Thirteenth Floor* (Josef Rusnak, 1999), a German and American coproduction. In David Cronenberg's *Eastern Promises* (2007), Mueller-Stahl plays against type, portraying the head of a Russian crime syndicate that traffics in child prostitution. The actor also appeared as the Israeli prime minister in four episodes during the fifth season of the television series *The West Wing* (2004). *See also* EAST

GERMAN FILM; HOLOCAUST IN FEATURE FILMS; *VERGAN-GENHEITSBEWÄLTIGUNGSFILM*.

MÜLLER, ROBBY (1940–). One of Germany's top cinematographers, Robby Müller began as a cameraman on the early films of **Wim Wenders**, later becoming the director's collaborator on some of his major films. The two men share a philosophy of filmmaking that includes the importance of location shooting, natural sound and lighting, appropriate use of space, and avoidance of camera tricks and filters. Among the films they have made together are *Im Lauf der Zeit* (*Kings of the Road*, 1976), *Der amerikanische Freund* (*The American Friend*, 1977), *Paris, Texas* (1984), and *Bis ans Ende der Welt* (*Until the End of the World*, 1991), which focus on landscape, environment, and travel. Whether filming in black and white, as in *Im Lauf der Zeit*, or in color, as in the other three films, Müller uses his sets as a backdrop within which the story develops rather than allowing it to overwhelm the story with its beauty. In *Der amerikanische Freund*, environmental setting becomes a lie at times, as when a miniature of the Eiffel Tower is used in a scene taking place in New York or when the protagonist is in a station in Paris but could be anywhere as there are no identifying features locating the scene. In *Paris, Texas* (1984), Müller captures the gritty character of Houston's back streets and thoroughfares, the tawdry nature of peep show parlors, and the expanse of the Texas desert, showing preference for extreme far shots. In one memorable scene, he films a man arguing to get off an airplane that has clearance for takeoff, giving the audience a field of vision that encompasses the expanse of the airstrip with the plane in the distance. Viewers hear but do not see the man, forcing focus on the nature of the environment.

In addition to his collaboration with Wenders, Müller has worked with some of Europe's and America's major independent directors. For Sally Potter's *The Tango Lesson* (1997), he fashions a nuanced film of black and white images, with infrequent use of color. As Potter and Pablo Verón, playing themselves in this fictional documentary, dance along the Seine, natural lights from the riverbank and festive lights from an excursion boat create a fairyland in which the dancing couple can fall in love. Müller has also had a long cinematic relationship with Jim Jarmusch, the Hungarian American independent filmmaker who has long been a cult figure in Germany. Among their mutual projects are *Down by Law* (1986), *Mystery Train* (1989), *Ghost Dog: The Way of the Samarai* (1999), and the *Coffee and Cigarettes* series. *Mystery Train*, filmed in the grittier parts of Memphis, illustrates what Müller means when he says that location is important but should never overwhelm the movie. While Memphis becomes a character in the film, interacting with the narrative of two Japanese teenagers looking for Elvis, it is never an aesthetic object, stopping the narrative while viewers marvel at its presentation.

Müller has also worked with **New German Cinema** directors **Hans W. Geissendörfer**, on *Jonathan* (*Jonathan*, 1970), a vampire movie, and **Peter Lilienthal**, on *Es herrscht Ruhe im Land* (*Calm Prevails over the Country*, 1976), a political drama set in a fictional South American country. In addition, he was cinematographer on Polish director Andrzej Wajda's *Korczak* (*Korczak*, 1990), about a wealthy headmaster who protects Jewish children from the Nazis but eventually perishes in the concentration camp with them. He also worked with Danish director Lars von Trier. Müller was perfectly suited to work with von Trier, one of the writers of the *Dogme 95* manifesto, whose tenets include natural lighting and sound, no special effects or camera gimmickry, and location shooting. Their collaborative efforts yielded *Breaking the Waves* (1996), the signature film of *Dogme 95*, and *Dancer in the Dark* (2000), a paradoxical mix of musical and *Dogme 95* realism.

MURNAU, FRIEDRICH WILHELM (1888–1931). In spite of his short career in films, Friedrich Wilhelm Murnau (born Friedrich Wilhelm Plumpe) left a legacy of some of the best-remembered and most critically acclaimed movies of Germany's silent film era, including *Nosferatu, eine Symphonie des Grauens* (*Nosferatu*, 1922), *Der letzte Mann* (*The Last Laugh*, 1924), and *Faust* (*Faust*, 1926). On the success and strength of these films, Murnau received a Hollywood contract, where he directed *Sunrise* (1927), a film that won three Academy Awards: for Murnau for Artistic Quality of Production, for Janet Gaynor for Best Actress, and for Charles Rosher and Karl Struss for Cinematography.

Murnau's *Der letzte Mann* was an innovative masterpiece of the silent era. Working closely with pioneer cameraman **Karl Freund** and screenwriter **Carl Mayer**, the director created a uniquely German tragedy of humiliation and degradation. Perceiving the *schadenfreude* (joy at the suffering of others) of his neighbors when he is demoted to lavatory attendant, a once proud doorman succumbs to his abject shame and collapses in the men's toilet. The strength of the film lies not in its plot, which is fairly standard for German melodrama, but in its fluid visual style. Murnau and his collaborators freed the camera from its tripod for this film, allowing it to swing and move freely as it captured the hero's psychological confusion at his fate. The fluidity of movement allows the story to be told without intertitles, until the end of the film, when a coda that provided a happy end to an otherwise bleak story is introduced through an ironic title. Film critic C. A. Lejeune wrote that, "It [the film] gave the camera a new dominion, a new freedom . . . . It influenced the future of motion picture photography."

Murnau's *Nosferatu* gave a sense of lyrical realism to an important staple of German cinema, the horror film. Subtitling his film *A Symphony of Horror*, Murnau freed the story from the claustrophobic studio look of *Das Cabinet des Dr. Caligari* (*The Cabinet of Caligari*, **Robert Wiene**, 1920). Rather than using highly stylized, expressionistic sets as popularized by Wiene's film, Murnau chose to shoot much of *Nosferatu* outdoors. The resulting atmospheric impressionism lends the film both a sense of realism and dreaminess. It is as if a shroud of mist and shadows prevents the characters from seeing the truth behind the evil of the vampire. Murnau and his film became the subject of *Shadow of the Vampire* (E. Elias Merhige, 2000), a fictional story about the making of *Nosferatu* which, because of its central conceit that the actor playing Nosferatu was a real vampire, has gained cult status.

Murnau's painterly style is again obvious in *Faust* (1926), which emphasizes horror over the philosophical dilemma of a man who sells his soul to the devil. Murnau's visuals capture the humor from the early scenes of Johann Wolfgang von Goethe's masterpiece, as when Mephistopheles and Martha make small talk in a garden as Faust seduces Gretchen. At the same time, they represent the majesty of angels, the depravity of witches, and the cunning of the devil. Some critics consider *Faust*, even more than *Der letzte Mann*, to be Murnau's crowning achievement. Regardless of which film is considered his best, it is clear that the pictorial quality of his images is like poetry, revealing more than the eye can see.

– N –

NEGRI, POLA (1894–1987). One of the first vamps of silent film, Pola Negri (born Barbara Apolonia Chalupiec) began acting in films in 1914 in her native Poland after ill health forced her to give up her intended career as a ballet dancer. Her success in Polish films led to film engagements in Germany, where she gained international fame after starring in two films directed by **Ernst Lubitsch**: *Carmen* (*Gypsy Blood*, 1918) and *Madame Dubarry* (*Passion*, 1919). Negri carried her screen persona of liberated woman into her off-screen life and became known as a vamp on and off screen. When *Madame Dubarry*, recut as *Passion* for the Hollywood film audience, became a success with American viewers apparently hungry for exotic stars, Negri received a lucrative contract from Hollywood. One of the first German actors to be lured away from Germany, Negri immigrated to the United States in 1923 and established herself as a seductress in over a dozen films, including *Forbidden Paradise*, also with Lubitsch (1924), and *A Woman of the World* (1925) and *Good and Naughty* (1926), both by Malcolm St. Clair.

At the height of her career in the silent era, Negri earned a fortune by cultivating the persona developed in Germany. She kept herself in the spotlight through affairs with leading actors, most notably Charlie Chaplin and Rudolph Valentino, ensuring the success of films that many consider inferior to the work she did with Lubitsch. Eventually, however, the public tired of Negri's publicity stunts. One in which she followed a train carrying Valentino's body across the country, fainting on cue for reporters at various stops, was particularly offputting to her fans. Coupled with the advent of sound, which revealed her thick, almost incomprehensible Polish accent, and Hollywood's downplaying of the seductress, Negri's publicity stunt ruined her American career and she returned to Germany.

In the 1930s she again acted in several films for **Universum Film AG** (Ufa) studio, now under the control of Joseph Goebbels and the National Socialists. Most notable of these was *Mazurka* (*Mazurka*, 1935) directed by **Willi Forst**, one of Germany's favorite actors at the time. The film reportedly became one of Adolf Hitler's favorites, leading to rumors that he was having an affair with Negri. Negri, who was part Jewish, fell out of favor with the Nazis, and she again emigrated from Germany to America in 1941. She never regained the stardom she had once had, but was offered the role of Norma Desmond in Billy Wilder's *Sunset Boulevard* (1950), a part she turned down and which made Gloria Swanson an instantly recognizable icon of film history.

NEW GERMAN CINEMA (NGC). The term refers to the renaissance of German filmmaking that began during the **Young German Cinema** movement established by the **Oberhausen Manifesto** and continued until the death of **Rainer Werner Fassbinder** in 1982. New German Cinema hardly constituted a formal school, and indeed the individualism and idiosyncrasies of the directors, rather than any similarities in style, are what unite their films.

The films of **Wim Wenders**, for example, are noted for their abstract geographical and psychological landscapes. Those of Fassbinder reveal a preoccupation with emotional insecurity, which the director presents either in a starkly realistic style or one of extreme opulence and luxury. The films of **Werner Herzog** are noted for their sensuous colors and exotic locales and those of **Volker Schlöndorff** for their craftsmanship. The works of these directors differ thematically as well. Wenders favors epics about lone existential heroes searching for identity, whether as angels, drifters, or cowboys. Fassbinder, on the other hand, dwells on the emotional repression by society of individuals who are different from the norm. Herzog focuses on the exceptional individual, studying the level of endurance before breaking. Finally, Schlöndorff is known for his adaptations of bestselling novels by respected writers.

Other directors of NGC include **Reinhard Hauff**, **Hans W. Geissendörfer**, and Hark Böhm, among others. United in the conviction that filmmaking was a highly individualistic enterprise, these directors overcame distribution difficulties by forming their own private company, the **Filmverlag der Autoren**. The name (Authors' Film Publishing Group) reveals their affinity to the auteur film movement in France.

NIELSEN, ASTA (1881–1972). Asta Nielsen was a popular silent film actress in the 1910s and 1920s. Although she began her film career in Denmark, Nielsen's main work was in Germany. Like **Fern Andra**, an American, and **Pola Negri**, a Pole, Nielsen found commercial success in the burgeoning German film industry by fulfilling a particular niche. Whereas Andra played sportive figures and Negri played femmes fatales, Nielsen was cast almost from the beginning as the wayward girl who either finds her way back into society or is banished or even dies. Before and during World War I, she worked mostly with her husband, Urban Gad.

During the war Nielsen returned to Denmark, but she resumed her German film career in the 1920s. Again playing wayward women, Nielsen became a public favorite. She preferred subtle movement over the wild gesticulation often associated with silent film acting, thereby bringing viewers into her films. In that regard, she was the opposite of **Henny Porten**, whose style gravitated toward spectacle, although both women played the same type of dramatic roles.

Unhappy with some of the parts offered her, Nielsen created her own company, Artfilm, and produced and acted in a number of literary classics. She adapted William Shakespeare's *Hamlet* (*Hamlet*, Sven Gade and Heinz Schall, 1921), playing the title character as a princess disguised as a man. She also appeared in adaptations of Frank Wedekind's *Die Büchse der Pandora* (*Pandora's Box*, Arzén von Cserépy, 1921), in the role later made famous by **Louise Brooks**; August Strindberg's *Fräulein Julie* (*Miss Julie*, Felix Basch, 1922); and Henrik Ibsen's *Hedda Gabler* (*Hedda Gabler*, Franz Eckstein, 1925), three of northern Europe's best-known tragedies.

***NOSFERATU, EINE SYMPHONIE DES GRAUENS* (1920).** Directed by **Friedrich Wilhelm Murnau** in 1920, *Nosferatu, eine Symphonie des Grauens* (*Nosferatu, a Symphony of Horror*) combines expressionist style, imagery of horror, and on-site locations to create a frightening vision of evil. One of many horror films to be produced in Germany in the 1910s and early 1920s (*see Das Cabinet des Dr. Caligari*; **Galeen, Henrik; Wegener, Paul; Wiene, Robert**), *Nosferatu* adapts the legend of Count Dracula as introduced to Victorian England by Bram Stoker's novel *Dracula* (1897). Aside from the basic outline of the novel, Murnau's film does not resemble Stoker's narrative. Murnau relocates the setting from 19th-century London to 18th-century northern Germany; he reduces the cast of characters or lessens their roles; he recasts the vampire as a hideous monster rather than a continental sophisticate; and he ignores some of the mythology surrounding the legend, including mirror imagery and death by a stake through the heart. Most important, he deemphasizes the subtext of sexual repression in *Dracula*, which reflected Victorian England's neurotic fears, and replaces it with a subtext reflecting Germany's physical and psychological misery following World War I. Murnau also changed names in order to avoid a lawsuit by Stoker's widow for infringement of copyright, but he failed to win the ensuing legal action against the film.

Nosferatu begins by telling the story of the novel. A man, Thomas Hutter, travels to Transylvania in search of adventure and fortune, leaving behind his beautiful bride, Ellen. In Transylvania, his visit to Count Orlak's castle concludes with the closing of a transaction to sell the count a building in Wisborg, his being bitten during the night by Orlak, and his captivity and eventual escape from the castle. Meanwhile, Count Orlak comes to Wisborg and people begin dying. But here Murnau changes the story. Instead of a melodrama that focuses on sexual repression and anxiety, Murnau offers a gothic tale of evil that focuses on death and sacrifice. In Murnau's version, people die not from bats flying in through windows but from the plague brought by infested rats. Murnau forgoes a suspenseful hunt for the vampire's coffin and heroic action by the men in the film. He replaces masculine bravura with feminine sacrifice. After Thomas's return, Ellen senses the connection between the count and the death of so many townspeople and in her husband's absence sacrifices herself by keeping Count Orlak at her bedside until sunrise, when he melts from the sun's rays.

Nosferatu is not a horror film in the conventional sense. Nothing jumps out at characters in the film to frighten viewers; no one is shown dying in a gruesome fashion; there is little suspense; and the only chase is a humorous interlude at the end when the vampire's factotum is tracked down. Moreover, the formal expressionist sets of other horror films at the time are replaced by actual locations. Murnau frightens viewers by placing evil in an ordinary world. When Thomas Hutter first visits Transylvania, he is picked up in the mountains by a fast-arriving coach that is seen in negative. When he gets to the castle, he enters through an archway that leads into a black void. When he looks out of his room in the castle, he looks down on a naturalist setting that he cannot get to because of the height of his bedroom. In Wisborg, which comprises only a short segment of the film, we see no one being killed. Exteriors and interiors are of dilapidated patrician houses, suggesting the death occurring everywhere but unseen. At one point, Ellen looks down out of her window onto a street that is deserted except for a long line of pallbearers carrying coffins.

As with **Metropolis** (*Metropolis*, **Fritz Lang**, 1927), another silent German classic, no definitive version of *Nosferatu* exists, although the British Film Institute has restored it as well as *Metropolis*. That no original master copy exists traces back to legal action brought against Murnau by Stoker's widow for copyright infringement. After she won her lawsuit, the courts ordered all copies of the film destroyed. Several copies remained, however, and the film had a New York premier in 1929. By the early 1940s the film was considered one of Murnau's masterpieces. Consequently, with the rise in popularity of cinema clubs and film societies, a number of 16mm prints became available, with various soundtracks. The numbers increased with the advent of VHS and DVD formats, so *Nosferatu* can be viewed with music that varies from jazz to electronic to 19th-century classical. There is even a version with music by O-Negative, an alternative rock band. What there is not is a version with Hans Erdmann's original score. The restoration by the British Film Institute (BFI) did, however, add back Murnau's color filters to indicate mood and time of day. *Nosferatu* received feature-length homage 80 years later in *Shadow of the Vampire* (E. Elias Merhige, 2000), whose central conceit is that Max Schreck, the actor who played Nosferatu, was a genuine vampire.

– O –

OBERHAUSEN MANIFESTO. In 1962, a group of 26 writers and directors at the Oberhausen Film Festival in Oberhausen, Germany, issued a statement proclaiming that the old cinema was dead. "The collapse of the commercial German film industry finally removes the economic basis for a mode of filmmaking whose attitude and practice we reject. With it, the new film has a chance to come to life . . . . The old cinema is dead. We believe in the new."

The leading spokesman for the new cinema was **Alexander Kluge**, a lawyer, writer, and documentary filmmaker. His efforts among government officials on behalf of the group led to the establishment of the **Kuratorium Junger Deutscher Film**, an agency to oversee the allocation of film subsidies, which was responsible for supporting the independent directors who came to be known as **Young German Cinema**. Other signatories prominent in German film include **Edgar Reitz**, who directed the critically acclaimed and popular miniseries *Heimat—eine deutsche Chronik* (*Heimat: A Chronicle of Germany*, 1984); Peter Schamoni, whose film *Schonzeit für Füchse* (*Close Season on Foxes*, 1966) was one of the first films of Young German Cinema; and Hansjürgen Pohland, who cast his film *Katz und Maus* (*Cat and Mouse*, 1967), based on Günter Grass's novel of the same name, with Lars and Peter Brandt, sons of then mayor of Berlin Willy Brandt, calling forth a storm of protest from conservatives in the nation's press.

OPHÜLS, MAX (1902–1957). Asked in 1936 what he considered his nationality to be, after fleeing into exile from the Nazis and directing films in France, Holland, and Italy, Max Ophüls (born Max Oppenheimer) answered, "I'll know tomorrow." Born into a German Jewish family in what is today the German Saarland—the Saarbrücken Film Festival awards an annual Max Ophüls prize to the most promising new director—Ophüls is also considered a French film director. It seems more accurate to count him as one of the many German Jewish exiles who enriched the international art world in the 1930s and after, especially when one considers that *Liebelei* (*Flirtation*, 1932), his first international success, based on the play of the same name by the Austrian writer Arthur Schnitzler, was a German production.

Ophüls also worked in radio and theater in German-speaking countries for at least some of his career. Moreover, although not Viennese, the mixture of melancholy and gaiety often found in the works of Austrian *fin de siècle* theater permeates many of his films.

Ophüls's masterpiece is without question *Lola Montès* (known in German as *Lola Montez*, 1955). Using unconventional narrative form, the film failed to attract a wide public, even after being reedited by the production studio. Indeed, the French audience at the premier was so disappointed in the film, which starred the popular fifties French sex symbol Martine Carol, that the police had to be called to quell a disturbance at the theater. Championed by Francois Truffaut and other members of the film publication *Cahiers du Cinéma*, today *Lola Montès* is considered an excellent example of auteur cinema. The film features all the elements of Ophüls's unmistakable style: constantly moving camera, often inaudible dialogue, characters speaking while moving—walking, dancing, climbing stairs—and placement of objects between the camera and the characters. The film also contains the director's favorite themes of romantic love, illusion, and morality. Ophüls critically examines society's moral codes, revealing his love for humanity and concern for the fate of individuals.

OSWALD, RICHARD (1880–1963). Richard Oswald (born Richard W. Ornstein), a successful director, producer, and writer of the 1910s and 1920s, specialized in detective films, literary adaptations, and sexual enlightenment films (*see* **Aufklärungsfilm**). Film historians view him as a natural talent, owing to the clarity of his screenplays. His precise descriptions of scenes and directions for filming influenced the industry, and also made filmmaking more economical.

Oswald had three distinct periods. In the 1910s, he directed melodramas, mysteries, and art films (literary adaptations). He created a series of mysteries first as theater plays and then screenplays based on Arthur Conan Doyle's *The Hound of the Baskervilles* (1902). The first episodes of the series were directed by Rudolf Meinert in 1914, but Oswald took over directing the films in 1915. At the time, he also created the detective Engelbert Fox. Another series of mysteries ran under the title *Das unheimliche Haus* (*The Eerie House*). In addition, he filmed *Hoffmans Erzählungen* (*Tales of Hoffmann*, 1916), based on the gothic tales of German author E. T. A. Hoffmann; *Das Bildnis des Dorian Gray* (*The Picture of Dorian Gray*, 1917), based on Oscar Wilde's novel of that title; and *Der lebende Leichnam* (*The Living Corpse*, 1918), based on a work by Leo Tolstoy.

In 1916 Oswald began producing *Es werde Licht* (*Let there Be Light*), the first of a number of sexual enlightenment films. Unlike many of the sex films that were being made at the time due to the lessening of censorship after the war, Oswald's films were a genuine attempt to seriously address sexual taboos of the time, influenced by the psychoanalytic theories of Sigmund Freud and the sexual research of Magnus Hirschfeld. *Es werde Licht* consisted of four parts: the first episodes are about venereal disease, the last is a plea to reform Paragraph 218, the law outlawing abortion in Germany, a topic throughout the 1920s. He also did films on prostitution and homosexuality, including *Anders als die Andern* (*Different from the Others*, 1919), which championed elimination of the laws against homosexual relationships.

In the 1920s Oswald again turned to literary adaptations, but because they proved less popular with the public than other genres, he switched to historical films, mysteries, and light entertainment. With the advent of sound, he was successful with *Der Hauptmann von Köpenick* (*The Captain of Köpenick*, 1931), based on Carl Zuckmayer's satire of the Prussian love of uniforms. Oswald also directed operettas, farces, and comedies. Film histories record that before he left Germany, he had the distinction of Joseph Goebbels attending a screening of his film *Ein Lied geht um die Welt* (*A Song Goes around the World*, 1933) and of having his *Ganovenehre* (*Crook's Honor*, 1932) be one of the first films banned when the Nazis got into power. *See also* AUSTRIAN CINEMA.

OTTINGER, ULRIKE (1942–). One of Germany's most original filmmakers, Ulrike Ottinger, like **Herbert Achternbusch** and **Werner Schroeter**, exemplifies the avant garde of **New German Cinema**. Her films combine **Rainer Werner Fassbinder**'s focus on the outsider, **Alexander Kluge**'s deliberate and minimal cinematic style, and **Werner Herzog**'s documents of strange and wonderful people and places. In the United States and elsewhere, Ottinger's films are known primarily through screenings sponsored by the Goethe Institute. In Germany, they play limited engagements in art house venues, at film festivals, or on the cultural television channels. In spite of the obscurity of her films, Ottinger enjoys an excellent reputation as director, writer, and producer of demanding films.

Freak Orlando (*Freak Orlando*, 1981), one of Ottinger's major successes, illustrates her focus on the marginal and bizarre. The opening scene disorients viewers as a woman clad in monk's garb walks across a desolate area up to a woman on a cross and then proceeds into town, entering under a neon sign proclaiming "Freak City." As she does in another of her open-ended tales, *Johanna d'Arc of Mongolia* (*Joan of Arc of Mongolia*, 1989), Ottinger forces viewers to confront the clichés of other films and change their perception of the outsider or so-called freak in society.

Ottinger has made a number of critically acclaimed documentaries. *Taiga* (*Taiga*, 1992) is a three-part, eight-hour epic of life among reindeer herders in the outer reaches of Mongolia. The film requires patience as the director rejects the usual narrative devices employed by documentary filmmakers: narration; engaging, sentimental images; and privileged point of view shots. She replaces them with long moments of silence, lingering shots, and an eavesdropper's point of view. For example, in one scene she places the camera in a corner of the yurt where a shaman is preparing a ceremony. On the one hand, the technique minimizes the disruption caused by the act of filming. On the other hand, it frustrates viewers' attempts to see what is going on.

Ottinger's *Exil Shanghai* (*Exile Shanghai*, 1997) documents the three waves of Jewish immigration to that Chinese city. In a series of interviews against a backdrop of still photos, archive footage, and newly shot material, Ottinger examines the Jewish impact on the city historically, but mostly she concentrates on the years 1937–1945, when thousands of Jews fled to the country because of its open policies on immigration. The director asks Jews who were living there at the time but no longer live there to comment on their experiences under Japanese occupation. In 2004, Ottinger showed a lighter side to her filmmaking, directing the comedy *Zwölf Stühle* (*Twelve Chairs*), based on the novel *12 stulev* (*12 Chairs*) by Russian writers Ilja Ilf and Jevgeni Petrov (1928) and filmed a number of times, including by Mel Brooks (*The Twelve Chairs*, 1970). *See also* MONTEZUMA, MAGDALENA.

– P –

PABST, GEORG WILHELM (1885–1967). Although his directing career spanned four decades, from the Weimar Republic to the postwar years, and his works include some of the most popular and critically acclaimed films of their day, Georg Wilhelm Pabst never gained the auteur reputation of many of his contemporaries. This lack of recognition may be due in part to his large output, which makes it difficult to find a unifying or auteur principle at work in all his films, particularly as they occurred over so many years. In part, it may be due to his inclination to make his films timely, thus relating them to contemporary sociopolitical problems rather than to his personal vision. Finally, there may be reluctance to grant Pabst his due for historical–political reasons. He returned to Austria after the Nazis had gained power there and made films for the National Socialists when he realized he could not return to the United States, thus opening himself up to charges of opportunism. Particularly troubling to some film historians is the fact that the two films he made for the Nazis, although escapist entertainment, nonetheless served the government's propaganda machine.

Pabst's most acclaimed films were made during the silent era. One of his earliest features, *Die freudlose Gasse* (*The Joyless Street*, 1925), introduced the legendary Greta Garbo to an international audience. The film exposes the growing misery of Vienna's middle class during the inflationary period at the hands of an exploitative black-marketeering elite. *Die freudlose Gasse* was one of a series of left-leaning films made in the Weimar Republic that documented for viewers the misery they were enduring outside the theater. The themes of sex, money, and power dominate in Pabst's work, which led authorities to censor his great silent films, particularly when shown in America. The director's *Die Büchse der Pandora* (*Pandora's Box*, 1929) made **Louise Brooks** an icon of German silent film. The film personifies sexuality in its main character, Lulu, German expressionist playwright Frank Wedekind's free-spirited and sensual creation, a femme fatale who destroys the men who love her until she herself is killed by Jack the Ripper. The success of *Die Büchse der Pandora* led to further collaboration between Pabst and Brooks. Their second film, *Das Tagebuch einer Verlorenen* (*Diary of a Lost Girl*, 1929), contains themes of rape, seduction, and unwed motherhood played out in the milieu of country home, reform school, and brothel.

Pabst's early sound films before the Nazi takeover reveal his wide range of social commitments. *Westfront 1918* (*Comrades of 1918*, 1930) is an antiwar epic that many consider more effective than Lewis Milestone's classic *All Quiet on the Western Front* (1930). Both films were despised by the National Socialists, who upon their release in 1930 disrupted showings through acts of hooliganism and finally suppressed them once Adolf Hitler took power. *Westfront 1918* was one of five Pabst films to make a list of 100 greatest German films ever, voted on by film critics, directors, and historians.

Pabst's version of **Bertolt Brecht**'s play *Die Dreigroschenoper* (*The Threepenny Opera*, 1931) captures much of Brecht's satire on the pretensions of capitalist society. Nonetheless Brecht was displeased with the film, taking the film company to court for compensation, a case he lost. Brecht's main objection, supported by most film historians but not all, was that the film watered down the playwright's parody of bourgeois self-righteousness and hypocrisy and perhaps even subverted his intention, supporting rather than criticizing the economic and political establishment. Pabst's *Kamaradschaft* (*Comradeship*, 1931) is a plea for international cooperation, which earned Pabst vilification at home in Germany but the Legion of Honor in France. Both *Die Dreigroschenoper* and *Kamaradschaft* were released in separate French-language versions, a common practice in the early years of sound.

After leaving Germany to pursue a career first in France and then Hollywood, Pabst returned to Germany and Austria for family matters. There he made two films, *Komödianten* (*The Comedians*, 1941), about the founding of a national theater in the 18th century, and *Paracelsus* (*Paracelsus*, 1943), about the Renaissance scientist whose methods of treating patients met with resistance from the public. Although neither film differs from film biographies of other countries, Pabst's work is criticized for drafting great historical figures— Paracelsus was actually born in Switzerland and not Germany—to serve Nazi ideology. Moreover, both films tell stories about misunderstood people who were ahead of their time, adding to the German genius cult that had built up around Hitler.

After the war, in what some consider an attempt to regain his reputation as a man with an active social conscience, Pabst directed two *Vergangenheitsbewältigungsfilme* films. *Der letzte Akt* (*The Last Ten Days*, 1954/1955) tells about Hitler's life in his Berlin bunker at the end of the war, shortly before his suicide, a theme also filmed by **Oliver Hirschbiegel** in *Der Untergang* (*The Downfall*, 2004) and by Hans-Christoph Blumenberg in *Die letzte Schlacht* (*The Last Battle*, 2005). *Es geschah am 20. Juli* (*The Jackboot Mutiny*, 1955, aka *It Happened on the 20th of July*) re-creates the best known of the assassination attempts on Hitler, which was carried out by a group of military officers led by Colonel Claus Schenk Graf von Stauffenberg.

The other Pabst films that made the list of "100 most significant German films" are all from his early work. They include *Kamaradschaft*, *Das Tagebuch einer Verlorenen*, *Die Büchse der Pandora*, *Die freudlose Gasse*, and *Die Dreigroschenoper*. Also on the list is *Die weiße Hölle vom Piz Palü* (*The White Hell of Pitz Palu*, 1929), a so-called *Bergfilm* or **mountain film**, directed by **Arnold Fanck**, for which Pabst directed the studio scenes. *See also* AUSTRIAN CINEMA.

PALMER, LILLI (1914–1986). After studying acting in Berlin in the early 1930s, Lilli Palmer left Germany in 1933, when the Nazis came to power, because of her Jewish heritage. She began her career in films therefore in the United Kingdom rather than Germany, appearing in nearly 20 feature films, including Alfred Hitchcock's *Secret Agent* (1936), before going to Hollywood with her first husband, the British actor Rex Harrison. In the United States, she starred on Broadway as well as in Hollywood, often with Harrison. Their major successes were *Bell Book and Candle* on Broadway and *The Four Poster* (Irving Reis, 1952) for Hollywood.

After divorcing Harrison, Palmer returned to Europe and starred in her first German film, *Feuerwerk* (*Fireworks*, **Kurt Hoffmann**, 1954), a musical comedy about the circus. As an indication of how international the film industry has always been, Palmer introduced the song *"O mein Papa"* ("Oh! My Pa-Pa") in the film. In turn it was covered by American pop idol Eddie Fisher and became a top-selling song in the United States. Between 1954 and 1986, Palmer appeared in another 20 films in her native country. One of the most memorable

of these is *Mädchen in Uniform* (*Girls in Uniform*, Géza von Radványi, 1958), a remake of Leontine Sagan's 1931 classic of the same
name. Although the film, which looks at latent homosexuality in a
girls' boarding school, was panned by many critics, it is noteworthy
for Palmer's performance as well as that of **Romy Schneider**, Germany's most popular female actor at the time. Also noteworthy
among Palmer's German films is *Lotte in Weimar* (*Lotte in Weimar*,
Egon Günther, 1974), an East German production based on the novel
of the same name by Thomas Mann. The film appeared at the same
time that a number of other films based on classical themes and literature appeared in the German Democratic Republic and was an attempt to give the film more commercial possibilities in the West.
Palmer's acting style was not integrated well into the ensemble of
East German actors, however, and the film did not achieve the hoped-
for critical and commercial success.

Known primarily for her portrayal of elegant women of the world,
Palmer played to type in most of her films, whether made in England,
the United States, or Germany. She also brought her elegance to
American and German television. In America, she appeared frequently during the so-called golden age of television drama, including
in productions of *Lux Video Theater* (1952), *U.S. Steel Hour* (1953),
and *Fourstar Playhouse* (1954). She also had her own shows, *The Lilli
Palmer Show* (1953) and *Lilli Palmer Theatre* (1956). Her later American films include *The Boys from Brazil* (Franklin Schaffner, 1978)
and the television miniseries *Peter the Great* (Marvin Chomsky,
1984–1985), which also starred **Hanna Schygulla** and **Maximilian
Schell**, among others.

Palmer's German film career mirrors her work in the United
States. There also she enjoyed success on television at the same
time as her feature film career. She appeared in television dramas as
well as in talk shows. In 1956 and 1957, she won Awards in Silver
for Outstanding Individual Achievement: Actress for her roles in
Teufel in Seide (*Devil in Silk*, Rolf Hansen) and *Anastasia: Die letzte Zarentochter* (*The Czar's Last Daughter*, Falk Harnack), and in
1976 an Award in Gold as a lifetime achievement award from the
German film industry. Palmer also has a star on Hollywood's Walk
of Fame.

PETERSEN, WOLFGANG (1941–). Although Wolfgang Petersen today directs big-budget action thrillers in Hollywood, he began his career working for German television. His early television credits for the series *Tatort* (*Scene of the Crime*, 1970–), for which he directed six episodes between 1971 and 1977, revealed early in his career his strength in creating psychologically taut dramas. His reputation as a director of suspense films was further enhanced by *Einer von uns Beiden* (*One of Us Two*, 1974), a thriller for which he received an Award in Gold as Best New Director from the German film industry. His made-for-television film *Die Konsequenz* (*The Consequence*, 1977), a sensitive portrayal of a homosexual relationship, caused a scandal in Germany—Bavarian television refused to broadcast the movie—but brought Petersen recognition as a talented director of auteur films in the vein of **New German Cinema**. The film starred then German heartthrob **Jürgen Prochnow**, who would again work for Petersen in the highly successful war film *Das Boot* (*The Boat*, 1981).

Das Boot propelled Petersen to international fame. One of the most costly movies in German film history at the time it was made, the film tells the story of submarine warfare from the side of the Germans. Although German directors had made **war films** before, showing the war from the point of view of the German combatants, none had had the emotional power of *Das Boot*. Moreover, none had compelled viewers through cinematic point of view to identify so strongly with the plight of men fighting not only for a doomed cause, but also for the wrong cause. Point of view notwithstanding, the film became very successful outside Germany, particularly in England and the United States, where it passed out of the so-called art house ghetto circuit to play in suburban multiplexes. The fact that English and American viewers accepted a film in which they essentially side with the enemy speaks for the film's emotional center. *Das Boot* is included on the list of the 100 most significant German films, voted on by critics, directors, and historians.

Die unendliche Geschichte (*The Neverending Story*, 1984), Petersen's second successful international production, is a children's movie based on Michael Ende's book of the same name. **Bernd Eichinger**, producer of the film, and Petersen made the film in English to ensure acceptance by an international audience, a practice since followed by German and French directors, including Germans **Volker Schlöndorff**, **Wim Wenders**, and **Werner Herzog** and Frenchmen Jean-Jacques Annaud and Luc Besson. *The Neverending Story* faithfully adapts Ende's novel, capturing the work's imagination and, more important, the story within a story that lends the novel and movie a depth not usually found in youth literature. Critics emphasize the film's special effects, which although they would become dated only a few years later, for the time delighted children and adults.

Petersen's success with *Das Boot* and *The Neverending Story* brought him to Hollywood, where he directed *Enemy Mine* (1985)—a film he shot at his former home studio in Bavaria—*Shattered* (1991), *In the Line of Fire* (1993), *Outbreak* (1995), *Air Force One* (1997), *The Perfect Storm* (2000), *Troy* (2004), and *Poseidon* (2006). *The Perfect Storm* and *Poseidon* are of particular interest as they reprise the trope of entrapment found in *Das Boot*, first on a fishing trawler lost in a tremendous storm and then on an ocean liner turned upside down. While the situation may change in each of these three films, the testing of characters within a confined situation is the same. This is also true of his nonmariner pictures: *Enemy Mine*, in which two enemies must rely on each other to survive on an alien world; *Outbreak*, in which a community is held prisoner within an internment camp to stop a plague; and *Air Force One*, in which a megalomaniac holds the president and his family hostage within the limited space of the presidential plane. *See also VERGANGENHEITSBEWÄLTIGUNGFILM.*

PIEL, HARRY (1892–1963). Harry Piel wrote, directed, produced, and acted in his own films. His first work, *Schwarzes Blut* (*Black Blood*, 1912), anticipated the rest of Piel's film career, which eschewed logical stories in favor of sensational footage. Piel became known for his use of explosives in action scenes in sci-fi, detective, and animal adventure films. Two of his detectives in the 1910s, Kelly Brown and Joe Deebs, were polar opposites in their approach to the law, but both Piel roles involved him in stunts in which he reportedly never used a double. As Kelly Brown, 1913–1917, Piel played an undercover cop who used even illegal means to trap the criminals. As Joe Deebs, whom he played from 1918–1919, he portrayed a law-abiding police officer, himself often the object of chases. Eventually he combined the two personas into Harry Peel the adventurer, a figure that captivated German and international audiences and led to a pulp fiction publication, with the actor as the hero. The violence and criminal topics in his films raised concern among educators about Piel's influence on youth, leading to a ban on their import into the United States as immoral. The Soviet Union also forbade their exhibition on the grounds they could lead to criminal activity.

Piel made the transition to sound easily, continuing to favor themes that showcased stunts and effects, often ignoring narrative logic: jungle adventures, circus films, and science fiction. *Der Herr der Welt* (*The Master of the World*, 1934) tells the story of a robotic machine whose rays will help the inventor become ruler over humankind. *Artisten* (*Performers*, 1935), which takes place in a circus, allows Piel to display his physical talents in capturing a rogue elephant and also chasing down a dangerous criminal. In another circus film, *Menschen, Tiere, Sensationen* (*Men, Animals, Sensations*, 1938), he has to subdue a tiger gone wild in an act. *Der Dschungel ruft* (*The Jungle Calls*, 1936) presents Piel as Bobby Roeder, a cross between Tarzan and medicine doctor, a man who lives in the Indian jungle with his animal friends. One day his world is disturbed by outsiders who shoot a white bull. Blamed for the killing, Bobby must run from local residents upset at the sacrilege until circumstances permit him to prove his innocence. The film closes as Roeder and a visiting American woman ride off into the jungle on an elephant. For his films in the 1930s, Piel relied on film effects to help create those stunts he was getting too old to perform.

After World War II, Piel was one of the few actors temporarily jailed for his involvement in the Third Reich. He was banned from working in films until 1950, and when he returned he was never able to regain his previous popularity.

POMMER, ERICH (1889–1966). The most important producer during the German film industry's so-called golden age in the 1920s, Erich Pommer helped develop **Universum Film AG** (Ufa) into an international production studio. His name is linked to many of the classics directed by some of Germany's best-known directors. Among the over 170 films that he produced are the silent classics *Das Cabinet* *des Dr. Caligari (The Cabinet of Dr. Caligari*, **Robert Wiene**, 1920), *Die Nibelungen (The Nibelungen*, **Fritz Lang**, 1924), *Der letzte Mann (The Last Laugh*, **Friedrich Wilhelm Murnau**, 1924), *Varieté (Jealousy*, **Ewald André Dupont**, 1925), and *Metropolis (Metropolis*, Lang, 1927). During the sound era he produced *Der blaue Engel (The Blue Angel*, Josef von Sternberg, 1930), *Die Drei von der Tankstelle (Three from the Gas Station*, Wilhelm Thiele, 1930), and *Der Krongreß tanzt (The Congress Dances*, Erik Charell, 1931)— three of the most critically and commercially successful of Ufa's sound films. Pommer is credited through these and other films with nurturing the careers of Germany's brightest talents, including writer **Carl Mayer** and actors **Emil Jannings** and **Marlene Dietrich**.

With a good sense of what the public wanted to see, Pommer is responsible for the framing device added to *Das Cabinet des Dr. Caligari* and the happy ending appended to *Der letzte Mann*. Carl Mayer and Hans Janowitz, the writers of *Dr. Caligari*, originally intended the film to play without a narrative frame, which would have indicted the psychiatric hospital headed by Dr. Caligari, a stand-in for German authority. Pommer, fearing that an attack on German institutions would limit the appeal of the film, included a narrative frame that revealed the events as the product of a madman's delusions and exonerated Dr. Caligari. Carl Mayer's original screenplay called for *Der letzte Mann* to end with the complete degradation of the demoted doorman played by Emil Jannings. Pommer's intervention added an ironic coda that transformed the destitute doorman into a millionaire and allowed audiences to leave the theater smiling.

Although his career continued into the 1950s, Pommer was never again to equal the success of the 1920s; all but a dozen or so of his films were made in the Weimar era. Nonetheless, he was able to achieve a critical success with the antiwar film *Kinder, Mütter, und ein General (Children, Mothers, and a General*, László Benedek, 1955), about a group of 14-year-old boys drafted in World War II. The film won international critical praise and received a Golden Globe in 1956 for Best Foreign Film but was less well-received in Germany and failed at the box office. The theme of drafting boys out of high school was taken up again in the more commercially successful *Die Brücke (The Bridge*, **Bernhard Wicki**, 1959).

PORTEN, HENNY (1888–1960). Described as "sturdy and blond" and reminiscent of "the Valkyries and the bronze statues in German town squares" by French film historian Georges Sadoul, Henny Porten personified the German Everywoman, even when playing non-German roles, such as Anne Boleyn in *Anna Boleyn* (*Anne Boleyn*, **Ernst Lubitsch**, 1920). She was a nonemotive actor, performing for the camera as spectacle. Rather than disappearing into the screen space of the story, she foregrounded herself as an object in front of the camera, a style she no doubt developed in her early films.

Porten acted in German films at the beginning of film history, appearing for the first time in *Meißner Porzellan* (*Meissen Porcelain*, 1906), a synchronized sound strip produced by **Oskar Messter** and directed by her father, Franz Porten, who directed most of her early work. In the 1910s she appeared in melodramas, often playing women suffering because of love. These films, including *Das Opfer* (*The Sacrifice*, 1913), *Die große Sünderin* (*The Sinner*, 1914), and *Um das Glück betrogen* (*Betrayed by Happiness*, 1914), and all directed by her husband, Curt A. Stark, promise a sentimental experience. After her husband's death in World War I, Porten preferred to be directed by **Rudolf Biebrach**, who had acted in many of the films she made for Stark. With Biebrach she continued to make schmaltzy fare. These films, often with screenplays written by **Robert Wiene**, include *Märtyrerin der Liebe* (*Martyr of Love*, 1915), *Abseits vom Glück* (*Flipside of Happiness*, 1916), *Gelöste Ketten* (*Loosened Chains*), and the comedy *Agnes Arnau und ihre drei Freier* (*Agnes Arnau and Her Three Suitors*, 1918).

In addition to the shorts, melodramas, and sentimental comedies made with Stark and Biebrach—and there are over 100 such early films—Porten also acted in more demanding and prestigious projects. She played opposite Emil Jannings in a comedy directed by Lubitsch, *Kohlhiesels Töchter* (*Kohhiesel's Daughters*, 1920), a satirical and cynical look at love. In *Anna Boleyn*, Porten plays the ill-fated wife of Henry VIII. In *Die Geierwally* (*Geierwally*, Ewald André Dupont, 1921), a popular tale of unrequited love, revenge, and suicide that has been the subject of films and theater in Germany, she plays the title character. The story is best known to non-Germans through the opera *La Wally* by Alfredo Catalani, whose main aria was used in the film *Diva* (*Diva*, 1981) by French director Jean-Jacques Beineix. Henny Porten also starred in one of the 1920s iconic street films, *Hintertreppe* (*Backstairs*, Leopold Jessner and Paul Leni, 1921), which like many of her films ends in tragedy brought about by misunderstanding.

Since Porten could play both dramatic and comedic parts, her popularity lasted throughout the 1920s. In addition to the films already mentioned, she made dozens more during the silent era, most with **Carl Froelich**, a director she again worked with during the Third Reich. Although she was worried at first about sound movies—her acting skills were based on short takes interrupted by black screen and intertitles—she easily converted to the continuous acting style required by sound films, starring in a remake of *Kohlhiesels Töchter* (Hans Behrendt, 1930), among other films. When the Nazis took control of Germany in 1933, Porten continued to act, but because she refused to divorce her Jewish husband, she received few roles. Among the roles she did receive were parts in films by Froelich, for whom she had made so many films during the Weimar Republic, and also **Georg Wilhelm Pabst**, who cast her in *Komödianten* (*The Comedians*, 1940/1941), a film about the birth of modern German theater in the 18th century. After the war, Porten got few roles in West Germany but signed a contract with **DEFA**, the East Germany film studio, and appeared in several films in the East, including *Das Fräulein von Scuderi* (*Mademoiselle Scuderi*, 1954), an adaptation of the E. T. A. Hoffmann novella of the same name.

POTENTE, FRANKA (1974–). Franka Potente captivated Germany, and eventually an international audience, with her role as Lola, a redheaded German Generation X-er who must find DM 100,000 for her slacker boyfriend Manni, in the film *Lola rennt* (*Run Lola Run*, **Tom Tykwer**, 1998). Able to break glass with her scream, run incredible distances in under 20 minutes, and regenerate her life when the outcome does not suit her, Lola gave Potente a chance to display her dramatic, comedic, and physical acting abilities.

Potente, who is one of a number of German actors who gained international recognition in the 1990s (*see also* **Bleibtreu, Moritz; Fürmann, Benno; Riemann, Katja; Schweiger, Til**), began her career on German television, often in roles showing an independent or rebellious spirit. In the romantic comedy *Nach Fünf im Urwald* (*It's a Jungle Out There*, Hans-Christian Schmid, 1995), she plays a runaway who gives her parents pause to remember their own spirited youth. In *Opernball* (*Opera Ball*, Urs Egger, 1997), based on Josef Haslinger's best-selling political novel, she's an independent-minded reporter. Her one misstep, according to critics, was her role as one of the three girls in *Die Drei Mädels von der Tankstelle* (*Babes' Patrol*, Michael F. Bringmann, 1997), a failed remake of the 1930 classic *Die Drei von der Tankstelle* (*Three from the Gas Station*, Wilhelm Thiele), which cast the three gas attendants as women rather than men.

Although she gained international fame for her red hair, which became known in Germany as "*Lola rot*" (Lola red), Potente has more naturally colored and less bizarre styles in her other films. In *Der Krieger und die Kaiserin* (*The Princess and the Warrior*, Tykwer, 2000), Potente plays a nurse who tracks down and pursues a man who has saved her life. Her performance is more nuanced than in *Lola rennt*, as she unravels not only the mystery of her savior but also of murder. On the basis of her German films, Potente received supporting roles in major Hollywood films. She plays opposite Johnny Depp as drug dealer George Jung's girlfriend in *Blow* (Ted Demme, 2001), and opposite Matt Damon in the spy movies *The Bourne Identity* (Doug Liman, 2002) and *The Bourne Supremacy* (Paul Greengrass, 2004). She has also appeared in *Bin ich schön?* (*Am I Beautiful?* **Doris Dörrie**, 1998) as a woman who travels through Spain pretending to be a deaf-mute, and in *Anatomie* (*Anatomy*, Stefan Ruzowitzky, 2000), as a medical student who helps to unravel a macabre murder mystery.

PROCHNOW, JÜRGEN (1941–). Jürgen Prochnow became an international star with his portrayal of a tough as nails U-boat captain with deep concern for his crew in **Wolfgang Petersen's** *Das Boot* (*The Boat*, 1981). In his character of "Der Alte," Prochnow perfectly captures the tense ambivalence created in viewers asked to identify with men fighting for a cause that history has condemned as evil. His humanity and his skepticism of the Nazi cause become apparent as the captain returns a Nazi salute, not with "Heil Hitler" but with a handshake. Prochnow's nuanced performance, his good physique, and his ruggedly handsome face, somewhat scarred but with high cheekbones and intense eyes, clearly helped viewers identify with the men's mission and hope for their success.

Das Boot brought Prochnow an international career by winning him numerous offers from Hollywood. But his German work had already made him well known in Germany. In *Die Verrohung des Franz Blum* (*The Brutalization of Franz Blum*, **Reinhard Hauff**, 1974), one of his early roles, Prochnow played a decent man sent to prison only to have the violence and dehumanized nature of prison life turn him into a criminal. He next played Ludwig Götten, an army deserter whose gentle nature seduces the title character in *Die verlorene Ehre der Katharina Blum* (*The Lost Honor of Katharina Blum*, **Volker Schlöndorff** and **Margarethe von Trotta**, 1975). When he leaves through the ventilation system the next day to escape the police, Katharina's life is turned upside down as the boulevard press paints her as a terrorist's girlfriend. Made at a time of political unrest in Germany caused by radicals, the film resonated with Germany's Left. In Petersen's *Die Konsequenz* (*The Consequence*, 1977), Prochnow portrays a homosexual prisoner seduced by the son of the prison's warden. When he is later released, social structures prevent them from making a life together.

In Hollywood, Prochnow continued to play characters on the wrong side of the system, but without the humanistic center of the characters found in his German films. Indeed, the roles seem stereotypes at times. In *The Seventh Sign* (Carl Schulz, 1988), he is a mysterious boarder; in *Robin Hood* (John Irwin, 1990), a made-for-television film of the tale, he plays bad guy Sir Miles Folcanet; and in *Interceptor* (Michael Cohn, 1992) he plays a terrorist. The most extreme example of the types of roles he often gets is undoubtedly his portrayal of a brutal police officer in *A Dry White Season* (Euzhan Palcy, 1989), a film about white brutality against blacks in South Africa. But Prochnow does get other roles as well, generally small in nature and often requiring the intensity of his acting. In *The Da Vinci Code* (Ron Howard, 2006), he again plays someone with dubious morals, but with a twist, as here his character is an effete snob, a relative weakling.

PULVER, LISELOTTE (1929–). Liselotte Pulver was an audience darling in the 1950s and early 1960s, appearing in dozens of West Germany's most popular films. She received recognition early in

Föhn (*The White Hell of Pitz Palu*, Rolf Hansen, 1950), in which she played Maria, the **Leni Riefenstahl** role, in this remake of *Die weiße Hölle des Piz Palü* (**Arnold Fanck** and **Georg Wilhelm Pabst**, 1929). Her next film, *Heidelberger Romanze* (*Heidelberg Romance*, **Paul Verhoeven**, 1951), displayed her talent for musical romances and lighter material. Subsequent to *Heidelberger Romanze*, Pulver appeared in a number of comedies, many directed by one of the 1950s most commercially successful directors, **Kurt Hoffmann**. Her films for Hoffmann included *Ich denke oft an Piroschka* (*I Often Think of Piroschka*, 1955), *Heute heiratet mein Mann* (*My Husband Is Getting Married Today*, 1956), *Bekenntnisse des Hochstaplers Felix Krull* (*Confessions of Felix Krull*, 1957), and *Das Wirtshaus im Spessart* (*The Spessart Inn*, 1958). Pulver was adept at playing perky, sprightly women, with a good sense of comedic timing—as, for example, in her role of an aspiring screenwriter in **Helmut Käutner's** *Die Zürcher Verlobung* (*The Zurich Engagement*, 1957). In that film, Pulver plays a Doris Day-like ingénue who must extradite herself from a case of mistaken identity in order to marry the man she loves.

Pulver also had a number of important dramatic roles. She appeared as the title character's lover in *Hanussen* (*Hanussen*, **Otto Wilhelm Fischer** and Georg Marischka, 1955), a film about proto-fascism as Adolf Hitler rises to power. In addition, **Douglas Sirk** cast her in his World War II love story *A Time to Love and a Time to Die* (1958), based on Erich Maria Remarque's best-selling novel. In 1959, she appeared in *Die Buddenbrooks* (*The Buddenbrooks*, Alfred Weidenmann), as the headstrong daughter in Thomas Mann's saga about the rise and fall of a patrician Lübeck family. In the 1970s and 1980s, Pulver could be seen on German television in variety shows and also as one of the human hosts on *Sesamstraße*, the German version of *Sesame Street*. In 1980, she received an Award in Gold (*see* **film awards**) for lifetime achievement in films and television.

– Q –

QUINN, FREDDY (1931–). In the 1950s and 1960s, Freddy Quinn appeared in a series of films as a singing traveler. The films are reminiscent in some ways of the singing cowboy films of America's

Gene Autry and Roy Rogers, in which an adventure-seeking loner falls in love with a pretty woman, confronts danger in the guise of ineffectual villains, sings some ballads, and then leaves to continue his adventures. They also resemble the formula of Elvis Presley's films in the late 1950s, with the story serving merely as the vehicle for songs, as suggested by the titles of the films: *Freddy, die Gitarre und das Meer* (*Freddy, the Guitar and the Sea*, Wolfgang Schleif, 1959), *Freddy und die Melodie der Nacht* (*Freddy and the Melody of the Night*, Schleif, 1960), *Freddy und der Millionär* (*Freddy and the Millionaire*, Paul May, 1961), and *Freddy und das Lied der Südsee* (*Freddy and the Song of the South Sea*, Werner Jacobs, 1962).

One of several singers-turned-actors (*see also* **Alexander, Peter; Backus, Gus; Froboess, Cornelia; Kraus, Peter**), Quinn had the most developed persona. He favored films that included adventure, romance, stunts, and singing. Film historian Peter Spiegel refers to him as the singing **Harry Piel**.

– R –

RAAB, KURT (1941–1988). Kurt Raab gained fame as a member of **Rainer Werner Fassbinder**'s ensemble players, working with him first in his *antiteater*, an actors' troupe that Fassbinder organized around the principle of minimalism in art. Later Raab, like others in the ensemble, became members of Fassbinder's film collective. Raab worked as a set decorator, winning an Award in Gold for Production Design from the German film industry for *Whity* (*Whity*, Fassbinder, 1971). He also had a small acting role in the film, a melodramatic, campy tale of the fall of a wealthy family in the late 19th-century American Southwest. The title refers to a light-skinned African American servant who tries to serve a dysfunctional family, including following instructions from some members to kill others.

Raab's slightly portly build, hangdog expression, and slumping shoulders predestined him to play the loser. His first major acting role was in Fassbinder's *Warum läuft Herr R. Amok?* (*Why Does Mr. R. Run Amok?* 1970), in which he played an ineffectual office worker who has a nervous breakdown and commits a multiple murder before killing himself. The film typecast him as a stressed out and uptight petit bourgeois, a role which he reprised in various forms during his career, in Fassbinder's *Satansbraten* (*Satan's Brew*, 1976) and *Bolwieser* (*The Stationmaster's Wife*, 1977) and other lesser known films. In *Satansbraten*, a dark comedy, Raab plays an untalented poet whose life spirals downward as he tries to cope with a loony brother, two mistresses, a lonely wife, and debts. In *Bolwieser*, he plays the title character, an ineffectual stationmaster, who is cuckolded frequently as his wife sleeps with other men in the town.

Raab split with Fassbinder in 1977 and, like **Hanna Schygulla**, another of the moody director's stock players, proved that a career was possible without his benefactor. From the time of leaving Fassbinder until his death from AIDS in 1988, Raab worked as an actor, set designer, and script writer for a number of German directors, including **Ulrike Ottinger**, Robert van Ackeren, and **Herbert Achternbusch**. In 1983, he directed *Die Insel der blutigen Plantage* (*Island of the Bloody Plantation*, 1983), a brutal drama of rape and torture set in a women's prison on an island. The film, for which Raab also wrote the screenplay, was a critical and commercial failure in Germany but enjoyed modest success in Asian countries. In the years before his death, Raab played small roles in several successful international films set in the years of Nazi Germany. Besides appearing in **Agnieszka Holland**'s *Bittere Ernte* (*Angry Harvest*, 1985), about a Jewish woman being hidden from the Nazis by a Polish farmer, and in *Escape from Sobibor* (Jack Gold, 1997), set in the infamous death camp, Raab played Adolf Hitler in *Mussolini: The Rise and Fall of Il Duce* (Alberto Negrin, 1985), a film produced by an international consortium that played on HBO.

After Fassbinder's death in 1982, Raab published *Die Sehnsucht des Rainer Werner Fassbinder*, the least flattering of a number of kiss and tell biographies by the filmmaker's associates. In his book, Raab details Fassbinder's insistence on total control of his actors, relating anecdotes meant to reflect on the director's cruelty. The book also details Fassbinder's heterosexual and homosexual affairs and serves as Raab's autobiographical confession of his own problems with alcohol, drugs, and pedophilia.

RABEN, PEER (1940–2007). Peer Raben wrote the music for a number of the films of **New German Cinema** directors and, until **Rainer Werner Fassbinder**'s death in 1982, was that director's preferred music collaborator. His credits include the score for well over half of Fassbinder's films. Raben has said that he wanted his music to add an emotional component to Fassbinder's generally ironic and satirical melodramas. As a result, the filmmaker's often cold and objective visuals unfold against a contrasting score of crescendos and other musical effects. In more elaborate films, such as *Die Ehe der Maria Braun* (*The Marriage of Maria Braun*, 1979) and *Lili Marleen* (*Lili Marleen*, 1981), Raben's dramatic music underscores Fassbinder's penchant for stylized visuals and choreographed movement. At the same time, the contrapunctal musical inserts fulfill a Brechtian function of distancing viewers from the events on the screen. *See also* BRECHT, BERTOLT.

RADDATZ, CARL (1912–2004). Carl Raddatz began his acting career with the National Socialist propaganda film *Urlaub auf Ehrenwort* (*Furlough on Recognizance*, Karl Ritter, 1938), in which he played an infantryman on leave during World War I. The film is often viewed by critics as an ode to military virtues. Raddatz's next few films eschewed overt propaganda in favor of entertainment. In *Sylvesternacht am Alexanderplatz* (*New Year's Eve on Alexanderplatz*, Richard Schneider-Edenkoben, 1939), for example, Raddatz plays a man who plans to commit suicide on New Year's Eve but changes his mind after a friend shows him people with truly miserable lives: a mother who dies in childbirth, a couple whose marriage is ending, and an ex-convict trying to rebuild his life.

Raddatz appeared in three of the National Socialist era's most egregiously propagandistic films of entertainment: *Das Wunschkonzert* (*Concert by Request*, Eduard von Borsody, 1940), a love story that starts in prewar Germany during the Olympic Games and continues to the start of World War II. *Das Wunschkonzert* glorifies the nationalist spirit and the ideal of self-sacrifice of those on the home front as well as those fighting the war. *Stukas* (*Stukas*, Karl Ritter, 1941) focuses on the air war against England, with multiple scenes of dive-bombing, destruction, and opportunities to die for Germany. In one of the strangest film moments ever made, Raddatz, leading a squadron on a raid to England, sings a song of the Stukas (the name of the planes they are flying) with his men about bombing England. The film cuts between the men's faces inside the bubbles of their planes and the squadron flying in formation, reminiscent of cardboard cutouts on a stage. Arguably the most notorious of Raddatz's roles was in *Heimkehr* (*Homecoming*, Gustav Ucicky, 1941), which set out to legitimize Germany's march into Poland as a return to a greater Germany. The film's penultimate scene shows a German woman cheering up fellow prisoners by reminding them they will one day be able to again breathe German air, hear the German language, listen to birds chirping in German, and be buried in German soil. The final scene suggests this will happen as soon as Adolf Hitler's troupes conquer Poland and make it part of Germany.

Raddatz acted in a number of nonpropagandistic films also. His portrayal of Reinhart in *Immensee* (*Bees' Lake*, **Veit Harlan**, 1943), Theodor Storm's 19th-century novella of unfulfilled romance, reveals his tender and romantic nature, as in *Wunschkonzert*, but without the overt political message. *Unter den Brücken* (*Under the Bridges*, **Helmut Käutner**, 1945) reveals Raddatz at his most vulnerable. Playing a man who is in love with a woman also loved by his best friend, his character must grapple with choosing one over the other. Raddatz displays the character's inner turmoil through music, comedy, and facial expression. Not released until after the war although made before its end, *Unter den Brücken* exists almost as an anomaly among the rest of the National Socialist film repertoire. Raddatz continued his career after the war, acting mostly in lesser-known films, although he did appear in Käutner's *Epilog: Das Geheimnis der Orplid* (*The Secret of the Orplid*, 1950), an allegory about the beginning of the Cold War, and *Jeder stirbt für sich allein* (*Everyone Dies His Own Death*, Alfred Vohrer, 1976), about a couple during World War II who begin opposing the Nazis after their son falls in battle.

REINHARDT, MAX (1873–1943). The fame of Max Reinhardt (born Max Goldmann) rests with theater rather than film. He directed only four films in Germany, all before 1914, and only one elsewhere, *A Midsummer Night's Dream* (1935), in Hollywood. Reinhardt nonetheless had an important impact on the look of German films in the 1920s. Known for his impressionistic, monumental style, with stress on ornamental and decorative sets, contrast lighting, and ensemble acting, Reinhardt influenced directors such as **Ernst Lubitsch** and **Fritz Lang**. Lang in particular owed the look of his film *Die Niblungen* (*The*

Nibelungen, 1924), with its massive architecture, crowds of extras, and precise movement, to Reinhardt's theater productions, which contrasted with the naturalist school of staging by presenting theater as spectacle. Reinhardt's school of acting also gave a start to many of Germany's most famous film actors. Reinhardt transferred his stagecraft to *A Midsummer Night's Dream*, which he had already staged successfully at the Hollywood Bowl. The film introduced 14-year-old Mickey Rooney as Puck. The actor went on to become one of the most beloved American actors in the 1930s and 1940s.

REINIGER, LOTTE (1899–1981). Lotte Reiniger, a pioneer of animation in German film, used a technique for animation that used silhouette puppets to create unique films, from the 1920s through the 1950s. Reiniger's method consisted of producing animation by making individual shots of silhouette figures as they are repositioned through attached wires. Much like the photographing of multiple cells to generate the illusion of movement in classical animation, Reiniger's method created animated shadow figures reminiscent of Chinese shadow plays. Initial success with short films in the early 1920s led to a feature-length project, *Die Abenteuer des Prinzen Achmed* (*The Adventures of Prince Achmed*, 1926), from one of the tales of *The Arabian Nights*, a work for which she had difficulty finding a distributor. Reiniger had more success with her next film, *Dr. Doolittle und seine Tiere* (*Dr. Doolittle and His Animals*, 1928), based on Hugh Lofting's novel, with music by Kurt Weill and Paul Hindemith. She continued to make films using silhouette animation throughout her career, directing over 40 projects, mostly but not exclusively fairy tales.

REINL, HARALD (1908–1986). Harald Reinl began his film career as a double for **Leni Riefenstahl** in the **mountain film** *Stürme über dem Mont Blanc* (*Avalanche*, **Arnold Fanck**, 1930). He later assisted Riefenstahl with the editing of her mountain film *Tiefland* (*Lowlands*, 1940–1944, released 1954), which tells a Carmen-like story of love between a mountain man and a gypsy. Riefenstahl's influence can be seen in Reinl's *Bergkristall* (*Mountain Crystal*, 1949), based on Adalbert Stifter's 19th-century novella of that name, which reveals a visual structure reminiscent of Riefenstahl's *Das blaue Licht* (*The Blue*

Light, 1932). Rather than continue in the atmospheric style of art films, however, Reinl began focusing on commercial projects. During the next three decades he directed films of every genre, following trends but also setting them.

Reinl directed **war films**, espionage thrillers, and German Westerns, among other genres. In the late 1950s, his war films *Die Grünen Teufel von Monte Cassino* (*The Green Devils of Monte Cassino*, 1958) and *U47—Kapitänleutnant Prien* (*U47: Lieutenant Commander Prien*, 1958) joined a host of others in looking back uncritically at the role of ordinary military men during World War II. In the 1960s, Reinl filmed a series of German Westerns based on the works of Karl May. The films starred Lex Barker, who had become famous as Tarzan in Hollywood films, as Old Shatterhand, a scout who often worked with Indian chief Winnetou to solve mysteries and right injustices (*see* **Winnetou films**). The films also led to a similar series in East Germany (*see* **East German film**), where more emphasis was placed on exploitation of the Indians by Americans than in Reinl's films. Reinl's craftsmanship as a director and master of action is also evident in his films on pulp fiction hero Jerry Cotton, such as *Dynamit in grüner Seide* (*Death and Diamonds*, 1968), a heist film taking place in Los Angeles. Late in his career, Reinl directed two documentaries. The first, *Botschaft der Götter* (*Mysteries of the Gods*, 1976), is based on the best-selling book by Erich von Däniken, in which the author theorizes that extraterrestrial beings seeded the earth's development. The second, *. . . und die Bibel hat doch Recht* (*. . . and the Bible Is Right After All*, 1977), looks at Werner Keller's research purporting to show the historical accuracy of the Bible.

REITZ, EDGAR (1932–). A signatory of the **Oberhausen Manifesto**, Edgar Reitz directed short films and industrial films before his first feature, *Mahlzeiten* (*Lust for Love*, 1967), which, together with **Volker Schlöndorff**'s *Der junge Törless* (*The Young Törless*, 1966) and **Alexander Kluge**'s *Abschied von gestern* (*Yesterday Girl*, 1966), helped usher in the era of **Young German Cinema**. Although this distanced look at the dissolution of a marriage was critically successful, Reitz's reputation at the time never equaled that of the other members of the new German wave of filmmaking, who in addition to

Kluge and Schlöndorff included **Rainer Werner Fassbinder** and **Werner Herzog**, among others.

Then, in 1984, Reitz directed *Heimat—eine deutsche Chronik* (*Heimat: A Chronicle of Germany*), a 15-hour, 11-episode television film (also shown theatrically) that *Variety* called "the fulfillment of all the hopes of the **New German cinema** over the past two decades." This epic series established Reitz as one of the most important filmmakers of the period, even though it was not released until 1984, several years after most film historians consider the movement to have been over. After the phenomenal success of *Heimat*, Reitz directed *Die zweite Heimat – Chronik einer Jugend* (*Heimat II: A Chronicle of a Generation*, 1992), *Heimat 3 – Chronik einer Zeitwende* (*Heimat 3: A Chronicle of Beginnings and Endings*, 2004) and *Heimat-Fragmente: Die Frauen* (*Heimat-Fragments: The Women*, 2006).

The first *Heimat* film is a national epic set in the Hunsrück region of Germany and follows the Simon family over six decades. Reitz weaves the story of the Simons, a village farm family, so vividly into Germany's history from 1919 to 1982 that tourists reportedly visited the Hunsrück area in search of the fictional village of Schabbach, the Simon's hometown or *Heimat*. The second *Heimat* film fills in background material for one of the characters of the first series. Hermann Simon, the youngest son of Maria Simon, the character who ties the first series together, leaves home in episode nine (1960) of the 11-episode epic to pursue a career in music. *Heimat II* follows his story during the 1960s in Schwabing, Munich's artist quarter, and the stories of the people that live in his commune. Whereas the first *Heimat* series presented the scope of German history from the time of World War I to 1982, the year Helmut Kohl came to power, signaling a turn to neoconservatism in Germany, the second series limits itself to the intellectual and professional growth of an individual character against a backdrop of student idealism and radicalism. The third set of episodes in *Heimat 3* examines Germany after the fall of the Berlin Wall and the reunification of the Federal Republic of Germany and the German Democratic Republic. In this series of films Hermann Simon again serves as the central character, whose life plays out against the historical events that are unfolding. The film ends as his daughter, Lulu, stares out a window as the 21st century begins, providing a fitting conclusion, as the series began when her grandmother Maria was 17 at the beginning of the 20th century. *Heimat-Fragmente: die Frauen* follows Lulu. It is a more introspective film than the others in the series. *See also* STÖCKL, ULA.

RIEFENSTAHL, LENI (1902–2002). Germany's most controversial, talented, and famous film director, Leni Riefenstahl produced her masterpieces during and in the service of the Third Reich. While many film critics consider Riefenstahl a genius, others refuse to forgive her collaboration with the Nazis. She is the only German film director of the Third Reich who, although twice exonerated by the courts, in 1948 and 1952, found it impossible to finish any of her film projects after the war.

Riefenstahl began her film career as an actor in the **mountain films** of **Arnold Fanck**. With her striking beauty and athletic figure (she was a dancer when Fanck first employed her), Riefenstahl presented a human counterpart to the physical majesty of the mountains, which functioned more as actor than backdrop in Fanck's films. She was at once sporty and natural, a symbol of the active, emancipated woman. Yet in spite of her emancipation, she was accepted in the male-dominated world of mountain climbing. In 1932, Riefenstahl directed her own mountain film, *Das blaue Licht* (*The Blue Light*), which combines everyday mountain life with lyrical symbols and tableaux. In addition, the film provides Riefenstahl an opportunity to indulge in romantic mysticism and display her physical beauty.

Riefenstahl's fame, however, results not from her acting, her physical appearance, or her early films, but rather from two films commissioned by Joseph Goebbels: *Triumph des Willens* (*Triumph of the Will*, 1935) and *Olympia* (*Olympia*, 1938). The documentary *Triumph des Willens* covers a National Socialist Party rally held in Nuremberg in 1934. Although it is not clear whether everything one sees is genuinely part of the rally, whether it was influenced by the fact of being filmed, or whether it was perhaps even staged for the film, three things are certain. First, the movie is a powerful piece of propaganda filmmaking, glorifying the political and military power of the Nazis. Riefenstahl uses the human form as architectural building blocks; elevates military marching into a religious ritual; and encloses and opens space with banners, flags, and columns. Second, the film's images and ideas have been quoted frequently in other films, including

Rocky Horror Picture Show (Jim Sharman, 1975), *Star Wars* (George Lucas, 1977), and *Jewel of the Nile* (Robert Zemeckis, 1985). Finally, Riefenstahl made a film of the 1933 Nuremberg rally, *Der Sieg des Glaubens* (*Victory of Faith*, 1933), in which she practiced many of the techniques that found their way into *Triumph des Willens*, which lends credence to critics who argue that the 1934 rally was orchestrated to conform to the filmmaker's vision.

Olympia consists of two parts, *Fest der Völker* (*Festival of the People*) and *Fest der Schönheit* (*Festival of Beauty*). This documentary of the 1936 Olympic Games in Berlin used 43 cameramen shooting from every conceivable angle in order to give Riefenstahl the material she needed to create her film. Long setting the standard of sports films, *Olympia* not only celebrates individual achievement, it glorifies the human body. It is at once intimate and informative.

After the defeat of Nazi Germany in World War II and the collapse of the Third Reich, Riefenstahl tried to continue her directing career. In 1954, she released *Tiefland* (*Lowlands*, 1940–1944), a film she had finished shooting before the end of the war. Two film projects on the Nuba in Africa remained unfinished, although a photo journal of her work there was published. In 2002, she released *Impressionen unter Wasser* (*Impressions under Water*), a work she began filming a decade earlier when she took up scuba diving at the age of 90, which documents the world in and beneath coral reefs and her still present athleticism. Over the years fascination for Riefenstahl has not ebbed, as evidenced perhaps by the highly negative essay by Susan Sonntag, "Fascinating Fascism" (*New York Times Review of Books*, 1975); a cover story in *Sports Illustrated* (1989); a three-hour documentary on her work and life, *Die Macht der Bilder: Leni Riefenstahl* (*The Wonderful, Horrible Life of Leni Riefenstahl*, Ray Müller, 1993); and numerous shorter documentaries in 2002, when she turned 100. *See also* ALLGEIER, SEPP.

RIEMANN, KATJA (1963–). Katja Riemann began working in German television before being recognized for her role as the emancipated woman looking for love in **Katja von Garnier**'s comedy *Abgeschminkt!* (*Making Up!* 1993). The film launched Riemann's career as Germany's top female actor of the 1990s. During the next few years she appeared in some of Germany's most successful film comedies, including *Der bewegte Mann* (*Maybe . . . Maybe Not*, Sönke Wortmann, 1994), *Stadtgespräche* (*Talk of the Town*, Rainer Kaufmann, 1995), *Bandits* (*Bandits*, von Garnier, 1996), and *Die Apothekerin* (*The Pharmacist*, Kaufmann, 1997). Riemann's romantic comic talents are particularly strong in *Der bewegte Mann*, a film that otherwise belongs to the male characters—her philandering boyfriend, his gay roommate, the gay roommate's queenly gay friend, and the butch lover of the last mentioned. In spite of the grimacing and campy acting of the men in the film, Riemann manages through facial expressions and naturally delivered lines to retain her dignity and achieve victory in the war of the sexes and love triangle that the film parodies.

Riemann is adept at the type of parody found in *Der bewegte Mann*, giving a fresh look to a generic stereotype, the strong woman in need of love. In *Stadtgespräche*, she plays a radio talk show host who dispenses advice to morning commuters but cannot find a man of her own. Helped in her search by her gay brother, she finds the man of her dreams only to find out he is the husband of her new best friend. *Bandits* allows Riemann to display her musical as well as comedic talents, playing an escaped prisoner on the road with a music group, trying to hide in plain sight. In *Die Apothekerin*, she may or may not be the cause of a number of people dying mysteriously in her presence. In Kai Wessel's *Goebbels und Geduldig* (*Goebbels and Geduldig*, 2001), Riemann plays Eva Braun with comedic flair. The film is a precursor to the 2007 film *Mein Führer – Die wirklich wahrste Wahrheit über Adolf Hitler* (*Mein Führer: The Truly Truest Truth about Adolf Hitler*, Dani Levy, 2007), a comedy about Adolf Hitler's last few months in power. Riemann again plays a small part as Eva Braun.

RÖKK, MARIKA (1913–2004). Singer, dancer, and actor, Marika Rökk was part of National Socialist Germany's film strategy to boost box office profits in Germany and also abroad. Rökk's physical style of dancing—she could tap, turn somersaults, and jump rhythmically—made her one of cinema's most athletic dancers at the time. Moreover, she had a pleasant but not overly strong voice, suited well to operettas, and also managed the coquettish style preferred by that genre. Her most demanding role was in *Kora Terry* (*Kora Terry*, Georg Jacoby, 1940), a film in which she plays two sisters, managing the nuanced differences in movement and singing style demanded to make her portrayal of the two women believable. In *Die Frau meiner Träume* (*The Woman of My Dreams*, Jacoby, 1944), Rökk plays a successful singer-dancer in stage revues who escapes the hectic pace of theater life and finds love in the countryside. The central love story, which shows Rökk's character falling in love with an engineer in a mountain village, showcases her charisma as she charms a lodge with her accordion playing and folk singing. The love story is framed by major production numbers that give Rökk an opportunity to tap, twirl, and leap around a stage that continually shifts its setting, similar to a Hollywood musical of the 1930s. After the war, Rökk continued appearing in films and on television in romantic musicals and revues.

RUBBLE FILMS. In the first years after World War II, German directors filmed in the ruins of Berlin and other cities that had been destroyed by bombing raids, the bombed structures serving as backdrop to stories about the war and reminders of Germany's defeat. These films came to be known as "rubble films" (Trümmerfilme). The best known of the rubble films, and also the first film to be made in postwar Germany, *Die Mörder sind unter uns* (*The Murderers Are among Us*, **Wolfgang Staudte**, 1946), focuses on guilt and responsibility, concluding that the perpetrators of Nazi crimes must and will be located and brought to justice. *Irgendwo in Berlin* (*Somewhere in Berlin*, Gerhard Lamprecht, 1946), in contrast, avoids the question of guilt and responsibility, emphasizing instead the need to confront pessimism, defeatism, and black market profiteering in order to rebuild the country. *In jenen Tagen* (*In Those Days*, **Helmut Käutner**, 1947) takes a third direction and tells the story of seven successive owners of an automobile during the years of the Third Reich, portraying how each owner was in some way duped or victimized by National Socialism.

Rubble films differ in overall style, depending on the director, but they have in common, given the physical conditions of the country, a dependence on the immediacy, spontaneity, and sentimentality of Italian neorealism, a film movement that also took to the streets for its stories. *Die Mörder sind unter uns* combines the shadows of German expressionism with the Italian style. We see its indebtedness to neorealism in a scene in a train station, with passengers hanging on to the cars and riding the engine, as if still escaping the turmoil of the war; we see it in the dilapidated building in which the main characters have their apartment, with broken windows and cracked walls. Finally, we see it in an extended sequence when the antihero of the film walks through a cityscape of rubble that resembles a desert of broken concrete, bricks, and stones. At other times, though, Staudte films through door and window frames, showing how the characters are still constricted by their past; he films shadows that lurk in the background, threatening the present; in the finale, he symbolizes Germany's dilemma by projecting the figures as shadows on the wall of a ruined building; and he ends the sequence by filming the villain through a grating that turns into prison bars.

Similarly, *Irgendwo in Berlin* shoots amid the ruins of buildings, streets, and workshops, but unlike Staudte, who emphasizes dark corners and shadows amid the rubble, Lamprecht uses lighting that allows natural contrasts. This difference reflects the film's optimism. Rather than look backward to who is guilty, it looks forward to rebuilding the lives of the living now that the war is over. Nowhere is the optimism more evident than in the closing sequence of the movie, which borrows from agitprop and social realist theater and film. Gustav, the young boy whose father is depressed because he has come home from war to find his workshop destroyed and thus his livelihood endangered, relates his father's worries to an older neighbor. The neighbor in turn tells of the loss of his son in war and how he has overcome his sorrow. Rather than dwell on the loss, he tries to make life for himself and those around him better. The facial expression of the boy, which has been registering worry, brightens as Gustav declares he "wants to make things better too." The next scene shows Gustav in the middle of a street strewn with rubble, whistling his friends into action; they appear from the ruins of various structures and converge on the father's workshop, which is actually just a huge pile of debris in the middle of a courtyard. When the father arrives he sees scores of Gustav's friends busily working the rock pile; as the film ends, he and his neighbor, who has taken off his suit coat, join the youth and work to remove the rubble of the past. The film, which was financed by the Soviet zone, which later became the German Democratic Republic (East Germany), anticipates the social realism that would later be the preferred style of **East German film**.

In jenen Tagen provides a third variation of how German directors mix neorealism with personal style preferences. Käutner does not pursue the guilty as a way of overcoming the past as Staudte does; nor does he advocate looking forward as a solution to conquering the past as Lamprecht does. Instead, he tells a tale of an automobile that covers the years 1933 through 1945, hoping his story will explain away guilt and responsibility. The tone of the film underscores the way it differs from the other two movies. Käutner adapts his preferred style of poetic realism to the neorealism found in the rubble films. Indeed, except that necessity forces the director to shoot amid ruins and rubble, the film is no different in style from the ones he made during National Socialism. During the last year of the Third Reich, Käutner had directed *Unter den Brücken* (*Under the Bridges*, 1945), whose story at times resembles the loosely told tales preferred by neorealists. Its soft focus and melancholy tone, like much of Käutner's work, though, resemble French poetic realism, which shows reality as filtered through the director's lens rather than being captured directly by it. When Käutner follows the car and its owners through the Third Reich, the lens ignores the political, as it ignores questions of guilt and responsibility. Instead, characters are shown to be ignorant of the state of affairs in Germany or to be antagonistic to the state of affairs; never are they responsible. In essence, *In jenen Tagen* belongs to the genre of rubble films only because of the frame in which the story of the car is told; the opening and closing shots show the car after the war in the middle of the bombed buildings of a city.

Rubble films are not without critics. The films generally avoid points of view that might implicate viewers in the past or move them to ask questions about responsibility. The protagonists, with whom viewers are clearly meant to identify, are free of involvement in events of the Third Reich, except as powerless bystanders. In this way, they offer viewers in the immediate aftermath of the war a degree of comfort in their fatalism: "What else could we have done?" At the end of *Die Mörder sind unter uns*, for example, the victim is spared the justice of a vigilante-style execution by the intervention of a righteous woman. In *Irgendwo in Berlin*, a young boy redeems his father's pride and spirit by organizing his friends to rebuild the father's workshop, thus offering the man hope for the future. *In jenen Tagen* turns the question of guilt on its head by making Germans the victims. Even the true victims, a half Jewish couple who at one time owned the car, seem surprised at the anti-Semitism evident in the Jewish pogrom on 9 November 1938, also called Kristallnacht or "Night of Broken Glass." They apparently had overlooked the Nuremberg laws that stripped German Jews of their rights and other manifestations of persecution. In the first film, although Staudte admits to the criminality of the Nazis, he seems to say that even if they walk among us, it wasn't us. In the second film, Lamprecht ignores criminality and responsibility, and focuses on the future. In the third film, Käutner suggests that Germans were surprised by Nazi power and policies, were ignorant at first of their criminality, and once they knew offered resistance. In spite of any subtexts that might exonerate the protagonists, and by extension German viewers, these three films show the destruction caused by the war, lending them the documentary realism of all rubble films, which although fiction offer a glimpse into the destruction present in Germany after the country's defeat in World War II.

RÜHMANN, HEINZ (1902–1994). Heinz Rühmann was one of Nazi Germany's most popular stars, appearing in over 35 films from 1933 to 1945. Yet because of his success with the public, Rühmann was able to keep his distance from the government's more egregious attempts at fusing film and ideology. Unlike other apolitical actors and directors, who also kept a distance but nonetheless appeared in or directed an occasional film with propaganda intent, Rühmann played in harmless comedies throughout the era, with one exception, *Quax, der Bruchpilot* (*Quax, the Stunt Pilot*, **Kurt Hoffmann**, 1941), a film that some critics interpret as a recruitment vehicle for the Air Force, but which when separated from the historical context might be seen as a harmless diversion.

Rühmann gained recognition for his role in the pre–National Socialist era film *Die Drei von der Tankstelle* (*Three from the Gas Station*, Wilhelm Thiele, 1930), a musical comedy in which he plays one of three down-on-their-luck men in love with the same rich girl. The film helped create Rühmann's persona of a likable, stable guy whose calm demeanor sees him through even the worst of situations.

Among the films Rühmann made during the National Socialist era are some of Germany's best-remembered comedies. He starred in

Der Mann, der Sherlock Holmes war (*The Man Who Was Sherlock Holmes*, **Karl Hartl**, 1937), in which he played a confidence man pretending to be Dr. Watson to **Hans Albers**'s Sherlock Holmes, and *13 Stühle* (*Thirteen Chairs*, E. W. Emo, 1938), based on the novel *Twelve Chairs* by Ilya Lif and Yevgeni Petrov, about the hunt for money hidden in one of 13 identical-looking chairs scattered around the country. The work has been adapted for film by Russian, British, Spanish, French, and American directors as well as **New German Cinema** director **Ulrike Ottinger**. Rühmann also played the lead in **Helmut Käutner**'s *Kleider machen Leute* (*Clothes Make the Man*, 1940), based on Gottfried Keller's 19th-century novella about a tailor mistaken for a count. Rühmann portrays the tailor with a quiet arrogance, wanting to extradite himself from pretending but also enjoying the perquisites the mistake in identity brings, including the attention of a young woman. When his identity is revealed during a humiliating skit put on by a neighboring town, Rühmann's emotional reaction produces feelings of compassion in viewers that only the best comedians can elicit.

Rühmann's most celebrated role during the Third Reich was as a man who returns to school to experience what homeschooling has deprived him of: the joys and sufferings of high school, which in retrospect produce feelings of nostalgia. *Die Feuerzangenbowle* (*Flaming Punch Bowl*, Helmut Weiss, 1944) was an immediate success and has since become a cult classic, turning up on German television with the regularity of *It's a Wonderful Life* (Frank Capra, 1946) on American television and also being shown by student clubs, especially around New Year's Eve, the traditional time to drink flaming punch. Because the film is critical of school authorities, Rühmann had to intervene on its behalf with Nazi authorities, who wanted to prevent its release.

Rühmann continued to have a successful film career after the war, both as leading man in comedies and in character parts. He played Father Brown in several German adaptations of G. K. Chesterton's stories about the detective in a cleric's robe. He also portrayed petty criminals, teachers, and imposed-upon fathers or husbands in dozens of comedies. His best-remembered film roles, however, are as Wilhelm Voigt, the shoemaker mistaken for an officer in *Der Haupmann von Köpenick* (*The Captain of Köpenick*, Käutner, 1956), and as Schwejk in *Der brave Soldat Schwejk* (*The Good Soldier Schweik*,

Axel von Ambesser, 1960). Schwejk is an early 20th-century Till Eulenspiegel (a court jester–like character from German folktales), who champions the little guy by playing the idiot and therefore fooling authority.

Rühmann sometimes broke from his comedic persona and took on challenging dramatic roles. He portrayed a retired detective chasing a serial killer in *Es geschah am hellichten Tag* (*It Happened in Broad Daylight*, Ladislao Vajda, 1958). The part required him to be cool and detached, as he uses a young girl as bait to catch a killer; but it also required moments of introspection and despair. The role was portrayed by Jack Nicholson in *The Pledge* (Sean Penn, 2001). He had one of his most demanding roles in *Mein Schulfreund*, (*My School Friend*, **Robert Siodmak**, 1960), as a man who stands up to the Nazis and writes to Hermann Göring to stop the war, after which he is institutionalized as insane. After the war, the man spends 15 years getting the authorities to declare him sane. The film was an effective exposé of how postwar West Germany was dealing, or not dealing, with its Nazi past (*see* **Vergangenheitsbewältigungsfilm**). For his role as a Jewish passenger in *Ship of Fools* (Stanley Kramer, 1965), Rühmann received a Golden Globe. Among other awards he received are the Award in Gold for Best Actor for his role as Father Brown in the Chesterton mystery *Das schwarze Schaf* (*The Black Sheep*, Helmut Ashley, 1960), and again for Best Actor as the shoemaker in *Der Hauptmann von Köpenick*. He also received a Bambi, Germany's version of the "People's Choice Award," a record 14 times. *See also* FILM AWARDS.

RUTTMANN, WALTER (1887–1941). Walter Ruttmann (1887–1941) was an avant-garde filmmaker, documentarist, and pioneer in German animation. Although he began his artistic career as a painter, he soon switched to films, declaring in 1918 that "it makes no sense to paint anymore. The painting must be set in motion." The results of setting his canvases in motion were the experimental animation films *Opus I-IV* (1921–1925) and the animated falcon sequence of **Fritz Lang**'s *Siegfrieds Tod* (*Siegfried's Death*, 1924), the first half of the epic film *Die Nibelungen* (*The Nibelungen*, 1924).

Ruttmann's best-remembered film is the documentary *Berlin – Sinfonie der Großstadt* (*Berlin: Symphony of a Great City*, 1927).

Originally planned as a coproduction with screenwriter **Carl Mayer**, who left because he felt the film was emphasizing beauty at the expense of social contrasts, *Berlin – Sinfonie der Großstadt* is a montage of big city rhythms. Influenced by the montage techniques of the Russian directors Dziga Vertov and Sergei Eisenstein, Ruttmann follows the life of Berlin from before the city awakens until it again sleeps. In spite of his indebtedness to the Russians, critics point out that the film lacks their social idealism. Nevertheless, the film is a landmark of German silent cinema. Ruttmann's newsreel-like realism offered a contrast to filmic expressionism and represented a cinematic version of the literary movement known as Neue Sachlichkeit (new objectivity). Eliminating subtitles completely, Ruttmann tells the story of a day in the life of Berlin in five acts, connecting the film's episodes through rhythmic movement of people, cars, trains, planes, and even amusement rides. Ruttmann's film was widely imitated at the time, leading to numerous city documentaries set to symphonic music. Its influence can also be found in nondocumentaries. A montage sequence of Northern European ports in **Helmut Käutner**'s *Unter den Brücken* (*Under the Bridges*, 1945) recalls similar montage overlays from Ruttmann's work.

Ruttmann's career continued under the Nazis. He wrote part of the screenplay for ***Triumph des Willens*** (*Triumph of the Will*, 1935), **Leni Riefenstahl**'s masterpiece of propaganda. Ruttmann reportedly wrote and directed the opening sequence of credits, which cast Adolf Hitler as Germany's savior. In addition, he realized numerous short documentaries for the Nazis that helped make up the Nazi cinema program of newsreel, cultural short, and feature film.

– S –

SANDER, HELKE (1937–). Like her contemporary **Alexander Kluge,** Helke Sander plays a larger role in German film from **New German Cinema** and beyond than the impact of her films at home and abroad would indicate. As founder, publisher, and writer for the periodical *Frauen und Film*, Sander promotes issues of women's equity in society, in the art world, and in the film industry. Sander's narrative films, feature-length documentaries, and shorts are often autobiographical, not necessarily about her personal life, however, and explore the difficulty women in public life have finding an identity that balances their private and public selves.

Although Sander focuses on making films about women for women, men are not excluded from her works. Men may even be the subject of the film's narrative, but they are never its subjectivity. Men may act as agents, but Sander's point of view or that of the feminist movement in general always deconstructs their agency, in effect negating its power. Her most powerful film in this respect is *Befreier und Befreite* (*Liberators and Liberated*, aka *Liberators Take Liberties*, 1992), a documentary about the women who were raped by Soviet soldiers as they marched into Berlin at the end of World War II. Sander interviews women who were raped, children conceived through rape, and soldiers of the Red Army. She exposes through her interviews the lies or hypocrisy of cultures that for centuries have accepted rape as the victors' right of conquest. The women talk about their helplessness, as they were raped multiple times in succession by soldiers waiting their turn; they talk about the shame that adheres to victims of rape and not to the rapist; and they talk about living and coping with the aftermath. The men talk about their needs, that men are inclined to require sexual release.

In contrast to the seriousness of *Befreier und Befreite*, Sander's *Die Deutschen und ihre Männer* (*The Germans and Their Men*, 1989) takes a lighter look at men. A woman seeking a husband comes to Bonn, at that time Germany's seat of government, making the city ideal to highlight the foibles and duplicities of political leaders. At the airport, she divides men into those with ties and those without. She further divides the former group into those whose ties have polka dots and those whose ties have stripes. Her conclusion and that of the film is that all men are the same: duplicitous creatures of habit.

Even though Sander occasionally moves men into the center of her work, for the most part they remain outside her scope of interest, except to show how male hegemony influences thinking and affects women's lives. Her first major success came with *Die allseitig reduzierte Persönlichkeit – REDUPERS* (*The All-Round Reduced Personality: Outtakes*, 1978). The film, whose title is a play on an East

German socialist slogan, "die allseitig verwirklichte sozialistische Persönlichkeit" (the all-around successfully realized socialist personality), details the difficult life of a woman who moves to Berlin as she tries to balance work and family. More important, the film shows how difficult it is for the woman to reconcile her view of being a good mother with society's expectations of what makes a good mother. Sander revisits this theme in a later documentary, *Mitten im Malestream* (*In the Midst of the Malestream*, 2005). Using the occasion of a feminist conference on the topic of the history of the women's movement, the filmmaker examines the narrowness of the media's coverage of feminist issues. She shows how at the start of the new women's movement in the 1970s the diversity of opinion in feminism was largely overlooked as media reported on the student movement, showing less interest in women's issues. *In Der subjektive Faktor* (*The Subjective Factor*, 1981), a fictionalized account of the start of a feminist group, Sander examines how women's identity grows out of the images the group constructs, which in turn are based on images provided by society. *See also FRAUENFILM*.

SANDER, OTTO (1941–). Although he has appeared in a number of internationally acclaimed films, Otto Sander remains relatively unknown outside Germany. This may be due partly to the modest parts he has in major films, but certainly also to his preference for theatrical work in Germany, where he is a major presence. Sander's film breakthrough came in *Sommergäste* (*Summer Folk*, aka *Summer Guests*, Peter Stein, 1976), a film adaptation of a stage play by Maxim Gorki, in which he transferred his critically well-received performance as a dissolute, cynical engineer from stage to film. His other films have included the role of the Marquise's brother in *Die Marquise von O.* (*The Marquise of O.*, Eric Rohmer, 1976), in which he played a self-righteous Prussian aristocrat, and the part of communist revolutionary Karl Liebknecht in *Die Geduld der Rosa Luxemburg* (*Rosa Luxemburg*, **Margarethe von Trotta**, 1986).

Sander is also an excellent comic, favoring broad, slapstick comedy over more subtle forms. In *Der Mann im Pyjama* (*The Man in Pajamas*, Christian Rateuke and Hartmann Schmige, 1981), he plays a man locked out of his apartment in only his pajamas, offering opportunities for the actor to display comic timing in a series of embarrassing situations. Sander received the Ernst Lubistsch award for Best Comedic Performance for the film. In *Wer spinnt denn da, Herr Doktor?* (*Who's Crazy, Doctor?* Rateuke and Stefan Lukschy, 1981), Sander plays over the top as a crazy patient, in a sketchlike satire of hospitals. He has a similarly satirical role in *Kondom des Grauens* (*Killer Condom*, Martin Walz, 1996), a grotesque comedy about a condom that terrorizes New York City.

Sander's international exposure occurred during a miniboom of success for German films abroad from the late 1970s and through the 1990s. During this time he had small but memorable parts in *Das Boot* (*The Boat*, **Wolfgang Petersen**, 1981), as a drunken, cynical captain in the film's prologue; in *Die Comedian Harmonists* (*The Harmonists*, Joseph Vilsmaier, 1997), as the Jewish agent of the singers; and in *Der Himmel über Berlin* (*Wings of Desire*, **Wim Wenders**, 1987), as the angel Cassiel. His supporting role was reprised and expanded in *In weiter Ferne, so nah!* (*Faraway, So Close!* Wenders, 1993), the sequel to *Der Himmel über Berlin*. In this film, Cassiel becomes human, but unlike Damiel, the angel turned human in the first film, who is able to find love and hope, Cassiel experiences despair: he lives as a homeless man and experiences the rightwing bashing of Jews and other minorities, a reflection on what happened immediately after the Berlin Wall fell and the two German states united.

SANDERS-BRAHMS, HELMA (1940–). Film historian Thomas Elsaesser once described Helma Sanders-Brahms as the least-loved filmmaker in Germany after **Hans-Jürgen Syberberg**. The director's lack of popularity notwithstanding, Sanders-Brahms's films are stylistically accomplished and thematically challenging, they speak to the social and political issues of the country at the time of their release, they have appeared in film festivals around the world, and they have won awards. For these reasons, most film critics are in general agreement about the importance of Sanders-Brahms for **New German Cinema** (NGC), especially in furthering its political, humanist, and feminist agenda. Her early shorts and features champion the dignity of the working class. *Shirins Hochzeit* (*Shirin's Wedding*, 1976) tells the tragic story of one of the many guest workers in Germany. *Heinrich* (*Heinrich*, 1977) tells of the life and suicide of Heinrich von

Kleist, a 19th-century German writer whose novellas and dramas were a favorite source of NGC directors because of their sensitive, rebellious heroes. The film won the top federal film prize, a prestigious *goldene Schale* (golden bowl), for best film of 1977 although it too awakened hostility in some, who viewed it as pretentious and an example of what was wrong with the film subsidy system.

Sanders-Brahms's most successful film internationally, *Deutschland bleiche Mutter* (*Germany Pale Mother*, 1980), received mixed reviews in Germany. Some critics felt that its look back at a marital relationship during the Third Reich was too nostalgic. Others felt that its mother–daughter relationship was exploiting a fashionable subject. Yet many found the strength of the movie to lie in its treatment of these two related themes and in its study of love, marriage, and family during the Nazi era and in the years following. Regardless of how one judges the tone Sanders-Brahms gives her film, there is no denying its power to evoke an era many Germans at the time of the film's release would have preferred to forget. *Deutschland bleiche Mutter* opens with a reading of the **Bertolt Brecht** poem that gives the film its title, a lament of the harm Germans have visited on their country themselves. The story then relates a young couple's courtship and marriage during the Third Reich, experiencing first happiness, then separation because of the war. The film reprises the trope of Germany's self-inflicted pain and suffering after the war ends, showing the woman walking through the bomb-scarred Berlin landscape and telling her young daughter the fairy tale of the "Robber Bridegroom." The tale, which is told against a backdrop of tall chimneys resembling those of crematoria, relates a communal gathering that invited a robber murderer into their midst only to discover too late who he was. Midway in the telling of the fairy tale, and central to another of Sanders-Brahms's themes, the woman is raped by soldiers liberating the city. Sanders-Brahms here touches on a topic many wanted to stay buried even as late as 1980, the year of the film's release: the rape of Germany's women by the conquering troops, some of them repeatedly. She thus approached a taboo subject almost 12 years before **Helke Sander** made it the topic of her documentary, *Befreier und Befreite* (*Liberators and the Liberated*, aka *Liberators Take Liberties*, 1992), which also caused controversy for dealing with an event many were not ready to admit occurred. **Edgar Reitz** had also alluded to the rape of German women in *Stunde Null* (*Zero Hour*, 1977), a film about immediate postwar Germany.

Many of Sanders-Brahms other films also deal with issues of feminism. *Flügel und Fesseln* (*The Future of Emily*, 1985) examines the life of a successful actress whose parents disapprove of her decision to raise her child without the father, who, however, remains in the actress's life. *Apfelbäume* (*Apple Trees*, 1992) explores the life of a couple immediately before and after the fall of the Berlin Wall 1n 1989. The story relates how the couple ends in prison because of machinations of the Stasi, East Germany's secret police, and how the problems caused before the fall of the Berlin Wall cannot be reconciled once it is gone. One of the more unusual films Sanders-Brahms has made is a 52-second short for *Lumière et compagnie* (*Lumière and Company*, 1996), for which 40 directors made shorts using the Cinematographe invented by Louis and August Lumière. *See also VERGANGENHEITSBEWÄLTIGUNGSFILM.*

SAß, KATRIN (1956–). One of East Germany's leading actors, Katrin Saß portrayed a variety of women in feature films and on television who were trying to realize personal fulfillment in a socialist society. She won recognition for her first film, *Bis dass der Tod euch scheidet* (*Until Death Do Us Part*, **Heiner Carow**, 1979), in which she plays Sonja, a young woman coping with married life, a new child, and a husband who believes she should devote herself to being mother and wife, rather than seeking identity within the larger socialist sphere. For her role as a single mother in *Bürgschaft für ein Jahr* (*Probationary Custody for One Year*, Herrmann Zschoche, 1981), she won a Silver Bear award as Best Actress at the **Berlin Film Festival.** As in her first film, Saß plays a woman who must reconcile her own desires with what society expects of her, but in this case she does not seek positive fulfillment within the greater socialist structure. Rather, she flees into a self-indulgent life, which threatens to result in her children being removed from the home.

Das Haus am Fluß (*The House on the River*, Roland Gräf, 1986) revealed Saß's range as an actress. In the film, which takes place in Nazi Germany, she plays a woman torn between her soldier husband and her Nazi supervisor. In Gräf's *Fallada – letztes Kapitel* (*Fallada: Last Chapter*, 1988), Saß plays Ursula Losch, Hans Fallada's morphine-addicted lover who contributes to the writer's downward spiral. In one of the last films made by **DEFA**, *Heute sterben immer nur die anderen* (*Nowadays It's Always the Others Who Die*, Siegfried Kühn, 1990), Saß comforts a friend dying of cancer while another turns away in fear. After the two German states unified, Saß played mostly on television in the 1990s. In 2003, she gained international recognition for her role as the mother in *Good Bye, Lenin!* (*Good Bye, Lenin!* Wolfgang Becker), a nostalgic look at the German Democratic Republic. Saß won a Bambi and a Film Award in Gold for her role in the film (*see* **film awards**). She followed her portrayal of the sympathetic mother with one of an opportunistic anti-Semite who betrays her Jewish neighbors to the Nazis, hoping to be given their house, but who loses her son instead (*Babij Yar* [*Babi Yar*, Jeff Kanew, 2003]). *See also* EAST GERMAN FILM.

SCHELL, MARIA (1926–2005). Maria Schell was one of the most successful German film stars of the 1950s. Her first role, in **Karl Hartl**'s *Der Engel mit der Posaune* (1948), which she remade in England as *The Angel with the Trumpet* (Anthony Bushell, 1950), brought Schell international recognition. She was an intensely dramatic actress whose range extended from quiet moods of introspection to great emotional outbursts. She acted in Austrian, German, French, Italian, English, and American films, appearing in dramas, comedies, Westerns, horror movies, and science fiction films. The films for which she gained her reputation, though, are best described as social-consciousness melodramas and literary adaptations.

Schell starred in several films dealing with Germany's troubled history, the first being the already mentioned *Der Engel mit der Posaune* and its English-language remake. The film follows an Austrian Jewish family from 1880 through the turbulent half-century of Austrian history, ending just after the close of World War II and the fall of Nazism. The movie is one of the few early postwar films to deal with Nazi policies against Jews, even if only to a limited degree. It is a historical irony that its star, Paula Wessely, plays the matriarch of a Jewish family only a few years after having starred in the propagandistic Nazi film about German racial identity, *Heimkehr* (*Homecoming*, Gustav Ucicky, 1941). In the mid-1950s, Schell played a German doctor in World War II who is abducted by Yugoslavian partisans. Slowly she begins to see the war from the perspective of her captors and in the end crosses a bridge, which gives the film its name and reinforces the film's central metaphor, *Die letzte Brücke* (*The Last Bridge*, **Helmut Käutner**, 1954), in order to distribute medicine to a group she no longer sees as the enemy. Schell's role as a mother who had had an affair with a Jewish neighbor in Klaus Emmerich's *Die erste Polka* (*The First Polka*, 1979) allowed Schell to reinforce her reputation for playing introspective characters.

Besides playing in movies that examined Germany's past, Schell also appeared in a number of literary adaptations, the best known being *Die Ratten* (*The Rats*, **Robert Siodmak**, 1955); *Rose Bernd* (*Rose Bernd*, **Wolfgang Staudte**, 1957); *Gervaise* (*Gervaise*, René Clément, 1956); *The Brothers Karamazov* (Richard Brooks, 1957); and *For Whom the Bell Tolls* (John Frankenheimer, 1959), a two-part movie made for the American television drama series *Playhouse 90*. The two German films were both based on plays by the German realist playwright Gerhart Hauptmann. The screenplay for *Die Ratten* brought the play, originally set in the 19th century, into the postwar period, thus allowing the theme of biological and adoptive motherhood to be set in the sociopolitical milieu of a divided Germany. *Rose Bernd* likewise relocates a German classic to postwar Germany, resettling the tragedy-fated heroine Rose from her home in Silesia to West Germany. *Gervaise*, based on Émile Zola's 19th-century realist novel *L'Assommoir* (*Drink*, 1877), added to Schell's repertoire of vulnerable working-class women. In a role reversal, Schell played the coquettish Grushenka in *The Brothers Karamazov*, a part for which American actress Marilyn Monroe reportedly campaigned. Her part as Maria in *For Whom the Bell Tolls* for American television suggests how wide the actress's popularity had become.

In the 1960s, with the advent of **New German Cinema**, Schell turned to television, the theater, and Hollywood genre films as the roles for which she was known went out of fashion. She played the role made famous by Greta Garbo in the remake of *Ninotchka* (Tom Donovan, 1960); appeared in the Westerns *The Hanging Tree* (Delmer Daves, 1959) and *Cimarron* (Anthony Mann, 1960), the horror movie *Il trono di fuoco* (*Throne of the Blood Monster*, Jesus Franco, 1970), and the thriller *The Odessa File* (Ronald Neame, 1974); made a cameo appearance in Richard Donner's *Superman, the Movie* (1978); and played the role of the mother in David Hemming's *Just a Gigolo* (1979), starring David Bowie. Including her television films, Schell played in 90 films. *See also* AUSTRIAN CINEMA; SCHELL, MAXIMILIAN.

SCHELL, MAXIMILIAN (1930–). Maximilian Schell began his career playing sensitive, disillusioned soldiers in German films. His first such role was in *Kinder, Mütter, und ein General* (*Children, Mothers, and a General*, László Benedek, 1955), a movie about drafting 15-year-old adolescents to fight on the front. Although not as well known as **Bernhard Wicki**'s *Die Brücke* (*The Bridge*, 1959), which tells a similar story, the film nonetheless depicts the insanity of continuing to fight a war that is lost. Schell's sensitivity in his portrayal of a young deserter disillusioned with fighting became a trademark of his acting. He played next in *Der 20. Juli* (*The Plot to Assassinate Hitler*, Falk Harnack, 1955), one of two movies about the same theme to come out in 1955. The other was **Georg Wilhelm Pabst**'s *Es geschah am 20. Juli* (*Jackboot Mutiny*, 1955). Schell plays a sensitive philosopher who is able to synthesize and reconcile the conflicting arguments surrounding the ethics of assassinating Adolf Hitler. Schell next received the starring role in **Helmut Käutner**'s *Ein Mädchen aus Flandern* (*A Girl from Flanders*, 1956), again playing a soldier tired of combat, but this time in World War I.

Schell's performance in German **war films** and his handsome looks won him a part in Edward Dmytryk's *The Young Lions* (1958). Playing opposite Marlon Brando and Montgomery Clift, an actor with whom he was favorably compared, Schell drew on his German film portrayals of young officers disillusioned with a war that no longer made sense. He next appeared in the television production *Judgment at Nuremberg* (George Roy Hill, 1959) as the defense attorney for the Germans in the Nuremberg trials that arose out of crimes committed by Germany in World War II. He later reprised the role in Stanley Kramer's 1961 film of the same name, for which he won an Oscar as best actor. As Hans Rolfe, Schell gives a bravura performance that indirectly removes the totality of guilt from his client generals by arguing that all Germans share a collective guilt for what happened during the war.

During a career that spans six decades, Schell has acted in over 90 films. Not surprisingly, his roles often have him playing German Nazis, scientists, or eccentrics, but he also plays German Jews or Israelis, indeed any role that calls for speaking English with a German-sounding or guttural accent. He has appeared in the war films *Counterpoint* (Ralph Nelson, 1968), *The Desperate Ones* (Alexander Ramati, 1968), *Cross of Iron* (Sam Peckinpah, 1977), and *A Bridge Too Far* (Richard Attenborough, 1977), and in the espionage thrillers *The Deadly Affair* (Sidney Lumet, 1966) and *The Odessa File* (Ronald Neame, 1974), in roles not too far removed from his first parts. But he has also acted in science fiction and horror films, including *The Black Hole* (Gary Nelson, 1979), *Deep Impact* (Mimi Leder, 1998), and *John Carpenter's Vampires* (John Carpenter, 1998). He played a gourmet chef in the comedy *The Freshman* and the understanding father of the Jewish adolescents in the dramas *The Diary of Anne Frank* (Boris Sagal, 1980) and *The Chosen* (Jeremy Kagan). He also gained recognition for his roles in *The Man in the Glass Booth* (Arthur Hiller, 1975), for which he received an Oscar nomination for best actor, and *Julia* (Fred Zinnemann, 1977), for which he received a nomination for best supporting actor. In a role that was completely outside his usual parts, Schell played the character "K," a man caught in a bureaucratic nightmare without the wits or will to free himself, in *Das Schloß* (*The Castle*, Rudolf Noelte, 1968), based on Franz Kafka's eponymous novel.

In addition to his success as an actor, Schell has had a distinguished career as a film director. His first film, *Erste Liebe* (*First Love*, 1970), was nominated for an Oscar as Best Foreign Film (Switzerland) and received an Award in Gold (*see* **film awards**) from the Germanl film industry. His 1973 film *Der Fußgänger* (*The Pedestrian*), about a West German industrialist who must face his National Socialist past, was nominated for an Oscar as Best Foreign Film (Germany) and won the *goldene Schale* (golden bowl), the highest honor given by the German film industry, the first time it had been awarded in 14 years. In 1975, he directed *Der Richter und sein Henker* (*End of the Game*, 1975), which is based on Friedrich Dürrenmatt's best-seller of the same name. Starring an international cast that included John Voight, Jacqueline Bisset, and Robert Shaw, the film was one of a number of European coproductions that came to be known as Euro pudding. It also showed the influence of the spy thriller trend then prevalent in

Hollywood movies, as Schell focused on the international mystery behind a series of murders, rather than on Dürrenmatt's complex question of guilt and divine justice.

Schell has directed two documentaries of movie legends, **Marlene Dietrich** and his sister, **Maria Schell**. For *Marlene Dietrich* (*Marlene*, 1984), Schell shot abundant footage, only to have Dietrich refuse to release any shots in which she appeared. By the time of the film, the once-glamorous movie star had retreated to her apartment. Schell solved the problem by using only the audio portion of the interviews, showing Dietrich from the back or in shadow and filling in the rest with scenes from her films. Schell's documentary *Meine Schwester Maria* (*My Sister Maria*, 2002) reverses the intimacy of the Dietrich biography, providing almost an exposé of his sister's mental and physical frailty. The film was made three years before Maria Schell's death, when she had already withdrawn from the world. Schell films his sister at her home in the Alps, at times highlighting her frailty through staged scenes, using a double when he shows her falling on ice. As in the Dietrich documentary, however, the director includes ample footage from his sister's films, important because some of the films are not readily available.

Schell's reputation as an actor of stature can be seen in the number of times he has played historical figures, roles usually afforded only to the world's top actors. Over the years he has portrayed Simón Bolívar (*Simón Bolívar*, Alessandro Blasseti, 1969), Peter the Great (*Peter the Great*, Martin J. Chomsky, 1968), Frederick the Great (*Young Catherine*, Michael Anderson, 1991), and Vladimir Lenin (*Stalin*, Ivan Passer, 1992). He has also played a pharaoh (*Abraham*, Joseph Sargent, 1994) for American television and Albert Einstein in *Giganten* (*Giants*), a series on German television about important people in German history, in the episode *Albert Einstein* (*Albert Einstein*, Gero von Boehm, 2007). In addition to the Oscars mentioned earlier, Schell received an honorary award from the German film industry, which, however, he refused to accept, and a Bambi (*see* **film awards**) in 1992 for lifetime achievement. *See also* AUSTRIAN CINEMA.

SCHLÖNDORFF, VOLKER (1939–). Volker Schlöndorff, one of the signatories to the **Oberhausen Manifesto** (1962), the document proclaiming the birth of a **New German Cinema** (NGC), directed what many film historians consider the first major film of the NGC, *Der junge Törless* (*The Young Törless*, 1966). Basing his film on the novel by Robert Musil, which takes place in the restrictive and repressive world of a boy's boarding school in pre–World War I Germany, Schlöndorff draws clear parallels between the sadism and latent fascism found in the boys and the origins of Nazism and the Third Reich.

Although Schlöndorff is one of the few members of the NGC who found commercial success, some critics feel that he never again approached the artistic vision he displayed in his first film. While recognizing his talents as a skilled craftsman and technician—he apprenticed under French directors Alain Resnais, Louis Malle, and Jean-Pierre Melville—his detractors criticize his failure to impose an individual style on his movies. Yet it is precisely Schlöndorff's ability to adapt his style to his material and not the material to his style that has made him a master of the cinematic adaptation.

Among the many pieces of literature that he has adapted for film is Heinrich Kleist's novella *Michael Kohlhaas* (1810). Schlöndorff's *Michael Kohlhaas–Der Rebell* (*Man on Horseback*, 1969) was a high budget international production that failed at the box office and temporarily set back his commercial film career but did not harm his artistic creation. In the following year, for example, he made what may be his quirkiest and most individualistic film, *Der plötzliche Reichtum der armen Leute von Kombach* (*The Sudden Wealth of the Poor People of Kombach*), an ironic **Heimatfilm** in which Schlöndorff uses **Brechtian** distancing to emphasize his political philosophy.

In addition to adapting literary masterpieces to the screen, Schlöndorff has made political films, the two best known being *Die verlorene Ehre der Katharina Blum* (*The Lost Honor of Katharina Blum*, 1975), codirected with **Margarethe von Trotta** and based on Heinrich Böll's political novella *Die verlorene Ehre der Katharina Blum oder: Wie Gewalt entstehen und wohin sie führen kann* (*The Lost Honor of Katharina Blum, or How Violence Develops and Where It Can Lead*), and *Deutschland im Herbst* (*Germany in Autumn*, 1978), a cooperative film about Germany's reaction to terrorist activities in fall 1977, for which he directed one episode. *Die verlorene Ehre der Katharina Blum* was remade for American television by CBS as the

Lost Honor of Kathryn Beck (Simon Langton, 1984) and starred Marlo Thomas and Kris Kristofferson.

Schlöndorff's *Die Blechtrommel* (*The Tin Drum*, 1979), based on the novel by Günter Grass, won the Golden Palm for best picture at Cannes in 1980 and also won the Oscar for best foreign film that same year. The movie epitomizes Schlöndorff's devotion to high production values. It displays exquisite sets, authentic historical details, and a prominent international cast. At the same time, it is one of the more entertaining and hence commercially successful attempts by German directors to come to terms with Germany's Nazi legacy.

Schlöndorff is sometimes criticized for his expensive international coproductions including *Die Blechtrommel*, *The Handmaid's Tale* (1989), *Homo Faber* (*Voyager*, 1991), and *Der Unhold* (*The Ogre*, 1996). In response to criticism that international productions are too homogenized, like pudding, Schlöndorff asks, "what is wrong with European pudding as long as it's tasty?" In 2000 he reprised the modest but political style of his earlier films in *Die Stille nach dem Schuss* (*Legend of Rita*), a film about German radicals and their afterlife in the German Democratic Republic. Clearly, his reputation in the filmmaking community is considerable, as he was appointed the head of the **Babelsberg Studios** in Potsdam, Germany, the former **DEFA** studio of the German Democratic Republic that was sold to a French conglomerate.

SCHMIDT, ECKHART (1938–). Eckhart Schmidt belonged to a group of young German filmmakers dubbed the Neue Münchner Gruppe (New Munich Group) by film critic Enno Patalas. They appeared about the same time that **Alexander Kluge** and **Edgar Reitz**, among others, were proclaiming in the **Oberhausen Manifesto** that grandpa's cinema was dead. Schmidt and the other members of the group—**Rudolf Thome**, Max Zihlmann, Klaus Lemke, and May Spils—made movies for the sheer joy of making movies. They wanted to appeal to a broad audience, in particular viewers under 30. As a result they subscribed more to the tenets of the Hollywood B picture, which encompassed action, accessible story, and erotic scenes. Schmidt's early works included the melodrama, *Mädchen – Mädchen* (*Girls, Girls*, Roger Fritz, 1966), about a father and son who both love the same woman and for which he wrote the screen-

Werner Krauß in Robert Wiene's Das Cabinet des Dr. Caligari (1920). Photograph courtesy of the Murnau-Stiftung and Transit Film

Hans Heinrich von Twardowski and Fern Andra in Robert Wiene's Genuine (1920). Photograph courtesy of the Murnau-Stiftung and Transit Film

Gustav Fröhlich in Fritz Lang's Metropolis *(1926). Photograph courtesy of the Murnau-Stiftung and Transit Film*

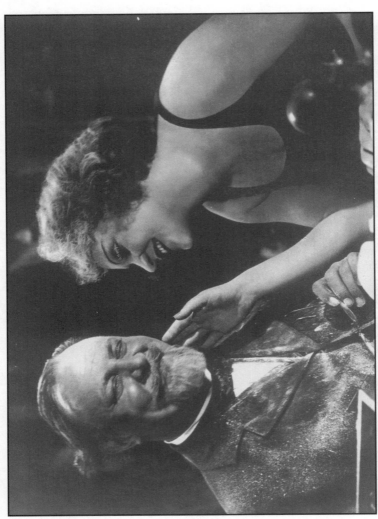

Marlene Dietrich and Emil Jannings in Josef von Sternberg's Der blaue Engel (1930). Photograph courtesy of the Murnau-Stiftung and Transit Film

Peter Lorre in Fritz Lang's M *(1931). Photograph courtesy of Deutsches Filminstitut—DIF*

Shot-putter Hans-Heinrich Siewert in Leni Riefenstahl's Olympia *(1938). Photograph courtesy of Leni-Riefenstahl Photo Archives*

Marianne Hoppe and Ferdinand Marian in Helmut Käutner's Romanze in Moll (1943). Photograph courtesy of the Murnau-Stiftung and Transit Film

Pierre Brice and Lex Barker in Harald Reinl's Der Schatz im Silbersee *(1962). Photograph courtesy of Rialtofilm*

Gojko Mitić in Josef Mach's Die Söhne der großen Bärin (1965). Photograph courtesy of Deutsches FilmInstitut—DIF

Scene from Konrad Wolf's Mama, ich lebe *(1977). Photograph courtesy of Progress-Film*

Winfried Glatzeder and Angelica Domröse in Heiner Carow's Die Legende von Paul und Paula (1973). Photograph courtesy of Progress-Film

The Kalinka Sisters in Ulrike Ottinger's Johanna d'Arc of Mongolia (1989). Photograph courtesy of Ulrike Ottinger Filmproduktion

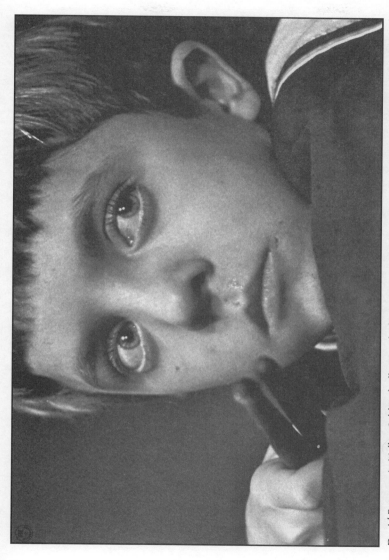

David Bennent in Volker Schlöndorff's Die Blechtrommel (1979). Photograph courtesy of Deutsches Filminstitut—DIF

Hanna Schygulla and Klaus Löwitsch in Rainer Werner Fassbinder's Die Ehe der Maria Braun (1978). Photograph courtesy of the Rainer Werner Fassbinder Foundation

Otto Sander (middle) in Wolfgang Petersen's Das Boot (1981). Photograph courtesy of the Deutsches Filminstitut—DIF

Franka Potente and Moritz Bleibtreu in Tom Tykwer's Lola rennt (1998). Photograph courtesy of X-Verleih and Deutsches Filminstitut—DIF

Donevan Gunia (l) and Alexandra Maria Lara in Oliver Hirschbiegel's Der Untergang (2004). Photograph courtesy of Deutsches Filminstitut—DIF

play, and *Die Flucht* (*Flight* 1966), a short about young gangsters, reminiscent of Jean-Luc Godard's *À bout de Souffle* (*Breathless*, 1959). In his first full-length film, *Jet Generation – Wie Mädchen heute Männer lieben* (*How Girls Love Men of Today*, 1968), Schmidt explores the sexual tension of young people on the make. In *Fantasie* (*Fantasy*), the third film of the multidirector trilogy *Erotik auf der Schulbank* (*Eroticism in High School*, 1968), he looks at the sexual fantasies that a boy going through puberty has about his teacher. *Männer sind zum Lieben da* (*The Girls from Atlantis*, 1970) follows a group of alien women who have come to earth to capture men to take back as sex slaves. *Der Fan* (*Trance*, 1982) tells the story of a girl so obsessed with a pop star that she murders him and saws him to pieces when he does not return her affection. Of his work, Schmidt remarked that he would sooner make films with naked women than ones with a lot of problem-laden dialogue. Since the mid-1990s, Schmidt has been making television documentaries.

SCHNEIDER, ROMY (1938–1982). Although she had a varied and successful acting career outside Germany, within Germany Romy Schneider (born Rosemarie Magdalena Albach) was typecast as a spirited, mildly rebellious young woman after appearing as the young queen Victoria in Ernst Marischka's *Mädchenjahre einer Königin* (*Maiden Years of a Queen*, 1954) and as Princess and then Empress Elizabeth of the Austro-Hungarian Empire in the highly successful *Sissi* trilogy. Through the films of this series—*Sissi* (1955), *Sissi – Die junge Kaiserin* (*Sissi: The Young Empress* (1956), and *Sissi – Schicksalsjahre einer Kaiserin* (*Sissi: Critical Years of a Young Empress*, 1957)—Schneider became identified with her portrayal of the empress as an independently minded woman whose charm and beauty enchanted everyone except her mother-in-law. The films also belonged to the **Heimatfilm** genre, a group of movies considered sentimental and overly sweet by many critics and film historians.

Schneider intentionally broke from the image she had developed in the *Sissi* and *Sissi*-like films by accepting roles in edgier films, most notably in *Monpti* (*Monpti*, **Helmut Käutner**, 1957) and *Mädchen in Uniform* (*Girls in Uniform*, Géza von Radványi, 1958). *Monpti* begins as an inconsequential romance, as a young woman pretends to be rich in order to impress a young Hungarian artist, played by **Horst**

Buchholz, a teenage idol at the time. As the movie progresses, ironic comments distance viewers from the story as it spirals downward in tone into a full-blown teenage love tragedy. Roles such as those in *Monpti* and her next film, *Mädchen in Uniform* (*Girls in Uniform*, Géza von Radvàney, 1958), a remake of the 1931 film about latent homosexuality (*Mädchen in Uniform*, Leontine Sagan), did not fully overcome the public's perception of Schneider as a star of light romances, and to escape her typecast image she left Germany to make films first in Italy and finally in France. She starred as the title character in *Christine* (*Christine*, Pierre Gaspard-Huit, 1958), a remake of **Max Ophüls**'s 1931 film *Liebelei* (*Flirtation*), based on Artur Schnitzler's drama of the same name. Although the movie is set in Austria in the late 1800s, the period of many of Schneider's costume romances, the film eschews sentimental nostalgia in favor of social criticism.

Schneider also had a brief career in English-language movies, including ones made for Hollywood. Her English-language films include *The Trial* (Orson Welles, 1962), based on the novel by Franz Kafka, *Good Neighbor Sam* (David Swift, 1963), and *What's New, Pussycat* (Clive Donner, 1965), for which Woody Allen wrote the screenplay. Schneider's American career never captured American viewers, perhaps because Hollywood saw her as a sexy European starlet rather than a dramatic actress. In France, in contrast, she often played the part of a cool, controlled woman in charge of her destiny. There she won the César, the French film industry award, as Best Actress for the film *L'Important c'est d'aimer* (*That Most Important Thing: Love*, Andrzej Zulowski, 1975), in which she played an actress in soft-core pornographic films, a character far from the innocent ingénues of her early career. She won another award for *Une histoire simple* (*A Simple Story*, 1978), which she made with Claude Sautet, the director who was mainly responsible for recasting her image and for whom she made five films. In 1977, she played the leading role in *Gruppenbild mit Dame* (*Group Portrait with Lady*, Aleksandar Petrovic), based on the novel of that name by Heinrich Böll, which reconstructs the life of a woman during World War II. The German film industry honored her for the role with the **Film Award** in Gold for Outstanding Individual Achievement by an Actress. *See also* AUSTRIAN CINEMA.

SCHRADER, MARIA (1965–). Maria Schrader is one of Germany's most productive actors, having completed 35 movies in fewer than 20 years. Playing a wide variety of roles, from bank robber to adulteress to lesbian seductress, Schrader refuses to be typecast, although the theme of love and friendship runs through all of her films. One of her first films, *I Was on Mars* (*I Was on Mars*, Dani Levy, 1992), a romantic comedy, finds her character in New York City. A fish out of water, barely understanding English, she is conned out of her money by an Italian grifter who eventually falls in love with her. In *Burning Life* (*Burning Life*, Peter Welz, 1994), a crime caper comedy, two women become friends during a bank robbery and set off on a cross-country crime spree during which they give their gains to the poor, endearing themselves to the populace. In *Keiner liebt mich* (*Nobody Loves Me*, **Doris Dörrie**, 1994), Schrader plays Fanny Fink, a woman who becomes neurotically obsessed with finding a husband before she is 30 and is helped by a gay African German to become more self-assertive.

In her later films, themes turn darker. *Stille Nacht* (*Silent Night*, Levy, 1995) is about a ménage à trois in which a woman is torn between her husband and a man with whom she had a brief affair. She plays an assertive lesbian in *Aimée & Jaguar* (*Aimee & Jaguar*, Max Färberböck, 1999), who seduces a married woman whose husband is at the war front. The two women retreat into their own world until they are eventually arrested by the Gestapo. In *Meschugge* (*The Giraffe*, Levy, 1998) and *Rosenstraße* (*Rosenstraße*, **Margarethe von Trotta**, 2003), Schrader plays women living in New York who go back to Germany searching for their Jewish past. Perhaps her most moving film has been *Schneeland* (*Snowland*, **Hans W. Geissendörfer**, 2005), a story of a woman whose husband dies in an auto accident; she plans to commit suicide although she has three children. In Lapland, where she has gone to relive the time she met her husband, she discovers a body frozen in snow. Flashbacks reveal a tender love story that changes her mind.

SCHROETER, WERNER (1945–). Film historian Thomas Elsaesser refers to Werner Schroeter as a filmmaker's filmmaker. Although he has won numerous awards; has influenced directors as different as

Hans-Jürgen Syberberg, Ulrike Ottinger, and **Rainer Werner Fassbinder**; and has even scored modest successes with the public with a few of his films, Schroeter remains relatively unknown outside Western European film circles, unlike other members of the **New German Cinema**.

Schroeter is a sensualist, with high camp sensibilities. His images of beauty captivate the imagination but also overload one's sensory receptors, leaving viewers astonished, mystified, or just plain baffled at their meaning. His early films, shot in 8mm, were highly experimental shorts, focusing on the extravagance of opera, the kitsch of popular music, or the affinity between the two. Many focused on the opera diva Maria Callas, ordering still photos into collages that suggested the emotion in her singing. In the three-minute short *Callas Walking Lucia* (*Callas Walking Lucia*, 1968), for example, the director offers a montage of shots of the opera singer performing Donizetti's *Lucia di Lammermoor* in order to suggest the emotion behind her crying.

Schroeter's first feature, *Eika Katappa* (*Eika Katappa*, 1969), shot in 16mm, eschews a narrative story line in favor of a series of high points from history and myth. It counterposes, as do almost all of his films, high and popular culture. During the 144-minute film Schroeter develops the experimental direction of his early 8mm films, juxtaposing seemingly unconnected images synchronized to operatic and rock music. His technique highlights those moments that are highly emotional in nature: death, love, sickness, despair. In *Der Tod der Maria Malibran* (*The Death of Maria Malibran*, 1972), also shot in 16mm, Schroeter creates a tour de force of allusions, referencing historical figures as distanced from each other as Johann Wolfgang von Goethe and Janis Joplin. Starring **Magdalena Montezuma**, an underground actress who appeared in many of Schroeter's films, the movie remains one of the director's favorites, perhaps because it embodies what he feels film should be about: "In my films I want to live out the very few basic human moments of expressivity to the point of musical and gestural excess–those few authentic feelings: life, love, joy, hatred, jealousy, and the fear of death, without psychologizing them."

In 1978 Schroeter turned to 35mm for his films, thereafter making the movies for which he is best known. These films approached and sometimes achieved commercial viability. In *Neapolitanische*

Geschichten (*The Kingdom of Naples*, aka *Neapolitanische Geschwister* [*Neapolitan Siblings*], 1978), Schroeter abandons the episodic, sometimes disjointed, style of his early work to tell in chronological order the history of a Neapolitan family from 1943 to 1972. At two-year intervals, a narrator fills in historical background, at first objectively distanced from the siblings but becoming more involved in their story as it progresses. The film won an Award in Gold (*see* **film awards**) from the German film industry, as did his *Tag der Idioten* (*Day of the Idiots*, 1981), a difficult study of the radical feminism and terrorism that had shocked German sensibilities in the 1970s. A feature made between these two, *Palermo oder Wolfsburg* (*Palermo or Wolfsburg*, 1980), which deals with the issue of Germany's immigrant workers, a topic also explored at the time by Fassbinder in *Angst essen Seele auf* (*Ali: Fear Eats the Soul*, 1974) and **Helma Sanders-Brahms** in *Shirins Hochzeit* (*Shirin's Wedding*, 1976), won a golden bear at the **Berlin Film Festival**. *Malina* (*Malina*, 1990), with French actress Isabelle Huppert, is based on a work by German author Ingeborg Bachmann and tells of the loneliness of love. The film won an Award in Gold as Best German Film of 1991 but was criticized by German feminists for its portrayal of the title character.

Schroeter has also directed several feature-length documentaries, including *Poussières d'amour – Abfallprodukte der Liebe* (*Love's Debris*, 1996), "a meditation on life, love, death and the human voice." As in his 16mm films and his shorts from the beginning of his career, the film is episodic, replacing the information one expects in a documentary with the emotional lyricism of the operatic voice and the pathos of the aging diva. He again examines the beauty of aging in *Die Königin – Marianne Hoppe* (*The Queen: Marianne Hoppe*, 2000) a documentary about **Marianne Hoppe**, one of Germany's most popular and gifted actors during the Third Reich, who also had a successful career after the war in German film and television.

SCHÜFFTAN, EUGEN (1893–1977). Eugen Schüfftan, who had a distinguished career in Germany and Hollywood as a cinematographer, particularly in the area of special effects, is best known for the camera effect that carries his name, the Schüfftan process. Used for the first time in *Metropolis* (*Metropolis*, **Fritz Lang**, 1927), where

Schüfftan used small-scale models to create Lang's vision of a futuristic city, the process involves using mirrors to reflect a model or landscape onto a visual field. By eliminating the necessity of location shooting or the building of full-scale architectural structures, the process saves money for the studio. Eventually Schüfftan's process was replaced by matte shots, a process that was easier and less expensive. Over the years Schüfftan worked as cinematographer and special effects supervisor on major films in Germany, France, and America. After *Metropolis*, he supervised camera effects on Abel Ganz's *Napoleon* (*Napoléon*, 1927), in which special effects give the film its dynamic movement. In 1937, he worked on Marcel Carné's *Le Quai des brumes* (*Port of Shadows*), his cinematography adding to the reputation of 1930s French poedtic realism, a cross between realism and atmospheric impressionism. In 1961, he won an Academy Award for his camera work on *The Hustler* (Robert Rossen). The German film industry honored Schüfftan in 1964 for his years of service to German film.

SCHWARZENBERGER, XAVER (1946–). Xaver Schwarzenberger, cinematographer and director, gained international recognition for his collaboration with **Rainer Werner Fassbinder**, in whose films he experimented with a series of lighting and filter effects, in black and white and color. His use of low contrast, filtered light on Fassbinder's ambitious undertaking, the 14-episode *Berlin Alexanderplatz* (*Berlin Alexanderplatz*, 1980), based on the novel by Alfred Döblin, confused and even angered viewers, who complained that they could not see the underlit images on their televisions no matter how much they adjusted the contrast controls. For Fassbinder's *Lili Marleen* (*Lili Marleen*, 1981), which Schwarzenberger referred to as a horror movie, the cinematographer punctuated scenes with sudden outbursts of light, matching the sudden musical bursts of the score by **Peer Raben**. Taken together, Schwarzenberger's cinematography and Raben's music lent a surreal look to an otherwise banal love story.

Schwarzenberger's expressive cinematography transforms two of Fassbinder's later films, *Lola* (*Lola*, 1981) and *Die Sehnsucht der Veronika Voss* (*Veronika Voss*, 1982). At the director's urging, Schwarzenberger took his experiments with color and light in *Lola* ad absurdum. In a scene that has become a classic example of use of color filters, Lola, the town's richest prostitute, and Bohm, the town's most upstanding citizen, are sitting in a car. She is bathed in pink light, he in blue. Suddenly they are illuminated by the headlights of a bus and are exposed for all to see within a garish yellow light. Such daring camera work had some critics gushing and others crying foul. **Kurt Raab,** a member of Fassbinder's film ensemble, sarcastically referred to the experiment as Goethe's *Farbenlehre*, an allusion to the color theories of Germany's most celebrated poet. Regardless of one's reaction, though, the filters helped recall the colors of 1950s movies, the years when the story is taking place. Moreover, they commented effectively on the hypocrisy of those engaged in rebuilding Germany and made it difficult to ignore the work of this team.

In *Die Sehnsucht der Veronika Voss*, Schwarzenberger devised a crisp black-and-white contrast that remained with viewers even as the story faded. The film, about an aging film diva addicted to drugs, references Billy Wilder's classic masterpiece *Sunset Boulevard* (1950). Commenting on the aesthetics of his black-and-white cinematography, Schwarzenberger remarked that he just wanted to avoid the gray-and-white style of French poetic realism and create true black-and-white contrasts: "grau mochte ich nie" ("I never liked gray"). For *Querelle* (*Querelle*, 1982), Fassbinder's filming of Jean Genet's work of the same name, Schwarzenberger filmed outdoor scenes in a garish yellow orange and indoor ones in blue-green, adding to the artificial world that Fassbinder portrayed in the movie. In all of the movies the men made together, Schwarzenberger's cinematography added to the distancing that is the hallmark of a Fassbinder film.

After Fassbinder's death in 1982, Schwarzenberger began to direct his own films. Among these are *Donauwalzer* (*Waltzes of the Danube*, 1984) and *Gewitter im Mai* (*Thunderstorms in May*, 1987), films in the *Heimatfilm* genre that avoid the usual sentimentality. Schwarzenberger also directed the enormously successful comedies *Otto – Der Film* (*Otto: The Film*, 1985) and *Otto – Der neue Film* (*Otto: The New Film*, 1987), starring popular German stand-up comic Otto Waalkes. The movies became the two largest grossing German films of the 1980s. Since the early 1990s Schwarzenberger has worked almost exclusively in television as a director who does his own cinematography. *See also* AUSTRIAN CINEMA.

SCHWEIGER, TIL (1963–). One of a group of actors who gained recognition in the 1990s, Til Schweiger is one of the most prolific of new German stars (*see also* **Bleibtreu, Moritz; Kretschmann, Thomas; Król, Joachim; Riemann, Katja**). He had won a number of fans, especially female, with his portrayal of an air force pilot in the popular German television series, *Lindenstraße* (*Lindenstrasse*, 1985–). Schweiger's breakthrough film was *Der bewegte Mann* (*Maybe . . . Maybe Not*, Sönke Wortmann, 1994), in which he plays Axel, a heterosexual rooming with a homosexual after his girlfriend throws him out of the house. Schweiger portrays Axel as a mix of machismo and vulnerability, creating a persona that he develops in his following movies. The movie made him a bankable star, equally adept in comedies, buddy films, and action movies. He followed *Der bewegte Mann* with the equally successful, *Männerpension* (*Jailbirds*, **Detlev Buck**, 1996), in which he plays a convict let out of prison to find a woman who will fall in love with him. He worked again with Wortmann in *Das Superweib* (*Superwife*, 1996), a divorce comedy, which was one of Germany's biggest box office hits of the year. That same year he had roles in *Das Mädchen Rosemarie* (*A Girl Called Rosemarie*, **Bernd Eichinger**) and *Die Halbstarken* (*The Hoologans*, Urs Egger), remakes of two popular 1950s films. In *Die Halbstarken*, he plays Freddy, the leader of the gang, a role played by **Horst Buchholz**, a 1950s heartthrob in the original. His follow-up film, *Knockin' on Heaven's Door* (*Knockin' on Heaven's Door*, Thomas Jahn, 1997), was again one of Germany's most successful films of the year. In the film, a sentimental crime comedy, Schweiger plays a dying man who sets out on a road trip with a friend who is also dying.

Schweiger's directorial debut, in which he plays the title role, was *Der Eisbär* (*The Polar Bear*, codirector Granz Henman, 1998), an homage to Quentin Tarantino's style of cool, ironic visuals to tell a hip gangster story. In his next film as director, *Barfuss* (*Barefoot*, 2005), in which he plays a hedonistic bachelor who falls in love with a mental patient, Schweiger again relies on his image as hard but sensitive romantic hero. One of the actor's best-received roles, in which he deviates from type, is Max Schmeling in *Joe and Max* (Steve James, 2002), the German boxer who first defeated and then lost to Joe Lewis during the late 1930s. Made for American television, the film follows the two fights but also focuses on Schmeling's reluctance to be a poster boy for the Nazis and on the friendship that develops between the two men. Schweiger's other appearances in American movies have been in minor roles, often as the bad guy. He plays villains in *The Replacement Killers* (Antoine Fuqua, 1996) and *Lara Croft Tomb Raider: The Cradle of Life* (Jan de Bont, 2003), and although he plays a German U-boat Captain in World War II in *In Enemy Hands* (Tony Giglio, 2004), his character is presented sympathetically.

SCHYGULLA, HANNA (1943–). In an interview in 2005, Hanna Schygulla rejected the idea that she is a museum relic of the bygone era of **New German Cinema** (NGC). Yet that critics and film historians see her as the quintessential actress of the films of **Rainer Werner Fassbinder**, NGC's leading filmmaker, has indeed imprinted her on film history as an icon of the 1970s. Schygulla met Fassbinder through their mutual involvement in the action-theater, of which she was a cofounder. She continued working with him when the action-theater evolved into Fassbinder's *antiteater*, which championed a minimalist approach to staging, acting, and sets that influenced the director's early films, in which Schygulla was a featured player. As the principal star of his film ensemble, Schygulla portrayed cool and pretty women without morals and feelings. Her star-quality looks raised her above the others in the cast, ensuring that the camera found and lingered on her in any scene in which she appeared. Even the otherwise intentionally static *Katzelmacher* (*Katzelmacher*, 1969), which later in his career Fassbinder referred to as "häßlich" (ugly), lights up when Schygulla enters the scene. In Fassbinder's *Fontane Effi Briest* (*Effi Briest*, 1974), Schygulla played against her developing persona of insensitive prostitute, winning recognition as the title character Effi Briest, the complex, isolated, and insecure young heroine from Fontane's novel, a work that was part of the school curriculum for generations and thus known to most German viewers.

Hoping to advance her career, Schygulla briefly left Fassbinder's ensemble after *Fontane Effi Briest*, appearing in *Falsche Bewegung* (*False Movement*, aka *The Wrong Movement*, 1975) directed by **Wim Wenders**, another of the young directors of New German Cinema. Loosely based on the classic novel *Wilhelm Meisters Lehrjahre* (*Wilhelm Meister's Apprenticeship*), by Johann Wolfgang von Goethe, the film's stilted style of acting suited Schygulla's preferred minimalist approach

to emotion, which she had shown in Fassbinder's films. Before returning to Fassbinder, she also appeared in *Ansichten eines Clowns* (*Faces
of a Clown*, Vojtěch Jasný, 1976), based on the novel of the same name
by the Nobel Laureate Heinrich Böll and a made for TV film, *Die Dä-
monen* (*The Possessed*, Claus Peter Witt, 1977), based on the late 19th-
century novel by Fyodor Dostoyevsky.

Schygulla's breakthrough to international fame came in 1979 after
she returned to Fassbinder and starred in **Die Ehe der Maria Braun**
(*The Marriage of Maria Braun*, 1979), as a woman driven by an obsession to build a successful life for herself and her husband. Believing her husband has died in the war, Maria engages in an affair with
a black American soldier, whom she kills when her husband reap-
pears and walks in on their lovemaking. As Hermann Braun sits in
prison for a crime Maria committed, she enters into a second affair,
striving to make a fortune that she and Hermann can enjoy once he is
released. Some critics saw Maria as a modern-day Mother Courage,
the antiheroine of **Bertolt Brecht**'s play *Mutter Courage*, who sacrifices personal happiness for economic gain. Others saw her as a
metaphor of 1950s Germany, personifying the striving Germans of
the postwar era who had no time for tears or sentiment as they rebuilt
their country. Still others viewed Maria as a reflection of German
women during and after the war, called upon to take on the roles of
men but then asked to step aside after the men returned from the
fighting. However one sees the film, there is no doubt that it tapped
directly into German viewers' self-doubts about the emotional and
psychological cost of the economic miracle that had transformed
West Germany in the 1950s and 1960s. They saw in those years, and
in the nightmare of the Third Reich that had preceded them, the cause
of the political repression of the 1970s and the coldness of the society that at the time surrounded them.

Schygulla's role as Maria Braun and a subsequent role as the title
figure in Fassbinder's *Lili Marleen* (*Lili Marleen*, 1981) assured
Schygulla of a career after the director's death in 1982. She has starred
in the films of some of the most respected directors in international
cinema, including **Volker Schlöndorff**'s *Die Fälschung* (*Circle of Deceit* 1981), about the war in Lebanon at the time of the movie's making; Ettore Scola's *La Nuit de Varennes* (*That Night in Varennes*,
1982), about the French Revolution; Jean-Luc Godard's *Passion* (*Go-*

dard's Passion, 1982); Carlos Saura's *Antonietta* (*Antonietta*, 1982); and Andrzej Wajda's *Eine Liebe in Deutschland* (*A Love in Germany*, 1983), a film set during World War II. *Eine Liebe in Deutschland* suggests how influential her role as Maria Braun may have been, for once again Schygulla found herself cast in a melodramatic love story set during World War II or its aftermath. Over the next decade she appeared in three more films about the Nazi era, *Miss Arizona* (*Miss Arizona*, Pál Sándor, 1987), set in a Budapest night club; *Abrahams Gold* (*Abraham's Gold*, Jörg Graser, 1990), set in a Bavarian village that discovers a chest full of gold fillings of victims of the Holocaust; and *Warszawa. Année 5703* (*Warsaw. Year 5703*, Janusz Kijowski, 1992), set in the Warsaw Ghetto in 1943. Schygulla has also appeared in a number of films by the noted and controversial Israeli director Amos Gitai, including *Golem, l'esprit de l'exile* (*Golem, the Spirit of Exile*, 1992), *Golem, le jardin pétrifié* (*Golem: The Petrified Garden*, 1993), and *Milim* (*Metamorphoses of a Melody*, 1996), films about Jewish legend and mystery. Schygulla also appeared on American television, in *Peter the Great* (Marvin J. Chomsky and Laurence Schiller, 1986), and in the cult Hungarian film by Béla Tarr and Ágnes Hranitzky, *Werckmeister harmóniák* (*Werckmeister Harmonies*, 2000), about the apocalypse. In 2007, she played in *Auf der anderen Seite* (*The Edge of Heaven*) by acclaimed Turkish–German director **Fatih Akim**.

SEYBOLD, KATRIN (1943–). Katrin Seybold's films document the outsider in German history and culture. Her early focus was the Sinti and Jews persecuted by the Nazis, but she also examines maltreatment of political dissidents and neglect of children. She and her consultant and codirector, Melanie Spitta, have produced four films on the Sinti and Roma. *Schimpft uns nicht Ziguener* (*Don't Call Us Gypsies*, 1980) and *Wir sind Sinti Kinder und keine Zigeuner* (*We Are Sinti Children and Not Gypsies*, 1981) identify contemporary discrimination against Sinti and Roma in Germany, visiting families in their homes and at their celebrations. *Es ging Tag und Nacht, liebes Kind – Zigeuner (Sinti) in Auschwitz* (*It Went on Day and Night, Dear Child: Gypsies (Sinti) in Auschwitz*, 1982) interviews a woman who had been imprisoned at Auschwitz. *Das falsche Wort* (*Calumny*, 1987) exposes historical discrimination and persecution which officially were still being denied at the time of the film's release.

Seybold has spoken out against discrimination of other groups as well. Her documentary *Seit ich weiß, dass ich nicht mehr lange lebe, bin ich stark* (*Since I Found Out That I Don't Have Much Longer to Live, I Am Strong*, 1987) includes interviews with people suffering from AIDS. Two other films look at persecution of the Jews during the Third Reich. In *Deutsch ist meine Muttersprache* (*German is my Native Language*, 1990), Seybold and codirector Emanuel Rund film German émigrés to Israel as they remember life among non-Jewish Germans. The documentary *Alle Juden raus! Juden Verfolgung in einer deutschen Kleinstadt 1933–1945* (*All Jews Out! The Persecution of the Jews in a Small German Town 1933–1945*), produced by Seybold and directed by Rund, accompanies the survivors of a Jewish family as they visit the small town of Göppingen in southern Germany, recalling the members of their family who perished in the Nazi concentration camps. She also directed *Nein! Zeugen des Widerstandes in München 1933–1945* (*No! Witnesses of the Resistance in Munich 1933–1945*, 1998), about the individuals and groups such as The White Rose, Sophie and Hans Scholl's resistance movement, who protested Nazi policies. *See also* HOLOCAUST IN FEATURE FILMS; *VERGANGENHEITSBEWÄLTIGUNGSFILM*.

SIODMAK, ROBERT (1900–1973). Robert Siodmak immigrated to the United States via France in the early 1930s to escape the Nazis. In his publicity biography, he thereafter claimed to having been born in Tennessee rather than Dresden, Germany, his true place of birth. But although he fabricated an American origin for himself, his movies, even those made in Hollywood, reveal his roots in German film. Remembered as one of the originators of the Hollywood film style known as film noir, Siodmak directed some of the genre's better known works, including *The Killers* (1946); *The Spiral Staircase* (1946), more a gothic murder mystery in the style of Alfred Hitchcock than a noir film; and *The File on Thelma Jordon* (1950). Influenced by the expressionism of the **Universum Film AG** (Ufa) studio style prevalent in the 1920s in Germany and brought to Hollywood by German émigrés, Siodmak created in his films a world that is dark, claustrophobic, and cynical and populated by urban dwellers governed by fate, passion, and obsession.

As important as his Hollywood films noirs are, Siodmak's reputation rests also on the films he made in Germany, both before and after his years directing movies for Hollywood. His first film, for example, *Menschen am Sonntag* (*People on Sunday*, 1930), the last great silent film made in Germany, follows the lives of six ordinary Germans as they relax on Sunday. Starring nonprofessional actors, the film melds the realist experimental camera work of such city films as *Berlin – Die Sinfonie der Großstadt* (*Berlin: Symphony of a Great City*, **Walter Ruttmann**, 1927) and *The Man with a Movie Camera* (Dziga Vertov, 1929) and storytelling fictions. Siodmak was one of four directors on the film, the others being his brother Curt Siodmak, Edgar G. Ulmer, and Fred Zinnemann, who all, like Siodmak, had successful careers in Hollywood, but who unlike him did not return after the war to again work in Germany. *Menschen am Sonntag* is a tour de force of experimental realism, which critics compare to both Italian neorealism of the 1940s and the French New Wave of the 1960s. Three other films that Siodmak made in Germany before leaving for Hollywood—*Der Mann der seinen Mörder sucht* (*The Man Who Seeks His Own Murderer*, 1931), *Stürme der Leidenschaft* (*Storms of Passion*, 1932), and *Brennendes Geheimnis* (*The Burning Secret*, 1933)—move beyond the realism of his first movie and anticipate the themes and style of his later work. *Brennendes Geheimnis* was condemned by Joseph Goebbels as a "corrupter of the German family" because of its theme of adultery.

After a successful career in Hollywood, Siodmak again directed films in Germany. Like two of his contemporaries, **Peter Lorre** and **Georg Wilhelm Pabst**, who also returned to Germany after the war to direct individual projects, Siodmak wanted to help Germans come to terms with the events of the Nazi regime. *Die Ratten* (*The Rats*, 1955) relocates Gerhart Haupmann's play to postwar Germany, allowing the bleak milieu of a war-scarred country to serve as metaphor for the scars of his characters. In *Nachts, wenn der Teufel kam* (*The Devil Strikes at Night*, 1957), he tells the story of a serial killer in Nazi Germany, focusing as much on the psychological state of mind of the Germans near the end of the war as on that of the killer. The story of mass murderer Bruno Ludke, whose crimes were covered up by the Gestapo, becomes a metaphor for the reign of terror of National Socialism. *Nachts, wenn der Teufel kam* won 10 national awards, including the coveted *goldene Schale* (golden bowl) of the German film industry as best picture. It was also nominated for an Academy Award as Best Foreign Film of 1958. Late in his career Siodmak also directed several German Westerns and adventure films starring Lex Barker, whose fame in the United States rested on following Johnny Weissmueller in the role of Tarzan, but who in Germany was known for starring in film versions of Western novels by German 19th-century author Karl May.

SIRK, DOUGLAS (1897–1987). Considered by many critics to be the master of kitsch and soap opera superficiality because of the melodramatic films he made in Hollywood in the 1950s, Douglas Sirk (born Detlev Sierck) was nonetheless an expert storyteller and masterful film stylist. The films Sirk made during his career in the Third Reich surpass the standard fare of other National Socialist directors in quality and popular success. Although he did not subscribe to Nazi ideology, Sirk's talent as a filmmaker ensured he could make films, perhaps because he left any subversive elements out of his films. Indeed, as critics of his films under National Socialism have pointed out, a conservative tone runs throughout his German work. Family, Germany, and tradition triumph in spite of the erotic attraction of the films' male and female characters. In *Zu neuen Ufern* (*To New Shores*, 1937), for example, **Zarah Leander**, whom this and her next film for Sirk, *La Habanera* (*La Habanera*, 1937), made a star, plays a dance hall diva who is willing to go to prison for her gambling, unethical lover. After being deported to a prison in Australia, she learns the true value of love and marriage through her relationship with an Australian rancher, but not before her former lover, in typical Sirkian melodrama, kills himself. The final scene in a church, which stresses tradition and the sanctity of marriage, anticipates the emotional endings of Sirk's Hollywood films. In similar fashion, *La Habanera* ends on an uplifting note, as the heroine sails for Europe, having initially been seduced by the Spanish rhythms of Puerto Rico. At one point in the film, Sirk contrasts the Latin sounds of the Habanera with the purity of German Christmas carols in a scene that must have endeared him to National Socialist ideologues, in spite of his otherwise liberal tendencies.

Sirk continued his preference for melodramatic love stories after relocating to Hollywood. His films often starred Rock Hudson, an American movie idol of the 1950s, and generally employed the talents of Frank Skinner for the soundtrack, Russell Mitty as cinematographer, Alexander Golitzen as art director, and Ross Hunter as producer. Sirk and his team developed a style that is uniquely Sirk's. Consisting of a symbolic color palette, a carefully constructed mise-en-scène that stresses framing devices and reflecting surfaces, stories that expose the contradictions of love relationships, and subtexts about the unhappiness of the privileged, Sirk's Hollywood films were widely popular in the 1950s, especially among women.

In the late 1960s film historians, led by critics such as Andrew Sarris and Jon Halliday, elevated Sirk to the status of auteur filmmaker. What many had considered Sirk's kitsch became Sirk's deconstructing irony, a way to distance viewers from the melodramatic emotion of the story in order to focus on the problems in American society. His simple plots, exaggerated characters, and closed world thus became a means to emphasize themes of repressed sexuality, corruption of love by money, and failed family relationships. In the early 1970s, German filmmaker **Rainer Werner Fassbinder**'s homage to Sirk's work, particularly to *All That Heaven Allows* (1956), further enhanced the director's reputation by highlighting the unhappiness supposedly hiding beneath the happy endings. For Sarris, Halliday, and Fassbinder, Sirk's sentimentalized images at the end of his movies became ironic comments on American values. Regardless of whether one sees him as the king of kitsch or a purveyor of **Brechtian**-like alienation, one cannot overlook Sirk's individual talent or his continued appeal to film audiences.

SKLADANOWSKY, MAX (1863–1939). Max Skladanowsky and his brother Emil were pioneers of film. Experimenting with motion picture technology at the same time as brothers Louis and Auguste Lumière, the Skladanowskys invented a two-camera projection system, the **Bioscop**, which by alternating exposure of the strip of film, created the illusion of movement. They gave a public performance of the apparatus two months before the Lumières demonstrated their single projector system. Because the Bioscop was more cumbersome than the single projector system, and moreover because it produced inferior quality projections, Max Skladanowsky abandoned his system. He continued however to produce and exhibit short films, mainly comedy shorts.

SÖDERBAUM, KRISTINA (1912–2001). Kristina Söderbaum, Swedish by birth, was one of the Third Reich's most visible actors, appearing in several of the regime's major productions. Her first successful role, as a young woman in **Veit Harlan**'s *Jugend* (*Youth*, 1938), was career setting in several ways for Söderbaum. It was the first film in which she was directed by Harlan, whom she later married, and for whom she worked exclusively throughout her career during the Third Reich and in postwar West Germany during the 1950s. Her portrayal of a vulnerable young girl seduced by her own emotional weakness and youthful desires created a type that she repeated in many films. She drowns in the final scene, a means of death repeated in other movies and which earned her the nickname *Reichswasserleiche* (The Official State Water Corpse).

Söderbaum's high-visibility roles included two of the Third Reich's major propaganda efforts. She plays Dorothea in *Jud Süß* (*Jew Süss*, Harlan, 1940), the narrative counterpart to the documentary *Der ewige Jude* (*The Eternal Jew*, Fritz Hippler, 1940), the Nazi's two most virulently anti-Semitic films. Dorothea is an innocent girl, engaged to be married, who is at first seduced by the cosmopolitan charm and swarthy good looks of Süß Oppenheimer, played by **Ferdinand Marian**. After she learns the truth of his treacherous nature, she cannot extricate herself from his influence, is raped, and commits suicide. In *Kolberg* (*Kolberg*, Harlan, 1945), one of the last films made in Nazi Germany, her character, Maria, learns the importance of giving one's life to a cause. In a final speech her father, played by **Heinrich George**, consoles her by telling her she too has helped the country through her sacrifice. The film is seen by many as another example of Propaganda Minister Joseph Goebbels policy of fighting to the death.

Other important films for Söderbaum were *Immensee* (*Bees' Lake*, 1943), in which she plays a woman who foregoes love rather than being unfaithful to her husband, even after he is dead, and *Opfergang* (*The Great Sacrifice*, 1944), in which she plays a woman who dies of a broken heart. After the war, Söderbaum continued to make films with Harlan, and after his death appeared in *Karl May* (*Karl May*, **Hans-Jürgen Syberberg**, 1974), as the wife of the 19th-century German author of novels about Indian life in America's West. *See also DURCHHALTUNGSFILM.*

SÖHNKER, HANS (1903–1981). Hans Söhnker appeared in over 100 movies during his five decades in film. He began his career in operetta in the 1930s but did not achieve recognition until **Helmut Käutner** cast him as Michael in *Auf Wiedersehen, Franziska! (Goodbye, Franziska!*, 1941), in which he plays a bon vivant cameraman who travels the world. The title refers to the frequency with which he says goodbye to his wife to follow another photographic story. Käutner also cast Söhnker in *Große Freiheit # 7 (Port of Freedom*, 1944), his film about sailors and nightlife in the Reeperbahn, Hamburg's red light district. After the war, Söhnker had a successful career first portraying leading men and later fathers, but always with the same mixture of head in the clouds exuberance and feet on the ground solidness. He appeared in *Film ohne Titel (Film without Title*, Rudolf Jugert, 1948), a postwar **rubble film** that suggests postwar Germany will need a new form of entertainment to address the past. In the 1960s and 1970s, he became a regular on German television, appearing in a number of popular series.

SPENGLER, VOLKER (1939–). One of the many actors in the repertoire troupe of **Rainer Werner Fassbinder**, Volker Spengler specialized in introverted, damaged, and decidedly odd characters. As the brother of a has-been poet in Fassbinder's *Satansbraten (Satan's Brew*, 1976), he portrays an imbecilic sexual pervert, who in one scene waves his penis over a visitor's food. His part in *Chinesisches Roulette (Chinese Roulette*, 1976) is less obscene, but again he plays a simpleton who is controlled by others. Spengler's first leading role for Fassbinder was in *In einem Jahr mit 13 Monden (In a Year with 13 Moons*, 1978), a black comedy about a bisexual man, played by Spengler, who undergoes a sex operation in order to get a man he met briefly to love him. Unlike his supporting roles, his part as Erwin/Elvira reveals the breadth of Spengler's emotional range. At times hysterical, at other times camp, Spengler also plays Erwin/Elvira as life-weary and damaged. Other Fassbinder films in which Spengler appears are *Eine Reise ins Licht – Despair (Despair*, 1978), in which he has an affair with his cousin; *Die dritte Generation (The Third Generation*, 1979), in which he plays an ineffectual terrorist; and *Die Ehe der Maria Braun (The Marriage of Maria Braun*, 1979), in which he has a very small role as a train conductor.

Since the character is conventional, Spengler wears an eye patch for the part, lending it the usual degree of oddity.

Spengler has also appeared in the films of other directors. He plays the lead, an accidental terrorist who is involved in a love triangle with a mother and her daughter in *Obszön – Der Fall Peter Herzl* (*Obscene: The Case of Peter Herzl*, Hans-Christof Stenzel, 1981) and Goebbels's brother-in-law, Fegelein, in *100 Jahre Adolf Hitler – die letzten Stunde im Führerbunker* (*100 Years of Adolf Hitler: The Last Hour in the Führer's Bunker*, Christoph Schlingensief, 1989), a film in which everyone goes mad as the end of the war nears. He again had a major role in **Volker Schlöndorff**'s *Der Unhold* (*The Ogre*, 1996), playing Hermann Göring as a blustering hunter who rubs moose droppings in his fingers and relieves tension by dipping his hands in mercury.

STAUDTE, WOLFGANG (1906–1984). Wolfgang Staudte ranks as one of the two most important film directors in the postwar period in German film (the other is **Helmut Käutner**). Making his most important movies for **DEFA**, the East German studio, Staudte turned a critical lens on the Nazi past and Germany's crimes. At the same time, he also showed understanding for ordinary German citizens during this period. Five of his films, *Die Mörder sind unter uns* (*The Murderers Are among Us*, 1946), *Rotation* (*Rotation*, 1949), *Rosen für den Staatsanwalt* (*Roses for the Prosecutor*, 1959), *Kirmes* (*The Fair*, aka *Death Carousel*, 1960), and *Zwischengleis* (*Between the Tracks*, 1978), deal specifically with the Third Reich and its legacy. A sixth film, *Der Untertan* (*The Kaiser's Lackey*, 1951), focuses instead on the elements in German culture prior to 1933 that gave rise to the Nazis.

Staudte began his film career as an actor, appearing in over 30 films, before turning to directing films during the Third Reich. Aside from two film documentaries in the mid-1930s, which could be seen as mildly propagandistic, his films made under National Socialist rule were comedies and romances, without propagandic intent. The best known of these is *Akrobat Schööön* (*Acrobat Schööön*, 1943), starring Charlie Rivel, a successful acrobatic clown of the era. At times reminiscent of the visual gags from the films of Charlie Chaplin, *Akrobat Schööön* tells the story of a clown who goes from stage hand to discovered star after he steps in for a missing act in a variety show.

Staudte's first postwar German film, *Die Mörder sind unter uns*, is a melodrama about a returning soldier who confronts a crisis of conscience when he meets his former commander, a man responsible for killing Polish hostages. Denied financing by authorities in the American, British, and French sectors of Berlin, Staudte finally received support from the Soviets after revising the ending of the movie, removing the vigilante justice his screenplay implied. *Die Mörder sind unter uns* is remarkable for its honesty in looking at personal and collective guilt for the war crimes committed by the Nazis. At one point in the movie, the man guilty of war crimes, who has become a respected citizen and integrated back into the community, eats lunch over a newspaper whose headline reads "2 Millionen vergast" (2 Million Gassed), the earliest narrative filmic reference to mass killings by the Nazis. Shot amid the ruins of Berlin, making it the first of the so-called **rubble films**, the film combines stylistic elements of Italian neorealism and Hollywood film noir. As in neorealism, Staudte films on location, capturing the misery of the people and the devastation caused by the war. Yet, as in film noir, he constructs a melodramatic thriller, replete with symbolic shadows, existentialist characters, and portentous music.

Although *Die Mörder sind unter uns* has become the major film of Staudte's legacy, his films made in the first 15 years after the war addressed Germany's past again and again. *Rotation* tells of a man who joins the Nazi Party at first in order to blend in and secure a living but who then actively opposes Nazism once he understands the direction the party is taking Germany. Turned in by his son as a traitor, he escapes execution by the arrival of Allied troops. In the end, his son also has a change of political heart and the two reconcile, providing the sentimental or happy end found in other Staudte films about the war. In *Rosen für den Staatsanwalt*, for example, Rudi, a soldier, is accused of a petty crime during the Third Reich and is sentenced to execution by Dr. Schramm, an overly zealous National Socialist judge. He escapes death and after the war meets the judge, now a prosecutor for the state. Rudi again ends up in front of Dr. Schramm at trial. This time, though, he is rescued from prison when Dr. Schramm exposes his Nazi sympathies by imploding in court and asking that Rudi be put to death for his petty crime. Staudte forgoes a happy end in *Kirmes*, a film about a deserter from the Nazi army, who kills himself in order not to endanger his family. When his body is found years later while a fair (Kirmes) is being set up, his family prefers to leave the past buried, a sentiment that many viewers in West Germany, the country where the film was produced, shared in 1960.

Staudte's most critically acclaimed movie is arguably *Der Untertan*, also an East German production, made for **DEFA** in 1951. Although set in the Wilhelmine period before the rise of the Nazis, the film is very much about the Third Reich and the character flaws, as seen by Heinrich Mann in his novel, on which the film is based, that led Germans to accept Adolf Hitler's dictatorship. The film follows the career of a small-minded man who learns early in his career that to get ahead he has to flatter and serve those above him and mistreat those below. The movie's biting satire may have been too much for West Germany at the time, which kept the film out of distribution for six years. *See also* EAST GERMAN FILM.

STÖCKL, ULA (1938–). In spite of her early work in films and her efforts on behalf of feminism, Stöckl has never been as well known among the general public as other women filmmakers in **New German Cinema**, such as **Margarethe von Trotta**, **Helma Sanders-Brahms**, and **Helke Sander**. Her films are nonetheless respected by film critics and directors in Germany and abroad. They do not receive wide theatrical distribution, but they appear often in solo or combined retrospectives of German film organized by the Goethe Institute, universities, or other agencies.

Stöckl was one of the first women to attend the Ulm School of Film (1963–1968) and also one of the first women to make films that deal subjectively with the feminine psyche and the difficulties women have functioning in a male-oriented society. Her first feature, *Neun Leben hat die Katze* (*The Cat Has Nine Lives*, 1968), looks at the way a group of women function within institutional structures. *Eine Frau mit Verantwortung* (*A Woman with Responsibility*, 1978) tells the story of a woman who feels responsibility for everyone but herself. Most often, though, when critics write about her contribution to feminist filmmaking, they cite *Der Schlaf der Vernunft* (*The Sleep of Reason*, 1984). Drawing on the Greek myth of Medea, Stöckl focuses on a woman's struggles to be independent of her husband, her mother, and her daughters. As with her other films, Stöckl includes ethical questions on individual, communal, or corporate behavior. Here, for example, she takes issue with the marketing of birth control pills without absolute proof of their safety.

Stöckl's most creatively experimental effort to date has been *Geschichten vom Kubelkind* (*Stories of a Dumpster Child*, 1971), which she codirected with **Edgar Reitz**. The film, which is actually 23 short films that range in length from 2 minutes to 20, was a response to the conformity required by distributors of filmmakers who wanted to get their films into theatrical release. Stöckl and Reitz conceived of their work as stand-alone episodes that could be ordered from a menu in a film café. The works relate the adventures of a person, born as a full-grown woman in a dumpster, who cannot fit comfortably into societal roles, nor does she wish to. Each episode in the series tells of the Kubelkind's inability to understand societal structures and strictures. At the end of each, she dies but is reborn in the next installment of the story. Each episode is also filmed in the style of a different genre, from sci-fi to Western, thriller to romance.

Stöckl was one of the first filmmakers to address German unification after the fall of the Berlin Wall in 1989, in her film *Das alte Lied* (*Same Old Song*, 1992). Here, a woman returns with her brother and family to Dresden, a city she had fled after the war. She has two goals, to reunite with an old lover, although she and her former lover are now both 70, and to reclaim a house that was appropriated by the Communists after she fled. In a series of lyrical and self-reflexive shots, punctuated by the verses of Germany's national anthem, the film deals with youthful angst deriving from the collapse of a system they had been taught to believe in, the dropping of incendiary bombs on Dresden by the Allies, the unethical if not immoral behavior of West Germans returning to the East to reclaim homes, the Stasi, and unification in general, among other problems. When the film ends, viewers are left feeling anxious about the future, but the absolute pessimism of her earlier films has been replaced by a ray of hope that maybe young people will not repeat the mistakes of the past. Although a number of films have been set in the East since the Berlin Wall fell, most of these have been situation comedies, nostalgic satires, or sentimental dramas. *Das alte Lied* remains one of only a few post–Berlin Wall films to deal sensitively and honestly with the end of the German Democratic Republic. Two others are *Das Versprechen* (*The Promise*, von Trotta, 1995) and *Vergiss Amerika* (*Forget America*, Vanessa Jopp, 2000).

STOLZE, LENA (1956–). Lena Stolze plays primarily supporting roles, but she has also appeared in two of Germany's most internationally successful films, *Die weiße Rose* (*The White Rose*, 1982) and *Das schreckliche Mädchen* (*The Nasty Girl*, 1990), both directed by **Michael Verhoeven**. In *Die weiße Rose*, she plays Sophie Scholl, who together with her brother Hans prints and distributes broadsides against National Socialist policies. When caught they are summarily tried and executed, along with others who were part of the underground movement. Stolze portrays Sophie as a young woman full of life, given to having fun, but also as a courageous woman, not afraid of authorities. In the same year, Stolze portrayed Scholl in another movie, *Fünf letzte Tage* (*Five Last Days*, aka *The Last Five Days*, **Percy Adlon**). Because Adlon focuses on the period after Sophie's capture, the role gave Stolze more opportunity for introspection as she discusses motivations with her cell mate and debates the prosecutor. In *Das schreckliche Mädchen*, Stolze shows her lighter side in a serious role. Playing Sonja, a young woman who as a schoolgirl began investigating her town's involvement in Nazism, she flirts with her teacher, argues with town bureaucrats for access to materials, and insists on exposing the lies of her town. Stolze's strength is to combine capriciousness with determination, using facial expressions and body movement to suggest her various moods. *See also VERGANGENHEITSBEWÄLTIGUNGSFILM*.

STRAUB, JEAN-MARIE (1933–), AND DANIÈLE HUILLET (1936–2006). Jean-Marie Straub and his partner Danièle Huillet made over 20 films together. Born in France, they immigrated to Germany in the 1960s and began making films during the era known as **New German Cinema** (NGC). Their work at this time paradoxically had a profound influence on NGC and at the same time had the weakest reception by both public and critics of the movement's directors. Yet their minimalist style influenced the films of **Rainer Werner Fassbinder**, **Werner Schroeter**, and **Herbert Achternbusch**.

Straub and Huillet are film purists, reducing cinema to its essentials, unenhanced and unadorned image and sound. Their cinematic style adapts the theater principles of **Bertolt Brecht** to film and may also be found in Fassbinder's *antiteater*, a style that eschews dramatic conventions in favor of play readings. Wanting to prevent viewers from identifying with characters and stories, Straub and Huillet prefer simple décor; Brechtian acting, a style in which the actors stand outside their rolls; and natural sound. Furthermore, they avoid linear stories, narrative logic, and heightened drama. The one constant in their films is a continuous deconstruction or breaking down of the cinematic process. For viewers, the result is not only an extreme experience of alienation from the movie but also a feeling of frustration at never being allowed a comfortable place from which to enjoy the story.

Straub and Huillet's best-known film is *Chronik der Anna Magdalena Bach* (*Chronicle of Anna Magdalena Bach*, 1968), for which Straub won a Bambi in Germany and an award for Best Film from the British Film Institute in 1968 (*see* **film awards**). The directors also wrote the screenplay and edited the final product. *Die Chronik der Anna Magdalena Bach* uses letters and other contemporary texts, read from the point of view of Anna Magdalena Bach, to tell about the life of her husband, Johann Sebastian Bach. Straub and Huillet's major innovation in the film was that they used music as aesthetic material, not as accompaniment to or commentary on screen action. During extended takes, Bach's music is the only focus. Although a chamber orchestra is visible, there is no audience in the film world listening to the music, leaving movie viewers to react without the usual outside influence.

When filmmaker and critic Jean-Luc Godard remarked that Straub and Huillet's film lacked relevance to contemporary problems, Straub replied that it was his "contribution to the fight of the South Vietnamese against the Americans." This seeming non sequitur and yet quite serious answer characterizes not only this film but other projects as well. *Nicht versöhnt oder Es hilft nur Gewalt, wo Gewalt herrscht* (*Not Reconciled*, 1965), based on the Heinrich Böll novel *Billard um halb 10* (*Billiards at Half Past Nine*), is an austere film that examines Germany's collective guilt for the crimes of the Third

Reich by studying a German family over a period of 50 years. Their film *Der Bräutigam, die Komödiantin und der Zuhälter* (*The Bridegroom, the Actress and the Pimp*, 1968) documents Fassbinder's truncated *antiteater* production of Ferdinand Bruckner's *Krankeit der Jugend* (*Sickness of Youth*, 1930) at the same time that it opens the work beyond the confines of static scenery to pan through countryside and sleazy neighborhoods.

Straub and Huillet left Germany in 1969 to make films in Italy. They resumed making films in Germany, usually French and German coproductions, in the 1980s. *Klassenverhältnisse* (*Class Relations*, 1983), their adaptation of Franz Kafka's unfinished novel *Amerika*, reflects the love of experimentation and provocation found in their earlier films. Actors remain outside the characters, sets are minimal and reflect no particular era, and costumes symbolically refer to a character's societal position. In 2000, the couple again started making their films outside Germany, in Italy and France.

SYBERBERG, HANS-JÜRGEN (1935–). Hans-Jürgen Syberberg never gained the lasting fame of his contemporaries in the **New German Cinema** (NGC), although at the time his films were released, critics and filmmakers discussed them at length. They won awards, received praise from critics, especially those outside Germany, and otherwise enjoyed the same publicity and public acknowledgment given the films of other NGC directors, such as **Rainer Werner Fassbinder**, **Werner Herzog**, and **Volker Schlöndorff**. Fassbinder included three of Syberberg's best-known films on a list of Germany's worst movies; he called *Karl May* (*Karl May*, 1974), a film about Germany's beloved 19th-century author of novels about the American West, one of the 10 most disgusting films of NGC. He listed *Ludwig – Requiem für einen jungfräulichen König* (*Ludwig: Requiem for a Virgin King*, 1972) and *Hitler, ein Film aus Deutschland* (*Hitler: A Film from Germany*, 1977) as 2 of the 10 most insignificant German movies. What caused Fassbinder's dislike is difficult to say, but along with many of Germany's critics, he found the films ponderous and laden with undifferentiated collective guilt for the crimes of the past. While NGC directors were certainly critical of Germany's destructive force in 20th-century history, they applied guilt more selectively. Syberberg, in contrast, found the evil of Adolf

Hitler and the Nazis in everything and everyone German and applauded himself for his insight.

Syberberg's fame rests primarily on the seven-hour-plus documentary *Hitler, ein Film aus Deutschland*. Conceived in the manner of a Wagnerian opera—even the viewing was to take place all on the same day with a dinner break in the middle, as is the case with Wagner's longer operas—the film overwhelms the senses with optical and acoustic impressions as it attempts to answer the question, "How did Hitler gain power?" To the dismay of mainly German critics, Syberberg does not concern himself with the actual or historical figure. Rather, continuing the investigations begun in *Ludwig – Requiem für einen jungfräulichen König* and *Karl May*, he characterizes the myths, the history, and the popular conceptions that created Hitler. The result is a pastiche that confused but enthralled viewers, particularly outside Germany. The critic for the Paris weekly *Le Monde* called it *Faust III*, referring to Johann Wolfgang von Goethe's dramatic masterpiece of sin and redemption, and American critic Susan Sontag described it as "one of the great works of art of the 20th century." The British Film Institute (BFI) named it best picture of 1978. The German film industry awarded **Peter Kern**, who played multiple parts in the film, its top prize for acting.

Hitler, ein Film aus Deutschland is a difficult film to digest, and not merely because it lasts seven hours. The difficulty lies not in its length but in the emotional involvement that viewing the film causes. Although much of the film takes place on a soundstage cluttered with memorabilia of the past, employs elaborate marionettes in the likeness of key National Socialist officials, and avoids cinematic illusion, viewers are not distanced from the film; rather, they are drawn into the world Syberberg creates, through dreamlike visuals, opulent music, and imaginative sets. One is truly emotionally exhausted after sitting through the work in its entirety, a reaction similar to that which one experiences at Richard Wagner's operas, particularly *Götterdämmerung*, whose theme of final destruction writers began using as metaphor for the Third Reich soon after Germany's defeat. *See also VERGANGENHEITSBEWÄLTIGUNGSFILM*.

SZABÓ, ISTVÁN (1938–). István Szabó is a Hungarian director who in the 1980s directed a trilogy of three of Germany's major movies about protofascism and Nazism: *Mephisto* (*Mephisto*, 1981), *Oberst Redl* (*Colonel Redl*, 1985), and *Hanussen* (*Hanussen*, 1988). *Mephisto* is based on the novel of that title by Klaus Mann, which is a thinly veiled exposé of **Gustaf Gründgens**, who enjoyed an opportunistic career under Nazi rule. The book, written in 1936, was not published in Germany until 1965. *Oberst Redl* is set during the Austro-Hungarian Empire and tells of the rise of Redl, an ordinary man, through the ranks of the security police, until an act of treason on his part leads to his death. *Hanussen* is about the notorious charlatan who in his stage act performed tricks of mind reading and off stage held séances with the Weimar Republic's elite. He also advised Adolf Hitler, which was to prove Hanussen's downfall. **Klaus Maria Brandauer** starred in all three films as the title character, playing each man as larger than life, brought down by his hubris. Szabó showcases Brandauer's physical style of acting and his range of emotion in facial expression. The camera follows the actor through his dance calisthenics and stage appearances in *Mephisto* and *Hanussen*, capturing the actor's animal energy. It lingers in close up on Brandauer's face, revealing subtle and exaggerated emotion. Szabó privileges the mise-en-scène and uses classic camera placement, objects, and people to symbolize the seduction and dangers of fascistic power. In *Mephisto*, he films the protagonist Höfgen captured by a spotlight, no longer able to get free of Nazi control. In *Hanussen*, he films the psychic from a distance, foregrounding his vulnerability.

Szabó's other films have been either for the Hungarian film industry or American independent productions. In these also he shows interest in Europe's anti-Semitic past. *Sunshine* (1999) tells of three generations of a Hungarian Jewish family, which served the Austro-Hungarian Empire, changed its name to assimilate better into the population, and yet suffered the Holocaust nonetheless. *Taking Sides* (2001) is a film biography of Wilhelm Furtwängler, the controversial conductor who was conductor of the Berlin Philharmonic during the Third Reich. *See also VERGANGENHEITSBEWÄLTIGUNGSFILM.*

– T –

THALBACH, KATHARINA (1954–). Katharina Thalbach began as a child actor on East German television, appeared in East German the-

ater in her teens, and had her first major film role as Lotte in *Die Leiden des jungen Werthers* (*The Sorrows of the Young Werther*, Egon
Günther, 1976), based on Johann Wolfgang von Goethe's late 18th-
century novel. Subsequently Thalbach moved from East to West Germany and had supporting roles in *Das zweite Erwachen der Christa
Klages* (*The Second Awakening of Christa Klages*, **Margarethe von
Trotta**, 1978), an early feminist film about a band of bank robbers
who use the proceeds for women's issues; *Winterspelt* (*Winterspelt*,
Eberhard Fechner, 1978), a critical look at the Battle of the Bulge;
and *Die Blechtrommel* (*The Tin Drum*, **Volker Schlöndorff**, 1979),
based on Günter Grass's satirical novel about ordinary citizens during
the Third Reich. Thalbach brought to her roles a combination of innocence and eroticism. Her portrayal of Maria in *Die Blechtrommel* was
particularly emblematic of her appeal. As a young woman brought to
the Matzerath household to care for the man-child Oskar, Maria has
affairs both with Oskar and his father. Her sexual games with Oskar
led to controversy in the United States when the state of Oklahoma declared the movie obscene because it intimated a sexual relationship
between Oskar, who was 16 in the film but was being played by a 12-
year-old boy, and Maria, who was a teenager being played by a 26-
year-old actress.

Thalbach, who has appeared in over 80 theatrical and television
films, generally plays supporting roles. Her portrayal of a young
woman in *Paradies* (*Paradise*, **Doris Dörrie**, 1986) who is seduced
by the husband of a friend and ends up as a prostitute reveals once
again Thalbach's quality of innocent sexuality, even as a 30-year-
old. One of her major lead roles came as a reporter in *Der achte Tag*
(*The Eighth Day*, Reinhard Münster, 1990), a sci-fi thriller about
biogenetic research. In *Sonnenallee* (*Sonnenallee*, Leander Haußmann, 1999), a coming-of-age film set in East Berlin before the fall
of the Berlin Wall, Thalbach had a featured role as a scatter-brained
mother; it was a part that revealed her comic timing and yet also had
the same mixture from her earlier films of innocence and seductive
beauty.

THOME, RUDOLF (1939–). Rudolf Thome was a member of a group
of young German filmmakers active in Schwabing, Munich's Greenwich Village, known as the Neue Münchner Gruppe (New Munich
Group) or Schwabing Group. Although they started making films

about the same time that the directors of **Young German Cinema** were reviving Germany's film reputation, Thome and his fellow filmmakers, **Eckhart Schmidt**, Max Zihlmann, Klaus Lemke, and May Spils, made movies to appeal to a broad audience, resulting in an emphasis on young people and sex. *Rote Sonne* (*Red Sun*, 1970), for which Zihlmann wrote the screenplay, for example, is an erotic mix of sci-fi and male fantasy about a world in which women kill men if they want to prolong a sexual relationship into something more meaningful. Thome recognized the limit that his filmmaking in Schwabing placed on his creativity and moved to Berlin in the 1980s.

Thome's work in Berlin reveals him as auteur, still with a keen interest in erotic stories, but focusing more on the philosophical underpinnings of relationships. *Der Philosoph* (*The Philosopher*, 1989) examines the causal nature of sex between a student, his girlfriend, and her friends. *Paradiso – Sieben Tag mit sieben Frauen* (*Paradise: Seven Days with Seven Women*, 2000) likewise seems a male fantasy as it tells about a man who celebrates his 60th birthday (Thome's age when he made the film) with his present wife, his former wives, and his lovers. Like all of Thome's Berlin films, *Paradiso* emphasizes talk over action, analyzing human relationships. It is also about generational reconciliation, as the conflict at the heart of the story is not the various love liaisons but the return of the man's son after 20 years. In *venus.de – Die bewegte Frau* (*Venus Talking*, 2001), Thome looks at the ambivalent nature of technology in our lives. An author agrees to allow a camera to record her writing her next novel, unaware that others have also set up cameras to spy on her. The film looks at all aspects of our technological world, the insight it gives into the creative process but also the intrusion into privacy. At the same time, Thome questions whether the filmed image is the truthful image.

Rauchzeichen (*Smoke Signals*, 2006) is paradigmatic of Thome's films. It examines a group of people on the island of Sardinia, far from life and outsiders in this world. Critics often compare Thome to Eric Rohmer, the French director, and his examination of the existential crises of the bourgeoisie. Thome's characters talk, becoming mouthpieces for philosophizing about life, love, and death. Very little happens and stories remain minimal. This may explain why his films are successful with critics, but generally do not do well at the box office.

TOBIS-FILM. Second in size only to **Universum Film AG** (Ufa), Tobis-Film was founded in 1928 as a means to capitalize on sound technology (Tobis is an acronym of *Ton-Bild-Syndikat* [Sound-Image Syndicate]). Hollywood film studio Warner Brothers had released *The Jazz Singer* in 1927, using the Vitaphone sound system, which synchronized image to sound on a disc. Tobis, in contrast, had access to a process developed by Tri-Ergon Musik AG, which placed the sound directly on the filmstrip, a technique the company had developed in the early 1920s but didn't immediately pursue. Tobis signed an agreement with Klangfilm to merge into Tobis-Klangfilm and also signed an agreement with Ufa, which led to Germany's successful entry into sound film production. Eventually the film industries in Germany and Hollywood agreed to carve up the market, Germany getting German-speaking lands and Hollywood America.

Under the Nazis (1933–1945), Tobis-Film produced over 100 films, including the propaganda movies *Ich klage an* (*I Accuse*, **Wolfgang Liebeneiner**, 1941) and *Ohm Krüger* (*Ohm Krüger*, Hans Steinhoff, 1941), the latter starring **Emil Jannings**; the musicals of **Paul Verhoeven**; and the comedies of **Kurt Hoffmann**. After the war, Tobis became a part of Ufa, but was dissolved in 1962 along with its parent company.

TRENKER, LUIS (1892–1990). Luis Trenker, an impassioned mountain climber, began his film career as a consultant on **Arnold Fanck**'s **mountain film** *Berg des Schicksals* (*Mountain of Destiny*, 1924). Fanck cast him in a small part, but by the next Fanck film, *Der heilige Berg* (*The Sacred Mountain*, 1926), Trenker played lead. Appearing opposite **Leni Riefenstahl**, who was starring as Diotima in her first Trenker film, he was part of a love triangle, in which both he and his rival for Diotima die in a fall from a mountain. In Fanck's *Der große Sprung* (*The Big Jump*, 1927), mountaineer Trenker must again vie for Riefenstahl's love against a sophisticated flatlander.

After his success with Fanck, and in the mountain films of Italian directors Mario Bonnard and Nunzio Malasomma, Trenker started directing his own mountain films. *Berge in Flammen* (*Mountains on Fire*, 1931), codirected with **Karl Hartl**, tells of two friends on opposite sides during World War I who must each defend the same mountain peak. Trenker also made an English-language version, released as

Doomed Battalion. In *Der Rebell* (1932), codirected with Edwin H. Knopf and also released in an English-language version, *The Rebel*, Trenker creates the persona that endeared him to the National Socialists when they came to power the following year: the loner or outsider whose heroic sacrifice serves the fatherland. Trenker directed and acted in nine films for the Nazis, including *Der verlorene Sohn* (*The Prodigal Son*, 1934), in which he plays a young man who leaves his small mountain village to seek love and fortune in New York City only to realize that happiness is at home, and *Der Kaiser von Kalifornien* (*The Emperor of California*, 1936), in which he plays Johann Suter, the German American on whose property gold was discovered, which set off the 1849 gold rush.

After the war Trenker had no trouble continuing his career in spite of his favored status among Nazi officials. On the one hand, he had grown leery of Nazi policies and retired to Italy. On the other hand, his films had never been laden with propaganda and outside of the National Socialist context could be viewed as neutral, if conservatively oriented, entertainment. In the 1950s, he made a number of mountain documentaries and then several feature films. Never achieving his theatrical success of the 1930s, he moved to television, where he had several series that featured his work. These, as well as his mountain novels, gained a wide following.

TREUT, MONIKA (1954–). With her films *Die Jungfrauenmaschine* (*The Virgin Machine*, 1988) and *My Father Is Coming* (*My Father Is Coming*, 1990), Monika Treut became a cult favorite on American college campuses, in New York's and San Francisco's gay communities, and in the German alternative film scene. *Die Jungfrauenmaschine* follows a young German woman's search for romantic love in San Francisco. *My Father Is Coming* tells of a young German woman in the porn industry in New York who worries because her father is coming to visit. But the stories of these two films are merely Treut's device to film San Francisco's and New York's underworld of sex, to interview performance artists such as Susie Sexpot and Annie Sprinkle, and to introduce acts of erotica into her movies.

Treut's eye for striking images and her sense of humor only partially ameliorate the soft-core pornographic content of her films. At times, the images sabotage her clearly militant feminist intent, as in

Die Jungfrauenmaschine, in which a lengthy scene of lesbian love-making fetishizes the women into erotic objects that could be found in male pornography as well. The same effect is noticeable in *Verführung: die grausame Frau* (*Seduction: The Cruel Woman*, 1985) and "Taboo Parlor," a segment of the omnibus film *Erotique* (1994). Both films dramatize Hamburg's sadomasochist district by focusing on the spectral quality of the acts of cruelty rather than their psychological or sociological meaning. The result is that viewers are captivated by the cruelty, perhaps even participating in it, rather than being distanced from the act.

In spite of erotic images sometimes becoming pornographic, Treut often captures the good and bad, the erotic and absurd of love relationships, thus rescuing her material from the merely salacious. In addition to narrative features that function as documentaries of the sex underworld, Treut has also made genuine documentaries exploring alternative sexual preferences. *Gendernauts – Eine Reise ins Land der neun Geschlechter* (*Gendernauts: A Journey through Shifting Identities*, 1999) explores female to male transsexuals, those who undergo physical transformation and those who undertake hormonal treatments, but stop short of becoming physically male.

TRISSENAAR, ELISABETH (1944–). Elisabeth Trissenaar was a well-established stage actor before her portrayal of the lusty, petit bourgeois wife in **Rainer Werner Fassbinder**'s *Bolwieser* (*The Stationmaster's Wife*, 1977) brought her international recognition. Her deep voice and physicality make Trissenaar ideally suited for roles that require understated eroticism. In Fassbinder's *Die Ehe der Maria Braun* (*The Marriage of Maria Braun*, 1979), she plays against type as Maria's best friend, for here she is a bit plump and a bit dull-witted, unable to please her husband. In her next part for Fassbinder, she again was playing an erotic woman, appearing as Lena, one of Franz Biberkopf's lovers, in the television miniseries *Berlin Alexanderplatz* (*Berlin Alexanderplatz*, 1980), based on Alfred Döblin's novel of the same name.

Trissenaar has made several films about persecution during the Third Reich. In addition to acting in *Eine Liebe in Deutschland* (*A Love in Germany*, 1983), by Polish director Andrzej Wajda, she played a persecuted Jewish woman who allows herself to be first protected then seduced by a Polish peasant in order to save herself from the Nazis in *Bittere Ernte* (*Angry Harvest*, 1985), by Polish director **Agnieszka Holland**. In *Charlotte*, by Dutch director Frans Weisz (*Charlotte*, 1984), Trissenaar plays the mother of the title character as a woman filled with the joy of life. In **Doris Dörrie**'s *Keiner liebt mich* (*Nobody Loves Me*, 1994), she trades on her erotic persona by playing the heroine's mother, an oversexed, self-centered woman who writes soft-core pornographic novels. Trissenaar has also appeared in numerous shows on German television, both in classical plays and crime dramas.

TRIUMPH DES WILLENS. *Triumph des Willens* (*Triumph of the Will*, **Leni Riefenstahl**, 1935), a classic example of the documentary as propaganda, is also one of the most controversial documentaries ever made. The film records the Nationalist Socialist Party rally held in Nuremberg in 1934, and was the second film Riefenstahl had made of the Nuremberg meetings. The first had been filmed the previous year and released as *Der Sieg des Glaubens* (*Victory of Faith*, 1933). The notoriety that *Triumph des Willens* brought its director followed her throughout the remainder of her life, preventing her, in her opinion, from pursuing a meaningful film career after World War II. At the heart of the controversy is whether the documentary or parts of it had been staged and whether Riefenstahl made the film out of ideological commitment or if it was, as she claimed, an aesthetic exercise on her part. History has also asked to what extent the film was financed by the National Socialists; Riefenstahl maintained throughout her life that *Triumph des Willens* was just a commission.

From the film's release, critics, among them **Siegfried Kracauer** and Susan Sontag, alleged that the documentary was staged, that is, that the rally was meant as a propaganda event to manipulate public opinion about National Socialism and to serve as a hagiography of Nazi Germany's leader, Adolf Hitler. Certainly it is true that the massive architecture at locations for the various events; the elaborate ceremonies focusing on Germany's regional differences, ordinary citizens, and history; and the rhythmic marching and evocative torchlight parades all speak to orchestration. Yet in all probability these would have occurred with or without Riefenstahl's cameras, documented in some other fashion. Events of the nature of the Nuremberg rally were staged to impress the masses; the technology of film merely allows the staging to achieve another level and be further disseminated.

To anyone who has seen *Triumph des Willens*, Riefenstahl's commitment to Nazi ideology is not in doubt. How could a director make such a powerful statement about a movement she did not believe in? The opening shots, for example, present Hitler as a savior coming to Nuremberg to redeem the suffering imposed by the Allies in the Versailles Treaty, which marked the end of World War I. Riefenstahl herself, however, never deviated from her official statement about the film: "A commission was proposed to me. Good. I accepted. Good. I agreed, like so many others, to make a film. . . . It is history. A pure historical film. . . . It reflects the truth as it was then."

Audiences today might find the film tedious. The marching and speech-making seem to have no end. Yet to contemporary viewers, especially German viewers, the film introduced a charismatic leader who would lead the country to recapture its past greatness. To non-German viewers, it presented a people united to face the world. The National Socialists as led by Hitler offered peace and prosperity to the Germans but made clear that the world would respect them for their military might.

Riefenstahl's strength as director is her love of motion, creating movement through a mise-en-scène of never static objects or through rhythmic editing that changes the scene at regular intervals. Even during speeches, the camera moves, speakers move, and point of view changes. Speaking about the film's power, Riefenstahl said: "It's a feeling for links between images, a connection between one picture and the next . . . or from one visual color-range, say from grey tones, to another. It's like a musical composition. It's very important to put a climax at the right point in a film . . . so that there's a continuous build-up."

Triumph des Willens consists of 12 to 16 sequences (depending on how one divides the segments). After the opening sequence, which shows Hitler's arrival in Nuremberg, there is an aerial pan of Nuremberg in the morning, the shot capturing a shadow of the plane carrying Hitler and reinforcing the imagery of Hitler as savior. These are followed by workers at revelry and at play, and finally by men in a choral performance. At that point, Hitler mounts a podium to speak to them, and it is here that Riefenstahl's power as director is most noticeable;

she cuts between individual men and the assembled group, suggesting how each part is related to the greater whole. And when she makes the association with the whole, she cuts to Hitler or the Nazi flag or both. To reinforce the relationship, the cuts to the flag or to Hitler are accompanied by the word Führer (literally "leader," and Hitler's title) or the word Deutschland. The sequences also illustrate Riefenstahl's understanding of the importance of rhythm. Brightly lit sequences are followed by torchlight parades and assemblies. Jubilation is followed by seriousness, speeches by movement.

Riefenstahl saw the main themes of her film as work and peace. She admitted liking Hitler's program when she first was introduced to it, and to her he was a guarantor of prosperity and peace. Thus the film emphasizes worker brigades, industriousness, and speeches calling for peace. Yet buried not very deeply in all of this is the symbolic text that Germany was betrayed during World War I and that Hitler and the Nazis would repair the damage done to the nation by its enemies. The film played to the emotions of those in Germany who felt defeated and to those whom the Nazis and Hitler had successfully convinced they were betrayed by the previous government. It is thus difficult if not impossible to believe that Riefenstahl did not subscribe to the film's message. *See also* ALLGEIER, SEPP.

TYKWER, TOM (1965–). With the release of *Winterschläfer* (*Winter Sleepers*, 1997) and *Lola rennt* (*Run Lola Run*, 1998) within a year and a half of each other, Tom Tykwer became an overnight sensation, viewed as the savior of German film, both domestically and abroad. In both films, Tykwer experiments with narrative style, demonstrates technical skill, and tells stories that appeal to younger audiences without alienating older viewers. *Winterschläfer* begins as a fairy tale, introducing four people who are in their late twenties and a man in his fifties as they wake up. A tragic accident in the first 10 minutes provides the catalyst for a sequence of coincidences that lead to a fatal but hopeful ending. Tykwer uses colors, camera tricks, and plot devices to tie his characters together, so that the ending seems the only logical conclusion to the beginning. It also seems to comment on the nature of film narratives, which once put on film can have only the outcome placed there.

In *Lola rennt*, Tykwer comments differently about the nature of film. According to the movie, there are any number of outcomes to a narrative. The story of the film is simple: A woman in her early twenties must raise DM 100,000 in 20 minutes or her boyfriend will die. She begins her quest three times, starting over when she does not like the conclusion of the previous search. As in *Winterschläfer*, Tykwer experiments with style, shooting on film and video; bathing intimate bedroom scenes, which signal the start of the next episode, in red; and interspersing series of sequenced still images that intimate alternate futures for characters. The film was a phenomenon in Germany, becoming the year's highest grossing film and also one of the most successful international movies in decades. The film's actress, **Franka Potente**, gained international star status with her portrayal of the self-confident, dedicated Lola. Her bizarrely colored hair spawned a fad for "Lola-red." A mayoral candidate used posters in which he is shown running like Lola, with the slogan "Diegpen rennt für Berlin" (Diegpen Runs for Berlin). The film's techno soundtrack, written by Tykwer, as is the music in most of his films, became a best-seller.

Tykwer's style and themes were influenced by the work of Polish director Krzysztof Kieslowski (1945–1996), whose Polish and French films focused on the element of chance in relationships. *Przypadek* (*Blind Chance*, 1987) has similarities to *Lola rennt*, in that it tells a story, which is preceded by a man running three times, each time with a different outcome. Whereas Kieslowski uses the device to analyze the political situation in Poland at the time of the Solidarity movement, Tykwer employs it to muse about chaos and game theory. The opening sequence in *Lola rennt*, in which a narrator reduces life's philosophy to a 90-minute soccer game, sets the hip, ironic tone of the film.

Winterschläfer and *Lola rennt* combine the element of coincidence, as found in German fairy tales, with the dreamlike aspect of Spanish magic realism. Even when in control of their situations, the protagonists need help from the outside. This mix of influence appears in his later movies as well. In *Der Krieger und die Kaiserin* (*The Princess and the Warrior*, 2000), a young woman is saved from dying by a man fleeing the police; she falls in love with him, but until he can be rid of memories of a death for which he feels guilty, he rejects her. His healing moment comes in a reenactment of the tragic moment haunting him, in which a mysterious double dies, releasing him from his torment and allowing for a happily ever after ending in a distant lighthouse. *Heaven* (*Heaven*, 2002) ends literally with a deus ex machina, a helicopter that rescues a man and a woman fleeing Italian authorities. Based on a screenplay Kieslowski had wanted to film before his death, *Heaven*, as are the other Tykwer films, is about forgiveness and redemption.

Tykwer deviates from his usual themes and happy ending in *Perfume: The Story of a Murderer*, 2006). Based on Patrick Süskind's novel *Das Parfum* (*Perfume*, 1985), whose so-called unfilmability had been the subject of the satirical *Rossini* (*Rossini*, **Helmut Dietl**, 1997), *Das Parfum* tells the story of a serial killer with a sense of smell that is perfect for making new and enticing scents but who has no scent of his own. In addition to the problem of finding a way to make the sense of smell visible, Tykwer also had to find the visual equivalent of the novel's baroque language, which clusters nouns and adjectives into metaphoric descriptions of love and death, sex and decay, fragrance and smell. Tykwer accomplishes the supposedly impossible by packing the mise-en-scène as tightly with objects as Süskind packs his sentences with nouns and by forcing viewers through his evocative images of rotting flesh and fish to smell the stench of late 18th-century Paris sewers.

Tykwer also directs short films. *Because* (*Because*, 1990), anticipating *Lola rennt*, gives three different endings to a story; *Epilog* (1992), in a continuous take, focuses on the breakup of a love affair; and *True* (*True*, 2004), a segment in the omnibus film *Paris, je t'aime* (*Paris, I Love You*, 2006), tells of the end of an affair between a woman and a man who is blind, the film reliving the affair through the man's memories. The segment was retitled "Faubourg Saint-Denis" for the Omnibus film.

Tykwer is one of Germany's most honored directors, having been nominated for or won almost 40 awards at various European venues. He won the Bavarian Film Award for Best Direction by a Young Filmmaker for his first feature *Die tödliche Maria* (*Deadly Maria*, 1993) and won again for direction for *Perfume*. He won an Award in Gold (*see* **film awards**) from the German film industry for *Lola rennt* and *Der Krieger und die Kaiserin* and an Award in Silver for *Winter-*

schläfer. For *Perfume*, he was also honored with a Bambi, Germany's people's choice award.

– U –

UNIVERSUM FILM AG (UFA). Universum-Film AG, usually referred to as Ufa, was Germany's major film studio from its establishment in 1917 until the end of the Third Reich in 1945. Although the name was revived in another company in the late 1950s, the new Ufa went bankrupt a few years later. The name continues on in the Ufa theater chain, with many major cities in Germany and other European countries having a multiscreen Ufa-Palast (Ufa palace).

Even before World War I had ended in defeat for Germany, Ufa was intended as a means for jump-starting a viable German film industry. A consortium of businessmen under the leadership of Emil Georg von Strauß, an eminent banker at the time, bought a 50 percent interest in the new company and eventually owned production, distribution, and exhibition facilities throughout Germany, Austria, and Switzerland. The other 50 percent of the incubation funds came from the German Ministry of War, as the new company was also to help the war effort. Ufa quickly became the most important studio in Germany and in the early 1920s bought a controlling share of Decla-Bioscop, Germany's other major studio (*see* **Bioscop GmbH Berlin**). Size and bad business judgments, including investing too heavily in prestige films, brought the company to the edge of bankruptcy several times. It was rescued by American studios Metro-Goldwyn-Mayer and Paramount, which with Ufa formed Parafumet, a consortium whose partnership agreement obligated Ufa to play American films in its theaters in return for the American studios distributing and playing German films in America. The agreement made Ufa's financial situation worse, and it had to be rescued a second time, by Alfred Hugenberg, a conservative German who owned a hugely influential media conglomerate.

After the Nazis came to power in 1933, they gradually took control of the studio. Minister of Propaganda Joseph Goebbels believed strongly in the power of films to influence public perceptions of reality and thus nurtured the German film industry but also put strict controls on what studios could produce. At first, control came through censorship at all stages of production. Eventually, though, the government bought controlling interest in the studios, bringing them under a central trust. Ufa became the studio under which everything was eventually subsumed. By 1937, the government owned over 70 percent of the company and by 1942 had total control.

– V –

VALENTIN, BARBARA (1940–2002). Barbara Valentin (born Ursula Ledersteger) was one of the many voluptuous actresses in vogue in Europe in the 1950s and 1960s who wanted to capitalize on the popularity of Marilyn Monroe, Jayne Mansfield, and Bridgette Bardot. Valentin's career was in German B movies, mostly sexploitation films that showcased her statuesque figure. Titles such as *Ein Toter hing im Netz* (*Horrors of Spider Island*, Fritz Böttger, 1960), *In der Hölle ist noch Platz* (*There's Still Room in Hell*, Ernst R. von Theumer, 1961), *The Festival Girls* (Leigh Jason, 1962), and *In Frankfurt sind die Nächte heiß* (*Playgirls*, Rolf Olsen, 1966) reflect Valentin's persona in the films: a pouty, buxomy blonde with loose values.

In the 1970s she became a member of **Rainer Werner Fassbinder**'s repertory troupe of actors. She appeared in eight of his films, including *Angst essen Seele auf* (*Ali: Fear Eats the Soul*, 1973). This film is about an older German woman, Emmi, who marries a dark-skinned Moroccan, Ali, 20 years younger than she. Valentin plays the owner of a bar frequented by immigrant workers, in which Emmi and Ali meet. Her tight clothes, pouty expression, and sultry attempts at seducing Ali are meant to remind viewers of Valentin's origins as a B actress in the 1960s. After Fassbinder's death, Valentin continued her career, primarily in supporting parts.

VAN EYCK, PETER (1911–1969). Peter van Eyck (born Götz von Eyck) played in more than 90 movies between 1943 and 1969. His blond good looks and muscular physique made him ideal as a German officer, a role he played in German as well as Hollywood films. Primarily a supporting actor, he became a leading man in the 1960s in a number of German and international coproductions. Among these were the crime thrillers *Scotland Yard jagt Dr. Mabuse* (*Scotland Yard Hunts Dr. Mabuse*, aka *Dr. Mabuse vs. Scotland Yard*, Paul May, 1963) and *Die Todesstrahlen des Dr. Mabuse* (*The Death Ray of Dr. Mabuse*, aka *The Secret of Dr. Mabuse*, 1964), B-movie attempts to capitalize on the popularity of the **Fritz Lang** Mabuse films, one of which had been released in 1960.

VEIDT, CONRAD (1893–1943). Conrad Veidt acted in more than 110 films during his career, 75 of them during the silent film era. His most recognizable and memorable role is that of Cesare, the sleepwalking monster in *Das Cabinet des Dr. Caligari* (*The Cabinet of Dr. Caligari*, **Robert Wiene**, 1920). His portrayal of the tall, mute monster, walking with arms extended, influenced the stiff, jerky gait a decade later of Boris Karloff, the monster in *Frankenstein* (James Whale, 1931). Another notable role was Süss Oppenheimer in *Jew Süss* (Lothar Mendes, 1934), the British version of the story of an 18th-century Jew who became finance minister in the German duchy of Wüttemberg and whose hubris led to his execution. In contrast to a Nazi version of the story (*see* **Jud Süß**), in which Süß Oppenheimer becomes the focus of Nazi Germany's anti-Semitism, Veidt plays Oppenheimer sympathetically, revealing the psychological motivation behind his treason. In 1942, Veidt played the title character and his twin American brother in *Nazi Agent* (Jules Dassin). He also had a role as a German officer in Michael Curtiz's cult classic *Casablanca* (1942).

VERBOTSFILME. *See* EAST GERMAN FILM.

VERGANGENHEITSBEWÄLTIGUNGSFILM. The term *Vergangenheitsbewältigung* refers to the process of coming to terms with the past, in particular the Nazi past. A *Vergangenheitsbewältigungsfilm* engages its viewers in the events leading to, occurring during, or ensuing from the Third Reich and National Socialist Germany. To many, the reference suggests a critical confrontation with the horrors of Nazi Germany, including the abrogation of basic human rights for all; the denial of personal freedoms and human dignity to German Jews; the killing in extermination camps of millions of Europe's

Jews; the persecution and murder of the Sinti and Roma peoples, homosexuals, the severely handicapped, and other minorities; and the starting and continued fighting of a destructive war that devastated Germany and the rest of Europe and killed millions of Germans and non-Germans. Not all of the films, though, are critical of the past. Films in this category can call forth guilt, denial, or a vow not to let it happen again, without necessarily bringing viewers to honestly confront or assess what occurred, whether they were complicit or not.

A few early films addressed the past forthrightly, among them *Die Mörder sind unter uns* (*The Murderers Are among Us*, **Wolfgang Staudte**, 1946) and *Ehe im Schatten* (*Marriage in the Shadows*, **Kurt Maetzig**, 1947), both productions from the Soviet-controlled East Zone that was to become East Germany. By the 1950s, especially in West Germany, films about the past avoided confronting viewers with images that were too harsh.

For the most part, West German films dealing with the Nazi past focused on non-Holocaust topics such as the lives of ordinary citizens as they coped with the hardships of war. *Wir Wunderkinder* (*Aren't We Wonderful*, **Kurt Hoffmann**, 1959), for example, follows two men from childhood through middle age, showing how one supported the regime and one silently opposed it. The only mention of Jewish persecution is when a Jewish friend of the silent German is forced to emigrate, joins the American army, and returns as a liberator. *08/15* (Paul May, 1954–1955) follows soldiers from the early days of the war until final defeat. It avoids depicting the atrocities committed by the army. which Staudte's film had addressed as early as 1945. *08/15* focuses on the bravery of common soldier, thus supporting West Germany's rearming and joining NATO in the 1950s. These films, among others, offered escapist fare while at the same time expressing a message of warning against repeating the past. The exception to avoiding the past again came from directors in East Germany, but not until the 1960s and 1970s. **Frank Beyer**'s *Nackt unter Wölfen* (*Naked among Wolves*, 1963) takes place in an extermination camp and *Jakob der Lügner* (*Jacob the Liar*, 1974), takes place in a Jewish Ghetto. East German directors, however, dissembled the facts by suggesting a direct link between fascism and capitalism, thus avoiding involving the East German citizenry and military in the atrocities of the past.

The release in Germany of the American series *Holocaust* (1978) occasioned public debate about how honestly German institutions were dealing with the past. Film and television produced a number of narrative features, some decidedly more honest than others, and some of them no more forthright than those in the 1950s and 1960s. Joseph Vilsmaier's *Herbstmilch* (*Autumn Milk*, 1989), for example, focuses on rural life during the Third Reich, showing how peasants were affected by the war years and yet also suggesting they kept their distance. The director's *Stalingrad* (*Stalingrad*, 1995), a remake of *Hunde, wollt ihr ewig leben?* (*Dogs, Do You Want to Live Forever?* **Frank Wisbar**, 1959) corrects some of the more egregious pandering to the German military found in the original while making a strong statement about the folly of war. Several of the episodes of **Edgar Reitz**'s epic miniseries **Heimat – Eine deutsche Chronik** (*Heimat: A Chronicle of Germany*, 1984) follows the inhabitants of a fictional village in the Eifel region of Germany during the Third Reich. As in *Herbstmilch*, Nazism seems to come more from the outside than to be something that grew within Germany, and here too the Holocaust is ignored. None of the films by German directors addressed the Holocaust or confronted viewers with the horrors of the past in the way that films from non-German countries did—for example, *Shoah* (Claude Lanzman, 1985), an eight-hour documentary on the Holocaust produced in France.

The 60th anniversary of the end of the war brought another spate of films dealing with the Third Reich and helping Germans to come to terms with the past three generations later. *NaPoLa* (*Before the Fall*, Dennis Gansel, 2004) follows the life of a young man in an elite Nazi school. *Sophie Scholl – die letzten Tage* (*Sophie Scholl: The Final Days*, Marc Rothemund, 2005) revisits one of Germany's favorite stories of resistance about brother and sister Hans and Sophie Scholl, who were beheaded by the Nazis as traitors. The story is told from Sophie's perspective in her final days in prison, the same method used by **Percy Adlon** in *Fünf letzte Tage* (*Five Last Days*, 1992) and **Michael Verhoeven** in *Die weiße Rose* (*The White Rose*, 1982). Verhoeven expands the story, constructing a thriller around the clandestine protests of the students. In *Der Untergang* (*The Downfall*, 2004), **Oliver Hirschbiegel** tells of Adolf Hitler's last 10 days as Berlin was under siege, characterizing the Nazi leader as a madman, capable of tenderness one moment and exploding the next. *Mein Führer – Die wirklich wahrste Wahrheit über Adolf Hitler* (*Mein Führer: The Truly Truest Truth about Adolf Hitler*, Dani Levy, 2007), breaks a taboo of sorts by using humor to depict Hitler, the Nazis, and the Holocaust. The film is a comedy about a Jewish actor, who is released from Sachsenhausen to help a depressed Adolf Hitler work on a speech to rally the German people as the country faces imminent defeat. *See also* HOLOCAUST IN FEATURE FILMS.

VERHOEVEN, MICHAEL (1938–). Michael Verhoeven is the conscience of German film, revisiting in his movies again and again the atrocities committed by the Germans during National Socialist rule. Before making his name as a director, Verhoeven acted in films, including *Der Pauker* (*The Crammer*, Axel von Ambesser, 1958) and *Der Jugendrichter* (*The Juvenile Judge*, 1960), the latter directed by his father, **Paul Verhoeven**, and both starring one of Germany's most popular actors, **Heinz Rühmann**. He also earned a medical degree and practiced medicine for a few years. In 1967, he directed the film *Paarungen* (*The Dance of Death*), based on August Strindberg's play, followed by two light sex comedies, in vogue at the time in West Germany: *Engelchen macht weiter – hoppe, hoppe Reiter* (*Up the Establishment*, 1969) and *Der Bettenstudent oder Was mach' ich mit den Mädchen?* (*Student of the Bedroom* aka *What Do I Do with the Girls?* 1970).

In 1970, in addition to directing *Der Bettenstudent*, Verhoeven found his political voice in pictures and directed *o.k.* (*o.k.*), a dramatization of an actual occurrence during the Vietnam War, the rape of a Vietnamese girl by four soldiers while a fifth watched and did nothing. The film scandalized the jury at the **Berlin Film Festival** because of its theme and also because of its Brechtian distancing. Verhoeven set the incident in the Bavarian forest, thus, even if only indirectly, indicting the Germans in the atrocities on screen, and more important, calling up the horrors of Germany's own war past. Years later, Brian de Palma filmed the occurrence in *Casualties of War* (1989).

In 1980 Verhoeven examined the brutalization of war on Germany's children. *Sonntagskinder* (*Sunday Children*) tells the story of a girl and her friends during World War II. The film's themes of rape, suicide, and disfigurement attest to the inhumanity of war, any war. In *Die weiße Rose* (*The White Rose*, 1982), Verhoeven condemns the Third Reich and its judiciary but also shows the pockets of resistance to National Socialist atrocities. The film follows the activities of Sophie and Hans Scholl, two students at the University of Munich who secretly distributed a newsletter, *Die weiße Rose*, critical of the Third Reich and its National Socialist leaders, until captured and executed by guillotine. Verhoeven structured *Die weiße Rose* as a suspenseful spy thriller which, together with the popularity of a tale about youthful and fearless war protesters, led to its becoming the most successful German film of 1982. It was also the most controversial; the closing credits announce that the Scholls and the other members of their resistance group had still not been fully exonerated because the present-day judicial system had yet to repudiate the verdicts of National Socialist trials, a statement that suggested to many Germans that Germany was still not dealing forthrightly with its past. Thus, although the film won Verhoeven an Award in Silver (*see* **film awards**) for Directing and an Award in Gold for its lead actress, **Lena Stolze**, the government refused to allow its distribution abroad by the Goethe Institute. Two years later, however, the NS people's courts were declared illegal, thus validating Verhoeven's criticism. In an interview at the San Francisco Jewish Film Festival, the director remarked that this was the first time "that a film in combination with a proclamation changed anything political. This is a very important thing" (quoted in *San Francisco Chronicle*, July 25, 1997).

In *Das schreckliche Mädchen* (*The Nasty Girl*, 1990), Verhoeven again cast Stolze, who had played Sophie Scholl, as a woman who earns the hatred of her townspeople when she researches their activities in the Third Reich. The film was a surprise success in the United States, even receiving considerable exposure on cable television, in spite of its use of **Brechtian** alienation techniques, including back projection, voice over, and alternation of scenes in black and white with those in color. Stolze again won an Award in Gold for her performance. The film won awards as best picture from several critics' associations and was nominated that year for an Oscar as Best Foreign Film. The success of the film also led to a closer examination of personal guilt in the crimes of the Third Reich.

Verhoeven continued examining Germany's past in *Mutters Courage* (*My Mother's Courage*, 1995), a film about German Hungarian playwright George Tabori's mother and how, in 1944, she escaped the roundup of Jews in Budapest for deportation to Auschwitz. As in *Das schreckliche Mädchen*, Verhoeven relies on Brechtian techniques of distancing, including having Tabori enter into scenes as a commentator who interacts with the characters. The style of acting also derives from Brechtian theories, in which the actor stays outside his role. In the interview for the *San Francisco Chronicle* cited above, Verhoeven explained, "I can't imagine doing a film about [Nazism] which lets the audience forget that this is only a performance."

After a decade of directing for German television, including the comedic miniseries *Die schnelle Gerdi* (*Fast Gerdi*, 1989–2004), which starred his wife **Senta Berger**, and several episodes of the popular police drama *Tatort* (*Scene of the Crime*, 1970–), Verhoeven returned to examining the past in the feature-length documentary *Der unbekannte Soldat* (*The Unknown Soldier*, 2006). Verhoeven's film documents a controversy that began in 1995 with the opening of the photographic exhibit "Vernichtungskrieg: Verbrechen der Wehrmacht 1941–1944" ("War of Extermination: Crimes of the Armed Services 1941–1944"). Consisting of 15,000 photographic documents showing members of the German military committing crimes of violence against prisoners of war, Jews, and villagers in Eastern Europe, the touring exhibit ran counter to the widely held belief that even if Adolf Hitler and his ministers, the High Command and other high-ranking officers, the Gestapo, and the Schutzstaffel (SS) had committed atrocities, the ordinary members of the military had behaved honorably. Fictionalized and actual biographies from the 1950s, some made into films (*see* **Vergangenheitsbewältigungsfilm**), had created a myth that the armed services were above reproach for their actions. Belief in the myth was further strengthened by films such as **Wolfgang Petersen**'s *Das Boot* (*The Boat*, 1981), which draws a clear distinction between being Nazi and being a member of the submarine's crew. Even Joseph Vilsmaier's *Stalingrad* (*Stalingrad*, 1993), which highlights some of the atrocities of the German military, drew a clear distinction between the ordinary soldiers and their officers.

Verhoeven began documenting the exhibit (which eventually visited 33 cities in Germany and Austria before being withdrawn in 1999 for redesign) at a demonstration in Munich, when thousands of neo-Nazis clashed with supporters of the documentation. Verhoeven filmed the exhibit itself; showed reactions of visitors; examined reasons for the controversy; interviewed witnesses in Germany, the Ukraine, and the United States, among other places; and in this way created an informative and objective film about the exhibit and the controversy. Released in 2006, the film was preceded by the redesigned exhibit, which expands the story being told about the military by including positive photos and images as well.

VERHOEVEN, PAUL (1901–1975). Paul Verhoeven, the father of director **Michael Verhoeven**, began his career in theater as an actor and director. He started acting in films during the Nazi era, appearing mainly in small roles, such as the bartender in **Luis Trenker**'s *Der Kaiser von Kalifornien* (*The Emperor of California*, 1936), and as a director's secretary in his own movie, *Der große Schatten* (*The Big Shadow*, 1944). He also had starring roles, as in *Herr Sanders lebt gefährlich* (*Mr. Sanders Lives Dangerously*, Robert A. Stemmle, 1944), in which he plays the author of crime novels. In addition, he appeared in son Michael Verhoeven's *Paarungen* (*The Dance of Death*, 1967), based on the August Strindberg drama of the same title, as the pathological Edgar.

As director, Verhoeven was adept in many genres, including dramas, thrillers, adventures, comedies, and musicals. He gained recognition for his romantic comedies, of which *Heidelberger Romanze* (*Heidelberg Romance*, 1951) is the best known. The film plays with the motifs of the love triangle, mistaken identity, and parental interference to craft a classic of the *Heimatfilm*, a genre in vogue after World War II. *Heidelberger Romanze* trades on the nostalgia associated with that city, romanticized in Wilhelm Meyer-Förster's play *Alt Heidelberg* (1903), replacing the original's fairy tale story of a servant girl marrying a prince with a conventional love story set in the upper middle class. As was the case with many German directors of the 1930s, 1940s, and 1950s, Verhoeven ended his career as a director of made-for-television films.

VOGLER, RÜDIGER (1942–). Rüdiger Vogler has appeared in over 130 films in four decades but remains relatively unknown outside Germany. His major roles have been in the films of **Wim Wenders**, having played in nine of the director's movies, four times as photojournalist Phillip Winter. His first film as Winter was *Alice in den Städten* (*Alice in the Cities*, 1974), which established his persona of sympathetic loner and outsider. Winter, who seems a reincarnation of the 1940s and 1950s existential hero, seems driven by nothing more than a need to accumulate experience, which includes positive interactions with others but without long-term commitment. He reprised Winter in smaller roles in *Bis ans Ende der Welt* (*Until the End of the World*, 1991) and *In weiter Ferne, so nah!* (*Faraway, So Close!* 1993). In *Lisbon Story* (*Lisbon Story*, 1994), Winter is again the focus when he goes to Lisbon to help a friend having trouble finishing a silent film about the city. He stays to record sound images for the film his friend is making and helps him finally finish the film. Vogler also has the lead in two other Wenders movies. In *Falsche Bewegung* (*False Movement*, 1975), based on Johann Wolfgang von Goethe's *Wilhelm Meisters Lehrjahre* (*Wilhelm Meister's Apprenticeship*), Vogler portrays the title character of the novel. Set in the present, his Wilhelm drifts through a series of encounters with characters that help him grow as an actor but with whom he forms no lasting bonds. In *Im Laufe der Zeit* (*Kings of the Road*, 1976), Vogler plays a repairman who travels through small towns repairing film projectors for old theaters. He meets another man, with whom he travels for a time, in homage to Hollywood buddy films, but from whom he separates after an argument.

Vogler's films for other directors have offered him mainly supporting roles. For example, he plays the boyfriend of the conservative sister in *Die bleierne Zeit* (*Marianne and Juliane*, **Margarethe von Trotta**, 1981), a film about terrorism in 1970s Germany, and he plays a Hungarian general in **István Szabó**'s *Sunshine* (*Sunshine*, 1999), a family saga spanning the political turmoil of the 20th century. He has also appeared in numerous made-for-television movies and in series television.

VON BÁKY, JOSEF (1902–1966). One of a number of Hungarian-born filmmakers who pursued a film career in Germany, Josef von Báky is best known for *Münchhausen* (*The Adventures of Baron Munch-hausen*, 1943) made during the Third Reich to celebrate the studio's 25th anniversary. Starring **Hans Albers** as the Baron prone to exaggeration, von Báky created a fantasy filled with special effects and magical moments that can still charm viewers, in spite of its age and in spite of its origin as a film produced under National Socialism. After the war, von Báky directed films in most genres, including the **rubble film** . . . *und über uns der Himmel* (*And Above Us the Sky*, 1947), again starring Albers. The film centers on a returning soldier who survives by trading on the black market, a recurring theme in films about the postwar years. Von Báky also contributed to a wave of teenage rebel films in the 1950s, an international film phenomenon. *Die Frühreifen* (*The Rowdies*, 1957) is reminiscent of such Hollywood films as *The Wild One* (László Benedek, 1953) and *Rebel without a Cause* (Nicholas Ray, 1955) and followed the successful West German film *Die Halbstarken* (*Teenage Wolfpack* aka *The Hooligans*, Georg Tressler, 1956). Von Báky also directed the comedy *Das doppelte Löttchen* (*Two Times Lotte*, 1950), about twins who try to get their separated parents back together. The film is based on the Erich Kästner novel of that name, which provided the source for both versions of Walt Disney Studio's *The Parent Trap* (David Swift, 1961, and Nancy Meyers, 1998) and for Joseph Vilsmaier's *Charlie & Louise – Das doppelte Löttchen* (*Charlie & Louise*, 1994). An animated version of *Das doppelte Löttchen*, directed by Toby Genkel, appeared in 2007.

VON GARNIER, KATJA (1966–). Katja von Garnier's career seems a contradiction. Although she directed two of Germany's more domestically and internationally successful films in the 1990s, her output remains small. On the one hand, this may be by choice. On the other, it may be the difficulty in assigning the films a genre. *Abgeschminkt!* (*Making Up!*, 1993) and *Bandits* (*Bandits*, 1997) are both comedies. At the same time, they are women's films (*see* **Frauenfilm**) that do not compromise von Garnier's feminist perspective for the sake of a laugh or to appeal to a wider male audience. *Abgeschminkt* runs 55 minutes and was the director's graduate thesis from film school.

Von Garnier looks at relationships exclusively from the side of the women in the film, relegating male figures to sex objects, similar to the way the American television show *Grey's Anatomy* portrays men.

The film *Bandits* tells the story of four female rock musicians who break out of jail on their way to a benefit concert at which they are to perform. Because of its theme of women on the run, the film has reminded critics of *Thelma & Louise* (Ridley Scott, 1991). *Bandits*, however, distinguishes itself by its light touch. Moreover, one does not feel like a male genre has been grafted onto a women's film, as is the case with *Thelma & Louise*.

Von Garnier's success in Germany brought her to America, where she directed the HBO movie *Iron Jawed Angels* (2004), a dramatization of the struggles of the suffragist movement in America. *Blood and Chocolate* (2007), a modestly budgeted special effects film about werewolves, tells the usually male-oriented werewolf's tale from the perspective of a young woman, reminiscent of the fashion in which other legends and urban myths have been appropriated to appeal to a female audience through identification and to the male audience through attractive actresses.

VON HARBOU, THEA (1888–1954). Thea von Harbou was one of Germany's most important and prolific screenwriters. Her strength as screenwriter was her ability to adapt both classical and popular literature. She was also sought after as a script doctor, someone who fixes other writers' screenplays. Von Harbou's name appears in the credits of many of Germany's best-known classic films, including those of **Friedrich Wilhelm Murnau**, Joe May, **Ewald André Dupont**, and **Fritz Lang**.

Von Harbou's most successful collaboration was with Lang, to whom she was briefly married. Together they worked on some of the best-known films of the silent film's golden age. Their collaboration produced the gothic tale *Der müde Tod* (*Destiny*, 1921) and the Dr. Mabuse films, *Dr. Mabuse, der Spieler* (*Dr. Mabuse, the Gambler*, 1922) and *Das Testament des Dr. Mabuse* (*The Testament of Dr Mabuse*, 1933). They also collaborated on *Die Nibelungen: Siegfrieds Tod* (*Siegfried's Death*, 1924) and *Die Nibelungen: Kriemhilds Rache* (*Kriemhild's Revenge*, 1924)—both based on the classic medieval Germanic legend *The Lay of the Nibelungen*—and *Metropolis* (*Metropolis*, 1927), based on an original idea by Lang and von Harbou. In the sound film era, they worked together on the classic thriller *M* (*M*, Fritz Lang, 1931), the film that made **Peter Lorre** a star.

Lang left for Hollywood in 1934 in the wake of the growing strength of the National Socialists. He was part Jewish and sensed danger if he stayed, particularly after *Das Testament des Dr. Mabuse* was banned by the government as too critical of National Socialism. Von Harbou, however, remained in Germany, joining the Nazi Party in 1932, a year before Adolf Hitler came to power, and continued having success as a screenwriter, working with some of the most important directors of the Third Reich, including Hans Steinhoff, Gustav Ucicky, **Wolfgang Liebeneiner**, and **Veit Harlan**. In retrospect, it is easy to recognize fascist leanings in her novels and other literature, in which she stresses self-sacrifice. Likewise, it is possible to read protofascist sentiments into her and Lang's screenplay of *Metropolis*, based on her novel. Although critics and the public have marveled at the visual masterpiece that the film is, many have been baffled by its fusion of the industrialist owner's mind and the union worker's hand through the rebellious son's heart.

VON PRAUNHEIM, ROSA (1942–). Rosa von Praunheim (born Holger Mischwitzki) caused a minor scandal in Germany with the release of *Nicht der Homosexuelle ist pervers, sondern die Situation, in der er lebt* (*It Is Not the Homosexual Who Is Perverse but the Society in Which He Finds Himself*, 1970), a story of a gay marriage in which one of the partners seeks solace, after being rejected by his lover, in parks and men's toilets. West German television at first refused to broadcast the film. Later, when it was shown, Bavarian television refused to pick up the broadcast. Von Praunheim has not softened his approach to homosexual themes. *Ein Virus kennt keine Moral* (*A Virus Has No Morals*, 1985) angered the gay and lesbian community in both Germany and the United States by depicting the homosexual protagonists not as the men next door, normal in every way except for sexual orientation, but as sexual outlaws who make no excuses for their lifestyle. In both of these films, von Praunheim's intentionally amateurish style and penchant for kitsch and bad taste serve to enlighten and provoke his audiences about the gay lifestyle, regardless of viewers' political views or sexual orientation.

Von Praunheim comes from the Berlin Underground, a collection of artists and filmmakers whose work recalls the underground cinema of New York artists such as Andy Warhol. And like Warhol, von Praunheim's status as an auteur filmmaker, his refusal to compromise to suit mainstream taste, and his ability to film cheaply ensure not only that his pictures get made but that they receive attention at film festivals and in art houses.

Some of von Praunheim's films have managed to appeal to mainstream audiences. *Ich bin meine eigene Frau* (*I Am My Own Woman*, 1992) documents the story of Charlotte von Mahlsdorf (b. Lothar Berfelde) and her attempts to live freely as a woman first in Nazi Germany and then in the former German Democratic Republic. The film depicts events from von Mahlsdorf's life within the historical and personal contexts that helped her develop her sexual identity. *Der Einstein des Sex* (*The Einstein of Sex*, 1999) is a biography of Magnus Hirschfeld, a late 19th- and early 20th-century doctor who studied homosexuality in order to establish its sexual normalcy. In an uncharacteristically emotional and unironic scene, von Praunheim shows Hirschfeld watching a newsreel, looking on as Nazis destroy his life's work. *Für mich gab's nur noch Fassbinder* (*Fassbinder's Women*, 2000) interviews the women (and some men) in **Rainer Werner Fassbinder**'s films, documenting the charisma of the filmmaker. *Männer, Helden, schwule Nazis* (*Men, Heroes and Gay Nazis*, 2005) documents homosexuality among present-day neo-Nazi groups and during the Third Reich, particularly within the Sturmabteilung (SA), Adolf Hitler's private army headed by Ernst Röhm. The film examines the appeal of fascism even for homosexuals, who were often National Socialism's victims. In *Dein Herz in meinem Hirn* (*Your Heart in My Brain*, 2005), von Praunheim dramatizes the bizarre story of Bernd Jürgen Brandes and Armin Meiwes, who met after Brandes answered Meiwes's Internet ad seeking someone who would let Meiwes cannibalize him.

Von Praunheim's style and themes preclude his rising above cult status. As *Dein Herz in meinem Hirn* reveals, even in a film that could attract a larger audience because of the theme, von Praunheim bewilders that audience through campy interludes, kitschy sentiment, and low production values. In one of his earlier films, *Die Bettwurst* (*The Bed Sausage*, 1971), critics surmise that the actors, playing the lead couple finding love late in life, were given no directions at all, resulting in a film that is almost incomprehensible. And yet von Praunheim has definite cinematic sensibility. In *Anita – Tänze des Lasters* (*Anita: Dances of Lust*, 1987), which takes place both in the Weimar Republic and the present, von Praunheim alternates color and black and white, but not as one might suspect. In flashbacks to the Weimar years, a woman's imaginings of being the famed erotic dancer Anita Berber are filmed in color, offering compositions reminiscent of Otto Dix paintings. The woman's present day is black and white or, as critics have noted, washed-out gray. Although such use of color and black and white is a cinematic cliché, it suggests von Praunheim's cinematic eye but also that the clumsiness his films sometimes display is intentional.

VON TROTTA, MARGARETHE (1942–). One of several women directors of the **New German Cinema** who gained recognition for their skill and artistry as filmmakers, Margarethe von Trotta began her film career as a screenplay writer for **Volker Schlöndorff** and as an actress in the films of Schlöndorff, **Rainer Werner Fassbinder**, and **Herbert Achternbusch**. Her first feature film as director, *Die verlorene Ehre der Katharina Blum* (*The Lost Honor of Katharina Blum*, 1975), codirected with Schlöndorff, has been her most commercially successful film to date. Based on a novel by Heinrich Böll, it tells the story of a vulnerable young woman who is vilified by a rightist-controlled newspaper for unknowingly harboring a leftist radical. The paper, *Die Zeitung*, was an obvious reference to the conservative *Bildzeitung*, published by Axel Springer, the bête noire of German radicals. The film introduces two themes—women's issues and radical politics—that were to form the core of von Trotta's later films. *Die verlorene Ehre der Kathrina Blum* became a cult film of Germany's leftist community and also created a stir among Germany's conservative establishment, which accused the film of the same support for terrorism that they had seen in Böll's novel.

Das zweite Erwachen der Christa Klages (*The Second Awakening of Christa Klages*, 1978), von Trotta's first solo feature, asks whether a good deed justifies breaking the law. The film's main character robs a bank to finance a daycare facility and is supported even by those who may not agree with her actions. Von Trotta's most critically successful film, *Die bleierne Zeit* (*Marianne and Juliane*, 1981), searches for the root cause of radicalism among Germany's Left, locating it in the oppressive bourgeois political structures of postwar Germany. The film's German title, which translates literally as "leaden times," refers to a poem by Friedrich Hölderlin, a German romantic poet, and equates Germany's malaise in the 1970s to the misguided politics of the 1950s, a theme also popular with other New German Cinema directors. *Die bleierne Zeit*, which won seven awards, including Best Picture, at the Venice Film Festival in 1977, tells of two sisters, one rebellious and one obedient in their youth, who reverse roles when older, the more rebellious one becoming a journalist, the quieter one becoming a radical leftist. The suicide of the rebellious sister in prison alludes to Gudrun Ensslin's mysterious death in Stammheim prison in 1977. Ensslin and her sister were members of the Baader-Meinhof terrorist organization, a group responsible for robberies and killings during Germany's turbulent 1970s. The death was also one of the subjects of the omnibus film *Deutschland im Herbst* (*Germany in Autumn*, 1978).

Although all of von Trotta's films focus on women, not all concern themselves with radical politics. *Schwestern oder die Balance des Glücks* (*Sisters or the Balance of Happiness*, 1979) and *Heller Wahn* (*Sheer Madness*, 1983), for example, are dramas of inner turmoil. They focus on relationships between women to study the delicate balance between life and psyche, living and emotional well-being. Between 1988 and 1993 von Trotta directed three films in Italy, among them *Il Lungo silenzio* (*The Long Silence*, 1993), a film in which a woman finds the courage to oppose the mafia.

In *Das Versprechen* (*The Promise*, 1994), von Trotta returned to directing in Germany and to focusing on the relationship between political reality and personal happiness. The film tells the story of a young couple who get separated after the Berlin Wall is built, the woman escaping to West Germany and the man remaining in East Germany. The couple reunites in 1968, during "the Prague Spring," a time when Soviet communism seemed to be easing its hold on satellite countries. They resume their affair, which this time results in the woman's pregnancy, but once again they are separated as the Soviets march into Czechoslovakia and end the country's liberalization of communism. They meet one more time when the Berlin Wall is torn down and the two German states are united, but the film leaves open whether they can finally achieve a lasting relationship.

The political past is also the subject of von Trotta's *Rosenstraße* (*Rosenstreet*, 2003), starring **Katja Riemann** and **Maria Schrader**, two of Germany's more popular and successful actors in the 1990s. The film was von Trotta's first film to devote itself entirely to the Holocaust, although Germany's National Socialist legacy had formed the backdrop of earlier films. *Rosenstraße* relates the true events surrounding a protest vigil by women in front of a prison in the Rosenstraße (a street in Berlin) in which their Jewish husbands had been incarcerated. Told in flashback to the daughter of one of the women, the film unfolds as a personal quiet narrative, without the high drama often found in films on the subject of the Holocaust. In *Ich bin die andere* (*I Am the Other Woman*, 2006), von Trotta again moves away from the political and historical to film a psychodramatic thriller. At times psycho thriller and at other times bordering on satire, the film stars one of Germany's top actors of the 1980s and 1990s, **Armin Mueller-Stahl**, who plays the father of a woman (Riemann) who vacillates between seductress and wholesome woman.

Von Trotta is not without detractors. Some critics find her films too programmatic, too didactic, arguing that she is unfair in her portrayal of men or overly subjective in advancing a feminist agenda. While it is true that all of the films mentioned above concern women, with men almost always in parts that make them reflections of the women and without their own voices, her portrayals are as fair as films about men in which women are portrayed negatively and as inferiors. Moreover, there is no doubt that von Trotta was the most visible of women directors in Germany in the 1970s and 1980s, that she raised and continues to raise feminist consciousness, and that she does not compromise ideas for commercial success. *See also FRAUENFILM*.

– W –

WAR FILMS. It might seem strange that German directors addressed the war barely 10 years after Germany's defeat in World War II. As early as the mid-1950s, however, West German filmmakers focused attention on the average soldier and marine, highlighting their military

virtues—bravery, sacrifice, humanity, and camaraderie—while obscuring the Nazi cause for which they were fighting. The films were
first and foremost vehicles for entertainment, fitting in well with the
other movies of the time, films of nostalgia (*see* **Heimatfilm**), romantic comedies, musicals, and mysteries. Yet they also served a dual purpose of focusing on the recent past and rehabilitating the military for
the present.

As films that focused on the past (*see* **Vergangenheitsbewältigungsfilm**), the West German war films failed to engage viewers critically. On the one hand they may have presented an antiwar message:
Paul May's trilogy *08/15* (*08/15*, 1954–1955), the title refers to a term
used similarly to the American military expression GI, admonishes
viewers at the end to never let the events in the film happen again.
Kinder, Mütter, und ein General (*Children, Mothers, and a General*,
László Benedek, 1955) depicts 15-year-old boys riding off to the front
as their mothers look on. **Bernhard Wicki** likewise focused on youth
in war. As his film *Die Brücke* (*The Bridge*, 1959) ends, one of seven
youths remains alive. The last scene shows him dragging a comrade
across the bridge, letting go, and continuing toward the camera. The
camera, however, stays focused on the dead youth on the bridge. *Haie
und kleine Fische* (*Sharks and Small Fish*, **Frank Wisbar**, 1957)
films the bodies of a group of sailors who have escaped their boat and
are floating in the water waiting to be rescued. *Hunde, wollt ihr ewig
leben?* (*Dogs, Do You Want to Live Forever?* Wisbar, 1959) asks if the
disaster at Stalingrad will finally make men learn and cynically suggests it won't. On the other hand, as harsh as the images are, the films
present an ambivalent message about war. The men and boys in the
film possess those virtues considered necessary for war and to which
society and the films give added value, lessening the meaninglessness
of their deaths by focusing on their heroism.

The antiwar sentiment of the war films is further diminished by the
films' structure, which absolves the participants from wrongdoing.
The stories make clear that the soldiers were merely doing what good
soldiers do, following orders. The culprits in these films are cowardly
officers; bureaucratic mix-ups; a misguided High Command; and an
uncaring, cold leader, Adolf Hitler. Critics of the films have pointed
out that West Germany's war films exonerated the military at the time
Konrad Adenauer was negotiating entry into the North Atlantic

Treaty Organization (NATO), requiring a German military presence in the country. The 1950s war films thus reflected the official public policy of the need for a strong and reliable military. In the films at least, there was no need to suspect the motives of the enlisted men. Interestingly, two films made much later, *Das Boot* (*The Boat*, **Wolfgang Petersen**, 1981) and *Stalingrad* (*Stalingrad*, Joseph Vilsmaier, 1993), widely seen by critics and the public as strong antiwar films, follow the same formula of the films of the 1950s. They, too, depict ordinary fighting men doing their duty while also having to deal with cowardly leaders and an immoral High Command.

WEGENER, PAUL (1874–1948). Actor and director Paul Wegener is a pioneer of German film, known for his integration of fantasy into his movies. In *Der Student von Prag* (*The Student of Prague*, 1913), his first production, which he codirected with Stellan Rye, he plays a man who has sold his mirror reflection to the devil. The film was a success in Germany and abroad, anticipating the future development of German film during the Weimar Republic (1918–1933). Wegener's next production *Der Golem* (*The Golem*, 1915), codirected with **Henrik Galeen**, tells of a clay statue come to life that wreaks havoc on his community. Based on a Jewish legend, the film's popularity led to two sequels by Wegener, *Der Golem und die Tänzerin* (*The Golem and the Dancer*, codirector Rochus Gliese, 1917) and *Der Golem, wie er in die Welt kam* (*The Golem: How He Came into the World*, codirector Carl Boese, 1920). The ancient Jewish legend has also been the subject of films in France, Italy, and America and was lampooned in an episode of *The Simpsons*, "Treehouse of Horror XVII" (2006).

Wegener's other directorial works at the time also favored dark fantasy; his favorite sources for material being German fairy tales and legends. His acting roles included mostly screen heavies, typecasting that continued into the Third Reich, when he played a friend of the title figure in the early Nazi propaganda film *Hans Westmar* (*Hans Westmar*, Franz Wenzler, 1933), a fictionalized biography of Horst Wessel, the writer of the Nazi anthem bearing his name. At the end of the regime, he played a cowardly town mayor in the propaganda film *Kolberg* (*Kolberg*, **Veit Harlan**, 1945).

In addition to the gothic films of the silent era and the few films under Nazi rule, Wegener also had a career-long interest in Far Eastern philosophy, prompting him to create such films as *Der Yoghi* (*The Yogi*, codirector Gliese, 1916), *Lebende Buddhas* (*Living Buddhas*, 1925), and *Der große Mandarin* (*The Great Mandarin*, 1949).

WENDERS, WIM (1945–). One of the founders of the **Filmverlag der Autoren**, Wim Wenders is one of only a few directors (**Volker Schlöndorff** is another) of **New German Cinema** who continues to enjoy critical and commercial success, even getting his films distributed beyond the arthouse circuit. Wenders, a film auteur or practitioner of *autoren-kino*, has explored and expanded his considerable talent as filmmaker while staying true to his belief that films are primarily visual works of art rather than plot-driven stories.

Wenders gained recognition early in his career for his use of long takes, traveling camera, and sparse dialogue to tell loose, rambling stories of searching and of odyssey. Although his later films place more importance on dialogue, they continue to tell loosely constructed stories, focusing more on characters and their search for identity and also on being a means to connect once again with reality.

From early films such as *Alice in den Städten* (*Alice in the Cities*, 1974) to later works such as *In weiter Ferne, so nah* (*Far Away, So Close!*, 1993), Wenders relies on spatial metaphors to tell his tales of individuals adrift in an environment of continual image bombardment, traversing geographical landscapes that mirror the characters' psychological states. In *Angst des Tormanns beim elf Meter* (*Anxiety of the Goalie at the Free Kick*, 1972), based on a story by Austrian writer **Peter Handke**, Wenders presents an existential study of a soccer player who has committed murder. In *Alice in den Städten*, he follows the odyssey of a photographer and a young girl as they search for the child's grandmother.

Wenders's *Im Lauf der Zeit* (*Kings of the Road*, 1976) is the director's ultimate film of odyssey. Almost three hours long, the film follows a technician as he travels through small towns along the border between East and West Germany, repairing projectors in old movie houses. After meeting a disillusioned man who has just broken up with his wife, the two men travel together, providing an occasion for male bonding, philosophizing about life, and the little tension the movie has. Wenders's next film, *Der amerikanische Freund* (*The American Friend*, 1977), based on Patricia Highsmith's *Ripley's*

Game, tells the story of a German framemaker (played by **Bruno Ganz**) befriended by an American con artist whom the framemaker has insulted. Thematically, the film escalates Wenders's preoccupation with searching, chance friendships, and existential angst. The irony in the title reveals itself in the way the American Ripley, played by Dennis Hopper, ingratiates himself into the framemaker's life, as the two men bond through a contract killing.

Der amerikanische Freund and *Im Lauf der Zeit* reflect Wenders's growing fascination with technology, especially the technical reproduction of images. In the latter film, the technician travels from town to town, visiting old movie houses that barely manage to exist anymore. His friend is running away from a past that includes having worked as a typesetter, another job vanishing from the landscape. *Der amerikanische Freund* includes self-reflexive elements such as art forgery, Polaroid photos, surveillance cameras, pornographic film production, a camera obscura, X-ray pictures, and picture frames, among others. Both films also anticipate Wenders's later films critical of American culture. The technician in *Im Lauf der Zeit* remarks that America has colonized German culture, a reflection of European intellectual thinking, which laments the negative influence of America's popular culture on German life. Tom Ripley can be understood as a metaphor of that colonization, a relationship in which the American Ripley's overtures to the German Jonathan seduce him with friendship and coerce him into acting against his own interests.

Wenders's greatest critical and commercial successes to date have been *Paris, Texas* (1984) and *Der Himmel über Berlin* (*Wings of Desire*, 1987). *Paris, Texas* exhibits Wenders's signatory style: long takes, sparse dialogue, and landscapes that consume the characters as images take on life of their own. The themes of male bonding and redemption are familiar from earlier films too, highlighted by Sam Shepard's screenplay, which stresses how such themes play out between estranged relations. In the film, two brothers, Travis, a psychologically damaged, recovering alcoholic, and Walt, a sensible, stable man who has been raising his brother's son, must reconcile their love for each other and their concern for the boy. Travis, who wants to assume responsibility for his son and reunite him with Jane, Travis's estranged wife, hopes this act will give him the forgiveness he needs to achieve closure in a life plagued by painful memories of being set afire by his wife. In a striking scene of reconciliation, Jane and Travis, each on opposite sides of a one-way mirror at a peep show where Jane works, relate their love story: how they met, the happiness they enjoyed, and how their love died.

Die Himmel über Berlin builds on Wenders's themes of reconciliation and love. A guardian angel, played by Ganz, falls in love with a trapeze artist in the city of Berlin and learns from an angel turned man, played by Peter Falk playing himself, how he can become human. The film is a cinematographic marvel, switching between black and white and color as angels hover over the divided city of Berlin, eavesdropping on their charges, but unable to intervene and meaningfully help them with their lives. Yet even if the angels cannot intervene, the film offers hope in the way the camera captures Berlin from the sky, prophetically showing it as one city, in spite of the division caused by the Berlin Wall. Further solace comes from the film's quiet confrontation with the past: Homer, the storyteller, played by Jewish actor **Curt Bois**, emphasizes both through his story and through the actor the importance of remembering the past. That importance is reinforced through Peter Falk, who is in Berlin to film a movie about the Holocaust. The film received a number of awards from various organizations, including one for Best Director from the Cannes Film Festival and an Award in Gold (*see* **film awards**) for its cinematographer, Henri Alekan, from the German film industry. Wenders's sequel to *Die Himmel über Berlin*, *In weiter Ferne, so nah*, again follows an angel who becomes human. Although the film did not achieve the critical or commercial success of its predecessor, it nonetheless was also honored with numerous awards, including the Grand Jury Prize from Cannes and an Award in Gold for the cinematographer Jürgen Jürges.

Wenders's later films continue his preoccupation with using American culture as a backdrop for observing dysfunction. They display also his penchant for self-reflexive statements about film: *The End of Violence* (1997), *The Million Dollar Hotel* (2000), and *Don't Come Knocking* (2005) examine violence, the decadence of American culture, and male midlife crisis in the same expansive, rambling way of his earlier movies. For Wenders, images have always been more important than narrative coherence. *The End of Violence* concocts a loosely told story of abduction, government sanctioned spying, love, and murder, while asking what role film plays in America's violence-prone culture. *The Million Dollar Hotel* examines a murder in a flophouse while introducing the numerous offbeat characters that such a setting allows. Finally, *Don't Come Knocking* parodies the American Western as it follows an actor who tires of his roles and goes off in search of himself. All three productions were shot in English, a practice Wenders began with *Paris, Texas*, and star recognizable Hollywood actors.

In addition to feature narrative films, Wenders has also made music videos and has directed a number of documentaries. *Aufzeichnungen zu Kleidern und Städten* (*A Notebook on Clothes and Cities*, 1989) documents conversations between the director and fashion designer Yohji Yamamoto, examining the relationship between designing clothes and making movies. The music video *Willie Nelson at the Teatro* (1998) films the singer in a small theater. Wenders's best-known documentary of music is undoubtedly *Buena Vista Social Club* (1999), which films the efforts of Ry Cooder, who composed the soundtrack to *Paris, Texas*, and his initiative to reunite a group of Havana musicians for an album. Wenders filmed interviews with the musicians and Cooder while spotlighting the music.

WERNER, OSKAR (1922–1984). Oskar Werner began his acting career on the stage in Austria and throughout his career alternated between theater and film. From his first roles in film he gained a reputation as a sensitive aesthete, during an era when men of action dominated the screen. Although he had acted in a few Austrian and German films during the Third Reich, when the Nationalist Socialists controlled film production, his film career began in earnest with the German and English productions of *Der Engel mit der Posaune* and *The Angel with the Trumpet* (**Karl Hartl**, 1948 and 1950, respectively). In the film, which is about a family of piano makers over several generations, Werner adopts the persona that followed him through most of his career. In 1950, he gained international recognition in the American war film *Decision before Dawn* (Anatole Litvak), playing a sensitive prisoner of war who volunteers to aid the Allies in obtaining information by spying on his country.

Werner by his account turned down over 300 roles during his 30-year career because they did not suit his character. In retrospect, he chose his movies well, as many have become classics or cult favorites. He worked with French director Francois Truffaut on the quintessential new wave film *Jules et Jim* (*Jules and Jim*, 1962) about two friends who fall in love with the same woman, and the film version of Ray Bradbury's successful science fiction novel *Fahrenheit 451* (1966). In addition, he appeared in Stanley Kramer's *Ship of Fools* (1965), for which he received a New York Film Critics' award and an Oscar nomination for his role as the ship's melancholic and ill doctor. In his last film role, in *Voyage of the Damned* (1976), he plays one of the many Jewish refugees who after the "Night of Broken Glass" or Kristallnacht, a pogrom against Jews in Germany in 1938, sailed from Germany on the *St. Louis*, only to be turned away first by Cuba and then by the United States before having to return to Europe.

WICKI, BERNHARD (1919–2000). Although he had a long and distinguished career as actor and filmmaker, Bernhard Wicki is best known for *Die Brücke* (*The Bridge*, 1959), his first major film as director. Among its many awards, the film won the *goldene Schale* (golden bowl); an Award in Gold, the top prize of the German film industry; a Golden Globe for best picture; an Oscar nomination for Best Foreign Film; and a United Nations peace prize. In 1989, the film received a special award at a German film industry retrospective, "40 Years of German Film" (*see* **film awards**).

Die Brücke is an antiwar film that follows the exploits of a group of seven 15- and 16-year-old boys who are drafted to defend a nonstrategic bridge in the closing days of World War II. Although not without its detractors, who see in the film the same glorification of war as more conventional **war films**, most critics agree that the film strongly condemns not only the Third Reich but war itself. The closing shot of one of the boys lying dead on the bridge has become an icon of German films of the 1950s.

Wicki often took on roles and assignments with a theme of *Vergangenheitsbewältigung*, or "coming to terms with the past," in films known as *Vergangenheitsbewältigungsfilm*. He appeared as Graf von Stauffenberg in *Es geschah am 20. Juli* (*The Jackboot Mutiny*, **Georg Wilhelm Pabst**, 1955). The film relates the 1944 attempt on Adolf Hitler's life by a small group in the German military. He played an officer in *Kinder, Mütter, und ein General* (*Children, Mothers, and a*

General, László Benedek, 1955), a forerunner to Wicki's *Die Brücke*, which like that film tells about a group of adolescents who are drafted into the war near its close. Wicki's imposing stature and deep voice won him supporting roles in some of Germany's and Europe's classic auteur films, including *La Notte* (*The Night*, Michelangelo Antonioni, 1961), *Eine Reise ins Licht – Despair* (*Despair*, **Rainer Werner Fassbinder**, 1978), *Eine Liebe in Deutschland* (*A Love in Germany*, Andrzej Wajda, 1983), and *Paris, Texas* (**Wim Wenders**, 1984).

In addition to *Die Brücke*, Wicki directed numerous films about fascism and World War II for Hollywood and German studios. *Morituri* (1965) is a conventional war thriller starring two of Hollywood's biggest stars at the time, Yul Brynner and Marlon Brando. The German sequences Wicki directed for *The Longest Day* (1961), a multistar and multidirector epic about the landing of Allied forces at Normandy on D-Day, contribute to that film's semidocumentary quality. Some of his films about fascism are based on well-known German sources. Following Wolfgang Kohlhasse's radio play of the same name, *Die Grünstein-Variante* (*The Grünstein-Variant*, 1984) functions as a metaphor for memory, as well as a character study of three men (a Greek, a Jew, and a German) who shared a prison cell in 1939, as one of the men tries to remember a chess move from that time. *Sansibar oder Der letzte Grund* (*Zanzibar or The Last Cause*, 1987), based on a 1957 Alfred Andersch novel of that title, brings together several characters, including a Jewish woman, a priest, and a student, who are trying to preserve freedom, flee Nazism, and save a forbidden sculpture by the banned artist Ernst Barlach. In his last film, *Das Spinnennetz* (*The Spider's Web*, 1989), based on the 1923 Joseph Roth novel of that name and for which Wicki received an Oscar nomination for Best Foreign Film, the director explores the origins of fascism as he focuses on 1920s Germany. The film stars **Klaus Maria Brandauer** and **Armin Mueller-Stahl** before their success in Hollywood films.

Wicki's best-known film without a National Socialist theme is *Der Besuch* (*The Visit*, 1964) with Ingrid Bergman and Anthony Quinn, based on *Der Besuch der alten Dame* (*The Visit of the Old Lady*, 1956) by Friedrich Dürrenmatt. Critics pretty much agreed that the film's casting of the still beautiful Bergman as an embittered, old woman with prosthetic limbs violated the play's absurdist basis and led to the film's commercial and critical failure, as did the addition of a happy end.

WIENE, ROBERT (1873–1938). Without question Robert Wiene is best known for the expressionist film *Das Cabinet des Dr. Caligari* (*The Cabinet of Dr. Caligari*, 1920). The film was a group project by writers Hans Janowitz and **Carl Mayer**, who created a psychological horror tale of intrigue and murder, and production designers Walter Reimann, Walter Röhrig, and Hermann Warm, who tapped into German expressionism to fashion sets that reflected the psychological turmoil of the characters. Wiene's contribution was to oversee the entire film, but most important to guide his cast through an appropriately expressionistic way of acting. Characters stare vaguely ahead, walk arms extended through the sets, and interact with each other hardly at all. The result is a film that reflected the state of Germany after World War I, a tortured, unfriendly landscape. It may also explain the phenomenal success of the movie, which Wiene had difficulty repeating when external conditions improved.

Wiene began his career as director of comedies, thrillers, and melodramas for **Oskar Messter**, a pioneer of German film. In the late 1910s, he wrote a number of screenplays for **Henny Porten**, then Germany's top actor, who worked closely with Messter. Wiene's success in 1920 with *Das Cabinet des Dr. Caligari* precipitated a change in his work, positioning him as a director of dark-themed films. *Genuine* (*Genuine*, 1920), starring American-born German film star **Fern Andra** at the peak of her popularity, was written by Mayer and is a love story involving possible vampires. *Raskolnikow* (*Crime and Punishment*, 1923) is again an exercise in expressionism, as Wiene films Fyodor Dostoyevsky's psychological novel. In *I.N.R.I.* (*Crown of Thorns*, 1923), Wiene draws parallels between the passion of Christ and the martyrdom of a young communist. *Orlacs Hände* (*The Hands of Orlac*, 1924) tells the bizarre tale of a pianist whose injured hands are replaced with those of a convicted murderer and who himself is charged with the murder of his father. As one of his first sound movies, Wiene filmed *Der Andere* (*The Other*, 1930), a remake of the 1913 classic by Max Mack, loosely based on the novel *Dr. Jekyll and Mr. Hyde* (Robert Louis Stevenson, 1886). As the Nazis gained control of Germany, Wiene immigrated to France hoping to do a sound remake of *Dr. Caligari*, but he died before the project was realized. The film he was working on at the time of his death, *Ultimatum* (*Ultimatum*, 1938), a love story set in Sarajevo in 1914 shortly before the assassination of Archduke Franz Ferdinand of Austria, was finished by **Robert Siodmak**.

WINKLER, ANGELA (1944–). Angelika Winkler is a successful German stage actor who has also found success in several of Germany's most important movies. Her feature film debut was in *Jagdszenen aus Niederbayern* (*Hunting Scenes from Lower Bavaria*, **Peter Fleischmann**, 1969), one of the early films of **New German Cinema**. Winkler plays the female lead in the film, a village prostitute who befriends a young man taunted by the townsfolk because of his homosexuality. Winkler portrays the woman as sympathetic and strong, vulnerable, yet willing to assert herself, qualities she brings to her other roles as well. The film also anticipated Winkler's preference for political or historically significant parts.

Winkler has worked twice for director **Volker Schlöndorff**. She played Katharina Blum in the director's political broadside against Germany's boulevard press, *Die verlorene Ehre der Katharina Blum* (*The Lost Honor of Katharina Blum*, codirector **Margarethe von Trotta**, 1975). Winkler's Katharina is a paradigm of the 1970s German woman, making tentative steps to free herself from male domination and achieve self-realization. In the shot/countershot scene that leads up to her killing the reporter whose harassment has been characterized as rape, Winkler's facial expression exudes coldness and yet a moral conscience as it flinches with each pull of the trigger. She received an Award in Gold (*see* **film awards**) as Best Actress for the part. In *Die Blechtrommel* (*The Tin Drum*, 1979), she portrays Agnes Matzeroth, the protagonist Oskar's mother, a sensual woman torn between two men, one who can satisfy her material wants and the other her sexual needs. Winkler's Agnes bursts the simple erotic confines of the role, placing the character in the list of cinematic liberated women.

Other roles reveal equally strong women. In *Deutschland im Herbst* (*Germany in Autumn*, 1978), an omnibus film about the government crackdown on terrorism without regard to civil rights, Winkler portrays Antigone, a woman who pays with her life when she buries her brother against the king's decree. In *Ediths Tagebuch* (*Edith's Diary*, **Hans W. Geissendörfer**, 1983), she plays a woman who escapes more and more into her daily journal until she can no longer distinguish fantasy from reality. She costarred with **Hanna Schygulla** in *Heller Wahn* (*Sheer Madness*, von Trotta, 1983) as a woman who struggles to get out from under the influence of her husband, eventually succeeding. *Benny's Video* (*Benny's Video*, **Michael Haneke**, 1992) represents a slight departure for Winkler. The film is about a boy who brutalizes animals and then kills his friend; Winkler portrays the boy's mother as disaffected by events. Her detachment raises the horror of the boy's brutality to another level.

WINNETOU FILMS. The term *Winnetou films* refers to a series of West German films about the American West based on pulp adventure novels by 19th-century author Karl May. East Germany had its own series of films about the American West, usually referred to as *Indianerfilme*, and usually based on historical figures.

Winnetou, an Apache Chieftain, and Old Shatterhand, his blood brother, appeared in 10 films in the 1960s. The first of these films, *Der Schatz im Silbernsee* (*Treasure of Silver Lake*, 1962), was the phenomenon of the year. Its success led to nine more films during the decade, all starring French actor Pierre Brice as Winnetou and most starring Lex Barker, who was known for his role as Tarzan in Hollywood films, as Old Shatterhand. The stories are interchangeable, generally revolving around a treasure, a misunderstanding between settlers and Indians, and bandits trying to stir things up and steal the loot. The stories turned out well in the end; Indians and whites reached an understanding. The films ennobled the Indians and treated the white settlers benignly. Problems that arose were always precipitated from the outside.

The East German Indianerfilme were a reaction to the success of the Winnetou series in the West. Rather than copy the formula of May's novels, however, East German directors reached for differentiated plots. Starring Yugoslav actor Gojko Mitic, who had appeared as an Indian in a Winnetou film, the East German works focused on different Indian leaders such as Tecumseh, Osceola, and Ulzana. The films also emphasized the policy of White European settlers of driving the Indians out of territories they wished to settle themselves. *Die*

Söhne der großen Bärin (*The Sons of the Great Mother Bear*, Josef Mach, 1965) tells of one tribe's refusal to move to a reservation, and the many perils of their flight to Canada. In *Ulzana* (*Ulzana*, Gottfried Kolditz, 1973), Indian Chieftain Ulzana has to defend his people's land against the Europeans, who oppose their communal farming methods. In *Apachen* (*Apaches*, Gottfried Kolditz, 1973), Ulzana avenges the near genocide of his tribe by the American Army. Mitic made 10 Indianer films for **DEFA**, one a year. *See also* EAST GERMAN FILM.

WISBAR, FRANK (1899–1967). Frank Wisbar (also Wysbar) directed some of the 1950s most memorable **war films**. After an unremarkable career in Nazi Germany, Wisbar fled the country in 1941 and immigrated to America, becoming a U.S. citizen. He was active in American television, directing films for *Fireside Theater*. In the mid-1950s, he returned to Germany to direct a series of war films, among them *Haie und kleine Fische* (*Sharks and Small Fish*, 1957), *Nacht fiel über Gotenhafen* (*Night Fell on Gotenhafen*, 1959), *Hunde, wollt ihr ewig leben?* (*Dogs, Do You Want to Live Forever?* 1959), and *Fabrik der Offiziere* (*Officer Factory*, 1960).

Wisbar is often accused of stripping German history of its context, making his characters too sympathetic, and otherwise avoiding a critical confrontation with the past. *Haie und kleine Fische*, for example, closes with a song of a sailor's lament of homesickness, as several men who have escaped from a submarine form a circle as they float in life preservers awaiting rescue, the war and the cause the men were fighting for totally forgotten. *Nacht fiel über Gotenhafen* tells of an Allied attack on a ship that is being used as a safe haven for women and children. Since it is based on a true event, it is unfair to criticize the movie for its relativism, that is, for its point of view that the other side killed innocent people also. The most often criticized of Wisbar's films, *Hunde, wollt ihr ewig leben?* and *Fabrik der Offiziere*, mitigate soldiers' actions by setting up a polarity between good German soldiers and bad Nazi officers. While it is true that soldiers have to follow orders, the films fail to differentiate between those ordinary men who were following orders and those who supported the Nazi ideology. Moreover, as the Wehrmachtausstellung (German Military Exhibition) of the mid-1990s revealed, ordinary soldiers were far from the benign fighting men depicted in 1950s German novels, autobiographies, and films.

WOLF, KONRAD (1925–1982). Although he made fewer than 20 films during his career, Konrad Wolf is East Germany's most critically successful and respected filmmaker. (*See* **East German film**.) His work to a great extent is autobiographical, reflecting the influence of his father, Friedrich Wolf, a communist dramatist of the 1920s, and his experiences in the Soviet Union, to which the family, communist and Jewish, immigrated after the Nazis came to power. Wolf joined the Soviet Army as a 17-year-old to fight against Germany.

Wolf's films concern themselves with Germany's past, with the dangers of misjudging or ignoring politics, and with the raising of moral consciousness. *Genesung* (*Recovery*, 1956) begins at the start of World War II, when a medical student has to interrupt his studies. The story then jumps to postwar East Germany, where the student is working as a doctor under an assumed name. When he is discovered, he is saved from prosecution by a judge whom he had helped escape the Nazis, illuminating the double meaning in the title, referring to the man's profession but more importantly to the healing of wounds from the past. *Lissy* (*Lissy*, 1957) begins before the Nazis come to power. As a member of the working class, Lissy's allegiance is to the communists, but after 1933 her husband and her brother both switch allegiance to the National Socialists, as does Lissy. Only when her brother is shot does she recognize the need to leave her Nazi husband and return to the communists. The film is reminiscent of Wolf's father's agit-prop dramas about conversion; in which primarily women learn through the course of a play the necessity of siding with the Left. Awakening of awareness is also the subject of *Sterne* (*Stars*, 1959), which relates the story of a Nazi soldier who falls in love with a Jewish woman being deported to Auschwitz and as a result has a political conversion. The following year Wolf again took up the theme of belated insight, this time from the side of a Jewish doctor. *Professor Mamlock* (*Professor Mamlock*, 1960), based on a play by his father, tells of a doctor in 1933 Germany who refuses to believe that the Nazis pose a danger to the Jews. Even after he is forced to terminate Jewish employees and his daughter has to leave high school, he persists in his optimism. Only when he has been reduced to a figurehead in his department does he recognize the truth and commit suicide.

Two of Wolf's films reflect his personal coming to terms with his Germanness, even as a Jew and a Soviet citizen. *Ich war neunzehn (I Was Nineteen*, 1968) is a war film, set at the close of World War II. A Soviet unit approaches Berlin and a young officer, German by birth, is made commandant of Bernau, a suburb. The young man must confront the mistrust of his fellow Russian comrades and the opinions of the townsfolk, who see him as a traitor. The film examines the German attitudes that could have led to Adolf Hitler's rise and poses the question of how anything German, the land of poets and thinkers, can ever be normal again. *Mama, ich lebe (Mama, I'm Alive*, 1977) follows four German soldiers who are captured and join the Soviets in the war against the Germans, their countrymen. When forced to shoot at fellow German soldiers, three are unable to do so. Although set during the war, the film suggests that 20 years after the war's end, having the Soviets present in their country was something many East Germans still had to work through.

Not all of Wolf's films deal with the past. *Der geteilte Himmel (Divided Heaven*, 1964) examines acceptance of a divided Germany only a short time after the building of the Berlin Wall. A chemist, who is having difficulties realizing his ambitions in the East, flees to the West, followed by his girlfriend. The woman, however, returns to the East, unable to abandon the socialist project of building a new social order in the East. *Der nackte Mann auf dem Sportplatz (The Naked Man on the Athletic Field*, 1973) is one of Wolf's few comedies, although he had presented a comedy as his thesis project in film school. The film satirizes prudish morality as townspeople object to the placement on their sports field of a statue depicting a naked runner. They would have preferred a clothed soccer player. *Solo Sunny (Solo Sunny*, 1980) examines everyday life in East Germany, focusing on a mediocre singer trying to have a successful career in Berlin.

Wolf's commitment to humanistic themes runs throughout his films. It is clear his sympathies lie with communism and the East German experiment to craft a new society; he was after all the son of a communist, raised in the Soviet Union, and the brother of Markus Wolf, the head of the notorious East German Stasi. Nonetheless, from *Genesung* to *Solo Sunny*, his focus is on individuals trying to exist within a system of controls. Whether the controls are seen as imposed from without by a dictator (Nazi Germany) or from within (belief in the socialist cause), they constrict the individual psyche. *Cinema verité* elements of natural sound, lighting, and acting reinforce the effect that the films are dealing with real people coming to terms with actual problems. *See also VERGANGENHEITSBEWÄLTIGUNGS-FILM.*

– Y –

YOUNG GERMAN CINEMA. Disappointed with the films of the 1950s and early 1960s, a group of directors proclaimed the **Oberhausen Manifesto** in 1962, inaugurating the movement known as Young German Cinema. Although the films coming out of the movement are as diverse as the filmmakers who signed the manifesto— **Alexander Kluge**, **Edgar Reitz**, Peter Schamoni, among others— they are characterized by the elliptical narrative style and choppy editing of the French new wave (*nouvelle vague*). This French cinematic movement influenced their work and their philosophy of filmmaking. Like the *nouvelle vague*, Young German Cinema championed works that emphasized the creative role of the filmmaker over all other aspects of movie production. More important, they viewed their films as works of art, important in their own right, rather than as commodities whose purpose was to sell tickets for the film industry. Young German Cinema filmmakers received government subsidies for their films under a short-lived system established in 1967, administered by the **Kuratorium Junger Deutscher Film** (Young German Film Board).

Directors of the Young German Cinema and their films are often subsumed under the rubric **New German Cinema**, a term that describes the film movement that succeeded Young German Cinema in the 1970s and refers especially to the films distributed by the **Filmverlag der Autoren.**

– Z –

ZIEMANN, SONJA (1926–). Sonja Ziemann could be called the queen of the *Heimatfilm*. After appearing as Bärbel in **Hans Deppe**'s *Schwarzwaldmädel* (*The Black Forest Girl*, 1950) and *Grün ist die Heide* (*The Heath Is Green*, 1951), Ziemann became Germany's favorite actress in the 1950s. In both films, she plays a young innocent, girl-next-door type, who has to overcome obstacles before she can marry the man she loves. The first is set in Germany's romantic Black Forest, the setting of many fairy tales, and the second takes place on the picturesque Lüneburg Heath. The love stories of both films are set against an atmosphere of nostalgia, historical in the *Schwarzwaldmädel* and political in *Grün ist die Heide*. As she grew out of her role as ingénue, Ziemann became a popular character actress on German television.

ZILLE-FILMS. Named for graphic artist Heinrich Zille (1858–1929), who specialized in scenes of the unemployed, prostitutes, petty criminals, and the underclass in general, the films foregrounded life among Germany's poor. The two most noted examples of the genre are *Die Verrufenen* (*Slums of Berlin*, literal title, *The Disreputable*, Gerhard Lamprecht, 1925), about misery among the underclass in Berlin's alleys, and *Mutter Krausens Fahrt ins Glück* (*Mother Krause's Journey to Happiness*, Phil Jutzi, 1929), about the despair that leads the urban poor to commit suicide. Jutzi's film was produced by Prometheus-Film GmbH, a company that financed works to counterbalance the middle-class and bourgeois themes that the communists saw in mainstream movies. It was one of the first films banned when the Nazis came to power.

The 100 Most Significant German Films

In 1995, on the occasion of the 100th anniversary of the birth of motion pictures, the Stiftung Deutsche Kinemathek, an organization similar to the American Film Institute (AFI), which has its own list of 100 most significant American films, released a list of the 100 most significant German films. A group of industry experts, which included film historians, journalists, editors, and filmmakers, nominated films based on their artistic, political, or social significance. Among the jurors were former East German filmmakers Frank Beyer and Kurt Maetzig; avant garde director Herbert Achternbusch; feminist and New German Cinema filmmaker Margarethe von Trotta; and NGC directors Wim Wenders, Volker Schlöndorff, and Edgar Reitz. Nondirectors included journalists Peter Buchka, Peter W. Jansen, and Hellmuth Karasek, and film historians Ulrich Gregor, Enno Patalas, and Karsten Witte. A complete report on the process of selection and synopses of the films can be found in *Kino*, a quarterly publication of the Export-Union of German Film, beginning with the second issue of 2001, and also in the annual edition of *Kino,* beginning in 2001.

1. *M* (*M*, Fritz Lang, 1931)
2. *Das Cabinet des Dr. Caligari* (*The Cabinet of Dr. Caligari*, Robert Wiene, 1920)
3. *Berlin – Die Sinfonie der Großstadt* (*Berlin: Symphony of a City*, Walter Ruttmann, 1927)
4. *Nosferatu, eine Symphonie des Grauens* (*Nosferatu*, Friedrich Wilhelm Murnau, 1922)
5. *Menschen am Sonntag* (*People on Sunday*, Robert Siodmak et al., 1930)
6. *Die Mörder sind unter uns* (*The Murderers Are among Us*, Wolfgang Staudte, 1946)

7. *Der blaue Engel* (*The Blue Angel*, Josef von Sternberg, 1930)
8. *Metropolis* (*Metropolis*, Fritz Lang, 1927)
9. *Die freudlose Gasse* (*Street Joyless*, Georg Wilhelm Pabst, 1925)
10. *Der Untertan* (*The Kaiser's Lackey*, Wolfgang Staudte, 1951)
11. *Kuhle Wampe oder Wem gehört die Welt?* (*Kuhle Wampe*, aka *Whither Germany?*, Slatan Dudow, 1932)
12. *Der Student von Prag* (*The Student of Prague*, Stellan Rye and Paul Wegener, 1913)
13. *Die Brücke* (*The Bridge*, Bernhard Wicki, 1959)
14. *Abschied von gestern* (*Yesterday Girl*, Alexander Kluge, 1966)
15. *Mutter Krausens Fahrt ins Glück* (*Mother Krause's Journey to Happiness*, Phil Jutzi, 1929)
16. *Der Golem, wie er in die Welt kam* (*The Golem: How He Came into the World*, Paul Wegener and Carl Boese, 1920)
17. *Dr. Mabuse, der Spieler* (*Dr. Mabuse, the Gambler*, Fritz Lang, 1922)
18. *Unter den Brücken* (*Under the Bridges*, Helmut Käutner, 1945)
19. *Die Nibelungen: Siegfrieds Tod* [Teil 1] (*Siegfried's Death* [Part I]); *Die Nibelungen: Kriemhilds Rache* [Teil 2] (*Kriemhild's Revenge* [Part II], Fritz Lang, 1924)
20. *Der letzte Mann* (*The Last Laugh*, Friedrich Wilhelm Murnau, 1924)
21. *Der müde Tod* (*Destiny*, Fritz Lang, 1921)
22. *Liebelei* (*Liebelei* aka *Flirtation*, Max Ophüls, 1933)
23. *Spur der Steine* (*Trace of Stones*, Frank Beyer, 1966)
24. *Das Wintergartenprogramm der Gebrüder Skladanowsky* (*The Skladanowsky Brothers' "Wintergarten Programme,"* Max Skladanowsky, 1895)
25. *Lola Montez* (*Lola Montés*, Max Ophüls, 1955)
26. *Faust* (*Faust*, Friedrich Wilhelm Murnau, 1926)
27. *Heimat – Eine deutsche Chronik* (*Heimat: A Chronicle of Germany*, Edgar Reitz, 1984)
28. *Deutschland im Herbst* (*Germany in Autumn*, Collective of Directors, 1978)
29. *Madame Dubarry* (*Passion*, Ernst Lubitsch, 1919)
30. *Berlin – Alexanderplatz* (*Berlin-Alexanderplatz*, Phil Jutzi, 1931)
31. *Die Ehe der Maria Braun* (*The Marriage of Maria Braun*, Rainer Werner Fassbinder, 1979)

32. *Münchhausen* (*The Adventures of Baron Munchausen*, Josef von Báky, 1943)
33. *Die Büchse der Pandora* (*Pandora's Box*, Georg Wilhelm Pabst, 1929)
34. *Die Blechtrommel* (*The Tin Drum*, Volker Schlöndorff, 1979)
35. *Das Testament des Dr. Mabuse* (*The Testament of Dr. Mabuse*, Fritz Lang, 1933)
36. *Im Lauf der Zeit* (*Kings of the Road*, Wim Wenders, 1976)
37. *Triumph des Willens* (*Triumph of the Will*, Leni Riefenstahl, 1935)
38. *Der junge Törless* (*Young Törless*, Volker Schlöndorff, 1966)
39. *Katzelmacher* (*Katzelmacher*, Rainer Werner Fassbinder, 1969)
40. *Große Freiheit Nr. 7* (*Port of Freedom*, Helmut Käutner, 1944)
41. *Rotation* (*Rotation*, Wolfgang Staudte, 1949)
42. *Wir Wunderkinder* (*Aren't We Wonderful?*, Kurt Hoffmann, 1958)
43. *Das Wachsfigurenkabinett* (*Waxworks*, Paul Leni and Leo Birinsky, 1924)
44. *Mädchen in Uniform* (*Girls in Uniform*, Leontine Sagan, 1931)
45. *Varieté* (*Jealousy*, Ewald André Dupont, 1925)
46. *Rosen für den Staatsanwalt* (*Roses for the Prosecutor*, Wolfgang Staudte, 1959)
47. *Alice in den Städten* (*Alice in the Cities*, Wim Wenders, 1974)
48. *Die Halbstarken* (*Teenage Wolfpack*, aka *The Hooligans*, Georg Tressler, 1956)
49. *Die verlorene Ehre der Katharina Blum* (*The Lost Honor of Katharina Blum*, Volker Schlöndorff and Margarethe von Trotta, 1975)
50. *Westfront 1918* (*Comrades of 1918*, Georg Wilhelm Pabst, 1930)
51. *Die Dreigroschenoper* (*The Threepenny Opera*, Georg Wilhelm Pabst, 1931)
52. *Solo Sunny* (*Solo Sunny*, Konrad Wolf, 1980)
53. *Angst essen Seele auf* (*Ali: Fears Eats the Soul*, Rainer Werner Fassbinder, 1974)
54. *Der Verlorene* (*The Lost One*, Peter Lorre, 1951)
55. *Die Drei von der Tankstelle* (*Three from the Gas Station*, Wilhelm Thiele, 1930)
56. *In jenen Tagen* (*Seven Journeys* aka *In Those Days*, Helmut Käutner, 1947)

57. *Olympia. Teil I: Fest der Völker, Teil II: Fest der Schönheit* (*Olympia. Part I: Festival of the People, Part II: Festival of Beauty*, Leni Riefenstahl, 1938)
58. *Jud Süß* (*Jew Süss*, Veit Harlan, 1940)
59. *Der geteilte Himmel* (*Divided Heaven*, Konrad Wolf, 1964)
60. *Der Himmel über Berlin* (*Wings of Desire*, Wim Wenders, 1987)
61. *Nicht versöhnt oder Es hilft nur Gewalt, wo Gewalt herrscht* (*Not Reconciled or Only Violence Helps Where Violence Rules*, Jean-Marie Straub, 1965)
62. *Vampyr* (*The Vampire*, Carl Theodor Dreyer, 1932)
63. *Tagebuch einer Verlorenen* (*Diary of a Lost Girl*, Georg Wilhelm Pabst, 1929)
64. *Der Prozeß – Eine Darstellung des Majdanek-Verfahrens in Düsseldorf* (*The Trial: Presentation of the Majdanek Concentration Camp Trial in Düsseldorf* , Eberhard Fechner, 1984)
65. *Der Händler der vier Jahreszeiten* (*The Merchant of Four Seasons*, Rainer Werner Fassbinder, 1972)
66. *Romanze in Moll* (*Romance in a Minor Key*, Helmut Käutner, 1943)
67. *Ehe im Schatten* (*Marriage in the Shadows*, Kurt Maetzig, 1947)
68. *Die Legende von Paul und Paula* (*The Legend of Paul and Paula*, Heiner Carow, 1973)
69. *Chronik der Anna Magdalena Bach* (*Chronicle of Anna Magdalena Bach*, Jean-Marie Straub and Danièle Huillet, 1968)
70. *Aguirre, der Zorn Gottes* (*Aguirre, the Wrath of God*, Werner Herzog, 1972)
71. *Ich war neunzehn* (*I Was Nineteen*, Konrad Wolf, 1968)
72. *Die Abenteuer des Prinzen Achmed* (*The Adventures of Prince Achmed*, Lotte Reiniger, 1926
73. *Sterne* (*Stars*, Konrad Wolf, 1959)
74. *Die bleierne Zeit* (*Marianne and Juliane*, Margarethe von Trotta, 1981)
75. *Die Straße* (*The Street*, Karl Grune, 1923)
76. *Germania anno zero* (*Germany Year Zero*, Roberto Rossellini, 1948)
77. *Kameradschaft* (*Comradeship*, Georg Wilhelm Pabst, 1931)
78. *Emil und die Detektive* (*Emil and the Detectives*, Gerhard Lamprecht, 1931)

79. *Berlin – Ecke Schönhauser* (*Berlin: Schönhauser Corner*, Gerhard Klein, 1957)
80. *Berlin Alexanderplatz* [14 Teile] (*Berlin Alexanderplatz* [14 Parts], Rainer Werner Fassbinder, 1980)
81. *Der Kongreß tanzt* (*Congress Dances*, Erik Charell, 1931)
82. *Das Kaninchen bin ich* (*I Am the Rabbit*, Kurt Maetzig, 1965)
83. *Die Artisten in der Zirkuskuppel – Ratlos* (*Artists under the Bigtop: Perplexed*, Alexander Kluge, 1968)
84. *Fontane Effi Briest* (*Effi Briest*, Rainer Werner Fassbinder, 1974)
85. *Der amerikanische Freund* (*The American Friend*, Wim Wenders, 1977)
86. *Asphalt* (*Asphalt*, Joe May, 1929)
87. *Jakob der Lügner* (*Jacob the Liar*, Frank Beyer, 1974)
88. *Jeder für sich und Gott gegen alle* (*The Enigma of Kaspar Hauser*, Werner Herzog, 1974)
89. *Nachts, wenn der Teufel kam* (*The Devil Strikes at Night*, Robert Siodmak, 1957)
90. *Die Mysterien eines Frisiersalons* (*The Mysteries of a Hairdresser's Shop*, Bertolt Brecht and Erich Engel, 1923)
91. *Die weiße Hölle vom Piz Palü* (*The White Hell of Pitz Palu*, Georg Wilhelm Pabst and Arnold Fanck, 1929)
92. *Das Mädchen Rosemarie* (*The Girl Rosemarie*, Rolf Thiele, 1958)
93. *Aus einem deutschen Leben* (*Death is My Trade*, Theodor Kotulla, 1977)
94. *Viktor und Viktoria* (*Viktor and Viktoria*, Reinhold Schünzel, 1933)
95. *Das Boot* (*The Boat*, Wolfgang Petersen, 1981)
96. *Jagdszenen aus Niederbayern* (*Hunting Scenes from Lower Bavaria*, Peter Fleischmann, 1969)
97. *Lebensläufe* (*Biographies, the Story of the Children of Golzow*, Winfried Junge, 1981)
98. *Berliner Ballade* (*The Ballad of Berlin*, Robert A. Stemmle, 1948)
99. *Mephisto* (István Szabó, 1981)
100. *Die zweite Heimat – Chronik einer Jugend* (*Heimat II: Chronicle of a Generation*, Edgar Reitz and Robert Busch, 1992)

Bibliography

German film presents scholars a complex subject for research both diachronically and synchronically. The topic spans over 110 years, German filmmakers having been among the pioneers of the projected moving image. Political events have produced distinct film epochs: the early films of the Wilhelmine period (1895–1918), the golden age of German film during the Weimar Republic (1918–1933), the conservative and controlling images of the Third Reich (1933–1945) and of the East German regime (1949–1989), and the commercial as well as art house or auteur cinema of West Germany from 1945 to the present time. The topic of German film must also travel along tracks emerging from different national film industries, two of which, the German and the Austrian, have separations between them that are not well defined and borders where crossings are frequent. The two well-defined German national industries, those of the Federal Republic of Germany (West Germany) and the German Democratic Republic (East Germany), could not cross the borders separating them. Changes in film policies, technological innovations, and audience preferences during the multiple eras of German film have produced differentiated film cultures. Moreover, cinema has always been a global phenomenon. Actors, directors, cinematographers, and composers embrace the international nature of their art. Thus the question of defining German cinema is indeed complex and open to debate.

The bibliography that follows is intended to offer scholars of German film points of departure for exploration of a rich and exciting body of knowledge. It is not exhaustive, as that would require all the pages of this volume. Rather it encompasses essential works, from general introductory volumes to specialized works on specific eras, personalities, and concepts. Included are Internet sites that offer a wealth of information to the practiced user of electronic publications. Much specific and detailed knowledge comes from German-language sites, which offer some, but unfortunately not all, of their information in English.

It is now virtually impossible to exhaust the scholarly literature when researching German film, so abundant are the offerings. Yet it was not always so. German academics came relatively late to film scholarship. To be sure, German scholars wrote about film as soon as movies were displayed for public viewing, but regularly produced academic film scholarship dates to the early 1970s when a volume of screen plays, *Masterworks of the German Cinema* (1973), with an introduction by Roger Manville, awakened interest in classic German films. A book that became a standard reference for Germany's new wave cinema, John Sandford's *The New German Cinema,* was published in 1979. In the 1980s, slowly at first and then with ever-increasing speed, German film scholarship exploded, precipitated primarily by three film scholars, Eric Rentschler, Anton Kaes, and Thomas Elsaesser. Their names appear multiple times in this bibliography, not only because they have written on German film more than any other German film scholars, but also because their works have influenced and encouraged others to explore the fields they have opened. Elsaesser has produced groundbreaking work on early cinema and the German new wave, including *A Second Life: German Cinema's First Decades* (1996) and *New German Cinema: A History* (1989). Rentschler in effect introduced the new wave to the American academic curriculum. Among his many books are *West German Film in the Course of Time: Reflections on the Twenty Years since Oberhausen* (1984) and *West German Filmmakers on Film: Visions and Voices* (1988). Kaes's work *From Hitler to Heimat: The Return of History as Film* has become a standard on film historiography as applied to German cinema. It is important to note here also that Rentschler and Kaes offered annual seminars financed by the Deutsche Akademische Austauschdienst on introducing German film into the university curriculum.

Serious scholars should be familiar with a number of works that predate the boom in German film scholarship. Siegfried Kracauer's *From Caligari to Hitler: A Psychological History of the German Film* (1947) is an important starting point for any excursion into the cinema of the Weimar Republic. Although his work has many critics, there are none who fail to acknowledge his contribution to film analysis. Equally important for exploring the expressionist elements in Weimar cinema is Lotte Eisner's *The Haunted Screen: Expressionism in the German Cin-*

ema and the Influence of Max Reihardt (1969), a translation of her *L'écran démoniaque* (1952). Whereas Kracauer and Eisner are indispensable for psychological analyses of Weimar film, Curt Riess's *Das gab's nur einmal: Die große Zeit des deutschen Films* is the standard for behind-the-scenes history of the major productions of the 1920s. David Stewart Hull's *Film in the Third Reich: A Study of the German Cinema, 1933–1945* was the standard reference for work in cinema of the Third Reich and remains important for research into the topic. Although it has been superseded by later works, in particular Rentschler's *The Ministry of Illusion: Nazi Cinema and Its Afterlife* (1996) and Linda Schulte-Sasse's *Entertaining the Third Reich: Illusions of Wholeness in Nazi Cinema* (1996), it is still the best source for an overview of Nazi cinema. In recent years Sabine Hake, Mary-Elizabeth O'Brien, and Robert Reimer have contributed volumes on individual films of the period.

Although New German Cinema traces back to the Oberhausen Manifesto of 1962, its impact on American academics was not noticed until several important works of the early 1980s. James C. Franklin's *New German Cinema: From Oberhausen to Hamburg* for the Twayne series on film detailed the beginnings of the new wave, the importance of the subsidy system, and the initial cool reception by critics for the films. Klaus Phillips's edited volume, *New German Filmmakers: From Oberhausen through the 1970s*, discussed the more prominent directors such as Werner Herzog and Rainer Werner Fassbinder, but more important, included essays on directors whose work was not as widely distributed or written about: Ula Stöckl, Peter Lilienthal, and May Spils. Timothy Corrigan's *New German Film: The Displaced Image* situated the films within their sociohistorical context, reflecting the shift in film programs at the time to a more theoretical approach to film.

Politics of the Cold War kept the films of the German Democratic Republic (East Germany) from being widely distributed in the West, and therefore scholarship was limited mainly to German-language essays on the country's major works, the films of Konrad Wolf, or the works dealing with anti-Semitism, such as *Jakob der Lügner* or *Nackt unter Wölfen*. In 1990, however, the University of Massachusetts entered into a cooperative agreement with DEFA, the East German film studio, to distribute the studio's films on VHS and DVD. Spearheaded by Barton Byg, the opening of a DEFA film library at the University of Massachusetts included symposia and also summer seminars similar to those directed for

West German film by Rentschler and Kaes. In addition to multiple essays by Byg on DEFA film, works such as Joshua Feinstein's *The Triumph of the Ordinary: Depictions of Daily Life in the East German Cinema* have raised the profile of East German cinema in academic circles.

While the films and those engaged in film production of the Weimar era, the Third Reich, the New German Cinema and, if belatedly, East Germany, are described, discussed, and analyzed in dozens of books and hundreds of essays, the film industry of the 1950s remains relatively under-researched, although that is certainly changing. Heide Fehrenbach's *Cinema in Democratizing Germany: Reconstructing National Identity after Hitler* (1995) details film structure in postwar Germany and through the 1950s. Robert Shandley's *Rubble Films: German Cinema in the Shadow of the Third Reich* (2001), while not about the 1950s per se, discusses the postwar period, which was so important for the reestablishment of a German film industry in the 1950s. Moreover, there are two standard works on the 1950s written in German: Claudius Seidl's *Der deutsche Film der fünfziger Jahre* (1987) and Micaela Jary's *Traumfabriken Made in Germany: die Geschichte des deutschen Nachkriegsfilms 1945–1960* (1993). Analyses of individual works from the period can also be found in general histories such as Sabine Hake's *German National Cinema* (2002) or Robert Reimer and Carol Reimer's *Nazi-retro Film: How German Narrative Cinema Remembers the Past* (1992).

There are likewise few general works devoted entirely to the Austrian film industry. An essential text is Robert von Dassanowsky's *Austrian Cinema: A History* (2005), which offers chapters that cover Austrian film from 1895 to the present. Willy Riemer's *After Postmodernism: Austrian Literature and Film in Transition* (2000) has analyses of individual filmmakers and films. Eric Rentschler's volume, *The Films of G. W. Pabst: An Extraterritorial Cinema*, (1990) contains papers from a symposium on the Austrian director, who actually made only a few of his films in Austria. Indeed, that is the difficulty when writing about Austrian film: so much of it is subsumed by German cinema. For unlike literature, which retains the national identity of the author, even when published abroad or in another language, film works are collaborations, and the national identity of the originator is thus difficult to discern. Major film anthologies often include a rubric for Austrian film and also discuss individual personalities. Thus it can be more successful to research under individual names such as Pabst, Valie Export, Michael

Haneke, Klaus Maria Brandauer, Maximilian Schell, Maria Schell, and Xaver Schwarzenberger, to name but a few. Also, the *International Film Guide*, edited by Peter Cowie, offers summaries of the year's production in Austrian film for isolated years.

German film literature is particularly diverse in thematic areas. Of the many feminist publications, Julia Knight's *Women and the New German Cinema* (1992) and Susan E. Linville's *Feminism Film Fascism: Women's Auto/biographical Film in Postwar Germany* (1998) cover the major and also experimental works of the 1960s–1980s. *Frauen und Film*, founded by filmmaker Helke Sander, contains interviews, reviews, retrospective essays, and film analyses in German and English. Germany's past is also well represented in the literature on film. In addition to Kaes's book on historiography cited earlier, Eric L. Santner's *Stranded Objects: Mourning, Memory and Film in Postwar Germany* (1990) has become the standard text for beginning research on how Germany has, or has not, used film to come to terms with its past. In *The Cinema's Third Machine: Writing on Film in Germany 1907–1933* (1993), Sabine Hake offers a thorough examination of the role of film criticism in shaping reception and understanding of film in the early years as well as during the Weimar Republic. In *The New German Cinema: Music, History, and the Matter of Style* (2004), Caryl Flynn analyses the role of music in film, an often overlooked aspect of film analysis. Even more specialized volumes look at themes within periods. Patrice Petro focuses on the tragic melodramas of Weimar cinema in *Joyless Streets: Women and Melodramatic Representation in Weimar Germany* (1989), and Leonie Naughton examines German films in *That Was the Wild East: Film Culture, Unification, and the "New" Germany* (2002). The volume deals with how a united Germany has assimilated the culture of East Germany after the fall of the Berlin Wall.

Germany's federal system fosters decentralization of support facilities for film research. Each state has its own *Landesbildstelle*, or film office, which lends films to schools, archives pedagogical material, and holds photo collections, among other services. Important film archives are found in Berlin, Berlin-Potsdam, Wiesbaden, Koblenz, Munich, Frankfurt, and Vienna, among other locations, requiring advanced planning when writing on German film. Yet researching German film has been made easier of late through CineGraph, a nonprofit film institute that publishes the most comprehensive encyclopedia of film available, some of it online and some of it in English. The institute holds film congresses and at cinegraph.de provides links to museums, archives, festivals, and thematic databases. A second site that is invaluable to research in German film is filmportal.de, which offers filmographies, bibliographies, and biographies of the major and minor participants in German film history. The site is in German but has many entries in English translation. Filmportal.de also offers an extensive photo gallery of movie stills with links to the companies that hold the publication rights. Moreover, it offers a comprehensive time line of German cinema from 1895 to the present and includes brief online essays on the many facets of German film. Although not as extensive as filmportal.de, Filmarchiv.at offers similar information for Austrian film. Of the many sites for reviews, one of the most comprehensive for German films is www.artechock.de/film/index.htm. The reviews are in German but are valuable because of their analytical insights into popular German films and the analyses of non-German films by German critics. Three other general sites that include reviews and essays of German and Austrian works are Entertext at http://people.brunel.ac.uk, kinoeye.org, and sensesofcinema.com.

German film schools, film archives, sociopolitical organizations, and museums publish their own yearbooks and journals on film, offering a rewarding collection on German film from the beginning to the present. *KINtop*, an annual of the origins of film as entertainment, is invaluable for scholars researching the first 25 years of German film. The quarterly issues of *Kino: Films of the Federal Republic of Germany* are collected into an annual volume. In addition to the detailed information in quarterly volumes covering all movies produced in Germany, the annual lists all films produced in Germany since 1946, including distribution rights when this information is available. The *DEFA-Jarhbuch* (*Apropos: Film . . .: Das Jahrbuch der DEFA-Stiftung*) is devoted to presenting the history of the film industry in East Germany. In addition to the yearbooks, Germany produces a number of important film journals: The periodical *Frauen und Film* represents women in the German film industry, offering interviews, reviews, and essays on Germany's and Austria's commercial, auteur, and avant-garde women directors. *Film-Dienst*, first published in 1948 by Das Katholische Institut für Medieninformation, provides nondogmatic reviews of films and DVDs from a Catholic perspective, as well as essays on personalities, films, and related film topics. The journal *epd Film* is the Protestant counterpart to the *Film-Dienst*. Other periodicals cover specialized topics such as *FilmExil*, which appears twice yearly and covers directors who fled Nazi Germany; and *New German Critique*, whose special issues discuss German film and filmmakers. The *Film-Kurier-Index* is a series that began in 1991 to publish reprints of the more than 7,000 numbers of *Film-Kurier*, the most important film publication for the industry from 1919 to 1944.

The bibliography that follows is by nature of the undertaking incomplete. Nonetheless it presents those works important to appreciate the diversity, vitality, and controversy of German film. The divisions covering Wilhelmine Germany, the Weimar Republic, the Third Reich, the postwar period to the Oberhausen Manifesto (New German Cinema), East German cinema, and the post-Oberhausen and postunification cinema are not arbitrary. They represent political, historical, and aesthetic disjunctures reflected in the films of the respective periods. Yet they should not suggest discontinuity from one period to the next, for as with any historical and cultural phenomenon, influences from one period or movement appear in those following it or those existing beside it. Therefore, following the division into periods, the bibliography is also divided into themes to afford deeper insight into the richness of German film scholarship.

CONTENTS

REFERENCE AND GENERAL WORKS

Alter, Nora M. *Projecting History: German Nonfiction Cinema, 1967–2000*. Ann Arbor: University of Michigan Press, 2002.

Arnheim, Rudolf. *Film as Art*. Berkeley and Los Angeles: University of California Press, 1957. Originally published in German as *Film als Kunst*. Berlin: Ernst Rowohlt Verlag, 1932.

Bandmann, Christa, and Joe Hembus. *Klassiker des deutschen Tonfilms, 1930–1960*. Munich: Wilhelm Goldmann Verlag, 1980.

Barlow, John D. *German Expressionist Film*. Boston: Twayne, 1982.

Baxter, John. *The Hollywood Exiles*. New York: Taplinger Publishing, 1976.

Bergfelder, Tim, Erica Carter, and Deniz Göktürk, eds. *The German Cinema Book*. London: BFI Publishing, 2002.

Boa, Elizabeth. *Heimat: A German Dream; Regional Loyalties and National Identity in German Culture, 1890–1990*. New York: Oxford University Press, 2000.

Bock, Hans-Michael, ed. *CineGraph: Lexikon zum deutschsprachigen Film*. 6 vols. Munich: edition text + kritik, 1984–.

Bock, Hans-Michael, and Michael Töteberg, eds. *Das Ufa-Buch: Kunst und Krisen, Stars und Regisseure, Wirtschaft und Politik*. Frankfurt am Main: Verlag Zweitausendeins, 1992.

Bourget, Jean Loup. *Douglas Sirk*. Paris: Edilig, 1984.

Brennicke, Ilona, and Joe Hembus. *Klassiker des deutschen Stummfilms, 1910–1930*. Munich: Wilhelm Goldmann Verlag, 1983.

Cook, David A. *A History of Narrative Film*. 4th ed. New York: W. W. Norton, 2004.

Dassanowsky, Robert von. *Austrian Cinema: A History*. Jefferson, N.C.: McFarland, 2005.

DelGaudio, Sybil. *Dressing the Part: Sternberg, Dietrich, and Costume*. Rutherford, N.J.: Fairleigh Dickinson University Press; Cranbury, N.J.: Associated University Presses, 1993.

Deutsches Filminstitut–DIF, eds. *Die Vergangenheit in der Gegenwart Konfrontationen mit den Folgen des Holocaust im deutschen Nachkriegsfilm*. Munich: edition text + kritik, 2000.

Dokumentation: 30 Jahre Internationale Filmwoche Mannheim, 1951–1981. Edited by Internationale Filmwoche Mannheim and Klaus Hofmann. Mannheim: Internationale Filmwoche Mannheim, 1981.

Elsaesser, Thomas. *European Cinema: Face to Face with Hollywood*. Amsterdam: Amsterdam University Press, 2005. Distributed in the U.S. by the University of Chicago Press.

Elsaesser, Thomas, Jean-Francois Lyotard, and Edgar Reitz. *Der zweite Atem des Kinos*. Edited by Andreas Rost. Frankfurt am Main: Verlag der Autoren, 1996.

Elsaesser, Thomas, and Michael Wedel. *The BFI Companion to German Cinema*. London: BFI Publishing, 1999.

Felix, Jürgen, ed. *Unter die Haut: Signaturen des Selbst im Kino der Körper*. St. Augustin, Germany: Gardez! Verlag, 1998.

"Film and Exile." Special Issue. *New German Critique*, no. 89 (Spring–Summer): 1–189.

"German Film History." Special Issue. *New German Critique*, no. 60 (Autumn 1993): 1–191.

"German Media Studies." Special Issue. *New German Critique*, no. 78 (Autumn 1999): 1–192.

Gersch, Wolfgang. *Film bei Brecht: Bertolt Brechts praktische und theoretische Auseinandersetzung mit dem Film*. Berlin: Henschel, 1975.

Ginsberg, Terri, and Kirsten Moana Thompson. *Perspectives on German Cinema*. New York: G. K. Hall; London: Prentice Hall International, 1996.

Hake, Sabine. *German National Cinema*. New York: Routledge, 2002.

Halle, Randall, and Margaret McCarthy, eds. *Light Motives: German Popular Film in Perspective*. Detroit: Wayne State University Press, 2003.

Hanisch, Michael. *Auf den Spuren der Filmgeschichte: Berliner Schauplätze*. Berlin: Henschel, 1991.

"Heimat." Special Issue. *New German Critique*, no. 36 (Autumn 1985): 1–276.

Helt, Richard C., and Marie E. Helt. *West German Cinema, 1985–1990: A Reference Handbook*. Metuchen, N.J.: Scarecrow Press, 1992.

Helt, Richard C., and Marie E. Helt. *West German Cinema since 1945: A Reference Handbook*. Metuchen, N.J.: Scarecrow Press, 1987.

Henseleit, Felix, ed. *Die Internationalen Filmfestspiele Berlin von 1951–1974 im Zeitraffer*. Berlin: Internationale Filmfestspiele Berlin, 1975.

Hohnstock, Manfred, and Alfons Bettermann, eds. *Deutscher Filmpreis, 1951–1980*. Bonn: Bundes Innenministerium, 1980.

Holba. Herbert, Günter Knorr, and Peter Spiegel. *Reclams deutsches Filmlexikon: Filmkünstler aus Deutschland, Österreich und der Schweiz*. Stuttgart: Reclam, 1984.

Hölzl, Gebhard, and Thomas Lassonczyk. *Armin Mueller-Stahl: Seine Filme, sein Leben*. Munich: Wilhelm Heyne, 1992.

Horak, Jan-Christopher. *Fluchtpunkt Hollywood: Eine Dokumentation zur Filmemigration nach 1933*. 2nd ed. Münster: MakS Publikationen, 1986.

Humphries, Reynold. *Fritz Lang: Genre and Representation in his American Films*. Baltimore: Johns Hopkins University Press, 1989.

Jacobsen, Wolfgang, ed. *Babelsberg: das Filmstudio.* 3rd ed. Berlin: Stiftung Deutsche Kinemathek; Berlin: Argon, 1994.

Jacobsen, Wolfgang, Anton Kaes, Hans Helmut Prinzler, and Filmmuseum Berlin-Deutsche Kinomathek. *Geschichte des deutschen Film.* 2nd ed. Stuttgart: J. B. Metzler, 2004.

Jacobsen, Wolfgang, and Volker Noth. *Berlin im Film: Die Stadt, die Menschen.* Berlin: Argon, 1998.

Jacobsen, Wolfgang, and Hans Helmut Prinzler. *Siodmak Bros.: Berlin-Paris-London-Hollywood.* Berlin: Argon, 1998.

Kaes, Anton. *From Hitler to Heimat: The Return of History as Film.* Cambridge: Harvard University Press, 1989.

Kaltenbach, Christiane. *Frauen Film Handbuch.* Berlin: Verband der Filmarbeiterinnen, 1983.

Kanzog, Klaus. *Staatspolitisch besonders wertvoll: Ein Handbuch zu 30 deutschen Spielfilmen der Jahre 1934 bis 1945.* Munich: Verlag Schaudig und Ledig, 1994.

Klaus, Ulrich J. *Deutsche Tonfilme: Filmlexikon der abendfüllenden deutschen und deutschsprachigen Tonfilme nach ihren deutschen Uraufführungen.* 12 vols. Berlin: Kalus-Archiv, 1988.

Koebner, Thomas, ed. *Idole des deutschen Films: Eine Galerie von Schlüsselfiguren.* Munich: edition text + kritik, 1997.

Koepnick, Lutz P. *The Dark Mirror: German Cinema between Hitler and Hollywood.* Berkeley and Los Angeles: University of California Press, 2002.

Kolker, Robert Phillip. *The Altering Eye: Contemporary International Cinema.* New York: Oxford University Press, 1983.

Kracauer, Siegfried. *Theory of Film: The Redemption of Physical Reality.* Princeton, N.J.: Princeton University Press, 1997.

Kramer, Thomas, ed. *Reclams Lexikon des deutschen Films.* Stuttgart: Reclam, 1995.

Kramer, Thomas, and Martin Prucha. *Film im Lauf der Zeit: 100 Jahre Kino in Deutschland, Österreich und der Schweiz.* Vienna: Ueberreuter, 1994.

Kreimeier, Klaus. *Kino und Filmindustrie in der BRD: Ideologieproduktion und Klassenwirklichkeit nach 1945.* Kronberg: Scriptor Verlag, 1973.

——. *Die UFA Story: Geschichte eines Filmkonzerns.* Munich: Carl Hanser, 1992.

——. *The Ufa Story: A History of Germany's Greatest Film Company, 1918–1945.* Translated by Robert Kimber and Rita Kimber. New York: Hill and Wang, 1996.

Kuzniar, Alice A. *The Queer German Cinema.* Stanford, Calif.: Stanford University Press, 2000.

Laufer, Elisabeth. *Skeptiker des Lichts: Douglas Sirk und seine Filme.* Frankfurt am Main: Fischer Taschenbuch, 1987.

Lellis, George L. *Bertolt Brecht, Cahiers du Cinéma and Contemporary Film Theory.* Ann Arbor, Mich.: UMI Research Press, 1982.

Marquardt, Axel, ed. *Internationale Filmfestspiele Berlin, 1951–1984: Filme, Namen, Zahlen.* Berlin: Internationale Filmfestspiele Berlin, [1985].

McCormick, Richard W., and Alison Guenther-Pal, eds. *German Essays on Film.* New York: Continuum, 2004.

Meurer, Hans Joachim. *Cinema and National Identity in a Divided Germany, 1979–1989: The Split Screen.* Lewiston, N.Y.: Edwin Mellen Press, 2000.

Michel, Gabriele. *Armin Müller-Stahl: Die Biografie.* Munich: Paul List Verlag, 2000.

Miersch, Annette. *Schulmädchen-Report: Der deutsche Sexfilm der 70er Jahre.* Berlin: Bertz Verlag, 2003.

Moltke, Johannes von. *No Place Like Home: Locations of Heimat in German Cinema.* Berkeley and Los Angeles: University of California Press, 2005.

Mühl-Benninghaus, Wolfgang. "Verbotene Leinwand: Filmzensur." *Film und Fernsehen* 6 (1987): 46–52.

Müller, Heinz, ed. *Film in der Bundesrepublik Deutschland.* Berlin: Henschel, 1990.

Murray, Bruce A., and Christopher J. Wickham, ed. *Framing the Past: The Historiography of German Cinema and Television.* Carbondale: Southern Illinois University Press, 1992.

Neumann, Hans-Joachim. *Der deutsche Film heute: Die Macher, das Geld, die Erfolge, das Publikum.* Frankfurt am Main: Ullstein, 1986.

Noltenius, Johanne. *Die Freiwillige Selbstkontrolle der Filmwirtschaft und das Zensurverbot des Grundgesetzes.* Göttingen: Verlag Otto Schwarz, 1958.

Nowell-Smith, Geoffrey, ed. *Oxford World History of Cinema.* New ed. Oxford: Oxford University Press, 1996.

Ott, Frederick W. *The Great German Films: From before World War I to the Present.* Secaucus, N.J.: Citadel, 1986.

Paech, Anne. *Kino zwischen Stadt und Land: Geschichte des Kinos in der Provinz: Osnabrück.* Marburg: Jonas, 1985.

Pflaum, Hans Günther. *Germany on Film: Theme and Content in the Cinema of the Federal Republic of Germany.* Edited by Robert Picht. Translated by Richard C. Helt, and Roland Richter. Detroit: Wayne State University Press, 1990.

Prinzler, Hans Helmut. *Chronik des deutschen Films, 1895–1994.* Stuttgart: J. B. Metzler, 1995.

———. *Das Jahr 1945: Filme aus fünfzehn Ländern.* Berlin: Stiftung Deutsche Kinemathek, 1990.

Prodolliet, Ernest. *Nosferatu: Die Entwicklung des Vampirfilms von Friedrich Wilhelm Murnau bis Werner Herzog.* Freiburg, Switerland: Universitatsverlag, 1980.

Projektgruppe deutscher Heimatfilm. *Der deutsche Heimatfilm: Bildwelten und Weltbilder; Bilder, Texte, Analysen zu 70 Jahren deutscher Filmgeschichte.* Tübingen: Tübinger Vereinigung für Volkskunde, 1989.

Quart, Barbara Koenig. *Women Directors: The Emergence of a New Cinema.* New York: Praeger Publishers, 1988.

Rauh, Reinhold, and Edgar Reitz. *Film als Heimat.* Munich: W. Heyne, 1993.

Reimer, Robert C., and Carol J. Reimer. *Nazi-retro Film: How German Narrative Cinema Remembers the Past.* New York: Twayne, 1992.

Rentschler, Eric, ed. *German Film and Literature: Adaptations and Transformations.* New York: Methuen, 1986.

Rhiel, Mary. *Re-viewing Kleist: The Discursive Construction of Authorial Subjectivity in West German Kleist Films.* New York: Peter Lang, 1991.

Santner, Eric L. *Stranded Objects: Mourning, Memory, and Film in Postwar Germany.* Ithaca, N.Y.: Cornell University Press, 1990.

Schenk, Ralf, and Helga Hartmann. *Mitten ins Herz: 66 Liebesfilme.* Berlin: Henschel, 1991.

Schmitt, Heiner. *Kirche und Film: Kirchliche Filmarbeit in Deutschland von ihren Anfängen bis 1945.* Schriften des Bundesarchivs, no. 26. Boppard am Rhein: Harald Boldt Verlag, 1979.

"Siegfried Kracauer." Special issue. *New German Critique,* no. 54 (Autumn 1991): 1–189.

Silberman, Marc. *German Cinema: Texts in Context.* Detroit: Wayne State University Press, 1995.

Siodmak, Robert. *Zwischen Berlin und Hollywood: Erinnerungen eines großen Filmregisseurs.* Munich: F. A. Herbig, 1980.

Sirk, Douglas. *Sirk on Sirk: Conversations with Jon Halliday.* New and rev. ed. Boston: Faber and Faber, 1997.

Spangenberg, Eberhard. *Karriere eines Romans: "Mephisto," Klaus Mann und Gustav Gründgens; Ein Dokumentarischer Bericht aus Deutschland und dem Exil 1925–1981.* Munich: Edition Spangenberg im Ellerman Verlag, 1982.

Spurgat, Günter. *Theodor Storm im Film: Die Kino- und Fernsehverfilmungen seiner Werke.* Lübeck: Graphische Werkstätten, 1987.

Stern, Michael. *Douglas Sirk.* Boston: Twayne, 1979.

Thompson, Kristin. *Herr Lubitsch Goes to Hollywood: German and American Film after World War I.* Amsterdam: Amsterdam University Press, 2005. Distributed in the U.S. by the University of Chicago Press.

Traub, Hans, and Hanns Wilhelm Lavies, eds. *Das deutsche Filmschrifttum: Eine Bibliographie der Bücher und Zeitschriften über das Filmwesen.* Leipzig: Hiersemann, 1940.

Verband der Filmarbeiterinnen. *Frauen Film Handbuch*. Berlin: Verband der Filmarbeiterinnen, 1984.

Verfassungsklage: 35 Filmarbeiterinnen gegen Regierung der Bundesrepublik Deutschland. Cologne: Verband der Filmarbeiterinnen, 1988.

Vogel, Amos. *Film as a Subversive Art*. New York: Random House, 1974. Reprint. London: C. T. Editions. Distributed in the U.S. by D.A.P.

Vogt, Guntram. *Die Stadt im Film: deutsche Spielfilme, 1900–2000*. Marburg: Schüren, 2001.

Werner, Paul. *Die Skandalchronik des deutschen Films*. Frankfurt am Main: Fischer Taschenbuch, 1990.

Wolf, Steffen. *Filmförderung oder Zensur?: Von "Der dritte Mann" bis "Otto der Film": Gedanken zum Film, zur Filmbewertung, und zur Filmforderung. 35. Jahre Filmbewertungsstelle Wiesbaden (FBW), 1951–1986*. Ebersberg: Edition Achteinhalb Lothar Just, 1986.

Wollenberg, Hans H. *Fifty Years of German Film*. Translated by Ernst Sigler. London: Falcon Press, 1948. Reprint. New York: Arno Press, 1972.

Zahlmann, Stefan. *Körper und Konflikt: Filmische Gedächtniskultur in BRD und DDR seit den sechziger Jahren*. Berlin: Arno Spitz, 2001.

Zander, Peter. *Thomas Mann im Kino*. Berlin: Bertz + Fischer, 2005.

Zglinicki, Friedrich von. *Die Wiege der Traumfabrik: Von Guckkästen, Zauberscheiben und bewegten Bildern bis zur Ufa in Berlin*. Berlin: Transit, 1986.

Zimmermann, Peter, and Gebhard Moldenhauer. *Der geteilte Himmel: Arbeit, Alltag und Geschichte im ost- und westdeutschen Film*. Konstanz: UVK Medien, 2000.

WILHELMINE ERA: 1895–1918

Barkhausen, Hans. *Filmpropaganda in Deutschland im Ersten und Zweiten Weltkrieg*. Hildesheim: Olms Presse, 1982.

Belach. Helga, ed. *Henny Porten: Der erste deutsche Filmstar 1890–1960*. Berlin: Haude und Spener, 1986.

Bergstrom, Janet Lynn. "Asta Nielsen's Early German Films." In *Before "Caligari": German Cinema, 1895–1920*, edited by Paolo Cherchi Usai and Lorenzo Codelli, 162–85. [Pordenone]: Edizioni Biblioteca dell'Immagine, 1990.

Birett. Herbert. *Lichtspiele: Das Kino in Deutschland bis 1914*. Munich: q-Verlag, 1994.

———. "Standortverzeichnis früher deutscher Filmzeitschriften." In *KINtop: Jahrbuch zur Erforschung des frühen Films*, vol. 1, *Früher Film in Deutschland*, edited by Frank Kessler, Sabine Lenk, and Martin Loiperdinger, 136–44. Frankfurt am Main: Stroemfeld/Roter Stern, 1993.

Birett. Herbert, ed. *Das Filmangebot in Deutschland, 1895–1911.* Munich: Winterberg, 1991.
————. *Verzeichnis der in Deutschland gelaufenen Filme: Entscheidungen der Filmzensur.* Berlin: K. G. Saur, 1980.
Brennicke, Ilona, and Joe Hembus. *Klassiker des deutschen Stummfilms, 1910–1930.* Munich: Wilhelm Goldmann Verlag, 1983.
Bretschneider, Jürgen, Bärbel Dalichow, and Filmmuseum Potsdam. *Babelsberg: Gesichter einer Filmstadt/Babelsberg: Faces of a Film Metropolis.* Berlin: Henschel, 2005.
Cherchi Usai, Paolo, and Lorenzo Codelli, eds. *Before "Caligari": German Cinema, 1895–1920.* [Pordenone]: Edizioni Biblioteca dell'Immagine, 1990.
Chronik der Karl Geyer-Filmfabrik. Vol. 1, *1911–1921* [held at the Stiftung Deutsche Kinemathek, Berlin].
Curry, Ramona. "How Early German Film Stars Helped to Sell the War(s)." In *Film and the First World War*, edited by Karel Dibbets and Bert Hogenkamp, 139–48. Amsterdam: Amsterdam University Press, 1995.
Curtis, Scott. "The Taste of a Nation: Training the Senses and Sensibility of Cinema Audiences in Imperial Germany." *Film History* 6 (Winter 1994): 445–69.
Dagrada, Elena. "Filmsprache und Filmgeschichte: Das Beispiel *Eine Fliegenjagd, oder Die Rache der Frau Schultze* von Max und Eugen Skladanowsky." In *KINtop: Jahrbuch zur Erforschung des frühen Films*, vol. 4, *Anfänge des dokumentarischen Films*, edited by Frank Kessler, Sabine Lenk, and Martin Loiperdinger, 143–62. Frankfurt am Main: Stroemfeld/Roter Stern, 1995.
Dahlke, Günther, and Karl Günther, eds. *Deutsche Spielfilme von den Anfängen bis 1933: Ein Filmführer.* Berlin: Henschel, 1986.
Diederichs, Helmut H. "Die Anfänge deutschen Filmpublizistik 1895 bis 1909: Die Filmberichterstattung der Schaustellerzeitschrift 'Der Komet' und die Gründung der Filmfachzeitschriften." *Publizistik* 1 (1985): 55–71.
————. *Anfänge deutscher Filmkritik.* Stuttgart: Verlag Robert Fischer and Uwe Wiedleroither, 1986.
————. *Der Filmtheoretiker Herbert Tannenbaum.* Frankfurt am Main: Deutsches Filmmuseum, 1987.
————. *Frühgeschichte deutscher Filmtheorie: Ihre Entstehung und Entwicklung bis zum Ersten Weltkrieg.* Habilitationsschrift, FB Gesellschaftswissenschaften der J. W. Goethe-Universität, Frankfurt, 1996. www.soziales.fh-dortmund.de/diederichs/pdfs/habil.pdf
————. "The Origins of the 'Autorenfilm.'" In *Before "Caligari": German Cinema, 1895–1920*, edited by Paolo Cherchi Usai and Lorenzo Codelli, 380–401. [Pordenone]: Edizioni Biblioteca dell'Immagine, 1990.
Dupont, E. A. *Wie ein Film geschrieben wird und wie man ihn verwertet.* Berlin: G. Kuhn, 1919. Reprinted as "Ewald André Dupont: Anleitung für

Filmschriftsteller; Wie ein Film geschrieben wird und wie man ihn verwertet," in *Ewald André Dupont: Autor und Regisseur*, edited by Jürgen Bretschneider. Munich: edition text + kritik, 1992.

Elsaesser, Thomas. *Early Cinema: Space, Frame, Narrative*. London: BFI Publishing, 1990.

———. "Early German Cinema: Audiences, Style and Paradigms." *Screen* 33, no. 2 (Summer 1992): 205–14.

———. "Filmgeschichte - Firmengeschichte - Familiengeschichte: Der Übergang vom Wilhelminischen zum Weimarer Film." In *Joe May: Regisseur und Produzent*, edited by Hans-Michael Bock and Claudia Lenssen, 11–30. Munich: edition text + kritik, 1991.

———, ed. *A Second Life: German Cinema's First Decades*. Amsterdam: Amsterdam University Press, 1996. Distributed in the U.S. by the University of Chicago Press.

———. "Wilhelminisches Kino: Stil und Industrie." In *KINtop: Jahrbuch zur Erforschung des frühen Films*. Vol. 1, *Früher Film in Deutschland*, edited by Frank Kessler, Sabine Lenk, and Martin Loiperdinger, 10–28. Frankfurt am Main: Stroemfeld/Roter Stern, 1993.

Elsaesser, Thomas, and Michael Wedel, eds. *Kino der Kaiserzeit*. Munich: edition text + kritik, 2002.

Fischli. Bruno. "Das Goldene Zeitalter der Kölner Kinematographie (1896–1918)." In *Vom Sehen im Dunkeln: Kinogeschichten einer Stadt*, edited by Bruno Fischli and Rolf-Dieter Lavier, 7–38. Cologne: Prometh Verlag, 1990.

Garncarz, Joseph. "Warum gab es im Stummfilmkino keine deutschen Kinderstars?" In *KINtop: Jahrbuch zur Erforschung des frühen Films*. Vol. 7, *Stummes Spiel, sprechende Gesten*, edited by Frank Kessler, Sabine Lenk, and Martin Loiperdinger, 99–112. Frankfurt am Main: Stroemfeld/Roter Stern, 1998.

Gehler, Fred. "Pioniere und Visionäre 1912–1933." In *Filmstadt Babelsberg: Zur Geschichte des Studios und seiner Filme*, edited by Axel Geiss. Potsdam: Filmmuseum Potsdam; Berlin: Nicolai, 1994.

Geiss, Axel, ed. *Filmstadt Babelsberg: Zur Geschichte des Studios und seiner Filme*. Potsdam: Filmmuseum Potsdam; Berlin: Nicolai, 1994.

Gökturk. Deniz. "Market Globalization and Import Regulation in Imperial Germany." In *Film and the First World War*, edited by Karel Dibbets and Bert Hogenkamp, 188–97. Amsterdam: Amsterdam University Press, 1995.

Hake, Sabine. *The Cinema's Third Machine: Writing on Film in Germany, 1907–1933*. Lincoln: University of Nebraska Press, 1993.

———. *Passions and Deception: The Early Films of Ernst Lubitsch*. Princeton, N.J.: Princeton University Press, 1992.

——. "Self-referentiality in Early German Cinema." *Cinema Journal* 31 (Spring 1992): 37–55.

Hansen, Miriam. "Early Silent Cinema: Whose Public Sphere?" The Origins of Mass Culture: The Case of Imperial Germany. *New German Critique*, no. 29 (Spring–Summer 1983): 147–84.

——. "Reinventing the Nickelodeon: Notes on Kluge and Early Cinema." Special Issue on Alexander Kluge: Theoretical Writings, Stories, and an Interview. *October* 46 (Autumn 1988): 178–98.

Hennigsen, Wiltrud. *Die Entstehung des Kinos in Münster: Versuch einer Historiographie.* Münster: Hennigsen, 1990.

Herbst, Helmut. "Oskar Messter: Forgotten Pioneer of German Cinema." *Historical Journal of Film, Radio and Television* 15, no. 4 (October 1995): 569–74.

Heuwinkel, Christiane. "Die Metamorphose der Tagespresse: Der Filmkritiker E. A. Dupont." In *Autor und Regisseur*, edited by Jürgen Bretschneider and Ewald André Dupont. Munich: edition text + kritik, 1992.

Hoppe, Hans. *Die Zukunft des Kinos.* Stettin: Hessenland, 1912.

Hunt, Leon. "Frühgeschichte des deutschen Films: Licht am Ende des Tunnels." In *Geschichte des deutschen Films*, edited by Wolfgang Jacobsen, Anton Kaes, and Hans Helmut Prinzler, 13–38. Stuttgart: J. B. Metzler, 1993.

——. *"The Student of Prague:* Division and Codification of Space." In *Early Cinema: Space, Frame, Narrative*, edited by Thomas Elsaesser, 389–402. London: BFI Publishing, 1990.

Jacobsen, Wolfgang. "The Flying Producer: Notes on Erich Pommer." In *Before "Caligari": German Cinema, 1895–1920*, edited by Paolo Cherchi Usai and Lorenzo Codelli, 186–201. [Pordenone]: Edizioni Biblioteca dell'Immagine, 1990.

Jochum, Norbert, ed. *Das wandernde Bild: Der Filmpionier Guido Seeber.* Berlin: Stiftung Deutsche Kinemathek; Berlin: Elephanten Press, 1979.

Jung, Uli. "Local Views: A Blind Spot in the Historiographie of Early German Cinema." *Historical Journal of Film, Radio, and Television* 22, no. 3 (2002): 253–73.

Jung, Uli, and Walter Schatzberg. "Robert Wiene's Film Career before *"Caligari."* In *Before "Caligari": German Cinema, 1895–1920*, edited by Paolo Cherchi Usai and Lorenzo Codelli, 292–311. [Pordenone]: Edizioni Biblioteca dell'Immagine, 1990.

Kaes, Anton. "The Debate about Cinema: Charting a Controversy (1909–1929)." Special Issue on Weimar Film Theory. *New German Critique*, no. 40 (Winter 1987): 7–33.

——, ed. *Kino-Debatte: Texte zum Verhältnis von Literatur und Film, 1910–1929.* Tübingen: Max Niemeyer Verlag; Munich: Deutscher Taschenbuchverlag, 1978.

Kessler, Frank. "A Highway to Film Art?" In *Before "Caligari": German Cinema, 1895–1920*, edited by Paolo Cherchi Usai and Lorenzo Codelli, 438–51. [Pordenone]: Edizioni Biblioteca dell'Immagine, 1990.

Kessler, Frank, Sabine Lenk, and Martin Loiperdinger, eds. *KINtop: Jahrbuch zur Erforschung des frühen Films*. Vol. 1, *Früher Film in Deutschland*. Frankfurt am Main: Stroemfeld/Roter Stern, 1992.

———. *KINtop: Jahrbuch zur Erforschung des frühen Films*. Vol. 3, *Oskar Messter: Erfinder und Geschäftsmann*. Frankfurt am Main: Stroemfeld/Roter Stern, 1994.

Kinter, Jürgen. *Arbeiterbewegung und Film (1895–1933)*. Hamburg: Medienpädagogik-Zentrum, 1985.

KINtop: Jahrbuch zur Erforschung des frühen Films, edited by Frank Kessler, Sabine Lenk, and Martin Loiperdinger. Basel and Frankfurt am Main: Stroemfeld/Roter Stern, 1992– .

Koebner, Thomas. "Der Film als neue Kunst - Reaktionen der literarischen Intelligenz: Zur Theorie des Stummfilms (1911–1924)." In *Literaturwissenschaft-Medienwissenschaff*, edited by Helmut Kreuzer, 1–31. Heidelberg: Quelle and Meyer, 1977.

Koerber, Martin. "Oskar Messter, Film Pioneer: Early Cinema between Science, Spectacle, and Commerce." In *A Second Life: German Cinema's First Decades*, edited by Thomas Elsaesser, 51–61. Amsterdam: University of Amsterdam Press, 1996. Distributed in the U.S. by the University of Chicago Press.

Lamprecht, Gerhard. *Deutsche Stummfilme 1903–1931*. 9 vols. Berlin: Deutsche Kinemathek, 1966–1970.

Lange, Konrad. *Nationale Kinoreform*. Mönchengladbach: Volksvereinsverlag, 1918.

Lenk, Sabine. "Filmverrückt oder Wie es wirklich im Kino zugeht: Kurzfilmographie zum Thema 'Das Kino auf der Stummfilmleinwand'." In *KINtop: Jahrbuch zur Erforschung des frühen Films*. Vol. 5, *Aufführungsgeschichten*, edited by Frank Kessler, Sabine Lenk, and Martin Loiperdinger, 161–70. Frankfurt am Main: Stroemfeld/Roter Stern, 1996.

Lichtenstein, Manfred. "The Brothers Skladanowsky." In *Before "Caligari": German Cinema, 1895–1920*, edited by Paolo Cherchi Usai and Lorenzo Codelli, 312–25. [Pordenone]: Edizioni Biblioteca dell'Immagine, 1990.

Loiperdinger, Martin. "Erhaltene Spielfilme aus der Messter-Produktion, 1909–1918." In *KINtop: Jahrbuch zur Erforschung des frühen Films*. Vol. 3, *Oskar Messter: Erfinder und Geschäftsmann*, edited by Frank Kessler, Sabine Lenk, and Martin Loiperdinger, 209–12. Frankfurt am Main: Stroemfeld/Roter Stern, 1994.

———, ed. *KINtop: Schriften*. Vol. 2, *Oskar Messter: Filmpionier der Kaiserzeit*. Frankfurt am Main: Stroemfeld/Roter Stern, 1994.

MacMahon, Alison. "Stummfilmgeschichte im Licht der Tonbilder." In *KIN-top: Jahrbuch zur Erforschung des frühen Films*. Vol. 8, *Film und Projek-tionskunst*, edited by Frank Kessler, Sabine Lenk, and Martin Loiperdinger, 141–58. Frankfurt am Main: Stroemfeld/Roter Stern, 1999.

Murray, Bruce A. "An Introduction to the Commercial Film Industry in Germany from 1895 to 1933." In *Film and Politics in the Weimar Republic*, edited by Thomas G. Plummer et al., 23–33. New York: Holmes and Meier, 1982.

Narath, Albert. *Oskar Messter: Der Begründer der deutschen Kino- und Fil-mindustrie*. Berlin: Deutsche Kinemathek, 1966.

Oksiloff, Assenka. *Picturing the Primitive: Visual Culture, Ethnography, and Early German Cinema*. New York: Palgrave, 2001.

Païni, Dominique. "Der frühe Film zwischen Bühne und Zufall." In *KINtop: Jahrbuch zur Erforschung des frühen Films*. Vol. 5, *Aufführungsgeschichten*, edited by Frank Kessler, Sabine Lenk, and Martin Loiperdinger, 150–54. Frankfurt am Main: Stroemfeld/Roter Stern, 1996.

Pehla, Karen. "Joe May und seine Detektive: Der Serienfilm als Kinoerlebnis." In *Joe May: Regisseur und Produzent*, edited by Hans-Michael Bock and Clauia Lenssen, 61–72. Munich: edition text + kritik, 1991.

Prawer, S. S. *Between Two Worlds: Jewish Presences in German and Austrian Film, 1910–1933*. New York: Berghahn Books, 2005.

Quaresima, Leonardo. "'Dichter heraus!': The Autorenfilm and German Cin-ema of the 1910's." *Griffithiana* 13, nos. 38–39 (October 1990): 101–26.

Rother, Rainer. "*Bei unseren Helden an der Somme*: Eine deutsche Antwort auf die Entente-Propaganda." In *KINtop: Jahrbuch zur Erforschung des frühen Films*. Vol. 4, *Anfänge des dokumentarischen Films*, edited by Frank Kessler, Sabine Lenk, and Martin Loiperdinger, 123–42. Frankfurt am Main: Stroem-feld/Roter Stern, 1995. Also published as *"Bei unseren Helden an der Somme* (1917): The Creation of a 'Social Event'." *Historical Journal of Film, Radio and Television* 15, no. 4 (October 1995): 525–42.

Schlüpmann, Heide. "Cinema as Anti-Theater: Actresses and Female Audi-ences in Wilhelminian Germany." *Iris*, no. 11 (Summer 1990): 77–93. Also published in *In Silent Film*, edited by Richard Abel. New Brunswick, N.J.: Rutgers University Press, 1996.

———. "Cinematographic Enlightenment versus 'The Public Sphere': A Year in Wilhelminian Cinema." *Griffithiana*, no. 50 (March 1994): 75–85.

———. "Early German CinemaMelodrama: Social Drama." In *Popular Euro-pean Cinema*, edited by Richard Dyer, and Ginette Vincendeau, 206–19. New York: Routledge, 1992.

———. " 'Die Erziehung des Publikums': Auch eine Vorgeschichte des Weimarer Kinos." In *KINtop: Jahrbuch zur Erforschung des frühen Films*. Vol. 5, *Auf-führungsgeschichten*, edited by Frank Kessler, Sabine Lenk, and Martin Loiperdinger, 133–46. Frankfurt am Main: Stroemfeld/Roter Stern, 1996.

———. *"Ich möchte kein Mann sein*: Ernst Lubitsch, Sigmund Freud und die frühe deutsche Komödie." In *KINtop: Jahrbuch zur Erforschung des frühen Films*. Vol. 1, *Früher Film in Deutschland*, edited by Frank Kessler, Sabine Lenk, and Martin Loiperdinger, 75–92. Frankfurt am Main: Stroemfeld/ Roter Stern, 1993.

———. *Unheimlichkeit des Blicks: Das Drama des frühen deutschen Kinos.* Frankfurt am Main: Stroemfeld/Roter Stern, 1990.

———. "Wahrheit und Lüge im Zeitalter der technischen Reproduzierbarkeit: Detektiv und Heroine bei Joe May." In *Joe May: Regisseur und Produzent*, edited by Hans-Michael Bock and Claudia Lenssen, 45–60. Munich: edition text + kritik, 1991.

Seidel, Renate, and Allan Hagedorff, eds. *Asta Nielsen: Ihr Leben in Fotodokumenten, Selbstzeugnissen und zeitgenössischen Betrachtungen,* Berlin: Henschel, 1981.

"Skladanowsky und die Nebelbilder." In *KINtop: Jahrbuch zur Erforschung des frühen Films*. Vol. 8, *Film und Projektionskunst*, edited by Frank Kessler, Sabine Lenk, and Martin Loiperdinger, 83–100. Frankfurt am Main: Stroemfeld/Roter Stern, 1999.

Sturm, Georges. *Die Circe, der Pfau und das Halbblut: die Filme von Fritz Lang, 1916–1921.* Trier: Wissenschaftlicher Verlag Trier, 2001.

Thomas, Douglas B. *The Early History of German Motion Pictures, 1895–1935.* Washington, D.C.: Thomas International, 1999.

Thomas, Paul. "Fassbinder: The Poetry of the Inarticulate." *Film Quarterly* 30, no. 2 (Winter 1976–1977): 2–17.

Weinstein, Valerie. "Anti-Semitism or Jewish 'Camp'?: Ernst Lubitsch's *Schuhpalast Pinkus* (1916) and *Meyer Aus Berlin* (1918)." *German Life and Letters* 59, no. 1 (January 2006): 101–21.

Welch, David. "A Medium for the Masses: Ufa and Imperial German Film Propaganda during the First World War." *Historical Journal of Film, Radio, and Television* 6, no. 1 (1986): 85–91.

Zglinicki, Friedrich von. *Die Wiege der Traumfabrik: Von Guckkästen, Zauberscheiben und bewegten Bildern bis zur Ufa in Berlin.* Berlin: Transit, 1986.

Zimmerschied, Karl. *Die deutsche Filmindustrie: Ihre Entwicklung, Organisation und Stellung im deutschen Staats- und Wirtschaftsleben.* Stuttgart: Poeschel, 1922.

WEIMAR REPUBLIC: 1918–1933

Adkinson, Robert V. *"The Cabinet of Dr. Caligari": A Film by Robert Wiene, Carl Mayer and Hans Janowitz.* Translated by Robert V. Adkinson. New York: Simon & Schuster, 1972.

Allen, Jerry C. *Conrad Veidt: From "Caligari" to "Casablanca".* Rev. ed. Pacific Grove, Calif.: Boxwood Press, 1993.

Allgeier, Sepp. *Die Jagd nach dem Bild: 18 Jahre als Kameramann in Arktis und Hochgebirge.* Stuttgart: J. Engelhorns, 1931.

Alter, Nora M. "The Politics and Sounds of Everyday Life in *Kuhle Wampe*: Reconsidering Brecht's Film Theory." In *Sound Matters: Essays on the Acoustics of German Culture*, edited by Nora M. Alter and Lutz Koepnick, 79–90. New York: Berghahn Books, 2004.

Amann, Frank, Ben Gabel, and Jürgen Keiper. *Revisited: Der Fall Dr. Fanck: Die Entdeckung der Natur im deutschen Bergfilm (1992).* Frankfurt am Main: Stroemfeld /Roter Stern, 1992.

Andriopoulos, Stefan. "Spellbound in Darkness: Hypnosis as an Allegory of Early Cinema." *Germanic Review* 77, no. 2 (Spring 2002): 102–16.

Armour, Robert A. *Fritz Lang.* Boston: Twayne, 1978.

Aspetsberger, Friedbert, ed. *Der Berg Film, 1920–1940.* Innsbruck: Studien Verlag, 2003.

Atwell, Lee. *G. W. Pabst.* Boston: Twayne, 1977.

Aurich, Rolf, Wolfgang Jacobsen, and Cornelius Schnauber, with Nicole Brunnhuber und Gabriele Jatho. *Fritz Lang: Leben und Werk; Bilder und Dokumente* [*Fritz Lang, His Life and Work: Photographs and Documents*]. Translated into English by Robin Benson. Berlin: Jovis Verlag, 2001.

Bachmann, Holger. "The Production and Contemporary Reception of *Metropolis*." In *Fritz Lang's "Metropolis": Cinematic Views of Technology and Fear*, edited by Michael Minden and Holger Bachmann, 3–46. Rochester, N.Y.: Camden House, 2000.

Barlow, John D. *German Expressionist Film.* Boston: Twayne, 1982.

Barsacq, Leon. *Caligari's Cabinet and Other Grand Illusions: A History of Film Design.* Rev. ed. Edited by Elliott Stein. Translated by Michael Bullock. New York: New American Library, 1978.

Battle, Pat Wilks. "Conrad Veidt." *Films in Review* 44, nos. 3–4 (March–April 1993): 74–87.

Beicken, Peter. "Faust in Film: The Case of Dr. Caligari." In *Doctor Faustus: Archetypal Subtext at the Millenium*, by Peter Werres, James Campbell, and Peter Beicken, 43–67. Morgantown: West Virginia University Press, 1999.

Bellour, Raymond. "On Fritz Lang." *Sub-Stance,* no. 9 (1974): 25–34.

Benesch, Klaus. "Technology, Art, and the Cybernetic Body: The Cyborg as Cultural Other in Fritz Lang's *Metropolis* and Philip K. Dick's *Do Androids Dream of Electric Sheep?*" *Amerikastudien-American Studies* 44, no. 3 (1999): 379–92.

Bergstrom, Janet Lynn. "Expressionism and *Mabuse*." *Iris,* nos. 14–15 (Autumn 1992): 85–98.

———. "The Logic of Fascination: Fritz Lang and Cinematic Conventions." PhD diss., University of California at Los Angeles, 1980.

———. "Murnau, Movietone and Mussolini." *Film History* 17, nos. 2–3 (2005): 187–204.

———. "Psychological Explanation in the Films of Lang and Pabst." In *Psychoanalysis and Cinema*, edited by E. Ann Kaplan, 163–80. New York: Routledge, 1989.

———. "Sexuality at a Loss: The Films of F. W. Murnau." *Poetics Today* 6, nos. 1–2 (1985): 185–203. Also published in *The Female Body in Western Culture: Contemporary Perspectives*, edited by Susan Rubin Suleiman, 242–61. Cambridge: Harvard University Press, 1986.

Biro, Matthew. "The New Man as Cyborg: Figures of Technology in Weimar Visual Culture." *New German Critique*, no. 62 (Spring–Summer 1994): 71–110.

Bloch, Robert. "The Master and *Metropolis*." In *Omni's Screen Flights/ Screen Fantasies: The Future According to Science Fiction Cinema*, edited by Danny Peary, 85–90. Garden City, N.Y.: Doubleday, 1984.

Bloom, Suzanne, and Ed Hill. "Dark Wonder: Fritz Lang's *Metropolis* and New Technical Wonders." *Artforum* 27, no. 10 (Summer 1989): 86–91.

Bogdanovich, Peter. "Fritz Lang." In *Who the Devil Made It*, 170–234. New York: Knopf, 1967.

———. *Fritz Lang in America.* London: Studio Vista, 1967.

Boivert, Nancy, and Low Taylor. "Fritz Lang's *M*: A Study in Criminality; Proceedings of Fourth Annual International Film Conference of Kent State University, April 16, 1986." In *Crime in Motion Pictures*, edited by Douglas Radcliff-Umstead, 90–95. Kent, Ohio: Romance Language Department, Kent State University, 1986.

Bond, K. "Ernst Lubitsch." *Film Culture*, nos. 63–64 (1977): 139–53.

Bongartz, Barbara. *Von Caligari zu Hitler, von Hitler zu Dr. Mabuse? eine psychologische Geschichte des deutschen Films von 1946 bis 1960.* Münster: MakS Publikationen, 1992.

Brandt, Hans Jürgen. "Walter Ruttmann: Vom Expressionismus zum Faschismus." Parts 1–3. *Filmfaust*, no. 49 (1985): 38–46; no. 50 (1985): 45–54; no. 51, (1986): 42–54.

Bratton, Susan Power. "From Iron Age Myth to Idealized National Landscape: Human-Nature Relationships and Environmental Racism in Fritz Lang's *Die Nibelungen*." *Worldviews: Environment, Culture, Religion* 4, no. 3 (November 2000): 195–212.

Braudy, Leo. "The Double Detachment of Ernst Lubitsch." *MLN* 98, no. 5 (December 1983): 1071–84. Also published in *Native Informant: Essays on Film, Fiction, and Popular Culture*, 67–76. New York: Oxford University Press, 1991.

Brennan, Matthew C. "Repression, Knowledge, and Saving Souls: The Role of the 'New Woman' in Stoker's *Dracula* and Murnau's *Nosferatu*." *Studies in the Humanities* 19, no. 1 (June 1992): 1–10.

Brennicke, Ilona, and Joe Hembus. *Klassiker des deutschen Stummfilms, 1910–1930*. Munich: Wilhelm Goldmann Verlag, 1983.

Brewster, Ben. "Brecht and the Film Industry." *Screen* 16, no. 4 (Winter 1975–1976): 16–33. Also published as "Brecht and the Film Industry: On *The Threepenny Opera* Film and *Hangmen Also Die!*" In *Perspectives on German Cinema*, edited by Terri Ginsberg and Kirsten Moana Thompson. New York: G. K. Hall; London: Prentice Hall International, 1996.

———. "The Fundamental Reproach: Bertolt Brecht and the Cinema." In *Explorations in Film Theory: Selected Essays from Ciné-tracts*, edited by Ron Burnett, 191–200. Bloomington: Indiana University Press, 1991.

Brodnax, Mary. "Man a Machine: The Shift from Soul to Identity in Lang's *Metropolis* and Ruttmann's *Berlin*." In *Peripheral Visions: The Hidden Stages of Weimar Cinema*, edited by Kenneth S. Calhoon, 73–93. Detroit: Wayne State University Press, 2001.

Bronfen, Elisabeth. "Seductive Departures of Marlene Dietrich: Exile and Stardom in *The Blue Angel*." Film and Exile. *New German Critique,* no. 89 (Spring–Summer 2003): 9–31.

———. "Vertreibung aus dem vertrauten Heim: *Der blaue Engel* (Josef von Sternberg)." In *Heimweh: Illusionsspiele in Hollywood,* 95–142. Berlin: Volk und Welt, 1999.

Budd, Mike. "Authorship as Commodity: The Art Cinema and *The Cabinet of Dr. Caligari*." *Wide Angle* 6, no. 1 (1984): 12–19.

———. "The *Cabinet of Doctor Caligari*: Production, Reception, History." In *Close Viewings: An Anthology of New Film Criticism*, edited by Peter Lehman, 333–52. Tallahassee: Florida State University Press, 1990.

———. "Retrospective Narration in Film: Re-reading *The Cabinet of Dr. Caligari*." *Film Criticism* 4, no. 1 (Fall 1979): 35–43.

Budd, Mike, ed. *"The Cabinet of Dr. Caligari": Texts, Contexts, Histories*. New Brunswick, N.J.: Rutgers University Press, 1990.

Burch, Noël. "Dr. Mabuse: Terror and Deception of the Image." *German Quarterly* 78, no. 4 (Fall 2005): 481–95.

———. "Fritz Lang: German period." In *In and Out of Synch: The Awakening of a Cine-Dreamer*, translated by Ben Brewster, 3–31. London: Scolar, 1991.

———. "Notes on Fritz Lang's first *Mabuse*." In *In and Out of Synch: The Awakening of a Cine-Dreamer*, translated by Ben Brewster, 205–27. London: Scolar, 1991.

Calhoon, Kenneth Scott. "F. W. Murnau, C. D. Friedrich, and the Conceit of the Absent Spectator." *MLN* 120, no. 3 (April 2005): 633–53.

———, ed. *Peripheral Visions: The Hidden Stages of Weimar Cinema.* Detroit: Wayne State University Press, 2001.

Cardullo, Bert. "Expressionism and *Nosferatu.*" *San Jose Studies* 11, no. 3 (Fall 1985): 25–33.

———. "Expressionism and the Real Cabinet of Dr. Caligari." *Film Criticism* 6, no. 2 (Winter 1982): 28–34.

Carringer, Robert L., and Barry Sabath. *Ernst Lubitsch: A Guide to References and Resources.* Boston: G. K. Hall, 1978.

Carroll, Noel. "Lang, Pabst and Sound." *Ciné-Tracts* 2, no. 1 (Autumn 1978): 15–23.

Chang, Joseph. "*M*: A Reconsideration." *Literature/Film Quarterly* 7, no. 4 (1979): 300–308.

Clark, Jill. "Scientific Gazing and the Cinematic Body Politic: The Demonized Cyborg of *Metropolis.*" *Intertexts* 3, no. 2 (Fall 1999): 168–79.

Coates, Paul. *The Gorgon's Gaze: German Cinema, Expressionism, and the Image of Horror.* Cambridge: Cambridge University Press, 1991.

Collier, Jo Leslie. *From Wagner to Murnau: The Transposition of Romanticism from Stage to Screen.* Ann Arbor, Mich.: UMI Research Press, 1988.

Coulson, Anthony. "Entrapment and Escape: Readings of the City in Karl Grune's *The Street* and G. W. Pabst's *The Joyless Street.*" In *Expressionist Film–New Perspectives*, edited by Dietrich Scheunemann, 187–200. Rochester, N.Y.: Camden House, 2003.

Crawford, Ronald L. "The Reaffirmation of Germanic Values: Fritz Lang's *Die Nibelungen:* Proceedings of Seventh Annual International Film Conference of Kent State University, April 11 & 12, 1989." In *Varieties of Filmic Expression,* edited by Douglas Radcliff-Umstead, 2–5. Kent, Ohio: Romance Languages Department, Kent State University 1989.

Currie, Hector. "Fritz Lang's *M*: Symbol of Transformation." In *Cinema Drama Schema: Eastern Metaphysics in Western Art,* 149–58. New York: Philosophical Library, 1985.

Dadoun, Roger. "Metropolis: Mother-City–'Mittler'–Hitler." Translated by Arthur Goldhammer. *Camera Obscura,* no. 15 (Fall 1986): 137–63. Reprinted in: *Close Encounters: Film, Feminism, and Science Fiction,* edited by Constance Penley, Elizabeth Lyon, Lynn Spigel, and Janet Bergstrom, 133–59. Minneapolis: University of Minnesota Press, 1991.

Dahlke, Günther, and Karl Günther, eds. *Deutsche Spielfilme von den Anfängen bis 1933: Ein Filmführer.* Berlin: Henschel, 1986.

Dalle Vacche, Angela. "Murnau's *Nosferatu*: Romantic Painting as Horror and Desire in Expressionist Cinema." *Post Script* 14, no. 3 (Summer 1995): 25–36.

Dassanowsky, Robert von. "Der Einfluß Arnold Fanck und Leni Riefenstahl im zeitgenössischen amerikanischen Film." In *Der Bergfilm, 1920–1940,* edited by Friedbert Aspetsberger, 113–24. Innsbruck: Studien Verlag, 2002.

Deppermann, Maria. "Femme Machine: Zum Filmischen Code in Fritz Langs *Metropolis*. In *Semiotik der Geschlechter*, edited by Jeff Bernard, Theresia Klugsberger, and Gloria Whitlan, 157–68. Stuttgart: Akademischer Verlag, 1989.

Dickos, Andrew. "German Expressionism and the Roots of the Film Noir." In *Street with No Name: A History of the Classic American Film Noir*. Lexington: University Press of Kentucky, 2002.

Diethe, Carol. "Anxious Spaces in German Expressionist Films." In *Spaces in European Cinema,* edited by Myrto Konstantarakos, 52–63. Portland, Oreg.: Intellect, 2000.

———. "Beauty and the Beast: An Investigation into the Role and Function of Women in German Expressionist Film." In *Visions of the "Neue Frau": Women and the Visual Arts in Weimar Germany*, edited by Marsha Meskimmon and Shearer West. Aldershot, England: Scolar Press; Brookfield, Vt.: Ashgate, 1995.

Dimendberg, Edward. "From Berlin to Bunker-Hill: Urban Space, Late Modernity, and Film-noir in Fritz Lang's and Joseph Losey's *M*." *Wide Angle,* 19, no. 4 (October 1997): 62–93.

Doane, Mary Ann. "The Erotic Barter: *Pandora's Box* (1929)." In *Femmes Fatales,* 142–63. New York: Routledge, 1991.

Dolgenos, Peter. "The Star on C. A. Rotwang's Door: Turning Kracauer on its Head." *Journal of Popular Film and Television* 25, no. 2 (Summer 1997): 68–75.

Donahue, Neil H. "Unjustly Framed: Politics and Art in *Das Cabinet des Dr. Caligari*." *German Politics and Society,* no. 32 (Summer 1994): 76–88.

Donahue, William Collins. "The Shadow Play of Religion in Fritz Lang's *Metropolis*." *New England Review* 24, no. 4 (Fall 2003): 207–21.

Durgnat, Raymond. "From *Caligari* to Hitler." *Film Comment* 16, no. 4 (July–August 1980): 59–70.

Dyer, Richard. "Less and More Than Women and Men: Lesbian and Gay Cinema in Weimar Germany." Special Issue on Weimar Mass Culture. *New German Critique,* no. 51 (Autumn 1990): 5–60.

———. "Weimar: Less and More Like the Others." In *Now You See It: Studies on Lesbian and Gay Film,* 2nd ed., 23–62. New York: Routledge, 2003.

Eisner, Lotte H. *Fritz Lang.* New ed. Edited by David Robinson. Translated by Gertrud Mander. London: Secker and Warburg, 1976. Reprint. New York: Da Capo, Press, 1986.

———. *The Haunted Screen: Expressionism in the German Cinema and the Influence of Max Reinhardt.* Translated by Roger Greaves. Berkeley and Los Angeles: University of California Press, 1973. Originally published in French, 1952.

———. "Lubitsch and the Costume Film." In *The Haunted Screen: Expressionism in the German Cinema and the Influence of Max Reinhardt*, translated from the French by Roger Greaves, 75–88. Berkeley and Los Angeles: University of California Press, 1973.

———. *Murnau*. Rev. and enl. ed. Berkeley and Los Angeles: University of California Press, 1973.

Eksteins, Modris. "War, Memory, and Politics: The Fate of the Film *All Quiet on the Western Front*." *Central European History* 13, no. 1 (1980): 60–82.

Elsaesser, Thomas. "Cinema: The Irresponsible Signifier: Siegfried Kracauer's Film (of) History." Special Issue on Weimar Film Theory. *New German Critique*, no. 40 (Winter 1987): 65–89.

———. "Film History and Visual Pleasure: Weimar Cinema." In *Cinema Histories, Cinema Practices*, edited by Patricia Mellencamp and Philip Rosen. Frederick, Md.: University Publications of America, 1984.

———. "Fritz Langs Fallen für Geist und Auge: *Dr. Mabuse, der Spieler* und andere Verkleidungskünstler." In *Das Weimarer Kino - aufgeklärt und doppelbödig*, 97–136. Berlin: Vorwerk 8, 1999.

———. "A German Ancestry to Film Noir?" *Iris* (Paris), no. 21 (Spring 1996): 129–44.

———. "Germany: The Weimar Years." In *Oxford World History of Cinema*, new ed., edited by Geoffrey Nowell-Smith, 136–50. Oxford: Oxford University Press, 1999.

———. "Going 'Live': Body and Voice in Some Early German Sound Films." In *Le son en perspective: nouvelles recherches/New Perspectives in Sound Studies*, edited by Dominique Nasta and Didier Huvelle, 155–68. New York: Peter Lang, 2004.

———. "Innocence Restored? Reading and Rereading a 'Classic'." In *Fritz Lang's "Metropolis": Cinematic Views of Technology and Fear*, edited by Michael Minden and Holger Bachmann. Rochester, N.Y.: Camden House, 2000.

———. "Lulu and the Meter Man: Pabst's *Pandora's Box* (1929)." *Screen* 24, nos.4–5 (July-October 1983): 4–36. Also published in *German Film and Literature: Adaptations and Transformations*, edited by Eric Rentschler, 40–59. New York: Methuen, 1986.

———. "*Metropolis*." London: BFI Publishing, 2000.

———. "Secret Affinities: F. W. Murnau." *Sight and Sound*, no. 58 (Winter 1988–1989): 33–39.

———. "Six Degrees of *Nosferatu*." *Sight and Sound* 11, no. 2 (February 2001): 2–15.

———. "Social Mobility and the Fantastic. In *"The Cabinet of Dr. Caligari": Texts, Contexts, Histories*, edited by Mike Budd, 171–89. New Brunswick, N.J.: Rutgers University Press, 1990.

——. "Transparent Duplicities: *The Threepenny Opera*." In *The Films of G. W. Pabst: An Extraterritorial Cinema,* edited by Eric Rentschler, 103–15. New Brunswick, N.J.: Rutgers University Press, 1990.

——. *Weimar Cinema and After: Germany's Historical Imaginary*. New York: Routledge, 2000.

——. "Weimar Cinema, Mobile Selves, and Anxious Males: Kracauer and Eisner Revisited." In *Expressionist Film: New Perspectives*, edited by Dietrich Scheunemann, 33–71. Rochester, N.Y.: Camden House, 2003.

——. *Das Weimarer Kino: aufgeklärt und doppelbödig*. Berlin: Vorwerk 8, 1999.

Elsaesser, Thomas, and Malte Hagener. "Walter Ruttmann: 1929." In *Das Jahr 1929: Beiträge zur Archäologie der Medien*, edited by Stefan Andriopoulos and Bernhard J. Dotzler, 316–49. Frankfurt am Main: Suhrkamp, 2002.

Esser, Michael. "Rooms of Felicity: Architektur und Geheimnis in den Filmen von Fritz Lang." *Filmbulletin,* no. 173 (1990): 22–35.

——. "Zombies im Zauberwald: *Die Nibelungen* von Fritz Lang. In *Das Ufa-Buch: Kunst und Krisen, Stars und Regisseure, Wirtschaft und Politik*, edited by Hans-Michael Bock und Michael Töterberg, 142–45. Frankfurt am Main: Verlag Zweitausendeins, 1992.

Exertier, Sylvain. "La lettre oubliee de *Nosferatu*." *Positif*, no. 228 (March 1980): 47–51.

Eyman, Scott. *Ernst Lubitsch: Laughter in Paradise*. Baltimore: Johns Hopkins University Press, 2000.

Faletti, Heidi. "Reflections of Weimar Cinema in the Nazi Propaganda Films *SA-Mann Brand, Hitlerjunge Quex*, and *Hans Westmar*." In *Cultural History through a National Socialist Lens*, edited by Robert C. Reimer, 11–36. Rochester, N.Y.: Camden House, 2000.

Fanck, Arnold. *Er führte Regie mit Gletschern, Stürmen und Lawinen: Ein Filmpionier erzählt*. Munich: Nymphenburger Verlagshandlung, 1973.

——. *Der Kampf mit dem Berge*. Berlin: Reimar Hobbing, 1931.

——. *"SOS Eisberg"! Mit Dr. Fanck und Ernst Udet in Grönland: Die Grönland-Expedition des Universal-Films*. Munich: Bruckmann, 1933.

——. *"Der weisse Rausch."* Stuttgart: Deutscher Bücherbund, 1973.

Firda, Richard Arthur. "Literary Origins: Sternberg's Film, *The Blue Angel*." *Literature/Film Quarterly* 7, no. 2 (1979): 126–36.

Fischer, Lucy. "Dr. Mabuse and Mr. Lang." *Wide Angle* 3, no. 3 (Winter 1980): 18–26.

Fisher, Peter S. *Fantasy and Politics: Visions of the Future in the Weimar Republic*. Madison: University of Wisconsin Press, 1991.

Fleishman, Avrom. "Dramatized Narration: *The Cabinet of Dr. Caligari* and *Hiroshima Mon Amour*." In *Narrated Films: Storytelling Situations in Cinema History*, 99–127. Baltimore: Johns Hopkins University Press, 1992.

Franju, Georges. "Le style de Fritz Lang." *Cahiers du cinéma,* no. 101 (November 1959): 16–22.

Franklin, James C. "Metamorphosis of a Metaphor: The Shadow in Early German Cinema." *German Quarterly* 53, no. 2 (March 1980): 176–88.

Friedberg, Anne. "An Unheimlich Maneuver between Psychoanalysis and the Cinema: *Secrets of a Soul* (1926)." In *The Films of G. W. Pabst: An Extraterritorial Cinema,* edited by Eric Rentschler, 41–51. New Brunswick, N.J.: Rutgers University Press, 1990.

Fuhrich, Angelika. "Woman and Typewriter: Gender, Technology, and Work in Late Weimar Film." *Women in German Yearbook: Feminist Studies in German Literature and Culture* 16 (2000): 151–66.

Fujiwara, Chris. "The Testaments of Fritz Lang." *Cineaste* 30, no. 2 (Spring 2005): 38–42.

Garncarz, Joseph. "Fritz Lang's *M:* A Case of Significant Film Variation." *Film History* 4, no. 3 (1990): 219–26.

———. "Warum gab es im Stummfilmkino keine deutschen Kinderstars?" In *KINtop: Jahrbuch zur Erforschung des frühen Films.* Vol. 7, *Stummes Spiel, sprechende Gesten,* edited by Frank Kessler, Sabine Lenk, and Martin Loiperdinger, 99–112. Frankfurt am Main: Stroemfeld/Roter Stern, 1998.

Gaughan, Martin. "Ruttmann's *Berlin*: Filming in a 'Hollow Space'." In *Screening the City,* edited by Mark Shiel and Tony Fitzmaurice, 41–57. New York: Verso, 2003.

Gay, Peter. "The Weimar Resemblance." *Horizon* 12, no. 1 (1970): 4–15.

Gehler, Fred. *Friedrich Wilhelm Murnau.* Berlin: Henschel, 1990.

———. "Pioniere und Visionäre 1912–1933." In *Filmstadt Babelsberg: Zur Geschichte des Studios und seiner Filme,* edited by Axel Geiss. Potsdam: Filmmuseum Potsdam; Berlin: Nicolai, 1994.

Gehler, Fred, and Ullrich Kasten. *Fritz Lang: Die Stimme von "Metropolis."* Berlin: Henschel, 1990.

Geiss, Axel, ed. *Filmstadt Babelsberg: Zur Geschichte des Studios und seiner Filme.* Potsdam: Filmmuseum Potsdam; Berlin: Nicolai, 1994.

Genova, Judith A. "Wittgenstein and *Caligari.*" *Philosophical Forum* n.s., 4, no. 2 (Winter 1972–1973): 186–98.

Geser, Guntram. *Fritz Lang: "Metropolis" und "Die Frau im Mond": Zukunftsfilm und Zukunftstechnik in der Stabilisierungszeit der Weimarer Republik.* Meitingen: Corian-Verlag Heinrich Wimmer, 1996.

Glass, Erlis. "Entrepreneurial Empowerment of Women in Brecht's *Dreigroschenoper*: Film versus Theaterstuck." *Anuario de Cine y Literatura en Espanol: An International Journal on Film and Literature,* no. 2 (1996): 81–91.

Gleber, Anke. *The Art of Taking a Walk: Flanerie, Literature, and Film in Weimar Culture.* Princeton, N.J.: Princeton University Press, 1999.

——. "Female Flanerie and the Symphony of the City." In *Women in the Metropolis: Gender and Modernity in Weimar Culture*, edited by Katharina von Ankum, 67–88. Berkeley and Los Angeles: University of California Press, 1997.

——. "The Woman and the Camera—Walking in Berlin: Observations on Walter Ruttmann, Verena Stefan, and Helke Sander." In *Berlin in Focus: Cultural Transformations in Germany*, edited by Barbara Becker-Cantarino, 105–24. Westport, Conn.: Praeger, 1996.

Goergen, Jeanpaul, ed. *Walter Ruttmann: Eine Dokumentation*. Berlin: Freunde der Dt. Kinemathek, 1989.

Gökturk, Deniz. "How Modern Is It? Moving Images of America in Early German Cinema." In *Hollywood in Europe: Experiences of a Cultural Hegemony*, edited by David W. Ellwood and Rob Kroes, 44–67. Amsterdam: Vrije Universiteit Press, 1994.

Goss, Mimi Tennyson. *The Democratic Spirit of the Weimar Cinema*. Cambridge, Mass.: Research Programs, John F. Kennedy School of Government, Harvard University, 1994.

Grafe, Frieda, Enno Patalas, and Hans Prinzler. *Fritz Lang*. Munich: Hanser, 1976.

Gramman, Karola, and Heide Schlüpmann. "Love as Opposition, Opposition as Love: Thoughts about Hertha Thiele." In *Herthe Thiele*, edited by Hans Helmut Prinzler. Berlin: Stiftung Deutsche Kinematek, 1983. Also published online as *Mädchen in Uniform*. Parts 1–2. Translated by Leoni Naughton. www.latrobe.edu.au/screeningthepast/reruns/thiele.html.

Greve, Ludwig, Margot Pehle, and Heidi Westhoff, eds. *"Hätte ich das Kino!" Die Schriftsteller und der Stummfilm; Eine Ausstellung des Deutschen Literaturarchivs im Schiller-Nationalmuseum Marbach a.N. von vom 24. April bis 31. Oktober 1976*. Munich: Kösel Verlag, 1976.

Grob, Norbert. "'Bringing the Ghostly to Life': Fritz Lang and His Early Dr. Mabuse Films." In *Expressionist Film: New Perspectives*, edited by Dietrich Scheunemann, 87–110. Rochester, N.Y.: Camden House, 2003.

Guerin, Frances. *A Culture of Light: Cinema and Technology in 1920s Germany*. Minneapolis: University of Minnesota Press, 2005.

Gunning, Tom. *The Films of Fritz Lang: Allegories of Vision and Modernity*. London: BFI Publishing, 2000.

Güttinger, Fritz. *Der Stummfilm in Zitat der Zeit*. Frankfurt am Main: Deutsches Filmmuseum, 1984.

Güttinger, Fritz, ed. *Kein Tag ohne Kino: Schriftsteller über den Stummfilm*. Frankfurt am Main: Deutsches Filmmuseum, 1984.

——. *Köpfen Sie mal ein Ei in Zeitlupe! Streifzüge durch die Welt des Stummfilms*. Zurich: NZZ Verlag, 1992.

Hake, Sabine. "Architectural Hi/Stories: Fritz Lang and *The Nibelungs.*" *Wide Angle* 12, no. 3 (July 1990): 38–57.

———. "Chaplin Reception in Weimar Germany." Special Issue on Weimar Mass Culture. *New German Critique,* no. 51 (Autumn 1990): 87–111.

———. *The Cinema's Third Machine: Writing on Film in Germany, 1907–1933.* Lincoln: University of Nebraska Press, 1993.

———. "Lubitsch's Period Films as Palimpsest: On Passion and Deception." In *Framing the Past: The Historiography of German Cinema and Television,* edited by Bruce A. Murray and Christopher J. Wickham, 68–98. Carbondale: Southern Illinois University Press, 1992.

———. *Passions and Deception: The Early Films of Ernst Lubitsch.* Princeton, N.J.: Princeton University Press, 1992.

———. "Urban Spectacle in Walter Ruttmann's *Berlin, Symphony of the Big City.*" In *Dancing on the Volcano: Essays on the Culture of the Weimar Republic,* edited by Thomas W. Kniesche and Stephen Brockmann, 127–42. Columbia, S.C.: Camden House, 1994.

Hales, Barbara. "Fritz Lang's *Metropolis* and Reactionary Modernism." *New German Review* 8 (1992): 18–30.

Hall, Kenneth E. "Von Sternberg, Lubitsch, and Lang in the Work of Manuel Puig." *Literature/Film Quarterly* 22, no. 3 (July 1994): 181–87.

Hansen, Miriam. "Decentric Perspectives: Kracauer's Early Writings on Film and Mass Culture." Special Issue on Siegfried Kracauer. *New German Critique,* no. 54 (Autumn 1991): 47–76.

Hantke, Steffen, ed. *Caligari's Heirs: The German Cinema of Fear after 1945.* Lanham, Md.: Scarecrow Press, 2006.

Hardt, Ursula. *From "Caligari" to California: Erich Pommer's Life in the International Film Wars.* New York: Berghahn Books, 1996.

Hauer, Stanley R. "The Sources of Fritz Lang's *Die Nibelungen.*" Silent Cinema Issue: D. W. Griffith, Fritz Lang, Erich von Stroheim, et al. *Literature/Film Quarterly* 18, no. 2 (April 1990): 103–10.

Hensley, Wayne E. "The Contribution of F.W. Murnau's *Nosferatu* to the Evolution of Dracula." *Literature/Film Quarterly* 30, no. 1 (2002): 59–64.

Hoeppner, Klaus. *Fritz Lang: Filmblatter, Filmografie, Bibliografie.* Berlin: Filmmuseum; Berlin: Internationale Filmfestspiele Berlin, 2001.

Hogue, Peter. "True Blue." [director's original cut of *The Blue Angel*] *Film Comment* 30, no. 2 (March–April 1994): 38–42.

Horak, Jan-Christopher. "Film History and Film Preservation: Reconstructing the Text of *The Joyless Street* (1925)." *Screening the Past,* no. 5 (November 16, 1998). www.latrobe.edu.au/screeningthepast/firstrelease/fir1298/jhfr5b.html

———. "The Pre-Hollywood Lubitsch." *Image* (Rochester, N.Y.) 18, no. 4 (1975): 19–29.

——. "Schadenfreude: Deutsche Filmkomödien und Karl Valentin." In *KIN-top: Jahrbuch zur Erforschung des frühen Films*. Vol. 1, *Früher Film in Deutschland*, edited by Frank Kessler, Sabine Lenk, and Martin Loiperdinger, 58–74. Frankfurt am Main: Stroemfeld/Roter Stern, 1993.

Horak, Jan-Christopher, with Gisela Pichler, eds. *Berge, Licht und Traum: Dr. Arnold Fanck und der deutsche Bergfilm*. Munich: Bruckmann, 1997.

Humphries, Reynold. *Fritz Lang: Genre and Representation in his American Films*. Baltimore: Johns Hopkins University Press, 1989.

Hunt, Leon. *"The Student of Prague:* Division and Codification of Space." In *Early Cinema: Space, Frame, Narrative*, edited by Thomas Elsaesser, 389–402. London: BFI Publishing, 1990.

Huyssen, Andreas. "The Vamp and the Machine: Technology and Sexuality in Fritz Lang's *Metropolis*." Special Double Issue on New German Cinema. *New German Critique*, nos. 24–25 (Autumn 1981–Winter 1982): 221–37. Also in *After the Great Divide: Modernism, Mass Culture, Postmodernism*, by Andreas Huyssen, 65–81. Bloomington: University of Indiana Press, 1986.

Isaacs, Neil D. "Lubitsch and the Filmed-play Syndrome." *Literature/Film Quarterly* 3, no. 4 (Autumn 1975): 299–308.

Jacobsen, Wolfgang. *G. W. Pabst*. Berlin: Argon, 1997.

——. *"Metropolis": Ein filmisches Laboratorium der modernen Architek-tur/"Metropolis": A Cinematic Laboratory for Modern Architecture*. Stuttgart: Edition Axel Menges, 2000.

Jacoby, Alexander. "Tartuff." *Senses of Cinema: An Online Film Journal Devoted to the Serious and Eclectic Discussion of Cinema*, no. 28 (September–October 2003). www.sensesofcinema.com/contents/cteq/03/28/tartuff.html

Jacques, Norbert. *"Dr. Mabuse, der Spieler": Roman, Film, Dokumente*. Edited by Günter Scholdt. St. Ingbert: W. J. Rohrig, 1987.

Jansen, Peter W., and Wolfram Schütte, eds. *Friedrich Wilhelm Murnau*. Munich: Carl Hanser, 1990.

Jansen, Wolfgang W. "Kino und Varieté." In *Das Varieté: Die glanzvolle Geschichte einer unterhaltenden Kunst*, 145–54. Berlin: Edition Hentrich. 1990.

Jason, Alexander. *Der Film in Ziffern und Zahlen: Die Statistik der Lichtspiel-häuser in Deutschland, 1895–1925*. Berlin: Deutsches Druck- und Ver-lagshaus, 1925.

Jelavich, Peter. *"Berlin Alexanderplatz": Radio, Film, and the Death of Weimar Culture*. Berkeley and Los Angeles: University of California Press, 2006.

Jenkins, Stephen, ed. *Fritz Lang: The Image and the Look*. London: BFI Pub-lishing, 1981.

Jensen, Paul M. *The Cinema of Fritz Lang*. New York: A. S. Barnes, 1969.

Jones, Nicholas. "Hamlet in Warsaw: The Antic Disposition of Ernst Lubitsch." Hamlet on Film: A Special Supplement. *EnterText: An Interactive Interdisciplinary E-Journal for Cultural and Historical Studies and Creative Work* 1, no. 2 (Spring 2001). http://people.brunel.ac.uk/~acsrrrm/entertext/hamlet/jones.pdf

Josse, Harald. *Die Entstehung des Tonfilms: Beitrag zu einer faktenorientierten Mediengeschichtsschreibung.* Munich: Alber, 1984.

Jubak, James. "Lang and Parole: Character and Narrative in *Doktor Mabuse, der Spieler.*" *Film Criticism* 4, no. 1 (Fall 1979): 25–34.

Jung, Uli, and Walter Schatzberg. *Beyond "Caligari": The Films of Robert Wiene.* New York: Berghahn Books, 1999.

———. "The Invisible Man Behind *Caligari*: The Life of Robert Wiene." *Film History* 5, no. 1 (March 1993): 22–35.

Kaes, Anton. "Cinema and Modernity: On Fritz Lang's *Metropolis.*" In *High and Low Cultures: German Attempts at Mediation,* edited by Reinhold Grimm and Jost Hermand, 19–35. Madison: University of Wisconsin Press for Monatshefte, 1994.

———. "The Debate about Cinema: Charting a Controversy (1909–1929)." Special Issue on Weimar Film Theory. *New German Critique,* no. 40 (Winter 1987): 7–33.

———. *M.* London: BFI Publishing, 2000.

———. "Mass Culture and Modernity: Notes Toward a Social History of Early American and German Cinema." In *America and the Germans: An Assessment of a Three-Hundred-Year History.* Vol. 2, *The Relationship in the Twentieth Century,* edited by Frank Trommler and Joseph McVeigh, 317–31. Philadelphia: University of Pennysylvania Press, 1990.

———. "Modernity and Its Discontents: Notes on Alterity in Weimar Cinema." Translated by David Levin. *qui parle: Literature, Philosophy, Visual Arts, History* 5, no. 2 (Spring–Summer 1992): 135–42.

———. "Silent Cinema." *Monatshefte* 82, no. 3 (1990): 246–56.

———. "Weimar Cinema: The Predicament of Modernity." In *European Cinema,* edited by Elizabeth Ezra, 59–77. Oxford: Oxford University Press, 2004.

Kaes, Anton, ed. *Kino-Debatte: Texte zum Verhältnis von Literatur und Film, 1910–1929.* Tübingen: Max Niemeyer Verlag; Munich: Deutscher Taschenbuchverlag, 1978.

Kaplan, E. Ann. *Fritz Lang, a Guide to References and Resources.* Boston: G. K. Hall, 1981.

———. "Fritz Lang and German Expressionism: A Reading of *Dr. Mabuse, der Spieler.*" In *Passion and Rebellion: The Expressionist Heritage,* edited by Stephen Eric Bronner and Douglas Kellner, 398–408. South Hadley, Mass.: J. F. Bergin, 1983.

Kappelhoff, Hermann. *Der moblierte Mensch: G.W. Pabst und die Utopie der Sachlichkeit.* Berlin: Vorwerk 8, 1994.

Kester, Bernadette. *Film Front Weimar: Representations of the First World War in German Films on the Weimar Period (1919–1933).* Amsterdam: Amsterdam University Press, 2003. Distributed in the U.S. by the University of Chicago Press.

Ketchiff, Nancy. "Dr. Caligari's Cabinet: A Cubist Perspective." *Comparatist: Journal of the Southern Comparative Literature Association* 8 (May 1984): 7–13.

Kinter, Jürgen. *Arbeiterbewegung und Film (1895–1933).* Hamburg: Medienpädagogik-Zentrum, 1985.

Koch, Gertrud. "Between Two Worlds: Von Sternberg's *The Blue Angel* (1930)." In *German Film and Literature: Adaptations and Transformations*, edited by Eric Rentschler, 60–72. New York: Methuen, 1986.

——. *Kracauer zur Einführung.* Hamburg: Junius, 1995.

——. *Siegfried Kracauer: An Introduction.* Translated by Jeremy Gaines. Princeton, N.J.: Princeton University Press, 2000.

Koebner, Thomas. "Caligaris Wiederkehr in Hollywood? Stummfilm-Expressionismus, 'Filmemigranten' und Film noir." In *Innen-Leben: Ansichten aus dem Exil: Ein Berliner Symposium*, edited by Hermann Haarmann, 107–19. Berlin: Fannei and Walz, 1995.

——. "Der Film als neue Kunst—Reaktionen der literarischen Intelligenz: Zur Theorie des Stummfilms (1911–1924)." In *Literaturwissenschaft-Medienwissenschaff*, edited by Helmut Kreuzer, 1–31. Heidelberg: Quelle and Meyer, 1977.

——. "Murnau-A Conservative Filmmaker? On Film History as Intellectual History." In *Expressionist Film—New Perspectives*, edited by Dietrich Scheunemann, 111–23. Rochester, N.Y.: Camden House, 2003.

Koll, Gerald. *Pandoras Schätze: Erotikkonzeptionen in den Stummfilmen von G. W. Pabst.* Munich: Diskurs Film Verlag, 1998.

Koller, Michael. "Faust." *Senses of Cinema: An Online Film Journal Devoted to the Serious and Eclectic Discussion of Cinema*, no. 28 (September–October 2003). www.sensesofcinema.com/contents/cteq/03/28/faust.html

——. "Nosferatu." *Senses of Cinema: An Online Film Journal Devoted to the Serious and Eclectic Discussion of Cinema*, no. 8 (July–August 2000). www.sensesofcinema.com/contents/cteq/00/8/nosferatu.html

Konigsberg, Ira. "Cinema, Psychoanalysis, and Hermeneutics: G. W. Pabst's *Secrets of a Soul*." In *The Movies: Texts, Receptions, Exposures*, edited by Laurence Goldstein and Ira Konigsberg, 11–39. Ann Arbor: University of Michigan Press, 1996.

Korte, Helmut, ed. *Film und Realität in der Weimarer Republik.* Munich: Carl Hanser, 1978.

——. "Die Welt als Querschnitt: *Berlin - Die Sinfonie der Großstadt* (1927)." In *Fischer Filmgeschichte.* Vol. 2, *Der Film als gesellschaftliche Kraft*, edited by Werner Faulstich and Helmut Korte, 75–91. Frankfurt am Main: Fischer Taschenbuch, 1991.

Kracauer, Siegfried. "The *Cabinet of Dr. Caligari.*" In *Film Theory and Criticism: Introductory Readings*, 6th ed., edited by Leo Braudy and Marshall Cohen, 154–65. New York: Oxford University Press, 2004.

——. "Cult of Distraction: On Berlin's Picture Palaces." Translated by Thomas Y. Levin. Special Issue on Weimar Film Theory. *New German Critique*, no. 40 (Winter 1987): 91–96.

——. *From "Caligari" to Hitler: A Psychological History of the German Film.* Princeton, N.J.: Princeton University Press, 1947.

——. *The Mass Ornament: Weimar Essays.* Translated by Thomas Y. Levin. Cambridge: Harvard University Press, 1995.

Kramer, Steven Phillip. "Fritz Lang's Definitive *Siegfried* and Its Versions." *Literature/Film Quarterly* 13, no. 4 (1985): 258–74.

Kreimeier, Klaus, ed. *Zur Metaphysik des Dekors: Raum, Architektur und Licht im klassischen deutschen Stummfilm.* Marburg: Schüren Verlag, 1994.

Lamprecht, Gerhard. *Deutsche Stummfilme 1903–1931.* 9 vols. Berlin: Deutsche Kinemathek, 1966–1970.

Lang, Fritz. *Fritz Lang: Interviews.* Edited by Barry Keith Grant. Jackson: University Press of Mississippi, 2003.

——. "Fritz Lang on Dr. Mabuse." *Monthly Film Bulletin* 45, no. 531 (April 1978): 80.

Leblans, Anne. "Inventing Male Wombs: The Fairy-tale Logic of *Metropolis.*" In *Peripheral Visions: The Hidden Stages of Weimar Cinema*, edited by Kenneth S. Calhoon, 95–119. Detroit: Wayne State University Press, 2001.

Leduc, Jacques, Andres Poirier, and Pierre Theberge. "Entretien avec Louise Brooks." *Positif,* no. 297 (November 1985): 6–11.

Levin, David J. *Richard Wagner, Fritz Lang, and the Nibelungen: The Dramaturgy of Disavowal.* Princeton, N.J.: Princeton University Press, 1998.

Liebman, Stuart. "Weimar Cinema's Greatest Hits." *Cineaste* 21, no. 3 (June 1995): 50–52.

Liebmann, Robert. *"The Blue Angel": An Authorized Translation of the German Continuity.* New York: Simon & Schuster, 1968.

Littau, Karin. "Refractions of the Feminine: The Monstrous Transformations of Lulu." *MLN* 110, no. 4 (September 1995): 888–912.

Loewy, Hanno. *"Das blaue Licht."* In *Béla Balazs: Märchen, Ritual und Film*, 320–50. Berlin: Vorwerk 8, 2003.

Luhr, William. *"Nosferatu* and Postwar German Film." *Michigan Academician* 14, no. 4 (Spring 1982): 453–58.

Lungstrum, Janet. "Metropolis and the Technosexual Woman of German Modernity." In *Women in the Metropolis: Gender and Modernity in Weimar Culture*, edited by Katharina von Ankum, 128–44. Berkeley and Los Angeles: University of California Press, 1997.

Mack, Michael. "Film as Memory: Siegfried Kracauers's Psychological History of German 'National Culture'." *Journal of European Studies* 30, no. 118 (2000 June): 157–81.

Macrae, David. "Ruttmann, Rhythm, and 'Reality': A Response to Siegfried Kracauer's Interpretation of *Berlin: The Symphony of a Great City*." In *Expressionist Film—New Perspectives*, edited by Dietrich Scheunemann, 251–69. Rochester, N.Y.: Camden House, 2003.

Madsen, Axel. "Lang." *Sight and Sound* 36, no. 3 (Summer 1967): 108–12.

Maibohm, Ludwig. *Fritz Lang, seine Filme—sein Leben*. Munich: Wilhelm Heyne, 1981.

Malone, Paul M. "Negotiating Modernity in Weimar Film Theory." *Film Philosophy* 3, no. 37 (September 1999).

Murnau, F. W., and Enno Patalas. *Südseebilder: Texte, Fotos und der Film Tabu*. Berlin: Bertz + Fischer, 2005.

Mayne, Judith. "Dracula in the Twilight: Murnau's *Nosferatu*." In *German Film and Literature: Adaptations and Transformations*, edited by Eric Rentschler, 25–39. New York: Methuen, 1986.

———. "Marlene Dietrich, *The Blue Angel*, and Female Performance." In *Seduction and Theory: Readings of Gender, Representation, and Rhetoric*, edited by Dianne Hunter, 28–46. Urbana: University of Illinois Press, 1989.

McCormick, Richard W. "From Caligari to Dietrich: Sexual, Social, and Cinematic Discourses in Weimar Film." *Signs: Journal of Women in Culture and Society* 18, no. 3 (Spring 1993): 640–68.

———. *Gender and Sexuality in Weimar Modernity: Film, Literature, and "New Objectivity."* New York: Palgrave, 2001.

———. "Private Anxieties/Public Projections: 'New Objectivity,' Male Subjectivity, and Weimar Cinema." *Women in German Yearbook: Feminist Studies in German Literature and Culture* 10 (1994): 1–18.

Mellencamp, Patricia. "Oedipus and the Robot in *Metropolis*." *Enclitic* 5, no. 1 (Spring 1981): 20–42.

Minden, Michael. "The City in Early Cinema: Metropolis, Berlin and October." In *Unreal City: Urban Experience in Modern European Literature and Art*, edited by Edward Timms and David Kelley, 193–213. Manchester, England: Manchester University Press, 1985.

———. "Lang's *Metropolis* and the United States." *German Life and Letters* 53, no. 3 (July 2000): 340–50.

———. "Politics and the Silent Cinema: The *Cabinet of Dr. Caligari* and *Battleship* Potemkin." In *Visions and Blueprints: Avant-Garde Culture and Rad-*

ical Politics in Early Twentieth-century Europe, edited by Edward Timms, and Peter Collier, 287–306. Manchester, England: Manchester University Press, 1988.

Minden, Michael, and Holger Bachmann, eds. *Fritz Lang's Metropolis: Cinematic Visions of Technology and Fear.* Rochester, N.Y.: Camden House, 2000.

Monaco, Paul. *Cinema and Society: France and Germany during the Twenties.* New York: Elsevier, 1976.

Murphy, Richard J. "Carnival Desire and the Sideshow of Fantasy: Dream, Duplicity and Representational Instability in the *Cabinet of Dr. Caligari.*" *Germanic Review* 66, no. 1 (Winter 1991): 48–56.

Murray, Bruce A. *Film and the German Left in the Weimar Republic: From "Caligari" to "Kuhle Wumpe."* Austin: University of Texas Press, 1990.

———. "An Introduction to the Commercial Film Industry in Germany from 1895 to 1933." In *Film and Politics in the Weimar Republic*, edited by Thomas G. Plummer et al., 23–33. New York: Holmes and Meier, 1982.

Myers, Tracy. "History and Realism: Representations of Women in G. W. Pabst's *The Joyless Street.*" In *Gender and German Cinema: Feminist Interventions.* Vol. 2, *German Film History/German History on Film*, edited by Sandra Frieden, Richard W. McCormick, Vibeke R. Petersen, and Laurie Melissa Vogelsang, 259–71. Providence, R.I.: Berg, 1993.

Naber, Hermann. "Ruttmann und Konsorten: Über die frühen Beziehungen zwischen Hörspiel und Film." *Rundfunk und Geschichte* 32, nos. 3–4 (2006): 5–20.

Nenno, Nancy P. "'Postcards from the Edge': Education to Tourism in the German Mountain Film." In *Light Motives: German Popular Film in Perspective*, edited by Randall Halle and Margaret McCarthy, 61–84. Detroit: Wayne State University Press, 2003.

Neumann, Dietrich, ed. *Film Architecture: Set Designs from "Metropolis" to "Blade Runner".* Munich: Prestel, 1996.

———. "The Urbanistic Vision in Fritz Lang's *Metropolis.*" In *Dancing on the Volcano: Essays on the Culture of the Weimar Republic*, edited by Thomas W. Kniesche and Stephen Brockmann, 143–62. Columbia, S.C.: Camden House, 1994.

Ott, Frederick W. *The Films of Fritz Lang.* Secaucus, N.J.: Citadel Press, 1979.

Pabst, G. W. *Pandora's Box (Lulu): A Film.* Rev. ed. Translated from the German by Christopher Holme. London: Lorrimer, 1984.

Papapetros, Spyridon. "Malicious Houses: Animation, Animism, Animosity in German Architecture and Film–from Mies to Murnau." *Grey Room*, no. 20 (Fall 2005): 6–37.

Patalas, Enno. *"Metropolis" in/aus Trummern: eine Filmgeschichte.* Berlin: Bertz, 2001.

——. *"Metropolis*, Scene 103." *Camera Obscura*, no. 15 (Fall 1986): 164–73. Also published in *Close Encounters: Film, Feminism, and Science Fiction*, edited by Constance Penley, Elisabeth Lyon, Lynn Spigel, and Janet Bergstrom, 161–70. Minneapolis: University of Minnesota Press, 1991.

Paver, Chloe E. M. " 'Als Hitler und der Tonfilm kamen': Cinematic, Technological, and Historical Narratives in Gert Hofmann's Der Kinoerzähler." *Modern Language Review* 97, no. 3 (July 2002): 32–52.

Pegge, C. Denis. *"Caligari*: Its Innovations in Editing." *Quarterly of Film, Radio, and Television* 11, no. 2 (Winter 1956): 136–48.

Pehla, Karen. "Joe May und seine Detektive: Der Serienfilm als Kinoerlebnis." In *Joe May: Regisseur und Produzent*, edited by Hans-Michael Bock and Clauia Lenssen, 61–72. Munich: edition text + kritik, 1991.

Perez, Gilberto. *"Nosferatu."* *Raritan: A Quarterly Review* 13, no. 1 (Summer 1993): 1–28.

Petrie, Graham. *Hollywood Destinies: European Directors in America after World War I, 1922–1931*. Rev. and updated ed. Detroit: Wayne State University Press, 2002.

Petro, Patrice. *Joyless Streets: Women and Melodramatic Representation in Weimar Germany*. Princeton, N.J.: Princeton University Press, 1989.

——. "Perceptions of Difference: Woman as Spectator and Spectacle." In *Women in the Metropolis: Gender and Modernity in Weimar Culture*, edited by Katharina von Ankum, 41–66. Berkeley and Los Angeles: University of California Press, 1997.

——. "World Weariness, Weimar Women, and Visual Culture." In *Aftershocks of the New: Feminism and Film History*, 95–123. New Brunswick, N.J.: Rutgers University, 2000.

Phillips, Gene D. "Fritz Lang Remembers." *Focus on Film*, no. 20 (Spring 1975): 43–51.

Pike, David L. "'Kaliko-Welt': The Großstädte of Lang's *Metropolis* and Brecht's *Dreigroschenoper*." *MLN* 119, no. 3 (Spring 2004): 474–505.

Plummer, Thomas G., Bruce A. Murrey, and Linda Schulte-Sasse, eds. *Film and Politics in the Weimar Republic*. New York: Holmes and Meier, 1984.

Poague, Leland A. *The Cinema of Ernst Lubitsch*. South Brunswick, N.J.: A. S. Barnes, 1978.

Pratt, David B. "'O Lubitsch, Where Wert Thou?': Passion, the German Invasion and the Emergence of the Name 'Lubitsch'." *Wide Angle* 13, no. 1 (January 1991): 34–70.

Prawer, S. S. *Between Two Worlds: Jewish Presences in German and Austrian Film, 1910–1933*. New York: Berghahn Books, 2005.

——. *"The Blue Angel."* London: BFI, 2002.

Prinzler, Hans Helmut, ed. *Herthe Thiele*. Berlin: Stiftung Deutsche Kinematek, 1983.

Prinzler, Hans Helmut, and Enno Patalas, eds. *Lubitsch.* Munich: C. J. Bucher.

Rapp, Christian. *Höhenrausch: Der Deutsche Bergfilm.* Vienna: Sonderzahl Verlag, 1997.

Renk, Herta-Elisabeth. *Ernst Lubitsch: mit Selbstzeugnissen und Bilddokumenten.* Reinbek bei Hamburg: Rowohlt, 1992.

Rentschler, Eric, ed. *The Films of G. W. Pabst: An Extraterritorial Cinema.* New Brunswick: Rutgers University Press, 1990.

——. "Hochgebirge und Moderne: Eine Standortbestimmung des Bergfilms." In *Berge, Licht und Traum: Dr. Arnold Fanck und der deutsche Bergfilm*, edited by Jan-Christopher Horak with Gisela Pichler, 85–102. Munich: Bruckmann, 1997.

——. "Mountains and Modernity: Relocating the Bergfilm." Special Issue on Weimar Mass Culture. *New German Critique,* no. 51. (Autumn 1990): 137–61.

Rich, B. Ruby. "From Repressive Tolerance to Erotic Liberation: *Girls in Uniform.*" *Jump Cut,* nos. 24–25 (March 1981): 44–50. Reprinted in *Re-vision, Essays in Feminist Film Criticism*, edited by Mary Ann Doane, Patricia Mellencamp, and Linda Williams, 100–130. Los Angeles: American Film Institute, 1984. Also published in *Gender and German Cinema: Feminist Interventions.* Vol. 2, *German Film History/German History on Film*, edited by Sandra Frieden, Richard W. McCormick, Vibeke R. Petersen, and Laurie Melissa Vogelsang, 61–96. Providence, R.I.: Berg, 1993.

Riefenstahl, Leni. *Kampf in Schnee und Eis.* Leipzig: Hesse and Becker, 1933.

Riess, Curt. *Das gab's nur einmal: Die große Zeit des deutschen Films.* 2 vols. Frankfurt am Main: Ullstein, 1985.

Rogowski, Christian. "From Ernst Lubitsch to Joe May: Challenging Kracauer's Demonology with Weimar Popular Film." In *Light Motives: German Popular Film in Perspective*, edited by Randall Halle and Margaret McCarthy, 1–23. Detroit: Wayne State University Press, 2003.

Roper, Katherine. "Looking for the German Revolution in Weimar films." *Central European History* 31, nos. 1–2 (Winter–Spring, 1998): 65–90.

Roth, Lane. "Dracula Meets the Zeitgeist: *Nosferatu* (1922) as Film Adaptation." *Literature/Film Quarterly* 7, no. 4 (1979): 309–13.

——. "Film, Society and Ideas: *Nosferatu* and Horror of Dracula." In *Planks of Reason: Essays on the Horror Film*, edited by Barry Keith Grant, 245–54. Metuchen, N.J.: Scarecrow Press, 1984.

——. "*Metropolis*, the Lights Fantastic: Semiotic Analysis of Lighting Codes in Relation to Character and Theme." *Literature/Film Quarterly* 6, no. 4 (1978): 342–46.

Rotondi, Cesar J. "The 1984 Review, the 1927 Review, Fritz Lang: The Maker of *Metropolis.*" *Films in Review* 35 (October 1984): 464–69.

Rubenstein, Lenny. "*Caligari* and the Rise of the Expressionist Film." In *Passion and Rebellion: The Expressionist Heritage*, edited by Stephen Eric Bronner and Douglas Kellner. South Hadley, Mass.: J. F. Bergin, 1983.

Ruppert, Peter. "Fritz Lang's *Metropolis* and the Imperatives of the Science Fiction Film." *Seminar: A Journal of Germanic Studies* 37, no. 1 (February 2001): 21–32.

Russell, Catherine. "Beyond Pleasure: Lang and Mortification." In *Narrative Mortality: Death, Closure, and New Wave Cinemas,* 31–66. Minneapolis: Minnesota University Press, 1995.

Rutsky, R. L. "The Mediation of Technology and Gender: *Metropolis*, Nazism, Modernism." Special Issue on German Film History. *New German Critique*, no. 60 (Autumn 1993): 3–32. Also published in *Fritz Lang's "Metropolis": Cinematic Views of Technology and Fear*, edited by Michael Minder and Holger Bachmann, 217–45. Rochester, N.Y.: Camden House, 2000.

Salber, Linde. *Marlene Dietrich.* Reinbek bei Hamburg: Rowohlt, 2001.

Salt, Barry. "From *Caligari* to Who?" *Sight and Sound* 48, no. 2 (Spring 1979): 119–23.

Sandford, John. "Chaos and Control in the Weimar Film." *German Life and Letters* 48, no. 3 (July 1995): 311–23.

Saunders, Thomas J. "Comedy as Redemption: American Slapstick in Weimar Culture." *Journal of European Studies* 17, no. 4 (December 1987): 253–77.

———. "Germany and Film Europe." In *Film Europe and Film America: Cinema, Commerce and Cultural Exchange, 1920–1939*, edited by Andrew Higson and Richard Maltby. Exeter, England: Exeter University Press, 1999.

———. "History in the Making: Weimar Cinema and National Identity." In *Framing the Past: The Historiography of German Cinema and Television*, edited by Bruce A. Murray and Christopher J. Wickham, 42–67. Carbondale: Southern Illinois University Press, 1992.

Sawyer, Andy. "More Than Metaphor: Double Vision in Lang's *Metropolis*." *Foundation: The Review of Science Fiction*, no. 64 (Summer 1995): 70–81.

Schaal, Hans Dieter. "Spaces of the Psyche in German Expressionist Film." *Architectural Design* 70, no. 1 (January 2000): 12–15.

Schanze, Helmut. "On Murnau's *Faust*: A Generic Gesamtkunstwerk?" In *Expressionist Film—New Perspectives*, edited by Dietrich Scheunemann, 223–35. Rochester, N.Y.: Camden House, 2003.

Scheunemann, Dietrich. "The Double, the Decor, and the Framing Device: Once More on Robert Wiene's *The Cabinet of Dr. Caligari*." In *Expressionist Film—New Perspectives*, edited by Dietrich Scheunemann, 125–56. Rochester, N.Y.: Camden House, 2003.

———, ed. *Expressionist Film—New Perspectives*. Rochester, N.Y.: Camden House, 2003.

Schindler, Stephan. "What Makes a Man a Man: The Construction of Masculinity in F. W. Murnau's *The Last Laugh*." *Screen* 37, no. 1 (Spring 1996): 30–40.

Schlemmer, Gottfried, Bernhard Riff, and Georg Haberl, eds. *G. W. Pabst*. Münster: MakS Publikationen, 1990.

Schlüpmann, Heide. "Wahrheit und Lüge im Zeitalter der technischen Reproduzierbarkeit: Detektiv und Heroine bei Joe May." In *Joe May: Regisseur und Produzent*, edited by Hans-Michael Bock and Claudia Lenssen, 45–60. Munich: edition text + kritik, 1991.

Schönfeld, Christiane "Modern Identities in Early German Film: *The Cabinet of Dr. Caligari*." In *Engaging Film: Geographies of Mobility and Identity*, edited by Tim Cresswell and Deborah Dixon, 174–90. Lanham, Md.: Rowman & Littlefield, 2002.

Schwarz, Alexander. *Der geschriebene Film: Drehbücher des deutschen und russischen Stummfilms*. Munich: diskurs film Verlag, 1994.

Seidel, Renate, and Allan Hagedorff, eds. *Asta Nielsen: Ihr Leben in Fotodokumenten, Selbstzeugnissen und zeitgenössischen Betrachtungen*, Berlin: Henschel, 1981.

"Siegfried Kracauer." Special issue, *New German Critique*, no. 54 (Autumn 1991): 1–189.

Siodmak, Robert. *Zwischen Berlin und Hollywood: Erinnerungen eines großen Filmregisseurs*. Munich: F. A. Herbig, 1980.

Smith, Evans Lansing. "Framing the Underworld: Threshold Imagery in Murnau, Cocteau, and Bergman." *Literature/Film Quarterly* 24, no. 3 (July 1996): 241–54.

Solomon, Stanley J. "*The Cabinet of Dr. Caligari*." In *The Classic Cinema; Essays in Criticism*, edited by Stanley J. Solomon. New York: Harcourt Brace Jovanovich, 1973.

Sorge, Ernst. *Mit Flugzeug, Faltboot und Filmkamera in den Eisfjorden Grönlands*. Berlin: Die Drei Masken Verlag, 1933.

Spaich, Herbert. *Ernst Lubitsch und seine Filme*. Munich: Wilhelm Heyne, 1992.

Spreng, Eberhard. "Propaganda als Unterhaltung? Drei Regisseure des deutschen Films, 1929–1945." In *Projekt, Spurensicherung: Alltag und Widerstand im Berlin der 30er Jahre*. Berlin: Elefanten Press, 1983.

Stevens, Dana. "Writing, Scratching, and Politics from *M* to *Mabuse*." *qui parle: Literature, Philosophy, Visual Arts, History* 7, no. 1 (Fall–Winter 1993): 57–80.

Stiles, Victoria M. "Fritz Lang's Definitive *Siegfried* and Its Versions." *Literature/Film Quarterly* 13, no. 4 (1985): 258–74.

———. "The Siegfried Legend and the Silent Screen: Fritz Lang's Interpretation of a Hero Saga." *Literature/Film Quarterly* 8, no. 4 (1980): 232–36.

Strathausen, Carsten. "The Image as Abyss: The Mountain Film and the Cinematic Sublime." In *Peripheral Visions: The Hidden Stages of Weimar Cinema*, by Kenneth S. Calhoon, 171–90. Detroit: Wayne State University Press, 2001.
——. "Uncanny Spaces: The City in Ruttmann and Vertov." In *Screening the City*, edited by Mark Shiel and Tony Fitzmaurice, 15–40. New York: Verso, 2003.

Sturm, Georges. *Die Circe, der Pfau und das Halbblut: die Filme von Fritz Lang, 1916–1921.* Trier: Wissenschaftlicher Verlag Trier, 2001.

Sudendorf, Werner. "Expressionism and Film: The Testament of Dr Caligari." In *Expressionism Reassessed*, edited by Shulamith Behr, David Fanning, and Douglas Jarman. Manchester, England: Manchester University Press, 1993.

Tatar, Maria. "The Killer as Victim: Fritz Lang's *M*." In *Lustmord: Sexual Murder in Weimar Germany*, 153–72. Princeton, N.J.: Princeton University Press, 1995.

Telotte, J. P. "The Seductive Text of *Metropolis*." *South Atlantic Review* 55, no. 4 (November 1990): 49–60.

Thomas, Douglas B. *The Early History of German Motion Pictures, 1895–1935.* Washington, D.C.: Thomas International, 1999.

Töteberg, Michael. *Fritz Lang mit Selbstzeugnissen und Bilddokumenten.* 4th ed. Reinbek bei Hamburg: Rowohlt, 2000.

Unrau, Rona. "Eine Symphonie des Grauens, or the Terror of Music: Murnau's *Nosferatu*." *Literature/Film Quarterly* 24, no. 3 (1996): 234–40.

von Sternberg, Josef, and Heinrich Mann. *"The Blue Angel": The Novel by Heinrich Mann, the Film by Josef Von Sternberg.* New York: Frederick Ungar, 1979.

Wager, Jans B. *Dangerous Dames: Women and Representation in the Weimar Street Film and Film Noir.* Athens: Ohio University Press, 1999.

Wagner, Geoffrey. *"The Blue Angel*: A Reconsideration." *Quarterly of Film, Radio and Television* 6, no. 1 (Autumn 1951): 48–53.

"Weimar Film Theory." Special Issue. *New German Critique,* no. 40 (Winter 1987): 1–240.

Weisstein, Ulrich. *"Professor Unrat* and *The Blue Angel*: Translations and Adaptations of Heinrich Mann's Novel in Two Media." *Film Journal* 1, nos. 3–4 (Fall–Winter 1972): 53–61.

Werner, Gösta. "Fritz Lang and Goebbels: Myth and Facts." *Film Quarterly* 43, no. 3 (Spring 1990): 24–27.

Williams, Alan. "Structures of Narrativity in Fritz Lang's *Metropolis*." *Film Quarterly* 27, no. 4 (Summer 1974): 17–24.

Williams, Andrew P. "The Silent Threat: A (Re)viewing of the 'Sexual Other' in *The Phantom of the Opera* and *Nosferatu*." *Midwest Quarterly* 38, no. 1 (Autumn 1996): 90–101.

Williams, Bruce. *"The Threepenny Opera." Senses of Cinema: An Online Film Journal Devoted to the Serious and Eclectic Discussion of Cinema*, no. 5 (April 2000). www.sensesofcinema.com/contents/cteq/04/32/threepenny_opera.html

Zglinicki, Friedrich von. *Die Wiege der Traumfabrik: Von Guckkästen, Zauberscheiben und bewegten Bildern bis zur Ufa in Berlin*. Berlin: Transit, 1986.

THE THIRD REICH: 1933–1945

Ahren, Yizhak, Stig Hornshøj-Møller, and Christoph B. Melchers. *"Der ewige Jude": Wie Goebbels hetzte: Untersuchungen zum nationalsozialistischen Propagandafilm*. Aachen: Alano, 1990.

Albrecht, Gerd. *Der Film im 3. Reich: [eine Dokumentation]*. Karlsruhe: Doku-Verlag, 1979.

———. *Nationalsozialistische Filmpolitik: Eine soziologische Untersuchung über die Spielfilme des Dritten Reiches*. Stuttgart: Ferdinand Enke, 1969.

Alter, Nora M. "Re/Fusing Past and Present: Cinematic Reunification under the Sign of Nationalism and Racism." In *Beyond 1989: Re-reading German Literature since 1945*, edited by Keith Bullivant, 129–52. Providence, R.I.: Berghahn Books, 1997.

"American Intelligence Report on Leni Riefenstahl—May 30th, 1945." *Film Culture*, no. 77 (Fall 1992): 34–38.

Arnold, Thomas, Jutta Schöning, and Ulrich Schröter. *"Hitlerjunge Quex": Einstellungsprotokoll*. Munich: Filmland-Presse; Frankfurt am Main: Institut für Historisch-Sozialwissenschaftiche Analysen, IHSA, 1980.

Ascheid, Antje. *Hitler's Heroines: Stardom and Womanhood in Nazi Cinema*. Philadelphia: Temple University Press, 2003.

———. "Nazi Stardom and the 'Modern Girl': The Case of Lilian Harvey." Special Issue on Nazi Cinema. *New German Critique*, no. 74 (Spring–Summer 1998): 57–89.

———. "A Sierkian Double Image: The Narration of Zarah Leander as a National Socialist Star." *Film Criticism* 23, nos 2–3 (Winter–Spring 1999): 46–73.

Bach, Steven. *Leni: The Life and Work of Leni Riefenstahl*. New York: Knopf, 2007.

Barkhausen, Hans. *Filmpropaganda in Deutschland im Ersten und Zweiten Weltkrieg*. Hildesheim: Olms Presse, 1982.

———. "Footnote to the History of Riefenstahl's *Olympia*." *Film Quarterly* 28, no. 1 (Fall 1974): 8–12.

Barsam, Richard Meran. *Filmguide to "Triumph of the Will."* Bloomington: Indiana University Press, 1975.

Bateson, Gregory. "An Analysis of the Nazi Film *Hitlerjunge Quex*." In *The Study of Culture at a Distance*, edited by Margaret Mead and Rhoda Métraux, 302–14. Chicago: University of Chicago Press, 1953.

Bathrick, David. "State of the Art as Art of the Nazi State: The Limits of Cinematic Resistance." In *Flight of Fantasy: New Perspectives on Inner Emigration in German Literature, 1933–1945*, edited by Neil H. Donahue and Doris Kirchner, 292–304. New York: Berghahn Books, 2003.

Bechdorf, Ute. *Wunsch-Bilder? Frauen im nationalsozialistischen Unterhaltungsfilm*. Tübingen: Max Niemayer Verlag, 1992.

Berg-Pan, Renata. *Leni Riefenstahl*. Boston: Twayne, 1980.

Berger, Eberhard. "Eine Augenblick der Freiheit oder Helmut Käutner's *Romanze in Moll*." In *Mitten ins Herz: 66 Liebesfilme*, edited by Helga Hartmann and Ralf Schenk, 170–73. Berlin: Henschel, 1991.

Berman, Russell A. "Written Right across Their Faces: Leni Riefenstahl, Ernst Jünger, and Fascist Modernism." In *Modern Culture and Critical Theory: Art, Politics, and the Legacy of the Frankfurt School*, 99–119. Madison: University of Wisconsin Press, 1989.

Bernstein, Sandra, and Michael MacMillian. "Leni Riefenstahl: A Selected Annotated Bibliography." *Quarterly Review of Film Studies* 2, no. 4 (November 1977): 439–57.

Blumenberg, Hans-Christoph. *"Das Leben geht weiter": Der letzte Film des Dritten Reichs*. Berlin: Rowohlt, 1993.

Bonnell, Andrew G. "Melodrama for the Master Race: Two Films by Detlef Sierck (Douglas Sirk)." *Film History* 10, no. 2 (1998): 208–18.

Brandt, Hans-Jürgen. *NS-Filmtheorie und dokumentarische Praxis: Hippler, Noldan, Junghans*. Tübingen: Max Niemayer Verlag, 1987.

———. "Der Propagandakern—*Ich klage an*." In *Widergänger: Faschismus und Antifaschismus im Film*, edited by Joachim Schmitt-Sasse, 15–37. Münster: MakS Publikationen, 1993.

Bräuninger, Werner. "Stählerne Romantik: Leni Riefenstahl und die ästhetisierung der Politik." In *Ich wollte nicht daneben stehen . . . : Lebensentwürfe von Alfred Baeumler bis Ernst Jünger, Essays,* 247–66. Graz: Ares Verlag, 2006.

Byg, Barton. "Nazism as Femme Fatale: Recuperations of Cinematic Masculinity in Postwar Berlin." In *Gender and Germanness: Cultural Productions of Nation*, edited by Patricia Herminghouse and Magda Mueller, 176–88. Providence, R.I.: Berghahn Books, 1997.

Cadars, Pierre, and Francis Courtade. *Geschichte des Films im Dritten Reich*. Munich: Carl Hanser, 1975.

Clooney, Nick. *"Triumph of the Will."* In *The Movies That Changed Us: Reflections on the Screen,* 217–28. New York: Atria Books, 2002.

Corliss, Richard. "Leni Riefenstahl: A Bibliography." *Film Heritage* 5, no. 1 (Fall 1969): 27–36.

Courtade, Francis and Pierre Cadars. *Geschichte des Films im Dritten Reich*. Translated from the original French by Florian Hopf. Munich: Wilhelm Heyne, 1975. Also published in an abridged German edition by Carl Hanser, 1975.

Culbert, David, ed. *Leni Riefenstahl's "Triumph of the Will."* Frederick, Md.: University Publications of America, 1986.

Culbert, David, and Martin Loiperdinger. "Leni Riefenstahl's *Tag der Freiheit*: The Nazi Rally Film." *Historical Journal of Film, Radio and Television* 12, no. 3 (1992): 3–40.

Dassanowsky, Robert von. " 'Wherever you may run, you cannot escape him': Leni Riefenstahl's Self-Reflection and Romantic Transcendence of Nazism in *Tiefland*." *Camera Obscura*, no. 35 (May 1995): 107–29.

Davidson, John E. "Cleavage: Sex in the Total Cinema of the Third Reich." Modernity and Postmodernity. *New German Critique*, no. 98 (Summer 2006): 101–33.

Downing, Taylor. *"Olympia."* London: BFI Publishing, 1992.

Drewniak, Boguslaw. *Der deutsche Film, 1938–1945: Ein Gesamtüberblick*. Düsseldorf: Droste, 1987.

Elsaesser, Thomas. "Leni Riefenstahl: The Body Beautiful, Art, Cinema and Fascist Aesthetics." In *Women and Film: A Sight and Sound Reader*, edited by Pam Cook and Philip Dodd, 186–97. Philadelphia: Temple University Press, 1993.

Everson, William K. *"Triumph of the Will."* In *The Documentary Tradition*, 2nd ed., edited by Lewis Jacobs, 138–40. New York: W. W. Norton, 1972.

Faletti, Heidi. "Reflections of Weimar Cinema in the Nazi Propaganda Films *SA-Mann Brand*, *Hitlerjunge Quex*, and *Hans Westmar*." In *Cultural History through a National Socialist Lens*, edited by Robert C. Reimer, 11–36. Rochester, N.Y.: Camden House, 2000.

Fox, Jo. *Filming Women in the Third Reich*. New York: Berg, 2000.

Friedman, Régine-Mihal. "Die Ausnahme ist die Regel: Zu *Romanze in Moll* (1943) von Helmut Käutner." *Frauen und Film*, no. 43 (December 1987): 48–58.

——— "Juden-Ratten—Von der rassistischen Metonymie zur tierischen Metapher in Fritz Hipplers Film *Der ewige Jude*." *Frauen und Film*, no. 47 (September 1989): 24–35.

———. *L'image et son Juif: Le Juif dans le cinéma Nazi*. Paris: Payot, 1983.

———. "Male Gaze and Female Reaction: Veit Harlan's *Jew Süss* (1940)." In *Gender and German Cinema: Feminist Interventions*. Vol. 2, *German Film History/German History on Film*, edited by Sandra Frieden, Richard W. McCormick, Vibeke R. Petersen, and Laurie Melissa Vogelsang, 117–33. Providence, R.I.: Berg, 1993.

Fürstenau, Theo. "Dr. Goebbels' Rede im Kaiserhof am 28. 3. 1933." In *Der Film im 3. Reich: [eine Dokumentation]*, edited by Gerd Albrecht, 26–31. Karlsruhe: Schauburg Fricker, 1979.

——. "Rede bei der ersten Jahrestagung der Reichsfilmkammer, 5. März 1937, in der Krolloper, Berlin." In *Nationalsozialistische Filmpolitik: Eine Soziologische Untersuchung über die Spielfilme im Dritten Reich*, edited by Gerd Albrecht, 447–63. Stuttgart: Ferdinand Enke, 1979.

——. "Rede des Reichsministers Dr. Joseph Goebbels auf der ersten Jahrestagung der Reichsfilmkammer am 5. März 1937 in der Krolloper, Berlin." In *Der Film im 3. Reich: [eine Dokumentation]*, edited by Gerd Albrecht, 32–63. Karlsruhe: Schauburg Fricker, 1979.

——. *Vom Kaiserhof zur Reichskanzlei*. Munich: Zentralverlag der N.S.D.A.P. Frz. Eher Nachf., 1934.

Giesen, Rolf. *Nazi Propaganda Films: A History and Filmography*. Jefferson, N.C.: McFarland, 2003.

——. *"Triumph of the Will*, the Odd Case of Leni Riefenstahl." In *Nazi Propaganda Films: A History and Filmography,* 10–34. Jefferson, N.C.: McFarland, 2003.

Graham, Cooper C. *Leni Riefenstahl and "Olympia."* Metuchen, N.J.: Scarecrow Press, 1986.

——. *"Olympia* in America, 1938: Rifenstahl, Leni, Hollywood, and the Kristallnacht." *Historical Journal of Film Radio and Television* 13, no. 4 (1993): 433–50.

Hake, Sabine. "The Melodramatic Imagination of Detlef Sierck: *Final Chord* and Its Resonances." *Screen* 38, no. 2 (Summer 1997): 120–48.

——. *Popular Cinema of the Third Reich*. Austin: University of Texas Press, 2001.

Haskins, Ekaterina V. "Time, Space, and Political Identity: Envisioning Community in *Triumph of the Will*." In *The Terministic Screen: Rhetorical Perspectives on Film*, edited by David Blakesley. Carbondale: Southern Illinois University Press, 2003.

Hattendorf, Manfred. "Der propagandistische Dokumentarfilm." *In Dokumentarfilm und Authentizität: Ästhetik und Pragmatik einer Gattung,* 2nd ed, 278–84. Konstanz: UVK Medien, 1999.

Heck-Rabi, Louise. "Leni Riefenstahl: A Crystal Grotto." In *Women Filmmakers: A Critical Reception*, 94–134. Metuchen, N.J.: Scarecrow Press, 1984.

Heinzelmann, Herbert. "Die Heilige Messe des Reichsparteitags: Zur Zeichensprache von Leni Riefenstahls *Triumph des Willens*." In *Faszination und Gewalt: Zur politischen Ästhetik des Nationalsozialismus*, edited by Bernd Organ and Wolfgang W. Weiß, 163–68. Nürnberg: Pädagogeschen Instituts, 1992.

Heller, Heinz-B. "'Stählerne Romantik' und Avantgarde: Beobachtungen und Anmerkungen zu Ruttmanns Industriefilmen." In *Triumph der Bilder: Kultur- und Dokumentarfilm vor 1945 im internationalen Vergleich*, edited by Peter Zimmermann and Kay Hoffmann, 105–18. Konstanz: UVK Verlags, 2003.

Hinton, David B. *The Films of Leni Riefenstahl*. 3rd ed. Metuchen, N.J.: Scarecrow Press, 2000.

———. *"Triumph of the Will*: Document or Artifice?" *Cinema Journal* 15, no. 1 (Autumn 1975): 48–57.

Hitchens, Gordon. "Leni Riefenstahl Comments on the U.S. Army Interrogation." *Film Culture,* no. 79 (Winter 1996): 31–34.

———. "Recent Riefenstahl Activities and a Commentary on Nazi Propaganda Filmmaking." *Film Culture,* no. 79 (Winter 1996): 35–41.

Hoffmann, Hilmar. *Mythos Olympia: Autonomie und Unterwerfung von Sport und Kultur; Hitlers Olympiade, olympische Kultur, Riefenstahls "Olympia"-Film.* Weimar: Aufbau Verlag, 1993.

———. *The Triumph of Propaganda: Film and National Socialism, 1933–1945.* Translated by John A. Broadwin and V. R. Berghahn. Providence, R.I.: Berghahn Books, 1996.

Horak, Jan-Christopher. "Luis Trenker's *The Kaiser of California*: How the West Was Won, Nazi Style." *Historical Journal of Film, Radio and Television* 6, no. 2 (1986): 181–88.

Hornshøj-Møller, Stig, and David Culbert. *"Der ewige Jude* (1940): Joseph Goebbels' Unequaled Monument to Anti-Semitism." *Historical Journal of Film, Radio, and Television* 12, no. 1 (1992): 41–67.

Hull, David Stewart. *Film in the Third Reich: A Study of the German Cinema, 1933–1945.* Berkeley and Los Angeles: University of California Press, 1969. Reprinted as *Film in the Third Reich; Art and Propaganda in Nazi Germany.* New York: Simon & Schuster, 1973.

Infield, Glenn B. *Leni Riefenstahl: The Fallen Film Goddess.* New York: Thomas Crowell, 1976.

Jary, Micaela. *Ich weiß, es wird einmal ein Wunder gescheh'n: Das Leben der Zarah Leander.* Berlin: Aufbau Verlag, 2001.

Kanzog, Klaus. "Der Dokumentarfilm als politischer Katechismus: Bemerkungen zu Leni Riefenstahl's *Triumph des Willens.*" In *Perspektiven des Dokumentarfilms,* edited by Manfred Hattendorf, 57–84. Munich: Verlag Schaudig und Ledig, 1995.

———. *Staatspolitisch besonders wertvoll: Ein Handbuch zu 30 deutschen Spielfilmen der Jahre 1934 bis 1945.* Munich: Verlag Schaudig und Ledig, 1994.

Kelman, Ken. "Propaganda as Vision—*Triumph of the Will.*" *Film Culture,* nos. 56–57 (1973): 168–71.

Kershaw, Ian. "How Effective Was Nazi Propaganda?" In *Nazi Propaganda: The Power and the Limitations,* edited by David Welch, 180–205. Totowa, N.J.: Barnes and Noble Books, 1983.

Kinkel, Lutz. *Die Scheinwerferin: Leni Riefenstahl und das "Dritte Reich."* Hamburg: Europa Verlag, 2002.

Knopp, Guido. "Leni Riefenstahl: Die Regisseurin." In *Hitler's Frauen und Marlene,* 149–206. Munich: C. Bertelsmann, 2001.

Knopp Daniel. *NS-Filmpropaganda: Wunschbild und Feindbild in Leni Riefenstahls "Triumph des Willens" und Veit Harlans "Jud Süß."* Marburg: Tectum, 2004.

Koepnick, Lutz P. *The Dark Mirror: German Cinema between Hitler and Hollywood.* Berkeley and Los Angeles: University of California Press, 2002.

———. "En-Gendering Mass Culture: The Case of Zarah Leander." In *Gender and Germanness: Cultural Productions of Nation,* edited by Patricia Herminghouse and Magda Mueller, 161–75. Providence, R.I.: Berghahn Books, 1997.

———. "Screening Fascism's Underground: Kurt Bernhardt's *The Tunnel.*" Special Issue on Nazi Cinema. *New German Critique,* no. 74 (Spring–Summer 1998): 151–78.

———. "Sirk and the Culture Industry: *Zu neuen Ufern* and *The First Legion.*" *Film Criticism* 23 nos. 2–3 (Winter–Spring 1999): 94–121.

Kuzniar, Alice A. "Zarah Leander and Transgender Specularity." *Film Criticism* 23, nos. 2–3 (Winter–Spring 1999): 74–93.

Kurowski, Ulrich. *Deutsche Spielfilme 1933–1945: Materialien.* 2nd ed. Munich: Stadtsmuseum München, 1978.

Labanyi, Peter. "Images of Fascism: Visualization and Aestheticization in the Third Reich." In *The Burden of German History, 1919–1945,* edited by Michael Laffan, 151–77. London: Methuen, 1988.

Leander, Zarah. *Es war so wunderbar: Mein Leben.* Hamburg: Hoffmann und Campe, 1973.

———. *So bin ich und so bleibe ich.* Edited by Roland Gööck. Gütersloh: C. Bertelsmann, 1958.

Leimgruber, Florian, ed. *Luis Trenker, Regisseur und Schriftsteller: Die Personalakte Trenkers im Berlin Document Center.* Bolzano: Frasnelli-Keitsch, 1994.

Leiser, Erwin. *Nazi Cinema.* Translated by Gertrud Mander and David Wilson. London: Secker and Warburg, 1974.

Liebe, Ulrich. *Verehrt, verfolgt, vergessen: Schauspieler als Naziopfer.* Weinheim: Beltz Quadriga, 1992.

Lippe, Adrian. *Leni Riefenstahl und die Macht der Bilder.* Munich: GRIN Verlag, 2000.

Loewy, Hanno. *"Das blaue Licht."* In *Béla Balazs: Märchen, Ritual und Film,* 320–50. Berlin: Vorwerk 8, 2003.

Loiperdinger, Martin. "Halb Dokument, halb Fälschung: Zur Inszenierung der Eröffnungsfeier in Leni Riefenstahls Olympia-Film *Fest der Völker.*" *Medium* 18, no. 3 (1988): 42–46.

——. "Hans Westmar": Einstellungsprotokoll. Munich: IHSA Arbeitspapiere im Verlag der Filmland Presse, 1980.

——. "Hans Westmar: Faschistische und kommunistische Öffentlichkeit kämpfen um den Besitz der Straße." In Märtyrerlegenden im NS-Film, edited by Martin Loiperdinger, 55–76. Opladen: Leske + Budrich, 1991.

——. Rituale der mobilmachung: Der Parteitagsfilm "Triumph des Willens" von Leni Riefenstahl. Opladen: Leske + Budrich, 1987.

——. "Sieg des Glaubens: Ein gelungenes Experiment nationalsozialistischer Filmpropaganda." In Formative Ästhetik im Nationalsozialismus: Intentionen, Medien und Praxisformen totalitärer ästhetischer Herrschaft und Beherrschung, edited by Ulrich Herrmann and Ulrich Nassen, 31–42. Basel: Beltz Verlag, 1994.

——. "Triumph des Willens": Einstellungsprotokoll. Frankfurt am Main: Filmland Presse, 1980.

Loiperdinger, Martin, ed. Märtyrerlegenden im NS-Film. Opladen: Leske + Budrich, 1991.

Loiperdinger, Martin, and David Culbert. "Leni Riefenstahl, the SA, and the Nazi Party Rally Films, Nuremberg 1933–1934: Sieg des Glaubens and Triumph des Willens." Historical Journal of Film, Radio and Television 8, no. 1 (1988): 3–38.

——. "Leni Riefenstahl's Tag der Freiheit: The Nazi Rally Film." Historical Journal of Film, Radio and Television 12, no. 3 (1992): 3–40.

Loiperdinger, Martin, and Klaus Schönekäs. "Die große Liebe: Propaganda im Unterhaltungsfilm." In Bilder schreiben Geschichte: Der Historiker im Kino, edited by Rainer Rother, 143–53. Berlin: Wagenbach, 1991.

Lowry, Stephen. Pathos und Politik: Ideologic in Spielfilmen des Nationalsozialismus. Tübingen: Max Niemeyer Verlag, 1991.

Mandell, Richard. "The Olympics Preserved." In The Nazi Olympics, 250–74. New York: Macmillan, 1971. Reprint: University of Illinois Press, 1987.

Marcorelles, Louis. "Käutner Le Dandy." Cahiers du Cinéma, no. 73 (July 1957): 26–29.

——. "The Nazi Cinema (1933–1945)." Sight and Sound, no. 25 (Autumn 1955): 65–69.

Marcus, Alan. "Reappraising Riefenstahl's Triumph of the Will." Film Studies, no. 4 (Summer 2004): 75–86.

Margry, Karel. "Theresienstadt (1944–1945): The Nazi Propaganda Film Depecting the Concentration Camp as Paradise." Historical Journal of Film, Radio and Television 12, no. 2 (1992): 145–62.

Meyer, Thomas. "'Gesichtsverlust' versus Resemantisierung: Überlegungen zum Gesicht des Arbeiters im Nationalsozialismus anhand einiger Filme von Walther Ruttmann." montage/av 13, no. 2 (2004): 75–91.

Moeller, Felix. *The Film Minister: Goebbels and the Cinema in the Third Reich.* Stuttgart: Edition Axel Menges, 2000.

Morgan, Ben. "Music in Nazi Film: How Different Is *Triumph of the Will?*" *Studies in European Cinema* 3, no. 1 (April 2006): 37–53.

Muhlen, Norbert. "The Return of Goebbels's Filmmakers." *Commentary* 11, no. 3 (March 1951): 245–50.

Müller, Ray. *Die Macht der Bilder Leni Riefenstahls (The Wonderful, Horrible Life of Leni Riefenstahl).* VHS. 2 vols. New York: Kino Video, 1993.

Nadar, Thomas R. "The Director and the Diva: The Film Musicals of Detlef Sierck and Zarah Leander; *Zu neuen Ufern* and La *Habanera*." In *Cultural History through a National Socialist Lens: Essays on the Cinema of the Third Reich*, edited by Robert C. Reimer, 65–83. Rochester, N.Y.: Camden House, 2000.

"Nazi Cinema." Special Issue. *New German Critique*, no. 74 (Spring–Summer 1998): 1–192.

Neale, Steve. "*Triumph of the Will*: Notes on Documentary and Spectacle." *Screen* 20, no. 1 (1979): 63–86.

Nowotny, Peter. *Leni Riefenstahl's "Triumph des Willens": Zur Kritik dokumentarischer Filmarbeit im NS-Faschismus.* Dortmund, 1981.

O'Brien, Mary-Elizabeth. *Nazi Cinema as Enchantment: The Politics of Entertainment in the Third Reich.* Rochester, N.Y.: Camden House, 2004.

Olivier, Antje, and Sevgi Braun. "Das Negative macht mich nicht kreativ— Leni Riefenstahl, die Regisseurin von Macht und Schönheit." In *Anpassung oder Verbot: Künstlerinnen und die 30er Jahre*, 263–94. Düsseldorf: Droste, 1998.

Petley, Julian. "Sirk in Germany." *Sight and Sound* 57, no. 1 (Winter 1987–1988): 58–61.

Petro, Patrice. "Nazi Cinema at the Intersection of the Classical and the Popular." Special Issue on Nazi Cinema. *New German Critique*, no. 74 (Spring–Summer 1998): 41–55. Also published in *Aftershocks of the New: Feminism and Film History*, 124–35. New Brunswick, N.J.: Rutgers University Press, 2002.

Peucker, Brigitte. "The Fascist Choreography: Riefenstahl's Tableaux." *Modernism/modernity* 11, no. 2 (April 2004): 279–97.

Reimer, Robert, ed. *Cultural History through a National Socialist Lens: Essays on the Cinema of the Third Reich.* Rochester, N.Y.: Camden House, 2000.

Rentschler, Eric. "The Elemental, the Ornamental, the Instrumental: *The Blue Light* and Nazi Film Aesthetics." In *The Other Perspective in Gender and Culture: Rewriting Women and the Symbolic*, edited by Juliet Flower MacCannell, 161–88. New York: Columbia University Press, 1990.

———. "Fatal Attractions: Leni Riefenstahl's *The Blue Light*." *October* 48 (Spring 1989): 47–68.

——. "Germany: Nazism and After." In *Oxford World History of Cinema*, new ed., edited by Geoffrey Nowell-Smith, 374–83. Oxford: Oxford University Press, 1999.

——. *The Ministry of Illusion: Nazi Cinema and Its Afterlife*. Cambridge: Harvard University Press, 1996.

——. "There's No Place Like Home: Luis Trenker's *The Prodigal Son* (1934)." Special Issue on German Film History. *New German Critique*, no. 60 (Autumn 1993): 33–56.

——. "The Triumph of Male Will: *Münchhausen* (1943)." *Film Quarterly* 43, no. 3 (Spring 1990): 14–23.

Rich, B. Ruby. "Leni Riefenstahl: The Deceptive Myth." In *Sexual Stategems: The World of Women in Film*, edited by Patricia Erens, 202–9. New York: Horizon Press, 1979. Also published in *Chick Flicks: Theories and Memories of the Feminist Film Movement*, 40–47. Durham, N.C.: Duke University Press, 1998.

Riefenstahl, Leni, "After a Half-Century, Leni Riefenstahl Confronts the U.S. Army That Exonerated Her of War Crimes." *Film Culture*, no. 79 (Winter 1996): 79–82.

——. *Kampf in Schnee und Eis*. Leipzig: Hesse and Becker, 1933.

——. *Leni Riefenstahl: A Memoir*. New York: Picador, 1995.

——. *Leni Riefenstahl: A Memoir*. New York: St. Martin's Press, 1992.

——. "*Olympia*." New York: St. Martin's Press, 1994.

——. *The Sieve of Time: The Memoirs of Leni Riefenstahl*. London: Quartet Books, 1992.

Romani, Cinzia. *Tainted Goddesses: Female Film Stars of the Third Reich*. Translated by Robert Connolly. New York: Sarpedon, 1992.

Roth, Karl H. "*Ich klage an*: Aus der Entsteheungsgeschichte eines Propagandafilms." In *Aktion T-4 1939–1945: Die Euthanasie-Zentrale in der Tiegartenstraße 4*, 2nd, enl. ed., edited by Götz Aly, 93–116. Berlin: Edition Hentrich, 1989.

Rother, Rainer. "*Bei unseren Helden an der Somme*: Eine deutsche Antwort auf die Entente-Propaganda." In *KINtop: Jahrbuch zur Erforschung des frühen Films*. Vol. 4, *Anfänge des dokumentarischen Films*, edited by Frank Kessler, Sabine Lenk, and Martin Loiperdinger, 123–42. Frankfurt am Main: Stroemfeld/Roter Stern, 1995. Also published as "*Bei unseren Helden an der Somme* (1917): The Creation of a 'Social Event'." *Historical Journal of Film, Radio and Television* 15, no. 4 (October 1995): 525–42.

——. *Leni Riefenstahl: Die Verführung des Talents*. Berlin: Henschel, 2000.

——. *Leni Riefenstahl: The Seduction of Genius*. Translated by Martin H. Bott. London: Continuum, 2002.

Sanders-Brahms, Helma. "Tyrannenmord: *Tiefland* von Leni Riefenstahl." In *Das Jahr 1945: Filme aus 15 Ländern,* by Hans Helmut Prinzler, 173–76. Berlin: Stiftung Deutsche Kinemathek ,1990.

——. "Zarah." In *Jahrbuch Film 81/82,* edited by Hans-Günter Pflaum, 165–72. Munich: Carl Hanser, 1981.

Sarkowicz, Hans, ed. *Hitler's Künstler: Die Kultur im Dienst des Nationalsozialismus.* Frankfurt am Main: Insel Verlag, 2004

Schaake, Erich, and Roland Bäurle. "Leni Riefenstahl: Triumph des schönen Scheins" In *Hitler's Frauen: Die willigen Helferinnen und ergebenen Mätressen des Führers.* Munich: Paul List Verlag, 2000.

Schaub, Hannah B. *Riefenstahls Olympia: Körperideale - ethische Verantwortung oder Freiheit des Künstlers?* Munich: Wilhelm Fink Verlag, 2003.

Schirach, Henriette von. "Leni Riefenstahl." In *Frauen um Hitler: Nach Materialien.* Munich: F. A. Herbig, 1983.

Schlüpmann, Heide. "Faschistische Trugbilder weiblicher Autonomie." *Frauen und Film,* nos. 44–45 (October 1988): 44–66. Also published in *Frauen und Faschismus in Europa: Der faschistische Körper,* edited by Leonore Siegele-Wenschkewitz and Gerda Stuchlik, 211–27. Pfaffenweiler: Centaurus, 1990.

——. "Trugbilder weiblicher Autonomie im nationalsozialistischen Film: Leni Riefenstahl: Triumph des weiblichen Willens?" In *Sport und Film: Bewegte Körper—bewegte Bilder,* by Annette C. Eckert. Berlin: Cine Marketing, 1993.

Schoeps, Karl-Heinz. *Literature and Film in the Third Reich.* Rochester, N.Y.: Camden House, 2004.

Schulte-Sasse, Linda. *Entertaining the Third Reich: Illusions of Wholeness in Nazi Cinema.* Durham, N.C.: Duke University Press, 1996.

Walter, Michael. "Die Musik des Olympiafilms von 1938." *Acta Musicologia* 62, no. 1 (January–February 1990): 82–113.

Welch, David, ed. *Nazi Propaganda: The Power and the Limitations.* Totowa, N.J.: Barnes and Noble Books, 1983.

——. *Propaganda and the German Cinema, 1933–1945.* New York: Oxford University Press, 1983.

Werner, Gösta. "Fritz Lang and Goebbels: Myth and Facts." *Film Quarterly* 43, no. 3 (Spring 1990): 24–27.

Winston, Brian. "*Triumph of the Will.*" *History Today* 47, no. 1 (January 1997): 24–28.

——. "Was Hitler There? Reconsidering *Triumph of the Will.*" *Sight and Sound* (Spring 1981): 102–7.

Witte, Karsten. "Die Filmkomödie im Dritten Reich." In *Die deutsche Literatur im Dritten Reich: Themen, Traditionen, Wirkungen,* edited by Horst Denkler and Karl Prümm, 347–65. Stuttgart: Reclam, 1976.

———. "The Indivisible Legacy of Nazi Cinema." Special Issue on Nazi Cinema. *New German Critique*, no. 74 (Spring–Summer 1998): 23–30.

———. *Lachende Erben, Toller Tag: Filmkomödie im dritten Reich*. Berlin: Vorwerk 8, 1995.

Wood, Robin. "Fascism/Cinema." *CinemAction*, no. 18 (Fall 1989): 45–50.

Wulf, Joseph. *Theater und Film im Dritten Reich*. Vienna: Ullstein, 1983.

Zonal Film Archives (Hamburg, Germany). *Catalogue of Forbidden German Feature and Short Film Productions Held in Zonal Film Archives of Film Section, Information Services Division, Control Commission for Germany, (BE)*. Original text by John F. Kelson. Westport, Conn.: Greenwood Press, 1996.

EAST GERMAN FILM AND DEFA: 1945–1990

Agde, Günter, ed. *Kahlschlag: das 11. Plenum des ZK der SED 1965: Studien und Dokumente*. Berlin: Aufbau Taschenbuch, 1991.

Alter, Nora M. "Excessive Pre/Requisites: Vietnam through the East German Lens." *Cultural Critique*, no. 35 (Winter 1996–1997): 39–79.

Bahr, Gisela. "Film and Consciousness: The Depiction of Women in East German Movies." In *Gender and German Cinema: Feminist Interventions*, vol. 1, *Gender and Representation in New German Cinema*, edited by Sandra Frieden, Richard W. McCormick, Vibeke R. Petersen, and Laurie Melissa Vogelsang, 125–40. Providence, R.I.: Berg, 1993.

Behn, Manfred, and Hans-Michael Bock, eds. *Film und Gesellschaft in der DDR*. 2 vols. Hamburg: CineGraph, 1988–1989.

Berghahn, Daniela. *Hollywood behind the Wall: The Cinema of East Germany*. Manchester, England: Manchester University Press, 2005.

———. "Liars and Traitors: Unheroic Resistance in Antifascist DEFA Films." In *Millennial Essays on Film and Other German Studies*, edited by Daniela Berghahn and Alan Bance, 19–36. New York: Peter Lang, 2002.

Beyer, Frank. *Wenn der Wind sich dreht: meine Filme, mein Leben*. Munich: Econ, 2001.

Blunk, Harry. *Die DDR in ihren Spielfilmen: Reproduktion und Konzeption der DDR-Gesellschaft im neueren Defa-Gegenwartsfilm*. Munich: Profil, 1984.

———, ed. *Filmland DDR: Ein Reader zu Geschichte, Funktion und Wirkung der DEFA*. Cologne: Verlag Wissenschaft und Politik, 1990.

Blunk, Harry, and Dirk Jungnickel, eds. *Filmland DDR: ein Reader zu Geschichte, Funktion und Wirkung der DEFA*. Colonge: Wissenschaft und Politik, 1990.

Bock, Hans-Michael. "East Germany: The DEFA Story." In *Oxford World History of Cinema*, new ed., edited by Geoffrey Nowell-Smith, 627–32. New York: Oxford University Press, 1999.

Byg, Barton. "DEFA and the Traditions of International Cinema." *The European Cinema Reader*, edited by Catherine Fowler, 153–61. London: Routledge, 2002.

———. "Generational Conflict and Historical Continuity in GDR Film." In *Framing the Past: The Historiography of German Cinema and Television*, edited by Bruce A. Murray and Christopher J. Wickham, 197–219. Carbondale: Southern Illinois University Press, 1992.

———. "What Might Have Been: DEFA Films of the Past and the Future of German Cinema." *Cineaste* 17, no. 4 (Summer 1990): 9–15.

Byg, Barton, and Betheny Moore, eds. *Moving Images of East Germany: Past and Future of DEFA Film*. Washington, D.C.: American Institute for Contemporary German Studies; Baltimore: Johns Hopkins University Press, 2002.

Claus, Horst. "Personal Memories of Change, Freedom and Opportunity: The Post-war Years in Wolfgang Kohlhaase's Films *Inge, April und Mai* and *Der Bruch*." In *1949/1989: Cultural Perspectives on Division and Unity in East and West*, edited by Clare Flanagan and Stuart Taberner, 245–57. Atlanta: Rodopi, 2000.

"East German Film." Special Issue, *New German Critique,* no. 82 (Winter 2001): 1–192.

Elsaesser, Thomas, and Michael Wedel. "Defining DEFA's Historical Imaginary: The Films of Konrad Wolf." East German Film. *New German Critique,* no. 82 (Winter 2001): 3–24.

Engelke, Henning, and Simon Kopp. "Der Western im Osten. Genre: Zeitlichkeit und Authentizität im DEFA- und im Hollywood-Western." In *Zeithistorische Forschungen/Studies in Contemporary History* (Online) 1, no. 2 (2004). www.zeithistorische-forschungen.de/16126041–Engelke-Kopp-2–2004

Feinstein, Joshua. *The Triumph of the Ordinary: Depictions of Daily Life in the East German Cinema, 1949–1989*. Chapel Hill: University of North Carolina Press, 2002.

Fellmer, Claudia. "The Communist Who Rarely Played a Communist: The Case of DEFA Star Erwin Geschonneck." In *Millennial Essays on Film and Other German Studies*, edited by Daniela Berghahn and Alan Bance. New York: Peter Lang, 2002.

Figge, Susan G., and Jennifer K. Ward. "(Sich) Ein genaues Bild zu machen: Jurek Becker's *Bronsteins Kinder* as Novel and Film." *Germanic Review* 70, no. 3 (Summer 1995): 90–98.

Filmarchiv Austria, ed. *"Der geteilte Himmel": Hohepunkte des DEFA-kinos 1946–1992*. Vol. 1, *Filme der Retrospektive*, edited by Helmut Pflügl. Vol. 2, *Essays zur Geschichte der DEFA und Filmografien von 61 DEFA-Regisseurinnen*, edited by Raimund Fritz. Vienna: Filmachiv Austria, 2001.

Finke, Klaus, ed. *DEFA-Film als nationales Kulturerbe?* Berlin: VISTAS, 2001.

———. *Politik und Mythos: Kader, Arbeiter und Aktivisten im DEFA-Film.* Oldenburg: Bis, Bibliotheks- und Informationssystem der Universität Oldenburg, 2002.

Fisher, Jaimey. "Who's Watching the Rubble-Kids? Youth, Pedagogy, and Politics in Early DEFA Films." East German Film. *New German Critique,* no. 82 (Winter 2001): 91–125.

Fritzsche, Karin, and Claus Löser, eds. *Gegenbilder: Filmische Subversion in der DDR, 1976–1989: Texte, Bilder, Daten.* Berlin: Janus Press, 1996.

Frölich, Margrit. "Behind the Curtains of a State-Owned Film Industry: Women Filmmakers at the DEFA." In *Triangulated Visions: Women in Recent German Cinema,* edited by Ingeborg Majer O'Sickey and Ingeborg von Zadow, 43–63. Albany: State University of New York Press, 1998.

Geiss, Axel, ed. *Repression und Freiheit: DEFA-Regisseure zwischen Fremd- und Selbstbestimmung.* Potsdam: Brandenburgische Landeszentrale für politische Bildung, 1997.

Gemünden, Gerd. "Between Karl May and Karl Marx: The DEFA Indianerfilme (1965–1983)." East German Film. *New German Critique,* no. 82 (Winter 2001): 25–38.

———. "Gone Primitive: The Indianerphantasien of Herbert Achternbusch." *Germanic Review* 73, no. 1 (Winter 1998): 32–49.

Georgi, Renate, and Peter Hoff, eds. *Konrad Wolf: Neue Sichten auf seine Filme; Ein Beitrag zur Kulturgeschichte der DDR.* Potsdam: Hochschule für Film und Fernsehen "Konrad Wolf"; Berlin: VISTAS, 1990.

Gerull, Brigitte, and DEFA Stiftung. *DEFA Dokumentarfilm, 1946–1992: Bestandsnachweis.* Potsdam: Hochschule für Film und Fernsehen "Konrad Wolf", Bibliothek/Zeitungsausschnittarchiv, 1996.

Giera, Joachim. *Kinderkino in Europa: der DEFA-Kinderfilm.* Edited by Holger Twele. Frankfurt am Main: Bundesverband Jugend und Film, 1993.

Glaß, Peter. *Kino ist mehr als Film: DEFA-Spielfilm, Kino und Kulturpolitik in der DDR, 1976–1990.* Berlin: Mariposa, 1996. Also published as *Kino ist mehr als Film: die Jahre 1976–1990 in der DDR.* Berlin: A. G. Verlag, 1999.

Greenberg, Alan, Herbert Achternbusch, and Werner Herzog. *Heart of Glass* [screenplay]. Munich: Skellig, 1976.

Gregson, Julie. "East or West: A Straight Choice? Representations of Masculinity and Constructions of National Identity in Wolfgang Kohlhaase and Gerhard Klein's *Berlin-Ecke Schönhauser.*" In *Millennial Essays on Film and Other German Studies,* edited by Daniela Berghahn and Alan Bance. New York: Peter Lang, 2002.

Guder, Andrea. *Genosse Hauptmann auf Verbrecherjagd: Der Krimi im Kino und Fernsehen der DDR.* Bonn: ARCult Media, 2003.

Habel, Frank-Burkhard. *Gojko Mitic, Mustangs, Marterpfähle: Die DEFA-Indianerfilme: das große Buch für Fans*. Berlin: Schwarzkopf und Schwarzkopf, 1997.

———. *Das große Lexikon der DEFA-Spielfilme: Die vollständige Dokumentation aller DEFA-Spielfilme von 1946 bis 1993*. Berlin: Schwarzkopf und Schwarzkopf, 2000.

———. *Zerschnittene Filme: Zensur im Kino*. Leipzig: Kiepenheuer und Witsch, 2003. [Zensur in Ost und West].

Habel, Frank-Burkhard, and Volker Wachter. *Das große Lexikon der DDR-Stars: Schauspieler aus Film und Fernsehen*. Berlin: Schwarzkopf und Schwarzkopf, 2002.

Heimann, Thomas. *DEFA, Künstler und SED-Kulturpolitik: zum Verhältnis von Kulturpolitik und Filmproduktion in der SBZ/DDR 1945 bis 1959*. Berlin: VISTAS, 1994.

———. *Erinnerung als Wandel: Kriegsbilder im frühen DDR-Film*. Cologne: Böhlau, 2000.

"Heimat." Special Issue. *New German Critique*, no. 36 (Autumn 1985): 1–276.

Heinze, Dieter, and Ludwig Hoffmann, eds. *Konrad Wolf im Dialog: Kunst und Politik*. Berlin: Dietz, 1985.

Holba, Herbert. "Deutsches Filmmelodram II: *Zu neuen Ufern*." *Filmjournal: F* (Ulm), no. 23 (May 1980): 39–43.

Holloway, Ronald, and Ralf Schenk. *Film and Cinema in Eastern Germany*. Berlin: PROGRESS Film-Verleih, 2000.

Hunt, Leon. "Frühgeschichte des deutschen Films: Licht am Ende des Tunnels." In *Geschichte des deutschen Films*, edited by Wolfgang Jacobsen, Anton Kaes, and Hans Helmut Prinzler, 13–38. Stuttgart: J. B. Metzler, 1993.

Infield, Glenn B. *Leni Riefenstahl: The Fallen Film Goddess*. New York: Thomas Crowell, 1976.

Jacobsen, Wolfgang, and Rolf Aurich. *Der Sonnensucher Konrad Wolf: Biographie*. Berlin: Aufbau-Verlag, 2005.

Jansen, Peter W., and Wolfram Schütte, eds. *Film in the DDR*. Munich: Carl Hanser, 1977.

Janssen, Herbert, and Reinhold Jacobi, eds. *Filme in der DDR 1945–86: Kritische Notizen aus 42 Kinojahren*. Cologne: Verlag Katholisches Institut für Medieninformation, 1987.

Jordan Günter. "Davidstern und roter Winkel: Das jüdische Thema in DEFA-Wochenschau und -Dokumentarfilm 1946–1948." In *Millennial Essays on Film and Other German Studies*, edited by Daniela Berghahn and Alan Bance. New York: Peter Lang, 2002.

———. *Erprobung eines Genres: Defa-Dokumentarfilme für Kinder, 1975–1990: Ein Nachlesebuch*. Remscheid, Germany: Kinder- und Jugendfilmzentrum in der Bundesrepublik Deutschland, 1991.

Jordan, Günter, and Ralf Schenk. *Schwarzweiß und Farbe: DEFA-Dokumentarfilme 1946–92*. Potsdam: Filmmuseum Potsdam; Berlin: Jovis Verlag, 1996.

Kannapin, Detlef. *Antifaschismus und Film in der DDR: die DEFA-Spielfilme 1945–1955/1956*. Cologne: Papyrossa, 1997.

Kersten, Heinz. *So viele Träume: DEFA-Film-Kritiken aus drei Jahrzehnten*. Edited by Christel Drawer. Berlin: VISTAS, 1996.

Koch, Gertrud. "On the Disappearance of the Dead among the Living: The Holocaust and the Confusion of Identities in the Films of Konrad Wolf." Special Issue on German Film History. *New German Critique*, no. 60 (Autumn 1993): 57–75.

König, Ingelore, Dieter Wiedemann, and Lothar Wolf, eds. *Arbeiten mit DEFA-Kinderfilmen*. Vol. 1, *Alltagsgeschichten*. Vol. 2, *Vergangene Zeiten*. Vol. 3, *Märchen*. Munich: KoPäd, 1998.

———. *Zwischen Bluejeans und Blauhemden: Jugendfilm in Ost und West*. Berlin: Henschel, 1995.

———. *Zwischen Marx und Muck: DEFA-Filme für Kinder*. Berlin: Henschel, 1996.

Leonhard, Sigrun D. "Testing the Borders: East German Film between Individualism and Social Commitment." In *Post New Wave Cinema in the Soviet Union and Eastern Europe*, edited by Daniel J. Goulding, 51–101. Bloomington: Indiana University Press, 1989.

Maetzig, Kurt. "Discussion with Kurt Maetzig." By Martin Brady. In *DEFA: East German Cinema, 1946–1992*, edited by Seán Allan and John Sandford, 77–92. New York: Berghahn Books, 1999.

Meyers, Peter. "Der DEFA-film: *Die Mörder sind unter uns*." In *Nationalsozialismus und Judenverfolgung in DDR-Medien*, 2nd enl. ed., 71–83. Bonn: Bundeszentrale für Politische Bildung, 1997.

Mittman, Elizabeth. "Fashioning the Socialist Nation: The Gender of Consumption in Slatan Dudow's *Destinies of Women*." *German Politics and Society* 23, no. 4 (Winter 2005): 28–44.

Mückenberger, Christiane. "The Anti-Fascist Past in DEFA Films." In *DEFA: East German Cinema, 1946–1992*, edited by Seán Allen and John Sandford, 58–76. New York: Berghahn Books, 1999.

———. "The Cold War in East German Feature Film." Special Issue: Media and the Cold War in Europe. *Historical Journal of Film, Radio and Television* 3, no. 1 (March 1993): 49–58.

———, ed. *Prädikat, Besonders schädlich: Filmtexte—"Das Kaninchen bin ich"; "Denk bloß nicht, daß ich heule"*. Berlin: Henschel, 1990.

Mückenberger, Christiane, and Günter Jordan. *"Sie sehen selbst, Sie hören selbst . . .": Eine Geschichte der DEFA von ihren Anfängen bis 1949*. Marburg: Hitzeroth, 1994.

Osterland, Martin. *Gesellschaftsbilder in Filmen: Eine soziologische Untersuchung des Filmangebots der Jahre 1949 bis 1964*. Stuttgart: Ferdinand Enke, 1970.

Palmer, Angela. "The Birth of Remembering: Wolfgang Staudte's *Die Mörder sind unter uns*. (The Murderers Are among Us, 1946)." *Kinoeye* 3, no. 11 (October 13, 2003). www.kinoeye.org/03/11/palmer11.php

Pflaum, Hans-Günther, and Hans Helmut Prinzler. *Film in der Bundesrepublik Deutschland: Der neue deutsche Film von den Anfängen bis zur Gegenwart; Mit einem Exkurs über das Kino der DDR*. New, ext. ed. Munich: Carl Hanser, 1992.

Poss, Ingrid, and Peter Warnecke, eds. *Spur der Film: Zeitzeugen über die DEFA*. Berlin: Ch. Links Verlag, 2006.

Ranga, Dana. *Unterhaltungsfilme der DEFA 1946–1965*. Berlin: Hochschule für Film und Fernsehen "Konrad Wolf" Berlin, 1993.

Rinke, Andrea. *Images of Women in East German Cinema, 1972–1982: Socialist Models, Private Dreamers and Rebels*. Lewiston, N.Y.: Edwin Mellen Press, 2006.

———. "Models or Misfits? The Role of Screen Heroines in GDR Cinema." In: *Triangulated Visions: Women in Recent German Cinema*, edited by Ingeborg Majer O'Sickey and Ingeborg von Zadow, 207–18. Albany: State University of New York Press, 1998.

Saß, Katrin. *Das Glück wird niemals alt*. Munich: Ullstein, 2003.

Schenk, Ralf. *Frauengestalten im Film und Fernsehen der DDR*. Bonn: Bundeszentrale für politische Bildung, 1997.

———. *Vor der Kamera: Fünfzig Schauspieler in Babelsberg*. Potsdam: Filmmuseum Potsdam; Berlin: Henschel, 1995.

Schenk, Ralf, ed. *Regie: Frank Beyer*. Potsdam: Filmmuseum Potsdam; Berlin: Edition Hentrich, 1995.

———. *Das zweite Leben der Filmstadt Babelsberg: DEFA Spielfilme 1946–1992*. Potsdam: Filmmuseum Potsdam; Berlin: Henschel, 1994.

Schenk, Ralf, and Erika Richter, eds. *apropros: Film . . . : Das Jahrbuch der DEFA-Stiftung*. Berlin: Das Neue Berlin, 2000– .

Schenk, Ralf, and Sabine Scholze, eds. *Die Trick-Fabrik: DEFA-Animationsfilme 1955–1990*. Dresden: DIAF, Deutschen Institut für Animationsfilme Dresden; Berlin: DEFA-Stiftung; Berlin: Bertz Verlag, 2003.

Schulz, Günter, ed. *Ausländische Spiel- und abendfüllende Dokumentarfilme in den Kinos der SBZ/DDR, 1945–1966: Filmografie*. Berlin: Bundesarchiv-Filmarchiv; DEFA-Stiftung, 2001.

Shandley, Robert R. "Coming Home through Rubble Canyons: *The Murderers Are among Us* and Generic Convention." In *Rubble Films: German Cinema in the Shadow of the Third Reich*, 25–46. Philadelphia: Temple University Press, 2001.

——. "Rubble Canyons: *Die Mörder sind unter uns* and the Western." *The German Quarterly* 74, no. 2 (Spring 2001): 132–47.

——. *Rubble Films: German Cinema in the Shadow of the Third Reich.* Philadelphia: Temple University Press, 2001.

Silberman, Marc. "Narrating Gender in the GDR: Hermann Zschoche's *Bürgschaft für ein Jahr* (1981)." *Germanic Review* 66, no. 1 (Winter 1991): 25–33.

——. "Remembering History: The Filmmaker Konrad Wolf." Special Issue on Alexander Kluge. *New German Critique*, no. 49 (Winter 1990): 163–91.

——. "'Semper Fidelis': Staudte's *The Subject* (1951)." In *German Film and Literature: Adaptations and Transformations*, edited by Eric Rentschler, 146–60. New York: Methuen, 1986.

Soldovieri, Stefan. "Socialists in Outer Space: East German Films—Venusian Adventure." *Film History* 10, no. 3 (1998): 382–98.

Sylvester, Regine. *The Forbidden Films*. Munich: Goethe-Institut, 1992.

Töteberg, Michael, ed. *Good bye, Lenin! ein Film von Wolfgang Becker: Drehbuch von Bernd Lichtenberg and Wolfgang Becker.* Berlin: Schwarzkopf and Schwarzkopf, 2003.

Trumpener, Katie. "DEFA: Moving Germany into Eastern Europe." In *Moving Images of East Germany: Past and Future of DEFA Film*, edited by Barton Byg and Betheny Moore, 85–104. Washington, D.C.: American Institute for Contemporary German Studies; Baltimore: Johns Hopkins University Press, 2002.

——. "'La guerre est finie': New Waves, Historical Contingency and the GDR 'Rabbit Films'." In *The Power of Intellectuals in Contemporary Germany*, edited by Michael Geyer, 113–37. Chicago: University of Chicago Press, 2001.

——. "Old Movies: Cinema as Palimpsest in GDR Fiction." East German Film. *New German Critique*, no. 82 (Winter 2001): 39–75.

Verband der Film- und Fernsehschaffenden der Deutschen Democratischen Republik. *"Berlin: Dossier einer Großstadt."* Special issue of *Film und Fernsehen* 6 (June 1987).

Waterkamp, Rainer, ed. *Kriminalität in den DDR-Medien.* Bonn: Bundeszentrale für Politische Bildung, 1998.

——. *Leit- und Feindbilder in DDR-Medien.* Bonn: Bundeszentrale für politische Bildung, 1997.

Zahlmann, Stefan. *Körper und Konflikt: Filmische Gedächtniskultur in BRD und DDR seit den sechziger Jahren.* Berlin: Arno Spitz, 2001.

Zilinski, Lissi, et al., eds. *Spielfilme der DEFA im Urteil der Kritik: Ausgewählte Rezensionen; Mit einer Bibliografie.* Berlin: Henschel, 1970.

Zimmermann, Peter, ed. *Deutschlandbilder Ost: Dokumentarfilme der DEFA von der Nachkriegszeit bis zur Wiedervereinigung.* Konstanz: UVK Medien, 1995.

Zimmermann, Peter, and Gebhard Moldenhauer. *Der geteilte Himmel: Arbeit, Alltag und Geschichte im ost- und westdeutschen Film*. Konstanz: UVK Medien, 2000.

Zschoche, Herrmann. *"Sieben Sommersprossen" und andere Erinnerungen*. Berlin: Verlag das Neue Berlin, 2002.

WEST GERMANY–POSTWAR/PRE-OBERHAUSEN: 1945–1962

Appel, Alfred, Jr. "Fritz Lang's American Nightmare." *Film Comment* 10, no. 6 (November–December 1974): 12–17.

Baker, Mark. " 'Trummerfilme:' Postwar German Cinema, 1946–1948." *Film Criticism* 20 (Fall–Winter 1995–1996): 88–101.

Barthel, Manfred. *So war es wirklich: Der deutsche Nachkriegsfilm*. Munich: F. A. Herbig, 1986.

Berger, Jürgen. "Bürgen heißt zahlen—und manchmal auch zensieren: Die Filmbürgschaften des Bundes, 1950–1955." In *"Zwischen Gestern und Morgen": Westdeutscher Nachkriegsfilm, 1946–1962*, edited by Hilmar Hoffmann and Walter Schobert, 80–97. Frankfurt am Main: Deutsches Filmmuseum, 1989.

Bessen, Ursula. *Trümmer und Träume: Nachkriegszeit und fünfziger Jahre auf Zelluloid; Deutsche Spielfilme als Zeugnisse ihrer Zeit; Eine Dokumentation*. Bochum: Dr. Brockmeier Verlag, 1989.

Bliersbach, Gerhard. *So grün war die Heide: der deutsche Nachkriegsfilm in neuer Sicht Thema-Film: Die gar nicht so heile Welt im Nachkriegsfilm*. Weinheim: Beltz Verlag, 1985. Reprinted as *So grün war die Heide: . . . Thema-Film: Die gar nicht so heile Welt im Nachkriegsfilm*. Weinheim: Psychologie Heute Taschenbuch, 1989.

Blumenberg, Hans-Christoph. *"Das Leben geht weiter": Der letzte Film des Dritten Reichs*. Berlin: Rowohlt, 1993.

Burghardt, Kirsten. "Moralische Wiederaufrüstung im frühen deutschen Nachkriegsfilm." In *Positionen deutscher Filmgeschichte: 100 Jahre Kinematographie; Strukturen, Diskurse, Kontexte*, edited by Michael Schaudig, 240–77. Munich: Schaudig und Ledig, 1996.

Cornelsen, Peter. *Helmut Käutner: Seine Filme—sein Leben*. Munich: Heyne, 1980.

Cramer, Heinz von. "Wer zahlt–darf tanzen: Versuch einer kritischen Biographie des deutschen Films." In *Bestandsaufnahme: Line deutsche Bilanz 1962*, edited by Hans Werner Richter, 517–42. Munich: Verlag Kurt Desch, 1962.

Culbert, David. "American Film Policy in the Re-education of Germany after 1945." In *The Political Re-education of Germany and Her Allies after World War II*, edited by Nicholas Pronay and Keith Wilson, 173–202. London: Croom Helm, 1985.

de Hadeln, Moritz. "Special Tribute: Berlin International Film Festival — Thirty-five Years of Dedication to Film." In *International Film Guide 1985*, 347–56. London: Tantivy Press, 1985.

Dokumentation: 30 Jahre Internationale Filmwoche Mannheim, 1951–1981. Edited by Internationale Filmwoche Mannheim and Klaus Hofmann. Mannheim: Internationale Filmwoche Mannheim, 1981.

Elsaesser, Thomas. "German Postwar Cinema and Hollywood." In *Hollywood in Europe*, edited by David Ellwood and Rob Kroes, 283–302. Amsterdam: Vrije Universiteit Press, 1994.

Fehrenbach, Heide. *Cinema in Democratizing Germany: Reconstructing National Identity after Hitler.* Chapel Hill: University of North Carolina Press, 1995.

———. "The Fight for the 'Christian West': German Film Control, the Churches, and the Reconstruction of Civil Society in the Early Bonn Republic." *German Studies Review* 14, no. 1 (February 1991): 39–63.

Fischer, Kurt J. "Die Krise des deutschen Films: Wirtschaftliche Tatsache und Möglichkeiten." *Politische Meinung* 10 (1957): 49–62.

Gandert, Gero. *Zur Retrospektive Wolfgang Staudte.* Berlin: Stiftung Deutsche Kinemathek, 1974.

Göttler, Fritz. "*Kolberg*: Nichts geht mehr." In *Das Jahr 1945: Filme aus fünfzehn Ländern*, edited by Hans Helmut Prinzler, 188–89. Berlin: Stiftung Deutsche Kinemathek, 1990.

Guback, Thomas. "Shaping the Film Business in Postwar Germany: The Role of the U.S. Film Industry and the U.S. State." In *The Hollywood Film Industry*, edited by Paul Kerr, 245–75. New York: Routledge, 1986.

Hartenian, Larry. "The Role of Media in Democratizing Germany: United States Occupation Policy, 1945–1949." *Central European History* 20, no. 2 (June 1987): 145–90.

Hauser, Johannes. *Neuaufbau der westdeutschen Filmwirtschaft, 1945–1955 und der Einfluß der US-amerikanischen Filmpolitik: Vom reichseigenen Filmmonopolkonzern (UFI) zur privatwirtschaftlichen Konkurrenzwirtschaft.* Pfaffenweiler: Centaurus, 1989.

Helt, Richard C., and Marie E. Helt. *West German Cinema since 1945: A Reference Handbook.* Metuchen, N.J.: Scarecrow Press, 1987.

Henseleit, Felix, ed. *Die Internationalen Filmfestspiele Berlin von 1951–1974 im Zeitraffer.* Berlin: Internationale Filmfestspiele Berlin, 1975.

Hobsch, Manfred. *Liebe, Tanz und 1000 Schlagerfilme.* Berlin: Schwarzkopf und Schwarzkopf, 1999.

Hoenisch, Michael. "Film as an Instrument of the U.S. Reeducation Program in Germany after 1945 and the Example of *Todesmühlen*." *Englisch-Amerikanische Studien* 4, nos. 1–2 (1982): 196–210.

Hoerschelmann, Olaf. " 'Memoria Dextera Est': Film and Public Memory in Postwar Germany." *Cinema Journal* 40, no. 2 (2001): 78–97.

Hoffmann, Hilmar, and Walter Schobert, eds. *"Zwischen Gestern und Morgen": Westdeutscher Nachkriegsfilm, 1946–1962*. Frankfurt am Main: Deutsches Filmmuseum, 1989.

Höfig, Willi. *Der deutsche Heimatfilm, 1947–1960*. Stuttgart: Ferdinand Enke, 1973.

Hohnstock, Manfred, and Alfons Bettermann, eds. *Deutscher Filmpreis, 1951–1980*. Bonn: Bundes Innenministerium, 1980.

Jacobsen, Wofgang, and Hans Helmut Prinzler, eds. *Käutner*. Berlin: Volker Spiess, 1992.

Jaeger, Klaus, and Helmut Regel. *Deutschland in Trümmern: Filmdokumente der Jahre, 1945–1949*. Oberhausen: Verlag Karl Maria Laufen, 1976.

Jary, Michaela. *Traumfabriken Made in Germany: Die Geschichte des deutschen Nachkriegsfilms, 1945–1960*. Berlin: Edition q, 1993.

Joseph, Robert. "Our Film Program in Germany: How Far Was It a Success?" *Hollywood Quarterly* 2, no. 2 (January 1947): 122–30.

Jung, Fernand. "Das Kino der frühen Jahre: Herbert Vesely und die Filmavantgarde der Bundesrepublik." In *"Zwischen Gestern und Morgen": Westdeutscher Nachkriegsfilm, 1946–1962*, edited by Hilmar Hoffmann and Walter Schobert, 318–37. Frankfurt am Main: Deutsches Filmmuseum, 1989.

Kalbus, Oskar. *Die Situation des deutschen Films: Ein aktueller Beitrag zur Analyse der Filmkrise von heute*. Wiesbaden: Film-Echo, 1956.

King, Alasdair. "Placing *Green Is the Heath* (1951): Spatial Politics and Emergent West German Identity." In *Light Motives: German Popular Film in Perspective*, edited by Randall Halle and Margaret McCarthy, 130–47. Detroit: Wayne State University Press, 2003.

Klär, Karl. *Film zwischen Wunsch und Wirklichkeit: Gespräche mit den Freunden des Films und seinen Gegnern*. Wiesbaden-Biebrich: Der neue Film Verlagsgesellschaft Feldt, 1957.

Knietzsch, Horst. *Wolfgang Staudte*. Berlin: Henschel, 1966.

König, Ingelore, Dieter Wiedemann, and Lothar Wolf, eds. *Zwischen Bluejeans und Blauhemden: Jugendfilm in Ost und West*. Berlin: Henschel, 1995.

Koschnitzki, Rüdiger. *Filmographie Helmut Käutner*. Wiesbaden: Deutsches Institut für Filmkunde, 1978.

Kreimeier, Klaus. *Kino und Filmindustrie in der BRD: Ideologieproduktion und Klassenwirklichkeit nach 1945*. Kronberg: Scriptor Verlag, 1973.

Kreuder, Thomas. "Ist die FSK verfassungswidrig? Bereits 1958 beantwortet Johanne Noltenius diese Frage mit Ja." *Frauen und Film*, no. 35 (October 1983): 78–87.

Krings, Hermann. *Was heißt wertvoll: Über Grundlagen und Maßstab der Filmbewertung.* 2nd ed. Wiesbaden-Biebrich: Filmbewertungsstelle Wiesbaden, 1961.

Leimgruber, Florian, ed. *Luis Trenker, Regisseur und Schriftsteller: Die Personalakte Trenkers im Berlin Document Center.* Bolzano: Frasnelli-Keitsch, 1994.

Loewenstein, Joseph, and Lynn Tatlock. "The Marshall Plan at the Movies: Marlene Dietrich and Her Incarnations." *German Quarterly* 65, nos. 3–4 (Summer–Fall 1992): 429–42.

Ludin, Malte. *Wolfgang Staudte.* Reinbeck bei Hamburg: Rowohlt, 1996.

Moltke, Johannes von. "Heimat and History: *Viehjud Levi*." Special Issue on Postwall Cinema. *New German Critique*, no. 87 (Autumn 2002): 83–106.

———. *No Place Like Home: Locations of Heimat in German Cinema.* Berkeley and Los Angeles: University of California Press, 2005.

———. "Trapped in America: The Americanization of the Trapp-Familie, or, 'Papas Kino' Revisited." *German Studies Review* 19, no. 3 (1996): 455–78.

Muhlen, Norbert. "The Return of Goebbels's Filmmakers." *Commentary* 11, no. 3 (March 1951): 245–50.

Netenjakob, Egon. *Staudte.* Edited by Eva Orbanz and Hans-Helmut Prinzler. Berlin: Volker Spiess, 1991.

Noltenius, Johanne. *Die Freiwillige Selbstkontrolle der Filmwirtschaft und das Zensurverbot des Grundgesetzes.* Göttingen: Verlag Otto Schwarz, 1958.

Orbanz, Eva, and Hans Helmut Prinzler, eds. *Staudte.* Berlin: Volker Spiess, 1991.

Osterland, Martin. *Gesellschaftsbilder in Filmen: Eine soziologische Untersuchung des Filmangebots der Jahre 1949 bis 1964.* Stuttgart: Ferdinand Enke, 1970.

Patalas, Enno. "Vom deutschen Nachkriegsfilm." In *Filmstudien: Beiträge des Filmseminars im Institut für Publizistik an der Universität Muenster*, Vol. 1, edited by Walter Hagemann, 13–28. Emsdetten: Verlag Lechte, 1952.

Pilgert, Henry P. *Press, Radio and Film in West Germany, 1945–1953.* [N.p.]: Historical Division, Office of the Executive Secretary, Office of the U. S. High Commissioner for Germany, 1953.

Pleyer, Peter. *Deutscher Nachkriegsfilm, 1946–1948.* Münster: Verlag C. J. Fahle, 1965.

Poore, Carol. "Who Belongs? Disability and the German Nation in Postwar Literature and Film." *German Studies Review* 26, no. 1 (February 2003): 21–42.

Prinzler, Hans Helmut. *Das Jahr 1945: Filme aus fünfzehn Ländern.* Berlin: Stiftung Deutsche Kinemathek, 1990.

Pütz, Karl Heinz. "Business or Propaganda? American Films and Germany, 1942–1946." *Englisch-Amerikanische Studien* 5, nos. 2–3 (1983): 394–415.

Regel, Helmut. "Der Film als Instrument alliierter Besatzungspolitik in Westdeutschland." In *Deutschland in Trümmern: Filmdokumente der Jahre 1945–1949*, edited by Klaus Jaeger and Helmut Regel, 39–50. Oberhausen: Verlag Karl Maria Laufen, 1976.

Reimer, Robert C., and Carol J. Reimer. *Nazi-retro Film: How German Narrative Cinema Remembers the Past.* New York: Twayne, 1992.

——. "Nazi-retro Filmography." *Journal of Popular Film and Television* 14, no. 2 (Summer 1986): 80–92.

Riess, Curt. *Das gibt's nur einmal: Das Buch des deutschen Films nach 1945.* Hamburg: Henri Nannen Verlag, 1958.

Ruther, Rainer. "Le Heimatfilm un genre typiquement teutonique." *Les cahiers de la cinémathèque* 32 (1981): 13–32.

Schmidt, Klaus M. *Lexikon Literaturverfilmungen: Verzeichnis deutschsprachige Filme, 1945–2000.* Stuttgart: J. B. Metzler, 2001.

Schmieding, Walter. *Kunst oder Kasse: Der Ärger mit dem deutschen Film.* Hamburg: Rütten und Loening, 1961.

Schnurre, Wolfdietrich. *Rettung des deutschen Films: Eine Streitschrift.* Stuttgart: Deutsche Verlags-Anstalt, 1950.

Schulberg, Stuart. "The German Film: Comeback or Setback?" *Quarterly of Film, Radio, and Television* 8 (Summer 1954): 400–404.

Schwab-Felisch, Hans. "Die Affäre Harlan." *Der Monat* 3, no. 28 (January 1951): 414–22.

Seidl, Claudius. *Der deutsche Film der fünfziger Jahre.* Munich: Wilhelm Heyne, 1987.

Shandley, Robert R. "Coming Home through Rubble Canyons: *The Murderers Are among Us* and Generic Convention." In *Rubble Films: German Cinema in the Shadow of the Third Reich,* 25–46. Philadelphia: Temple University Press, 2001.

——. *Rubble Films: German Cinema in the Shadow of the Third Reich.* Philadelphia: Temple University Press, 2001.

Staudte, Wolfgang, Hein Heckroth, and Günter Raguse. *Die Dreigroschenoper 63: Werkbuch zum Film.* Munich: Laokoon-Verlag, 1964.

Westermann, Barbel. *Nationale Identität im Spielfilm der fünfziger Jahre.* New York: Peter Lang, 1990.

WEST GERMANY–NEW GERMAN CINEMA: 1962–1982

Adair, Gilbert. "Fassbinder's Wristwatch." *Films and Filming,* no. 347 (August 1983): 13–16.

"Alexander Kluge." Special Issue. *New German Critique,* no. 49 (Winter 1990): 1–191.

Alter, Nora M. "The Political Im/perceptible in the Essay Film: Farocki's Images of the World and Inscriptions of War." Special Issue on Literature. *New German Critique,* no. 68 (Spring–Summer 1996): 165–92. Also published in *Harun Farocki: Working on the Sight-Lines,* edited by Thomas Elsaesser, 211–36. Amsterdam: Amsterdam University Press, 2004.

Armes, Roy. "Jean-Marie Straub: Strict Counterpoint." In *The Ambiguous Image: Narrative Style in Modern European Cinema,* 208–15. Bloomington: Indiana University Press, 1976.

Arnold, Heinz Ludwig, ed. *Rainer Werner Fassbinder.* Munich: edition text + kritik, 1989.

Atkinson, Michael. "The Wanderings of Werner Herzog." Critical Essay. *Film Comment* 36, no. 1 (January 2000): 16–19.

Bachmann, Gideon. "The Man on the Volcano: A Portrait of Werner Herzog." *Film Quarterly* 31, no. 1 (Fall 1977): 2–10.

Baer, Harry. *Schlafen kann ich, wenn ich tot bin: Das atemlose Leben des Rainer Werner Fassbinder.* Cologne: Kiepenheuer und Witsch, 1982.

Bammer, Angelika. "Through a Daughter's Eyes: Helma Sanders-Brahms's *Germany, Pale Mother.*" Special Issue on Heimat. *New German Critique,* no. 36 (Autumn 1985): 91–109.

Barg, Werner. *Erzählkino und Autorenfilm: Zur Theorie und Praxis filmischen Erzählens bei Alexander Kluge und Edgar Reitz.* Munich: Wilhelm Fink Verlag, 1996.

Beard, William. "American Madness: Concepts of Culture and Sanity in *The American Friend* and *Stroszek.*" *Yearbook of Comparative and General Literature* 40 (1992): 59–74.

Bennett, Edward. "The Films of Straub Are Not 'Theoretical'." *Afterimage* 7 (Summer 1978): 5–11.

Berling, Peter. *Die 13 Jahre des Rainer Werner Fassbinder.* Bergisch Gladbach: Lübbe, 1995.

Berman, Russell A. "Hans-Jürgen Syberberg: Of Fantastic and Magical Worlds." In *New German Filmmakers: From Oberhausen through the 1970s,* edited by Klaus Phillips, 359–78. New York: Frederick Ungar, 1984.

———. "The Recipient as Spectator: West German Film and Poetry of the Seventies." *The German Quarterly* 55, no. 4 (November 1982): 499–510.

Bettecken, Wilhelm. "25 Jahre Wandlungen des Kurzfilms." In *Sprache des Kurzfilms: Beispiel-25 Jahre Westdeutsche Kurzfilmtage Oberhausen,* edited by Johannes Horstmann, 124–45. Munich: F. Schoningh, 1981.

Bloom, Michael. "Woyzeck and Kaspar: The Congruities in Drama and Film." *Literature/Film Quarterly* 8, no. 4 (1980): 225–31.

Borchardt, Edith. "Leitmotif and Structure in Fassbinder's *Effi Briest.*" *Literature/Film Quarterly* 7, no. 3 (1979): 201–7.

Bourget, Jean Loup. *Douglas Sirk*. Paris: Edilig, 1984.

Bower, Kathrin. "Outing Hybridity: Polymorphism, Identity, and Desire in Monika Treut's *Virgin Machine.*" *European Studies Journal* 17, no. 1 (Spring 2000): 23–40.

Bowie, Andrew. "Alexander Kluge: An Introduction." *Cultural Critique,* no. 4 (Fall 1986): 111–18.

Braad Thomsen, Christian. *Fassbinder: The Life and Work of a Provocative Genius.* Translated by Martin Chalmers. Minneapolis: University of Minnesota Press, 2004.

Brady, Martin. "'Du Tag, wann wirst du sein . . .': Quotation, Emancipation and Dissonance in Straub/Huillet's *Der Bräutigam, die Komödiantin und der Zuhälter.*" *German Life and Letters* 53, no. 3 (2000): 281–302.

Brinckmann, Noll. "Schwere Zeiten für Schauspieler: Beobachtungen zu *Heller Wahn* und *Der Schlaf der Vernunft. Frauen und Film,* no. 40 (August 1986): 4–12.

Brockmann, Stephen. "Syberberg's Germany." *German Quarterly* 69, no. 1 (Winter 1996): 48–62.

Bromley, Roger. *From "Alice" to "Buena Vista": The Films of Wim Wenders.* Westport, Conn.: Praeger, 2001.

———. "Traversing Identity: Home Movies and Road Movies in *Paris, Texas.*" *Angelaki* 2, no. 1 (November 1995): 101–18.

Brown, Russell E. "Names in the Films of R. W. Fassbinder." *Names: Journal of the American Name Society* 41, no. 4 (December 1993): 239–47.

Bruck, Jan. "Brecht's and Kluge's Aesthetics of Realism." *Poetics: International Review for the Theory of Literature* 17, nos. 1–2 (April 1988): 57–68.

Brückner, Jutta. *Cinema regard violence.* Brussels: Cahiers du Grif, 1982.

———. Interview with Patricia Harbord. *Screen Education,* no. 40 (Autumn 1981–Winter 1982): 48–57.

———. "On Autobiographical Filmmaking." Translated by Jeannette Clausen. *Women in German Yearbook: Feminist Studies in German Literature and Culture* 11 (1995): 1–12.

———. "Recognizing Collective Gestures." Interview with Marc Silberman. *Jump Cut,* no. 27 (1982): 41–53.

———. "Women Behind the Camera." In *Feminist Aesthetics*, edited by Gisela Ecker,120–24. Boston: Beacon Press, 1986.

Brückner, Jutta, Margarethe von Trotta, and Geneviève Dormann. *"Le coup de grâce." L'avant-scène du cinéma* 181 (February 1, 1977): 3–23, 43–59.

Burns, Rob. "Fassbinder's *Angst essen Seele auf*: A Mellow Brechtian Drama." *German Life and Letters* 48, no. 1 (January 1995): 56–74.

——. "Social Reality and Stylization in *Fear Eats the Soul*: Fassbinder's Study in Prejudice." *New German Studies* 9, no. 3 (Autumn 1981): 193–206.

Byg, Barton. "German History and Cinematic Convention Harmonized in Margarethe von Trotta's *Marianne and Juliane*." In *Gender and German Cinema: Feminist Interventions*. Vol. 2, *German Film History/German History on Film*, edited by Sandra Frieden, Richard W. McCormick, Vibeke R. Petersen, and Laurie Melissa Vogelsang, 259–72. Providence, R.I.: Berg, 1993.

——. *Landscapes of Resistance: The German Films of Danièle Huillet and Jean-Marie Straub*. Berkeley and Los Angeles: University of California Press, 1995.

Caldwell, David, and Paul W. Rea. "Handke's and Wenders's *Wings of Desire*: Transcending Postmodernism." *German Quarterly* 64, no. 1 (Winter 1991): 46–54.

Caltvedt, Lester. "Herzog's *Fitzcarraldo* and the Rubber Era." *Film and History* 18, no. 4 (December 1988): 74–84.

Carroll, Noel. "Herzog, Presence, and Paradox." *Persistence of Vision*, no. 2 (Fall 1985): 30–40.

Casper, Kent. "Herzog's Quotidian Apocalypse: *La Soufrière*." *Film Criticism* 15, no. 2 (Winter 1991): 29–37.

——. "Romantic Inversions in Herzog's *Nosferatu*." *The German Quarterly* 64, no. 1 (Winter 1991): 17–24.

Castle, Robert. "Fritz Lang's Assumption Factory: Social Agreements and Schisms in *Fury, Modern Times,* and *A Clockwork Orange*." *Bright Lights Film Journal*, no. 38 (November 2002). www.brightlightsfilm.com/38/fury1 .htm

Chaffin-Quiray, Garrett. "An Adaptation with Fangs: Werner Herzog's *Nosferatu: Phantom der Nacht* (*Nosferatu the Vampyre*, 1979.)" *Kinoeye* 2, no. 20 (December 2002). www.kinoeye.org/02/20/chaffinquiray20.php

Cheesman, Tom. "Apocalypse Nein Danke-The Fall of Werner Herzog." In *Green Thought in German Culture: Historical and Contemporary Perspectives*, edited by Colin Riordan, 285–306. Swansea, UK: University of Wales Press, 1997.

Chipperfield, Alkan. "Murmurs from a Shadowless Land: Fragmentary Reflections on the Cinema of Werner Herzog." *Senses of Cinema: An Online Film Journal Devoted to the Serious and Eclectic Discussion of Cinema,* no. 15 (July–August 2001). www.sensesofcinema.com/contents/01/15/herzog_ alkan.html

Cleere, Elizabeth. "Three Films by Werner Herzog: Seen in the Light of the Grotesque." *Wide Angle* 3, no. 4 (1980): 12–19.

Collins, Richard, and Vincent Porter. *WDR and the Arbeiterfilm: Fassbinder, Ziewer, and Others*. London: BFI, 1981.

Cook, Roger F. "Angels, Fiction, and History in Berlin: *Wings of Desire*." In *The Cinema of Wim Wenders: Image, Narrative and the Postmodern Condition*, edited by Roger Cook and Gerd Gemünden, 163–90. Detroit: Wayne State University Press, 1997.

———. "Film Images and Reality: Alexander Kluge's Aesthetics of Cinema." *Colloquia Germanica* 18, no. 4 (1985): 281–99.

———. "Melodrama or Cinematic Folktale? Story and History in *Deutschland, bleiche Mutter*." *Germanic Review* 66, no. 3 (Summer 1991): 113–29.

Cook, Roger F., and Gerd Gemünden, eds. *The Cinema of Wim Wenders: Image, Narrative, and the Postmodern Condition*. Detroit: Wayne State University Press, 1996.

Corrigan, Timothy, ed. *The Films of Werner Herzog: Between Mirage and History*. New York: Methuen, 1986.

———. *New German Film: The Displaced Image*. Rev. ed. Bloomington: Indiana University Press, 1994.

———. "The Realist Gesture in the Films of Wim Wenders: Hollywood and the New German Cinema." *Quarterly Review of Film Studies* 5, no. 2 (Spring 1980): 204–16.

———. "The Temporality of Place, Postmodernism, and the Fassbinder Texts." Special Issue on Rainer Werner Fassbinder. *New German Critique,* no. 63 (Autumn 1994): 139–54.

———. "Types of History: Schlöndorff's *Coup de Grâce*." In *New German Film: The Displaced Image,* rev. ed., 54–73. Bloomington: Indiana University Press, 1994.

———. "Wenders' *Kings of the Road*: The Voyage from Desire to Language." Special Double Issue on New German Cinema. *New German Critique,* nos. 24–25. (Autumn 1981–Winter 1982): 94–107. Also published in *Perspectives on German Cinema*, edited by Terri Ginsberg and Kirsten Moana Thompson, 295–308. New York: G. K. Hall; London: Prentice Hall International, 1996.

———, ed. *Werner Herzog.* London, Methuen, 1986.

Covino, Michael. "Wim Wenders: A Worldwide Homesickness." *Film Quarterly* 31, no. 2 (Winter 1977–1978): 9–19.

Crimp, Douglas. "Fassbinder, Franz, Fox, Elvira, Armin, and All the Others." In *Queer Looks: Perspectives on Lesbian and Gay Film and Video*, edited by Martha Gever, Pratibha Parmar, John Greyson, 257–74. New York: Routledge, 1993.

Davidson, David. "Borne out of Darkness: The Documentaries of Werner Herzog." *Film Criticism* 5, no. 1 (1980): 10–25.

Davidson, John E. "As Others Put Plays upon the Stage: *Aguirre*, Neocolonialism, and the New German Cinema." Special Issue on German Film History. *New German Critique,* no. 60 (Autumn 1993): 101–30.

BIBLIOGRAPHY • 405

BIBLIOGRAPHY • 405

——. "Contacting the Other: Traces of Migrational Colonialism and the Imperial Agent in Werner Herzog's *Fitzcarraldo*." *Film and History* 24, nos. 3–4 (1994): 66–83.

——. *Deterritorializing the New German Cinema*. Minneapolis: University of Minnesota Press, 1999.

Dawson, Jan, ed. and comp. *The Films of Hellmuth Costard*. London: Riverside Studios, 1979.

——. "A Labyrinth of Subsidies: The Origins of the New German Cinema." *Sight and Sound* 50, no. 2 (Spring 1981): 102–7.

——. "The Sacred Terror—Shadows of Terrorism in the New German Cinema." *Sight and Sound* 48, no. 4 (Autumn 1979): 242–45.

——. *Wim Wenders*. New York: Zoetrope, 1976.

Delorme, Charlotte. "On the Film *Marianne and Juliane* by Margarethe von Trotta." *The Journal of Film and Video,* 37, no. 2 (Spring 1985): 47–51.

Dhein, Sabina. *Werner Schroeter: Regie im Theater.* Frankfurt am Main: Fischer Taschenbuch, 1991.

Dietrich, Christopher. "A Closet Full of Brutality: Volker Schlöndorff's *Der Junge Törless*." *Kinoeye* 2, no. 10 (May 27, 2002). www.kinoeye.org/02/10/dietrich10.html

Dost, Michael, Florian Hopf, and Alexander Kluge. *Filmwirtschaft in der Bundesrepublik Deutschland und in Europa: Götterdämmerung in Raten.* Munich: Carl Hanser, 1973.

Douglas, J. Yellowlees. "American Friends and Strangers on Trains." *Literature/Film Quarterly* 16, no. 3 (1988): 181–90.

Eckhardt, Bernd. *Rainer Werner Fassbinder in 17 Jahren 42 Filme: Stationen eines Lebens für den deutschen Film.* Munich: Wilhelm Heyne, 1982.

Eisner, Lotte H. "Herzog in Dinkelsbuehl." *Sight and Sound* 43, no. 4 (Autumn 1974): 212–13.

Elsaesser, Thomas. "American Friends: Hollywood Echoes in the New German Cinema." In *Hollywood and Europe: Economics, Culture, National Identities, 1945–95*, edited by Geoffrey Nowell-Smith and Steve Ricci, 141–55. London: BFI Publishing, 1998.

——. "American Graffiti: Neuer Deutscher Film zwischen Avantgarde und Postmoderne." In *Postmoderne-Zeichen eines kulturellen Wandels*, edited by A. Huyssen and K. Scherpe, 302–28. Reinbek bei Hamburg: Rowohlt, 1986.

——. "Antigone Agonistes: Urban Guerilla or Guerilla Urbanism? The RAF, *Germany in Autumn* and *Death Game*." In *Giving Ground, The Politics of Propinquity*, edited by Joan Copjec and Michael Sorkin, 267–302. London: Verso, 1999.

——. "*Berlin Alexanderplatz*: Franz Biberkopf'/S/Exchanges." *Wide Angle* 12, no. 1 (1990): 30–43. Also published in *Fassbinder's Germany: History,*

Identity, Subject, 217–36. Amsterdam: Amsterdam University Press, 1996. Distributed in the U.S. by the University of Chicago Press.

———. "From Anti-illusionism to Hyper-realism: Bertolt Brecht and Contemporary Film." In *Re-interpreting Brecht: His Influence on Contemporary Drama and Film*, edited by Colin Visser and Pia Kleber, 170–85. Cambridge, England: Cambridge University Press, 1990.

———. "Die Gegenwärtigkeit des Holocaust im Neuen Deutschen Film am Beispiel Alexander Kluge." In *Die Vergangenheit in der Gegenwart Konfrontationen mit den Folgen des Holocaust im deutschen Nachkriegsfilm*, edited by Deutsches Filminstitut–DIF, Claidia Dillmann, and Ronny Loewy, 54–67. Munich: edition text + kritik, 2001.

———. "Germany's Imaginary America: Wim Wenders and Peter Handke." In *European Cinema Conference Papers*, edited by Susan Hayward, 31–52. Birmingham, Ala.: Modern Languages Department: Aston University, 1985.

———. *Harun Farocki: Working on the Sight-Lines*. Amsterdam: Amsterdam University Press, 2004. Distributed in the U.S. by the University of Chicago Press.

———. "Historicizing the Subject: A Body of Work?" Special Issue on Rainer Werner Fassbinder. *New German Critique,* no. 63 (Autumn 1994): 10–33.

———. *A History of New German Cinema*. New Brunswick, N.J.: Rutgers University Press, 1989.

———. "'It Started with These Images'—Some Notes on Political Film-Making after Brecht in Germany: Helke Sander and Harun Farocki." *Discourse: Journal for Theoretical Studies in Media and Culture* 7 (Fall 1985): 95–120.

———. "Myth as the Phantasmagoria of History: H. J. Syberberg, Cinema and Representation." Special Double Issue on New German Cinema. *New German Critique,* nos. 24–25 (Autumn 1981–Winter 1982): 108–54.

———. *Der Neue Deutsche Film: Von den Anfängen bis zu den neunziger Jahren*. Munich: Wilhelm Heyne, 1994.

———. *New German Cinema: A History*. 2nd ed. New Brunswick, N.J.: Rutgers University Press, 1994.

———. "Primary Identification and the Historical Subject: Fassbinder and Germany." In *Narrative, Apparatus, Ideology*, edited by Philip Rosen, 535–49. New York: Columbia University Press, 1986.

———. *Rainer Werner Fassbinder.* Berlin: Bertz Verlag, 2001.

———. "A Retrospect on the New German Cinema." *German Life and Letters* 41, no. 3 (April 1988): 271–92.

———. "Tarnformen der Trauer: Herbert Achternbuschs Das letzte Loch." In *Lachen über Hitler - Ausschwitz-Gelächter? Filmkomödie, Satire und Holocaust*, edited by Margrit Frölich, Hanno Loewy, and Heinz Steinert, 155–80. Munich: edition text + kritik, 2003.

Ettl, Hubert. *Kurt Raab: Hommage aus der Provinz.* Viechtach: Edition Lichtung, 1989.

Farber, Manny, and Patricia Patterson. "Rainer Werner Fassbinder." *Film Comment* 11, no. 6 (November–December 1975).

Farocki, Harun. "History Is Not a Matter of Generations: Interview with Harun Farocki." *Camera Obscura,* no. 46 (May 2001): 47–75.

Fassbinder, Rainer Werner. *The Anarchy of the Imagination: Interviews, Essays, Notes.* Edited by Michael Töteberg and Leo A. Lensing. Translated from German by Krishna Winston. Baltimore: Johns Hopkins University Press, 1992.

———. *Fassbinder über Fassbinder: die ungekürzten Interviews.* Edited by Robert Fischer. Frankfurt am Main: Verlag der Autoren, 2004.

———. *Filme befreien den Kopf: Essays und Arbeitsnotizen.* Edited by Michael Töteberg. Frankfurt am Main: Fischer Taschenbücher, 1984.

———. "*Imitation of Life*: Über Douglas Sirk." *Fernsehen und Film* 2 (February 1971): 8–13. Reprinted in Fassbinder's *Filme befreien den Kopf,* 11–24, edited by Michael Töteberg. Frankfurt am Main: Fischer Taschenbücher, 1984. Also published as "Imitation of Life: On the Films of Douglas Sirk." In Fassbinder's *The Anarchy of the Imagination: Interviews, Essays, Notes—Rainer Werner Fassbinder,* edited by Michael Töteberg and Leo A. Lensing and translated by Krishna Winston, 77–89. Baltimore: Johns Hopkins University Press, 1992.

———. "*Katzelmacher.*" "*Preparadise Sorry Now.*" "*Bremer Freiheit.*" "*Blut am Hals der Katze*". 2nd ed. Berlin: Henschel, 1988.

———. *Die Kinofilme.* Munich: Schirmer/Mosel, 1987.

———. "A New Realism: Fassbinder Interviewed." By John Hughes and Brooks Riley. *Film Comment* 11, no. 6 (November–December 1975): 14.

———. *Plays.* Edited and translated by Denis Calandra. PAJ Playscripts. New York: PAJ Publications, 1992.

Fassbinder, Rainer Werner, and Harry Baer. *Der Film "Berlin Alexanderplatz": Ein Arbeitsjournal.* Frankfurt am Main: Verlag Zweitausendeins, 1980.

Feinstein, Howard. "BRD 1–2–3: Fassbinder's Postwar Trilogy and the Spectacle." *Cinema Journal* 23, no. 1 (Fall 1983): 44–56.

Fiedler, Theodore. "Alexander Kluge, Mediating History and Consciousness." In *New West German Filmmakers: From Oberhausen through the 1970s,* edited by Klaus Phillips, 195–229. New York: Frederick Ungar, 1984.

Finger, Ellis. "Kaspar Hauser Doubly Portrayed; Peter Handke's *Kaspar* and Werner Herzog's *Every Man for Himself and God Against All.*" *Literature/Film Quarterly* 7, no. 3 (1979): 235–43.

Fischetti, Renate. *Das neue Kino: Acht Porträts von deutschen Regisseurinnen: Helke Sander, Claudia von Alemann, Ula Stöckl, Helma Sanders-Brahms,*

Margarethe von Trotta, Jutta Brückner, Ulrike Ottinger, Doris Dörrie. Frankfurt am Main: Tende, 1992.

Fleming, Bruce E. "Thoughts and Their Discontents: *Törless*—Book to Film." *Literature-Film Quarterly* 20, no. 2 (April 1992): 109–14.

Flinn, Caryl. *The New German Cinema: Music, History, and the Matter of Style.* Berkeley and Los Angeles: University of California Press, 2004.

———. "Strategies of Remembrance: Music and History in the New German Cinema." In *Music and Cinema*, edited by James Buhler, Caryl Flinn, and David Neumeyer, 118–41. Hanover, N.H.: University Press of New England; Middletown, Conn.: Wesleyan University Press, 2000.

Forrest, Tara. "From History's Rubble: On the Future of the Past in the Work of Alexander Kluge." *Rethinking History* 9, no, 4 (December 2005): 429–48.

Franklin, James C. "Jean-Marie Straub/Danièle Huilette." In *New German Cinema: From Oberhausen to Hamburg,* 74–88. Boston: Twayne, 1983.

———. "Method and Message: Forms of Communication in Fassbinder's *Angst essen Seele auf.*" *Literature/Film Quarterly* 7, no. 2 (1979): 182–200.

———. *New German Cinema: From Oberhausen to Hamburg.* Boston: Twayne, 1983.

Freybourg, Anne Marie. *Bilder lesen: Visionen von Liebe und Politik bei Godard und Fassbinder.* Vienna: Passagen-Verlag, 1996.

Frieden, Sandra, Richard W. McCormick, Vibeke R. Petersen, and Laurie Melissa Vogelsang. *Gender and German Cinema: Feminist Interventions.* Vol. 1, *Gender and Representation in New German Cinema.* Vol. 2, *German Film History /German History on Film.* Providence: Berg, 1993.

Friedman, Lester. "Cinematic Techniques in *The Lost Honor of Katharina Blum.*" *Literature/Film Quarterly* 7, no. 3 (1979): 244–52.

Fritze, Ronald. "Werner Herzog's Adaptation of History in *Aguirre, the Wrath of God.*" *Film and History* 15, no. 4 (December 1985): 74–86.

Fuegi, John. "On Brecht's 'Theory' of Film." In *Ideas of Order in Literature and Film*, edited by Peter Ruppert, 107–18. Tallahassee: University Presses of Florida, 1980.

Gabrea, Radu. *Werner Herzog et la mystique rhenane.* Lausanne: L'Age d'Homme, 1986.

Geist, Kathe. "Mothers and Children in the Films of Wim Wenders." In *Gender and German Cinema: Feminist Interventions.* Vol. 1, *Gender and Representation in New German Cinema*, edited by Sandra Frieden, Richard W. McCormick, Vibeke R. Petersen, and Laurie Melissa Vogelsang, 11–22. Providence, R.I.: Berg, 1993.

———. "Wim Wenders: Wenders in the Cities." In *New German Filmmakers: From Oberhausen through the 1970's*, edited by Klaus Phillips, 379–404. New York: Frederick Ungar, 1984.

Gemünden, Gerd. "The Gangster Film and Melodrama of Rainer Werner Fassbinder." In *Framed Visions: Popular Culture, Americanization, and the Contemporary German and Austrian Imagination*, 89–107. Ann Arbor: University of Michigan Press, 1998.

———. "Gone Primitive: The Indianerphantasien of Herbert Achternbusch." *Germanic Review* 73, no. 1 (Winter 1998): 32–49.

———. "On the Way to Language: Wenders' *Kings of the Road*." *Film Criticism* 15, no. 2 (Winter 1991): 13–28.

———. "Re-Fusing Brecht: The Cultural Politics of Fassbinder's German Hollywood." Special Issue on Rainer Werner Fassbinder. *New German Critique*, no. 63 (Autumn 1994): 54–75.

Gentile, Mary C. "Helke Sander's *Redupers*: Personality-in-Process." *Film Feminisms: Theory and Practice*, 113–31. Westport, Conn.: Greenwood Press, 1985.

Gerulaitis, Renate. "Recurring Cultural Patterns: Werner Herzog's Film *Every Man for Himself and God against All, the Enigma of Caspar Hauser*." *Journal of Popular Culture* 22, no. 4 (Spring 1989): 61–69.

Gitlin, Todd. "*Fitzcarraldo*." *Literature/Film Quarterly* 37, no. 2 (1983–84): 50–54.

Gollub, Christian-Albrecht. "Volker Schlöndorff and Margarethe von Trotta: Transcending the Genres." In *New German Filmmakers: From Oberhausen through the 1970s*, edited by Klaus Phillips, 266–302. New York: Frederick Ungar, 1984.

Graf, Roman. " 'Alles ist verdächtig': Zum Thema der 'Homosexualität' in den Bearbeitungen der Kaspar-Hauser-Legende von Jakob Wassermann, Klaus Mann, and Werner Herzog." In *Der imaginierte Findling: Studien zur Kaspar-Hauser-Rezeption*, edited by Ulrich Struve, 103–19. Heidelberg: Carl Winter University, 1995.

Greenberg, Alan, Herbert Achternbusch, and Werner Herzog. *Heart of Glass* [screenplay]. Munich: Skellig, 1976.

Grenier, Richard. "Movies: Fassbinder & the Bloomingdale's Factor." *Commentary* 74, no. 4 (October 1982): 53–62.

———. "Why Herzog Differs." *Commentary* 74, no. 6 (December 1982): 59–67.

Grimm, Reinhold, and Henry J. Schmidt. "Bertolt Brecht and *Hangmen Also Die!*" *Monatshefte* 61, no. 3 (Fall 1969): 232–40.

Grisham, Therese. "Processes of Subjectification in Fassbinder's *I Only Want You to Love Me*." *Screen* 40, no. 4 (Winter 1999): 423–45.

Hainisch, Bernhard, and Thomas Pilz. "Werner Herzog's *Jeder fur sich und Gott gegen alle*: Ein Film." *Blimp*, no. 30 (Winter 1994): 16–22.

Hake, Sabine. "New German Cinema." *Monatshefte* 82, no. 3 (1990): 267–75.

——. "Review Essay: The New German Cinema; Problems of Historiography." *Quarterly Review of Film and Video* 12 (Sept 1991): 107–15.

Hall, Carol. "A Different Drummer: The *Tin Drum*, Film and Novel." *Literature/Film Quarterly* 18, no. 4 (1990): 236–44.

Hansen, Miriam. " Messages in a Bottle? Miriam Hansen Examines 'Frauen und Film': Women's Cinema and Feminist Film Theory in West Germany." *Screen* 28, no. 4 (Autumn 1987): 30–39.

——. "The Stubborn Discourse: History and Storytelling in the Films of Alexander Kluge." *Persistence of Vision*, no. 2 (Fall 1985): 19–29.

——. "Visual Pleasure, Fetishism and the Problem of Feminine/Feminist Discourse: Ulrike Ottinger's *Ticket of No Return*." West German Culture and Politics. *New German Critique*, no. 31 (Winter 1984): 95–108.

Haralovich, Mary Beth. "The Sexual Politics of *The Marriage of Maria Braun*." *Wide Angle* 12, no. 1 (January 1990): 6–16. Also published in *Perspectives in German Cinema*, edited by Terri Ginsberg and Kirsten Moana Thompson, 378–91. New York: G. K. Hall; London: Prentice Hall International, 1996.

Harcourt, Peter. "Adaptation through Inversion: Wenders' *Wrong Movement* (1974)." *Modern European Filmmakers and the Art of Adaptation*, edited by Andrew Horton and Joan Magretta, 263–77. New York: Frederick Ungar, 1981.

——. "*The Sudden Wealth of the Poor People of Kombach*." *Film Quarterly* 34, no.1 (1980): 60–63.

Hartsough, Denise. "Cine-Feminism Renegotiated: Fassbinder's *Ali* as Interventionist Cinema." *Wide Angle* 12, no. 1 (January 1990): 18–29.

Hayman, Ronald. *Fassbinder: Film Maker*. New York: Simon & Schuster, 1984.

Head, David. " 'Der Autor muss respektiert werden'—Schlöndorff-Trotta's *Die verlorene Ehre der Katharina Blum*." *German Life and Letters* 32, no. 3 (April 1979): 248–64.

Hembus, Joe. *Der deutsche Film kann gar nicht besser sein: Ein Pamphlet von gestern, Eine Abrechnung von heute*. Munich: Rogner und Bernhard, 1981.

Herzog, Werner. "*Cobra Verde*": *Filmerzählung*. Munich: Carl Hanser, 1987.

——. *Drehbücher*. Vol. 1, "*Lebenszeichen*," "*Auch Zwerge haben klein angefangen*," "*Fata Morgana*." Vol. 2, "*Aguirre, Der Zorn Gottes*," "*Jeder für sich und Gott gegen alle*," "*Land des Schweigens und der Dunkelheit*." Munich: Skellig, 1977.

——. *Drehbücher*. Vol. 3, "*Stroszek*," "*Nosferatu*": *Zwei Filmerzählungen*. Munich: Carl Hanser, 1979.

——. *Eroberung des Nutzlosen*. Munich: Carl Hanser, 2004.

——. "*Fitzcarrado*": *Erzählung*. Munich: Carl Hanser, 1982.

——. *"Fitzcarraldo": Filmbuch.* Munich: Schirmer/Mosel, 1982.
——. *"Fitzcarraldo": The Original Story.* Translated by Martje Herzog and Alan Greenberg. San Francisco: Fjord Press, 1982.
——. *Herzog on Herzog.* Edited by Paul Cronin. New York: Faber and Farber, 2003
——. *Of Walking in Ice: Munich–Paris, 23 November–14 December, 1974.* Translated by Marje Herzog and Alan Greenberg. London: Jonathan Cape, 1991.
——. *Screenplays.* Translated from the German by Alan Greenberg, and Martje Herzog. New York: Tanam Press, 1980.
——. "Tribute to Lotte Eisner." In *West German Filmmakers: Visions and Voices*, edited by Eric Rentschler, 115–18. New York: Holmes and Meier, 1988.
——. "Werner Herzog in Conversation with Geoffrey O'Brien." *Parnassus: Poetry in Review* 22, nos. 1–2 (Spring–Summer 1997): 40–54.
——. *"Wo die grünen Ameisen träumen": Filmerzählung.* Munich: Carl Hanser, 1984.
——. "The Wrath of Klaus Kinski: An Interview with Werner Herzog." By A. G. Basoli. *Cineaste* 24, no, 4 (1999): 32–35.
Hillman, Roger. "Narrative, Sound, and Film: Fassbinder's *The Marriage of Maria Braun*." In *Fields of Vision: Essays in Film Studies, Visual Anthropology, and Photography*, edited by Leslie Devereaux and Roger Hillman, 181–95. Berkeley and Los Angeles: University of California Press, 1995.
Holloway, Ronald. *O Is for Oberhausen: Weg zum Nachbarn.* Oberhausen: Verlag Karl Maria Laufen, 1979.
Horak, Jan-Christopher. "Werner Herzog's Ecran Absurde." *Literature/Film Quarterly* 7, no. 3 (1979): 223–37.
Hughes, John. "Why Herr R. Ran Amok: Fassbinder and Modernism." *Film Comment* 11, no. 6 (November–December 1975): 11–13.
Huillet, Danièle. "Das Feuer im Innern des Berges." Interview by Helge Heberle and Monika Funke Stern. *Frauen und Film*, no. 32 (June 1982): 4–12.
Hyams, Barbara. "Is the Apolitical Woman at Peace? A Reading of the Fairy Tale in *Germany, Pale Mother*." *Wide Angle* 10, no. 4 (1988): 40–51.
Iden, Peter. "The Sensation Maker: Rainer Werner Fassbinder and the Theater." *Wide Angle* 2, no. 1 (1978): 4–13.
Iden, Peter, Yaak Karsunke, Hans-Helmut Prinzler, Wilhelm Roth, and Wilfried Wiegand. *Rainer Werner Fassbinder.* Munich: Carl Hanser, 1975.
Jameson, Fredric. "'In the Destructive Element Immerse': Hans-Jürgen Syberberg and Cultural Revolution." The New Talkies. *October,* no. 17 (Summer 1981): 99–118. Also published in *Perspectives on German Cinema*, edited by

Terri Ginsberg and Kirsten Moana Thompson, 508–25. New York: G. K. Hall; London: Prentice Hall International, 1996.

Jansen, Peter W., and Wolfram Schütte, eds. *Herzog/Kluge/Straub.* Munich: Carl Hanser, 1976.

——. *Rainer Werner Fassbinder.* Munich: Carl Hanser, 1974.

——. *Werner Herzog.* Munich: Carl Hanser, 1979.

——. *Werner Schroeter.* Munich: Carl Hanser, 1980.

Johnson, Catherine. "The Imaginary and The Bitter Tears of Petra Von Kant." *Wide Angle* 3, no. 4 (1980): 20–25.

Johnston, Sheila. "The Author as Public Institution: The 'New' Cinema in the Federal Republic of Germany." *Screen Education,* nos. 32–33 (Winter 1979–1980): 67–78.

——. "A Star Is Born: Fassbinder and the New German Cinema." Special Double Issue on New German Film. *New German Critique,* nos. 24–25. (Autumn 1981–Winter 1982): 57–72.

Johnston, Sheila, and John Ellis. "The Radical Film Funding of ZDF." *Screen* 23, no. 1 (May–June 1982): 60–73.

Kaes, Anton. *Deutschlandbilder: Die Wiederkehr der Geschichte als Film.* Munich: edition text + kritik, 1987.

——. *From Hitler to Heimat: The Return of History as Film.* Cambridge: Harvard University Press, 1989.

——. "German Cultural History and the Study of Film: Ten Theses and a Postscript." Cultural History/Cultural Studies. *New German Critique,* no. 65 (Spring-Summer 1995): 47–58.

——. "History and Film: Public Memory in the Age of Electronic Dissemination." *History and Memory* 2 (Fall 1990): 111–29.

——. "History, Fiction, Memory: Fassbinder's *The Marriage of Maria Braun.*" In *German Film and Literature: Adaptations and Transformations,* edited by Eric Rentschler, 276–88. New York: Methuen, 1986.

——. "The New German Cinema." In *Oxford World History of Cinema,* new ed., edited by Geoffrey Nowell-Smith, 614–26. Oxford: Oxford University Press, 1999.

——. The Presence of the Past: Rainer Werner Fassbinder's *The Marriage of Maria Braun.*" In *From Hitler to Heimat: The Return of History as Film,* 73–103. Cambridge: Harvard University Press, 1989.

Kaiser, Gerhard. *Fitzcarraldo Faust: Werner Herzogs Film als postmoderne Variation eines Leitthemas der Moderne.* Munich: Carl Friedrich von Siemens Stiftung, 1992.

Kaltenbach, Christiane. *Frauen Film Handbuch.* Berlin: Verband der Filmarbeiterinnen, 1983

Kanzog, Klaus. "Wege zu einer Theorie der Literaturverfilmung am Beispiel von Volker Schlöndorffs Film *Michael Kohlhaas-Der Rebell.*" In *Methoden-*

probleme der Analyse verfilmter Literatur, edited by Joachim Paech, 23–52. Münster: MakS, 1984.

Kaplan, E. Ann. "Discourses of Terrorism, Feminism and the Family in von Trotta's *Marianne and Juliane*." *Persistence of Vision* 2 (1985): 61–68.

———. "Female Politics in the Symbolic Realm: Von Trotta's *Marianne and Juliane* [The German Sisters] (1981)." In *Women and Film: Both Sides of the Camera*, 104–12. New York: Methuen, 1983.

———. "The Search for the Mother/Land in Sanders-Brahms's *Germany, Pale Mother*." In *German Film and Literature: Adaptations and Transformations*, edited by Eric Rentschler, 289–304. New York: Methuen, 1986.

Kardish, Laurence, and Juliane Lorenz. *Rainer Werner Fassbinder.* New York: Museum of Modern Art, 1997; distributed by Harry N. Abrams.

Katz, Robert. *Love Is Colder Than Death: The Life and Times of Rainer Werner Fassbinder.* New York: Random House, 1987.

Keene, Judith. "Mothering Daughters: Subjectivity and History in the Work of Helma Sanders-Brahms's *Germany Pale Mother*." *Film Historia* 7, no. 1 (1997): 3–12.

Kinder, Marsha. "Ideological Parody in the New German Cinema: Reading *The State of Things*, *The Desire of Veronika Voss*, and *Germany Pale Mother* as Postmodernist Rewritings of *The Searchers*, *Sunset Boulevard* and *Blonde Venus*." *Quarterly Review of Film and Video* 7, nos. 1–2 (May 1990): 73–103.

Kirby, Lynne. "Fassbinder's Debt to Poussin." *Camera Obscura*, nos. 13–14 (Spring–Summer 1985): 5–27.

Kluge, Alexander. *Gelegenheitsarbeit einer Sklavin: Zur realistischen Methode.* Frankfurt am Main: Surkamp Verlag, 2002.

———. "On Film and the Public Sphere." Translated by Thomas Y. Levin and Miriam B. Hansen. Special Double Issue on New German Cinema. *New German Critique*, nos. 24–25 (Autumn 1981–Winter 1982): 206–20.

———. "Eine realistische Haltung müsste der Zuschauer haben, müßte ich haben, müßte der Film haben." Interview by Reiner Frey. *Filmfaust*, no. 20 (November 1980).

———. "Why Kluge." Special Issue on Alexander Kluge: Theoretical Writings, Stories, and an Interview by Stuart Liebman. *October* 46 (Autumn 1988): 4–22.

Knepper, Wendy. "Translation Theory, Utopia and Utopianism in *Paul et Virginie*, *Aguirre: Wrath of God*, *Candide* and *New Atlantis*." *Dalhousie French Studies* 37 (Winter 1996): 41–58.

Knight, Julia. *New German Cinema: Images of a Generation.* New York: Wallflower Press, 2004.

———. *Women and the New German Cinema.* New York: Verso, 1992.

Knopp, Daniel. *NS-Filmpropaganda: Wunschbild und Feindbild in Leni Riefenstahls "Triumph des Willens" und Veit Harlans "Jud Süß."* Marburg: Tectum, 2004.

Knopp, Guido. "Leni Riefenstahl: Die Regisseurin." In *Hitler's Frauen und Marlene,* 149–206. Munich: C. Bertelsmann, 2001.

Koch, Gertrud. " *Moses und Aron*: Musik, Text, Film und andere Fallen der Rezeption." In *Die Einstellung ist die Einstellung: Visuelle Konstruktionen des Judentums,* 30–52. Frankfurt am Main: Suhrkamp, 1992.

———. "Torments of the Flesh, Coldness of the Spirit: Jewish Figures in the Films of Rainer Werner Fassbinder." Translated by Andy Spencer and Miriam Hansen. In *Perspectives on German Cinema*, edited by Terri Ginsberg, and Kirsten Moana Thompson, 221–30. New York: G. K. Hall; London: Prentice Hall International, 1996. Originally published in *New German Critique,* no. 38 (Spring–Summer 1986): 28–38.

Koch, Kriscan. *Die Bedeutung des Oberhausener Manifests für die Filmentwicklung in der BRD.* New York: Peter Lang, 1985.

Koebner, Thomas, ed. *Autorenfilme: Elf Werkanalysen.* Münster: MakS Publikationen, 1990.

Koepnick, Lutz P. "Colonial Forestry: Sylvan Politics in Werner Herzog's *Aguirre* and *Fitzcarraldo*." Special Issue on German Film History. *New German Critique*, no. 60 (Autumn 1993): 133–59.

———. "Negotiating Popular Culture: Wenders, Handke, and the Topographies of Cultural Studies." Special Issue on Culture Studies. *German Quarterly* 69, no. 4 (Fall 1996): 381–400.

Kolker, Robert Phillip. *The Altering Eye: Contemporary International Cinema.* New York: Oxford University Press, 1983.

Kolker, Robert Phillip, and Peter Beicken. *The Films of Wim Wenders: Cinema as Vision and Desire.* Cambridge, England: Cambridge University Press, 1993.

Krause, Edith H. "Effi's Endgame." *Oxford German Studies,* no. 32 (2003): 155–84.

Kuhn, Anna K. "A Heroine for Our Time: Margarethe von Trotta's *Rosa Luxemburg*." In *Gender and German Cinema: Feminist Interventions.* Vol. 2, *German Film History/German History on Film,* edited by Sandra Frieden, Richard W. McCormick, Vibeke R. Petersen, and Laurie Melissa Vogelsang, 163–84. Providence, R.I.: Berg, 1993.

———. "Rainer Werner Fassbinder: The Alienated Vision." In *New German Filmmakers: From Oberhausen through the 1970's*, edited by Klaus Phillips, 76–123. New York: Frederick Ungar, 1984.

Kuhn, Annette. "Encounter between Two Cultures: A Discussion with Ulrike Ottinger." *Screen* 28, no. 4 (Autumn 1987): 74–79.

Kuzniar, Alice A. "Suture in/Suturing Literature and Film: Handke and Wenders." In *Intertextuality: German Literature and Visual Art from the Renaissance to the Twentieth Century*, edited by Ingeborg Hoesterey and Ulrich Weisstein, 201–17. Columbia, S.C.: Camden House, 1993.

Langford, Michelle. "Alexander Kluge." Great Directors: A Critical Database. *Senses of Cinema: An Online Film Journal Devoted to the Serious and Eclectic Discussion of Cinema,* no.27 (July–August 2003). www.sensesof cinema.com/contents/directors/03/kluge.html

———. *Allegorical Images: Tableau, Time and Gesture in the Cinema of Werner Schroeter.* Portland, Oreg.: Intellect, 2006.

———. "Film Figures: Rainer Werner Fassbinder's *The Marriage of Maria Braun* and Alexander Kluge's *The Female Patriot.*" In *Kiss Me Deadly: Feminism and Cinema for the Moment,* edited by Laleen Jayamanne, 147–79. Sydney: Power Publications, 1995.

———. "Werner Schroeter." Great Directors: A Critical Database. *Senses of Cinema: An Online Film Journal Devoted to the Serious and Eclectic Discussion of Cinema,* no. 24 (January–February 2003). www.sensesofcinema .com/contents/directors/03/schroeter.html.

LaValley, Al. "The Gay Liberation of Rainer Werner Fassbinder: Male Subjectivity, Male Bodies, Male Love." Special Issue on Rainer Werner Fassbinder. *New German Critique,* no. 63 (Autumn 1994): 108–37.

Lellis, George L. *Bertolt Brecht, Cahiers du Cinéma and Contemporary Film Theory.* Ann Arbor, Mich.: UMI Research Press, 1982.

Lewandowski, Rainer. *Die Filme von Alexander Kluge.* New York: Olms Press, 1980.

———. *Die Filme von Volker Schlöndorff.* New York: Olms Press, 1981.

Lichtenstein, Heiner, ed. *Die Fassbinder-Kontroverse, oder, Das Ende der Schonzeit.* Königstein im Taurnas: Äthenaum, 1986.

Liebman, Stuart. "On New German Cinema, Art, Enlightenment, and the Public Sphere: An Interview with Alexander Kluge." Special Issue on Alexander Kluge: Theoretical Writings, Stories, and an Interview. *October* 46 (Autumn 1988): 23–59.

Light, Andrew. "Wim Wenders and the Everyday Aesthetics of Technology and Space." Special Issue Perspectives on the Arts and Technology. *Journal of Aesthetics and Art Criticism* 55, no. 2 (Spring 1997): 215–29.

Limmer, Wolfgang. *Rainer Werner Fassbinder: Filmemacher.* Reinbek bei Hamburg: Rowohlt, 1981.

Linville, Susan E., and Kent Casper. "Romantic Inversions in Herzog's *Nosferatu.*" *The German Quarterly* 64, no. 1 (Winter 1991): 17–24.

Lode, Imke. "Terrorism, Sadomasochism, and Utopia in Fassbinder's *The Third Generation.*" In *Perspectives on German Cinema,* edited by Terri Ginsberg, and Kirsten Moana Thompson, 415–34. New York: G. K. Hall; London: Prentice Hall International, 1996.

Lorenz, Juliane, ed. *Chaos as Usual: Conversations about Rainer Werner Fassbinder.* New York: Applause Books, 2000.

Lorenz, Juliane, Herbert Gehr, and Marion Schmid, eds. *Das ganz normale Chaos: Gespräche über Rainer Werner Fassbinder.* Berlin: Henschel, 1995.

Lutze, Peter C. *Alexander Kluge: The Last Modernist.* Detroit: Wayne State University Press, 1998.

MacBean, James Roy. "Between Kitsch and Fascism: Notes on Fassbinder, Pasolini, (Homo)Sexual Politics, the Exotic, the Erotic and Other Consuming Passions." *Cineaste* 13, no. 4 (1984): 12–19.

———. "The Cinema as Self-Portrait: The Final Films of R. W. Fassbinder." *Cineaste* 12, no. 4 (1983): 9–16.

Magisos, Melanie. "*Not Reconciled*: The Destruction of Narrative Pleasure." *Wide Angle* 3, no. 4 (1980): 35–41. Also published in *Perspectives on German Cinema* by Terri Ginsberg and Kirsten Moana Thompson. New York: G. K. Hall; London: Prentice Hall International, 1996.

Magretta, William R., and Joan Magretta. "Story and Discourse: Schlöndorff and von Trotta's *The Lost Honor of Katharina Blum.*" In *Modern European Filmmakers and the Art of Adaptation*, edited by Andrew S. Horton and Joan Magretta, 278–94. New York: Frederick Ungar, 1981.

Mahoney, Dennis F. " 'What's Wrong with a Cowboy in Hamburg?' Narcissism as Cultural Imperialism in Wim Wenders' *The American Friend.*" *Journal of Evolutionary Psychology* 7, nos. 1–2 (March 1986): 106–16.

Marquardt, Axel, ed. *Internationale Filmfestspiele Berlin, 1951–1984: Filme, Namen, Zahlen.* Berlin: Internationale Filmfestspiele Berlin, [1985].

Mayne, Judith. "Fassbinder and Spectatorship." *New German Critique*, no. 12 (Autumn 1977) 61–74.

———. "Fassbinder's *Ali: Fear Eats the Soul* and Spectatorship." In *Close Viewings: An Anthology of New Film Criticism*, edited by Peter Lehman, 353–69. Tallahassee: Florida State University Press, 1990.

———. "Female Narration, Women's Cinema: Helke Sander's *The All- Round Reduced Personality/Redupers.*" Special Double Issue on New German Cinema. *New German Critique*, nos. 24–25 (Autumn 1981–Winter 1982): 155–71. Also published in *Issues in Feminist Film Criticism*, edited by Patricia Erens, 380–94. Bloomington: Indiana University Press, 1990.

McCarthy, Margaret. "Consolidating, Consuming, and Annulling Identity in Jutta Bruckner's *Hungerjahre.*" *Women in German Yearbook: Feminist Studies in German Literature and Culture* 11 (1995): 13–33.

McCormick, Richard W. "Cinematic Form, History, and Gender: Margarethe von Trotta's *Rosa Luxemburg.*" *Seminar: A Journal of Germanic Studies* 32, no. 1 (February 1996): 36–41.

———. "Confronting German History: Melodrama, Distantiation, and Women's Discourse in *Germany, Pale Mother.*" In *Gender and German Cinema: Feminist Interventions.* Vol. 2, *German Film History/German History on Film,* edited by Sandra Frieden, Richard W. McCormick, Vibeke R. Petersen, and Laurie Melissa Vogelsang, 185–207. Providence, R.I.: Berg, 1993.

———. "Wilhelm Meister Revisited: *Falsche Bewegung* by Peter Handke and Wim Wenders." In *The Age of Goethe Today: Critical Reexamination and Literary Reflection*, edited by Gertrud Bauer Pickar and Sabine Cramer, 194–211. Munich: Wilhelm Fink Verlag, 1990.

———. "The Writer in Film: *Wrong Move*." In *The Cinema of Wim Wenders: Image, Narrative, and the Postmodern Condition*, edited by Roger F. Cook and Gerd Gemünden, 89–109. Detroit: Wayne State University Press, 1997.

McCormick, Ruth. "Fassbinder and the Politics of Everyday Life-A Survey of His Films." *Cineaste* 8, no. 2 (Fall 1977).

———. "Fassbinder's Reality: An Imitation of Life." In *Imitations of Life: A Reader on Film and Television Melodrama*, edited by Marcia Landy, 586–95. Detroit: Wayne State University Press, 1991.

Meitzel, Matten. "A propos du nouveau Heimatfilm allemand: *La soudaine richesse des pauvres gens de Kombach*." *Les cahiers de la cinémathèque* 32 (1981): 133–37.

Mennel, Barbara. "Masochistic Fantasy and Racialized Fetish in Rainer Werner Fassbinder's *Ali: Fear Eats the Soul*." In *One Hundred Years of Masochism; Literary Texts, Social and Cultural Contexts*, edited by Michael C. Finke and Carl Niekerk, 191–205. Atlanta: Rodopi, 2000.

Michaels, Lloyd. "*Nosferatu*, or the Phantom of the Cinema." In *Play It Again, Sam: Retakes on Remakes*, edited by Andrew Horton and Stuart Y. McDougal, 239–49. Berkeley and Los Angeles: University of California Press, 1998.

Miersch, Annette. *Schulmädchen-Report: Der deutsche Sexfilm der 70er Jahre*. Berlin: ertz Verlag, 2003.

Mitgutsch, Waltraud. "Faces of Dehumanization: Werner Herzog's Reading of Büchner's *Woyzeck*." *Literature Film Quarterly* 9, no. 3 (1981): 152–60.

Moeller, Hans Bernhard. "Fassbinder's Use of Brechtian Aesthetics." *Jump Cut*, no. 35 (April 1990): 102–7.

———. "New German Cinema and Its Precarious Subsidy and Finance System." *Quarterly Review of Film Studies* 5, no. 2 (Spring 1980): 157–68.

Moeller, Hans-Bernhard, and George L. Lellis. *Volker Schlöndorff's Cinema: Adaptation, Politics, and the "Movie-Appropriate."* Carbondale: Southern Illinois University Press, 2002.

Moltke, Johannes von. "Camping in the Art Closet: The Politics of Camp and Nation in German Film." Special Issue on Rainer Werner Fassbinder. *New German Critique*, no. 63 (Autumn 1994): 77–106.

Monaco, Paul. "Across the Great Divide: Young German Cinema in the 1970s." *Mundus Artium* 11, no. 2 (1979): 42–51.

Mouton, Jan. "The Absent Mother Makes an Appearance in the Films of West German Directors." *Women in German Yearbook: Feminist Studies in German Literature and Culture* 4 (1988): 69–81.

——. "Werner Herzog's *Stroszek*: A Fairy-tale in an Age of Disenchantment." *Literature/Film Quarterly* 15, no. 2 (1987): 99–106.

Mueller, Roswitha. "Hans-Jürgen Syberberg's *Hitler*: An Interview-Montage." *Discourse: Journal for Theoretical Studies in Media and Culture* 2 (Summer 1980): 60–82.

Münzberg, Olav. "Schaudern vor der bleichen Mutter: Eine sozialpsychologische Analyse der Kritiken zum Film von Helma Sanders-Brahms." *Medium* 7 (July 1980): 34–37.

Murray, Bruce A., and Renate Möhrmann. "*Germany, Pale Mother*: On the Mother Figures in New German Women's Film." *Women in German Yearbook: Feminist Studies in German Literature and Culture* 11 (1995): 67–80.

"New German Cinema." Special double issue. *New German Critique,* nos. 24–25 (Autumn 1981–Winter 1982): 1–263.

Oksiloff, Assenka. "Eden Is Burning: Wim Wenders's Techniques of *Synaesthesia*." *German Quarterly* 69, no. 1 (Winter 1996): 32–47.

O'Toole, Lawrence. "The Great Ecstasy of the Filmmaker Herzog." *Film Comment* 15, no. 6 (November–December 1979): 33–39.

Ottinger, Ulrike. "Interview with Ulrike Ottinger." By Erica Carter. *Screen Education,* no. 41 (Winter–Spring 1982): 34–42.

——. "Interview with Ulrike Ottinger." By Roswitha Mueller. *Discourse: Journal for Theoretical Studies in Media and Culture* 4 (Winter 1981–1982): 108–26.

Paterson, Susanne F. "Fassbinder's *Ali: Fear Eats the Soul* and the Expropriation of a National Heim." *Post Script* 18, no. 3 (Summer 1999): 46–57.

Payne, Robert. "New German Cinema/Old Hollywood Genres." *Critical Studies* 5, no. 1 (Fall 1985): 8–11.

Penman, Ian. "Fassbinder: *Love Is Colder Than Death*." In *Vital Signs: Music, Movies and Other Manias,* 103–8. London: Serpent's Tail, 1998.

Perez, Gilberto. "Modernist Cinema: The History Lessons of Straub and Huillet." *Artforum* 17, no. 2 (October 1979): 46–55.

Perlmutter, Ruth. "Ghosts of Germany: Kaspar Hauser and Woyzeck." *Literature/Film Quarterly* 25, no. 3 (1997): 236–39.

——. "Wenders Returns Home on *Wings of Desire*." *Studies in the Humanities* 20, no. 1 (June 1993): 35–48.

Petzke, Ingo. *Der deutsche Experimentalfilm der 60er und 70er Jahre.* Munich: Goethe Institut, 1990.

Peucker, Brigette. "The Invalidation of Arnim: Herzog's *Signs of Life* (1968)." In *German Film and Literature: Adaptations and Transformations,* edited by Eric Rentschler, 217–30. New York: Methuen, 1986.

———. "Literature and Writing in the Films of Werner Herzog." In *Film und Literatur: literarische Texte und der neue deutsche Film*, edited by Sigrid Bauschinger, Susan L. Cocalis, and Henry A. Lea. Bern: Francke, 1984.

———. "Werner Herzog: In Quest of the Sublime." In *New German Filmmakers: From Oberhausen through the 1970's*, edited by Klaus Phillips, 168–84. New York: Frederick Ungar, 1984.

Pflaum, Hans Günther. *Rainer Werner Fassbinder: Bilder und Dokumente*. Munich: Edition Spangenberg im Ellerman Verlag, 1992.

———. *Werner Herzog*. Munich, Carl Hanser, 1979.

Pflaum, Hans Günther, and Rainer Werner Fassbinder. *Das bisschen Realität, das ich brauche: Wie Filme entstehen*. Munich: Carl Hanser, 1976.

Phillips, Klaus, ed. *New German Filmmakers: From Oberhausen through the 1970s*. New York: Frederick Ungar, 1984.

Plard, Henri. "Sur le film *Die Blechtrommel:* De Grass à Schlöndorff" *Etudes germaniques* 35 (January–March 1980): 69–84.

Plater, Edward M. V. "The Externalization of the Protagonist's Mind in Fassbinder's Despair." *Film Criticism* 11, no. 3 (Spring 1987): 29–43.

———. "Reflected images in Fassbinder's *Effi Briest*." *Literature/Film Quarterly* 27, no. 3 (July 1999): 178–88.

———. "Sets, Props and the 'Havanaise' in Fassbinder's *Fontane Effi Briest*." *German Life and Letters* 52, no. 1 (January 1999): 28–42.

Plater, Edward M. V., and, J. Yellowlees Douglas. "The Temptation of Jonathan Zimmermann: Wim Wenders' *The American Friend*." *Literature/Film Quarterly* 16, no. 3 (1988): 191–200.

Prager, Brad. "Beleaguered under the Sea: Wolfgang Petersen's *Das Boot* as a German Hollywood Film. In *Light Motives: German Popular Film in Perspective*, edited by Randall Halle and Margaret McCarthy, 237–58. Detroit: Wayne State University Press, 2003.

———. "The Face of the Bandit: Racism and the Slave Trade in Herzog's *Cobra Verde*." *Film Criticism* 28, no. 3 (2004): 2–20.

———. "Werner Herzog's Hearts of Darkness: *Fitzcarraldo*, *Scream of Stone* and Beyond." *Quarterly Review of Film and Video* 20, no. 1 (Winter 2003): 23–35.

Prandi, Julie D. "Point of View and the Possibility of Empathy: *Woyzeck*." *Literature/Film Quarterly* 13, no. 4 (October 1985): 210–14.

Prinzler, Hans-Helmut, and Eric Renschler, eds. *Der alte Film war tot: 100 Texte zum Westdeutschen Film, 1962–1987*. Frankfurt am Main: Verlag der Autoren, 2001.

———. *Augenzeugen: 100 Texte neuer deutscher Filmemacher*. Frankfurt am Main: Verlag der Autoren, 1988.

Quart, Barbara Koenig. *Women Directors: The Emergence of a New Cinema*. New York: Praeger Publishers, 1988.

Raab, Kurt. *Die Sehnsucht des Rainer Werner Fassbinder.* Munich: C. Bertels-mann, 1982.

"Rainer Werner Fassbinder." Special Issue. *New German Critique,* no. 63 (Autumn 1994): 1–192.

Rainer Werner Fassbinder Foundation, ed. *Rainer Werner Fassbinder: Dichter, Schauspieler, Filmemacher: Werkschau 28.5–19.7.1992.* Edited by Marion Schmid, and Herbert Gehr. Berlin: Argon, 1992.

Raskin, Richard. "What Is Peter Falk Doing in *Wings of Desire?*" *P.O.V: a Danish Journal of Film Studies,* no. 8 (December 1999): 141–56. http://pov.imv .au.dk/Issue_08/section_2/artc8A.html

Rayns, Tony, ed. *Fassbinder.* 2nd rev. and expanded ed. London: British Film Institute, 1980.

Reimer, Robert C. "Comparison of Douglas Sirk's *All That Heaven Allows* and R. W. Fassbinder's *Ali: Fear Eats the Soul*; or, How Hollywood's New England Dropouts Became Germany's Marginalized Other." *Literature/Film Quarterly* 24, no. 3 (1996): 281–87.

———. "Memories from the Past: A Study of Rainer Werner Fassbinder's *The Marriage of Maria Braun.*" *Journal of Popular Film and Television* 9, no. 3 (Fall 1981): 138–43.

Rentschler, Eric. "American Friends and the New German Cinema: Patterns of Reception." Special Double Issue on New German Cinema. *New German Critique,* nos. 24–25 (Autumn 1981–Winter 1982): 7–35.

———. "Deutschland im Vorherbst: Literature Adaptation in West German Film." *Kino: German Film,* no. 3 (Summer 1980): 11–19.

———. "From New German Cinema to the Post-Wall Cinema of Consensus." In *Cinema and Nation*, edited by Mette Hjort and Scott MacKenzie, 260–277. New York: Routledge, 2000.

———. "How American Is It: The U.S. as Image and Imaginary in German Film." *The German Quarterly* 57, no. 4 (Autumn 1984): 603–20.

———. "Kluge, Film History, and Eigensinn: A Taking of Stock from the Distance." West German Culture and Politics. *New German Critique,* no. 31 (Winter 1984): 109–24.

———. "Life with Fassbinder: The Politics of Fear and Pain." *Discourse: Journal for Theoretical Studies in Media and Culture* 6 (Fall 1983): 75–90.

———. "Remembering Not to Forget: A Retrospective Reading of Alexander Kluge's *Brutality in Stone.*" Special Issue on Alexander Kluge. *New German Critique*, no. 49 (Winter 1990): 23–41.

———. "Specularity and Spectacle in Schlöndorff's *Young Törless.*" In *German Film and Literature: Adaptations and Transformations*, edited by Eric Rentschler, 176–92. New York: Methuen, 1986.

———. "Terms of Dismemberment: The Body in-and-of Fassbinder's *Berlin Alexanderplatz* (1980)." *New German Critique,* no. 34 (Winter 1985): 194–208.

Also published in *German Film and Literature: Adaptations and Transformations*, edited by Eric Rentschler, 305–21. New York: Methuen, 1986.

——. "The Use and Abuse of Memory: New German Film and the Discourse of Bitburg." Special Issue on Heimat. *New German Critique,* no. 36 (Autumn 1985): 67–90.

——. "West German Film in the 1970's." Special Issue. *Quarterly Review of Film Studies* 5, no. 2 (Spring 1980).

——. *West German Film in the Course of Time: Reflections on the Twenty Years since Oberhausen.* Bedford Hills, N.Y.: Redgrave, 1984.

Rentschler, Eric, ed. *West German Filmmakers on Film: Visions and Voices.* New York: Holmes and Meier, 1988.

Rheuban, Joyce. *The Marriage of Maria Braun.* New Brunswick, N.J.: Rutgers University Press, 1986.

——. *"The Marriage of Maria Braun*: History, Melodrama, Ideology." In *Gender and German Cinema: Feminist Interventions.* Vol. 2, *German Film History/German History on Film*, edited by Sandra Frieden, Richard W. McCormick, Vibeke R. Petersen, and Laurie Melissa Vogelsang, 207–26. Providence, R.I.: Berg, 1993.

Rhiel, Mary. *Re-viewing Kleist: The Discursive Construction of Authorial Subjectivity in West German Kleist Films.* New York: Peter Lang, 1991.

Rickey, Carrie. "Fassbinder and Altman: Approaches to Filmmaking." *Performing Arts Journal* 2, no. 2 (Fall 1977): 33–48.

Riggs, Jeffery Alan. "The Faustian Theme in Fassbinder's *The Marriage of Maria Braun.*" *Studies in the Humanities* 16, no. 1 (June 1989): 24–32.

Rogers, Holly. "Fitzcarraldo's Search for Aguirre: Music and Text in the Amazonian Films of Werner Herzog." *Journal of the Royal Musical Association* 129, no. 1 (2004): 177–99.

Rogowski, Christian. " 'Der liebevolle Blick'? The Problem of Perception in Wim Wenders's *Wings of Desire.*" *Seminar: A Journal of Germanic Studies* 29, no. 4. (November 1993): 398–409.

——. " 'To Be Continued': History in Wim Wenders' *Wings of Desire* and Thomas Brasch's *Domino.*" *German Studies Review* 15, no. 3. (October 1992): 547–63.

Rosenbaum, Jonathon. "Jean-Marie Straub and Danièle Huillet." In *Film: The Front Line, 1984,* by David Ehrenstein. Denver: Arden Press, 1984.

Roth, Wilhelm. *Dreißig Jahre Oberhausen: Eine Kritische Retrospektive.* Oberhausen: Verlag Karl Maria Laufen, 1984.

Roud, Richard. *Jean-Marie Straub.* New York: Viking Press, 1972.

Ruffell, Jeff. "Rainer Werner Fassbinder." In *Great Directors: A Critical Database. Senses of Cinema: An Online Film Journal Devoted to the Serious and Eclectic Discussion of Cinema.* www.sensesofcinema.com/contents/directors/02/fassbinder.html

Rundell, Richard J. "Keller's *Kleider machen Leute* as Novelle and Film." *Die Unterrichtspraxis* 13, no. 2 (Fall 1980): 156–65.

Ruppert, Peter. "Fassbinder, Spectatorship, and Utopian Desire." *Cinema Journal* 28, no. 2 (Winter 1989): 28–47.

Sander, Helke. "Nimmt man dir das Schwert, dann greife zum Knüppel." *Frauen und Film*, no. 1 (July 1974): 12–48.

——. "There Should Be No Scissors in Your Mind: An Interview with Helke Sander." By Stuart Liebman. *Cineaste* 21, nos. 1–2 (1995): 40–42.

Sanders-Brahms, Helma. *Deutschland, bleiche Mutter: Film-Erzählung.* Reinbek bei Hamburg: Rowohlt, 1980.

——. "My Critics, My Films and I. (1980)." In *West German Filmmakers on Film: Visions and Voices*, edited by Eric Rentchler, 156–62. New York: Holmes and Meier, 1988.

——. "Tyrannenmord: *Tiefland* von Leni Riefenstahl." In *Das Jahr 1945: Filme aus 15 Ländern,* by Hans Helmut Prinzler, 173–76. Berlin: Stiftung Deutsche Kinemathek ,1990.

——. "Zarah." In *Jahrbuch Film 81/82*, edited by Hans-Günter Pflaum, 165–72. Munich: Carl Hanser, 1981.

Sanders-Brahms, Helma, with Peter Brunette. "Helma Sanders-Brahms: A Conversation." *Film Quarterly* 44, no. 2 (Winter 1990–1991): 34–42.

Sandford, John. *The New German Cinema.* New York: Da Capo Press, 1980.

Savage, Julian. "The Conscious Collusion of the Stare: The Viewer Implicated in Fassbinder's *Fear Eats the Soul." Senses of Cinema: An Online Film Journal Devoted to the Serious and Eclectic Discussion of Cinema,* no. 16 (September–October 2001). www.sensesofcinema.com/contents/cteq/01/16/fassbinder_fear.

Schidor, Dieter, and Rainer Werner Fassbinder. *Rainer Werner Fassbinder dreht "Querelle": "Ein Pakt mit dem Teufel."* Munich: Wilhelm Heyne, 1982.

Schlöndorff, Volker. *"Die Blechtrommel": Tagebuch einer Verfilmung.* 2nd ed. Neuwied: Luchterhand, 1979.

——. "Coming to Terms with the German Past: An Interview with Volker Schlöndorff." By Gary Crowdus and Richard Porton. *Cineaste* 26, no. 2 (March 2001): 18–23.

——. *"Der junge Törless." Film* (Velber) 4, no. 6 (1966): 45–56.

——. "The Legend of Volker Schlöndorff: *Rita* Director Goes Back to Basics." Interview by Anthony Kaufman. *indieWIRE* (January 31, 2001). www.indiewire.com/people/int_Volker_Schond_010131.html

——. *"The Tin Drum:* Volker Schlöndorff's 'Dream of Childhood'." Interview by John Hughes. *Film Quarterly* 35, no. 3 (Spring 1981): 2–10.

——. "Volker Schlöndorff: An Interview." By Barry Thomson and Greg Thomson. *Film Criticism* 1, no. 3 (Winter 1976–1977): 26–37.

Schlöndorff, Volker, and Günter Grass. *Die Blechtrommel als Film.* 4th ed. Frankfurt am Main: Zweitausendeins Verlag, 1979.

Schlumberger, Hella. "'I've Changed Along with the Characters in My Films': An Interview with Rainer Werner Fassbinder." *Performing Arts Journal* 14, no. 2 (May 1992): 1–23.

Schmid, Eva M. J. "'Das Leben ist viel zu kurz, um sich einen deutschen Film anzusehen': Ein Gespräch mit Eva M. J. Schmid." By Heide Schlüpmann. *Frauen und Film,* no. 35 (October 1983): 62–77.

Sharma, Shailja. "Fassbinder's *Ali* and the Politics of Subject-Formation." *Post Script* 14, nos. 1–2 (Fall–Winter–Spring 1994–1995): 104–16.

Shattuc, Jane. "Contra Brecht: R. W. Fassbinder and Pop Culture in the Sixties." *Cinema Journal* 33, no. 1 (Fall 1993): 35–54.

———. "R. W. Fassbinder as a Popular Auteur: The Making of an Authorial Legend." *Journal of Film and Video* 45, no. 1 (Spring, 1993): 40–57.

———. "R. W. Fassbinder's Confessional Melodrama: Towards Historicizing Melodrama within the Art Cinema." *Wide Angle* 12, no. 1 (January 1990): 44–59.

Shattuc, Jane, ed. "Special Issue on 'the Other Fassbinder'." *Wide Angle* 12, no. 1 (January 1990).

Sieglohr, Ulrike. "New German Cinema." In *The Oxford Guide to Film Studies,* edited by John Hill and Pamala Church Gibson, 466–70. Oxford: Oxford University Press, 1998.

Silberman, Marc. "Cine-Feminists in West Berlin." *Quarterly Review of Film Studies* 5, no. 2 (1980): 217–32.

———. "Film and Feminism in Germany Today." *Jump Cut,* no. 27 (1982): 41–53.

———. "German Film Women." *Jump Cut,* no. 29 (1984): 49–64.

———. "German Women's Film Culture." *Jump Cut,* no. 30 (1985): 63–69.

———. "Ula Stöckl: How Women See Themselves." In *New German Filmmakers: From Oberhausen through the 1970s,* edited by Klaus Phillips, 320–34. New York: Frederick Ungar, 1984.

———. "Women Filmmakers in West Germany: A Catalog." *Camera Obscura,* no. 6 (1980): 123–52.

———. "Women Filmmakers in West Germany: A Catalog (Part 2)." *Camera Obscura,* no. 11 (1983): 132–45.

Silverman, Kaja. "Fassbinder and Lacan." *Camera Obscura,* no. 19 (January 1989): 54–85. Also published in *Visual Culture: Images and Interpretations,* edited by Norman Bryson, Michael Ann Holly, and Keith Moxey, 272–301. Hanover, N.H.: University Press of New England; Wesleyan University Press, 1994.

———. "Helke Sander and the Will to Change." *Discourse: Journal for Theoretical Studies in Media and Culture* 6 (Fall 1983): 10–30.

————. "Kaspar Hauser's 'Terrible Fall' into Narrative." Special Double Issue on New German Cinema. *New German Critique*, nos. 24–25 (Autumn 1981–Winter 1982): 73–93.

Sinka, Margit M. "The Viewer as Reader: Werner Herzog's *Stroszek* in Film and Prose." *Post Script* 7, no. 3 (Summer 1988): 27–41.

Sontag, Susan. "Novel into Film: Fassbinder's *Berlin Alexanderplatz*." In *Where the Stress Falls: Essays,* by Susan Sontag, 123–31. New York: Farrar, Straus & Giroux, 2001.

Spaich, Herbert. *Rainer Werner Fassbinder: Leben und Werk.* Weinheim: Beltz Verlag, 1992.

Spector, Scott. "Wenders' Genders: From the End of the Wall to the End of the World." In *Triangulated Visions: Women in Recent German Cinema*, edited by Ingeborg Majer O'Sickey and Ingeborg von Zadow, 219–28. Albany: State University of New York Press, 1998.

Staskowski, Andrea. "Film and Phenomenology: Being-in-the-World of Herzog's *Aguirre, Wrath of God*." *Post Script* 7, no. 3 (Summer 1988): 14–26.

Steinborn, Bion, and Carola Hilmes."'Frieden' hat für uns Deutsche einen amerikanischen Geschmack': Ein Gespräch mit Marianne S. W. Rosenbaum." *Filmfaust,* no. 39 (May–June 1984): 27–31.

Stiles, Victoria M. "Fact and Fiction: Nature's Endgame in Werner Herzog's *Aguirre, the Wrath of God*." *Literature/Film Quarterly* 17, no. 3 (1989): 161–67.

————. "*Woyzeck* in Focus: Werner Herzog and His Critics." *Literature/Film Quarterly* 24, no. 3 (1996): 226–33.

Stöckl, Ula. "Gespräch mit Ula Stöckl and Reviews of Her Films." By Eva Hiller, Claudia Lenssen, and Gesine Strempel. *Frauen und Film,* no. 12 (June 1977): 3–23.

Straub, Jean-Marie. "'Andi Engel Talks to Jean-Marie Straub, and Danièle Huillet Is There Too'." *Enthusiasm*, no. 1 (1975): 1–25.

————. "Jean-Marie Straub." Interview by Barbara Bronnen. In *Die Filmemacher; zur neuen deutschen Produktion nach Oberhausen 1962,* by Barbara Bronnen and Corinna Brocher, 25–45. Munich: C. Bertelsmann, 1973.

Straub, Jean-Marie, and Danièle Huillet. "Moses and Aaron as an Object of Marxist Reflection." Interview by Joel Rogers. *Jump Cut,* nos. 12–13 (December 1976): 61–64.

Struve, Ulrich. "A Myth Becomes Reality: Kaspar Hauser as Messianic Wild Child." *Studies in Twentieth Century Literature* 22, no. 2 (Summer 1998): 273–94.

Syberberg, Hans Jürgen. "Germany's Heart: The Modern Taboo." Interview by Marilyn Berlin Snell. *New Perspectives Quarterly* 10, no. 1 (Winter, 1993):

20–25. Reprinted in *NPQ* 24, no. 2 (Spring 2007): 114–24. Also published in *At Century's End: Great Minds Reflect on Our Times*, edited by Nathan P. Gardels. La Jolla, Calif.: ALTI, 1995.

———. "Hans-Jürgen Syberberg: An Interview." By Betsy Erkkila. *Literature/Film Quarterly* 10, no. 4 (1982): 206–18.

———. *Hitler: A Film from Germany*. Translated by Joachim Neugroschel. New York: Farrar, Straus & Giroux, 1982.

Thomas, Paul. "Fassbinder: The Poetry of the Inarticulate." *Film Quarterly* 30, no. 2 (Winter 1976–1977): 2–17.

Thomsen, Christian. *Fassbinder: The Life and Work of a Provocative Genius*. Boston: Faber and Faber, 2000.

Thomson, David. "The Many Faces of Klaus Kinski." *American Film* (May 1980): 22–27.

Töteberg, Michael. "Fassbinder, Rainer Werner: A Bibliography of Primary and Secondary Literature." *Text und Kritik*, no. 103 (July 1989): 88–99.

———. *Rainer Werner Fassbinder*. Reinbek bei Hamburg: Rowohlt, 2002.

Tropiano, Stephen. "Fassbinder's Not-so-pretty Picture: Gay Life as Metaphor for Bourgeois Decay." *Gay and Lesbian Review* 8, no. 2 (March 2001): 18–20.

Trotta, Margarethe von. *Die bleierne Zeit*. Edited by Hans Jürgen Weber. Frankfurt am Main: Fischer Taschenbuch, 1981.

———. "Rebellinen wider eine bleierne Zeit: Ein Interview mit Margarethe von Trotta über ihren Film *bleierne Zeit*." By Reiner Frey and Christian Göldenboog. *Filmfaust*, no. 24. (October–November 1981): 29–36.

———. *Schwestern oder die Balance des Glücks: Ein Film*. Edited by Willi Bär and Hans Jürgen Weber. Frankfurt am Main: Fischer Taschenbuch, 1979.

———. "Working with Jutta Lampe. (1979)." In *West German Filmmakers on Film: Visions and Voices*, edited by Eric Rentchler, 178–90. New York: Holmes and Meier, 1988.

Trotta, Margarethe von, and Christiane Ensslin. *"Rosa Luxemburg": Das Buch zum Film*. Nördlingen: Greno, 1986.

Trotta, Margarethe von, and Luisa Francia. *"Das zweite Erwachen der Christa Klages"*. Frankfurt am Main: Fischer Taschenbuch, 1980.

Trotta, Margarethe von, Hans Jürgen Weber, and Carola Hembus. *"Heller Wahn": Ein Film von Margarethe von Trotta*. Frankfurt am Main: Fischer Taschenbuch, 1983.

Trotta, Margarethe von, Hans Jürgen Weber, and Ingeborg Weber. *"Die bleierne Zeit": Ein Film von Margarethe von Trotta*. Frankfurt am Main: Fischer Taschenbuch, 1981.

Turin, Maureen. "Jean-Marie Straub and Danièle Huillet: Oblique Angles on Film as Ideological Intervention." In *New German Filmmakers: From Oberhausen through the 1970s*, edited by Klaus Phillips, 335–58. New York: Frederick Ungar, 1984.

Van Wert, William F. "Hallowing the Ordinary, Embezzling the Everyday: Werner Herzog's Documentary Practice." *Quarterly Review of Film Studies* 5, no. 2 (Spring 1980): 183–92.

Varga, Darrell. "The Deleuzean Experience of Cronenberg's *Crash* and Wenders' *The End of Violence*. In *Screening the City*, edited by Mark Shiel and Tony Fitzmaurice, 262–83. New York: Verso, 2003.

Waldemer, Thomas P. "*Aguirre, the Wrath of God* and the Chronicles of Omagua and Dorado." *SECOLAS Annals: Journal of the Southeastern Council on Latin American Studies,* no. 26 (March 1995): 42–47.

Waller, Gregory A. "*Aguirre, the Wrath of God*: History, Theater, and the Camera." *South Atlantic Review*, 46, no. 2 (May 1981): 55–69.

Walsh, Martin. "Brecht and Straub/Huuillet: The Frontiers of Language, *History Lessons*." *Afterimage* 7 (Summer 1978): 12–32.

———. "The Complex Seer: Brecht and the Film." In *The Brechtian Aspect of Radical Cinema: Essays*, edited by Keith M. Griffiths. London: BFI, 1981.

———. "Introduction to Arnold Schoenberg's 'Accompaniment for a Cinematographic Scene': Straub/Huillet: Brecht: Schoenberg." *Camera Obscura*, no. 2 (Fall 1977): 34–49.

———. "*Moses and Aaron*: Straub-Huillet's Schoenberg." *Jump Cut*, nos. 12–13 (December 1976): 57–61.

Walter, Michael. "Die Musik des Olympiafilms von 1938." *Acta Musicologia* 62, no. 1 (January–February 1990): 82–113.

Ward, Jenifer K. "Enacting the Different Voice: *Christa Klages* and Feminist History." *Women in German Yearbook: Feminist Studies in German Literature and Culture* 11 (1995): 49–65.

Watson, Scott B. "'Harried by His Own Kind': Herzog and the Darker Dimensions of Icarus." *Arete: The Journal of Sport Literature* 3, no. 2 (Spring 1986): 71–78.

———. "Herzog's Healing Images: Mountain Climbing and Mankind's Degeneration." *Aethlon: The Journal of Sport Literature* 10, no. 1 (Fall 1992): 169–81.

Watson, Wallace Steadman. "'Sexuality Wanders Dark Paths': Fassbinder's Romanticism of *Berlin Alexanderplatz*." *Literature/Film Quarterly* 18, no. 4 (October 1990): 245–49.

———. *Understanding Rainer Werner Fassbinder: Film As Private and Public Art*. Columbia: University of South Carolina Press, 1996.

Waugh, Thomas. "Fassbinder Fiction: A New Biography." In *The Fruit Machine: Twenty Years of Writings on Queer Cinema*, 156–60. Durham, N.C.: Duke University Press, 2000.

———. "Rainer Werner Fassbinder." In *The Fruit Machine: Twenty Years of Writings on Queer Cinema,* by Thomas Waugh, 43–58. Durham, N.C.: Duke University Press, 2000.

Weinberger, Gabriele. "Marianne Rosenbaum and the Aesthetics of Angst (*Peppermint Peace*)." In *Gender and German Cinema: Feminist Interventions.* Vol. 2, *German Film History/German History on Film*, edited by Sandra Frieden, Richard W. McCormick, Vibeke R. Petersen, and Laurie Melissa Vogelsang, 227–40. Providence, R.I.: Berg, 1993.

———. *Nazi Germany and Its Aftermath in Women Directors' Autobiographical Films of the Late 1970: In the Murderers' House.* San Francisco: Mellen Research University Press, 1992.

Wenders, Wim. "Angels, History and Poetic Fantasy: An Interview with Wim Wenders." By Coco Fusco. *Cineaste* 16, no. 4 (1988): 14–17.

———. *Himmel über Berlin: ein Filmbuch.* Frankfurt am Main: Suhrkamp, 1990.

———. "An Interview with Wim Wenders." By Walter Donohue. *Sight and Sound* 1, no. 12 (April 1992): 8–13.

———. *My Time with Antonioni: The Diary of an Extraordinary Experience.* New York: Faber and Faber, 2000.

———. *On Film*: [Essays and Conversations]. New York: Faber and Faber, 2001.

———. "The Urban Landscape from the Point of View of Images." In *The Act of Seeing: Essays and Conversations,* 81–92. London: Faber and Faber, 1997.

Wenders, Wim, and Peter Handke. *Falsche Bewegung: Essays und Filmkritiken.* Frankfurt am Main: Suhrkamp, 1975.

Westdeutscher Kurzfilmtagen. *Dreißig Jahre Oberhausen: Eine kritische Retrospektive.* Oberhausen: Verlag Karl Maria Laufen, 1984.

Wickham, Christopher. "Heart and Hole: Achternbusch, Herzog and the Concept of Heimat." *Germanic Review* 64, no. 3 (Summer 1989): 112–20.

Wigod, Sheldon. "The Capitalist and the Lottery Queen: Sex and Politics in Fassbinder's *Fox and His Friends.*" In *Sex and Love in Motion Pictures*: *Proceedings of the Second Annual Film Conference of Kent State University, April 11, 1984*, 97–100. Kent, Ohio: Romance Languages Department, Kent State University, 1984.

Williams, Bruce. "'Life Is Very Precious, Even Right Now': (Un)happy Camping in the New German Cinema." *Post Script* 16, no. 3 (Summer 1997): 51–64.

Wings of Desire. Special issue. *P.O.V.: A Danish Journal of Film Studies*, December 8, 1999. http://pov.imv.au.dk/Issue_08/POV_8cnt.html

Wistrich, Robert S. "The Fassbinder Controversy." *Jerusalem Quarterly,* no. 50 (Spring 1989): 122–30.

Woodward, Katherine S. "European Anti-Melodrama: Godard, Truffaut, and Fassbinder." *Post Script* 3, no. 2 (Winter 1984): 34–47. Also published in *Imitations of Life: A Reader on Film and Television Melodrama*, edited by Marcia Landy, 586–95. Detroit: Wayne State University Press, 1991.

Wydra, Thilo. *Volker Schlöndorff und seine Filme*. Munich: Wilhelm Heyne, 1998.

Zipes, Jack. "The Political Dimensions of *The Lost Honor of Katharina Blum*." *New German Critique,* no. 10 (Winter 1977): 75–84.

Zwerenz Gerhard. *Die Ehe der Maria Braun: Roman [nach einem Film von Rainer Werner Fassbinder mit Hanna Schygulla in der Hauptrolle]*. Munich: Wilhelm Goldmann Verlag, 1979.

———. *Der langsame Tod des Rainer Werner Fassbinder, ein Bericht*. Munich: Schneekluth Verlag, 1982.

GERMANY–POST OBERHAUSEN/ POST UNIFICATION 1982–

Anderson, Susan C. "Outsiders, Foreigners, and Aliens in Cinematic or Literary Narratives by Bohm, Dische, Dörrie and Oren." *The German Quarterly* 75, no. 2 (Spring 2002): 144–59.

Bathrick, David. "Anti-Neonazism as Cinematic Practice: Bonengel's *Beruf Neonazi*." Legacies of Antifascism. *New German Critique,* no. 67 (Winter 1996): 133–46.

Berghahn, Daniela. "Fiction into Film and the Fidelity Discourse: A Case Study of Volker Schlöndorff's Re-interpretation of *Homo Faber*." *German Life and Letters* 49, no. 1 (1996): 72–87.

Birgel, Franz, and Klaus Phillips. *Straight through the Heart: Doris Dörrie, German Filmmaker and Author*. Lanham, Md.: Scarecrow Press, 2004.

Brady, Martin, and Helen Hughes. "German Film after the Wende." In *The New Germany: Social, Political and Cultural Challenges of Unification*, edited by John R. P. McKenzie and Derek Lewis, 279–85. Exeter, England: University of Exeter Press, 1995.

Brückner, Jutta. "Interview with Jutta Brückner." By Barbara Kosta and Richard W. McCormick. *Signs: Journal of Women in Culture and Society* 21, no. 2 (Winter 1996): 343–73.

Clarke, David. *German Cinema Since Unification*. New York: Continuum, 2006.

Combs, Richard. "Living in Never-Never Land: Michael Haneke Continues the Search for a New European Cinema." *Film Comment* 38, no. 2 (March–April 2002): 26–28.

Coury, David N. "Servus Deutschland: Nostalgia for Heimat in Contemporary West German Cinema." In *Moving Pictures, Migrating Identities*, by Eva Rueschmann, 72–89. Jackson: University Press of Mississippi, 2003.

Csicsery, George. "*Ballad of the Little Soldier*: Werner Herzog in a Political Hall of Mirrors." *Film Quarterly* 39, no. 2 (Winter 1985–1986): 7–15.

Davidson, John E. "A Story of Faces and Intimate Spaces: Form and History in Max Farberbock's *Aimee und Jaguar*." *Quarterly Review of Film and Video* 19, no. 4 (October–November 2002): 323–41.

Dörrie, Doris. "Searching for Stories in a Gray Germany (1978)." In *West German Filmmakers on Film: Visions and Voices*, edited by Eric Rentchler, 188–90. New York: Holmes and Meier, 1988.

Flinn, Caryl. "The Body in the (Virgin) Machine." *Arachne* 3, no. 2 (1996): 48–66.

Freyermuth, Gundolf S. *Der Übernehmer: Volker Schlöndorff in Babelsberg*. Berlin: Ch. Links Verlag, 1993.

Gemünden, Gerd. "National Identity and Americanization in the Unified Germany." In *Framed Visions: Popular Culture, Americanization, and the Contemporary German and Austrian Imagination*, 195–213. Ann Arbor: University of Michigan Press, 1998.

———. "Nostalgia for the Nation: Intellectuals and National Identity in Unified Germany." In *Acts of Memory: Cultural Recall in the Present*, edited by Mieke Bal, Jonathan Crewe and Leo Spitzer, 120–33. Hanover, N.H.: Dartmouth College, 1999.

———. "The Queer Utopia of Monika Treut." In *Framed Visions: Popular Culture, Americanization, and the Contemporary German and Austrian Imagination*, 177–94. Ann Arbor: University of Michigan Press, 1998.

Göktürk, Deniz. "Turkish Women on German Streets: Closure and Exposure in Transnational Cinema." In *Spaces in European Cinema*, edited by Myrto Konstantarakos, 64–76. Portland, Oreg.: Intellect, 2000.

Haase, Christine. "You Can Run, but You Can't Hide: Transcultural Filmmaking in *Run Lola Run*." In *Light Motives: German Popular Film in Perspective*, edited by Randall Halle and Margaret McCarthy, 395–415. Detroit: Wayne State University Press, 2003.

Halle, Randall. "German Film, Aufgehoben: Ensembles of Transnational Cinema." Special Issue on Postwall Cinema. *New German Critique*, no. 87 (Autumn 2002): 7–46.

———. "'Happy Ends' to Crises of Heterosexual Desire: Toward a Social Psychology of Recent German Comedies." *Camera Obscura*, no. 44 (2000): 1–39.

Halle, Randall, and Margaret McCarthy, eds. *Light Motives: German Popular Film in Perspective*. Detroit: Wayne State University Press, 2003.

Haneke, Michael. "Interview with Michael Haneke." By Lawrence Chua. *BOMB Magazine*, no. 80 (Summer 2002): 54–58.

——. "The World That Is Known: An Interview with Michael Haneke." By Christopher Sharrett. Translated by Jurgen Heinrichs. *Cineaste* 28, no. 3 (Summer 2003): 28–31.

Hart, Jonathan. "The Promised End: The Conclusion of Hoffman's *Death of a Salesman.*" *Literature/Film Quarterly* 19, no. 1 (1991): 60–65.

Hernandez, Tanya Kater. "*The Buena Vista Social Club*: The Racial Politics of Nostalgia." In *Latino/a popular culture*, edited by Michelle Habell-Pall'an and Mary Romero, 61–72. New York: New York University Press, 2002.

Holland, Agnieszka. "Interview with Agnieszka Holland." By Godana P. Crnkovic. *Film Quarterly* 52, no. 2 (Winter 1998–99): 2–9.

Kaes, Anton. *Deutschlandbilder: Die Wiederkehr der Geschichte als Film*. Munich: edition text + kritik, 1987.

——. *From Hitler to Heimat:The Return of History as Film*. Cambridge: Harvard University Press, 1989.

——. "German Cultural History and the Study of Film: Ten Theses and a Postscript." Cultural History/Cultural Studies. *New German Critique*, no. 65 (Spring-Summer 1995): 47–58.

——. "History and Film: Public Memory in the Age of Electronic Dissemination." *History and Memory* 2 (Fall 1990): 111–29.

——. "Leaving Home: Film, Migration, and the Urban Experience." Special Issue on Nazi Cinema. *New German Critique*, no. 74 (Spring-Summer 1998): 179–92.

McCarthy, Margaret. "Angst Takes a Holiday in Doris Dörrie's *Am I Beautiful?* (1998)." In *Light Motives: German Popular Film in Perspective*, edited by Randall Halle and Margaret McCarthy, 376–94. Detroit: Wayne State University Press, 2003.

——. "Teutonic Water: Effervescent Otherness in Doris Dörrie's *Nobody Loves Me.*" *Camera Obscura*, no. 44 (2000): 40–73.

Moller, Olaf. "Film Critic Olaf Moller Reflects on the Current State of German Cinema in the wake of *Run Lola Run.*" *Film Comment* 37, no. 3 (May–June 2001): 11–13.

Moltke, Johannes von. "Between the Young and the New: Pop Sensibilities and Laconic Style in Rudolf Thome's Rote Sonne." *Screen* 41, no. 3 (Autumn 2000): 257–81.

Naughton, Leonie. *That Was the Wild East: Film Culture, Unification, and the New Germany*. Ann Arbor: University of Michigan Press, 2002.

Neumann, Hans-Joachim. *Der deutsche Film heute: die Macher, das Geld, die Erfolge, das Publikum*. Frankfurt am Main: Ullstein, 1986.

O'Sickey, Ingeborg Majer. "Whatever Lola Wants, Lola Gets (Or Does She?): Time and Desire in Tom Tykwer's *Run Lola Run.*" *Quarterly Review of Film and Video* 19, no. 2 (April 2002): 123–31.

O'Sickey, Ingeborg Majer, and Ingeborg von Zadow, eds. *Triangulated Visions: Women in Recent German Cinema*. Albany: State University of New York Press, 1998.

Ottinger, Ulrike. "Encounter between Two Cultures: A Discussion with Ulrike Ottinger." By Annette Kuhn. *Screen* 28, no. 4 (Autumn 1987): 74–79.

———. "*Johanna d'Arc of Mongolia*: Interview with Ulrike Ottinger." By Janet A. Kaplan. *Art Journal* 61, no. 3 (Autumn 2002): 6–21.

Pally, Marcia. "Open Dörrie." *Film Comment* 22, no. 5 (September–October 1986): 42–45.

"Postwall Cinema." Special Issue, *New German Critique*, no. 87 (Autumn 2002): 1–191.

Powrie, Phil. "Marketing History: *Swann in Love*." *Film Criticism* 12, no. 3 (Spring 1988): 33–45.

Rauh, Reinhold, and Edgar Reitz. *Film als Heimat*. Munich: Wilhelm Heyne, 1993.

Reimann, Andrea. "New German Cinema's Boundaries Opened: Postmodern Authorship and Nationality in Monika Treut's Films of the 1980s." In *Writing against Boundaries: Nationality, Ethnicity and Gender in the German-speaking Context*, edited by Barbara Kosta and Helga Kraft, 177–96. New York: Rodopi, 2003.

Reimer, Robert C. "Picture-Perfect War: An Analysis of Joseph Vilsmaier's *Stalingrad* (1993)." In *Light Motives: German Popular Film in Perspective*, edited by Randall Halle and Margaret McCarthy, 304–25. Detroit: Wayne State University Press, 2003.

Richardson, Colin. "Monika Treut: An Outlaw at Home." In *A Queer Romance: Lesbians, Gay Men, and Popular Culture*, edited by Paul Burston and Colin Richardson, 167–85. New York: Routledge, 1995.

Schlöndorff, Volker. "Coming to Terms with the German Past: An Interview with Volker Schlöndorff." By Gary Crowdus and Richard Porton. *Cineaste* 26, no. 2 (March 2001): 18–23.

———. "The Legend of Volker Schlöndorff: *Rita* Director Goes Back to Basics." Interview by Anthony Kaufman. *indieWIRE* (January 31, 2001). www .indiewire.com/people/int_Volker_Schond_010131.html

Simon, Sunka. "Out of Hollywood: Monika Treut's *Virgin Machine* and Percy Adlon's *Bagdad Cafe*." In *Queering the Canon: Defying Sights in German Literature and Culture*, edited by Christoph Lorey and John L. Plews, 383–402. Columbia, S.C.: Camden House, 1998.

Töteberg, Michael, ed. *Good bye, Lenin! ein Film von Wolfgang Becker: Drehbuch von Bernd Lichtenberg and Wolfgang Becker*. Berlin: Schwarzkopf and Schwarzkopf, 2003.

Treut, Monika. "Female Misbehavior." In *Feminisms in the Cinema*, edited by Laura Pietropaolo and Ada Testaferri, 106–21. Bloomington: Indiana University Press, 1995.

———. "From *Taboo Parlor* to Porn and Passing: An Interview with Monika Treut." By Gerd Gemünden, Alice Kuzniar, and Klaus Phillips. *Film Quarterly* 50, no. 3 (Spring 1997): 2–12.

———. *Die grausame Frau: zum Frauenbild bei de Sade und Sacher-Masoch.* Basel: Stroemfeld/Roter Stern, 1984.

———. "Die Zeremonie der blutenden Rose." *Frauen und Film,* no. 36 (February 1984): 35–43.

Trumpener, Katie. "*Johanna d'Arc of Mongolia* in the Mirror of Dorian Gray: Ethnographic Recordings and the Aesthetics of the Market in the Recent Films of Ulrike Ottinger." Special Issue on German Film History. *New German Critique,* no. 60 (Autumn 1993): 77–99.

Vogel, Amos "Of Nonexisting Continents: The Cinema of Michael Haneke." *Film Comment* 32, no. 4 (July–August 1996): 73–75.

Wood, Robin. "In Search of the *Code Inconnu*." [Critical Essay]. *CineAction,* no. 62 (Summer 2003): 41–49.

AUSTRIAN CINEMA

Alter, Nora M. "Imaging (Post)Gender under Transnational Capital: Valie Export´s Perfect Pair." In *After Postmodernism: Austrian Literature and Film in Transition*, edited by Willy Riemer, 267–82. Riverside, Calif.: Ariadne Press, 2000.

Anker, Steve, Peter Tscherkassky, and Martin Arnold. *Austrian Avant-Garde Cinema, 1955–1993*. Vienna: Sixpackfilm; San Francisco: San Francisco Cinémathèque, 1994.

Barry, Thomas F. "The Weight of Angels: Peter Handke and *Der Himmel über Berlin*." *Modern Austrian Literature* 23, nos. 3–4 (1990): 53–64.

Beckermann, Ruth, and Christa Bluemlinger. *Ohne Untertitel: Fragmente einer Geschichte des österreichischen Kino*. Vienna: Sonderzahl Verlag. 1996.

Bilda, Linda, Ernst Schmidt, and Wiener Secession. *Ernst Schmidt Jr.: Drehen Sie Filme, aber keine Filme! Filme und Filmtheorie, 1964–1987*. Vienna: Triton Verlag, 2001.

Dassanowsky, Robert von. *Austrian Cinema: A History*. Jefferson, N.C.: McFarland, 2005.

Eifler, Margret. "Valie Export's *Invisible Adversaries*: Film as Text." In *Gender and German Cinema: Feminist Interventions*. Vol. 1: *Gender and Representation in New German Cinema*, edited by Sandra Frieden, Richard W. Mc-

Cormick, Vibeke R. Petersen, and Laurie Melissa Vogelsang, 241–55. Providence, R.I.: Berg, 1993.

Export, Valie. "Expanded Cinema as Expanded Reality." *Senses of Cinema: An Online Film Journal Devoted to the Serious and Eclectic Discussion of Cinema*, no. 28 (September–October 2003). www.sensesofcinema.com/contents/03/28/expanded_cinema.html

———. "Ein Interview mit Valie Export." By Ruth Askey. *High Performance*, no. 13 (Spring 1981): 14–19.

Export, Valie, and Peter Weibel, eds. *Wien: Bildkompendium Wiener Aktionismus und Film*. Frankfurt am Main: Kohlkunstverlag, 1970.

Frey, Mattias. "*Benny's Video*, Caché, and the Desubstantiated Image." *Framework* 47, no. 2 (Fall 2006): 30–36.

———. "Michael Haneke Spotlight." *Senses of Cinema: An Online Film Journal Devoted to the Serious and Eclectic Discussion of Cinema*, no. 27 (July–August 2003). www.sensesofcinema.com/contents/directors/03/haneke.html

Gemünden, Gerd. *Framed Visions: Popular Culture, Americanization, and the Contemporary German and Austrian Imagination*. Ann Arbor: University of Michigan Press, 1998.

Hampton, Howard. "Bored Silly—Violent Film *Funny Games*." *Artforum International* 36, no. 7 (March 1998): 19. Also published online at http://findarticles.com/p/articles/mi_m0268/is_n7_v36/ai_20572910

Haneke, Michael. "Beyond Mainstream Film: An Interview with Michael Haneke." By Willy Riemer. In *After Postmodernism: Austrian Literature and Film in Transition*, edited by Willy Riemer. Riverside, Calif.: Ariadne Press, 2000.

———. "*71 Fragments of a Chronology of Chance*: Notes to the Film." In *After Postmodernism: Austrian Literature and Film in Transition*, edited by Willy Riemer. Riverside, Calif.: Ariadne, 2000.

Horwath, Alexander, and Peter Tscherkassky, eds. *Crossing the Lines: Austrian Independent Film + Video*. Vienna: Sixpackfilm, 2001.

King, Homay. "Vision and Its Discontents: Valie Export's *Invisible Adversaries*." *Discourse: Journal for Theoretical Studies in Media and Culture* 22, no. 2 (Spring 2000): 25–45.

Lamb-Faffelberger, Margarete. "Austria's Feminist Avant-Garde: Valie Export's and Elfriede Jelinek's Aesthetic Innovations." In *Out from the Shadows: Essays on Contemporary Austrian Women Writers and Filmmakers*, edited by Margarete Lamb-Faffelberger, 229–41. Riverside, Calif.: Ariadne Press, 1997.

———. *Valie Export und Elfriede Jelinek im Spiegel der Presse: Zur Rezeption der feministischen Avantgarde Österreichs*. New York: Peter Lang, 1992.

Lamb-Faffelberger, Margarete, ed. *Literature, Film and the Culture Industry in Modern Austria*. New York: Peter Lang, 2002.

——. *Out from the Shadows: A Collection of Articles on Austrian Literature and Film by Women since 1945.* Riverside, Calif.: Ariadne Press, 1997.

Lehner, Wolfgang, and Bernhard Praschl. "Stellen sie sich einen österreichischen Film vor! Zur Entwicklung des Avantgarde-, Experimental- und Undergroundfilms in der 2. Republik." In *Medienkultur in Österreich*, edited by Hans H. Fabris and Kurt Luger, 199–250. Vienna: Böhlau, 1988.

MacDonald, Scott. "Valie Export." In *A Critical Cinema: Interviews with Independent Filmmakers.* [Vol. 1]. Berkeley and Los Angeles: University of California Press, 1988.

Mörth, Otto, ed. *Marc Adrian: Das Filmische Werk.* Vienna: Sonderzahl Verlag, 1999.

Österreichisches Filmmuseum. *Dietmar Brehm: Party* [Filme 1974–2003]. Edited by Alexander Horwath, 2003.

Prawer, S. S. *Between Two Worlds: Jewish Presences in German and Austrian Film, 1910–1933.* New York: Berghahn Books, 2005.

Rentschler, Eric, ed. *The Films of G. W. Pabst: An Extraterritorial Cinema.* New Brunswick, N.J.: Rutgers University Press, 1990.

Riemer, Willy. *After Postmodernism: Austrian Literature and Film in Transition.* Riverside, Calif.: Ariadne Press, 2000.

——. "Michael Haneke, *Funny Games*: Violence and the Media." In *Conference on Austrian Literature and Culture, Lafayette College, 2001: Visions and Visionaries in Contemporary Austrian Literature and Film*, edited by Margarete Lamb-Faffelberger and Pamela S. Saur. New York: Peter Lang, 2004.

Scheugl, Hans. *Erweitertes Kino: Die Wiener Filme der 60er Jahre.* Vienna: Triton Verlag, 2002.

Schlemmer, Gottfried, ed. *Dietmar Brehm: Perfekt.* Vienna: Sonderzahl Verlag, 2000.

——. "Heimelektronik und Heimnachteil: Michael Hanekes *Benny's Video.* In *Der Neue Österreichische Film,* 286–99. Vienna: Wespennest, 1996.

Schlemmer, Gottfried, Bernhard Riff, and Georg Haberl, eds. *G. W. Pabst.* Münster: MakS Publikationen, 1990.

Seeßlen, Georg. "Eine Frage der Einstellung: die Liebe, das Gerede, der Waffenhandel; Die Theorie des Spiel-Films Die Praxis der Liebe von Valie Export." In *Der neue österreichische Film*, edited by Gottfried Schlemmer. Vienna: Wespennest, 1996.

Sicinski, Michael. "Valie Export and Paranoid Counter-Surveillance." *Discourse: Journal for Theoretical Studies in Media and Culture* 22, no. 2 (Spring 2000): 71–91.

Tscherkassky, Peter. "Lord of the Frames: Kurt Kren." Translated by Elisabeth Frank-Großebner. Reprinted from exhibition catalog, *Kurt Kren at Wiener Secession,* 1996. www.hi-beam.net/mkr/kk/kk-bio.html

AVANT-GARDE AND EXPERIMENTAL GERMAN FILM

Alter, Nora M. "Imaging (Post)Gender under Transnational Capital: Valie Export´s Perfect Pair." In *After Postmodernism: Austrian Literature and Film in Transition*, edited by Willy Riemer, 267–82. Riverside, Calif.: Ariadne Press, 2000.

Anker, Steve, Peter Tscherkassky, and Martin Arnold. *Austrian Avant-Garde Cinema, 1955–1993*. Vienna: Sixpackfilm; San Francisco: San Francisco Cinémathèque, 1994.

Bilda, Linda, Ernst Schmidt, and Wiener Secession. *Ernst Schmidt Jr.: Drehen Sie Filme, aber keine Filme! Filme und Filmtheorie, 1964–1987*. Vienna: Triton Verlag, 2001.

Bower, Kathrin. "Outing Hybridity: Polymorphism, Identity, and Desire in Monika Treut's *Virgin Machine*." *European Studies Journal* 17, no. 1 (Spring 2000): 23–40.

Curry, Ramona. "The Female Image as Critique in the Films of Valie Export (*Syntagma*)." In *Gender and German Cinema: Feminist Interventions*. Vol. 1, *Gender and Representation in New German Cinema*, edited by Sandra Frieden, Richard W. Mc Cormick, Vibeke Petersen, and Laurie Melissa Vogelsang, 255–66. Providence, R.I.: Berg, 1993.

Dawson, Jan, ed. and comp. *The Films of Hellmuth Costard*. London: Riverside Studios, 1979.

del Rio, Elena. "Politics and Erotics of Representation: Feminist Phenomenology and Valie Export's *The Practice of Love*." *Discourse: Journal for Theoretical Studies in Media and Culture* 22, no. 2 (Spring 2000): 46–70.

Dhein, Sabina. *Werner Schroeter: Regie im Theater*. Frankfurt am Main: Fischer Taschenbuch, 1991.

Eifler, Margret. "Valie Export's *Invisible Adversaries*: Film as Text." In *Gender and German Cinema: Feminist Interventions*. Vol. 1: *Gender and Representation in New German Cinema*, edited by Sandra Frieden, Richard W. McCormick, Vibeke R. Petersen, and Laurie Melissa Vogelsang, 241–55. Providence, R.I.: Berg, 1993.

Elsaesser, Thomas. "American Graffiti: Neuer Deutscher Film zwischen Avantgarde und Postmoderne." In *Postmoderne-Zeichen eines kulturellen Wandels*, edited by A. Huyssen and K. Scherpe, 302–28. Reinbek bei Hamburg: Rowohlt, 1986.

Export, Valie. "Expanded Cinema as Expanded Reality." *Senses of Cinema: An Online Film Journal Devoted to the Serious and Eclectic Discussion of Cinema*, no. 28 (September–October 2003). www.sensesofcinema.com/contents/03/28/expanded_cinema.html

———. "Ein Interview mit Valie Export." By Ruth Askey. *High Performance*, no. 13 (Spring 1981): 14–19.

———. "Interview with Valie Export." By Margret Eifler and Sandra Frieden. In *Gender and German Cinema: Feminist Interventions.* Vol. 1, *Gender and Representation in New German Cinema*, edited by Sandra Frieden, Richard W. McCormick, Vibeke R. Petersen, and Laurie Melissa Vogelsang, 267–78. Providence, R.I.: Berg, 1993.

———. "The Real and Its Double: The Body." *Discourse: Journal for Theoretical Studies in Media and Culture* 11, no. 1 (Fall–Winter 1988–1989): 3–27.

———. "Valie Export: Interview by Andrea Juno." In *Angry Women*, edited by Andrea Juno and V. Vale, 186–93. San Francisco: Re/Search Publications, 1991.

Export, Valie, and Peter Weibel, eds. *Wien: Bildkompendium Wiener Aktionismus und Film.* Frankfurt am Main: Kohlkunstverlag, 1970.

Gemünden, Gerd. "The Queer Utopia of Monika Treut." In *Framed Visions: Popular Culture, Americanization, and the Contemporary German and Austrian Imagination,* 177–94. Ann Arbor: University of Michigan Press, 1998.

Gregor, Ulrich, ed. *The German Experimental Film of the Seventies.* Munich: Goethe-Institut, 1980.

Heller, Heinz-B. " 'Stählerne Romantik' und Avantgarde: Beobachtungen und Anmerkungen zu Ruttmanns Industriefilmen." In *Triumph der Bilder: Kultur- und Dokumentarfilm vor 1945 im internationalen Vergleich*, edited by Peter Zimmermann and Kay Hoffmann, 105–18. Konstanz: UVK Verlags, 2003.

Holmlund, Chris. "Feminist Makeovers: The Celluloid Surgery of Valie Export and Su Friedrich." In *Play It Again, Sam: Retakes on Remakes*, edited by Andrew Horton and Stuart Y. McDougal, 217–37. Berkeley and Los Angeles: University of California Press, 1998.

Horwath, Alexander, and Peter Tscherkassky, eds. *Crossing the Lines: Austrian Independent Film + Video.* Vienna: Sixpackfilm, 2001.

Jansen, Peter W., and Wolfram Schütte, eds.. *Werner Schroeter.* Munich: Carl Hanser, 1980.

Jung, Fernand. "Das Kino der frühen Jahre: Herbert Vesely und die Filmavantgarde der Bundesrepublik." In *"Zwischen Gestern und Morgen": Westdeutscher Nachkriegsfilm, 1946–1962*, edited by Hilmar Hoffmann and Walter Schobert, 318–37. Frankfurt am Main: Deutsches Filmmuseum, 1989.

Kapke, Barry. "Body as Sign: Performance and Film Works of Valie Export." *High Performance,* no. 45 (Spring 1989): 34–37.

Kiernan, Joanna. "Films by Valie Export." *Millenium Film Journal,* nos. 16–18 (Fall–Winter 1986–1987): 181–87.

King, Homay. "Vision and Its Discontents: Valie Export's *Invisible Adversaries.*" *Discourse: Journal for Theoretical Studies in Media and Culture* 22, no. 2 (Spring 2000): 25–45.

Klotz, Marcia. "The Queer and Unqueer Spaces of Monika Treut's Films." In *Triangulated Visions: Women in Recent German Cinema*, edited by Ingeborg Majer O'Sickey and Ingeborg von Zadow, 65–77. Albany: State University of New York Press, 1998.

Knight, Julia. "The Meaning of Treut?" In *Immortal, Invisible: Lesbians and the Moving Image*, edited by Tamsin Wilton, 34–51. New York: Routledge, 1995.

Kuzniar, Alice A. "Lesbians Abroad: The Queer Nationhood of Monika Treut et al." In *The Queer German Cinema*, by Alice A. Kuzniar, 157–73. Stanford, Calif.: Stanford University Press, 2000.

Lamb-Faffelberger, Margarete. "Austria's Feminist Avant-Garde: Valie Export's and Elfriede Jelinek's Aesthetic Innovations." In *Out from the Shadows: Essays on Contemporary Austrian Women Writers and Filmmakers*, edited by Margarete Lamb-Faffelberger, 229–41. Riverside, Calif.: Ariadne Press, 1997.

———. *Valie Export und Elfriede Jelinek im Spiegel der Presse: Zur Rezeption der feministischen Avantgarde Österreichs*. New York: Peter Lang, 1992.

Langford, Michelle. *Allegorical Images: Tableau, Time and Gesture in the Cinema of Werner Schroeter.* Portland, Oreg.: Intellect, 2006.

———. "Werner Schroeter." Great Directors: A Critical Database. *Senses of Cinema: An Online Film Journal Devoted to the Serious and Eclectic Discussion of Cinema*, no. 24 (January–February 2003). www.sensesofcinema.com/contents/directors/03/schroeter.html

Lehner, Wolfgang, and Bernhard Praschl. "Stellen sie sich einen österreichischen Film vor! Zur Entwicklung des Avantgarde-, Experimental- und Undergroundfilms in der 2. Republik." In *Medienkultur in Österreich*, edited by Hans H. Fabris and Kurt Luger, 199–250. Vienna: Böhlau, 1988.

Lippert, Renate. "Ein Millimeter schmerzfreie Zone: Valie Exports . . . Remote . . . Remote." *Frauen und Film*, no. 39 (December 1985): 73–80.

MacDonald, Scott. "Valie Export." In *A Critical Cinema: Interviews with Independent Filmmakers.* [Vol. 1]. Berkeley and Los Angeles: University of California Press, 1988.

Mennel, Barbara. "Wanda's Whip: Recasting Masochism's Fantasy; Monika Treut's *Seduction: The Cruel Woman*." In *Triangulated Visions: Women in Recent German Cinema*, edited by Ingeborg Majer O'Sickey and Ingeborg von Zadow, 153–62. Albany: State University of New York Press, 1998.

Mörth, Otto, ed. *Marc Adrian: Das Filmische Werk.* Vienna: Sonderzahl Verlag, 1999.

Mueller Roswitha. "Leinwandverkörperlichungen: Valie Exports Syntagma." In *Feminismus und Medien*, edited by G. J. Lischka and Peter Weibel, 164–81. Bern: Benteli Verlag, 1991.

———. "The Prosthetic Womb: Technology and Reproduction in the Work of Valie Export." In *Out from the Shadows: Essays on Contemporary Austrian*

Women Writers and Filmmakers, edited by Margarete Lamb-Faffelberger, 242–51. Riverside, Calif.: Ariadne Press, 1997.

——. "Screen Embodiments: Valie Export's *Syntagma*." *Discourse: Journal for Theoretical Studies in Media and Culture* 13, no. 2 (Spring–Summer 1991): 39–57.

——. "The Uncanny in the Eyes of a Woman." Special Issue from the Center for Twentieth Century Studies. *SubStance* (University of Wisconsin Press), nos. 37–38 (1983): 129–39.

——. *Valie Export: Bild-Risse*. Vienna: Passagen Verlag, 2002.

——. *Valie Export: Fragments of the Imagination*. Bloomington: Indiana University Press, 1994.

Österreichisches Filmmuseum. *Dietmar Brehm: Party* [Filme 1974–2003]. Edited by Alexander Horwath, 2003.

Petzke, Ingo. *Der deutsche Experimentalfilm der 60er und 70er Jahre*. Munich: Goethe Institut, 1990.

Prammer, Anita. *Valie Export: Eine multimediale Künstlerin*. Vienna: Wiener Frauenverlag, 1988.

Reimann, Andrea. "New German Cinema's Boundaries Opened: Postmodern Authorship and Nationality in Monika Treut's Films of the 1980s." In *Writing against Boundaries: Nationality, Ethnicity and Gender in the German-speaking Context*, edited by Barbara Kosta and Helga Kraft, 177–96. New York: Rodopi, 2003.

Richardson, Colin. "Monika Treut: an Outlaw at Home." In *A Queer Romance: Lesbians, Gay Men, and Popular Culture*, edited by Paul Burston and Colin Richardson, 167–85. New York: Routledge, 1995.

Schenk, Irmbert. "Zwischen Futurismus, Realismus und Faschismus: Anmerkungen zu Walter Ruttmanns *Acciaio*." In *Triumph der Bilder: Kultur- und Dokumentarfilm vor 1945 im internationalen Vergleich*, edited by Peter Zimmermann and Kay Hoffmann, 218–34. Konstanz: UVK Verlags, 2003.

Scheugl, Hans. *Erweitertes Kino: Die Wiener Filme der 60er Jahre*. Vienna: Triton Verlag, 2002.

Scheugl, Hans, and Ernst Schmidt Jr. *Eine Subgeschichte des Films*. Frankfurt am Main: Suhrkamp, 1974.

Schlemmer, Gottfried, ed. *Dietmar Brehm: Perfekt*. Vienna: Sonderzahl Verlag, 2000.

Seeßlen, Georg. "Eine Frage der Einstellung: die Liebe, das Gerede, der Waffenhandel; Die Theorie des Spiel-Films Die Praxis der Liebe von Valie Export." In *Der neue österreichische Film*, edited by Gottfried Schlemmer. Vienna: Wespennest, 1996.

Sicinski, Michael. "Valie Export and Paranoid Counter-Surveillance." *Discourse: Journal for Theoretical Studies in Media and Culture* 22, no. 2 (Spring 2000): 71–91.

Silberman, Marc, tr. "Invisible Adversaries (Valie Export)." *Camera Obscura*, nos. 3–4 (Summer 1979): 219–24.

Simon, Sunka. "Out of Hollywood: Monika Treut's *Virgin Machine* and Percy Adlon's *Bagdad Cafe*." In *Queering the Canon: Defying Sights in German Literature and Culture*, edited by Christoph Lorey and John L. Plews, 383–402. Columbia, S.C.: Camden House, 1998.

Steffensen, Jyanni. "Epistemological Sadism: Queering the Phallus in Monica Treut's *Seduction*." *Atlantis* 23, no. 1 (Fall 1998): 137–45.

Straayer, Chris. "Lesbian Narratives and Queer Characters in Monika Treut's *Virgin Machine*." *Journal of Film and Video* 45, nos. 2–3 (Summer–Fall 1993): 24–39.

Treut, Monika. "Female Misbehavior." In *Feminisms in the Cinema*, edited by Laura Pietropaolo and Ada Testaferri, 106–21. Bloomington: Indiana University Press, 1995.

———. "From *Taboo Parlor* to Porn and Passing: An Interview with Monika Treut." By Gerd Gemünden, Alice Kuzniar, and Klaus Phillips. *Film Quarterly* 50, no. 3 (Spring 1997): 2–12.

———. *Die grausame Frau: zum Frauenbild bei de Sade und Sacher-Masoch.* Basel: Stroemfeld/Roter Stern, 1984.

———. "Die Zeremonie der blutenden Rose." *Frauen und Film*, no. 36 (February 1984): 35–43.

Tscherkassky, Peter. "Lord of the Frames: Kurt Kren." Translated by Elisabeth Frank-Großebner. Reprinted from exhibition catalog, *Kurt Kren at Wiener Secession*, 1996. www.hi-beam.net/mkr/kk/kk-bio.html

Webber, Mark. "Counting the Waves: A Summary of Activity [Overview of Austrian Avant-Garde Cinema]." *Senses of Cinema*, no. 28 (September–October 2003). www.sensesofcinema.com/contents/03/28/counting_the_waves.html

Wilke, Sabine. "The Body Politic of Performance, Literature, and Film: Mimesis and Citation in Valie Export, Elfriede Jelinek, and Monika Treut." *Paragraph* 22, no. 3 (November 1999): 228–47.

———. "The Sexual Woman and Her Struggle for Sexuality: Cruel Women in Sade, Sacher-Masoch, and Treut." *Women in German Yearbook: Feminist Studies in German Literature and* Culture 14 (1999): 245–60.

HOLOCAUST AND REMEMBERING NAZI GERMANY THROUGH POSTWAR FILM

Avisar, Ilan. *Screening the Holocaust: Cinema's Images of the Unimaginable.* Bloomington: Indiana University Press, 1988.

Baker, Mark. " 'Trummerfilme:' Postwar German Cinema, 1946–1948." *Film Criticism* 20 (Fall–Winter 1995–1996): 88–101.

Bammer, Angelika. "Through a Daughter's Eyes: Helma Sanders-Brahms's *Germany, Pale Mother.*" Special Issue on Heimat. *New German Critique*, no. 36 (Autumn 1985): 91–109.

Bathrick, David. "Anti-Neonazism as Cinematic Practice: Bonengel's *Beruf Neonazi.*" Legacies of Antifascism. *New German Critique*, no. 67 (Winter 1996): 133–46.

Berghahn, Daniela. "Liars and Traitors: Unheroic Resistance in Antifascist DEFA Films." In *Millennial Essays on Film and Other German Studies*, edited by Daniela Berghahn and Alan Bance, 19–36. New York: Peter Lang, 2002.

Berman, Russell A. "Hans-Jürgen Syberberg: Of Fantastic and Magical Worlds." In *New German Filmmakers: From Oberhausen through the 1970s*, edited by Klaus Phillips, 359–78. New York: Frederick Ungar, 1984.

Burghardt, Kirsten. "Moralische Wiederaufrüstung im frühen deutschen Nachkriegsfilm." In *Positionen deutscher Filmgeschichte: 100 Jahre Kinematographie; Strukturen, Diskurse, Kontexte*, edited by Michael Schaudig, 240–77. Munich: Schaudig und Ledig, 1996.

Creekmur, Corey K. "The Cinematic Photograph and the Possibility of Mourning." *Wide Angle* 9, no. 1 (Winter 1987): 41–49.

Deutsches Filminstitut–DIF, eds. *Die Vergangenheit in der Gegenwart Konfrontationen mit den Folgen des Holocaust im deutschen Nachkriegsfilm.* Munich: edition text + kritik, 2000.

Elsaesser, Thomas. "Die Gegenwärtigkeit des Holocaust im Neuen Deutschen Film am Beispiel Alexander Kluge." In *Die Vergangenheit in der Gegenwart Konfrontationen mit den Folgen des Holocaust im deutschen Nachkriegsfilm*, edited by Deutsches Filminstitut–DIF, Claidia Dillmann, and Ronny Loewy, 54–67. Munich: edition text + kritik, 2001.

Farocki, Harun. "History Is Not a Matter of Generations: Interview with Harun Farocki" *Camera Obscura*, no. 46 (May 2001): 47–75.

Feinstein, Howard. "BRD 1–2–3: Fassbinder's Postwar Trilogy and the Spectacle." *Cinema Journal* 23, no. 1 (Fall 1983): 44–56.

Friedman,Régine-Mihal. *L'image et son Juif: Le Juif dans le cinéma Nazi.* Paris: Payot, 1983.

———. "Juden-Ratten—Von der rassistischen Metonymie zur tierischen Metapher in Fritz Hipplers Film *Der ewige Jude.*" *Frauen und Film*, no. 47 (September 1989): 24–35.

———. "Male Gaze and Female Reaction: Veit Harlan's *Jew Süss* (1940)." In *Gender and German Cinema: Feminist Interventions.* vol. 2, *German Film History/German History on Film*, edited by Sandra Frieden, Richard W. McCormick, Vibeke R. Petersen, and Laurie Melissa Vogelsang, 117–33. Providence, R.I.: Berg, 1993.

Gemünden, Gerd. "Space Out of Joint: Ernst Lubitsch's *To Be or Not to Be*." Film and Exile. *New German Critique,* no. 89 (Spring–Summer 2003): 59–80.

Hall, Carol. "A Different Drummer: The *Tin Drum*, Film and Novel." *Literature/Film Quarterly* 18, no. 4 (1990): 236–44.

Hansen, Miriam. "The Stubborn Discourse: History and Storytelling in the Films of Alexander Kluge." *Persistence of Vision,* no. 2 (Fall 1985): 19–29.

Harlan, Veit. *Im Schatten meiner Filme: Selbstbiographie.* Edited by H. C. Opfermann. Gütersloh: Mohn, 1966.

Hoffmann, Hilmar. *The Triumph of Propaganda: Film and National Socialism, 1933–1945.* Translated by John A. Broadwin and V. R. Berghahn. Providence, R.I.: Berghahn Books, 1996.

Holland, Agnieszka. "Interview with Agnieszka Holland." By Godana P. Crnkovic. *Film Quarterly* 52, no. 2 (Winter 1998–99): 2–9.

Hornshøj-Møller, Stig, and David Culbert. "*Der ewige Jude* (1940): Joseph Goebbels' Unequaled Monument to Anti-Semitism." *Historical Journal of Film, Radio, and Television* 12, no. 1 (1992): 41–67.

Huyssen, Andreas. "The Politics of Identification: 'Holocaust' and West German Drama." Special Issue 1: Germans and Jews. *New German Critique*, no. 19 (Winter 1980), 117–36. Reprinted in *After the Great Divide: Modernism, Mass Culture, Postmodernism,* by Andreas Huyssen, 94–114. Bloomington: Indiana University Press, 1986.

Insdorf, Annette. *Indelible Shadows: Film and the Holocaust.* New York: Vintage, 1983.

Jameson, Fredric. " 'In the Destructive Element Immerse': Hans-Jürgen Syberberg and Cultural Revolution." The New Talkies. *October,* no. 17 (Summer 1981): 99–118. Also published in *Perspectives on German Cinema*, edited by Terri Ginsberg and Kirsten Moana Thompson, 508–25. New York: G. K. Hall; London: Prentice Hall International, 1996.

Jordan, Günter. "Davidstern und roter Winkel: Das jüdische Thema in DEFA-Wochenschau und -Dokumentarfilm 1946–1948." In *Millennial Essays on Film and Other German Studies*, edited by Daniela Berghahn and Alan Bance. New York: Peter Lang, 2002.

Kaes, Anton. *Deutschlandbilder: Die Wiederkehr der Geschichte als Film.* Munich: edition text + kritik, 1987.

———. *From Hitler to Heimat:The Return of History as Film.* Cambridge: Harvard University Press, 1989.

———. "German Cultural History and the Study of Film: Ten Theses and a Postscript." Cultural History/Cultural Studies. *New German Critique,* no. 65 (Spring–Summer 1995): 47–58.

——. "History and Film: Public Memory in the Age of Electronic Dissemination." *History and Memory* 2 (Fall 1990): 111–29.

——. "History, Fiction, Memory: Fassbinder's The Marriage of Maria Braun." In *German Film and Literature: Adaptations and Transformations*, edited by Eric Rentschler, 276–88. New York: Methuan, 1986.

Kaplan, E. Ann. "Discourses of Terrorism, Feminism and the Family in von Trotta's *Marianne and Juliane*." *Persistence of Vision* 2 (1985): 61–68.

——. "Female Politics in the Symbolic Realm: Von Trotta's *Marianne and Juliane* [The German Sisters] (1981)." In *Women and Film: Both Sides of the Camera*, 104–12. New York: Methuen, 1983.

——. "The Search for the Mother/Land in Sanders-Brahms's *Germany, Pale Mother*." In *German Film and Literature: Adaptations and Transformations*, edited by Eric Rentschler, 289–304. New York: Methuen, 1986.

Keene, Judith. "Mothering Daughters: Subjectivity and History in the Work of Helma Sanders-Brahms's *Germany Pale Mother*." *Film Historia* 7, no. 1 (1997): 3–12.

Koch, Gertrud. "On the Disappearance of the Dead among the Living: The Holocaust and the Confusion of Identities in the Films of Konrad Wolf." Special Issue on German Film History. *New German Critique*, no. 60 (Autumn 1993): 57–75.

——. "Torments of the Flesh, Coldness of the Spirit: Jewish Figures in the Films of Rainer Werner Fassbinder." Translated by Andy Spencer and Miriam Hansen. In *Perspectives on German Cinema*, edited by Terri Ginsberg, and Kirsten Moana Thompson, 221–30. New York: G. K. Hall; London: Prentice Hall International, 1996. Originally published in *New German Critique*, no. 38 (Spring–Summer 1986): 28–38.

Lungstrum, Janet. "Foreskin Fetishism: Jewish Male Difference in *Europa, Europa*." *Screen* 39, no. 1 (Spring 1998): 53–66.

Margry, Karel. "*Theresienstadt* (1944–1945): The Nazi Propaganda Film Depicting the Concentration Camp as Paradise." *Historical Journal of Film, Radio and Television* 12, no. 2 (1992): 145–62.

Melehy, Hassan. "Lubitsch's *To Be or Not to Be*: The Question of Simulation in Cinema." *Film Criticism* 26, no. 2 (Winter 2001): 19–40.

Meyers, Peter. "Der DEFA-film: *Die Mörder sind unter uns*." In *Nationalsozialismus und Judenverfolgung in DDR-Medien*, 2nd enl. ed., 71–83. Bonn: Bundeszentrale für Politische Bildung, 1997.

Mückenberger, Christiane. "The Anti-Fascist Past in DEFA Films." In *DEFA: East German Cinema, 1946–1992*, edited by Seán Allen and John Sandford, 58–76. New York: Berghahn Books, 1999.

Mueller, Roswitha. "Hans-Jürgen Syberberg's *Hitler*: An Interview-Montage." *Discourse: Journal for Theoretical Studies in Media and Culture* 2 (Summer 1980): 60–82.

Münzberg, Olav. "Schaudern vor der bleichen Mutter: Eine sozialpsychologische Analyse der Kritiken zum Film von Helma Sanders-Brahms." *Medium* 7 (July 1980): 34–37.

Murray, Bruce A., and Renate Möhrmann. "*Germany, Pale Mother*: On the Mother Figures in New German Women's Film." *Women in German Yearbook: Feminist Studies in German Literature and Culture* 11 (1995): 67–80.

Murray, Bruce A., and Christopher J. Wickham, eds. *Framing the Past: The Historiography of German Cinema and Television.* Carbondale: Southern Illinois University Press, 1992.

Nash, Mark, and Steve Neal. "Film: 'History/Production/Memory'." *Screen* 18, no. 4 (Fall–Winter 1977–1978): 87–91.

Palmer, Angela. "The Birth of Remembering: Wolfgang Staudte's *Die Mörder sind unter uns*. (The Murderers Are among Us, 1946)." *Kinoeye* 3, no. 11 (October 13, 2003). www.kinoeye.org/03/11/palmer11.php

Plard, Henri. "Sur le film *Die Blechtrommel:* de Grass à Schlöndorff" *Etudes germaniques* 35 (January–March 1980): 69–84.

Prager, Brad. "Beleaguered under the Sea: Wolfgang Petersen's *Das Boot* as a German Hollywood Film. In *Light Motives: German Popular Film in Perspective*, edited by Randall Halle and Margaret McCarthy, 237–58. Detroit: Wayne State University Press, 2003.

Prawer, S. S. *Between Two Worlds: Jewish Presences in German and Austrian Film, 1910–1933.* New York: Berghahn Books, 2005.

Reimer, Robert C. "Memories from the Past: A Study of Rainer Werner Fassbinder's *The Marriage of Maria Braun*." *Journal of Popular Film and Television* 9, no. 3 (Fall 1981): 138–43.

———. "Nazi-retro Films: Experiencing the Mistakes of the Ordinary Citizen." *Journal of Popular Film and Television* 12, no. 3 (Fall 1984): 112–17.

Reimer, Robert C., and Carol J. Reimer. *Nazi-retro Film: How German Narrative Cinema Remembers the Past.* New York: Twayne, 1992.

———. "Nazi-retro Filmography." *Journal of Popular Film and Television* 14, no. 2 (Summer 1986): 80–92.

Rentschler, Eric. "Germany: The Past That Would Not Go Away." In *World Cinema since 1945*, edited by William Luhr, 208–51. New York: Frederick Ungar, 1987.

———. "Remembering Not to Forget: A Retrospective Reading of Alexander Kluge's *Brutality in Stone*." Special Issue on Alexander Kluge. *New German Critique*, no. 49 (Winter 1990): 23–41.

——. "The Use and Abuse of Memory: New German Film and the Discourse of Bitburg." Special Issue on Heimat. *New German Critique,* no. 36 (Autumn 1985): 67–90.

Rheuban, Joyce. *The Marriage of Maria Braun.* New Brunswick, N.J.: Rutgers University Press, 1986.

Robertson, Ritchie. "Varieties of Antisemitism from Herder to Fassbinder." In *The German-Jewish Dilemma: From the Enlightenment to the Shoah,* edited by Edward Timms and Andrea Hammel, 107–21. Lewiston, N.Y.: Edwin Mellen Press, 1999.

Rogowski, Christian. " 'Der liebevolle Blick'? The Problem of Perception in Wim Wenders's *Wings of Desire." Seminar: A Journal of Germanic Studies* 29, no. 4. (November 1993): 398–409.

——. " 'To Be Continued': History in Wim Wenders' *Wings of Desire* and Thomas Brasch's *Domino." German Studies Review* 15, no. 3. (October 1992): 547–63.

Rosenberg, Joel. "Shylock's Revenge: The Doubly Vanished Jew in Ernst Lubitsch's *To Be or Not to Be." Prooftexts: A Journal of Jewish Literary History* 16, no. 3 (September 1996): 209–44.

Rosenbaum, Marianne S. W. "'Frieden' hat für uns Deutsche einen amerikanischen Geschmack': Ein Gespräch mit Marianne S. W. Rosenbaum." By Bion Steinborn and Carola Hilmes. *Filmfaust,* no. 39 (May–June 1984): 27–31.

Sanders-Brahms, Helma. *Deutschland, bleiche Mutter: Film-Erzählung.* Reinbek bei Hamburg: Rowohlt, 1980.

Santner, Eric L. *Stranded Objects: Mourning, Memory, and Film in Postwar Germany.* Ithaca, N.Y.: Cornell University Press, 1990.

——. "The Trouble with Hitler: Postwar German Aesthetics and the Legacy of Fascism." *New German Critique,* no. 57 (Autumn 1992): 5–24.

Schlöndorff, Volker. "Coming to Terms with the German Past: An Interview with Volker Schlöndorff." By Gary Crowdus and Richard Porton. *Cineaste* 26, no. 2 (March 2001): 18–23.

——. "*The Tin Drum:* Volker Schlöndorff's 'Dream of Childhood'." Interview by John Hughes. *Film Quarterly* 35, no. 3 (Spring 1981): 2–10.

Silberman, Marc. "Remembering History: The Filmmaker Konrad Wolf." Special Issue on Alexander Kluge. *New German Critique,* no. 49 (Winter 1990): 163–91.

Sontag, Susan. "Fascinating Fascism." In *Under the Sign of Saturn,* 73–105. New York: Farrar, Straus & Giroux, 1980. Originally published in the *New York Review of Books,* February 6, 1977. www.history.ucsb.edu/faculty/marcuse/classes/33d/33dTexts/SontagFascinFascism75.htm

Stimmel, Joanna K. "Between Globalization and Particularization of Memories: Screen Images of the Holocaust in Germany and Poland." *German Politics and Society* 23, no. 3 (Fall 2005): 83–105.

Tegel, Susan. "Leni Riefenstahl's 'Gypsy Question'." *Historical Journal of Film, Radio and Television* 23, no. 1 (March 2003): 3–10.

Tifft, Stephen. "Miming the Führer: *To Be or Not to Be* and the Mechanisms of Outrage." *The Yale Journal of Criticism* 5, no. 1 (Fall 1991): 1–40.

Trotta, Margarethe von. *Die bleierne Zeit.* Edited by Hans Jürgen Weber. Frankfurt am Main: Fischer Taschenbuch, 1981.

———. "Rebellinen wider eine bleierne Zeit: Ein Interview mit Margarethe von Trotta über ihren Film *bleierne Zeit.*" By Reiner Frey and Christian Göldenboog. *Filmfaust*, no. 24. (October–November 1981): 29–36.

Trotta, Margarethe von, Hans Jürgen Weber, and Ingeborg Weber. *"Die bleierne Zeit": Ein Film von Margarethe von Trotta.* Frankfurt am Main: Fischer Taschenbuch, 1981.

Trumpener, Katie. "Theory, History, and German Film." *Monatshefte* 82, no. 3 (1990): 294–306.

Weckel, Ulrike. "The Mitläufer in Two German Postwar Films: Representation and Critical Reception." *History and Memory* 15, no. 2 (2003): 64–93.

Zonal Film Archives (Hamburg, Germany). *Catalogue of Forbidden German Feature and Short Film Productions Held in Zonal Film Archives of Film Section, Information Services Division, Control Commission for Germany, (BE).* Original text by John F. Kelson. Westport, Conn.: Greenwood Press, 1996.

WOMEN IN FILM/WOMEN AND FILM

Acker, Robert. "The Major Directions of German Feminist Cinema." *Literature/Film Quarterly* 13, no. 4 (1985): 245–49.

Alter, Nora M. "Imaging (Post)Gender under Transnational Capital: Valie Export´s Perfect Pair." In *After Postmodernism: Austrian Literature and Film in Transition*, edited by Willy Riemer, 267–82. Riverside, Calif.: Ariadne Press, 2000.

———. "Triangulating Performances: Looking after Genre, after Feature." In *Triangulated Visions: Women in Recent German Cinema*, edited by Ingeborg Majer O'Sickey and Ingeborg von Zadow, 11–27. Albany: State University of New York Press, 1998.

"American Intelligence Report on Leni Riefenstahl—May 30th, 1945." *Film Culture*, no. 77 (Fall 1992): 34–38.

446 • BIBLIOGRAPHY

Ascheid, Antje. *Hitler's Heroines: Stardom and Womanhood in Nazi Cinema.* Philadelphia: Temple University Press, 2003.

———. "Nazi Stardom and the 'Modern Girl': The Case of Lilian Harvey." Special Issue on Nazi Cinema. *New German Critique*, no. 74 (Spring–Summer 1998): 57–89.

———. "A Sierkian Double Image: The Narration of Zarah Leander as a National Socialist Star." *Film Criticism* 23, nos. 2–3 (Winter–Spring 1999): 46–73.

Bach, Steven. *Leni: The Life and Work of Leni Riefenstahl.* New York: Knopf, 2007.

———. *Marlene Dietrich: Life and Legend.* New York: Da Capo Press, 2000.

Bahr, Gisela. "Film and Consciousness: The Depiction of Women in East German Movies." In *Gender and German Cinema: Feminist Interventions.* Vol. 1, *Gender and Representation in New German Cinema*, edited by Sandra Frieden, Richard W. McCormick, Vibeke R. Petersen, and Laurie Melissa Vogelsang, 125–40. Providence, R.I.: Berg, 1993.

Bammer, Angelika. "Through a Daughter's Eyes: Helma Sanders-Brahms's *Germany, Pale Mother.*" Special Issue on Heimat. *New German Critique*, no. 36 (Autumn 1985): 91–109.

Barnwell, Kathryn, and Marni Stanley. "The Vanishing Healer in Doris Dörrie's *Nobody Loves Me.*" In *Women Filmmakers: Refocusing,* edited by Jaqueline Levitin, Judith Plessis, and Valerie Raoul, 119–26. Vancouver: University of British Columbia Press, 2003.

Baumann, Antje. *Von Kopf bis Fuss auf Bilder eingestellt—Zur Darstellung von Marlene Dietrich und Leni Riefenstahl in deutschen Zeitungen von 1946 bis 2002.* Tönning: Der Andere Verlag, 2005.

Baxter, Peter. "On the Naked Thighs of Miss Dietrich." *Wide Angle* 2, no. 2 (1978): 18–25.

Bechdorf, Ute. *Wunsch-Bilder? Frauen im nationalsozialistischen Unterhaltungsfilm.* Tübingen: Max Niemayer Verlag, 1992.

Belach. Helga, ed. *Henny Porten: Der erste deutsche Filmstar 1890–1960.* Berlin: Haude und Spener, 1986.

Berg-Pan, Renata. *Leni Riefenstahl.* Boston: Twayne, 1980.

Bergstrom, Janet Lynn. "Asta Nielsen's Early German Films." In *Before "Caligari": German Cinema, 1895–1920,* edited by Paolo Cherchi Usai and Lorenzo Codelli, 162–85. [Pordenone]: Edizioni Biblioteca dell'Immagine, 1990.

Bernstein, Sandra, and Michael MacMillian. "Leni Riefenstahl: A Selected Annotated Bibliography." *Quarterly Review of Film Studies* 2, no. 4 (November 1977): 439–57.

Birgel, Franz, and Klaus Phillips. *Straight through the Heart: Doris Dörrie, German Filmmaker and Author.* Lanham, Md.: Scarecrow Press, 2004.

Bower, Kathrin. "Outing Hybridity: Polymorphism, Identity, and Desire in Monika Treut's *Virgin Machine.*" *European Studies Journal* 17, no. 1 (Spring 2000): 23–40.

Bräuninger, Werner. "Stählerne Romantik: Leni Riefenstahl und die ästhetisierung der Politik." In *Ich wollte nicht daneben stehen . . . : Lebensentwürfe von Alfred Baeumler bis Ernst Jünger, Essays,* 247–66. Graz: Ares Verlag, 2006.

Brennan, Matthew C. "Repression, Knowledge, and Saving Souls: The Role of the 'New Woman' in Stoker's *Dracula* and Murnau's *Nosferatu.*" *Studies in the Humanities* 19, no. 1 (June 1992): 1–10.

Brinckmann, Noll. "Schwere Zeiten für Schauspieler: Beobachtungen zu *Heller Wahn* und *Der Schlaf der Vernunft. Frauen und Film,* no. 40 (August 1986): 4–12.

Bronfen, Elisabeth. "Seductive Departures of Marlene Dietrich: Exile and Stardom in *The Blue Angel.*" Film and Exile. *New German Critique,* no. 89 (Spring–Summer 2003): 9–31.

Brooks, Louise. "Entretien avec Louise Brooks." Interview by Jacques Leduc, Andres Poirier, and Pierre Theberge. *Positif,* no. 297 (November 1985): 6–11.

Brückner, Jutta. *Cinema regard violence.* Brussels: Cahiers du Grif, 1982.

———. Interview with Patricia Harbord. *Screen Education,* no. 40 (Autumn 1981–Winter 1982): 48–57.

———. "Interview with Jutta Brückner." By Barbara Kosta and Richard W. McCormick. *Signs: Journal of Women in Culture and Society* 21, no. 2 (Winter 1996): 343–73.

———. "On Autobiographical Filmmaking." Translated by Jeannette Clausen. *Women in German Yearbook: Feminist Studies in German Literature and Culture* 11 (1995): 1–12.

———. "Recognizing Collective Gestures." Interview with Marc Silberman. *Jump Cut,* no. 27 (1982): 41–53.

———. "Women Behind the Camera." In *Feminist Aesthetics*, edited by Gisela Ecker, 120–24. Boston: Beacon Press, 1986.

Brückner, Jutta, Margarethe von Trotta, and Geneviève Dormann. *"Le coup de grâce." L'avant-scène du cinéma* 181 (February 1, 1977): 3–23, 43–59.

Byg, Barton. "Extraterritorial Identity in the Films of Jeanine Meerapfel." In *Neue Welt-Dritte Welt: Interkulturelle Beziehungen Deutschlands zu Lateinamerika und der Karibik,* edited by Sigrid Bauschinger and Susan Cocalis, 229–41. Tübingen: Francke, 1994.

———. "German History and Cinematic Convention Harmonized in Margarethe von Trotta's *Marianne and Juliane.*" In *Gender and German Cinema: Feminist Interventions.* Vol. 2, *German Film History/German History on Film,* edited by Sandra Frieden, Richard W. McCormick, Vibeke R. Petersen, and Laurie Melissa Vogelsang, 259–72. Providence, R.I.: Berg, 1993.

———. "Nazism as Femme Fatale: Recuperations of Cinematic Masculinity in Postwar Berlin." In *Gender and Germanness: Cultural Productions of Nation*, edited by Patricia Herminghouse and Magda Mueller, 176–88. Providence, R.I.: Berghahn Books, 1997.

Clooney, Nick. "*Triumph of the Will.*" In *The Movies That Changed Us: Reflections on the Screen*, 217–28. New York: Atria Books, 2002.

Corliss, Richard. "Leni Riefenstahl: A Bibliography." *Film Heritage* 5, no. 1 (Fall 1969): 27–36.

Craig, J. Robert. "From *Triumph of the Will* to the *Mighty Ducks of Anaheim*: Riefenstahl Rocks by the Pond." *Popular Culture Review* 8, no. 1 (February 1997): 111–20.

Curry, Ramona. "The Female Image as Critique in the Films of Valie Export (*Syntagma*)." In *Gender and German Cinema: Feminist Interventions*. Vol. 1, *Gender and Representation in New German Cinema*, edited by Sandra Frieden, Richard W. Mc Cormick, Vibeke Petersen, and Laurie Melissa Vogelsang, 255–66. Providence, R.I.: Berg, 1993.

Davidson, David. "From Virgin to Dynamo: The 'Amoral Woman' in European Cinema." *Cinema Journal* 21, no. 1 (Fall 1981): 31–58.

Davidson, John E. "Cleavage: Sex in the Total Cinema of the Third Reich." Modernity and Postmodernity. *New German Critique*, no. 98 (Summer 2006): 101–33.

del Rio, Elena. "Politics and Erotics of Representation: Feminist Phenomenology and Valie Export's *The Practice of Love.*" *Discourse: Journal for Theoretical Studies in Media and Culture* 22, no. 2 (Spring 2000): 46–70.

DelGaudio, Sybil. *Dressing the Part: Sternberg, Dietrich, and Costume.* Rutherford, N.J.: Fairleigh Dickinson University Press; Cranbury, N.J.: Associated University Presses, 1993.

Delorme, Charlotte. "On the Film *Marianne and Juliane* by Margarethe von Trotta." *The Journal of Film and Video*, 37, no. 2 (Spring 1985): 47–51.

Diethe, Carol. "Beauty and the Beast: An Investigation into the Role and Function of Women in German Expressionist Film." In *Visions of the "Neue Frau": Women and the Visual Arts in Weimar Germany*, edited by Marsha Meskimmon and Shearer West. Aldershot, England: Scolar Press; Brookfield, Vt.: Ashgate, 1995.

Dietrich, Marlene. *Nehmt nur mein Leben . . . : Reflexionen.* Munich: C. Bertelsmann, 1979.

Doane, Mary Ann. "The Erotic Barter: *Pandora's Box* (1929)." In *Femmes Fatales*, 142–63. New York: Routledge, 1991.

Dörrie, Doris. "Searching for Stories in a Gray Germany. (1978)" In *West German Filmmakers on Film: Visions and Voices*, edited by Eric Rentchler, 188–90. New York: Holmes and Meier, 1988.

Eifler, Margret. "Valie Export's *Invisible Adversaries*: Film as Text." In *Gender and German Cinema: Feminist Interventions*. Vol. 1, *Gender and Representation in New German Cinema*, edited by Sandra Frieden, Richard W. McCormick, Vibeke R. Petersen, and Laurie Melissa Vogelsang, 241–55. Providence, R.I.: Berg, 1993.

Elsaesser, Thomas. "Leni Riefenstahl: The Body Beautiful, Art, Cinema and Fascist Aesthetics." In *Women and Film: A Sight and Sound Reader*, edited by Pam Cook and Philip Dodd, 186–97. Philadelphia: Temple University Press, 1993.

———. "Lulu and the Meter Man: Pabst's *Pandora's Box* (1929)." *Screen* 24, nos. 4–5 (July–October 1983): 4–36. Also published in *German Film and Literature: Adaptations and Transformations*, edited by Eric Rentschler, 40–59. New York: Methuen, 1986.

Export, Valie. "Ein Interview mit Valie Export." By Ruth Askey. *High Performance*, no. 13 (Spring 1981): 14–19.

———. "Interview with Valie Export." By Margret Eifler and Sandra Frieden. In *Gender and German Cinema: Feminist Interventions*. Vol. 1, *Gender and Representation in New German Cinema*, edited by Sandra Frieden, Richard W. McCormick, Vibeke R. Petersen, and Laurie Melissa Vogelsang, 267–78. Providence, R.I.: Berg, 1993.

———. "The Real and Its Double: The Body." *Discourse: Journal for Theoretical Studies in Media and Culture* 11, no. 1 (Fall–Winter 1988–1989): 3–27.

———. "Valie Export: Interview by Andrea Juno." In *Angry Women*, edited by Andrea Juno and V. Vale, 186–93. San Francisco: Re/Search Publications, 1991.

Export, Valie, and Peter Weibel, eds. *Wien: Bildkompendium Wiener Aktionismus und Film*. Frankfurt am Main: Kohlkunstverlag, 1970.

Fischetti, Renate. *Das neue Kino: acht Porträts von deutschen Regisseurinnen: Helke Sander, Claudia von Alemann, Ula Stöckl, Helma Sanders-Brahms, Margarethe von Trotta, Jutta Brückner, Ulrike Ottinger, Doris Dörrie*. Frankfurt am Main: Tende, 1992.

Flinn, Caryl. "The Body in the (Virgin) Machine." *Arachne* 3, no. 2 (1996): 48–66.

Fox, Jo. *Filming Women in the Third Reich*. New York: Berg, 2000.

Frewin, Leslie Ronald. *Dietrich: The Story of a Star*. Completely rev. ed. New York: Stein and Day, 1967.

Frieden, Sandra, Richard W. McCormick, Vibeke R. Petersen, and Laurie Melissa Vogelsang. *Gender and German Cinema: Feminist Interventions*. Vol. 1, *Gender and Representation in New German Cinema*. Vol. 2, *German Film History / German History on Film*. Providence, R.I.: Berg, 1993.

Friedman, Lester. "Cinematic Techniques in *The Lost Honor of Katharina Blum.*" *Literature/Film Quarterly* 7, no. 3 (1979): 244–52.

Friedman, Régine-Mihal. "Die Ausnahme ist die Regel: Zu *Romanze in Moll* (1943) von Helmut Käutner." *Frauen und Film,* no. 43 (December 1987): 48–58.

———. "Male Gaze and Female Reaction: Veit Harlan's *Jew Süss* (1940)." In *Gender and German Cinema: Feminist Interventions.* Vol. 2, *German Film History/German History on Film*, edited by Sandra Frieden, Richard W. Mc-Cormick, Vibeke R. Petersen, and Laurie Melissa Vogelsang, 117–33. Providence, R.I.: Berg, 1993.

Fuhrich, Angelika. "Woman and Typewriter: Gender, Technology, and Work in Late Weimar Film." *Women in German Yearbook: Feminist Studies in German Literature and Culture* 16 (2000): 151–66.

Geist, Kathe. "Mothers and Children in the Films of Wim Wenders." In *Gender and German Cinema: Feminist Interventions.* Vol. 1, *Gender and Representation in New German Cinema*, edited by Sandra Frieden, Richard W. Mc-Cormick, Vibeke R. Petersen, and Laurie Melissa Vogelsang, 11–22. Providence, R.I.: Berg, 1993.

Gemünden, Gerd. "The Queer Utopia of Monika Treut." In *Framed Visions: Popular Culture, Americanization, and the Contemporary German and Austrian Imagination,* 177–94. Ann Arbor: University of Michigan Press, 1998.

Gentile, Mary C. "Helke Sander's *Redupers*: Personality-in-Process." *Film Feminisms: Theory and Practice,* 113–31. Westport, Conn.: Greenwood Press, 1985.

Glass, Erlis. "Entrepreneurial Empowerment of Women in Brecht's *Dreigroschenoper*: Film versus Theaterstuck." *Anuario de Cine y Literatura en Espanol: An International Journal on Film and Literature,* no. 2 (1996): 81–91.

Gleber, Anke. "Female Flanerie and the Symphony of the City." In *Women in the Metropolis: Gender and Modernity in Weimar Culture*, edited by Katharina von Ankum, 67–88. Berkeley and Los Angeles: University of California Press, 1997.

———. "The Woman and the Camera—Walking in Berlin: Observations on Walter Ruttmann, Verena Stefan, and Helke Sander." In *Berlin in Focus: Cultural Transformations in Germany*, edited by Barbara Becker-Cantarino, 105–24. Westport, Conn.: Praeger, 1996.

Göktürk, Deniz. "Turkish Women on German Streets: Closure and Exposure in Transnational Cinema." In *Spaces in European Cinema*, edited by Myrto Konstantarakos, 64–76. Portland, Oreg.: Intellect, 2000.

Gramman, Karola, and Heide Schlüpmann. "Love as Opposition, Opposition as Love: Thoughts about Hertha Thiele." In *Herthe Thiele*, edited by Hans Helmut Prinzler. Berlin: Stiftung Deutsche Kinematek, 1983. Also published online as "*Mädchen in Uniform.*" Parts 1–2. Translated by Leoni Naughton. www.latrobe.edu.au/screeningthepast/reruns/thiele.html

Hake, Sabine. "*The Oyster Princess* and *the Doll*: Wayward Women of the Early Silent Cinema." In *Gender and German Cinema: Feminist Interventions*. Vol. 2, *German Film History/German History on Film*, edited by Sandra Frieden, Richard W. McCormick, Vibeke R. Petersen, and Laurie Melissa Vogelsang, 13–32. Providence, R.I.: Berg, 1993.

Halter, Regina, Eva Hiller, and Renate Holy. "Die Filmemacherin Helma Sanders-Brahms." *Frauen und Film,* no. 13 (October 1977): 21–43.

Hansen, Miriam. " Messages in a Bottle? Miriam Hansen Examines 'Frauen und Film': Women's Cinema and Feminist Film Theory in West Germany." *Screen* 28, no. 4 (Autumn 1987): 30–39.

——. "Visual Pleasure, Fetishism and the Problem of Feminine/Feminist Discourse: Ulrike Ottinger's *Ticket of No Return.* West German Culture and Politics. *New German Critique,* no. 31 (Winter 1984): 95–108.

Haralovich, Mary Beth. "The Sexual Politics of *The Marriage of Maria Braun.*" *Wide Angle* 12, no. 1 (January 1990): 6–16. Also published in *Perspectives in German Cinema*, edited by Terri Ginsberg and Kirsten Moana Thompson, 378–91. New York: G. K. Hall; London: Prentice Hall International, 1996.

Hartsough, Denise. "Cine-Feminism Renegotiated: Fassbinder's *Ali* as Interventionist Cinema." *Wide Angle* 12, no. 1 (January 1990): 18–29.

Heck-Rabi, Louise. "Leni Riefenstahl: A Crystal Grotto." In *Women Filmmakers: A Critical Reception,* 94–134. Metuchen, N.J.: Scarecrow Press, 1984.

Heinzlmeier, Adolf. *Marlene: Die Biografie.* Hamburg: Europa Verlag, 2000.

Herzog, Werner. "Tribute to Lotte Eisner." In *West German Filmmakers: Visions and Voices*, edited by Eric Rentschler, 115–18. New York: Holmes and Meier, 1988.

Hinton, David B. *The Films of Leni Riefenstahl.* 3rd ed. Metuchen, N.J.: Scarecrow Press, 2000.

Hitchens, Gordon. "Leni Riefenstahl Comments on the U.S. Army Interrogation." *Film Culture,* no. 79 (Winter 1996): 31–34.

——. "Recent Riefenstahl Activities and a Commentary on Nazi Propaganda Filmmaking." *Film Culture,* no. 79 (Winter 1996): 35–41.

Holland, Agnieszka. "Interview with Agnieszka Holland." By Godana P. Crnkovic. *Film Quarterly* 52, no. 2 (Winter 1998–99): 2–9.

Holmlund, Chris. "Feminist Makeovers: The Celluloid Surgery of Valie Export and Su Friedrich." In *Play It Again, Sam: Retakes on Remakes*, edited by Andrew Horton and Stuart Y. McDougal, 217–37. Berkeley and Los Angeles: University of California Press, 1998.

Hutchison, Nina. "Between Action and Repression: *The Piano Teacher.*" *Senses of Cinema: An Online Film Journal Devoted to the Serious and Eclectic Discussion of Cinema* 26 (May–June 2003). www.sensesofcinema.com/contents/03/26/piano_teacher.html

Huyssen, Andreas. "The Vamp and the Machine: Technology and Sexuality in Fritz Lang's *Metropolis.*" Special Double Issue on New German Cinema. *New German Critique*, nos. 24–25 (Autumn 1981–Winter 1982): 221–37. Also in *After the Great Divide: Modernism, Mass Culture, Postmodernism*, by Andreas Huyssen, 65–81. Bloomington: University of Indiana Press, 1986.

Hyams, Barbara. "Is the Apolitical Woman at Peace? A Reading of the Fairy Tale in *Germany, Pale Mother.*" *Wide Angle* 10, no. 4 (1988): 40–51.

Infield, Glenn B. *Leni Riefenstahl: The Fallen Film Goddess*. New York: Thomas Crowell, 1976.

Jary, Micaela. *Ich weiß, es wird einmal ein Wunder gescheh'n: Das Leben der Zarah Leander.* Berlin: Aufbau Verlag, 2001.

Johnson, Catherine. "The Imaginary and the Bitter Tears of Petra Von Kant." *Wide Angle* 3, no. 4 (1980): 20–25.

Kaltenbach, Christiane. *Frauen Film Handbuch*. Berlin: Verband der Filmarbeiterinnen, 1983.

Kapke, Barry. "Body as Sign: Performance and Film Works of Valie Export." *High Performance,* no. 45 (Spring 1989): 34–37.

Kaplan, E. Ann. "Discourses of Terrorism, Feminism and the Family in von Trotta's *Marianne and Juliane.*" *Persistence of Vision* 2 (1985): 61–68.

——. "Female Politics in the Symbolic Realm: Von Trotta's *Marianne and Juliane* [The German Sisters] (1981)." In *Women and Film: Both Sides of the Camera,* 104–12. New York: Methuen, 1983.

——. *Looking for the Other: Feminism, Film, and the Imperial Gaze*. New York: Routledge, 1997.

——. "The Search for the Mother/Land in Sanders-Brahms's *Germany, Pale Mother.*" In *German Film and Literature: Adaptations and Transformations,* edited by Eric Rentschler, 289–304. New York: Methuen, 1986.

Keene, Judith. "Mothering Daughters: Subjectivity and History in the Work of Helma Sanders-Brahms's *Germany Pale Mother.*" *Film Historia* 7, no. 1 (1997): 3–12.

Kellner, Douglas. "Fassbinder, Women, and Melodrama: Critical Interrogations." In *Triangulated Visions: Women in Recent German Cinema,* edited by Ingeborg Majer O'Sickey and Ingeborg von Zadow, 219–28. Albany: State University of New York Press, 1998.

Kiernan, Joanna. "Films by Valie Export." *Millenium Film Journal,* nos. 16–18 (Fall–Winter 1986–1987): 181–87.

King, Homay. "Vision and Its Discontents: Valie Export's *Invisible Adversaries*." *Discourse: Journal for Theoretical Studies in Media and Culture* 22, no. 2 (Spring 2000): 25–45.

Kinkel, Lutz. *Die Scheinwerferin: Leni Riefenstahl und das "Dritte Reich."* Hamburg: Europa Verlag, 2002.

Klotz, Marcia. "The Queer and Unqueer Spaces of Monika Treut's Films." In *Triangulated Visions: Women in Recent German Cinema*, edited by Ingeborg Majer O'Sickey and Ingeborg von Zadow, 65–77. Albany: State University of New York Press, 1998.

Kluge, Alexander. *Gelegenheitsarbeit einer Sklavin: Zur realistischen Methode*. Frankfurt am Main: Surkamp Verlag, 2002.

Knight, Julia. "The Meaning of Treut?" In *Immortal, Invisible: Lesbians and the Moving Image*, edited by Tamsin Wilton, 34–51. New York: Routledge, 1995.

———. *Women and the New German Cinema*. New York: Verso, 1992.

Knopp, Guido. "Leni Riefenstahl: Die Regisseurin." In *Hitler's Frauen und Marlene,* 149–206. Munich: C. Bertelsmann, 2001.

Koch, Gertrud. "Blindheit als Innenansicht." *Frauen und Film,* no. 46 (February 1989): 21–33.

Koepnick, Lutz P. "En-Gendering Mass Culture: The Case of Zarah Leander." In *Gender and Germanness: Cultural Productions of Nation*, edited by Patricia Herminghouse and Magda Mueller, 161–75. Providence, R.I.: Berghahn Books, 1997.

Kosta, Barbara. *Recasting Autobiography: Women's Counterfictions in Contemporary German Literature and Film*. Ithaca, N.Y.: Cornell University Press, 1994.

Krause, Edith H. "Effi's Endgame." *Oxford German Studies,* no. 32 (2003): 155–84.

Kreutzer, Hermann, and Manuela Runge. *Ein Koffer in Berlin: Marlene Dietrich–Geschichten von Politik und Liebe.* Weimar: Aufbau Verlag, 2001.

Kuhn, Anna K. "A Heroine for Our Time: Margarethe von Trotta's *Rosa Luxemburg*." In *Gender and German Cinema: Feminist Interventions.* Vol. 2, *German Film History/German History on Film*, edited by Sandra Frieden, Richard W. McCormick, Vibeke R. Petersen, and Laurie Melissa Vogelsang, 163–84. Providence, R.I.: Berg, 1993.

Kuzniar, Alice A. "Lesbians Abroad: The Queer Nationhood of Monika Treut et al." In *The Queer German Cinema,* by Alice A. Kuzniar, 157–73. Stanford, Calif.: Stanford University Press, 2000.

———. " 'Now I Have a Different Desire': Transgender Specularity in Zarah Leander and R. W. Fassbinder." In *The Queer German Cinema,* 57–87. Stanford, Calif.: Stanford University Press, 2000.

———. "Zarah Leander and Transgender Specularity." *Film Criticism* 23, nos. 2–3 (Winter–Spring 1999): 74–93.

Lamb-Faffelberger, Margarete. "Austria's Feminist Avant-Garde: Valie Export's and Elfriede Jelinek's Aesthetic Innovations." In *Out from the Shadows: Essays on Contemporary Austrian Women Writers and Filmmakers*, edited by Margarete Lamb-Faffelberger, 229–41. Riverside, Calif.: Ariadne Press, 1997.

———. *Valie Export und Elfriede Jelinek im Spiegel der Presse: Zur Rezeption der feministischen Avantgarde Österreichs*. New York: Peter Lang, 1992.

Lamb-Faffelberger, Margarete, ed. *Out from the Shadows: A Collection of Articles on Austrian Literature and Film by Women since 1945*. Riverside, Calif.: Ariadne Press, 1997.

Leander, Zarah. *Es war so wunderbar: Mein Leben*. Hamburg: Hoffmann und Campe, 1973.

———. *So bin ich und so bleibe ich*. Edited by Roland Gööck. Gütersloh: C. Bertelsmann, 1958.

Leblans, Anne. "Inventing Male Wombs: The Fairy-tale Logic of *Metropolis*." In *Peripheral Visions: The Hidden Stages of Weimar Cinema*, edited by Kenneth S. Calhoon, 95–119. Detroit: Wayne State University Press, 2001.

Levin, David. "This Cinema That Is Not One? Monika Treut and a Deterritorialized German Cinema." In *A New Germany in a New Europe*, edited by Todd Herzog and Sander L. Gilman, 131–39. New York: Routledge, 2001.

Linville, Susan E. "Agnieszka Holland's *Europa, Europa*: Deconstructive Humor in a Holocaust Film." *Film Criticism* 29, no. 3 (Spring 1995): 44–53.

———. "*Europa, Europa*: A Test Case for German National Cinema." *Wide Angle* 16, no. 3 (February 1995): 39–51.

———. *Feminism, Film, Fascism: Women's Auto/biographical Film in Postwar Germany*. Austin: University of Texas Press, 1998.

Lippe, Adrian. *Leni Riefenstahl und die Macht der Bilder*. Munich: GRIN Verlag, 2000.

Lippert, Renate. "Ein Millimeter schmerzfreie Zone: Valie Exports . . . Remote . . . Remote." *Frauen und Film*, no. 39 (December 1985): 73–80.

Littau, Karin. "Refractions of the Feminine: The Monstrous Transformations of Lulu." *MLN* 110, no. 4 (September 1995): 888–912.

Loewenstein, Joseph, and Lynn Tatlock. "The Marshall Plan at the Movies: Marlene Dietrich and Her Incarnations." *German Quarterly* 65, nos. 3–4 (Summer–Fall 1992): 429–42.

Loiperdinger, Martin, and David Culbert. "Leni Riefenstahl, the SA, and the Nazi Party Rally Films, Nuremberg 1933–1934: *Sieg des Glaubens* and *Triumph des Willens*." *Historical Journal of Film, Radio and Television* 8, no. 1 (1988): 3–38.

Loiperdinger, Martin, and Klaus Schönekäs. "*Die große Liebe*: Propaganda im Unterhaltungsfilm." In *Bilder schreiben Geschichte: Der Historiker im Kino*, edited by Rainer Rother, 143–53. Berlin: Wagenbach, 1991.

Lungstrum, Janet. "Metropolis and the Technosexual Woman of German Modernity." In *Women in the Metropolis: Gender and Modernity in Weimar Culture*, edited by Katharina von Ankum, 128–44. Berkeley and Los Angeles: University of California Press, 1997.

MacDonald, Scott. "Valie Export." In *A Critical Cinema: Interviews with Independent Filmmakers*. [Vol. 1]. Berkeley and Los Angeles: University of California Press, 1988.

Magretta, William R., and Joan Magretta. "Story and Discourse: Schlöndorff and von Trotta's *The Lost Honor of Katharina Blum*." In *Modern European Filmmakers and the Art of Adaptation*, edited by Andrew S. Horton and Joan Magretta, 278–94. New York: Frederick Ungar, 1981.

Mayne, Judith. "Female Narration, Women's Cinema: Helke Sander's *The All- Round Reduced Personality/Redupers*." Special Double Issue on New German Cinema. *New German Critique*, nos. 24–25 (Autumn 1981–Winter 1982): 155–71. Also published in *Issues in Feminist Film Criticism*, edited by Patricia Erens, 380–94. Bloomington: Indiana University Press, 1990.

———. "Marlene Dietrich, *The Blue Angel*, and Female Performance." In *Seduction and Theory: Readings of Gender, Representation, and Rhetoric*, edited by Dianne Hunter, 28–46. Urbana: University of Illinois Press, 1989.

McCarthy, Margaret. "Angst Takes a Holiday in Doris Dörrie's *Am I Beautiful?* (1998)." In *Light Motives: German Popular Film in Perspective*, edited by Randall Halle and Margaret McCarthy, 376–94. Detroit: Wayne State University Press, 2003.

———. "Consolidating, Consuming, and Annulling Identity in Jutta Bruckner's *Hungerjahre*." *Women in German Yearbook: Feminist Studies in German Literature and Culture* 11 (1995): 13–33.

———. "Teutonic Water: Effervescent Otherness in Doris Dörrie's *Nobody Loves Me*." *Camera Obscura*, no. 44 (2000): 40–73.

McCormick, Richard W. "Cinematic Form, History, and Gender: Margarethe von Trotta's *Rosa Luxemburg*." *Seminar: A Journal of Germanic Studies* 32, no. 1 (February 1996): 36–41.

———. "Confronting German History: Melodrama, Distantiation, and Women's Discourse in *Germany, Pale Mother*." In *Gender and German Cinema: Feminist Interventions*. Vol. 2, *German Film History/German History on Film*, edited by Sandra Frieden, Richard W. McCormick, Vibeke R. Petersen, and Laurie Melissa Vogelsang, 185–207. Providence, R.I.: Berg, 1993.

———. "From Caligari to Dietrich: Sexual, Social, and Cinematic Discourses in Weimar Film." *Signs: Journal of Women in Culture and Society* 18, no. 3 (Spring 1993): 640–68.

———. *Gender and Sexuality in Weimar Modernity: Film, Literature, and "New Objectivity."* New York: Palgrave, 2001.

———. "Gender, Film, and German History: Filmmaking by German Women Directors from Weimar to the Present." In *Facing Fascism and Confronting the Past: German Women Writers from Weimar to the Present*, edited by Elke P. Frederiksen and Martha Kaarsberg Wallach, 245–70. Albany: State University of New York Press, 2000.

———. *The Politics of the Self: Feminism and the Postmodern in West German Literature and Film*. Princeton, N.J.: Princeton University Press, 1991.

Mennel, Barbara. "Local Funding and Global Movement: Minority Women's Filmmaking and the German Film Landscape of the Late 1990s." *Women in German Yearbook: Feminist Studies in German Literature and Culture* 18 (2002): 45–66.

———. "Wanda's Whip: Recasting Masochism's Fantasy; Monika Treut's *Seduction: The Cruel Woman*." In *Triangulated Visions: Women in Recent German Cinema*, edited by Ingeborg Majer O'Sickey and Ingeborg von Zadow, 153–62. Albany: State University of New York Press, 1998.

Mittman, Elizabeth. "Fashioning the Socialist Nation: The Gender of Consumption in Slatan Dudow's *Destinies of Women*." *German Politics and Society* 23, no. 4 (Winter 2005): 28–44.

Moeller, Hans Bernard. "West German Women's Cinema: The Case of Margarethe von Trotta." *Film Criticism* 9, no. 2 (Winter 1984–1985): 51–66.

Möhrmann, Renate. *Die Frau mit der Kamera: Filmemacherinnen in der Bundesrepublik Deutschland; Situation, Perspektiven; 10 exemplarische Lebensläufe*. Munich: Carl Hanser, 1980.

Molsen, Barbara. *Zwischentöne: Gespräche mit Schauspielern und Regisseuren*. Berlin: Verlag Das Neue Berlin, 1996.

Mouton, Jan. "The Absent Mother Makes an Appearance in the Films of West German Directors." *Women in German Yearbook: Feminist Studies in German Literature and Culture* 4 (1988): 69–81.

Mueller, Roswitha. "The Mirror and the Vamp." *New German Critique,* no. 34 (Winter 1985): 176–93.

———. "The Prosthetic Womb: Technology and Reproduction in the Work of Valie Export." In *Out from the Shadows: Essays on Contemporary Austrian Women Writers and Filmmakers*, edited by Margarete Lamb-Faffelberger, 242–51. Riverside, Calif.: Ariadne Press, 1997.

———. "Screen Embodiments: Valie Export's *Syntagma*." *Discourse: Journal for Theoretical Studies in Media and Culture* 13, no. 2 (Spring–Summer 1991): 39–57.

———. "The Uncanny in the Eyes of a Woman." Special Issue from the Center for Twentieth Century Studies. *SubStance* (University of Wisconsin Press), nos. 37–38 (1983): 129–39.

———. *Valie Export: Bild-Risse.* Vienna: Passagen Verlag, 2002.

———. *Valie Export: Fragments of the Imagination.* Bloomington: Indiana University Press, 1994.

Müller, Ray. *Die Macht der Bilder Leni Riefenstahls (The Wonderful, Horrible Life of Leni Riefenstahl).* VHS. 2 vols. New York: Kino Video, 1993.

Münzberg, Olav. "Schaudern vor der bleichen Mutter: Eine sozialpsychologische Analyse der Kritiken zum Film von Helma Sanders-Brahms." *Medium* 7 (July 1980): 34–37.

Murray, Bruce A., and Renate Möhrmann. "*Germany, Pale Mother*: On the Mother Figures in New German Women's Film." *Women in German Yearbook: Feminist Studies in German Literature and Culture* 11 (1995): 67–80.

Myers, Tracy. "History and Realism: Representations of Women in G. W. Pabst's *The Joyless Street.*" In *Gender and German Cinema: Feminist Interventions.* Vol. 2, *German Film History/German History on Film*, edited by Sandra Frieden, Richard W. McCormick, Vibeke R. Petersen, and Laurie Melissa Vogelsang, 259–71. Providence, R.I.: Berg, 1993.

Olivier, Antje, and Sevgi Braun. "Das Negative macht mich nicht kreativ— Leni Riefenstahl, die Regisseurin von Macht und Schönheit." In *Anpassung oder Verbot: Künstlerinnen und die 30er Jahre,* 263–94. Düsseldorf: Droste, 1998.

O'Sickey, Ingeborg Majer. "Representing Blackness: Instrumentalizing Race and Gender in Rainer Werner Fassbinder's *The Marriage of Maria Braun.*" *Women in German Yearbook: Feminist Studies in German Literature and Culture* 17 (2001): 15–29.

O'Sickey, Ingeborg Majer, and Ingeborg von Zadow, eds. *Triangulated Visions: Women in Recent German Cinema.* Albany: State University of New York Press, 1998.

Ottinger, Ulrike. "Encounter between Two Cultures: A Discussion with Ulrike Ottinger." By Annette Kuhn. *Screen* 28, no. 4 (Autumn 1987): 74–79.

———. "Interview with Ulrike Ottinger." By Erica Carter. *Screen Education,* no. 41 (Winter–Spring 1982): 34–42.

———. "Interview with Ulrike Ottinger." By Roswitha Mueller. *Discourse: Journal for Theoretical Studies in Media and Culture* 4 (Winter 1981–1982): 108–26.

———. "*Johanna d'Arc of Mongolia*: Interview with Ulrike Ottinger." By Janet A. Kaplan. *Art Journal* 61, no. 3 (Autumn 2002): 6–21.

Pabst, G. W. *Pandora's Box (Lulu): A Film.* Rev. ed. Translated from the German by Christopher Holme. London: Lorrimer, 1984.

Pally, Marcia. "Open Dörrie." *Film Comment* 22, no. 5 (September–October 1986): 42–45.

Petro, Patrice. *Aftershocks of the New: Feminism and Film History.* New Brunswick, N.J.: Rutgers University Press, 2002.

———. "Film Censorship and the Female Spectator: The Joyless Street (1925)." In *The Films of G. W. Pabst: An Extraterritorial Cinema*, edited by Eric Rentschler, 30–40. New Brunswick, N.J.: Rutgers University Press, 1990.

———. *Joyless Streets: Women and Melodramatic Representation in Weimar Germany.* Princeton, N.J.: Princeton University Press, 1989.

———. "World Weariness, Weimar Women, and Visual Culture." In *Aftershocks of the New: Feminism and Film History*, 95–123. New Brunswick, N.J.: Rutgers University, 2000.

Quart, Barbara Koenig. *Women Directors: The Emergence of a New Cinema.* New York: Praeger Publishers, 1988.

Rentschler, Eric. "The Elemental, the Ornamental, the Instrumental: *The Blue Light* and Nazi Film Aesthetics." In *The Other Perspective in Gender and Culture: Rewriting Women and the Symbolic*, edited by Juliet Flower MacCannell, 161–88. New York; Columbia University Press, 1990.

Rheuban, Joyce. "*The Marriage of Maria Braun*: History, Melodrama, Ideology." In *Gender and German Cinema: Feminist Interventions.* Vol. 2, *German Film History/German History on Film*, edited by Sandra Frieden, Richard W. McCormick, Vibeke R. Petersen, and Laurie Melissa Vogelsang, 207–26. Providence, R.I.: Berg, 1993.

Rich, B. Ruby. "From Repressive Tolerance to Erotic Liberation: *Girls in Uniform.*" *Jump Cut*, nos. 24–25 (March 1981): 44–50. Reprinted in *Re-vision: Essays in Feminist Film Criticism*, edited by Mary Ann Doane, Patricia Mellencamp, and Linda Williams, 100–130. Los Angeles: American Film Institute, 1984. Also published in *Gender and German Cinema: Feminist Interventions.* Vol. 2, *German Film History/German History on Film*, edited by Sandra Frieden, Richard W. McCormick, Vibeke R. Petersen, and Laurie Melissa Vogelsang, 61–96. Providence, R.I.: Berg, 1993.

———. "Leni Riefenstahl: The Deceptive Myth." In *Sexual Stategems: The World of Women in Film*, edited by Patricia Erens, 202–9. New York: Horizon Press, 1979. Also published in *Chick Flicks Theories and Memories of the Feminist Film Movement*, 40–47. Durham, N.C.: Duke University Press, 1998.

———. "She Says, He Says: The Power of the Narrator in Modernist Film Politics." *Discourse: Journal for Theoretical Studies in Media and Culture* 6 (Fall 1983): 31–46. Also published in *Gender and German Cinema: Feminist Interventions.* Vol. 1, *Gender and Representation in New German Cinema*, edited by Sandra Frieden, Richard W. McCormick, Vibeke R. Petersen, and Laurie Melissa Vogelsang, 143–61. Providence, R.I.: Berg, 1993.

Richardson, Colin. "Monika Treut: An Outlaw at Home." In *A Queer Romance: Lesbians, Gay Men, and Popular Culture*, edited by Paul Burston and Colin Richardson, 167–85. New York: Routledge, 1995.

Riefenstahl, Leni. *Leni Riefenstahl: A Memoir*. New York: Picador, 1995.

———. *Leni Riefenstahl: A Memoir*. New York: St. Martin's Press, 1992.

———. *"Olympia."* New York: St. Martin's Press, 1994.

———. *The Sieve of Time: The Memoirs of Leni Riefenstahl*. London: Quartet Books, 1992.

Rinke, Andrea. *Images of Women in East German Cinema, 1972–1982: Socialist Models, Private Dreamers and Rebels*. Lewiston, N.Y.: Edwin Mellen Press, 2006.

———. "Models or Misfits? The Role of Screen Heroines in GDR Cinema." In: *Triangulated Visions: Women in Recent German Cinema*, edited by Ingeborg Majer O'Sickey and Ingeborg von Zadow, 207–18. Albany: State University of New York Press, 1998.

Romani, Cinzia. *Tainted Goddesses: Female Film Stars of the Third Reich*. Translated by Robert Connolly. New York: Sarpedon, 1992.

Rosenbaum, Marianne S. W. "'Frieden' hat für uns Deutsche einen amerikanischen Geschmack': Ein Gespräch mit Marianne S. W. Rosenbaum." By Bion Steinborn and Carola Hilmes. *Filmfaust*, no. 39 (May-June 1984): 27–31.

Rother, Rainer. *Leni Riefenstahl: Die Verführung des Talents*. Berlin: Henschel, 2000.

———. *Leni Riefenstahl: The Seduction of Genius*. Translated by Martin H. Bott. London: Continuum, 2002.

Salber, Linde. *Marlene Dietrich*. Reinbek bei Hamburg: Rowohlt, 2001.

Sander, Helke. "Nimmt man dir das Schwert, dann greife zum Knüppel." *Frauen und Film*, no. 1 (July 1974): 12–48.

———. "There Should Be No Scissors in Your Mind: An Interview with Helke Sander." By Stuart Liebman. *Cineaste* 21, nos. 1–2 (1995): 40–42.

Sanders-Brahms, Helma. *Deutschland, bleiche Mutter: Film-Erzählung*. Reinbek bei Hamburg: Rowohlt, 1980.

———. "Helma Sanders-Brahms: A Conversation." With Peter Brunette. *Film Quarterly* 44, no. 2 (Winter 1990–1991): 34–42.

———. "My Critics, My Films and I. (1980)." In *West German Filmmakers on Film: Visions and Voices*, edited by Eric Rentchler, 156–62. New York: Holmes and Meier, 1988.

———. "Tyrannenmord: *Tiefland* von Leni Riefenstahl." In *Das Jahr 1945: Filme aus 15 Ländern,* by Hans Helmut Prinzler, 173–76. Berlin: Stiftung Deutsche Kinemathek ,1990.

———. "Zarah." In *Jahrbuch Film 81/82*, edited by Hans-Günter Pflaum, 165–72. Munich: Carl Hanser, 1981.

Schaake, Erich, and Roland Bäurle. "Leni Riefenstahl: Triumph des schönen Scheins" In *Hitler's Frauen: Die willigen Helferinnen und ergebenen Mätressen des Führers.* Munich: Paul List Verlag, 2000.

Schenk, Ralf. *Frauengestalten im Film und Fernsehen der DDR.* Bonn: Bundeszentrale für politische Bildung, 1997.

Schirach, Henriette von. "Leni Riefenstahl." In *Frauen um Hitler: nach Materialien.* Munich: F. A. Herbig, 1983.

Schlüpmann, Heide. "Faschistische Trugbilder weiblicher Autonomie." *Frauen und Film,* nos. 44–45 (October 1988): 44–66. Also published in *Frauen und Faschismus in Europa: Der faschistische Körper,* edited by Leonore Siegele-Wenschkewitz and Gerda Stuchlik, 211–27. Pfaffenweiler: Centaurus, 1990.

———. *"Ich möchte kein Mann sein*: Ernst Lubitsch, Sigmund Freud und die frühe deutsche Komödie." In *KINtop: Jahrbuch zur Erforschung des frühen Films.* Vol. 1, *Früher Film in Deutschland,* edited by Frank Kessler, Sabine Lenk, and Martin Loiperdinger, 75–92. Frankfurt am Main: Stroemfeld/ Roter Stern, 1993.

———. "Trugbilder weiblicher Autonomie im nationalsozialistischen Film: Leni Riefenstahl: Triumph des weiblichen Willens?" In *Sport und Film:Bewegte Körper, bewegte Bilder,* edited by Annette C. Eckert and Thomas Til Radevagen, 102–7. Berlin: Cine-Marketing, 1993.

Schwartz, Nancy. "Lubitsch's Widow: The Meaning of a Waltz." *Film Comment* 11, no. 2 (March–April 1975): 13–17.

Schygulla, Hanna, and Rainer Werner Fassbinder. *Hanna Schygulla: Bilder aus Filmen von Rainer Werner Fassbinder.* Munich: Schirmer/Mosel, 1981.

Segeberg, Harro. "Hitler und Riefenstahl: Anmerkungen zu Leni Riefenstahl's *Triumph des Willens.*" In *Schauspielen und Montage: Schauspielkunst Im Film; Zweites Symposium (1998),* edited by Knut Hickethier, 31–45. St. Augustin, Germany: Gardez! Verlag, 1999.

Seidel, Renate, and Allan Hagedorff, eds. *Asta Nielsen: Ihr Leben in Fotodokumenten, Selbstzeugnissen und zeitgenössischen Betrachtungen.* Berlin: Henschel, 1981.

Seiter, Ellen. "The Political Is Personal: Margarethe von Trotta's *Marianne and Juliane.*" In *Films for Women,* edited by Charlotte Brunsdon, 109–16. London: BFI Publishing, 1986.

———. "Women's History, Women's Melodrama: *Deutschland, bleiche Mutter.*" *German Quarterly* 59, no. 4 (Fall 1986): 569–81.

Sicinski, Michael. "Valie Export and Paranoid Counter-Surveillance." *Discourse: Journal for Theoretical Studies in Media and Culture* 22, no. 2 (Spring 2000): 71–91.

Sigmund, Anna Maria. "Leni Riefenstahl: Die Amazonenkönigin." In *Die Frauen der Nazis,* 145–72. Munich: Wilhelm Heyne, 2000.

Silberman, Marc. "Cine-Feminists in West Berlin." *Quarterly Review of Film Studies* 5, no. 2 (1980): 217–32.

———. "Film and Feminism in Germany Today." *Jump Cut,* no. 27 (1982): 41–53.

———. "German Film Women." *Jump Cut,* no. 29 (1984): 49–64.

———. "German Women's Film Culture." *Jump Cut,* no. 30 (1985): 63–69.

———. "Ula Stöckl: How Women See Themselves." In *New German Filmmakers: From Oberhausen through the 1970s,* edited by Klaus Phillips, 320–34. New York: Frederick Ungar, 1984.

———. "Women Filmmakers in West Germany: A Catalog." *Camera Obscura,* no. 6 (1980): 123–52.

———. "Women Filmmakers in West Germany: A Catalog (Part 2)." *Camera Obscura,* no. 11 (1983): 132–45.

———. "Zarah Leander in the Colonies." In *Medien/Kultur: Schnittstellen zwischen Medienwissenschaft, Medienpraxis und gesellschaftlicher Kommunikation,* edited by Knut Hicketier and Siegfried Zielinski, 247–53. Berlin: Volker Spiess, 1991.

Silberman, Marc, tr. "Invisible Adversaries (Valie Export)." *Camera Obscura,* nos. 3–4 (Summer 1979): 219–24.

Silverman, Kaja. "Helke Sander and the Will to Change." *Discourse: Journal for Theoretical Studies in Media and Culture* 6 (Fall 1983): 10–30.

Simon, Sunka. "Out of Hollywood: Monika Treut's *Virgin Machine* and Percy Adlon's *Bagdad Cafe.*" In *Queering the Canon: Defying Sights in German Literature and Culture,* edited by Christoph Lorey and John L. Plews, 383–402. Columbia, S.C.: Camden House, 1998.

Staskowski, Andrea. *Conversations with Experience: Feminist Hermeneutics and the Autobiographical Films of German Women.* New York: Peter Lang, 2004.

Steffensen, Jyanni. "Epistemological Sadism: Queering the Phallus in Monica Treut's *Seduction.*" *Atlantis* 23, no. 1 (Fall 1998): 137–45.

Stöckl, Ula. "Gespräch mit Ula Stöckl and Reviews of Her Films." Interview by Eva Hiller, Claudia Lenssen, and Gesine Strempel. *Frauen und Film,* no. 12 (June 1977): 3–23.

Straayer, Chris. "Lesbian Narratives and Queer Characters in Monika Treut's *Virgin Machine.*" *Journal of Film and Video* 45, nos. 2–3 (Summer–Fall 1993): 24–39.

Studlar, Gaylyn. *In the Realm of Pleasure: Von Sternberg, Dietrich, and the Masochistic Aesthetic.* Urbana: University of Illinois Press, 1988.

Taschen, Angelika. *Leni Riefenstahl: Five Lives.* Cologne: Taschen, 2000.

Tegel, Susan. "Leni Riefenstahl's 'Gypsy Question'." *Historical Journal of Film, Radio and Television* 23, no. 1 (March 2003): 3–10.

Thompson, Rick. "He and She: Weimar Screwballwerk." [Discusses *Viktor und Viktoria*] *Senses of Cinema: An Online Film Journal Devoted to the Serious and Eclectic Discussion of Cinema,* no. 22 (September–October 2002). www.sensesofcinema.com/contents/cteq/02/22/viktor.html

Treut, Monika. "Female Misbehavior." In *Feminisms in the Cinema*, edited by Laura Pietropaolo and Ada Testaferri, 106–21. Bloomington: Indiana University Press, 1995.

——. "From *Taboo Parlor* to Porn and Passing: An Interview with Monika Treut." By Gerd Gemünden, Alice Kuzniar, and Klaus Phillips. *Film Quarterly* 50, no. 3 (Spring 1997): 2–12.

——. *Die grausame Frau: zum Frauenbild bei de Sade und Sacher-Masoch.* Basel: Stroemfeld/Roter Stern, 1984.

——. "Die Zeremonie der blutenden Rose." *Frauen und Film,* no. 36 (February 1984): 35–43.

Trimborn, Jürgen. *Leni Riefenstahl: A Life.* Translated by Edna McCown. New York: Faber and Faber, 2007.

——. "Ein Meister der subjectiven Kamera: Karriere im Windschatten Leni Riefenstahl." In *Das Auge des Dritten Reiches: Hitlers Kameramann und Fotograf Walter Frentz*, edited by Hans Georg Hiller von Gaertringen, 69–81. Munich: Deutscher Kunstverlag, 2007.

——. *Riefenstahl: Eine deutsche Karriere: Biographie.* Berlin: Aufbau-Verlag, 2002.

Trotta, Margarethe von. *Die bleierne Zeit.* Edited by Hans Jürgen Weber. Frankfurt am Main: Fischer Taschenbuch, 1981.

——. "Rebellinen wider eine bleierne Zeit: Ein Interview mit Margarethe von Trotta über ihren Film *bleierne Zeit.*" By Reiner Frey and Christian Göldenboog. *Filmfaust,* no. 24. (October–November 1981): 29–36.

——. *Schwestern oder die Balance des Glücks: Ein Film.* Edited by Willi Bär and Hans Jürgen Weber. Frankfurt am Main: Fischer Taschenbuch, 1979.

——. "Working with Jutta Lampe. (1979)." In *West German Filmmakers on Film: Visions and Voices*, edited by Eric Rentchler, 178–90. New York: Holmes and Meier, 1988.

Trotta, Margarethe von, and Christiane Ensslin. *"Rosa Luxemburg": das Buch zum Film.* Nördlingen: Greno, 1986.

Trotta, Margarethe von, and Luisa Francia. *"Das zweite Erwachen der Christa Klages".* Frankfurt am Main: Fischer Taschenbuch, 1980.

Trotta, Margarethe von, Hans Jürgen Weber, and Carola Hembus. *"Heller Wahn": Ein Film von Margarethe von Trotta.* Frankfurt am Main: Fischer Taschenbuch, 1983.

Trotta, Margarethe von, Hans Jürgen Weber, and Ingeborg Weber. *"Die bleierne Zeit": Ein Film von Margarethe von Trotta.* Frankfurt am Main: Fischer Taschenbuch, 1981.

Verband der Filmarbeiterinnen. *Frauen Film Handbuch.* Berlin: Verband der Filmarbeiterinnen, 1984.

Verfassungsklage: 35 Filmarbeiterinnen gegen Regierung der Bundesrepublik Deutschland. Cologne: Verband. der Filmarbeiterinnen, 1988.

von Papen, Manuela. "Opportunities and Limitations: New Woman in Third Reich Cinema." *Women's History Review,* 8, no. 4 (December 1999): 693–728.

Wager, Jans B. *Dangerous Dames: Women and Representation in the Weimar Street Film and Film Noir.* Athens: Ohio University Press, 1999.

Wallace, Peggy Ann. "The Most Important Factor Was the 'Spirit': Leni Riefenstahl During the Filming of *The Blue Light.*" *Image* 17, no. 1 (March 1974): 16–28.

Ward, Jenifer K. "Enacting the Different Voice: *Christa Klages* and Feminist History." *Women in German Yearbook: Feminist Studies in German Literature and Culture* 11 (1995): 49–65.

Weinberger, Gabriele. "Marianne Rosenbaum and the Aesthetics of Angst (*Peppermint Peace*)." In *Gender and German Cinema: Feminist Interventions.* Vol. 2, *German Film History/German History on Film,* edited by Sandra Frieden, Richard W. McCormick, Vibeke R. Petersen, and Laurie Melissa Vogelsang, 227–40. Providence, R.I.: Berg, 1993.

——. *Nazi Germany and Its Aftermath in Women Directors' Autobiographical Films of the Late 1970s: In the Murderers' House.* San Francisco: Mellen Research University Press, 1992.

Wiebrecht, Ulrike. *Blauer Engel aus Berlin: Marlene Dietrich.* Berlin: be.bra, 2001.

Wilke, Sabine. "The Body Politic of Performance, Literature, and Film: Mimesis and Citation in Valie Export, Elfriede Jelinek, and Monika Treut." *Paragraph* 22, no. 3 (November 1999): 228–47.

——. "The Sexual Woman and Her Struggle for Sexuality: Cruel Women in Sade, Sacher-Masoch, and Treut." *Women in German Yearbook: Feminist Studies in German Literature and* Culture 14 (1999): 245–60.

Zipes, Jack. "The Political Dimensions of *The Lost Honor of Katharina Blum.*" *New German Critique,* no. 10 (Winter 1977): 75–84.

Zucker, Carole. *The Idea of the Image: Josef von Sternberg's Dietrich Films.* Rutherford: Fairleigh Dickinson University Press; Cranbury, N.J.: Associated University Presses, 1988.

——. "Some Observations on Sternberg and Dietrich." *Cinema Journal* 19, no. 2 (Spring 1980): 17–24.

PERIODICALS

Cahiers du cinéma
Camera Obscura
Cineaste
Cinema Journal
Commentary
Discourse: Journal for Theoretical Studies in Media and Culture
Entertext: An Interactive Interdisciplinary E-Journal for Cultural and Histori-
    cal Studies and Creative Work
Film and History
Film Comment
Film Criticism
Film Culture
Film History
Film Quarterly
Film und Fernsehen
Filmfaust
Filmkritik
Films in Review
Frauen und Film
Gay and Lesbian Review
German Life and Letters
German Politics and Society
German Quarterly
Germanic Review
German Studies Review
Historical Journal of Film, Radio, and Television
History and Memory
Iris
Journal of Film and Video
Journal of Popular Film and Television
Jump Cut
Kino: Films of the German Republic (after 2004, published as *German Films:*
    Yearbook)
Kino: German Film
Kinoeye
KINtop: Jahrbuch zur Erforschung des frühen Films
Literature/Film Quarterly
MLN
Monatshefte

montage a/v
New German Critique
October
Positif
Post Script
Quarterly of Film, Radio, and Television
Quarterly Review of Film and Video
Quarterly Review of Film Studies
Screen
Senses of Cinema: An Online Film Journal Devoted to the Serious and Eclectic Discussion of Cinema
Sight and Sound
Wide Angle
Women in German Yearbook: Feminist Studies in German Literature and Culture

WEBSITES

http://cinegraph.de (links to German film sites)
http://defafilmlibrary.com (extensive library of East German films)
http://filmarchiv.at/ (Austrian film site)
http://film-dienst.kim-info.de/ (subscription necessary for some material: articles)
http://www.filmportal.de (comprehensive source for information on German films)
http://filmref.com/ (reviews of international films)
http://german.about.com/library/blfilm_reviews.htm (reviews of German films)
http://pov.imv.au.dk/ (A Danish journal of film studies)
http://verdantmetropolis.homestead.com/links.html (metropolis fan site with links)
http://web.uvic.ca/geru/439/oberhausen.html (Oberhausen Manifesto)
http://www.artechock.de/film/index.htm (A German language film magazine)
http://www.bambi.de (Popular culture awards site)
http://www.bavaria-film.de/ (One of Germany's oldest film companies)
http://www.bpb.de/publikationen (cultural pedagogy)
http://www.deutsche-filmakademie.de (official industry site)
http://www.deutscher-tonfilm.de/ (hard to find facts on classic German sound films)
http://www.deutsches-filmhaus.de (photos, facts and more)
http://www.deutsches-filminstitut.de/ (major film site with links and articles)

http://www.djfl.de/ (Popular film site for star biographies and reviews)
http://www.dradio.de (short film recorded reviews)
http://www.filmbesprechungen.de/ (mostly commercial film site)
http://www.filmmuseum-berlin.de/ (biographies, exhibitions, archives)
http://www.filmreference.com/ (film reviews)
http://www.filmzentrale.com/ (extensive archive of film reviews)
http://www.germanfilms.de (pr site for German film)
http://www.germanhollywood.com/ (actors/directors across the ocean)
http://www.goethe.de/kue/flm/ (links to film topics)
http://www.helke-sander.de/ (personal web site)
http://www.kiez-ev.de/film/ (film reviews)
http://www.kinoeye.org/index_04_05.php (reviews)
http://www.kinofenster.de/ (film pedagogy)
http://www.kurt-maetzig.de/indexm.html (personal site)
http://www.marlenedietrich.org/ (official Dietrich site)
http://www.prisma-online.de/ (film summaries)
http://www.programmkino.de/cms/news.php?bereich=10 (reviews on art house films)
http://www.schnitt.de/ (general reviews)
http://www.sensesofcinema.com/ (general film reviews)
http://www.ula-stoeckl.com/ (personal web site)
http://www.zlb.de/medien-film.htm (Berlin state film library)

About the Authors

Robert C. Reimer, Ph.D., is chair of the Department of Languages and Culture Studies and professor of German at the University of North Carolina–Charlotte. He has a B.A. from the University of Wisconsin–Madison and an M.A. and Ph.D. from the University of Kansas–Lawrence. From 2001 to 2007, he directed the interdisciplinary Film Studies Program at UNC Charlotte. He is the coauthor of *Nazi-Retro Film: How German Narrative Cinema Remembers the Past* (Twayne Publishers, 1992), editor of *Cultural History through a National Socialist Lens: Essays on the Cinema of the Third Reich* (Camden House, 2000), and coauthor of the textbooks *German Culture through Film: An Introduction to German Cinema* (Focus Publishers, 2005) and *Arbeitsbuch zu German Culture through Film* (Focus Publishers, 2006). He is vice president of the Charlotte Film Society and serves as a juror in the Charlotte Film Festival.

Carol J. Reimer, M.L.S., is gifts coordinator and collection development associate in the J. Murrey Atkins Library at the University of North Carolina–Charlotte. She has a B.A. from UNC Charlotte and an M.L.S. from the University of Wisconsin–Milwaukee. She is the coauthor of *Nazi-retro Film: How German Narrative Cinema Remembers the Past* (Twayne Publishers, 1992) and has published articles on film in *The Journal of Popular Film and Television* and *Sightlines*.